Praise for *Stalin's Agent*:

'A titanic effort ... I would venture to suggest that not a few historians of note will have to review their opinions in light of this book.'

Professor Ángel Viñas, Complutense University of Madrid

'The book's combination of exhaustive research and riveting detail make it a turning point in the historiography of the Spanish Civil War as well as providing a fascinating insight into the failures of both the CIA and the KGB.'

Professor Paul Preston, London School of Economics and Political Science

'*Stalin's Agent* is a major contribution to the history of Soviet intelligence and foreign policy in its most paranoid phase.'

Professor Christopher Andrew, Official Historian of the Security Service MI5, *Literary Review*

'Russian intelligence operations are a seam of 20th century European history that can no longer be ignored ... Volodarsky enhances our understanding. His is not the last word – we'll never get there – but it is a significant and valuable addition.'

Alan Judd, writer, former personal assistant to the chief of SIS, *The Spectator*

'Volodarsky debunks the many self-constructed myths of "Stalin's agent". He does not stint of detail: this book is 800-plus pages long, with 190 pages of endnotes, 56 pages of bibliography, seven pages of abbreviations and acronyms, two forewords, three appendices, a brief history of the KGB and an introduction. The result is a mammoth.'

Andre van Loon, *The Australian*

'Meticulously researched and based on a variety of archival records from Russian, European and American depositories, Volodarsky's book is focused on major and minor details of the inter-war Soviet spy games: dates, names, and events ... Volodarsky is all over Soviet espionage history: from secret police operations against Ukrainian nationalists in the 1930s to Leopold Trepper's anti-Nazi underground Red Capella during the Second World War in the 1940s. Had I the opportunity to retitle his erudite study, instead of using the "life and death" publishers' cliché, I would have called it "Stalin's Agent: Alexander Orlov and the World of Early Soviet Espionage". This would better convey the format of this informative encyclopedia-type book, which is the most comprehensive text so far on the topic of Soviet espionage in the inter-war period.'

Professor Andrei Znamenski, *Review in History*

'*Stalin's Agent* is a must read for anyone seriously interested in the history of modern espionage, the Soviet aspect especially, and the history of the Spanish Civil War. It is likely to stand as a basic reference work for many years to come.'

Professor Richard B. Spence,
Slavonic and East European Review

'My purpose is to congratulate you on your Orlov book which I finished for the second time yesterday – and it is on the second reading that it is really possible to appreciate the truly enormous amount of research behind the book, and enjoy the precision in your writing. It is an excellent work of a rare quality in a difficult genre.'

Alf R. Jacobsen, The Norwegian Broadcasting
Corporation (NRK), letter to the author

The Birth of the
Soviet Secret Police

A NEW HISTORY OF THE KGB

The Birth of the Soviet Secret Police

Lenin and History's Greatest Heist, 1917–1927

Boris Volodarsky

FRONTLINE BOOKS

First published in Great Britain in 2023 by
Frontline Books
An imprint of Pen & Sword Books Limited
Yorkshire – Philadelphia

ISBN 978 1 52679 225 9

A CIP catalogue record for this book is
available from the British Library

Typeset by Mac Style
Printed in the UK by CPI Group (UK) Ltd, Croydon, CR0 4YY.

Pen & Sword Books Limited incorporates the imprints of After
the Battle, Atlas, Archaeology, Aviation, Discovery, Family History,
Fiction, History, Maritime, Military, Military Classics, Politics,
Select, Transport, True Crime, Air World, Frontline Publishing, Leo
Cooper, Remember When, Seaforth Publishing, The Praetorian Press,
Wharncliffe Local History, Wharncliffe Transport, Wharncliffe True
Crime and White Owl.

For a complete list of Pen & Sword titles please contact

PEN & SWORD BOOKS LIMITED
47 Church Street, Barnsley, South Yorkshire, S70 2AS, England
E-mail: enquiries@pen-and-sword.co.uk
Website: www.pen-and-sword.co.uk
or
PEN AND SWORD BOOKS
1950 Lawrence Rd, Havertown, PA 19083, USA
E-mail: Uspen-and-sword@casematepublishers.com
Website: www.penandswordbooks.com

Contents

Председателю О.Г.П.У.
Ф.Э. Дзержинскому

После происшедших с В.А. Стырне разговоров, я выражаю свое согласіе дать Вам вполне откровенныя показанія и свѣдѣнія по вопросамъ интересующимъ О.Г.П.У. относительно организаціи и состава Великобританской разведки и по скольку мнѣ извѣстно такія-же свѣдѣнія относительно Американской разведки, а также тѣхъ лицъ въ русской эмиграціи съ которыми мнѣ пришлось имѣть дѣло.

Москва, Внутренняя Тюрьма
30-го Окт. 1925. Сидней Рейли

A letter, allegedly by Sidney Reilly, 'the ace of spies', from the internal Lubyanka prison dated 30 October 1925 and addressed to the OGPU chairman Felix Dzerzhinsky. In this letter or note, originally written in Russian, Reilly gives his explicit agreement to disclose information about British and American secret services, their structure and staff, as well as about his contacts among the Russian émigré community.

They [our distant descendants in the twenty-first century] will come to the Pantheon of the revolution, they will rise, bowing their heads before the grey, majestic, wonderful walls of the Kremlin, and will look long upon the marble of funeral slabs, at the bronze death masks and bas-reliefs which, with time, will decorate the sepulchral bays.

Izvestia, 20 July 1936, marking the tenth anniversary of the death of Felix Dzerzhinsky

The problems of 'telling truth to power' haven't changed fundamentally over the last few thousand years. Because of the pressure to tell authoritarian regimes only what they wish to hear, they always have been and always will be second-rate when it comes to the understanding of intelligence.

Christopher Andrew

Despotic leaders do not rule alone.
From publishers' promo to Anne Applebaum,
Twilight of Democracy (1921)

List of Plates

1. Okhrana, St Petersburg Directorate, January 1905. (*Public domain*)
2. Nicholas II, tsarina and HIH tsarevich Aleksey N. Romanov. (*Public domain*)
3. Grand Duke Kirill Vladimirovich Romanov, 1924.
4. Carriage of the Imperial Train stationed in the town of Pskov where Nicholas II was forced by revolutionaries to abdicate the Russian throne on 2 March 1917 (Old Style).
5. Postcard with Bolshevik revolution heroes, Petrograd, October 1917. (*Lockhart, R. mss., 1906–1969, Collection No. LMC 1674*)
6. GPU/OGPU special forces (OSNAZ) in training.
7. Bolsheviks, members of the Ural regional Soviet who sentenced the former Russian tsar and his family to death.
8. The British Naval Campaign in the Baltic, 1918–19. Rear Admiral Hugh Sinclair lands in Reval (Tallinn), January 1918. (Public domain)
9 & 10. American soldier in Archangel, 1918, and Archangel in 2022.
11 & 12. Moscow, Lubyanka Square in 1900 and below – the OGPU headquarters in the same square in 1922.
13. Dzerzhinsky and first Cheka officers.
14. Dzerzhinsky in various tsarist jails in Russia.
15. A draft of the Order of Dzerzhinsky for Soviet intelligence personnel.
16. Dzerzhinsky chervonets 10 roubles.
17. Trotsky and Lenin, 1917. (*Public domain*)
18. Chicherin and Krestinsky, Berlin 1925.
19. Alexander Shliapnikov, Soviet trade-union leader, and Leonid Krasin in front of the Soviet embassy in Paris, 1924.
20. At least ten attempts were mounted by different revolutionary fractions seeking to assassinate Pyotr Arkadyevich Stolypin. (*Keystone/Getty Images*)
21. Boris Savinkov at the Supreme Tribunal in Moscow, 1924.
22. Robert H. Bruce Lockhart, 1920. (*Image UGC*)
23. Denys Norman Garstin, member of the British Intelligence Mission in St Petersburg 1917.
24. DeWitt Clinton Poole, arrived as the US consul in Moscow in September 1917. (*Courtesy of the National Archives, photo No. 152776*)

The Evolution of the KGB 1917–2017

November 1917   **NKVD**

Narodnyi komissariat vnutrennikh del (NKVD), People's Commissariat for Internal Affairs superseded the Interior Ministry of the previous regime right after the Bolshevik revolution of October 1917. It was initially tasked with conducting regular police work and overseeing prisons. It was disbanded in 1930 with its functions transferred to other government departments.

December 1917   **Cheka and VeCheka**

Chrezvychainaya Komissiya (Cheka), Extraordinary Commission for Combating Counter-Revolution and Sabotage, and from 1918 now VeCheka – All-Russian Extraordinary Commission for Combating Counter-Revolution, Profiteering and Corruption.

February 1922   **GPU and OGPU**

Gosudarstvennoe Politicheskoe Upravlenie (GPU), State Political Directorate, part of the *Narodnyi Komissariat Vnutrennikh Del* (NKVD), People's Commissariat for Internal Affairs of the Russian Federation, and from November 1923 *Ob'edinennoe Glavnoe Politicheskoe Upravlenie* (OGPU), Joint State Political Directorate under direct control of the Council of People's Commissars (Sovnarkom).

July 1934   **NKVD**

On 10 July the NKVD of the USSR was established as the country's police and security force.

July 1934   **GUGB**

Glavnoe Upravlenie Gosudarstvennoi Bezopasnosti (GUGB), Chief Directorate for State Security, now part of the NKVD.

February 1941–July 1941   **NKGB**

Narodnyi Komissariat Gosudarstvennoi Bezopasnosti (NKGB), People's Commissariat for State Security. During this period the GUGB was briefly transformed into a separate ministry (Commissariat), then was placed again under the NKVD, and finally from 14 April 1943 became the NKGB again.

March 1946   **MGB**
On 18 March 1946 all People's Commissariats were renamed Ministries and accordingly the NKGB became *Ministerstvo Gosudarstvennoi Bezopasnosti* (MGB).

May 1947–November 1951   **KI**
Komitet Informatsyi (KI), Committee of Information. Both political intelligence (MGB) and military intelligence (GRU) were united in one service; in the summer of 1948 all military personnel were returned to the General Staff of the Red Army; branches dealing with the new Eastern Bloc countries and the émigrés were returned to the MGB in late 1948; the KI was dismantled in 1951.

March 1953   **MVD**
Ministerstvo Vnutrennikh Del (MVD), Ministry for Internal Affairs. On 5 March 1953 the Ministry for State Security (MGB) became part of the enlarged MVD.

March 1954–November 1991   **KGB**
Komitet Gosudarstvennoi Bezopasnosti (KGB), Committee for State Security of the USSR Council of Ministers.

After the August 1991 Coup   **MSB, TsSR** and **KOGG**
After the collapse of the coup d'état attempt (19–22 August), all Communist Party activities on Soviet territory were terminated and banned, and the Committee for State Security of the USSR (KGB USSR) was dismantled and ceased to exist. Its first successor agencies were *Mezhrespublikanskaya Sluzhba Bezopasnosti* (MSB), the Inter-Republican Security Service; *Tsentralnaya Sluzhba Razvedki* (TsSR), Central Intelligence Service; and *Komitet po Okhrane Gosudarstvennoi Granitsy* (KOGG), State Border Protection Commiteee. The Specialist Protection Branch of the former KGB, the Government Protection Service, formerly known as 9th Directorate, became part of the Presidential Administration while the former KGB's 8th Chief Directorate (Code & Cipher), 16th Directorate (ELINT) and Government Communication Service were combined into the Government Communication Committee reporting to the President.

November 1991   **FSK**
The *Federalnaya Sluzhba Kontrrazvedki* (FSK) was a direct predecessor of the FSB and one of the successor agencies of the KGB. It existed from 1991 to 1995.

December 1991–March 2003   **FAPSI**

The *Federalnoe Agentstvo Pravitelstvennoi Svyazi i Informatsyi* (FAPSI), Federal Agency of Government Communication and Information, created by merging several specialist services of the former KGB, was responsible for providing signals intelligence (SIGINT) and secure protection of the government communications. In March 2003 the agency became one of the services of the FSB with some of its elements incorporated into the FSO in August 2004.

December 1991   **SVR**

After the collapse of the Soviet Union, the first 'Law on Foreign Intelligence' was adopted in August 1992, replacing the Central Intelligence Service with the *Sluzhba Vneshnei Razvedki* (SVR) which, in turn, became a successor of the First Chief Directorate (PGU) of the KGB. The SVR is the foreign intelligence service tasked mainly with the covert overseas collection of secret intelligence. A new law 'On Foreign Intelligence' was signed by President Boris Yeltsin on 10 January 1996. The SVR director is appointed by and accountable to the President. Since 2012 President Putin can personally issue any secret order to the SVR without consulting the State Duma (the lower house) and the Federation Council (the upper house) of the Federal Assembly of Russia. Since June 1972 the SVR headquarters has been in Yasenevo, a Moscow district which is also the site of two campuses of the British International School.

November 1993   **SBP**

The *Sluzhba Bezopasnosti Presidenta* (SBP) was created after the collapse of the Soviet Union as a Specialist Protection Command of the first Russian president Boris Yeltsin, part of the FSO. Since May 2000 it has been constantly expanding to become one of the world's most expert and well-armed protection services with the staff of about 3,000 officers. The Service has its own analytical department with the staff seconded from all branches of the Russian national intelligence machinery.

December 1993   **PS**

The *Pogranichnaya Sluzhba* (PS) was a Russian border guard service whose history dates back to 1571. Following the collapse of the Soviet Union the Russian Border Force was established as a separate government agency.

January 1994   **GUSP**

Glavnoe upravlenie spetsialnykh programme presdient RF (GUSP), the Chief Directorate for Special Programmes. It is a paramilitary government organisation, a successor of the combined 15th Chief Directorate (wartime government command centres) and Mobilisation Department of the former KGB, and former 5th department of the Russian Cabinet Office. Since its formation and until the time of writing, the agency's chiefs have been former high-ranking security service officers. Its head office is located in Moscow at number 2 Staraya Ploschad (Old Square), while the Presidential Administration occupies number 4, which since the 1920s housed the CPSU Central Committee.

April 1995   FSB

The *Federalnaya Sluzhba Bezopasnosti* (FSB) is the Russian domestic counter-intelligence and security agency also responsible for protecting Russian economic interests and counter-terrorism and espionage within the Russian Federation. It is directed by the President, headed by the FSB director and bound by the law 'On the Federal Security Service' of 1995 with its powers expanded in July 2010 by President Dmitry Medvedev. According to the same law the FSK was reorganised into the FSB. Since 1999 the FSB has also been tasked with intelligence-gathering on the territory of the former Soviet Union. Its head office is located in the former KGB building on Lubyanka Square in downtown Moscow. Today the FSB incorporates the previously independent Border Guard Service and a major part of the abolished Federal Agency of Government Communication and Information (FAPSI).

May 1996   FSO

After several failed and successful assassination attempts on the members of the Russian royal family, the Okhrana was formed in the Russian Empire in 1881 to defend the monarchy. 'Okhrana' literally means 'protection'. The Okhrana was identified by the Bolsheviks with Tsarist repression and after the October Revolution of 1917 was replaced by the bodyguard section of the Cheka. The Federal Protection Service was formed in May 1996 replacing the Chief Protection Directorate which traced its origin to the 9th Chief Directorate of the KGB.

March 1997   Zaslon

Special operations unit *Zaslon* (Shield) was formed within the SVR on 23 March 1997 by a secret presidential decree. It is the elite squadron of individually selected operatives tasked with supporting SVR operations. The unit ranges in size from 280 to 300 personnel commanded by a colonel who reports to the SVR director. The squadron has a wide range of responsibilities similar to those of the British Special Air Service (SAS) but unlike the SAS, which is a Special Forces unit of the British Army, Zaslon is part of the SVR's own security department. Similar to the SAS, the unit undertakes a number of roles including covert reconnaissance, direct action, close protection and hostage rescue. Much of the information regarding *Zaslon* is highly classified and is not commented on by the government.

March 2003   **PS**

On 11 March 2003 the Russian president Vladimir Putin changed the independent status of the Russian Border Force, transforming it into the Border Guard Service within the FSB. In July 2014 Ukraine filed a criminal case against the head of the Border Guard Service of the FSB accusing him of financing 'illegal military groups in Eastern Ukraine'.

April 2016   **Rosgvardiya**

The National Guard of Russia (Rosgvardiya) is a group of Special Forces and an independent law-enforcement agency accountable only to the president. The National Guard numbers about 340,000 personnel and is separate from the Russian Armed Forces although its units are formed from the élite Special Forces of the police and the army. The first director of the National Guard was and at the time of writing remains General of the Army Victor Zolotov, who has served as Putin's personal bodyguard for two decades.

February 2020   **SBRF**

Soviet Bezopasnosti Rossiiskoi Federatsyi (SBRF), the Security Council of Russia, was formed in April 1991 together with the new post of the President of the Russian Federation. Like the US National Security Council, the Security Council of Russia is the principal forum used by the President, who is also the supreme commander-in-chief of the armed forces, for consideration of national security, military, and foreign policy matters with senior government and state officials. Since its inception under new regulations decreed by President Putin on 16 January 2020, the SBRF includes twelve permanent members. The SBRF is chaired by the President. Its statutory attendees are the Deputy Chairman (a new post especially established for Dmitry Medvedev), the Head of the Presidential Administration, chairpersons of both chambers of the Federal Assembly, Minister of Defence, Minister for Foreign Affairs, Minister for Internal Affairs, Director of the FSB, Director of the SVR, Director of the National Guard, and Secretary of the Security Council. The SBRF meets at the Moscow Kremlin's Senate building.

Functions

The functions of the Russian security apparatus, unlike those of the Soviet and then Russian foreign intelligence service, remained (and will certainly continue to remain) relatively constant at least throughout the period 1826–2026. In July 1826 the Russian Emperor Nicholas I (Nikolai Pavlovich) founded the Third Section of His Imperial Majesty's Chancery. The Third Section ran a huge network of spies, collaborators and informers with the help of the Corps of Gendarmerie, a law enforcement and state security force. The Emperor placed a Baltic German cavalry general, Alexander Graf von Benckendorff, in charge of both. These were mighty organisations for the secret supervision of the whole Russian Empire, in fear of which, contemporaries report, not only private citizens but all other government departments trembled. The Third Section was disbanded in 1880 to be replaced by the Police Department and the Okhrana. Under different names, the system remained the same during communist rule until the collapse of the Soviet Union.

In the period between 1917 and 1991 members of the Russian secret political police described themselves as the Chekists, demonstrating that they were the heirs of Lenin's Cheka with 'clean hands, warm heart and cool head'. After 2000 this tradition was renewed to a certain extent. For reasons further described in this book, in the past few years the term *razvedchik*, which at the same time means 'prospector', 'scout' and 'secret service agent', became more popular.

The acronym KGB is often used to denote the internal security and foreign intelligence services of the USSR during the Cold War, which is basically correct although officially the KGB existed only from 1954 to 1991.

Headquarters

After the October Revolution (the exact date is not recorded), the imposing building of the All-Russia Insurance Company on Lubyanka Square in downtown Moscow was requisitioned to house the Cheka. In those days, positioned at the south-eastern part of the square was a fountain with a horse-carriage stand nearby. In 1958 the fountain was replaced by a statue of Felix Dzerzhinsky, the founder of the Cheka.

For 55 years this building housed both the Foreign Intelligence Service (First Chief Directorate, PGU) and the Security Service (Second Chief Directorate), both parts of the KGB, alongside other directorates, departments and services. It was generally known as the Centre especially among officers of the PGU. In June 1972 the foreign intelligence directorate moved to

Yasenevo, now part of Moscow, with a new Church of Intercession opened in 2015. The SVR compound, known internally as 'Les' ('Forest'), initially consisted of the main building and several auxiliary facilities plus bungalows for visitors and a better one for the chief. The Service doesn't give public tours of its headquarters buildings, but in December 2018 an exception was made for Nailah (Nailya) Asker-zade and a cameraman who were allowed to shoot a documentary there with the Service director playing the host. The film is available on YouTube.

In 1991 the first (and only) democratically-elected Mayor of Moscow, Gavriil Popov, ordered the dismantling of the 11-ton statue of The Iron Felix. On the night of 22 August, the statue in front of the KGB building was toppled and removed to the cheers of a crowd of about 10,000 people, hours after Michael Gorbachev resigned as the General Secretary of the CPSU.

Unlike those who locked themselves in the building helplessly watching the scene, many thought it was the beginning of a new era. Without doubt it was. But one junior colleague of those officers in the Lubyanka building, now the President of the new Russia, speaking to the nation in his annual address on 29 April 2005, used these words to describe his country's fate over the past 14 years: 'The collapse of the Soviet Union was the biggest geopolitical catastrophe of the century,' Putin said. 'For the Russian people, it became a real drama.' After another 15-plus years of his rule, 'new' Russia turned into a true monster much worse than its old communist predecessor.

Felix Dzerzhinsky is still around, now in the Muzeon sculpture park alongside many other former Soviet monuments. A short time ago, polling conducted by the Russian Levada Centre revealed that 51 per cent of Moscow residents support restoring the statue to its former location.

Abbreviations and Acronyms

AFP	Agence France-Press
Amtorg	American-Soviet Trading Corporation, first Soviet trade company established in New York
Arcos	All-Russian Co-operative Society, Anglo-Russian trade organisation
BKP	B'lgarska Komunisticheska Partiya ('Bulgarian Communist Party')
BRD	Bundesrepublik Deutschland ('Federal Republic of Germany'), West Germany
BVT	Bundesamt für Verfassungsschutz und Terrorismusbe kämpfung ('Federal Office For the Protection of the Consitution'), Austrian security agency until 2021
CEDA	Confederación Nacional de Derechas Autónomas ('Confederation of the Autunomous Right'), Spain
Centre	HQ of the KGB, their predecessors and their successor SVR, previously Lubyanka, now Yasenevo a.k.a. Les ('Forest')
Cheka	Chrezvychainaya Komissiya ('Extraordinary Commission for Combating Counter-revolution and Sabotage')
CIA	Central Intelligence Agency, the Agency, USA
CNT	Confederación Nacional del Trabajo ('National Confederation of Labour'), Spain
Comintern	Communist International, also known as the Third International (1919–43)
CPGB	Communist Party of Great Britain
CPSU	Communist Party of the Soviet Union
CPUSA	Communist Party of the USA
CRIMINT	Criminal Intelligence
DDR	Deutsche Demokratische Republik ('German Democratic Republic'), East Germany
DEDIDE	Departamento Especial de Información del Estado, one of several Spanish Republican intelligence services
DGS	Dirección General de Seguridad ('Directorate General of Security'), Spain

DGSE   Direction Générale de la Sécurité Extérieure ('General Directorate for External Security'), foreign intelligence agency, France

DGSI   Direction Générale de la Sécurité Intérieure ('General Directorate for Internal Security'), French security agency responsible for counter-espionage, counter-terrorism, countering cybercrime and any other homeland security threats

DI   Defence Intelligence, military intelligence, part of the Ministry of Defence (since 2009), UK

DIS   Defence Intelligence Staff (1964–2009), successor of military intelligence (DMI), Air Intelligence (AI) and Naval Intelligence (NID), UK

DLB   dead letter box

DRG   Diversionno-razvedyvatelnaya gruppa ('sabotage and reconnaissance group'), USSR/RF

DSN   Direktion Staatsschutz und Nachrichtendienst ('Directorate for State Protection and Intelligence Service'), since 2021 – part of the General Directorate for Public Security of the Interior Ministry and successor to the BVT, Austria

DST   Direction de la Surveillance du Territoire ('Directorate of Territorial Surveillance'), French counter-intelligence and security service (1944–2008)

ECCI   Executive Committee of the Communist International – the governing authority of the Comintern between the World Congresses

ECHELON   Worldwide SIGINT collection and analysis programme operated by the NSA assisted by appropriate government agencies of Australia, Canada, New Zealand and the UK

ELINT   'Electronic intelligence', covert intelligence gathering by electronic means

EM   Estado Mayor ('General Staff'), Spain

FAI   Federación Anarquista Ibérica ('Iberian Anarchist Federation')

FBI   Federal Bureau of Investigations, the Bureau, USA

FCD   First Chief Directorate (see PGU), KGB's foreign intelligence branch

FCDO   Foreign, Commonwealth and Development Office, UK

FCO   Foreign and Commonwealth Office, UK (from 1968 to September 2020). It merged with the Department for International Development to create FCDO

FI   Fourth International, revolutionary socialist organisation of Trotskyists
FO   Foreign Office, UK
FSB   Federalnaya Sluzhba Bezopasnosti ('Federal Security Service'), RF
FSO   Federalnaya Sluzhba Okhrany ('Federal Protection Service'), RF
FVEY   The Five Eyes alliance is an intelligence-sharing agreement between Great Britain and the USA with Australia, Canada and New Zealand
GC&CS   Government Code and Cipher School, UK (until 1946)
GCHQ   Government Communications Headquarters, UK
GPU   Gosudarstvennoe Politicheskoe Upravlenie ('State Political Directorate'), USSR
GRU   Glavnoe Razvedupravlenie, Soviet and Russian Military Intelligence
GUGB   Glavnoe Upravlenie Gosudarstvennoi Bezopasnosti ('Chief Directorate of State Security'), USSR
GULAG   Glavnoe Upravlenie Lagerei ('Chief Directorate of Corrective Labour Camps')
GUPVO   Glavnoe Upravlenie Pogranichnoi i Vnutrennei Okhrany ('Chief Directorate of the Border Guards and Internal Troops')
HUMINT   Human intelligence (obtained from human sources)
ILS   International Lenin School, Moscow (1926–91)
INO   Inostrannyi Otdel ('Foreign Intelligence Department'), Cheka-OGPU, 1920–34
INS   Immigration and Naturalisation Service, USA
JIC   Joint Intelligence Committee, UK
Kempeitai   Military Police Corps, Japanese intelligence and counter-intelligence service
KGB   Komitet Gosudarstvennoi Bezopasnosti ('Committee for State Security'), USSR
KI   Komitet Informatsyi ('Committee of Information'), Soviet foreign intelligence agency
KIM   Kommunisticheskii International Molodiozhy ('Communist International of Youth')
KJVD   Kommunistischer Jugend Verband Deutschlands ('The Young Communist League of Germany')
KPD   Kommunistische Partei Deutschlands ('Communist Party of Germany')

KPÖ	Kommunistische Partei Österreichs ('Austrian Communist Party')
KRO	Kontr-razvedyvatelnyi otdel ('Counter-intelligence department'), OGPU, until 1930
KSČ	Komunistická strana Československa, Czech and Slovak Communist Party
KUNMZ	Kommunistichesky Universitet Natsionalnykh Menshinstv Zapada ('The Communist University of the National Minorities of the West')
MGB	Ministerstvo Gosudarstvennoi Bezopasnosti ('Ministry of State Security'), USSR
MI5	British security service
MI6	Alternative designation for SIS, British foreign intelligence service
MI1c	Secret Intelligence Service, predecessor of MI6
MID	Military Intelligence Division, until March 1942 under the General Staff of the US Army
MBP	Ministerstwo Bezpieczeństwa Publicznego, the Ministry of Public Security of Poland
MOPR	Mezhdunarodnaya Organisatsyia Pomoschi Rabochim ('International Workers Aid Organisation'), better known as International Red Aid, Comintern/USSR
MOTsR	Monarkhicheskaya Organisatsyia Tsentralnoi Rossii ('Monarchist Organisation of Central Russia')
MVD	Ministerstvo Vnutrennikh Del ('Ministry of Internal Affairs'), USSR
NCSC	National Cyber Security Centre, UK, established in 2016 as part of the GCHQ, located in London
NKGB	Narodnyi Komissariat Gosudarstvennoi Bezopasnosti ('People's Commissariat for State Security'), Soviet Russia
NKID	Narodnyi Komissariat Inostrannykh Del ('People's Commissariat for Foreign Affairs'), Soviet Russia
NKVD	Narodnyi Komissariat Vnutrennikh Del ('People's Commissariat for Internal Affairs'), Soviet Russia
NKVT	Narodnyi Komissariat Vneshnei Torgovli (People's Commissariat for Foreign Trade'), Soviet Russia
NSA	National Security Agency, USA
ÖGB	Österreichischer Gewerkschaftsbund ('Austrian Trade-Union Federation')
OGPU	Ob'edinennoe Glavnoe Politicheskoe Upravlenie ('Unified Main Political Directorate'), Soviet intelligence and security service, successor of the VcheKa

OKDVA	Osobaya Krasnoznamyonnaya Dalnevostochnaya Armiya ('Special Red-Banner Far Eastern Army'), Soviet Russia
Okhrana	Tsarist security service, Russian Empire, 1881–1917
OKW	Oberkommando der Wehrmacht, Supreme Command of the German Armed Forces
OKW/Chi	Oberkommando der Wehrmacht Chiffrierabteilung, Signal Intelligence Branch of the Supreme Command of the German Armed Forces
OMS	Otdel Mezhdunarodnykh Svyazei ('International Liaison Department'), the intelligence branch of the Comintern
OMSBON	Otdelnyi Motostrelkovyi Batalion Osobogo Naznacheniya ('Special Motorised Battalion'), NKVD
OSINT	Open-source intelligence, information collected from publicly-available sources
OSS	Office of Strategic Services, USA
OUN	Organisation of Ukrainian Nationalists
OVRA	Organizzazione per la Vigilanza e la Repressione dell'Antifascismo ('Organisation for Vigilance and Repression of Anti-Fascism'), Italy
PCE	Partido Comunista de España ('Spanish Communist Party')
PCF	Parti Communiste Français ('French Communist Party')
PCM	Partido Comunista Mexicano ('Mexican Communist Party')
POUM	Partido Obrero de Unificación Marxista ('Workers' Party of Marxist Unification'), Spain
PSOE	Partido Socialista Obrero Español ('Spanish Socialist Workers' Party')
PSUC	Partit Socialista Unifacat de Catalunya
RAF	Royal Air Force, UK
RF	Russian Federation
RKKA	Raboche-Krestyanskaya Krasnaya Armiya ('The Workers-Peasants Red Army'), Soviet Russia
RSDLP	Russian Special Democratic Labour Party, a socialist political party founded in March 1898 in Minsk, then part of the Russian Empire
RSHA	Reichssicherheitshauptamt, the Chief Directorate of Security of Nazi Germany
ROVS	Rossiisky Obschevoiskovoi Soyuz ('Russian Combined Services Union')
RU	Razvedupr, Soviet military intelligence, later GRU
RUSI	The Royal United Services Institute for Defence and Security Studies, a British think tank founded in 1831. At

	the time of writing RUSI was chaired by William Hague, Baron Hague of Richmond, who used to serve as Secretary of State for Foreign and Commonwealth Affairs (2010–14), with Vice Chairman Sir John Scarlett, former chairman of the Cabinet Office Joint Intelligence Committee (2001–04) and Chief of SIS (2004–09)
SAJ	Sozialistische Arbeiter-Jugend ('Socialist Workers Youth'), Austria, Germany
SB	Służba Bezpieczeństwa, Polish security and intelligence service
SBU	Sluzhba Bezpeky Ukrayiny, the Security Service of Ukraine
SCD	Second Chief Directorate, KGB's internal security branch
SDECE	Service de Documentation Extérieure et de Contre-Espionnage ('External Documentation and Counter-Espionage Service'), French foreign intelligence service, 1944–82
Second International	Organisation of socialist and labour parties (1889–1916)
SGON	Spetsyalnaya Gruppa Osobogo Naznacheniya ('Special Group for Special Purposes'), NKVD
SIGINT	Signals intelligence (derived from interception and analysis of signals)
SIM	Servicio de Información Militar, Spanish Republican military counter-intelligence service
SIS	Secret Intelligence Service, UK
SNK	Sovet Narodnykh Komissarov, Council of People's Commissars, Soviet Russia
SOCMINT	Social Media Intelligence
SOE	Special Operations Executive, UK
SPEKO	Spetsyalnyi kriptograficheskii otdel OGPU, Special Cryptographic Department
Spetsnaz	Special Forces, USSR/RF
SR	Socialist Revolutionary
SS	Sluzhba Svyazi ('Communication Service'), predecessor of the OMS
SS	Schutzstaffel, paramilitary organisation in Nazi Germany (1925–45)
SSOD	Soyuz Sovetskikh Obshchestv Druzhby i Kulturnoi Svyazi s Zarubezhnymi Stranami ('Union of Soviet Societies for Friendship and Cultural Relations with Foreign Countries'), KGB front

S&T	Scientific & Technical Intelligence
StaPo	Staatspolizei, Austrian security police (until 2002)
Stasi	Common name for MfS, Ministerium für Staatssicherheit ('Ministry for State Security'), DDR
StB	Státní bezpečnost, Czechoslovak security and intelligence service
SVR	Sluzhba Vneshnei Razvedki ('Foreign Intelligence Service of Russia'), also known by its Russian acronym as PGU
TUC	Trade Union Congress, UK
UGT	Unión General de Trabajadores ('General Union of Workers'), Spain
UKUSA	Originally the UK-USA agreement for joint signal intercept networks between the GCHQ and NSA at the beginning of the Cold War, it has developed into a multilateral agreement for cooperation in signals intelligence between the Five Eyes (FVEY)
ULTRA	Wartime signals intelligence obtained by breaking high-level encrypted enemy radio and teleprinter communications, GC&CS/UK
UME	Unión Militar Española ('Spanish Military Union')
UNIT 8200	Israeli equivalent of the British GCHQ and American NSA – a signals intelligence unit, part of Israeli Military Intelligence (Aman), that also controls cryptography and cryptanalysis. According to some experts, it is probably the foremost technical intelligence agency in the world
UPA	Ukraińska Powstańcza Armia ('The Ukrainian Insurgent Army')
VChKa	All-Russian Cheka, the immediate successor of the Cheka and predecessor of the GPU-OGPU
VOKS	Vsesoyuznoe Obschestvo Kulturnoi Svyazi (s zagranitsei), All-Union Society for Cultural Relations (with foreign countries), NKVD front
WOSTWAG	West-East-European Trade Exchange Joint Stock Society, legitimate trade organisation and Soviet military intelligence front with head office in Paris and branches in Berlin, New York, Ulan Bator, Guangzhou and Tientsin (Tianjin)
Z Organisation	Top-secret, semi-autonomous intelligence organisation within SIS, set up and headed by Lieutenant Colonel Claude Dansey, 1936–45

Transliteration of Russian Names

The author and the editors followed the method of transliteration of Russian, Belarusian and Ukrainian names used by the Joint Technical Language Service (JTLS), part of the British GCHQ, which is based on British Standard. British Standard 2979 (1958) is the main system of the Oxford University Press – see Anne Waddingham, *New Hart's Rules: The Oxford Style Guide* (OUP, 2014). In cases where a specific English version of names of well-known individuals and historical figures has become firmly established, we have in most cases retained that version, for example: Vasili (instead of Vasiliy or Vasily, see Vasili Mitrokhin), *Izvestia* (instead of *Izvestiya*), or Beria (instead of Beriya). At the same time, we have used Lugovoy (instead of 'Lugovoi') and Iosif (instead of 'Joseph') Stalin.

Preface

by Alan Judd

Boris Volodarsky's three earlier books, *Stalin's Agent*, *The KGB's Poison Factory* and *Assassins*, are rightly valued for their meticulous and revealing research into some of the murkiest waters of intelligence history. *Stalin's Agent*, indeed, is uniquely revealing of Russian intelligence activities in the 1930s, especially in the Spanish Civil War. Now, in this volume, the first of a planned six, Volodarsky takes a deep dive into parts of the ocean where no light has ever penetrated. True, many writers have written about the history of the KGB (a term used here as shorthand for Russia's security and intelligence apparatus from 1917) but few if any have combined the perspectives of a former practitioner with that of a Western academic. The result is probably as detailed a mapping of that hidden seabed as we are likely to get, short of the mass transfer of Russian archives to the British Library.

This volume takes the story from the revolution of October 1917 and the formation of the Cheka to Stalin's eviction of Trotsky from the Central Committee of the Communist Party, and from the Party itself, in November 1927. Volodarsky sensibly takes us back to the nineteenth-century origins of the Okhrana, secret police and protection service to successive Tsars, in order to compare and contrast with the Soviet Cheka that followed it. Comparisons are in order because some of the individuals and methods were simply carried over, but the contrasts are more striking. The Okhrana was probably the smallest of Tsarist government agencies, never numbering more than about 1,100 staff and 600 reporting agents. The Cheka, however, was baptised with Lenin's credo to establish 'a special system of organised violence' in order to bring about the dictatorship of the proletariat; mass surveillance and terror were not Stalin's inventions but were there from the start. Anyone contemplating President Putin's multi-layered security and intelligence apparatus now – the widely-known FSB, SVR and GRU, along with the lesser-known Presidential Security Service (about 3000), the Federal Protection Service (about 20,000 Kremlin troops) and the National Guard (340,000) – might recall what Gerry Adams of Sinn Fein ominously said of the IRA: 'They haven't gone away, you know.'

In charting the reactions of British governments in particular and Western governments in general to the Soviet Union in the 1920s, Volodarsky makes a plausible case for his judgment that there was significant over-reaction to the perceived threat from exported communist revolution, culminating in the infamous ARCOS raid on the Soviet Trade Delegation in London in 1927. He argues that early Comintern and Cheka operations overseas were more amateurish than their targets appreciated and that aspirations and intentions were often mistaken for achievements. Along the way he points out burrows and neglected byways where it would be tempting to spend more time – the remarkable similarity of phrasing, for instance, between Lenin's definition of subversion and that enshrined in Britain's Security Service Act of 1989, or the role of the Okhrana in propagating the anti-Semitic libel *The Protocols of the Elders of Zion*, or the likelihood or otherwise that Lenin died not of a stroke but of syphilis.

It would be an understatement to say that Volodarsky makes good use of his manifold sources, Russian and Western. Any student of this subject – or the period in general – will find in this volume valuable pointers to further research. He makes particularly good use of Christopher Andrew's work with Vasili Mitrokhin, a KGB archivist who defected to Britain with a treasure trove of notes from KGB files described by the FBI as 'the most complete and extensive intelligence ever received from any source'. *The Mitrokhin Archive*, along with the informed commentary of this volume, gives us the most complete picture of those early Chekist days we are likely to see for a very long time, if ever. If any contemporary Russian intelligence officers take an interest in their own history, they'll learn more here than they are permitted to know at home.

Foreword and Acknowledgements

Before the collapse of the Soviet empire, which, let us recall it again, the Russian President Vladimir Putin called 'the greatest geopolitical catastrophe of the century' at the end of his first term in office, the KGB had seemed to outsiders a deeply mysterious and fearful organisation. All Soviet governments, from Lenin to Gorbachev, intended it to be so. The first attempt to tell its 'inside story' to the Western world, to present a more or less comprehensive picture of its foreign operations, dates back to 1990.

The main problem confronting all historians who had tried to research the history of the KGB – including journalists and writers like Julian Semenov, Genrikh Borovik or Evgeny Vorobiov, especially hired to produce hagiographic portraits of its intelligence heroes – had been the total inaccessibility of the KGB archives. The efforts of Western scholars to interpret specific historical subjects related to the activities of Russian Intelligence Services (RIS) or to describe various RIS operations or personalities were based, with only a few exceptions, on books by Soviet defectors (usually ghostwritten) and memoirs of former British and sometimes other intelligence officers and agents. The first attempts to write some historical accounts of the KGB predecessors became obsolete even before they were published. The breakthrough came in 1986 when Professor Christopher Andrew of Cambridge University met a recent Soviet defector of whom he had never heard previously. Or so he says.

The circumstances of their first meeting remain unknown but Professor Andrew had always insisted that although this top-level defector – it was Oleg Gordievsky – actively collaborated with both MI6 and MI5, no one ever suggested that together they should write a book about the KGB. Their joint effort, the first ever history of the KGB 'from Lenin to Gorbachev', came out four years later on New Year's Eve 1990.

Of course, to get involved in such a project Oleg required encouragement and approval. His unique position as a former acting head of the KGB station in London and more, as a long-term British agent and accordingly a prime British intelligence asset within the KGB, secured him access to the very top of the British intelligence community. Gordievsky's first address was Sir Arthur Antony Duff, Director General of the Security Service whose office was at the 6th floor of a ten-storey building at 140 Gower Street also housing K and B Branches.

By the time the Prime Minister, Margaret Thatcher, decided to offer Sir Antony this post, he had been known to her as a war hero, ex-ambassador, former chairman of the Joint Intelligence Committee and Intelligence Coordinator in the Cabinet Office. In less than a month, on 20 February 1985, he would also be 65 – over the Service retirement age. Nevertheless, she decided he would be the best choice at least for a short period like two or two-and-a-half years.

Antony Duff remained in this post until January 1988 when he was succeeded by Patrick Walker (later Sir). During his time at the helm of the British Security Service, Sir Antony made at least two contributions to the history of the KGB: he supervised the successful running in London and the later exfiltration from Russia of Oleg Gordievsky, the most famous British double agent in the KGB. And, after Gordievsky's debriefing and resettlement were completed, a productive collaboration between the Soviet defector and the British professor resulted in the first-ever academic history of the Soviet secret service, which until the dissolution of the Soviet Union was combining under one roof a variety of services that are now independent agencies and organisations.

Gordievsky's long and intensive debriefing had not yet been finished when Christopher Andrew's important book, *Secret Service: The Making of the British Intelligence Community*, was published in October 1985. In it, in what Professor Andrew modestly calls 'an uncharacteristic moment of clairvoyance', he writes that after a famous double agent Oleg Penkovsky, who provided secret information from the GRU (Soviet military intelligence), there should be another, even more successful agent-in-place, this time in the KGB. The formalities over, the foundation was laid for a productive collaboration between a high-ranking KGB officer and a British academic. With Gordievsky's advice and knowledge and a little help from the Service and FCO historians, the first public history of the KGB in English was published.

It was a huge success and all of its 800 pages were quickly translated into Russian (not to mention other languages) and the book came out in Moscow unabridged in 1992. It was a symbolic year because in February Stella Rimington, then DDG, who had worked in all three branches of the Security Service and before her appointment visited Moscow to make the first, as she thought, friendly contact between the British secret services and the KGB, became Director General of MI5.

As it happens, the publication in Moscow of *KGB: The Inside Story* by Andrew and Gordievsky coincided with yet another important event in the history of this organisation which was initially planned as the sword and shield of the Bolshevik revolution. In 1992 the British SIS exfiltrated from Russia another defector whose presence in the West had remained secret for seven years. His name was Vasili Mitrokhin.

For almost 30 years Mitrokhin worked in the foreign intelligence archives of the KGB, and in 1972 supervised their move to the new headquarters in Yasenevo near Moscow. As a senior archivist, he had unrestricted access to the most secret documents and had a chance to copy, or make notes, from the files that hardly anyone had an opportunity to see or work with. The best that was available even for the highest-ranking KGB or party officials were brief summaries of selected cases. What became known as the Mitrokhin Archive, which extends from the Bolshevik revolution to the 1980s, was described as 'the most complete and extensive intelligence ever received from any source'. This may be an exaggeration, but not too far off.

With Mitrokhin, everything was played by the book. In October 1995 Andrew was invited to the SIS head office at Vauxhall Cross where probably none other than 'C', Sir David Spedding, himself briefed him on what he describes as one of the most remarkable intelligence coups of the late twentieth century. 'When I first saw Mitrokhin's archive a few weeks after the briefing,' Professor Andrew recalls, 'both its scope and secrecy took my breath away.'

Unsurprisingly, by the time Andrew's two volumes of *The Mitrokhin Archive* came out, his first KGB history published nine years earlier had become outdated. The book, which is still hailed in Russia as 'the most comprehensive history of the KGB from Lenin to Gorbachev', now seems obsolete, containing some erroneous claims, false facts and misleading statements. However, although a careful analysis of new sources available three decades after its publication (including copies made by Mitrokhin and the documents uncovered by the Russian society Memorial plus research undertaken by other authors) would show that while some details and names in the Andrew and Gordievsky KGB history are confused and tangled, it still has value and should not be dismissed outright. Suffice it to say that almost everything that Soviet and Russian intelligence officers and historians know about their own service comes from this book.

* * *

Like much else in the study of intelligence, the history of Soviet and Russian secret services, their internal and foreign operations and their influence on Russian policy-making require regular reassessment. Partly, it is because from time to time previously classified or even never heard of documents somehow find their way out of the archives into the public domain. In such cases, and this concerns all government records, one should be very careful in making conclusions because even primary sources and especially secret documents usually contain factual errors not to mention the occasional clanger, bias, misinterpretation or an intentional untruth of those who produce them. As a result, the interpretation of some secret doings can quickly coagulate in false patterns.

Sometimes, writers deprived of access to fresh facts and original documents tend to copy what others have written, though that may be largely guesswork, misinformation and speculation. It is like writing the history of the Dark Ages when few events were documented and most of the witnesses illiterate or incapable of or prevented from knowing, much less describing, the historical events or figures of their time. Any such surviving fragmentary detail gains value because no other is recorded, even though it may stem from ignorance or partisanship and by repetition it gains credibility and becomes history.[1] This is accidental deception, self-deception or delusion when someone is deceived but there was no intention to deceive.

Another story is purposeful deception. One example is the biography of the Soviet NKVD deserter who became known as 'General Alexander Orlov'. His heroic life was artfully fabricated by the KGB and presented to the world in a book written by the Soviet KGB Colonel Oleg Tsarev in collaboration with the British writer John Costello. This book, called *Deadly Illusions* (1993) and hailed as 'the first book from the KGB archives' with various subtitles like 'The KGB secrets the British government doesn't want you to read' (the UK edition) or 'The KGB Dossier Reveals Stalin's Master Spy' (the American edition), might be best of all described as 'The KGB secrets the KGB does want you to read', an expression coined by Donald Cameron Watt.

Contemporary historians tend to forget that Tsarev was a KGB operative working in London under the cover of a journalist and expelled from Britain in the early 1980s. He was then employed by the Press and Public Relations office of the KGB in Moscow. Costello was a British journalist and writer, who was neither able to speak nor read Russian but was willing to accept documents given to him by the KGB archivists at face value, expecting fame and fortune to follow. As one reviewer noted, 'the book is a joint work of a clever KGB hardliner and John Costello, about whose historical abilities perhaps the less I say the better'. Nevertheless, it became an international bestseller and is still being quoted as an indisputable source by many intelligence writers although it had long been exposed as a fake history, a KGB deception.

Another example is a no less famous book *The Crown Jewels*, published in the United Kingdom in 1998 by HarperCollins and in the United States a year later by Yale University Press. This is Tsarev's second book based on the precis from the KGB files and written in collaboration with a Western author, in this case Nigel West. D.C. Watt labelled the book 'spy faction' and Sheila Kerr contributed a long review to an academic journal entitled 'Oleg Tsarev's Synthetic KGB Gems' (for whatever reason forgetting to mention the British co-author).

In the interwar period, the earlier part of which (1917–27) is the main subject of this volume, there were several important defections of OGPU, Red Army and CPSU officials. Perhaps the most important and valuable of them was Georges Agabekov, a young man who at the peak of his Cheka-GPU/OGPU career used to serve as head of its Eastern Section. With his command of three languages, Armenian, Turkish and Farsi, Agabekov previously operated undercover in several republics of Central Asia, Afghanistan, Persia and the Near East, and was well informed about Soviet agent networks there as well as about the organisational structure and personnel of the OGPU, which combined the functions of Soviet political police and overseas intelligence agency. However, Agabekov was almost completely ignored by British secret services although he was eager to share his knowledge and published two excellent books about Soviet intelligence operations and agents in several countries. Seven years after his defection Agabekov, who had settled in Belgium, was murdered by Soviet agents.

Another Soviet intelligence agent, Walter Krivitsky, who defected in France in 1927, was also completely ignored by both the British and French secret services. Only after the Byelorussian-born American journalist and writer Isaac Don Levine presented Krivitsky to the world as a 'general and former chief of Soviet Military Intelligence in Western Europe' did he attract attention of MI5. On behalf of the defector, Don Levine wrote several articles published in the *Saturday Evening Post* and a book *In Stalin's Secret Service* (UK title – *I was Stalin's Agent*) that came out in November 1939. Krivitsky was not even able to read it, let alone correct factual errors and inventions scattered in the manuscript, because his English was very poor. Nevertheless, early in 1940 Krivitsky was secretly brought to the UK to testify. The first female officer of the Security Service, Jane Sissmore (after marriage known as Kathleen Archer), its main Soviet expert, interviewed Krivitsky at length at the Langham Hotel in Portland Place. 'Her interrogation of the Russian defector Walter Krivitsky,' according to the authorised history of MI5, 'was a model of its kind – the first really professional debriefing of a Soviet intelligence officer on either side of the Atlantic.'[2]

Giving due credit to Mrs Archer's skills, with the exception of one case 'Krivitsky's information on Soviet agents still operating in Britain was too muddled to make identification possible'.[3] That as a result of extensive debriefing not a single other Soviet agent was identified had been perfectly in line with the Service's policy of the day because as recently as January 1939, Vernon Kell, the DG, confidently declared that '[Russian] activity in England is non-existent, in terms of both intelligence and political subversion'.[4] By that time many Soviet spies (moles like Kim Philby and his Cambridge friends) had already penetrated all levels of the British political, economic and scientific establishments.

Seven decades later it turned out that another name mentioned by Krivitsky proved too sensitive to include in the report on his debriefing. Jane Archer, who drew up the report, assured her superiors that she had left out all references to a current SIS agent.

During an interview Krivitsky recalled that while working for SIS in the Netherlands, one Bill Hooper asked Han Pieck, a Soviet agent-recruiter in the Hague, to find him work with Soviet intelligence. William John 'Bill' Hooper, a British subject born in Rotterdam, had been listed as a secretary to the British Passport Control Office (PCO, a SIS front) there since at least December 1928 or earlier, having later moved with this office, headed by Ernest Dalton, to The Hague. His younger brother, Herbert 'Jack' Hooper, had been a member of the PCO staff from 1933 to 1937. Bill Hooper met Pieck in early 1935, and already on 30 January submitted a report on communism in Holland and Pieck. Hooper's statement to that effect had been duly written down and filed in October 1939.[5] As a result, Valentine Vivian, head of SIS Section V, as well as his successor had every reason to believe Hooper was acting in the Service's interests and were thus anxious that he should not be incriminated in Archer's report.

In August 1945, the new Director-General of MI5, Sir David Petrie, informed the Chief of MI6: 'With the exception of one incident involving rather serious indiscretions with a woman and a general tendency to high expense claims, I have had no trouble with Hooper and have no reason to suspect that he has been acting other than in the interests of this country. His work, which has been carefully supervised, has in fact been extremely good.'[6]

Hooper's MI5 file PF 48890/V1-4 was declassified and released to the National Archives in November 2017 (KV 2/4346-4349). Christopher Andrew commented that Hooper was the only MI5 and SIS officer who had also worked for both Soviet and German intelligence. Recent research suggests that Bill Hooper had actually been able to pull the wool over everybody's eyes, including the Dutch security service, the BVD.[7] Hooper's name and pre-war adventures, usually with numerous factual errors, are mentioned in many books like Ladislas Farago's *The Game of the Foxes* (1971) or Nigel West's *MI6: British Secret Intelligence Service Operations 1909-45* (1983 and 2019), although already in 1986 the Dutch maritime historian

Karel Bezemer wrote that 'from September 1939 he [Hooper] was re-employed [by SIS] and succeeded in being recruited as a paid agent by both the German and Soviet-Russian secret services, but forwarded important information to the British'.[8] When Hooper was recruited as an MI5 agent in 1941, Felix Cowgill, head of SIS Section V – counter-intelligence – 'said that, above everything, he [Cowgill] is certain that he [Hooper] is absolutely loyal'.[9] With this, Hooper's name is not even mentioned in the traditional back-of-the-book index of the official history of MI6.

When the authorised history of MI5 was published, it had not yet been definitely proved that almost everything that Krivitsky said to Mrs Archer was either hearsay or an invention, although both his MI5 and FBI files have long been declassified and available for public use. His biographer, Gary Kern, has also published Krivitsky's *MI5 Debriefing and Other Documents on Soviet Intelligence* (2014) as a separate book. Therefore, Christopher Andrew states, somewhat misleadingly, that 'despite Krivitsky's inability to provide clear leads during his debriefing to any current Soviet agents or intelligence personnel in Britain, he none the less transformed the Security Service's understanding of the nature and extent of Soviet intelligence operations'.[10] No wonder articles like 'Still Perplexed About Krivitsky' (Earl M. Hyde Jr) continue to appear in peer-reviewed academic journals.

* * *

Just like the history of the British Security Service, the first century of the KGB (with its multiple predecessors and successors) falls into six periods which reflect its changing priorities both in and outside of the former USSR and what remained of it after August 1991. Remarkably, the new Russian foreign intelligence service, the SVR, also decided to publish its history 'from the ancient times to 2005', Putin's second term as president. By accident or design, they have also packed it in six books probably because in numerology the number six represents service, both divine and human. Putin is a former KGB officer and the SVR was formerly the First Chief Directorate of the KGB, which after the collapse of the Soviet Union became a separate organisation. Its first director, Yevgeny Primakov (1991–96), headed the editorial board of this semi-official collection of essays praising Soviet spies and their agents. Although its authors, many of whom are former and serving intelligence officers, claim that their stories are based on the KGB documents, they are highly unreliable if not profoundly misleading.

This volume covers the first decade from the Bolshevik revolution of October 1917 and the formation of the Cheka, the Soviet political police, to the time Stalin was able to concentrate all political power in his own hands by first removing Trotsky, his main opponent, from the Central Committee and then expelling him from the Communist Party altogether in November 1927. For seven decades the KGB in its various incarnations acted as the sword and shield first of the Bolshevik revolution and then the Communist Party of the Soviet Union. Initially, it set out to defend the revolution and exercise the dictatorship of the proletariat over all other classes by forcefully supressing the 'exploiters and various bourgeois elements', which also meant the intelligentsia. Other important tasks were to identify and destroy counter-revolution within and outside, and secure the diplomatic recognition of the country. Following the civil war, other tasks facing the Soviet leadership were the post-war reconstruction of agriculture, industry and economy where the Cheka and its successors, the GPU and OGPU, had the lead role in counter-subversion and counter-espionage. This has always been understood as 'activities threatening the safety or well-being of the first socialist state and intended to undermine or overthrow the Soviet government by political, industrial or violent means'.[11] Today's FSB, which draws a direct line of descent from the Cheka, GPU, NKVD and the KGB's Second Chief Directorate still operating from the old Lubyanka headquarters, has an incomparably wider remit.

The resistance to the sovietisation in Central Asia and other places, massive peasant rebellions plus a perceived threat of another foreign intervention contributed to the continued militarisation of Soviet society leading to fierce debates on how to reorganise the Red Army after the civil war. The unconventional nature of this war created new criteria for military merit. Several of prominent Bolshevik and Red Army leaders, like Stalin and Kliment Voroshilov, emphasised revolutionary ideology and guerrilla warfare over professionalism and training. The main argument was that if Marxism had completely reconsidered the concept of war, revolutionary experience and ideological rectitude would far outweigh experience of the former Tsar's General Staff.

With all this a matter of debates at the 10th Party Congress (8–16 March 1921), the devastated Soviet economy could only support a small army of 562,000 men. Here, on the thorny issue of military discipline and party democracy, David Stone writes, 'various opposition groups urged a relatively independent and bottom-up network of Communists within the military, both as a means of checking any counter-revolutionary efforts by military specialists and combating the Bolshevik party's own tendencies to ossification and authoritarianism ... The practical solution was a strong and tightly controlled Political Directorate.'[12] Known in Russian as PUR, Political Directorate of the Revolutionary Military Council of the Repubic (RVSR), it was established in May 1919 but was soon subordinated to both the RVSR and the party leadership. Already in January 1921, within the newly created Secret-Operational Directorate (SOU) of the VCheka, functions of the Special Department (OO) were expanded to include 16th section headed by Yakov Agranov and responsible for counter-intelligence and security in the Red Army, and 17th section headed by Nikolai Kalinin for counter-espionage work among former Tsarist officers now serving in the Red Army. Thus, parallel to the Communist Party control of the armed forces through political commissars, the VCheka special departments (OOs) were established within all large military units to counter subversion, detect and thwart enemy espionage as well as monitor and combat political dissent.

Before official trade and diplomatic relations were established with the capitalist powers, the Cheka was neither able nor interested to send its officers abroad except on short missions. These missions were usually related to the activities of anti-Bolshevik White Guard organisations conspiring with and supported by Western intelligence services. After permanent Soviet representations were established in foreign countries, the Cheka's foreign department, the INO, started sending its most trusted and capable operatives either as 'illegals' or, more often, under diplomatic cover as members of the Soviet diplomatic missions. Their task was not what traditionally is understood as 'espionage', that is 'the process of obtaining information that is not normally publicly available, using human sources (agents) or technical means'. The aim of the illegals was to penetrate the White Guard organisations planning political or terrorist actions against the newly established USSR or its representatives. Those operating under legal cover concentrated all their efforts on learning the Western governments' and their secret services' plans directed against their country because of the war scare that swept the Soviet Union in late 1926 and 1927. 'The available data,' according to John Sontag, 'suggests both that in 1926 the Soviet government was genuinely concerned that the Western powers were planning forcible territorial changes in Eastern Europe and that subsequent events in 1927 intensified Moscow's fear.'[13] The whole work of the Cheka and INO was concentrated on either confirming or refuting those fears.

What in Britain, France and other countries became known as communist propaganda, subversion, sedition and even Soviet espionage was in reality the amateurish but enthusiastic work of the Comintern and its agents. The Comintern, of course, was under the full control of the CPSU leadership and its agents were often combining the tasks given to them by the OMS (the International Liaison Department of the ECCI) with the secret work for the INO and (G)RU. In their turn, officers and agents of the Cheka and (G)RU posted abroad often acted as the Comintern's OMS representatives which resulted in confusion and misunderstanding by Western security services who based their assessments of the adversary's actions and intentions on the activities of their own secret intelligence services. Such errors of judgement and false beliefs (delusions) were typical of British secret services (SIS, MI5 and Special Branch) in the interwar period. This misunderstanding, combined with the lack of reliable material and sometimes simple negligence, has been fully reflected in the works of many intelligence historians in both Great Britain and the USA. The task of a historian today will be to change established patterns thanks to the unprecedented before availability of primary and secondary sources.

* * *

It is always a great challenge to write a history of a secret service and it had been my dream for at least three decades to produce a new history of the KGB correcting many errors and misconceptions of previously published volumes. I have done my best to find and study all published and unpublished material in English, Russian, German and French pertinent to the topic. My private archive and 'files' include my personal interviews with Soviet defectors, Russian, British and American former and serving intelligence officers and sometimes their families and children. There are letters, emails and manuscripts, photos, copies of unclassified documents in addition to a selected impressive library of books and other secondary sources in many languages that I rely on in my research.

I thank everybody who helped me, but first of all my wife Valentina who has always been the first reader and critic of all my works. I am also extremely grateful to my late friend Pete – Dr Tennent H. Bagley, a former high-ranking CIA officer and scholar who had opened to me, albeit for only a few years, a complex world of American intelligence.

Cambridge Professor Christopher Andrew has been at the forefront of the study of intelligence for over 50 years. During this time, he has produced a series of landmark works that have transformed our knowledge and understanding of the role of intelligence, as correctly noted by Mark Phythian in an exclusive interview with Chris in July 2016 for *Intelligence and National Security*, the leading academic journal that Andrew had co-founded. Besides his most significant contribution to the development of intelligence studies, Professor Andrew's great achievement is his discovery of a 'missing dimension' of international history, an area of academic inquiry dealing with the role the intelligence plays in political decision making. But probably Andrew's greatest achievement so far is his magisterial work *The Secret World: A History of Intelligence* (2018), which is a kind of an intelligence Bible no one else would be able to write.

My history teacher, best adviser and academic supervisor is Professor Sir Paul Preston of the London School of Economics and Political Science. Paul is a unique historian, helpful friend and a great man whose books even dealing with such cruel and violent subjects as the Spanish Holocaust, civil war and betrayal are full of his genuine interest in the people he is writing about. A native-level Spanish speaker, Professor Preston is the leading world expert on the history of Spain, especially contemporary history. During his long academic career, Sir Paul has become not only an outstanding British historian, Fellow of the British Academy, but also a prominent and influential Spanish historian. Beyond his own published works, Paul's commitment to mentoring subsequent generations of academics helps to ensure a steady stream of important history books.

I am very grateful to William A. Tyrer, a Hollywood filmmaker and producer who in the course of his research also became a historian of the interwar Soviet operations in Europe and America. Having worked with the papers of Vasili Mitrokhin at the Churchill College Archive Centre in Cambridge, he was able to locate and share with me important archival material and documents pertaining to this book project.

The editorial, production and marketing team of my British publisher, Frontline Books, an imprint of Pen & Sword, deserve my special thanks. I must make particular mention of Martin Mace, the publisher and himself a military historian and author who has been involved in writing and publishing military history for more than two decades. I thank Martin for his courage and trust because it was his decision to commission the writing of a new history of the KGB from a single author. I am immensely grateful to Lisa Hooson with whom I have had fruitful collaboration over many years, as well as to John Grehan, Stephen Chumbley, Jon Wilkinson, Olivia Camozzi-Jones and many others who enthusiastically worked on this first volume and thanks to whose efforts this book has been born.

There are many other people – historians, academics, researchers, librarians and archivists – to all of whom I must express my profound gratitude, and I can't afford not to mention the names of Mark Dunton, Principal Records Specialist – Contemporary, The National Archives in Kew, Richmond, Surrey; Ingrid Tanzberger of the Austrian National Library and a small group of professional men and women in Moscow, London and Washington whose names unfortunately cannot be named here.

Albeit planned to be in six volumes, my brief history of the KGB, the name this sinister organisation – both Soviet secret political police, counter-intelligence and foreign intelligence service – had during the most interesting period of the Cold War (from March 1954 until it was officially dissolved on 3 December 1991), cannot pretend to give a full account of a true monster born by Lenin's fevered brain. Another monster was the Soviet state itself. With a history spanning over 100 years this is a difficult task for one person, especially what concerns its past two decades under Russian President Vladimir Putin when the KGB split into many agencies giving birth to new monsters like, for example, Rosgvardiya or Presidential Security Service (SBP), together about 350,000 secret agents who serve as Mr Putin's Praetorian Guard. My mission is to give scholars, researchers, journalists and students of intelligence better understanding of its organisational structure, personnel, secret operations, mentality and motivations that constitute a 'missing dimension' of international history otherwise little known, totally unknown or not properly understood. This is not so much to change history, but to make it a bit more precise.

Boris B. Volodarsky,
Vienna-London, December 2022

Introduction: From the Okhrana to the National Guard

Alexander II, the Emperor of Russia who was also the King of Poland and the Grand Duke of Finland, better known in Russia simply as the Tsar, created the first special security department after an assassination attempt in 1866. It was a small organisation located at Number 16 on Fontanka Quay in St Petersburg, then the capital of the Russian Empire. Nothing happened after another failed attempt in 1879 but following the third one, in August 1880, the Tsar created the Department of State Police within the Ministry of the Interior and transferred part of the Special Corps of Gendarmes and the Third Section of the Imperial Chancellery to the new body. This department had a unit known as the Special Section which dealt with political crimes and sensitive investigations. This Special Section, or *Osoby Otdel* (OO) in Russian, formally commanded the Okhrana, which is the short form of *Okhrannoe Otdelenie*, the division which became better known by its diminutive Okhranka with a subtle, sneering expression of contempt. Its official full name was the Department for Protecting Public Security and Order.

Created to combat political terrorism and left-wing political activity, the Okhrana operated in the whole territory of the Russian Empire that included Poland, Finland and large parts of Transcaucasia but contrary to the claims of many Soviet and satellite publications it was probably the smallest government agency. According to Aleksei Vassilyev, its last chief, the Okhrana never had more than a thousand men.[1] Its head office in St Petersburg had fewer than 200 employees and the Moscow branch was even smaller. It also had two overseas agencies or centres known as Zagranichnaya Agentura. The first and most important was in Paris, opened in June 1883, which also oversaw the less important Berlin, London, Geneva and Warsaw stations. The second was in Bucharest. Together the Paris and Bucharest offices ran all intelligence and counter-intelligence operations worldwide.

The Okhrana's first official representative in Paris was a secret agent of the police department by the name of Petr Vasilievich Korvin-Krukovsky (who had served with the rank of titular councillor in the Ministry of the

Interior).[2] To those not taken into his confidence, he was known as a reporter, playwright and translator. After marrying a French actress, Korvin-Krukovsky lived and worked in Paris representing the ultra-nationalist Sacred Squad, a short-lived Russian underground monarchist organisation. It was formed immediately following the assassination of the Russian Emperor Alexander II in March 1881 to counter revolutionary terrorism. Two years later, after the dissolution of the Squad, Petr Korvin-Krukovsky was appointed the first chief of the Zagranichnaya Agentura. Accused of unprofessionalism, negligence and embezzling money from the secret funds, he was dismissed in March 1884. His successor, Petr Rachkovsky, a former prosecutor sent to Paris on a special secret mission in January 1884, replaced him, taking over the Paris Centre on 20 May. For a while Korvin-Krukovsky continued to work for him as an auxiliary agent later moving to Angers in western France where he died in 1899.

Rachkovsky was given two rooms in a side wing of the Hôtel d'Estrées, the residence of the Russian Ambassador Baron Arthur von Mohrenheim at 79 rue de Grenelle, with a separate entrance. He employed two people as his assistants and they remained his only permanent staff for eight years. Rachkovsky, or, as he had been known in Parisian high society, Monsieur Pierre, was a colourful personality about whom a lot has been written,[3] but perhaps one of the most interesting discoveries back in 1999 was documentary evidence found in the Russian archives showing that the notorious anti-Semitic forgery known as *The Protocols of the Elders of Zion* was the work of one of Rachkovsky's agents in Paris, of which there had been suspicions all along.

Matvei Golovinsky, the opportunistic scion of an aristocratic family and a former law student, joined the Holy Brotherhood, an anti-Semitic secret society which used forgery as a tool against the revolutionaries, publishing phoney newspapers and political tracts. His active role there got him a job in the government press department where Golovinsky acted as a spin doctor, placing articles in compliant newspapers and paying fees to journalists with ingrained 'habits of obedience'. Uncovered and publicly denounced as an informer, he moved to Paris and got in touch with Rachkovsky who used him to plant *The Protocols* in the French press. They were later sent as the genuine stuff to General Peter Orzhevsky, Commander of the Special Corps of Gendarmes and Deputy Minister of the Interior, beginning their inglorious journey around the world despite having been exposed as a 'base forgery' and a 'recrudescence of medieval bigotry and stupidity'. And despite the definitive scholarly debunking of *The Protocols* already in the early 1920s, it became perhaps the most influential forgery of the twentieth century.

During his 18 years at the helm of the Paris Centre of the Okhrana, Rachkovsky actively used against the revolutionary émigrés all fundamental counter-intelligence methods that the KGB later employed and all its successors in modern Russia continue to use.[4] Like the Okhrana within the Russian Empire, its centres and outposts abroad practised 'external surveillance' by hiring local plainclothes detectives, paying maîtres d'hôtel, concierges and cab drivers, and getting access to the local security services' files. Two other favourite methods were penetration by recruiting informers or sending penetration agents, and the use of agent provocateurs. The definition comes from French meaning 'inciting', somebody who provokes, persuades or encourages others to act in a violent or unlawful way. Among well-known examples is the blowing up of the printing shop in Geneva used by the Russian terrorist anti-government organisation Narodnaya Volya (People's Will), which the Rachkovsky agents succeeded looking like the work of disaffected revolutionaries. Another provocation was the unmasking of a bomb-making conspiracy by Russian émigrés in Paris.

The agent provocateur who played the leading role in this operation was known among the conspirators as Abraham Landezen, born in the Pinsk province of White Russia as Avraam-Aron Heckelmann. A student in St Petersburg, he was arrested for taking part in Narodnaya Volya underground political activities and recruited as a police informer. In 1890 Landezen was one of the organisers of the factory for the production of improvised explosive devices in Paris. When the bombs were ready and hidden in the premises rented by the plotters, on Rachkovsky's instructions Landezen informed the Sûreté and twenty-seven members of the organisation were arrested. Among others, he was also sentenced by a Paris tribunal to five years imprisonment as a terrorist, but managed to escape abroad. In 1893 he was baptised in the St Elizabeth's Russian Orthodox Church in Wiesbaden and became Arkady Mikhailovich Heckelmann, changing his family name to Harting and his place of birth to St Petersburg three years later.

Arkady Mikhailovich Harting (spelt Garting in Russian) made a dizzying career ascent from moonlighting as a confidential police informant, known as a seksot in Russian, to becoming a royal guard accompanying Nikolai Aleksandrovich Romanov to Coburg in Germany where the future Tsar Nicholas II proposed to Princess Alix of Hesse-Darmstadt. Later, in charge of the royal protection detail, Harting travelled with the Tsar and his family to Europe and Scandinavia, also visiting England and France. Starting from December 1900, he headed the Berlin station and then, in August 1905, was transferred to assume control of the Paris Centre of the Okhrana. Four years later, thanks to the information provided by an Okhrana defector, he was uncovered by Russian revolutionaries. On Thursday, 1 July 1909, Vladimir Burtsev wrote to the French Minister of Justice Aristide Briand (who would soon succeed Clemenceau as prime minister):

I have the honour to inform you of the following. In 1890 a certain Landezen, real name Gekkel'man, was sentenced *in absentia* by a French Court to five years in prison for his role as organiser of a dynamite plot. At that time I had been acquainted with Landezen for a year. I now wish to inform you that the individual calling himself Garting, aka Petrovsky, Beire etc. who is currently living in Paris, who is personally acquainted with M. Hamard, Head of the Sûreté, with M. Ruichard [*sic*] and with many other high-ranking officials, and who currently holds the post of Head of the Russian secret police in Paris is, in reality, none other than said Landezen, of which fact I can supply proof. I therefore ask that you issue an order for the arrest of the said Landezen-Garting-Petrovsky-Beire. I am at your service and willing and ready to supply evidence.[5]

The story broke for the first time a week later on the front pages of *L'Humanité*, at the time the paper of the SFIO (Section française de l'Internationale ouvrière), a political party founded by Jean Jaurès, a French socialist leader. The scandal quickly reached Russia and was reported, as it was said, 'in some detail and with a certain degree of balance'. The London *Times* also decided to react, describing Burtsev as 'the revolutionary writer who is daily filling the columns of the sensational press' and stressing that 'whatever antecedents of this mysterious personage [Harting] may have been, he rendered good service in the office to which he was appointed by the police authorities'.[6]

Nevertheless, the effect of this exposure resonated through Europe. In France, the National Assembly voted unanimously to stop such criminal activities and to expel all foreign police representatives. In Britain, the issue was raised in the House of Commons by a Labour MP, who demanded that the Liberal government put an end to the unwholesome practices of secret policemen. In Paris, Burtsev received wide acclaim and in their version of the story *Le Journal* described him as the 'Sherlock Holmes de la revolution russe' – a sobriquet which would stick to him for the rest of his life.[7]

While the scandal was unfolding, Harting was in Brussels preparing for the Tsar's state visit to France, thus evading arrest. He was hurriedly recalled to Russia, narrowly missing the opportunity to be awarded the Legion of Honour to which he had been admitted.[8] Promoted to Actual (Deistvitelny) State Councillor, a civil rank equal to those of Major General in the Army or Rear Admiral in the Navy, in 1913, during the First World War he served as head of Russian counter-intelligence in France and Belgium. Together with his wife, a very wealthy Belgian woman from Liège, after the war Harting returned to Brussels where he permanently settled, suddenly becoming a banker. What happened to him later is unknown.

When back in 1900 the Prussian Secret Police (Geheimpolizei) was initially approached about developing permanent liaison with the Okhrana, they hesitated until it was officially announced that the Berlin station would be headed by Harting, a person close to the Tsar. And indeed, as one historian notes, they never regretted it because, after having settled down at the number 4 on Friedrichstrasse opposite a nice park, Harting never forgot that a little extra inducement might result in a more conscientious approach to his needs on the part of his German colleagues. This tactic never failed and a well-bribed German police commissioner did his best to keep tabs on the Russian anarchists and revolutionaries. Altogether, Harting maintained in Germany some half-dozen penetration agents, his best man being Jacob Zhitomirsky who, as a student at Berlin University collaborated with the local police before he was picked up by the Okhrana in 1902. Zhitomirsky (party alias 'Otsov', Okhrana aliases 'André and 'Daudet') was able to get into the confidence of the Leninist revolutionary party group, where he was active until 1907, when the German authorities expelled them and he moved to France reporting to Harting. In May, Zhitomirsky, by that time a close associate of Lenin, attended the 5th Party Congress in London. When he was finally uncovered by Burtsev as a police infiltrator, Zhitomirsky managed to escape to South America.

One of Harting's major contributions to counter-intelligence was the introduction of a personal filing system on all revolutionaries and political suspects and a reference catalogue for operational planning, verification of data and intelligence reporting. And it was in Belgium after Harting's marriage, the CIA report states, that the Okhrana developed the most comprehensive exchange of information with the Belgian Sûreté Générale that lasted until the outbreak of war in 1914. According to the CIA estimates, by the end of 1908, the Okhrana Paris Centre had over forty men and women placed in Russian revolutionary organisations abroad.[9] Harting's penetration operations became a classic that would be studied in detail in the KGB High School.

However, by far the greatest success was achieved in Russia with the recruitment of Roman Malinovsky as a seksot. In June 1912, Stepan Beletsky, director of the Interior Ministry's Department of Police, flatly ordered that every union of workers in the country must have a secret police informant. Malinovsky, a Russified Pole, would become his most prized possession. He had a criminal record, having served a prison term for burglary. Upon his release Malinovsky joined the workers' movement and became the founder and later secretary of the St Petersburg Metal Workers' Union. To protect his connection with the St Petersburg police, he was arrested on a specious pretext and 'exiled' to Moscow, where his personal case officer was the chief of the Okhrana Pavel Zavarzin.

The Okhrana instructed Malinovsky to join Lenin's Bolsheviks and he was soon elected to the Moscow party committee and then nominated as a candidate for election to the State Duma. In January 1912 with Lenin's support he joined the Central Committee at the Prague Party Conference and in autumn was elected to the Duma. After the Prague conference Lenin decided to take over the popular newspaper *Pravda* making it the party's official and legal mouthpiece and moving its editorial board from Vienna, where it had been edited by Trotsky, to St Petersburg. When the first issue under Lenin's leadership was published on 22 April (New Style: 5 May) 1912, one of its editors was an Okhrana agent Miron Chernomazov while Malinovsky was involved, albeit briefly, in the business side of the paper's operation.[10]

With his election to the State Duma and especially after he became a member of the Central Committee of the Bolshevik party, the historians of the Petersburg Okhranka write, 'Beletsky had assumed personal control of Malinovsky and met him in the private dining-rooms of the most expensive restaurants', reviewing his agent's speeches, the drafts of some of which had been written by Lenin. For two years Malinovsky had remained the principal spokesman for the Leninist group in Russia, also leading the Bolshevik faction in the Duma.[11] On 4 May 1914, still a fully-fledged agent, Malinovsky suddenly resigned and left Russia with a 6,000-rouble annual pension (the average salary of a worker was about 300 roubles a year). After the Bolshevik revolution he suddenly returned to Russia and after a brief trial was executed by firing squad in November 1918.

The Paris Centre did not limit itself to collection of information on revolutionary suspects. It also pioneered a wide variety of what the KGB later called 'active measures',[12] a system of distribution of false or misleading information as well as black propaganda, better known today as covert psychological operations or psychological warfare, designed to influence foreign governments and public opinion both in its own country and abroad. Rachkovsky routinely paid French journalists like Gaston Calmette from *Le Figaro*, Charles Maurras, an organiser and principal philosopher of Action Française, and even Jules Hansen, an international mediator, lobbyist, writer and journalist of Danish descent, for pro-Russian articles and reviews. In the first decades of the twenty-first century this developed into the Kremlin's persistent attempts to use its secret services in covert operations 'to influence the world by unseen means – the hidden hand'.[13] This is exactly what Christopher Andrew and other leading intelligence historians describe as the 'missing dimension' to most studies of international relations and diplomacy.

The chiefs of Zagranichnaya Agentura were also active in foreign policy matters. Rachkovsky was a committed advocate of an alliance with France, diplomatically isolated after her defeat in the Franco-Prussian War. He was regularly used as secret intermediary in negotiations for the Franco-Russian Dual Alliance in 1891–4, establishing what became later known as a back channel between Western governments and Russia. In the autumn of 1891, he was as usual summoned to Fredensborg during the Tsar's annual vacation at the palace of his mother-in-law, the Queen of Denmark, to act as head of royal protection and security, when his agent Jules Hansen arrived.

Born in Denmark as Jens Julius 'Jules' Hansen (nicknamed 'Shrew'), since March 1864 he had been used as a Danish agent of influence in France, later becoming a French national and getting the diplomatic rank of embassy counsellor. Hansen played a role during negotiations between Denmark, Prussia and France and from 1890 between France and Russia. When he met Rachkovsky in the Fredensborg Palace in September 1891, he had with him a secret letter from the French Prime Minister and at the same time Minister of War, Charles de Freycinet, proposing close military consultations between France and Russia.[14] With all this in mind, the most important contribution by the Okhrana to the making of Tsarist foreign policy was, according to a historian, its pioneering role in the development of signals intelligence (SIGINT) 'derived from intercepting and where possible decrypting other governments' communications'.[15]

The back channel, first established by the Tsarist secret police at the end of the nineteenth century, would be successfully used for secret contacts between Soviet officials and foreign governments outside of the formal diplomatic machinery. Some scholars call it the black market of negotiations.[16] It is still used by the Kremlin today. A good example of such clandestine diplomacy was an unprecedented visit to Washington of the directors of three Russian secret services – SVR, FSB and GRU – in January 2018. Two of them, Naryshkin of the foreign intelligence service (SVR) and General Korobov of the military intelligence directorate (GRU), were among several Russian officials barred from entering the US under existing sanctions. So far, a series of guesses and speculations about the reasons and possible results of their visit has led to nothing.

With three 'official' secret services in the front line, another three truly clandestine Russian services usually remain in the shadow. These are the FSO, SPB and the National Guard of Russia (Rosgvardiya). One common element among them is the political figure who personifies the meaning of their existence. It is the President of Russia Vladimir Putin. Never since the new Russian Emperor, Nicholas I, established the office of the Chief of Gendarmes in July 1826 and appointed a Baltic German cavalry general Count Alexander von Benckendorff to head it, had there existed such a multilevel security architecture and personal protection service for the country's leader.

Shortly after a group of insurgent officers and their sympathisers supported by some 3,000 soldiers rebelled a few months before in what became known as the Revolt of the Decembrists, the Tsar formed two comparatively small law enforcement and state security organisations – gendarmerie units of the Special Corps of the Internal Guard (a decade later transformed into the Special Corps of Gendarmes), and the Third Section of the Imperial Chancellery, both under Benckendorff. Since its formation, only the most competent and well-educated army officers with noble titles could be appointed to the Corps of Gendarmes.

In Soviet Russia it was all different of course and a worker-peasant pedigree was essential for any civil servant or bureaucrat but even more so for a member of the communist secret police, Lenin's Cheka, not to mention the Red (body)Guards protecting new rulers of the new Russia.

After the collapse and disintegration of the Soviet Union, the first commander and actual founder of the Presidential Security Service of the new Russia was Alexander Korzhakov, the son of a factory worker and a weaver. After his compulsory military service which he spent in the ranks of the Kremlin Regiment, Korzhakov was recruited to the 9th Directorate of the KGB that specialised in personal security providing close protection to the top party and government officials. He was lucky to become one of Boris Yeltsin's personal bodyguards when the latter headed the Moscow (Communist) Party committee. When Yeltsin became the President of Russia, Korzhakov was appointed head of his security service.

In a rather short period of time, from September 1991 to June 1996, this man managed to become one of the most influential figures in the country, a puppeteer with enormous powers. Remarkably, as the years went by, Korzhakov more and more resembled an overweight male shrew still capable of delivering a venomous bite. His role model was Nikolai Vlasik who had headed Stalin's personal security for over 20 years. Like Vlasik, Korzhakov was dismissed from the service with the rank of lieutenant general, now writing books and even getting small parts in movies.

Among Korzhakov's presidential security team during Yeltsin's first term was one Victor Zolotov, who could be spotted among Yeltsin's close protection detail during the tumultuous days of the August 1991 putsch. Very much like his former boss and predecessor as head of the SBP, Zolotov came from a working-class family. A low-skilled steelworker before he was drafted into the army, Zolotov was recruited to the KGB serving in the 9th Directorate as a member of the protection division. Sent by Korzhakov to Leningrad, later St Petersburg, to guard the city's first post-Soviet mayor, Zolotov became close to two individuals who would play a decisive role in his life. One of them was Vladimir Putin, the mayor's adviser on external and international affairs. Another was a man named Roman Tsepov.

Together with Putin, Zolotov moved to the Kremlin and from May 2000 assumed control of the Presidential Security Service (SPB) at the same time being appointed deputy director of the Federal Protective Service (FSO) while remaining President Putin's personal bodyguard. He kept this position through all Putin's reigns well into the third presidential term, justifying his success with competence. Zolotov's security officers became semi-jokingly known as 'Men in Black' but not because, like in the popular American comic book series or science fiction action comedy, they were dressed in black suits and wore sunglasses. No. But these non-uniformed government agents have licence to harass, threaten or assassinate anybody who stands in Putin's way. On 5 April 2016, General of the Army Zolotov was appointed Director of the National Guard of Russia and a week later became a permanent member of the Security Council.

Alas poor Yorick! Count Benckendorff could not even dream of such power. From a rank-and-file member of a small close protection team to the head of the SBP with about 3,000 personnel and the FSO controlling some 20,000 Kremlin troops, and from there to the director of the National Guard having over 340,000 elite forces under his command, Zolotov's is an impressive feat. To compare, the Third Section of His Imperial Majesty's Chancellery under Benckendorff had sixteen junior officers in four tiny departments called 'expeditions', and only seventy-two before it was closed down in 1880;[17] the Special Corps of Gendarmes responsible for law enforcement and state security employed about 5,200 men; and the Okhrana total staff was never more than 1,100 with 200 agents at headquarters in St Petersburg. According to recent research, only 600 informants reported to the Okhrana at any one time.[18]

A quarter of a century ago, the newly formed Foreign Intelligence Service of Russia (SVR) issued a compact disc with the title *Russian Foreign Intelligence: VChK (Cheka)-KGB-SVR*, which claimed to give 'for the first time … a professional view on the history and development of one of the most powerful secret services in the world'. Professor Andrew later commented that 'nothing better illustrates the continuity between the Soviet and Russian foreign intelligence services than the attempt by the SVR to reclaim its KGB past'.[19] In the first decades of the twenty-first century the situation appears somewhat remote from past experience.

In Putin's Russia all is different. The current director of the SVR is the former head of the Presidential Administration under Medvedev, formerly Putin's campaign manager. The director of the FSB is the former chief of the Leningrad KGB directorate where Putin used to serve. The leading Kremlin hawk, the secretary of the Security Council is a former FSB director and former Putin's Leningrad KGB colleague while the deputy chairman of the

Security Council is Medvedev, formerly Putin's short-term substitute as President of Russia. The real power in Russia today is in the hands of the most devoted and trusted men around the national leader. Putin's personal friends and bodyguards have become the Golden Circle, the new King's Men,[20] the biggest private landowners and dollar billionaires who usually do not figure in the *Forbes* lists. Ye are the salt of the Russian earth, the new Russian 'nobility' and chieftains of the underground economy. Exactly as predicted in their old anthem, 'They have been naught–they shall be all'.[21] The only question is for how long.

ПРИКАЗ

Всероссийской Чрезвычайной Комиссии
№ 169.

Москва 20-го Декабря 1920 г

§ 1

1   Иностранный Отдел Особого Отдела ВЧК расформировать и организовать Иностранный Отдел ВЧК

2   Всех сотрудников, инвентарь и дела Иностранному Отделу ООВЧК передать в распоряжение вновь организуемого Иностранного Отдела ВЧК

3. Иностранный Отдел ВЧК подчинить Начальнику Особотдела тов. **Менжинскому.**

4   Врид Начальником Иностранного Отдела ВЧК назначается тов **Давыдов,** которому в недельный срок представить на утверждение Президиума штаты Иностранного Отдела

5   С опубликованием настоящего приказа все сношения с за границей, Наркоминделом, Наркомвнешторгом, Центроэваком и Бюро Коминтерна всем Отделам ВЧК производить только через Иностранный Отдел

Председатель ВЧК **ДЗЕРЖИНСКИЙ**

Сов.Секретно.

Тов. ДЗержинскому лично.

ПОЛОЖЕНИЕ

О

ЗАКОРДОННОЙ ЧАСТИ ИНОСОУГПУ.

А.

Зарубежная работа.

I.Общие положения.

1/ Закордонная часть ИНОГПУ является организационным центром, сосредотачивающим все руководство и управление зарубежной работой разведывательного и контр-разведывательного характера, проводимой Г.П.У.

III. Система организации.

I. Для выполнения всех вышеизложенных задач заграницей в определенных пунктах по схеме, вырабатываемой Закордонною Частью ИНО Г.П.У., имеют местопребывание уполномоченные, именующиеся - р е з и д е н т а м и.

НАЧЕНОГПУ:

Chapter 1

Origins of the Cheka

Six weeks after the October Revolution, on 7 December 1917,[1] a working group of seven prominent Bolsheviks under the chairmanship of Felix Dzerzhinsky (Feliks Dzierżyński in his native Polish), a professional revolutionary Marxist, gathered at Number 2 Gorokhovaya Street in Petrograd, now St Petersburg. Their leader came from a middle-class Polish-Jewish family. First arrested for his revolutionary activities at the age of 20, Felix would spend most of his early years behind bars, having only been freed from jail after the February Revolution of 1917.

The business at hand was the creation of the Extraordinary Commission copying a similar body set up by the Provisional Government only two days after the abdication of Nicholas II. That first pre-Bolshevik Commission, announced on 4 March, was a working group initially called the Supreme Investigatory Commission. It became better known as the Extraordinary Commission and was officially charged with 'the investigation of malfeasance in office of former ministers, chief administrators, and other persons in high offices of both the civil and the military and naval services'.[2] The objective of the Provisional Government's Extraordinary Commission was to investigate the use of provocateurs such as Evno Azef, the censorship of the press and the interception of private mail, ministerial incompetence and corruption during the war and many other things. As one of its historians noted, 'judicial legality rather than a desire for revolutionary vengeance governed its proceedings'.[3] With the new Bolshevik Extraordinary Commission, the Cheka, it was vice versa.

The address on Gorokhovaya Street was not chosen at random. It was a solid house built in the eighteenth century for Baron von Vietinghoff-Scheel, after his death turned into St Petersburg City Gradonachalstvo (Municipality), which then housed the City Police Administration. At the time of that memorable meeting in December 1917, Dzerzhinsky was sitting at a massive wooden desk with a green leather top that once belonged to Vyacheslav von Plehve, Minister of the Interior, whose horse-drawn coach had been blown apart by a terrorist bomb.[4] Several decades later, in 1974, this meeting room would be turned into an improvised museum of the Cheka's first days. After the collapse of the Soviet Union the building was refurbished and a small exhibition space on the first floor became the Museum of the History of the Russian Political Police, part of the much larger Political History Museum. The Gorokhovaya-2 branch of the museum, the Cheka commemorative room, was closed down in November 2019.

Eight revolutionaries gathered in the former office of the police chief following Lenin's request to Dzerzhinsky to propose a decree 'On measures to combat counter-revolutionary saboteurs' to be adopted at the Council of People's Commissars (or Sovnarkom, as the first Bolshevik government was known) meeting that evening. The draft had been written by Lenin who had also served as the Sovnarkom chairman. Apart from Dzerzhinsky, the others were Ivan Ksenofontov, Vasily Averin, Grigory 'Sergo' Ordzhonikidze, Karl Peterson (Kārlis Pētersons), Jacob Peters (Jēkabs Peterss), Dmitry Yevseyev and Valentin Trifonov.

Ksenofontov would be later promoted to Cheka deputy chairman in charge of the special tribunal, taking an active part in the violent crackdown on the open rebellion of the Red sailors from the naval base of Kronstadt against the Bolshevik government in March 1921, also called the Kronstadt Mutiny. Like Dzerzhinsky, Ksenofontov would die in 1926. The Red Army units suppressing the uprising were commanded by the 28-year-old former Tsarist officer Mikhail Tukhachevsky, who once shared a German prison cell with a French captain by the name of Charles de Gaulle. Because his soldiers showed great sympathy with the protesters, Tukhachevsky had to rely on the cadets, Cheka and the Red Guard troops. Russian historians still fail to produce exact figures for the casualties but it is estimated that among the rebels there were around 600 dead, 1,000 wounded and 2,500 prisoners,[5] most of them shot on the spot with or without trial.

Averin, a country boy like most of them, after December 1917 would serve as a member of the Cheka Collegium and later Commissar for Internal Affairs of Ukraine, member of the Central Party Committee, and Commissioner of the Defence Council of Ukraine to combat counter-revolution and banditry. Before his arrest in October 1937, Averin had been heading the Lena River Shipping Company in Yakutsk. Sentenced to 25 years as 'the enemy of the people', he died in the GULAG in 1945.

Sergo Ordzhonikidze, a Georgian Bolshevik, came of an impoverished noble family and joined the Russian Social Democratic Labour Party in 1903 at the age of 17. For the next few years he was mostly involved in the underground work for the Bolshevik faction of the party, during which time he was arrested several times and had to flee abroad to avoid trial. Imprisoned again upon his return, he knew little of the world and was quite unaware of his own extraordinary luck when in October 1907 he shared a prison cell with a fellow Georgian revolutionary named Ioseb Jughashvili (the future

Stalin). After his fourth arrest, the Bolsheviks reassigned him to Persia where they hoped to launch a revolution.

Since August 1907, this large area which also included Afghanistan and Tibet was divided by the Anglo-Russian Convention into northern and southern Persia, the latter recognised by Russia as part of the British sphere of interests. The Germans, in turn, hoped to create a wedge between Russia and Britain and established their Intelligence Bureau for the East to dismantle the Anglo-Russian Entente. The Bolsheviks were unable to gain sufficient support in Persia and Ordzhonikidze returned to Baku, 'the city of oil wells', the present capital and commercial hub of Azerbaijan. In 1911 he travelled to France where he attended lectures at the Longjumeau Party School founded by Lenin in the small town of Longjumeau near Paris. At the time of the revolution, when the Bolsheviks seized power in October 1917, Ordzhonikidze was in Petrograd. In the 1920s and 1930s, Sergo chaired the Central Control Commission of the party and was promoted to lead the Workers' and Peasants' Inspectorate (to ensure the proper functioning of Soviet economy), moving to Moscow where he was soon elected a member of the Politburo at the same time serving as People's Commissar of Heavy Industry. He shot himself in Moscow in February 1937 for reasons never properly explained.

Peterson, a member of the Red Latvian Riflemen reserve from Riga, with an unfinished secondary education but exemplary revolutionary background, after five months in the Cheka was appointed political commissar of the Latvian division. For the next five years, from 1921 to his death from tuberculosis, Peterson served as the People's Commissariat for Foreign Affairs' plenipotentiary in Novorossiysk, the country's main port on the Black Sea.

Peters, the son of a Latvian farm worker, accused of the attempted murder of a factory director, was arrested shortly after his 20th birthday. Acquitted by the Riga military court, he emigrated to England and in London joined a group of Latvian Social Democrats also becoming a member of the British Socialist Party. The BSP was a Marxist organisation which later joined forces with the communists to establish the Communist Party of Great Britain (CPGB). One of the leading figures there was Theodore (actually Fedor Aronovich) Rothstein, a Russian émigré, British journalist and close comrade of Lenin. In London Peters worked as a tailor's presser. Arrested just before Christmas 1910 on suspicion of the Houndsditch murders when three City of London Police officers were shot dead whilst trying to prevent a burglary at a jeweller's in Houndsditch, he remanded in custody but was acquitted.[6] In 1916 Peters married the daughter of a London banker but in May 1917 returned to Russia alone. Having moved to Petrograd later that year, he actively participated in the October Revolution. After the Cheka was established, he served as its deputy chairman and briefly, in July–August 1918, as acting chairman. Peters participated in the fast-track investigation of the so-called Lockhart plot, the Cheka's swoop on a group of Western diplomats including Robert Bruce Lockhart appointed as Britain's unofficial envoy to the Bolshevik regime, and in several Red Terror campaigns against counter-revolutionaries.[7] When his British wife and daughter joined him in Petrograd, they found out Peters had taken up with another woman and started another family. During the Great Purge he was arrested as a member of what they called the Latvian espionage ring and executed by the NKVD in April 1938. His English daughter was not allowed to return to the UK and died in the Soviet Union.

Among the Cheka founders, Yevseyev was one of the youngest. Coming from a family of a low-paid worker and with an uncompleted primary education, he became a trade-union leader arrested for revolutionary activities in 1915 and exiled to Siberia. Yevseyev moved to Petrograd in the spring of 1917 and in October, as a member of the revolutionary-military council, took part in street fighting against anti-revolutionary forces, mainly young cadets, known as 'junkers' in Imperial Russia after the German 'Junker' or junger Herr. In December, shortly after his 25th birthday, Yevseyev became one of the members of the Cheka Collegium and was appointed Dzerzhinsky's deputy at the same time serving at the corps headquarters of the Cheka troops. From March to August 1918, he had briefly headed several Cheka departments and from September moved to serve with the Cheka troops. In spite of his lack of any basic education, Yevseyev was accepted to the Red Army Academy where he studied intermittently, finally graduating in January 1922. Having never been engaged in trade or any business, after a brief spell in a cotton trust he was sent to Berlin as a member of the WOSTWAG board. WOSTWAG stood for West-Osteuropäische Warenaustausch Gesellschaft (West-East European Trading Company Ltd, later a public corporation or AG) established in 1922 in Berlin as a front for the Russian Intelligence Services (RIS). Its 'trading' primarily concentrated on illegal acquisition of Western arms, ammunition and military technology for the Red Army at the same time supplying Russian weapons and military equipment to the 'revolutionary' armies and groups in China, Mongolia, Afghanistan, and other places encouraging pro-Soviet and anti-capitalist foreign policy.[8] By the end of 1927, Yevseyev was transferred to the Soviet trade delegation in Berlin in charge of the department selling Russian art and antiques. In October 1941, terminally ill, he was evacuated to Tashkent where he died four months later.[9] As it turned out, in the whole group of the Cheka founders he was one of only two who actually managed to survive until the age of 50.

Referring to Vasili Mitrokhin's notes made in the KGB archive, Christopher Andrew quotes Yevseyev as the author of two of the Cheka's earliest operational manuals, *Basic Tenets of Intelligence* [Service] and *Brief Instructions for the Cheka On How to Conduct Intelligence* [Operations].[10] Unfortunately, these two manuals allegedly written by Yevseyev based on his detailed study of Okhrana tradecraft are not to be found anywhere. But his keynote address to the delegates of the First All-Russia Conference of the Chekas on its closing day, 14 June 1918, was recorded. 'If we do not have hidden eyes and ears in [their] aristocratic salons, embassies, missions and the like,' Yevseyev said, 'we will not be informed of all insidious plots being hatched by the enemies of the Soviet power against us.'

Valentin Trifonov was another Cheka founder who almost lived to see his 50th birthday. He was also the father of Yuri Trifonov, a Soviet writer, the author of *The House on the Embankment*, a novel that made him famous. Trifonov senior, who was born in 1888, joined the party at the age of 16. At the time of the Bolshevik uprising in Petrograd, he served as secretary of the Bolshevik faction of the Petrograd Soviet, spent the Russian Civil War on different fronts as a member of the Revolutionary Military Council, a supreme military authority, and was appointed the first chairman of the Military Collegium of the Supreme Court after the war. The Collegium had jurisdiction to deal with cases involving higher military and political personnel of the Red Army and Navy.[11] In 1926 he was sent to Finland as a Soviet trade representative. Before his arrest in June 1937, Valentin Trifonov had served as the last chairman of the Main Concession Committee, the Soviet government authority in charge of granting permissions to set up enterprises with full or partial foreign capital, the so-called foreign concessions. By the time of his arrest, most of those concessions had been unilaterally terminated by the USSR. Trifonov's case was investigated by the young lieutenant Victor Abakumov, who would become Minister of State Security of the USSR. Sentenced to death as a Trotskyist, Valentin Trifonov was shot in March 1938. His wife spent eight years in a labour camp for not denouncing her husband. Slightly over a decade later, in 1951, their son was awarded the Stalin Prize for literature.

Those seven revolutionary fanatics headed by Dzerzhinsky gathered to establish the All-Russian Extraordinary Commission for Combating Counter-Revolution and Sabotage reporting to the Council of People's Commissars or Sovnarkom,[12] an eighteen-member Bolshevik governing body headed by Lenin (Vladimir Ilyich Uliyanov), the architect of the Soviet system. None of the Cheka founders held a law degree or had ever been involved in investigative work. They were just dilettantes. And they had no clue about what is now known as tradecraft, that is, they knew nothing about the techniques and methods of spying or counter-espionage although many had sufficient experience in underground party work. The initial idea of the Commission was to defend the revolution and annihilate its real or perceived opponents as well as internal and external enemies.

Although the Cheka's early priorities were overwhelmingly domestic, in the first months of 1918 Dzerzhinsky decided to undertake the first tentative steps towards foreign intelligence collection. Within days of the foundation of the Cheka, the Commissar for Education Anatoly Lunacharsky sent to him one Aleksei Frolovich Filippov who before the Revolution graduated from the Faculty of Law of Moscow University but made a career as a publisher and even managed to work at a bank. First recruited as a secret agent to report on everything that he heard in industrial, banking and particularly in conservative circles in Petrograd, after the civil war broke out in Finland in January 1918 Filippov was sent to Helsingfors (now Helsinki) on intelligence assignment under cover as a Russian newspaper correspondent.

In this former Grand Duchy of the Russian Empire that Filippov had visited several times before the Revolution, the war was fought between the 'Reds' led by a pro-Soviet section of the Social Democratic Party, and the conservative 'Whites' for the leadership of Finland during the country's transition to independence. The leader of the Reds was Kullervo Achilles Manner, a Finnish journalist and politician. Filippov was to approach Manner and report about his plans and chances to seize and hold power from his position as chairman of the Finnish People's Delegation in the parliament.

But political control over their northern neighbour had only secondary importance for the Bolsheviks at the time. The real problem was the Russian Baltic Fleet based in Finland. After an armistice with the Central Powers (Germany, Austria-Hungary, Bulgaria and the Ottoman Empire) was signed in December 1917,[13] the ensuing peace negotiations were deadlocked in the face of Germany's severe demands. In February, the Central Powers launched an offensive that compelled the Bolsheviks to submit to the German terms. According to the Treaty of Brest-Litovsk finally signed on 3 March 1918, Russia was obliged either to keep its ships in Russian ports until the end of the war or disarm them immediately. This placed the greater part of the Baltic Fleet, locked in the ice of Helsingfors, under immediate threat since the 'White' Finns, supported by the Germans, were fast approaching. The situation was resolved with the help of Manner who was subsequently appointed commander-in-chief of the Red Guards as well as Prime Minister of a short-lived government by organising a series of evacuations assisted by icebreakers, the famous 'Ice Passage', that brought all the big ships and most of the smaller ones to Kronstadt between March and April 1918. 'The Baltic Fleet's ships thereafter did nothing of note,' Stephen MacLaughlin writes, 'aside from laying defensive minefields to the west of Kronstadt in August 1918; these were meant to deter the Germans, if they were tempted by Russian weakness to seize the ships or Petrograd itself. With that, the naval war in the Baltic came to an end – at least until the arrival of British forces in 1919.'[14]

After the civil war Manner fled to Soviet Russia where he was welcomed by his fellow Finn Otto Wille Kuusinen, the former commissar for education in his government. A year later both became high officials of the Comintern representing the Finnish Communist Party. In 1935 Manner was arrested and sentenced to ten years – he died in January 1939 in one of the forced-labour camps in the Komi republic.

The Finnish odyssey was Filippov's one and only assignment abroad. In March he returned to Petrograd and in December 1920 moved to Moscow where the Cheka established its new headquarters. First, he had served at the section dealing with speculation and criminal offences related to positions of authority or job-related crimes, later to be transferred to the so-called Special Group attached to the Presidium under the control of Dzerzhinsky. He then held a senior position in the Secret Department.[15] At the same time, Filippov acted as chairman of the Executive Committee of the Clergy (Ispolkomdukh) that started in Moscow with active support from the authorities and encouragement from the secret police.

The Sovnarkom that was to direct and control all activities of the Cheka was responsible for the 'general administration of the affairs of the state' with its chairman acting as the head of government where ministers had been substituted by people's commissars. Thus, the People's Commissar for Foreign Affairs was Trotsky (Lev Davidovich Bronstein), for Education Lunacharsky (Anatoly Alexandrovich Antonov), for Social Welfare Kollontai (Alexandra Mikhailovna Domontovich), for Nationalities Stalin (Ioseb Besarionis dze Jughashvili), and so on. Exactly half of those first Sovnarkom commissars were executed by the Cheka's successor, the People's Commissariat for Internal Affairs (NKVD). One, Trotsky, was assassinated, one was tortured to death in custody and many were executed during the Great Terror. The chairman of the Sovnarkom, Lenin, died in January 1924, aged 53, paralysed and dumb suffering from syphilis caught from a Parisian prostitute (and not from a stroke as has always been believed) during his years in exile.[16] His mistress as well as closest associate and friend, Inessa Armand, passed away four years before him.

Ivan Pavlov, a celebrated Russian scientist awarded the Nobel Prize in Physiology, concluded in his report, which remained secret for almost a century, that 'the revolution was made by a madman with syphilis of the brain'. After Lenin's death, Pavlov wrote to Stalin, 'On account of what you are doing to the Russian intelligentsia – demoralizing, annihilating, depraving them – I am ashamed to be called a Russian!' That was in 1927, a comparatively peaceful period of Soviet history when the ideological struggle within the party leadership was helping Stalin to finally concentrate undisputed power in his hands. In January 1928, Trotsky began his internal exile in Kazakhstan, by the summer other leading members of the opposition had been defeated, and the next January the great revolutionary heretic was expelled from the Soviet Union outright. Trotsky was murdered in Mexico City in August 1940 by an NKVD assassin.

The Cheka, transformed into VeCheKa (or VChK) and then GPU (later OGPU), the Chief Political Directorate, although formally headed by the Pole Vyacheslav Menzhinsky (Wiesław Mężyński in Polish), was actually commanded by his first deputy and Stalin's acolyte by the name of Enoch Yehudah, better known in Russia as Genrikh Yagoda.

Menzhinsky, whom Donald Rayfield calls 'the exquisite inquisitor' and about whom Trotsky wrote that he 'seemed like a poor sketch of an unfinished portrait', is praised in the KGB history as 'a polyglot and a man of culture' who presided over a series of successful GPU-OGPU deception operations against the counter-revolution imposed on the regime from without, as well as against 'dastardly saboteurs, plotters and spies' from within, repressing peasants and intellectuals and staging the first show trials. Well-travelled, 'he roamed France, Italy, and Britain and even the USA for eleven years', Rayfield writes, at one period working as a bank clerk for Crédit Lyonnais in Paris and as a teacher at the party school in Bologna. Shortly after the Treaty of Brest-Litovsk was signed between Germany and Soviet Russia, he was sent to Berlin with a delegation headed by Adolf Joffe. Six months later the whole Soviet delegation was expelled from the country on charges of preparing a communist uprising in Germany. 'Without Menzhinsky's shrewdness,' Professor Rayfield notes, 'Stalin could not have in the 1920s defeated his enemies abroad and at home; without Menzhinsky's ruthlessness, Stalin could not have pushed through collectivization.'[17]

Yagoda, an outright scoundrel, among other terrible crimes against humanity supervised the arrests, show trials and executions of the 'first wave' of the so-called Old Bolsheviks, who had masterminded and made the revolution. Yagoda became Dzerzhinsky's deputy shortly after the Russian Civil War, in September 1923. Stalin appointed him People's Commissar for Internal Affairs, a position that included the oversight of the regular (militia) and the secret police (Chief Directorate of State Security, GUGB), in July 1934, two months after Menzhinsky's death.

The son of a Jewish jeweller, Yagoda was able to carry on for only two years. Like photographs of other Stalin's secret police chairmen, his portrait does not decorate the walls of the KGB Museum, the historical showroom of the Federal Security Service of Russia, now closed to visitors. Several of them had been executed after being found guilty of horrific crimes that are gradually becoming known albeit to a very small extent: Yagoda and Agranov in 1938, Yezhov and Frinovsky in 1940, and Beria, Merkulov and five others in 1953. The first post-war chief – Abakumov – was executed in 1954.[18] At least two of their successors committed suicide – after the collapse of the Soviet Union in 1991 Boris Pugo, the Interior Minister and former Latvian KGB chairman, blew his brains out and in 2012 Leonid Shebarshin, former head of Soviet foreign intelligence, shot himself dead with his own gun.

'Whoever fights monsters should see to it that in the process he does not become a monster', Friedrich Nietzsche wrote in his famous philosophical treatise *Beyond Good and Evil* (1886). Alas, the intelligence chiefs do not read Nietzsche's works.

Chapter 2

Lenin, Trotsky, and
His Majesty's Secret Service

While the Central Powers, and especially Germany, with enthusiasm for the war visibly waning, insisted on an immediate peace, during 1917 both Britain and the United States wanted to keep Russia on the battlefield. From September 1914, MI1c or Military Intelligence Section 1c of the Secret Service Bureau (later British Secret Intelligence Service, SIS or MI6) was represented in Petrograd by Captain Archibald Campbell. Campbell's mission was scarcely clandestine and had no direct involvement with espionage. 'Reflecting in 1917 on the wartime development of intelligence work in Russia,' the official history of SIS states, 'General [Sir George] Macdonogh, the Director of Military Intelligence, described Campbell as "an officer of considerable ingenuity, ability and push, but of singularly unattractive personality"'.[1] On his assignment Campbell was accompanied by Victor Ferguson and Lieutenant Stephen Alley, who had been born and brought up in Russia and spoke the language fluently. The British Intelligence Mission, as it was called, was given a spacious room in the western wing of the General Staff Building on Palace Square in Petrograd, in front of the Winter Palace.

In May 1915 Campbell was replaced by Major Cudbert 'Cud' Thornhill, a 'first class Russian scholar', and during the next year there was another change when Thornhill was transferred to the embassy as assistant military attaché and Sir Samuel Hoare, a 36-year-old Member of Parliament (MP) and the scion of a wealthy banking family, was appointed in his place, taking over in July 1916. Hoare was instructed to 'obtain information from Russian unofficial sources, taking care that you shall never appear to be doing anything prejudicial to their interests or that could be in any way mistaken for espionage'.[2] Which in other words meant that what he should have been most concerned about was the 'plausible deniability' of his clandestine activities.

'Most of the order of battle intelligence was collected by Thornhill,' Michael Smith writes in his unofficial history of MI6. 'He was assisted by another MI1c officer, Captain Leo Steveni, a member of pre-war St Petersburg's

British expatriate community. Steveni's mother was the daughter of a Tsarist nobleman and minister. His father was a British citizen who before the war ran the largest firm of timber exporters based in St Petersburg and was a member of an expatriate community of some 2,000 Britons with their own shops, tailors, shirtmakers and an Anglican church.'[3] Moscow also had its own British community led from 1911 by the Rev. Frank North who had served as Chaplain of St Andrew's Anglican Church, Moscow.

By February 1917 the foreign intelligence section of the British Secret Service Bureau had eighteen staff in Russia (including Hoare). There were nine commissioned officers and nine civilians including one female, Winifred Spink. Half of them were operating in Petrograd supervised by Ernest Boyce, who had worked in the Russian mining industry before the war. Under Boyce were Stephen Tomes, a civilian under consular cover, Lieutenant Maurice Mansfield and Frank Urmston, another expatriate brought up in Russia. The intelligence work was organised along three lines. Military Section under John Scale was collecting military information of which the most important was the identification of enemy units on the Russian front (a standing requirement from General Macdonogh). Military Control Section under Alley was responsible for counter-espionage of every kind, liaison with Russian secret services and control of all travel from Russia to England and France,[4] and the War Trade Section under Hoare was collecting information on wartime trade and breaches of the blockade.

Hoare's other mission was commercial and economic intelligence. As Frank Stagg, who handled Russian information at Head Office, had explained to him before he left, 'We are now throwing a network of Commercial Intelligence System all over the world'. 'Above all,' he said, in was necessary to 'get a firm footing' in Russia, hoping Hoare would be able to produce 'sufficient information to serve some tempting dishes not merely to the British Govt but to big financial and commercial interests in the City'.[5] In late March 1917, before his next permanent posting in Rome, Hoare was back in London preparing a general survey of intelligence possibilities in Russia.

He was replaced by John Scale, promoted to major and awarded the DSO in April, who after the Bolshevik seizure of power was given accommodation inside the British embassy. On 6 April the United States declared war on Germany and shortly after a cable from New York described 'Leon Trotzki' as advocating the overthrow of the new Russian government (the Provisional Government established in March) and 'the starting of revolution in England and Germany'.

As Russia was moving from one political crisis to another, the Allied governments strove to keep it in the war. One part of this effort was an intelligence operation entrusted to the MI1c's representative in the United States, Sir William Wiseman.

* * *

Captain Sir William Wiseman, established in New York as head of the semi-official MI1c's North American organisation since January 1916, insisted the operation 'has to be entirely unofficial', very secretly organised and deniable. Having got London and Washington each to allocate $75,000 to his scheme, in June 1917 Wiseman persuaded the British author Somerset Maugham, recruited as a secret agent two years before, to go to Russia. 'Supplied with $21,000 [approximately $350,000 today] for expenses and travelling from the west coast of the United States, through Japan and Vladivostok,' Keith Jeffery writes, 'Maugham reached Petrograd in early September 1917.'[6] He fails to mention, however, that the British had first sent the writer to Switzerland where he studied Russian for six months before arriving in Vladivostok, a rather strange route. There, Maugham was lucky to catch the last regular Trans-Siberian train to cross the country from the Far East to the extreme north-west of Russia travelling together with a group of American consuls headed by DeWitt Clinton Poole. The US diplomat, who had himself been sent to Russia on an intelligence mission, later remembered that during their long travel across Russia he and Maugham saw each other a lot and that Maugham was 'on the way to Petrograd to do some secret work'. According to the official history of MI6, a review of Maugham's mission after his return reveals that it had been part of a broad plan 'to start an Intelligence and Propaganda service in Russia'. His real mission, however, was to help keep the Provisional Government and Russia in the war by countering German pacifist propaganda. Maugham's reports, signed with the cover name 'Somerville' and shared by Wiseman with the State Department, had been credited with providing the best political intelligence the Americans had about Russia at the time, which is no great surprise. Maugham had stayed in Russia for two and a half months before the Bolsheviks staged the Revolution and ultimately signing a peace treaty with Germany, so in the end his mission turned out to be a failure.

Maugham was not a random choice. Besides being Wiseman's relative by marriage, in London he had a mistress whose name was Alexandra Petrovna Kropotkina, the only child of Petr Kropotkin, a famous Russian writer, revolutionary, scientist, geographer and philosopher who advocated anarcho-communism. Born in London where her family was living in exile and better known in the West as Sasha Kropotkin, she returned to Russia with her father in 1917 after the February Revolution. Aged 30 and already married, she was delighted to see Maugham and was happy to introduce him to Alexander Kerensky, the Minister of War and the influential figure in the newly-formed socialist-liberal coalition government, soon to be elected the Prime Minister of what became known as the Provisional Government of Russia. Days before the October Revolution, Kerensky told Maugham that his government needed arms and ammunition and Maugham rushed back to London with the message, but it was too late.

Another well-known British writer who worked for British intelligence during the first months and years of the Revolution was Arthur Ransome, codenamed S/76. In 1913 Ransome left his wife and daughter and went to Russia, subsequently publishing *Old Peter's Russian Tales* (1916). He later became a foreign correspondent and covered the war on the Eastern Front for the London *Daily News*, a national daily newspaper before it merged with the *Daily Chronicle* resulting in the *News Chronicle*, the paper that became famous for its anti-Franco stance during the Spanish Civil War. In Petrograd Ransome was spending a great deal of time with Ariadna Tyrkova and her husband, the English journalist Harold Williams.

Tyrkova was a former socialist revolutionary and an old friend of Nadezhda Krupskaya, the wife of Lenin,[7] and of Peter Struve, whom she had met in exile in Germany and who would become Minister for Foreign Affairs in the Provisional Government. According to one of Ransome's biographers, 'To Tyrkova, meanwhile, he owed not only many pleasant weekends at the Tyrkov estate, but a first-hand account of the deep internal divisions that would eventually tip the Russian empire into revolution and civil war'.[8] She and Williams arranged for Ransome to be introduced to Sir George Buchanan, the British Ambassador, and Robert Bruce Lockhart (later Sir), a British diplomat with whom Ransome became good friends.

Lockhart, who is barely mentioned in the official history of MI6, was a great womaniser, having a lot of problems because of his affairs. He had been serving in Russia since 1912 first as Vice-Consul and then Consul General in Moscow, being recalled from time to time on account of his adulterous adventures and then coming back again. At the outbreak of the First World War the British government established the secret War Propaganda Bureau headed by Charles Masterman,[9] whose work was soon reinforced by a new Section MI7b of the Secret Service. Bernard Pares, Professor of Russian History at Liverpool University, who had been appointed official observer to the Russian army and had introduced Ransome to Williams, became aware of its activities and suggested to Lockhart to set up a similar organisation in Russia to control reports on the Eastern Front. After discussing the idea with Ransome and Harold Williams in January 1916, Lockhart submitted a proposal to the ambassador who approved it after a consultation with the

Foreign Office. The project became known as the International News Agency or the 'Anglo-Russian Bureau' but also, unofficially, as the British Propaganda Mission. Lockhart organised the Moscow branch from the British Consulate while its Petrograd outfit was headed by Ransome's friend Hugh Walpole, another British writer and journalist who had joined the Russian Red Cross. Leaving for Petrograd, Walpole took with him Denis Garstin who had taken up a tutorship in Russia and could speak the language.[10] Funded by the Foreign Office, the Bureau was engaged in placing pro-British stories in Russian newspapers.

After the Bolshevik October Revolution (New Style: 7 November 1917), Sir Mansfield Cumming, the founding Chief of the Service, began to work on 'an entirely new' Secret Service organisation in Russia. In January 1918 he proposed to General Macdonogh that this work might be organised from one of the Scandinavian neighbours of Russia, either Norway or Sweden. It was eventually agreed that Finland, Estonia and Latvia would be best suited for this and the SIS's Baltic area Inspectorate was established with Major Scale, temporary attached to the SIS station in Stockholm, appointed to head it. He combined the post of attaché with that of Military Control Officer. One of his men there (from March to September) was Oswald Rayner who had also served in Petrograd under Hoare together with Major Henry Vere Fane Benet who was awarded the CBE in 1918 for services in Russia. And following the British government's decision to adhere to the Anglo-French convention of 23 December 1917,[11] it was also decided that Lockhart, who had left shortly before the revolution, must return to Russia as an 'unofficial [diplomatic] agent' in charge of the British government's special mission to the Soviet government. He was accompanied by Captain William Hicks, the Moscow businessman Edward Birse as the mission's commercial expert and Edward J. Phelan of the Ministry of Labour (who later became Director-General of the International Labour Office). In March Phelan returned to London.

Before leaving for Russia in mid-January 1918, Lockhart met his Bolshevik counterpart, Maxim Litvinov, for lunch. The meeting was arranged by Reginald 'Rex' Leeper who had just moved from the Intelligence Bureau of the Department of Information to the newly created Political Intelligence Department of the Foreign Office. At a Lyon's Corner House luncheon table, they were joined by Theodore Rothstein, a Russian Jew turned British journalist writing for the *Daily News* and *The Manchester Guardian*. Litvinov (born Meir Henoch Wallach-Finkelstein) had resided in London almost permanently since the 5th RSDLP Congress held there in 1907 and was married to Ivy Low, the daughter of a Jewish university professor. Litvinov handed Lockhart a letter of introduction to Trotsky,[12] a prominent member of the Sovnarkom and People's Commissar for Foreign Affairs, which consequently opened plenty of doors for the British envoy when he and his party arrived in Petrograd on 30 January.

By the end of February, the British embassy (like most other foreign embassies and legations) left, taking with them about sixty members of the British colony in Petrograd and Moscow. The last official to depart was Francis Lindley CBE (later Sir), who had served as Counsellor and Ambassador Buchanan's semi-official replacement, leaving Lockhart as senior diplomat in charge with the staff that besides himself, Hicks, Birse and Phelan included Alfred Ferdinand Hill, formerly of the Black Watch (Royal Highlanders), who had served in Petrograd from 1916. He later moved to Moscow as part of Lockhart's mission. Captain Francis Cromie, a naval attaché representing the Naval Intelligence Division of the Admiralty War Staff, after the embassy staff left remained in Petrograd as well as Consul Arthur Woodhouse, Major R. McAlpine and Captain Charles Schwabe of General Poole's mission (Rusplycom).

Lockhart, still 30 then, later described those days in his *Memoirs of a British Agent* (1932): 'It was at this time that I first met Moura, who was an old friend of Hicks and Garstin [as well as Cromie and Edward Cunard of the shipping family who was serving as secretary of the British embassy] and a frequent visitor to our flat. She was then twenty-six ... I found her a woman of great attraction whose conversation brightened my daily life.' As it turned out, Moura Budberg, the name by which she would become famous,[13] was not the only Russian woman close to the British delegation in the revolutionary Petrograd.

In the meantime, Scale began to build up a team. On 15 March he 'introduced Mr. Reilly who is willing to go to Russia for us' to Cumming.[14] 'Very clever,' Cumming recorded in his diary, 'will take out £500 in notes and £750 in diamonds which are at a premium. I must agree tho' it is a great gamble as he will visit all our men in Vologda, Kief [sic], Moscow, etc.'[15] The Chief of SIS would soon note that there were still at least a dozen British intelligence officers stationed in Russia at the time.

Contrary to what is stated in the official history of MI6, it was almost certainly not Norman Thwaites in New York, 'who appears to have provided [for Reilly] the link to Scale and the opportunity to work for MI1c', as both Jeffery and Thwaites himself claim, but rather Leo Steveni, one of the officers who had served in Hoare's mission and was sent by Scale to Canada 'to enlist & instruct agents for Russia'.[16] Given the codename ST/1, before the end of March Reilly set off for the Russian port of Archangel.

There is a common myth enthusiastically and unanimously supported by almost every Russian, British and American author writing about him asserting that this Jew from Odessa became the British 'Ace of Spies'. This is of course thanks to Bruce Lockhart and his son Robin, who first hailed this 'man from nowhere' as undoubtedly the world's most extraordinary British spy regardless of the fact that upon closer examination his Russian adventures oscillate between high fantasy and low farce.[17] Despite a series of colourful exploits, this adventurous British agent obtained little if any intelligence of value.

Although no any definite documentary proof exists, Sigmund (Shlomo) Rosenblum – the future Sidney George Reilly – was almost certainly born in Odessa in 1873. Although who exactly was his father had not been established with certainty, his place of birth and nationality, usually united in one word meaning both, determined all his future life. An Odessite is not a usual demonym that identifies residents or natives of a particular place. In Odessa, 'where theft is often a virtue, where bandits become folk heroes', the historical intersection of Jewishness, adventurism and urban criminality is an old tradition. Even the language they speak is a fancy mix of Russian, Ukrainian, Yiddish and thieves' cant that often requires a dictionary to be properly understood. In the Soviet film *The Art of Living in Odessa* (1989), based on Isaak Babel's stories, Reb Arye-Leib faithfully forewarns Benya Krik, a gangster, of an impending police raid illustrating how in Odessa the devout work for the deviant. Old Odessa suffered from the assault unleashed by the Bolsheviks, having gained notoriety as a legendary city of Jewish gangsters and swindlers, a frontier boomtown mythologised for the adventurers, criminals and merrymakers who flocked there to seek easy wealth and lead lives of debauchery and excess, Jarrod Tanny writes in his brilliant book *City of Rogues and Schnorrers* (2011). 'The builders of socialism vowed to decimate its bandits and prostitutes, and the ideologues of socialist culture yearned to eradicate its music and humour ... Communism inflicted damage upon the essence of old Odessa, upon the souls of its people.'[18] So the Odessans rose against it. 'I have lately had some disagreements with Soviet power,' a famous literary character says. 'They want to build socialism, but I don't.' All this was, of course, in the past. As Mikhail Zhvanetsky once observed, Odessa no longer lives there.

Even before the revolution came to this largest Ukrainian port on the Black Sea, Shlomo Rosenblum left for Paris, later moving to New York. On 7 May 1918 he arrived in Moscow in full dress uniform as Lieutenant Reilly of the RAF and headed immediately for the Kremlin demanding to see Lenin personally. Amazingly, he was actually admitted, getting as far as meeting Sovnarkom's Secretary himself. (In describing this meeting in his report to London, Reilly confused Vladimir Dmitrievich Bonch-Bruyevich with his brother, General Mikhail Dmitrievich Bonch-Bruyevich, appointed by the

Bolsheviks to head the Supreme Military Council of Soviet Russia.) The Sovnarkom Secretary, a senior official, took Reilly for a special envoy of the British government but after a brief interview asked Lev Karakhan, deputy Commissar for Foreign Affairs, to check Reilly's credentials. Summoned to the Kremlin later that day, Bruce Lockhart was astonished to hear the news and, in his turn, summoned Boyce, demanding an explanation. 'The sheer audacity of the man,' Lockhart writes in his memoirs, 'took my breath away. Although he was years older than me, I dressed him down like a schoolmaster and threatened to have him sent home.'[19] Nonetheless, Reilly met Bonch-Bruyevich again several times, of which he regularly informed London,[20] although the main SIS representative in Russia at the time was Ernest Boyce.

During the first months of the Revolution, Dzerzhinsky and his Chekists did not care much about Allied military and intelligence personnel and even less about foreign civilians resident in the former Russian Empire. As the new regime faced large-scale protests, anti-government demonstrations and growing opposition to its measures, Lenin concluded that 'a special system of organised violence' would be necessary to establish the dictatorship of the proletariat predicted by Marxist philosophy as the intermediate stage between a capitalist economy and a lasting communist society. The original measures approved by the first Bolshevik government, the Council of People's Commissars (Sovnarkom), on 20 December 1917 for use by the newly established Extraordinary Commission in their struggle with the forces of counter-revolution were the seizure of property, resettlement, deprivation of ration cards for food, publication of lists of enemies of the people, and so on. The Cheka's main weapon, however, for the long period of 20 years after the Revolution and up to the Second World War (and beyond, until the death of Stalin) was to be terror.

Another effective technique in destroying opposition to the new Bolshevik regime became agent penetration borrowed from the Okhrana tradition of agents provocateurs, well-known to the revolutionaries. By the beginning of 1918, members of the Cheka were already 'regularly undertaking such dangerous operations' as agent penetrations: 'The situation of the tense class struggle demanded quick actions in exposing the nests of the counter-revolution. Any careless step could cost the Chekist his life. But courage and valour were his natural traits.'[21] As Professor Andrew notes, the greatest peacetime terror in European history and the largest-scale penetration of foreign government bureaucracies ever achieved by any intelligence service were the most striking accomplishments of the Soviet secret police. They were first tested during the period of 1918–23. But that was not all.

* * *

By early March 1918, when the Treaty of Brest-Litovsk was signed ending Russia's participation in the First World War, opposition to Bolshevik rule was constantly growing and the opinion in London (as well as in other Allied capitals) had been increasingly moving towards military intervention in the country, 'providing political and military support for anti-revolutionary elements'.[22] After taking part in the Russian-German negotiations, the Austrian-born Graf Wilhelm von Mirbach-Harff, who previously served at the German embassy in St Petersburg, was appointed the new German ambassador to Soviet Russia. Three months later, on 6 July 1918, he would be assassinated in Moscow following a decision of the Central Committee of the Left Socialist-Revolutionaries, the SRs, who, like the Allies, endeavoured to keep Russia in the war with Germany. Now historians refer to this as the second phase of the Allied strategic objectives in Russia covering the period after the Bolshevik revolution to the armistice on the Western Front, when the Allies 'tried first to prevent the Bolsheviks from making a separate peace with the Central Powers and, failing that, to re-establish an Eastern Front'.[23] This plan didn't work either.

One British agent who arrived in Moscow in March 1918 was Captain George Hill. He had been sent to Petrograd as a member of the Royal Flying Corps (RFC) mission to Russia two months before the Revolution and later was engaged in some semi-intelligence assignments in the south of Russia and Ukraine seconded to Major-General Frederick Poole, Commander of the British Military Equipment Section. Poole assigned him to work with Lieutenant Colonel Joe Boyle.

Joseph Whiteside Boyle turned 50 when the American Committee of Engineers in London decided to send him and Colonel Macdonell to Petrograd to report on the situation and assist in solving the problem of the Russian railways chaos that prevented the supply and transportation of troops to the front. Starting from the Stavka, Russian military headquarters in Mogilev, Byelorussia, the pair embarked upon a series of adventures.

When they reached Petrograd, their first target was the Smolny Institute, a boarding school for the daughters of the nobility – 'the female Eton of Russia' as Hill described it in his memoirs. At the Smolny, the pair presented their credentials to Adolf Joffe of a wealthy Karaite family who used his family's resources to support the Bolshevik newspaper. He was arrested, exiled to Siberia, and in October 1917 served as the Chairman of the Petrograd Military Revolutionary Committee. While Boyle and Hill were trying to persuade him that only they could keep the Russian trains running, Lenin ambled in with Karakhan in his wake. According to Hill:

The outward appearance of the Dictator was that of a strong and simple man of less than middle height with a Slavonic cast of countenance, piercing eyes, and a powerful forehead. He shook hands with us. His manner was not friendly, nor could it be said to be hostile; it was completely detached. He listened to what Joffe and Karahan [*sic*] had to say about us, and when they had finished, nodded his head two or three times and said, 'Of course, they must be given full facilities for the work they are doing' … Then bowing to us strolled away with his hands behind his back.[24]

Among other things, the pair exploited their relationship with Joffe to remove the Romanian treasures. In December 1916 a train with twenty-one carriages full of gold bars and gold coins travelled from Jassy to Moscow to deposit this gold load for safekeeping in the Kremlin. Seven months later, in the summer of 1917, as the war situation was getting worse for Romania, another transport was sent to Moscow containing the crown jewels, the archives of the Romanian academy and many antique treasures surpassing the value of the first train. Although Hill claims that he and Boyle were granted permission to remove the Romanian treasures and managed to smuggle the jewels back to Romania, this is quite certainly an exaggeration. As of 2020, only part of the objects – and none of the 91.5 tonnes of gold reserves – have been returned to Romania. At the time this book was sent to press, the problem with the Romanian treasure remained unresolved.

Joe Boyle OBE DSO died in England in April 1923.[25] Before that, he and George Hill acted as King's Messengers (diplomatic couriers) taking diplomatic bags from the British embassy in Petrograd to Romania travelling back and forth between Romania, South and North Russia, and Ukraine as part of the Russia Supply Committee, known in internal correspondence as RUSPLYCOM, which rapidly developed an intelligence role. Finally, according to his report to the Director of Military Intelligence, Captain Hill arranged for the safe passage of 'five echelons of Allied Military Missions evacuating from Roumania [*sic*]', coming to Moscow in March.[26] At that time Hill was collecting intelligence and reporting to London independently of other intelligence officers in Russia. Nevertheless, when he heard that the 4th Extraordinary All-Russian Congress of Soviets was about to meet in Moscow to ratify the Brest-Litovsk peace treaty, he decided to attend after having previously consulted with the British Consul General Sir Oliver Wardrop who concurred that it was advisable to be there. The British consul introduced Hill to Lieutenant Lionel Reid of MI1c, one of Boyce's assistants, who was also attending the Congress, which opened on 14 March and lasted three days (in his report to London Hill wrote 'five'). Lockhart and his mission arrived on 20 March.

After the Congress, Hill reported, he got into close touch with Lockhart and the Bolshevik leaders, among whom was Trotsky, who resigned as Commissar for Foreign Affairs one day before the Congress to be appointed People's Commissar of Army and Navy Affairs and Chairman of the Supreme Military Council, gaining full control of the Red Army. Hill also met Georgy Chicherin, the new Commissar for Foreign Affairs (who would serve until 1930), his deputy Karakhan (arrested and shot in 1937), and Vatslav Vorovsky (Wacław Worowski), Soviet representative to Scandinavia based in Stockholm, and later to Italy. Vorovsky was assassinated by a White Russian émigré during a diplomatic mission to Geneva in May 1923.

In May Hill 'amalgamated with MI1c Department for identifications', as he had put it, which means he began cooperating with MI1c's station chief, Boyce and his officers Urmston, Captain Victor Small and Lieutenant Reid in obtaining and sending to London identifications of enemy units on the Eastern Front. In June Hill started working primarily for Cumming's organisation although his MI1c designation remains unknown while his declared codename IK8 may be an invention. The documents reveal that between May and October 1918 he was working for both DMI and MI1c. In June, he reported, and especially in July, 'systematic recruiting started'. He also claimed that 'a small destruction gang was organised in July'.

* * *

A year before, Paul Dukes (later Sir), a talented musician who was to become ST/25 working undercover for the British Secret Service, was standing on the Nevsky Prospect in Petrograd watching the first revolutionary regiments come out. He witnessed the sacking of the arsenal by the infuriated mob and saw the soldiers breaking into the Kresty Prison. Dukes had been living in Russia since 1908, studying music at the conservatory, and was later hired by Albert Coates as assistant conductor at the Imperial Mariinsky Opera. He was also nominally in the service of the British Foreign Office as a Silver Greyhound or King's Messenger and after the revolution attached himself to the American YMCA, training a detachment of Boy Scouts in Samara. Then, one day, already in Moscow, he was handed a telegram from the Foreign Office urgently summoning him to London. On 29 July 1918 Mansfield Cumming noted in his diary, 'Mr Dukes arrived from Russia unexpectedly'.[27] This sounds strange because immediately upon arriving at King's Cross he was chauffeured to the Chief's office to be offered, without equivocation, 'a somewhat responsible post in the Secret Intelligence Service'. By the time of his meeting with the first 'C', the Political Intelligence Department (PID) of the Foreign Office had already been established and was handling the reports from Cumming's Bureau.

In the foreword to his memoirs first published in London in 1922, Dukes claims that he went to Russia 'not to conspire but to inquire'. However, his intelligence brief when he had first arrived at 2 Whitehall Court, Westminster, then the headquarters of the Smith-Cumming's organisation, was:

> We want you to return to Soviet Russia and to send reports on the situation there. We wish to be accurately informed as to the attitude of every section of the community, the degree of support enjoyed by the Bolshevist Government, the development and modification of its policy, what possibility there may be for an alteration of the regime or for a counter-revolution, and what part Germany is playing.[28]

Sir Paul does not say who instructed him, but nine decades later it transpired this was Sir Robert Nathan. He had worked closely with William Wiseman in the USA when the latter persuaded Somerset Maugham to go to Russia. According to Paul Dukes, after telling him briefly what the Service desired, Sir Robert, who headed the Political Section V, concluded: 'As to the means whereby you gain success to the country, under what cover you will live there, and how you will send out reports, we shall leave it to you, being best informed as to conditions, to make suggestions.' Three weeks later, he set out for Russia after a farewell interview with the chief. On the way, he was briefed by Major Scale in Stockholm and with forged documents identifying him as Iosif Ilyich Afirenko, a Ukrainian Cheka member, returned to Petrograd through Finland in December 1918 to take over the spy networks from an expatriate British businessman John Merrett.

By the time Dukes was escorted to the sanctum of the Chief's office at the top of the roof-labyrinth on a sunny August day, the remaining Allied diplomats stranded in Moscow, the new Soviet capital, were conspiring with the Bolsheviks' opponents, while the British, French, American and Japanese governments had begun military intervention where Britain acted as the driving force. 'What we are involved in,' Lenin announced in July, 'is a systematic, methodical and evidently long-planned military and financial counterrevolutionary campaign against the Soviet Republic, which all the representatives of Anglo-French imperialism have been preparing for months.'[29] This statement of the leader of the revolution unleashed a new (for the Cheka) campaign against 'imperialist powers abroad' plotting new attacks against the young Soviet state. Thus, 'foreign spies, saboteurs, terrorists and other subversive elements' sent by Western intelligence services under the cover of various official missions to undermine the world's first socialist state became – in addition to the continuous use of violence and intimidation by state officials and institutions against the citizens to gain their submission to authoritarian rule – the third pillar upon which the whole modus operandi of the Cheka, and later the GPU and NKVD would be based for years. It remained unchanged until the Nazi attack on the Soviet Union.

Lenin's anti-Allied rhetoric was the Bolshevik response to the United States sending 5,000 troops, which became known as the North Russia Expeditionary Force (nicknamed the Polar Bear Expedition) to Archangel as part of the Allied intervention in North Russia while another 8,000 American soldiers, organised as the Expeditionary Force Siberia, were shipped to Vladivostok. General Poole, to whom George Hill was officially seconded and who had previously spent two years in Russia, was appointed to lead the British part of the expedition to Archangel. The French, besides their Colonial Forces, sent a North Russian Battalion of the Foreign Legion composed of anti-Bolshevik Russian volunteers. It was inevitable that the intervention would lead the British, French and American intelligence officers openly operating in Russia being forced to leave the country. By that time Hill had already established a well-functioning courier service and was closely working with Reilly who, disappointed and bored by working under the official cover as an RFC officer and British government representative, went underground and, according to Hill's report, was providing excellent information. In his turn, Jeffery quotes an unnamed source that Reilly was 'obtaining very satisfactory results'. With this, the official history states quite boldly that 'Reilly's main value for SIS was his knowledge of Russian affairs'[30] as if other intelligence officers operating in Russia for years possessed less knowledge than this pretty imprudent impostor and adventurer from Odessa.

Reilly had several safe houses in Moscow and Petrograd where he resided under different guises, using what is now known as 'sexpionage' as the main element of his tradecraft. In Moscow, he stayed at the apartment of Dagmara Karozus, a dancer at the Moscow Art Theatre, at 3, Sheremetevsky Lane. She was one of the mistresses of the illustrious Count Alexander Sheremetev, who had served as aide-de-camp to Tsar Nicholas II. Karozus shared the apartment with other Russian dancers among whom was the 22-year-old Elizaveta Otten who soon began to sleep with Reilly, who was now posing as a Greek businessman. Besides being Reilly's mistress, Otten also became his chief courier.

Two days before the murder of the German Ambassador Count Mirbach, Reilly attended the 5th All-Russian Congress of Soviets where Left Socialist Revolutionaries (LSR) accounted for almost 30 per cent of all delegates. Somehow Reilly had managed to get an invitation and there in the Bolshoi

Theatre met Olga Starzhevskaya, an attractive 28-year-old typist working for the administrative section of the VTsIK.[31] He introduced himself as Konstantin Pavlovich Massino and soon they started dating, meeting at her apartment and in public gardens, sometimes dining at the famous Moscow restaurant Prague. He gave her 20,000 roubles to refurbish the apartment and they began living together. Reilly also used the services of Maxim Trester who was employed as garage manager of the Moscow Military District and when necessary drove 'Comrade Massino' around Moscow in the service auto. In Petrograd he used the apartment of his pre-war acquaintance, Elena Boyuzhovskaya, at 10, Torgovaya Street, as his accommodation address.

The Cheka knew nothing about the activities of the Allied diplomats and intelligence agents, but having gained access to the British diplomatic codes it is possible that they had been monitoring Lockhart's, Boyce's and Cromie's communications with London since at least May.[32] With a lot of problems to deal with, the Cheka didn't seem at all bothered. But in late June, Dzerzhinsky and his deputy Jacob Peters decided to use against their opponents the tactics of penetration and provocation that had so successfully been employed by the Okhrana against the revolutionaries. Two young Chekists, former Latvian officers named Jan Buikis and Jan Sprogis, using the aliases 'Schmidtchen' and 'Briedis', names of real persons, were dispatched to Petrograd with orders to infiltrate the local anti-Bolshevik underground.[33] It didn't take them long to come across agent networks set up by Captain Cromie and Reilly. Both amateurs in what concerned professional tradecraft, the naïve naval attaché and adventurous SIS lieutenant were happy to seize the opportunity of attracting Red Latvian Riflemen to their side and suggested that the two Letts should travel to Moscow to meet Bruce Lockhart. Cromie was happy to provide the dangles, as such provocateurs are known today, with an appropriate letter of introduction to the British government's envoy.

In early July Lockhart enthusiastically reported to London about a new anti-Bolshevik organisation called 'the Centre' (All-Russian National Centre, VNTs) which had contacts with both Savinkov's Union for the Defence of Motherland and Freedom (SZRS) and the Volunteer Army of Generals Mikhail Alekseyev and Anton Denikin fighting against the Bolsheviks in South Russia. A researcher specialising in the period notes that 'during July and August, the British agent [Lockhart] contributed substantial sums to the financial support of the anti-Bolsheviks and became deeply engaged in their counterrevolutionary machinations'.[34] This, however, was only part of what later became known as the Lockhart Plot.

Even more important to the history of the Lockhart Plot were the British envoy's increased contacts with the chief representatives of the other allied powers resident in Russia in 1918. Prompted by a directive from London, these contacts led Bruce Lockhart to establish regular communications with Fernand Grenard and DeWitt C. Poole, the Consul-General in Moscow of France and the United States respectfully. By the same token, but less directly, the British agent also became aware of French and American intelligence operations in Russia which were headed, in turn, by Colonel 'Henri' de Vertement [sic] and Xenophon Kalamatiano.[35]

For the Cheka it was also important to find out that Lockhart maintained regular contacts with a very extensive network of British and other Allied intelligence operatives in Russia, centred in Moscow and Petrograd and controlling intelligence officers and agents throughout the country. From the British side such networks were set up, expanded and controlled by Ernest Boyce and Captain Francis Cromie in Petrograd, as well as George Hill, Sidney Reilly and later Paul Dukes, the latter three operating under cover and always on the move.

By the time Buikis and Sprogis arrived in Moscow in early August, Dzerzhinsky was in self-imposed retirement (from 8 July to 21 August) allegedly because of his failure to prevent the assassination of the German Ambassador von Mirbach and an armed counter-revolutionary insurrection in Moscow. The acting Cheka chairman was Jacob Peters who initiated the investigation after a consultation with Nikolai Skrypnik, a member of the Cheka Collegium who had briefly headed its department for combating counter-revolution and sabotage. Buikis and Sprogis were instructed to meet Lockhart and elicit as much information as possible about his anti-Soviet activities, contacts, and about British spies and their agents operating in Russia. This became especially important because of the imminent Allied intervention in Archangel.

Meanwhile, things were developing quickly, going well beyond anything previously contemplated by the Cheka. Buikis and Sprogis introduced to Lockhart (and then Reilly) Eduards Berzin, the commander of the Special Light Artillery Detachment, then on duty guarding the Kremlin, as their co-conspirator. On 17 August Lockhart issued to all of them free passes stating that 'the bearer of this has an important mission to British Headquarters in Russia – please expedite his free passage and assist him in every way' while the headstrong Reilly made several large cash payments to the Letts and suggested 'to stage a counter-revolution in Moscow'. Having in mind that the Allied intervention in Archangel, which by then had been revealed as essentially small scale, was not such a great concern for the Cheka leadership any more, Dzerzhinsky (who returned to his post on 21 August) and his deputy Peters decided to use the situation to expose and destroy the entire foreign and domestic counter-revolutionary network in the country.[36] What would become known as subversion in London, was called counter-revolution in Soviet Russia.

On 24 August, Consuls Poole and Grenard convened a meeting at the US Consulate in Moscow, also attended by the French military attaché, head of the French Military Mission General Jean Guillaume Lavergne. Lockhart was not there. It was agreed that after the imminent departure of the Allied diplomatic staff from Russia, espionage and sabotage would be conducted by stay-behind intelligence agents: Reilly for the British SIS, Martial-Marie-Henri de Verthamon for the French Service de Renseignement, one of the country's military intelligence services, and Xenophon Blumental Kalamatiano, an American of Russian-Greek descent, for the United States. Among those present at the meeting was René Marchand, correspondent of *Le Figaro* in Russia also acting as an official agent of the French consulate.[37] Marchand knew Russia well having first come here before the war. In 1912 he published a book *Les Grands problèmes de la politique intérieure russe*, then took part in the war, was wounded, and later served as a Russian interpreter at the embassy accompanying Ambassador Joseph Noulens on his official trips. Ten days after the meeting at the US Consulate Marchand wrote a letter addressed to the president of France describing everything that he had heard.

It is not known whether this letter had ever reached Paris. According to several sources, it was found during a search in the French Military Mission at 5 Denezhny Lane, which had served as a residence for General Lavergne and Consul Grenard.[38] Anyway, it was published in *Izvestia* on 24 September 1918 under the headline 'Anglo-French Bandits'.

On 29 August the house of Henri de Verthamon of the Service de Renseignement was raided by the Cheka. The raid was made with a view, George Hill writes in his memoirs published 14 years later, to obtaining evidence of the conspiracy, which traitors in the French service had revealed to the Cheka. In his report to the War Office, Hill also mentioned that 'Commandant Devertement [*sic*]' managed to escape. Indeed, before the Cheka came to arrest him, de Verthamon had managed to leave Russia.

Only a few weeks earlier, on 20 June 1918, Volodarsky (real name Moisei Markovich Goldstein, no relation to this writer), a member of the Central Executive Committee and editor of *Red Gazette* in Petrograd, was murdered by an SR terrorist. On 17 August Moisei Uritsky, chairman of the Petrograd Cheka, was assassinated in front of the Cheka headquarters and on 30 August Lenin was shot and wounded. The moment was ripe to set off a wave of reprisals against the opposition and 'foreign counterrevolutionary plotters'.

On the afternoon of Saturday, 31 August, formally responding to the murders of the Bolshevik leaders and an attempt on the life of Lenin, the Cheka stormed the British embassy in Petrograd, killing Commander Cromie, who apparently put up resistance, firing his pistol at the attackers, and was shot dead. Arthur Woodhouse Jr., a long-serving consul in St Petersburg (and then Petrograd) was arrested and escorted to the prison in the Trubetskoy Bastion of the Peter and Paul Fortress. The British Intelligence Mission offices on Moika Embankment were also raided, which the official history of MI6 does not mention, and Ernest Boyce, Stephen Tomes, Guy Tamplin, Lawrence Webster and Charles Schwabe were imprisoned in the same Peter and Paul Fortress. Schwabe managed to escape while others were crammed into a small cell. Michael Smith, the author of the unofficial history of Britain's Secret Intelligence Service, notes that 'the spell spent in jail was not totally unproductive for the Service' – there Boyce met Nikolai Bunakov, a former Russian Army officer arrested for being 'politically unreliable'.[39] Bunakov would become ST/28. He was to play a prominent role in SIS operations against the Soviet Union for many years to come.

Reilly and Hill managed to escape and went underground. On 1 September details of the 'Lockhart Plot' were sensationally published by *Izvestia* and as a special flyer containing a brief account of the plot 'to overthrow Soviet government' with the title 'Allied invasion of Russia to suppress Workmen's Revolution and re-establish Tsarism' signed by Chicherin, Commissar for Foreign Affairs, distributed to the Allied troops in Archangel. Reilly turned up in Moscow three days after Lockhart's arrest, staying at Olga Starzhevskaya's apartment between 3 and 4 September. He managed to arrange a rendezvous with Hill, took Hill's cover document in the name of 'George Bergmann' and on Sunday, 8 September, left Moscow aboard a sleeper train bound for Petrograd. Spending about ten days in Petrograd, he left for Reval (now Tallinn), and from there to Helsingfors, Stockholm and London, arriving there on 8 November.[40] Elizaveta Otten, Reilly's lover and courier, was arrested on 1 September, after the raid on the embassy, and his other mistress, Starzhevskaya, was apprehended a week later. Otten was soon acquitted but Starzhevskaya sentenced to three months' imprisonment. A year later, on 12 December 1919, she was arrested again and placed in the Butyrka prison.

On the same Saturday night, 31 August, Lockhart and his assistant Captain Hicks were detained and briefly held at the Lubyanka internal prison in Moscow but released a few hours later. Hill spent a week in hiding having enough time to wind up his network and dispatch his 'girls' – his former secretary Evelyn Pediani, referred to in his reports as H.1, and her sister Mabel – who escaped across the Finnish border to Sweden and further to England. Evelyn would become Hill's second wife and give birth to their daughter Una. 'The little girl,' writes Hill's latest biographer, 'he hardly saw until she was eleven years old.'[41] After a minor clash with the British Consul General Sir Oliver Wardrop, who found it impossible to put him on the official list because he had been a secret agent working under cover, he resumed his legal status as Captain G.A. Hill of the Manchester Regiment and the RAF and joined his colleagues at the Finland railway station on their way to freedom. Hours before their departure, Captain Hicks hastily married his mistress Lyuba Malinina, the niece of former Moscow mayor Mikhail Chelnokov, who had been a good friend of Lockhart during his earlier days at the Moscow consulate. In the meantime, Henry J. 'Benji' Bruce, First Secretary under Ambassador Buchanan who had left Petrograd with the embassy staff, came back to take with him to London Tamara Karsavina, a beautiful Russian prima ballerina who was a principal dancer of the Imperial Russian Ballet and later of the Ballets Russes in Paris.[42] Bruce Lockhart was leaving Russia alone and his Russian mistress Moura was staying in Petrograd with only enough money to live for a few weeks.

There was a lot of unfinished business. Gerald 'Jim' Gillespie from the British consulate in Kherson took control of the intelligence networks left behind and began setting in place a fallback plan. Reilly and Hill were awarded the Military Cross on C's recommendation and Hill was also made a Companion of the Distinguished Service Medal. They were then sent into southern Russia under cover as British merchants.[43] Jacob Peters, Dzerzhinsky's deputy and one of the key figures in the Cheka's first clandestine operation against Russia's former allies, was arrested during the Great Purge as part of the so-called Latvian Operation. He was executed on 25 April 1938 at the Kommunarka shooting ground.

Eduards Berzin, commanding the Red Latvian Riflemen units, contributed to the Red Army's defeat of General Denikin's Armed Forces of South Russia in October 1919. After a brief spell in the intelligence department (Registrupr) of the army and the Executive Committee of the Comintern, Berzin joined the Cheka (later the GPU/OGPU) in February 1921. In the 1930s, he had headed the Dalstroi set up to manage the mining of gold and strategically important minerals and develop previously uninhibited territories of the Soviet Far and North-East regions. In March 1935 Berzin was awarded the Order of Lenin, the highest Soviet decoration. During the trial held *in camera* on 1 August 1938, Berzin was accused to have plotted, together with the enemy of the people Peters, the overthrow of the Soviet regime in collusion with British secret agents. He was additionally accused of planning various terrorist and subversive acts together with other former Chekists and of working for the German and Japanese secret services. Berzin was sentenced to death and immediately shot.

For the next two years or so, with direct military intervention and sustained support for the anti-Bolshevik White movement in the Russian Civil War, sixteen Allied coalition partners and Soviet Russia were openly at war. The Allied Powers withdrew in 1920 and on 16 March 1921 the Anglo-Soviet Trade Agreement was concluded making Britain the first Western power to start business with the Bolsheviks. In December 1984, the British Prime Minister would again say about Russia, 'We can do business together'. Margaret Thatcher invited Mikhail Gorbachev to visit Britain because she wanted to form her own personal opinion about the future leader of the Soviet Union. Ironically, preparing for bilateral negotiations both Mrs Thatcher and Comrade Gorbachev were advised by one and the same man, codenamed 'Gornov' by the KGB and 'Felix' by SIS.

Chapter 3

The Russian Civil War, Foreign Intervention, the Fate of the Romanovs, and British-American Intelligence

Within a few weeks after the Revolution, the Cheka became a punitive institution exclusively involved in purging political enemies real and imagined. Besides the decree 'On Red Terror' issued on 5 September 1918 which legitimised coercion, repression, violence and executions, it employed the Okhrana tactics of agent penetration first into domestic and then foreign anti-Bolshevik and counter-revolutionary organisations. After discovering, quite by chance, the 'Lockhart Plot' as it quickly became known, the Cheka leaders realised that it would be beneficial for the 'sword and shield of the revolution' also to penetrate foreign governments' missions sent to Russia under various pretexts. Such missions were sometimes operating openly, declaring themselves as legitimate representatives of foreign intelligence services; or covertly, under the cover of other official positions such as diplomatic or consular staff, trade missions, or military and economic advisers. What today is known as non-official cover when intelligence officers are not declared to the host country but pose as businessmen, journalists or students, or when professionally-trained people – men and women – operate under 'deep cover', sometimes in disguise using false names and nationalities, was then unknown to the mostly young dilletantes from the Cheka. But they were learning quickly.

The Allied strategic objectives in Russia changed over the course of the Great War and the Russian Civil War. For the last three years, from 1918 to 1920, Britain remained the driving force for intervention despite Prime Minister Lloyd George's opposition to armed conflict.[1] The US President Woodrow Wilson agreed to send 13,000 troops but warned his generals: 'Watch your step; you'll be walking on eggs loaded with dynamite.' Now historians tend to see Wilson's determination to send troops to Russia as one of his worst wartime decisions. 'It didn't really achieve anything — it was ill-conceived,' James Carl Nelson, author of *The Polar Bear Expedition* (2019), concludes.

In the meantime, the new Bolshevik state had to fight a two-front war. The Red Army was embroiled in a civil war against the White Armies plus the Allied intervention in the northern ports of Murmansk and Archangel, in the Caucasus and southern Russia, and in Siberia and Vladivostok, the largest Russian port on the Pacific coast.[2] The Cheka, in its turn, had to deal with countering the subversion actively assisted and sometimes inspired by British, French and American secret agents in addition to combating Russian counter-revolution, sabotage and speculation. If compared to British secret service machinery of the time, the Cheka combined MI5's investigative functions of tracking foreign espionage; Scotland Yard's Special Branch's right to search, arrest, cross-examine, interrogate and prosecute suspects; Basil Thomson's (Home Office) Directorate of Intelligence's responsibility to counter subversion (in the British case – Bolshevik-inspired civilian subversion and 'revolutionary movements'); the Old Bailey's power to impose punishments; and, finally, Wandsworth Prison's role to carry out executions. The Cheka did it all while no executive or legislative body responsible for coordination and oversight like, for example, the Secret Service Committee (SSC) or Joint Intelligence Committee (JIC), existed to execute control over its activities.

In the first half of 1918, the Extraordinary Commission (Cheka) under the Bolshevik version of the Cabinet Office, the Council of People's Commissars in the Soviet newspeak, was a comparatively small organisation. Its top brass included the Bureau, the Collegium, the Presidium and the chairman (always Dzerzhinsky until his death in July 1926) assisted by two deputies: Alexandrovich and Zaks, both Left SRs.

Vyacheslav Alexándrovich Alexandróvich (real name Vyacheslav Alekseyevich Dmitriyevsky) had served as deputy chairman from January to July 1918. Born to a noble Russian family in the Ryazan province, he had been a member of the Left SR party (internationalists). During the First World War Alexandrovich, party alias 'Pierre d'Orage' ('Storm Stone'), worked in the underground in Petrograd. Member of all the Cheka governing bodies, he had also headed the department to combat work-related crime. As the right-hand man of the chairman, Alexandrovich had the power to sign and a Cheka seal to stamp any document to show it was certified and agreed upon by the leadership. In July 1918 Alexandrovich took part in the Left SR uprising in Moscow against the Bolsheviks. One of the aims of the uprising was to resume the war with Germany. He was later accused of issuing a letter of introduction to the two Chekists, Yakov Blyumkin and Nikolai Andreyev, requesting an audience for them with the German ambassador von Mirbach, who was shot at the embassy at point-blank range on 6 July. One of the assassins, Blyumkin, was, like Reilly, born into a Jewish family in Odessa. After the assassination, Alexandrovich and his party comrades arrested Dzerzhinsky and his detail, calling for a revolt against the Bolsheviks.

Grigory Davydovich Zaks, born in Odessa in 1882, could not finish primary school and received his elementary education later. Grigory began his working career as a bookbinder and when he was barely 20 years old joined the SR party. He took part in the revolution of 1905, was arrested and exiled in Siberia. Two years later he emigrated to France living and working there with some intervals until 1912. Conscripted into the Imperial Russian Army upon his return, Zaks managed to dodge the draft and settled in Petrograd where he got a job as a metalworker, at the same time being active in the SR party. All this played a positive role in his career after the revolution when he was promoted first to several minor party posts having been later elected to the Presidium of the Petrograd Military-Revolutionary Committee and in December 1917 appointed Deputy People's Commissar of Education. In spring 1918 Zaks was delegated to work in the Cheka first heading its investigative section and then as one of Dzerzhinsky's deputies and member of the Collegium. He knew about his party's decision to assassinate Mirbach and did not oppose it but after the uprising wrote a letter to Dzerzhinsky in which he announced his disagreement with the Central Committee of the SRs. In November 1918 he joined the Bolsheviks, then briefly studied in the Red Army General Staff Academy and during the last years of the civil war served in military intelligence. In 1924–5 Zaks was posted as the Soviet military attaché to Estonia.

The former Cheka deputy chairman was first arrested in March 1935 but soon released. He had worked in Moscow as a consultant to Soyuzsnabprom, a supply organisation, when the NKVD arrested him for the second time in October 1937. Accused of spying for Japan, Zaks was sentenced to death and shot in December, two days before the New Year.[3]

The Left SR uprising was quickly crushed with the help of the Red Latvian Riflemen. As expected, Lenin, Trotsky and the Sovnarkom accused their opponents of treason, claiming that they were staging a mutiny to draw Russia into a new war against Germany and to overthrow the workers' and peasants' government, an accusation which the Left SRs consistently denied. Mass persecutions against the rebels started immediately with thirteen persons, including Alexandrovich, executed immediately without trial and others either sentenced to various terms or, as a minimum punishment, dismissed from all government positions.[4] Andreyev managed to flee to Ukraine and Blyumkin disappeared but soon resurfaced. He was pardoned and returned to his duties in the Cheka. On 8 July Lenin granted an interview to *Izvestia* expressing himself categorically as always: 'Their criminal terrorist act and revolt have fully and completely opened the eyes of the broad masses to the abyss into which the criminal tactics of the Left Socialist-Revolutionary adventurers are dragging Soviet Russia, the Russia of the people.'[5] Joachim Vatsetis (born Jukums Vācietis), who led the Latvian Riflemen loyal to the Bolsheviks, was arrested in November 1937 as a member of the alleged 'Latvian Fascist organisation within the Red Army', and executed on 28 July 1938.

Concerning the assassination of the German ambassador, historian George Katkov offers a different version.[6] He believes that the traditional view is false but came to prevail because it suited tthe Bolsheviks, the Germans and the Left SRs. Basing his arguments on a wealth of evidence, Katkov seeks to prove that the crime was in fact instigated by Lenin himself as a means (a) of eliminating Mirbach after Mirbach shifted to support anti-Bolshevik elements, and (b) of providing a pretext for crushing the Left SRs.

About ten days before the assassination, Mirbach wrote:

> After two months' careful observation, I can now no longer give Bolshevism a favourable diagnosis. We are unquestionably standing by the bedside of a dangerously ill man, who might show apparent improvement from time to time, but who is lost in the long run …
>
> One day we might therefore be faced with what for us would be the most undesirable state of affairs possible, i.e. Soviet Revolutionaries, financed by the entente and equipped with Czechoslovak arms, quite openly leading a new Russia back into the ranks of our enemies.

Mirbach saw the best solution in establishing in Russia a regime which, he wrote, 'would be favourable to *our* design and interests' composed of the moderates from the right wing, 'especially as such a combination would ensure that we had a large percentage of the influential men of the industrial and banking worlds serving our essential economic interests'.[7] This was against Lenin's plans and he could easily see the way out by killing two birds with one stone: getting rid of the German representative who was becoming too presumptuous and crushing the Socialist Revolutionaries who represented a challenge to the Bolsheviks seeking to establish what Marx called the dictatorship of the proletariat. (As it happens, the term had actually been coined by a socialist revolutionary named Joseph Weydemeyer and later adopted by Marx, Engels and Lenin.)

* * *

One of the most audacious Bolshevik crimes in this early period and quite certainly one of the most shameful chapters in Russian history was the barbarous murder of the Romanov family: the Emperor of All Russia Nicholas II, his wife Empress Alexandra, and their five children – Olga (22), Tatiana (21), Maria (19), Anastasia (17), and Alexei (13), – all shot and bayoneted to death. Also killed on the night of 16/17 July 1918 were retainers who had accompanied them: Yevgeny Botkin, the physician to the royal household; Anna Demidova, personal maid in service to Empress Alexandra; Aloise Lauris Trūps, a Latvian, better known in Russia as Aleksei Trupp, first footman in the royal household; and Ivan Kharitonov, head chef of the royal household.

In March 1917 the revolutionary wave in Petrograd reached the point when it became necessary for Nicholas II to abdicate the throne. In the morning of 2 March (Old Style), he made a decision, but in the afternoon reconsidered his initial intention to abdicate in favour of his son Alexei and decided that his brother, Mikhail Alexandrovich, Grand Duke Michael, should become the new Emperor of All Russia.

However, the next day the former Tsar wrote in his diary: 'So Misha has [also] abdicated. His manifesto ends with a call for the election of a Constituent Assembly in six months. God knows what possessed him to sign such a vile thing!'[8] The Provisional Government decreed that the imperial family should be held under house arrest in the Alexander Palace in Tsarskoe Selo, the imperial residence south of Petrograd. This proved to be a prelude to a lengthy wandering to Tobolsk, the historic capital of Siberia, which they finally reached by mid-August travelling by river ferries. There they settled in the former governor's mansion renamed the 'House of Freedom' after the revolution, living in considerable comfort. Nicholas II asked the Provisional Government for permission to remain there until his children recovered, planning then to proceed to Murmansk and from there to England.

At the end of March 1918, the Sovnarkom decided to remove the Romanovs to Yekaterinburg, the fourth largest city in Russia east of the Ural Mountains, where the family arrived at the end of April. They were imprisoned in the so-called Ipatiev House which was designated 'The House of Special Purpose'. The family was kept there in strict isolation. On 4 July the new commandant of the house was appointed. His name was Yurovsky.

Yakov Yurovsky was born in 1878 to an Orthodox Jewish family in the Siberian city of Tomsk. Some say he later converted to Lutheranism which, if true, would be a short-lived association with the Church. After the Russian Revolution of 1905, he joined the Bolsheviks, became an atheist, and was sent to work in the Cheka in December 1917. God knows what brought him to Yekaterinburg in July 1918 as a member of the local Cheka collegium, but he became the sole organiser and chief executioner of the Russian Imperial family.

By the end of the twentieth century this crime had been meticulously investigated, painstakingly documented and even Yurovsky's own account of the killing found and published.[9] It is backed by the testimonies of three other Cheka members who also took part in the execution. Numerous well-researched books highlighting different aspects of this tragic story have also been published.[10] But back in 1918 for Russia and the world the ex-Tsar and his family had simply vanished. Yurovsky later moved to Moscow, still serving in the Cheka/OGPU while seconded to the Gokhran, a Soviet repository of precious metals, precious stones, pearls and other valuables (which the

Bolsheviks obtained by looting banks, the Church, and robbing whole categories of people) but spent his last years working as director of the Polytechnical Museum. He died, according to the official version, of a stomach problem (a perforated duodenal ulcer) in 1938, which has not been confirmed by any documentary evidence.

In the summer of 1918 rumours began to circulate in Europe that Nicholas II, incarcerated with his family in Yekaterinburg, had been murdered by the Bolsheviks. According to Richard Pipes, it was possible that the Soviet government was intentionally spreading such rumours to test Western reaction to the contemplated execution of the former tsar. A Danish daily *Nationaltidende* telegrammed Lenin on 16 July 1918. 'Rumours here going,' the text read, 'that the oxszar [ex-tsar] has been murdered. Kindly wire facts.' Lenin responded in English on the same telegraphic blank. Lenin's denial – 'Rumour not true exczar safe all rumours are only lie of capitalist press' – was cabled when preparations for the massacre were already under way, just hours before the whole Imperial Family, along with its retainers, were brutally murdered (Richard Pipes, *The Unknown Lenin*, 46 and 48. RGASPI, f.2, op. 1, d. 6, l. 601).

Within days of the execution, the White forces marched into Yekaterinburg and after the initial clumsy inquiries by two inspectors appointed by the military command, Nikolai Sokolov, Investigating Magistrate for Cases of Special Importance of the Omsk Tribunal, was instructed to conduct a detailed investigation. Sokolov interviewed all witnesses who had managed to survive and examined all available physical evidence. It turned out that from the Romanovs' close entourage and household only Sidney Gibbes, the English tutor, and Pierre Gilliard, a Swiss academic and the French language tutor, survived while all others had been murdered by the Bolsheviks. Sir Thomas Preston, the Acting British Consul in Yekaterinburg (and later British Consul in Yekaterinburg, Vladivostok and Leningrad), who lived right near the Ipatiev House, provided help and was the first to inform the British government about the fate of the Romanovs.[11] To sort all material evidence and witness testimonies out, Sokolov formed a small group.

The findings of the Sokolov Commission became important state documents and were carefully preserved through the chaos of the civil war. Sokolov personally smuggled them to Paris, where he wrote a book, *Ubiistvo Tsarskoi Sem'i* (The Murder of the Imperial Family), based on his research and investigation material, which was first published posthumously in 1925.[12] Seven of the original eight case folders that belonged to Sokolov are now part of the Harvard University collection. Another set of documents, the depositions of eyewitnesses, was taken out of Russia by Professor George Telberg who, after publishing them in 1920, donated the documents to the Law Library of Congress in Washington, DC, along with a large collection of material related to the last years of Romanov rule.

From the moment that Nicholas's death was announced, people began to make conjectures as to what had become of him. Only Lenin was indifferent when Yakov Sverdlov broke the news on the evening of 18 July, during the Sovnarkom meeting. Lenin had obviously been informed earlier that day and was annoyed that the execution did not happen as he planned.

'I have to say,' Sverdlov began in his customary even tones, 'that we have had a communication that at Ekaterinburg, by a decision of a Regional Soviet, Nicholas has been shot. Nicholas wanted to escape. The Czecho-Slovaks were approaching. The Presidium of the All-Russian Central Executive Committee has resolved to approve.'

Silence from everyone.

'Let us now go on to read the draft [of the new law on health services] clause by clause,' suggested Ilych [Lenin] …

Lenin, Trotsky and other Bolshevik leaders realised that killing the ex-Tsar should have finished with autocracy and the imperial family for good. But it turned out that the manner of their death and the way it was presented had quite the opposite effect: it fuelled a stream of contradictory stories and gave Nicholas and his family a restless immortality, as Wendy Slater states in her book.[13] Unfortunately, like Pontius Pilate, a Roman governor of Judaea, forever stained with the blood of Jesus Christ, the chief executioner of the Romanovs also became immortal thanks to books and films commemorating the last Russian tsar.

Unlike Soviet intelligence operations, where *all* details will probably never be known, the evidence of this Bolshevik crime committed by the bestial and barbaric Chekists and dumb 'soldiers of the revolution' leaves no doubt. Still there is one pressing question: who ordered the murders?[14] Just as Sokolov, Telberg and Robert Wilton, the authors of the first published accounts of this crime realised how important it was for posterity that all documentary evidence about the murder of the Romanov family be preserved, so too the Bolshevik leaders who ordered the execution understood that what had not been recorded could not be proved and, therefore, the question of acting on it would not arise.

Remarkably, according to the survey published in April 2017, 100 years after the October Revolution, 56 per cent of Russians believed Lenin played a positive role in their country's history. Yet, three years later, on Lenin's sesquicentennial, the RFE/RL correspondents reported, 'the country he created no longer exists and its successor state – Russia – seems decidedly uninterested in marking 150 years since his birth. Even before the coronavirus pandemic hit, only the most diehard Communists remaining in Russia seemed even to have noticed the anniversary.'[15] And this is not to mention Russian schoolchildren who hardly know who Lenin, Trotsky or Sverdlov, the man who had most likely authorised the Urals Soviet to execute the Romanovs and later endorsed the shooting, were.

Eighty-five years after the execution of the former Russian imperial family, Russian President Vladimir Putin arrived in Yekaterinburg to meet a German Chancellor. Together they visited the site of the Ipatiev House, demolished by Putin's predecessor many years ago. For those who lived until the next decade, the incredible irony of the situation was to see a former KGB officer hailed by *Time* magazine as their person of the year with a frontpage article claiming 'A Tsar is Born'. To hear that a KGB agent became the Patriarch of Moscow and Primate of the Russian Orthodox Church. And to learn that a former German Chancellor who had been together with Putin in Yekaterinburg was appointed chairman of the board of the largest Russian oil company, becoming one of the chief promoters of Russian interests in Germany.

* * *

Neither the British Foreign Office nor the government in general understood the Bolsheviks' goals. At the same time, suspicious of their wartime allies, Britain sought a peace settlement that would ensure that with their main adversary, Germany, defeated, neither Russia nor France became sufficiently powerful to threaten the British Empire and its hold on the rest of the world.

At the end of the war, Sir Henry Wilson, the Chief of the Imperial General Staff, declared that 'our real danger now is not the Boch[e]', meaning the Germans, 'but Bolshevism'. This determined the attitude of both SIS and the Security Service (MI5) towards Russia for many years that followed – at least until the next World War both Services were mainly preoccupied with the challenge of international communism. Taking advantage of the post-revolutionary turmoil in Russia, Cumming authorised a number of adventurous operations in an effort to find out what was going on.[16] But that was only one part of the plan. British secret agents went to Russia not only to inquire, to paraphrase Paul Dukes' words, but also to conspire with various anti-Bolshevik organisations now operating underground. According to its official history, Russia was the second largest SIS commitment after Holland (for Germany), which also inevitably included much anti-Bolshevik work and anti-Soviet operations.

While Vladivostok and the Far East were generally disregarded, SIS activities in Russia concentrated on the north and the south. The south was rather well covered. After Reilly's return from Petrograd and then Hill's arrival in Britain on Armistice Day, 11 November 1918, they received decorations – a Military Cross (MC) for Reilly and a Distinguished Service Order (DSO) for Hill – and were sent on leave. However, their leave was interrupted and in mid-December they were summoned to the Cumming's Whitehall Court office (Hill was meeting the chief for the first time) and tasked with a new Russian mission for SIS.

In the meantime, between 25 November and 3 December 1918, the Revolutionary Tribunal in Moscow was hearing the Lockhart case with twenty-three individuals arrested and charged with committing espionage and terrorist activity on behalf of the Allied governments. Already in early September, *Pravda* and *Izvestia* released sensational frontpage stories announcing the liquidation of an apparently vast Anglo-French conspiracy centred in Moscow led by the chief of the special British mission to Russia. Four of the accused including Lieutenant Reilly were tried and convicted in absentia: Robert H. Bruce Lockhart; Fernand Grenard, French consul general; and Colonel 'Henri' de Vertemont, a 'French citizen', as he was identified in the protocol while this French officer's name was actually spelt as 'Verthamon'. They were declared outlawed, that is, 'deprived themselves of the protection of the law of the RSFSR' – a euphemism hiding the most extreme punishment amounting to a death sentence. The fifth, Xenophon Dmitrievich Kalamatiano, the head of the US intelligence Moscow cell, was sentenced to death by shooting together with his best agent, Lieutenant Colonel Alexander Friede (ST/26). The chief of the Petrograd ring, Vice-Consul Robert Witney Imbrie, who had been the sole US representative in the northern capital for five months, learned of his imminent arrest and fled to Finland with false papers thanks to the help of the Norwegian embassy in August 1918. Early next year he settled in Vyborg, tracking the movements of the White Army and sending regular reports to the Secretary of State.

In June 1920, after the failure of the White Army offensive in the north, Robert Imbrie left Finland. By then he had been tried in absentia by the Bolsheviks and sentenced to death while several of his accomplices had been captured.[17] Imbrie was then posted to Crimea, where he arrived in December by which time the White forces under General Wrangel had already collapsed and evacuated to Turkey. Having nothing more to do there, Imbrie was reassigned to Constantinople. Together with his wife, Katherine, he then moved to Ankara serving there as the new informal US representative – a position arranged by Admiral Mark Bristol, American High Commissioner based in Constantinople since 1919.

Kalamatiano, who was born in Vienna and whose stepfather, Pavel Blumenthal, was a young Jewish lawyer from St Petersburg, was recruited to work for the US Military Intelligence Division, first called the Military Intelligence Section, when the family emigrated to America. He served as assistant to the US commercial attaché, William C. Huntingdon, who was both his boss and intelligence controller while the whole secret work was supervised by Maddin Summers, the US Consul-General. Kalamatiano's official job was to collect information rather than intelligence, but he had nevertheless managed to set up several spy networks in Russia and Ukraine supplying both Huntingdon and Dewitt C. Poole, first Consul and then, after a sudden death of Summers at the end of April 1918, Consul-General in Moscow, with valuable military intelligence. His death senetence was replaced by 20 and then 5 years in prison and in August 1921 Kalamatiano and several other Americans were released and expelled to the USA.

'Of the four American journalists arrested in Russia in 1920-21 on suspicion of espionage,' Liz Atwood writes, 'two are known to have been working for the Military Intelligence Division and a third confessed to spying, although intelligence officials adamantly denied his claim.'[18] Among the known agents, Marguerite Harrison became the most famous and at the same time the most controversial. At the end of the First World War Harrison, working as a theatre and music critic for the *Baltimore Sun*, wrote to the head of the US Army's Military Intelligence Division (MID), asking to be sent abroad as a spy. In October 1919, MID Director Brigadier General Marlborough Churchill made his decision assigning Harrison a cipher book and the uncomplicated code name 'B' (based on Baker, her name at birth). Her destination was Russia where she arrived in February 1920 as an Associated Press correspondent, also contributing articles to the *Baltimore Sun* and the *New York Evening Post*.

It is believed that when Marcel Rosenberg, who had until March 1918 was employed by the American Red Cross Mission to Russia headed by Lieutenant Colonel Raymond Robins and now served as Chicherin's secretary, was meeting her and her companion at the Alexandrovsky train station in Moscow, the Cheka already knew that Harrison had been sent to Russia as a spy. This, however, may or may not be true.

On 4 March 1920 she was arrested on charges of espionage but agreed to work as a double agent signing the pledge of allegiance to the OGPU and the Soviet Republic after two days of interrogations at Lubyanka.[19] For the six months that she had been at large, Harrison duly provided information on foreigners resident in Moscow requested by her new Soviet handlers. Among others, one of her victims was Stan Harding, a British correspondent for the *New York World*, whom Harrison said was a British spy.[20] Harding was arrested on 25 June 1920, incarcerated in Lubyanka prison and sentenced to death, but released in November.[21] At the same time, as the Cheka appeared unsatisfied with her reports, Harrison was arrested again on 20 October and placed in the same Lubyanka prison. On 15 July 1921 Lenin sent a letter to Chicherin with a copy to Unszlicht, deputy head of the Cheka, referring to his recent meeting with Senator Joseph I. France, a Maryland Republican who had vouched for Harrison's good intentions. 'He was not begging to release her,' Lenin wrote, 'but asked whether anything could be done.'[22] In two weeks she was set free.

Arriving in Riga a few days after her release, Harrison dictated what resulted in a twenty-page report to the MID. In this document she asserted that the Bolsheviks were firmly entrenched in power and argued that the United States should recognise Soviet Russia. In another report, sent a week later from Berlin, she confirmed that she would continue her espionage work and volunteered to keep an eye on Senator France, who she believed had been fooled by Soviet propaganda.[23] In June 1922 Harrison was at the Far East, first in Japan and later in China, attending the Changchun Conference between representatives of the Japanese, Soviet and Chita governments held in September to consider Japanese demands for economic rights in the Russian territory of northern Sakhalin which Japan then occupied.

Travelling through China, Harrison spent two weeks in Beijing where she duly applied to the Soviet diplomatic mission, then headed by Adolf Joffe, for visas to visit Soviet Russia. Her application got to Aristarkh Rigin, alias 'Rylsky', INO head of station in China operating under the cover of attaché and head of the consular section. He immediately informed the Lubyanka headquarters. As soon as Harrison reached Chita with the intention to travel to Moscow by the Trans-Siberian Railway, on 22 November 1922 she was arrested and after a brief interrogation brought to the Soviet capital without any comfort and under armed escort. Two months later, having told her interrogators all she knew, she was released and allowed to leave the country.

In spite of a few dubious 'first' titles – Harrison was the first female secret agent sent to Russia by the Military Intelligence Division of the United States Army and the US Department of War, and the first US female spy to be incarcerated by the Bolsheviks – she retained her profound admiration for the country which excited her by its revolutionary fervour. 'The books and articles Harrison wrote on her return to the USA,' Sheldon Bart notes, 'and her many lectures provided American audiences with an accurate and thoughtful account of the history and geopolitics of a land that fascinated her and of the people for whom she felt the deepest affinity.'[24]

As always in such cases, Harrison's memoirs should be read with a pinch of salt. All her recollections about the circumstances of her first arrest on 4 March and second, on 20 October 1920, are to a great extent invented.[25] This is what Commissar for Foreign Affairs Chicherin wrote in a confidential cablegram to Ludwig Martens, Soviet Russia's representative to the United States, on 7 January 1921:

> Marguerite Harrison professional spy employed by American Military Intelligence Department. Was illegally smuggled into Russia last spring by the Polist [sic, Polish] authorities on the request of the American representative in Warsaw. Gathered military information forwarding it to Poles and Americans. Arrived in Moscow, her identity was established and she was arrested. Confronted with overwhelming evidence she confessed and offered her services to the Russian Extraordinary Commission [Cheka], revealing American and British spies as evidence of loyalty. Worked for the Extraordinary Commission until October when she was rearrested as it became evident that, while she gave some valuable and correct information, she continued to sell herself to our enemies. She cannot be released.[26]

Before US Military Intelligence got involved in Russia, Reilly and Hill set off together in mid-December 1918 travelling from Waterloo Station via Paris to Sevastopol, the largest city on the Crimean Peninsula and a major Black Sea port founded in 1783 as a naval base by Rear Admiral Thomas MacKenzie, a native Scot in Russian service. Because they were to operate under non-official cover, they adopted the guise of businessmen accredited by the Board of Trade. Their status was reinforced by a letter from Mansfield Cumming introducing them to Sir John Picton Bagge, Commercial Secretary, 1st Grade, responsible for South Russia who was returning to Odessa to resume his diplomatic duties as consul-general. According to John Aisnworth, Reilly would later form a close association with Bagge when Odessa became his base of operation early in February 1919.[27] In the meantime, he had other plans.

The British were actively supporting General Anton Denikin, the commander of the anti-Bolshevik Volunteer Army who had recently launched a highly successful campaign giving him control over the entire area between the Black and Caspian Seas. A few months earlier, in March, Trotsky started the reorganisation of the Red Army approved by the Central Committee having created the Supreme Military Council which was headed by Mikhail Bonch-Bruyevich, former chief of the Imperial General Staff. On 13 March Trotsky was appointed People's Commissar in full control of the Red Army and Navy while the post of commander-in-chief was abolished.

Throughout late 1918 and early 1919, there were a number of attacks on Trotsky's leadership of the army inspired by Stalin who had clashes with him over the reorganisation. In January 1919, Denikin's Volunteers defeated the Red Army in North Caucasus. At the same time, French troops, Poles and Czechs were occupying Odessa and Sevastopol. Nonetheless, it did not prevent Trotsky in March being elected one of only a handful of full members of the Politburo together with Lenin and Stalin. In the meantime, the Supreme Military Council was abolished and Trotsky appointed Joachim Vatsetis of the Red Latvian Riflemen who had formerly led his men against the Left SRs in Moscow and the Eastern Front against the Czechoslovak Legion to be commander-in-chief of the Red Army. Trotsky himself became chairman of the newly-formed Revolutionary Military Council and retained overall control over the military.

The two British secret agents met General Denikin on 10 January, two days after he was reconfirmed as Commander-in-Chief of the Armed Forces of South Russia. The following day Reilly reported to London that Denikin was heavily reliant on the assistance of the Allies and not only in material supplies but also troops which, the general assessed, 'will move behind us holding territories which we will reconquer'. Reilly was also convinced that the Bolshevik element in the Crimea 'can only be contained by presence [of] Allied forces'.[28] Remarkably, at the very moment Reilly and Hill were meeting Denikin, Major-General Sir George Milne, British officer in charge of the Army of the Black Sea, was touring the Caucasus.

With a single division under his command, Milne was to protect the oilfields around Baku on the Caspian Sea. The greatest anxiety of the British forces, Peter Day writes in his new biography of George Hill, 'was to keep the Bolsheviks out of this area; promoting General Denikin's cause further north was a secondary consideration.' Milne is quoted as reflecting on his experience in Russia's vast southern territories amid a bloody conflict between Armenia and Azerbaijan over several regions including Karabakh: 'The country and the inhabitants are equally loathsome and we seem to be accepting an enormous responsibility for no very great reason ... I cannot see that the world would lose much if the whole of the country cut each other's throats. They are certainly not worth the life of one British soldier.'[29] The conflict between the two independent states, Armenia and Azerbaijan, over Nagorno-Karabakh, which is a portion of the historic region of Karabakh, had not been resolved when this work was being written.

At the end of January Reilly, Second Lieutenant RAF, and Hill, Lieutenant 4th Battalion, Manchester Regiment, received news that they were both to be awarded the Military Cross 'for distinguished services rendered in connection with military operations in the field'. The official announcement appeared in the Supplement to the *London Gazette* on 12 February 1919, by which time Hill had already left Odessa where they had arrived on the last leg of their second mission together. Now operating alone, Reilly's dispatches were chiefly about the situation in his native town.

Controlled by the White forces, Southern Russia was divided into two operational zones by the Allies. The so-called eastern zone was British and the western zone French. The city of Odessa had a French garrison of some 60,000 men, whom Reilly in his dispatches criticised for their 'decidedly unfriendly' attitude towards the Volunteer Army. On the one hand, he accused the French of 'treating Russian staff officers with a total lack of elementary courtesy and even with insulting rudeness', and of converting Odessa 'into one of the worst administered and least safe cities in the world'. On the other, echoing the anti-Semitic element of the Denikin camp, he was blaming the French command in Odessa and especially Colonel Henri Freydenberg, Chief-of-Staff to General d'Anselme, described as 'mostly Jewish and ... pro-German', for the disdainful attitude towards the Volunteers, obstructing their efforts to supply, mobilise and operate their own forces.[30] On 21 February Reilly requested to be recalled home considering his further stay in Russia a waste of time. Walford Selby (later Sir), private secretary to Lord Robert

Cecil (Parliamentary Under-Secretary of State for Foreign Affairs), marked a copy of Reilly's above-mentioned dispatch no. 13, concerning the state of affairs in Odessa, as 'Circulated to the king and War Cabinet'.

Reilly's next assignment together with Hill would be in France to attend the Paris Peace Conference. At the end of March, Hill was sent back to South Russia and Reilly headed for New York on board the White Star Line's SS *Olympic*, finally getting there on 21 April.

* * *

At the time when members of both unofficial British diplomatic and official Military Intelligence missions were arrested while agents working undercover managed to flee, Gerald 'Jim' Gillespie took control of the intelligence networks. However, feeling that he himself would not last long, Gillespie handed over all remaining contacts to John Merritt, a British businessman based in Petrograd. Merritt had been working for the British Engineering Company of Russia and Siberia formed in 1915 to coordinate the export to Russia of products ordered by the Russian Government Supply Committee in London. Like many other British businessmen, he was happy to help his country's secret services. Unsuspected by the Cheka, Gillespie managed to get out to Finland where he was to take over the British passport control office in the Finnish Lapland town of Tornio. Known in Swedish as Torneå, it was an important border crossing to its twin municipality Haparanda on the Swedish side. Reports coming from Russia landed with Gillespie who then forwarded them to Major Scale in Stockholm for reporting on to London.

'I had assisted Mr Gillespie, the last of the intelligence officers, and on it becoming too dangerous for him to remain longer, I undertook on his request to keep on foot the various organisations started by Captain Cromie and other British officers,' Merritt later said. 'The work entailed considerable danger for myself, and involved my actual arrest on one occasion by the Red Guards.'[31] As he managed to flee, his Russian wife Lydia was arrested and interrogated in the Cheka offices in Gorokhovaya Street. If she had not been rescued in time, she could have been shot.

Dukes was sent to Russia to take over the spy networks from John Merritt. 'Dukes was given the designation ST25,' Michael Smith explains, 'as he was to be run by John Scale in Stockholm. Cumming told him that he had to find Merrett [*sic*] and pick up the reins of the agent networks set up in Petrograd and Moscow by Stephen Alley, Ernest Boyce, Scale and Jim Gillespie, as well as those run by the now-dead naval attaché Francis Cromie.'[32] In order to keep in touch with Dukes, Cumming personally organised two high-performance motor boats under Lieutenant Augustus Agar, designated

ST/34, to be stationed at the Terijoki (now Zelenogorsk, Russia) Yacht Club on the Gulf of Finland close to the then Russian border.[33] One of the first operations successfully carried out by Dukes was to smuggle John Merritt and his wife to Finland using escape lines that Merritt had himself set up to help Allied subjects, particularly British, to flee the country. 'Mr Merritt was certainly acting under circumstances of grave personal danger,' Dukes later wrote to the Foreign Office. 'Very little is generally known of the great services he rendered in the autumn of 1918.'[34]

The first reports from Dukes arrived in London on Christmas Day and contained high-grade intelligence based on dispatches between Trotsky and Commander-in-Chief of the Soviet Naval Forces Rear-Admiral Vasili Altvater. Altvater, then aged 35, had been born in Warsaw to a noble Baltic German family and joined the Bolsheviks after the revolution. Together with Trotsky he participated in peace negotiations in Brest-Litovsk as a naval adviser to the Soviet delegation. In his dispatches to Trotsky Altvater complained on the dire state of the Red Navy and warned that the Royal Navy might be able to support Finnish volunteers and the Estonian national army against the 7th Red Army offensive. By the time Dukes's reports arrived, this had indeed happened. A Royal Navy squadron under Rear-Admiral Edwyn Alexander-Sinclair, a formidable force consisting of 'C'-class cruisers and 'V&W'-class destroyers, at the time the most powerful and advanced ships of their type in the world, sailed into Estonian and Latvian ports sending in troops and supplies.

Although slightly delayed, this was important information for the British campaign in the Baltics codenamed Operation RED TREK. The British intervention was essential in preserving the independence of the Baltic states of Latvia and Estonia and assisting General Nikolai Yudenich, leader of the White movement in north-west Russia, to fight the Bolsheviks.

In revolutionary Petrograd Dukes worked with a number of Russian agents, the most important of whom was Nadezhda Vladimirovna Petrovskaya (née Wolfson).[35] Petrovskaya was a doctor by education and a Socialist Revolutionary (party pseudonym 'Maria Ivanovna Semyonova') by vocation. Duke, whose mistress she quickly became, called her 'Miss'. When Lenin was arrested in St Petersburg in December 1895, Petrovskaya, pretending to be his fiancé, visited him in prison, of which she reminded him in a letter when she herself was arrested by the Cheka.

Rem Krasilnikov, a KGB general famous for his counter-intelligence operations against American agents in the USSR in the 1980s, in his book *KGB Against MI6* (2000) did not bother to look into the files, confusing names and events while describing Paul Dukes' agents and adventures in Russia. The same is typical to other Russian sources which the Wikipedia article about Dukes refers to. Thus, Krasilnikov names Colonel Lundqvist, chief of staff of the 7th Red Army that defended Petrograd, as one of Dukes' agents, while the former Tsarist officer Vladimir Hjalmar Lundqvist was a member of the anti-Bolshevik underground organisation 'The National Centre' that had been preparing a revolt in Petrograd in anticipation of an attack by Yudenich's troops. Another 'agent' named by Krasilnikov is 'Alexander Bankau, an employee of the political department of the 7th Red Army'. In reality, 'Alexander Bankau, a soldier in the Automobile Section of the 8th Army' was one of the aliases of Paul Dukes.

Dukes, who generously paid for his information from the funds provided by another expatriate businessman, George Gibson, who had agreed to bankroll his activities, obtained his intelligence from many sources all of whom, of course, were fiercely opposed to the Bolsheviks. The British agent was usually meeting his Russian informers in the apartment that belonged to Ilya Kürz-Giedroyc (in some publications written 'Gedroitz', using its phonetic spelling).

Ilya Kürz, born in Paris in 1873, was an illegitimate son of Prince Romuald Władysław Giedroyc. Before the revolution he had worked in St Petersburg as a French journalist (some sources claim that in February 1910 René Marchand, who represented *Le Figaro*, after a perceived affront demanded satisfaction from Kürz in a duel), used to be a secret agent of the Okhrana in France and served as a counter-intelligence officer on the southern front. One of the couriers used by Dukes to send his reports to Stockholm was Peter Sokolov (codenamed ST/65, aliases 'Colberg' and 'Goalkeeper'), previously a famous Russian footballer (wingback), champion of Russia and St Petersburg (1912), who took part in the Summer Olympics in Stockholm. Sokolov later finished an officer candidate school and was commissioned in the rank of ensign serving in the Russian counter-intelligence unit in Tornio, Finland. Recruited in August 1918 by Ernest Boyce, he would become one of the most important British agents in the interwar period.

Petrovskaya was detained on 2 June 1919. From her prison cell she managed to send a letter to Lenin reminding him of their meetings two decades before. Lenin could not remember her name but responded with a copy to the Petrograd Cheka. Nikolai Yudin, a young Cheka investigator, had to release Petrovskaya after Lenin's intervention, but she was arrested again in November that year, charged with committing espionage and sentenced to death by shooting.[36] Petrovskaya was pardoned and released three years later, this time with Maxim Gorky's wife vouching for her. Her elder son Pavel, who had served in the political department of the 7th Red Army and who had been helping Dukes to collect intelligence, was arrested and executed in 1920 together with Colonel Lundqvist. Pictured in his book as 'Maria', John

Merritt's housekeeper, Petrovskaya was released from prison around the same time that Dukes's *Red Dusk and the Morrow* was first published in London.

Sensing that the Cheka was closing in on him, in August 1919 Dukes began to prepare his escape. On Monday, 25 August (a bad day for such an enterprise), Lieutenant Agar made a final effort to pick him up in Kronstadt but failed. Instead, Peter Sokolov managed to exfiltrate the agent through the Finnish border to Helsingfors. Back in England Dukes was rewarded with a knighthood – the only member of the Service, according to its official history, to be thus rewarded for work in the field in its first 40 years.

The last British agent who remained in Petrograd after Paul Dukes left Russia was the writer Arthur Ransome. In the official history of MI6 Ransome is mentioned only in passing, while there is considerable literature devoted to the writer's intelligence exploits as well as his private life and literary accomplishments. As Shelepina and Ransome, who had been married but effectively separated from his first wife, became increasingly close during the early part of 1918,

> The British saw an opportunity to use their relationship to their own advantage. Lockhart and the British chargé d'affaires, Sir Francis Lindley, went out of their way to encourage Ransome to get close to the Bolshevik leadership in order to obtain intelligence that could assist in their reporting back to London. It would be naïve to imagine that Shelepina was unaware of the risks she ran in passing documents to Ransome, who then passed them on to Lockhart, Lindley or Ernest Boyce, another MI1c officer who was to become a close personal friend of the reporter.[37]

During that visit to Russia, Ransome also became friendly with Lenin and other Bolshevik leaders. At the end of 1917, while interviewing Trotsky, at the time People's Commissar for Foreign Affairs, Ransome met his private secretary, Eugenia 'Zhenya' Shelepina, a 'tall jolly woman' with whom he fell deeply in love. As Brue Lockhart observed to the Foreign Office, Shelepina had been 'working with Ransome in connexion with MI1c and was incidentally instrumental in getting out of Russia the numerous Bolshevik papers and literature which Ransome sent to you'.[38] In December 1918 Cumming admitted to William Tyrrell, head of the Political Intelligence Department of the Foreign Office, that Ransome was 'probably the one person available to go openly to Moscow and Petrograd, and to give us first-hand information of the condition of things, and at any rate the ostensible policies that are being pursued there'.[39]

The plan to go to Russia, agreed between Ransome and Major John Scale in Stockholm (in Ransome's agent designation S.76, 'S' stood for Stockholm), was approved and the writer spent six weeks in Moscow in Petrograd in February-March 1919.

According to the official history of the Service, 'there is no evidence that he was able to supply much – or any – useful intelligence during this period'. But according to the unofficial history, Ransome's mission was a great success. He had interviewed Lenin three times, and had a number of meetings with Trotsky and other leading Bolsheviks. Finally, to Ransome's great satisfaction, he was able to attend the founding Congress of the Communist International, that would become known as the Comintern, held in Moscow on 2-6 March.

Yevgenia and Ransome left Moscow together on 28 October 1919, arriving in the Estonian capital of Tallinn (known as Reval until 1918) on 5 November. Three days before their departure and less than a week after the White Army commanded by Yudenich reached the outskirts of Petrograd, Shelepina was summoned to the office of Boris Kantorovich, executive secretary of the NKID. Following the instructions of Commissar Chicherin and his deputy Karakhan, Kantorovich handed over to Shelepina 35 diamonds weighing from 4.45 to 13.20 carats each plus three strings of pearls (altogether 206 pearls) amounting to an estimated sum of 1,039,000 roubles.[40] The treasures, handed to Soviet agents in Estonia, would have found its way to England where they would be used to finance trade unions and pro-Bolshevik publications including the *Daily Herald*, a newspaper published in London from 1912, one of whose founding members was William Norman Ewer, known as 'Trilby'.

Yudenich's offensive collapsed in late October and in Petrograd Trotsky was triumphant as the 7th and 15th Red Armies drove the White forces back to Estonia to be evacuated by British destroyers. Moscow secured a separate armistice with Tallinn on 3 January by promising to recognise Estonian independence. At the end of January, Yudenich was arrested as he tried to escape to Western Europe with North-western Army funds. Following diplomatic pressure by the Allies, the general was released and settled with his wife in France on the Côte d'Azur.

The Treaty of Tartu was signed on 2 February 1920 stipulating that Russia renounced in perpetuity all rights to the territory of Estonia, including the city of Narva with Jaanilinn (St John's Town, now known as Ivangorod) across the river.

The Latvian War of Independence ended on 11 August 1920 when the Treaty of Riga was signed, with Soviet Russia's recognition of the independence of Latvia 'for all future time'.

After the Bolshevik revolution and during the civil war of 1918–20, foreign intelligence collection had not even been considered by the Cheka, whose role was clearly defined as combatting counter-revolution and assisting the victory of the Red Army over its enemies. In the autumn of 1919, Dzerzhinsky's Extraordinary Commission proudly claimed that during the first 19 months of its existence it had discovered and neutralised '412 underground anti-Soviet organisations'.[41] As noted by Professor Andrew, the Cheka's most effective method of dealing with opposition was terror. At the same time, witnesses and victims were forced to give information and evidence because of the perceived or actual intimidation or threats against themselves or their loved ones, including threats against lives. During only its first four years the Cheka enormously outstripped the Okhrana in both the scale and the ferocity of its onslaught on political opposition as well as real or perceived adversaries. 'In 1901,' Christopher Andrew writes, '4,113 Russians were in internal exile for political crimes, of whom only 180 were on hard labour. Executions for political crimes were limited to those involved in actual or attempted assassinations. During the civil war, by contrast, Cheka executions probably numbered as many as 250,000, and may well have exceeded the number of deaths in battle.'[42] On 6 February 1922, Lenin proposed to the 9th Congress of the Soviets to abolish the Cheka, which was replaced by the State Political Directorate (GPU), with its powers of summary justice transferred to the People's Commissariat of Justice and the prosecutor's office attached to it.

The new GPU became one of the chief directorates of the People's Commissariat of Internal Affairs (NKVD) with Dzerzhinsky being appointed both the NKVD Commissar and Chairman of the GPU. In this role, Dzerzhinsky was assisted by seven individuals all of whom would play a prominent part in the history of the Soviet secret political police.[43] Except Menzhinsky, who died in May 1934, all of them were executed during the Great Terror.

In the first volume of *The Mitrokhin Archive* Christopher Andrew suggests that at the time of the October Revolution 'it had never occurred to Lenin that he and the Bolshevik leadership would be responsible for the rebirth of the Okrana in a new and far more terrible form'. Andrew refers to what Lenin believed to be his most important contribution to debates about politics, his pamphlet *The State and Revolution*, written in August-September 1917. In *The State and Revolution*, Andrew writes, Lenin claimed that there would be no need for a police force, let alone political police, after the people had taken power into their own hands. This is not entirely correct and rather refers to the translator's introduction to the English edition than to Lenin's words. As a matter of fact, the founder of the Soviet state never mentioned political police in this work.

Writing about the state, bourgeois right (by which he meant law), and repression shortly before the revolution, Lenin stated:

> Democracy is a form of the state, one of its varieties. And, consequently, it is like every state in representing the organized systematic use of violence against persons ... But democracy is by no means a boundary not to be over-stepped; it is only one of the stages on the road from feudalism to capitalism, and from capitalism to communism ... Of course, bourgeois right inevitably presupposes the existence of the *bourgeois state*, for right is nothing without an apparatus capable of *enforcing* the observance of the norms of right ... We are not utopians, and do not in the least deny the possibility and inevitability of excesses on the part of *individual persons* or equally the need to supress *such* excesses. But in the first place, no special machine, no special apparatus of suppression is needed for this; this will be done by the armed people it-self ... The dictatorship of the proletariat imposes a series of exclusions from freedom in relation to the oppressors, the exploiters, the capitalists. We must supress them in order to free humanity from wage slavery; their resistance must be crushed by force: it is clear that where there is suppression, where there is coercion, there is no freedom and no democracy.[44]

In his introduction to Lenin's work, Robert Service recalls that the Bolsheviks won less than a quarter of the votes in the universal-suffrage elections to the Consituent Assembly in late November 2017, the first free elections in Russian history. Alas, the Assembly only met for a single day the following January before being dissolved by the Bolsheviks. Five days before the elections, the Cheka was established. At that time Lenin was sending his pamphlet to the printers, simultaneously doing his best to ensure that the Cheka's powers were unrestricted. All other leaders of this vast country, from Stalin to Putin, faithfully followed Lenin's example.

Chapter 4

Comintern: Secret Soldiers of the Revolution

The 'internationalisation' of the work of the Cheka/GPU began gradually with the creation of the Soviet-dominated Communist International (Comintern), sometimes referred to as the Third International. Its founding congress was held in Moscow on 2–6 March 1919, opening with a tribute to Karl Liebknecht and Rosa Luxemburg, recently executed during the Spartacist uprising in Berlin.[1] Fifty-two delegates representing thirty-four political parties and organisations gathered in the Kremlin to form 'the general staff of the world revolution'.

Several important international events preceded the creation of the Comintern, two of them being the Peace Conference at the Quai d'Orsay in Paris which began on 18 January 1919 attended by thirty-eight nations, and the Polish-Ukrainian War, a conflict between the Second Polish Repubic and Ukrainian forces that lasted from November 1918 until July 1919.

The main aim of the Paris Conference dominated by the 'Big Four' – British Prime Minister David Lloyd George, French Prime Minister Georges Clemenceau, US President Woodrow Wilson and Italian Prime Minister Vittorio Emanuele Orlando, who made all major decisions before they were ratified – was to shape the future of the world after the Great War. Among its major decisions was the creation of the League of Nations, founded on 10 January 1920; signing of the peace treaties with the defeated states, of which the most important was the Treaty of Versailles with Germany (28 June 1919); the awarding of German and Ottoman overseas territories chiefly to Britain and France; the impositions of reparations upon Germany; and the drawing or drafting of new national borders. Soviet Russia was not formally invited because it had already signed a peace treaty with the Central Powers, but the Provisional Government of Alexander Kerensky, overthrown in October 1917, was represented by the former Foreign Minister of the Russian Empire Sergey Sazonov who had also served as the foreign minister of the anti-Bolshevik government of Admiral Kolchak.

One of the proposals at the conference was a new demarcation line between the Second Polish Republic and Soviet Russia, which became known as the Curzon Line, suggested for consideration by the British Foreign Secretary George Curzon to the Supreme War Council in 1919. It may be recalled that in the second half of the nineteenth century, Russian Tsar Alexander II incorporated Poland directly into Russia, partitioning it into ten provinces each headed by a military governor under the control of the Governorate-General in Warsaw. Before the Central Powers occupied the area in 1915 and the Kingdom of Poland was established, the last Russian Governor General of Warsaw was Prince Pavel Nikolayevich Yengalychev. Following the Treaty of Brest-Litovsk (March 1918), Bolshevik Russia ceded all Polish territories to the German Empire and the Dual Monarchy of Austria-Hungary. While the Paris Conference did not make a definitive ruling regarding Poland's borders, it accepted the Curzon Line proposal as a provisional boundary in December 1919 for the re-established Polish state. As a result of the Polish-Soviet War (February 1919–October 1920), the border between Poland and the RSFSR was determined with Poland gaining territory of about 200km east of the Curzon Line including the Vilnius region. With this, more than one million Poles remained in the territories that two years later became part of the Soviet Ukraine and Soviet Byelorussia. They were systematically persecuted by Soviet authorities for political, economic and religious reasons. In spite of the fact that many Poles and Polish Jews occupied prominent positions in the Cheka and its successors as well as in Soviet military intelligence, a great number of them became victims of what would be known as the Polish operation of the NKVD, launched in the 1930s.

In early 1919, Poland's Chief of State Józef Piłsudski, seeing himself as a descendent of the culture and traditions of the Polish-Lithuanian Commonwealth, felt the time was ripe to expand the borders of Poland as far east as possible. Lenin, on the contrary, saw Poland as a bulwark against Western imperialism and at the same time a bridge or corridor the Red Army had to cross to assist Europe-wide communist revolutions. And although up to the time of the Second Congress the main arena of the Bolsheviks' efforts was Europe with the primary revolutionary target and aspiration focusing on Germany,[2] the second socialist state in the world to be formed appeared to be Hungary with the proclamation of the Hungarian Soviet Republic on 21 March with Sándor Garbai as president and prime minister and Béla Kun as commissar for foreign affairs. Lenin personally instructed Kun to establish the 'dictatorship of the proletariat' and transform Hungary into a communist state. Immediately the Red Guard was organised under the command of Mátyás Rákosi (born Rosenfeld) with mobile punitive squads known as 'Lenin Boys' to supress counter-revolution. The communist government also set up revolutionary tribunals, starting the Red Terror campaign with intimidation, arrests, violence and mass executions.

* * *

In his attempt to write the first-ever academic history of the KGB, Christopher Andrew asserted that the founding congress of the Comintern was 'a mostly fraudulent piece of Russian revolutionary theatre' with 'only five delegates' arriving from abroad while the 'remainder were handpicked by the Bolshevik Central Committee from its foreign supporters in Moscow'.[3] This allegation probably came from Oleg Gordievsky, Professor Andrew's co-author. In reality, nineteen delegations (thirty-four delegates) with full or decisive votes and thirteen delegations (eighteen delegates) with consultative votes attended the Founding (First) Congress. And although this congress was obviously staged and artificial, and contact with member parties during the first few months was irregular, the initial period of Comintern activity was far more important than has been recognised.[4] Some experts even consider the creation of the Comintern as 'the most daring organisational venture Moscow ever undertook', which may very well be true.

The invitations were sent through couriers. According to Jakob Reich ('Comrade THOMAS'), who was among those few who helped to organise the First Congress, all couriers were former prisoners of war anxious to get home. They were given money and letters written on silk and sewn into their clothes, having been only asked to deliver those letters to their destination. Out of twenty-four couriers sent, Reich recalls, only three or four complied.

'One of the first persons to conduct a mission abroad specifically for the International was Beatrice Rutgers,' James Hulse comments, 'a Dutch woman who had travelled to Russia with her husband via America and Japan, arriving in the fall of 1918.' While her husband became a delegate to the Congress, she received an assignment to return to the Netherlands to invite Dutch Communists and revolutionaries from other Western European groups to come to Moscow. 'She reached Amsterdam safely but belatedly,' the historian adds, 'the document appeared in the Amsterdam Communist newspaper only on March 4, two days after the Congress opened.'[5]

The Russian Communist Party (Bolsheviks) was represented in both delegations, the main group including Lenin, Trotsky, Zinoviev, Stalin (there are, however, doubts that he actually participated), Nikolai Bukharin, the editor of *Pravda*, and Georgy Chicherin, People's Commissar for Foreign Affairs. Two more Russian delegates had consultative votes. For most foreign delegates a trip to Moscow to attend the Congress turned into a challenging adventure.

Lenin had certain misgivings about the German Spartacists who, he feared, could oppose his plans. Rosa Luxemburg, hailed at the Congress, had no confidence in Lenin, justly fearing that the communists of Western Europe might become prisoners of the Russian Bolsheviks. Their delegate, Hugo Eberlein, arrived in Moscow with a mandate to oppose the creation of a new communist organisation. Reich notes that as soon as he arrived, he told Lenin he had come only as an observer and under no circumstances would he associate himself with the new International. A second delegate, Gustav Klinger, a German from the Volga region who had never had any connection to the Kommunistische Partei Deutschlands (KPD), was held in reserve.

The Communist Party of German Austria was represented by Karl Steinhardt who was born in Hungary but later moved with his parents to Vienna. He had lived in Hamburg and travelled around the world, having managed to get a job as a printer on a large passenger steamer. As a member of a Marxist group in London in 1909–10, Steinhardt had been editing a newspaper *The People* before returning to Vienna, where he was elected general secretary of the KP(D)Ö at its first congress on 9 February 1919. His arrival in Moscow enlivened the conference proceedings.

Steinhardt chose the alias 'J. Gruber' and his appearance on the platform was picturesque and well stage-managed:

> In the middle of a boring speech the door was flung open; preceded by an attendant, a man in Austrian military uniform made his entry. With a shaggy beard, and a soldier's cap in shreds, he went straight to the rostrum: 'I'm the delegate of the Austrian Communists!' He produced a knife and cut open his cap, from which he withdrew a mandate. He began speaking, describing, almost in tears, what he had endured crossing the lines on the Ukrainian front. It made everyone tremble. Then, as he was about to finish, someone on the platform whispered to him: 'Shout: "Long Live the Congress of the Communist International!"' This the Austrian did on the spot. Thus were the words 'Congress of the Communist International' uttered for the first time.[6]

Steinhardt's adventures did not end there. On his return from Moscow his plane was shot down and he was taken prisoner by the Romanian police and sentenced to death for espionage. After the intervention of the International Red Cross, he was able to return to Vienna in January 1920.

The so-called Balkan Revolutionary Federation of Bulgaria-Romania was represented by Christian Rakovsky (born Krastyo Georgiev Stanchev in Bulgaria), who at the time served as Chairman of the Provisional Revolutionary Government of the Workers and Peasants of Ukraine. Arthur Ransome mentions Rakovsky in his work *Six Weeks in Russia in 1919*, published in London in June 1919. Rakovsky was very active as a revolutionary in Romania where he had inherited his father's estate on the Black Sea near Mangalia, long before he moved to Petrograd in the spring of 1917.[7] His diplomatic career began in February 1922 when he was sent to Berlin to negotiate with Germany and then was part of the official delegation to the Genoa Economic and Financial Conference. Two years later, as the Labour Party minority government came to power in Britain, Rakovsky and the Prime Minister Ramsay MacDonald negotiated the de jure recognition of Soviet Russia and agreed on a possible Anglo-Soviet General Treaty and a British loan to the Soviet Union. The scandal caused by what became known as the Zinoviev Letter provoked the fall of the MacDonald government and brought an end to all further talks. Rakovsky then served as the Soviet ambassador to France (October 1925–7), replacing Leonid Krasin. Christian Rakovsky was arrested in 1937 and shot by the NKVD with over 150 other political prisoners in the Medvedev Forest massacre in September 1941.

Finland was represented at the Congress by a five-member delegation of the former leaders of the Finnish Revolution and the Finnish Civil War: Yrjö Sirola, Kullervo Manner, Otto Wille Kuusinen, and brothers Jukka and Eino Rahja. The first three of them would become founding members of the Communist Party of Finland (Suomen Kommunistinen Puolue, SKP) in exile in the Soviet Union. Kuusinen would briefly serve as head of the short-lived Finnish Democratic Republic, Stalin's puppet regime during the three months of the Winter War in 1939–40. He had to return to Moscow after the peace treaty was signed in March. Despite his being a staunch Stalinist, Kuusinen managed very well under Khrushchev's 'de-Stalinisation' campaign, becoming Secretary of the CPSU Central Committee and even a member of the Politburo, the highest policymaking authority of the Soviet Union.

Emil Stang, a lawyer, came from Norway where he had practised as a barrister in Kristiania (now Oslo) from 1911, joining the Norwegian Labour Party in the same year. Elected its chairman in 1918, he was sent to Moscow to take part in the Congress, later becoming one of the founders of the Communist Party of Norway (NKP). Having been appointed a Supreme Court judge in 1937, which is a lifetime appointment, during the war he was arrested by the Nazis and held at the Sachsenhausen concentration camp in Germany. Stang survived and after the war was appointed Chief Justice of the Supreme Court of Norway.

Józef Unszlicht (in Russia: Iosif Stanislavovich Unshlikht) represented Poland and its Communist Party. Born in Mława, Płock Governorate in December 1879, an electrician by education and profession, Unszlicht had been an old Bolshevik, arrested many times for his revolutionary activities and spending years in prison and Siberian exile before the revolution. Later a member of the Petrograd Soviet, from February 1919 he had served as Commissar for War of the equally short-lived Lithuanian-Byelorussian Soviet Socialist Republic. Unszlicht was appointed member of the Provisional Polish Revolutionary Committee during the Polish-Soviet War in 1920 and in April 1921 succeeded Ivan Ksenofontov as Dzerzhinsky's

Cheka deputy. Donald Rayfield notes that as a trusted friend of Dzerzhinsky from the Warsaw underground in the 1900s, Unszlicht 'was to command the Cheka's 300,000 paramilitaries, an army of "special purpose units" which came into existence despite Trotsky's opposition to splitting up the armed forces and fell upon rebellious civilians, obstreperous peasants, Cossacks and routed soldiers'.[8] In August 1923 Unszlicht was promoted to member of the Revolutionary Military Council and chief of the Red Army supply. In June 1937 he was arrested, sentenced to death as a Polish spy and saboteur and shot in July 1938. His successor as Dzerzhinsky's deputy was Menzhinsky, another Pole.

The Swiss Communist Party was represented at the Founding Congress by Fritz Platten, who accompanied Lenin on the sealed train from Zurich to Sassnitz, and then on the ferry route known as Kungsleden (The King's Route) to the ferry port of Trelleborg, the southernmost town in Sweden, and from there through the whole country to the Russian border at Haparanda-Tornio, the northerly extreme of the Swedish coastline. In Trelleborg, the new elegant steamship *Drottning Victoria* (*Queen Victoria*) with Lenin, Platten, Armand and the rest of the party was greeted by a young left-wing socialist Otto Grimlund, who, like Platten, would become its country's sole representative (with three votes) at the Congress.

The Bolshevik British Communist Group in Russia was represented by Joe Fineberg, a Polish Jew who lived in the UK where he joined a Jewish section of the BSP in London's East End. In July 1918 Fineberg moved to Russia and became a translator for the Comintern, translating works of Lenin, Trotsky, Alexander Bogdanov and later Russian and Soviet writers including Lev Tolstoy and Ilya Ehrenburg. Fineberg acknowledged that as a non-voting delegate he had no mandate, was representing the British Socialist Party and endorsed the decisions of the Congress in its name.

One of the consultative delegates representing the French Communist Group (La Section Française du Parti Communiste [Bolchevik] Russe), was Jacques Sadoul, a former member of the French military mission in Moscow. Having decided not to return to France during the Russian Civil War, Sadoul assisted Trotsky in setting up the Red Army, becoming an instructor there. After the Allied embassies had left Russia, Sadoul was sent to Ukraine to instigate mutinies among the French intervention troops, and then to Germany to assist the KPD. In July 1919 Christian Rakovsky, then head of the Ukrainian Council of the People's Commissars, assigned Sadoul to negotiate an exchange of French prisoners in Odessa. In October, he was tried in absentia for collaborating with the enemy and acts of sedition, and on 7 November sentenced to death in France. In 1924, when France recognised Soviet Russia, Sadoul returned, was acquitted upon retrial and joined the

PCF. Failing to win any elections, however, he was employed by *Izvestia* as its correspondent in France. Sadoul was also a leading figure in the Society for Franco-Soviet Friendship and in 1927 was decorated by Klim Voroshilov with the Order of the Red Banner which was a clear demonstration of Sadoul's ties with Soviet military intelligence. The Germans arrested him during the occupation of France but he was eventually freed in exchange for his collaboration with the Vichy regime. Following the Allied liberation of France, Sadoul was elected Mayor of Sainte-Maxime in April 1945. Two years later he lost his mayor's office and spent the last nine years in retirement. His wife Yvonne survived him by almost five decades.

The First Congress did not elect an executive committee, which was done at the Second Congress in July–August 1920. Grigory Zinoviev (born Hirsch Apfelbaum) was elected Chairman (some incorrectly say 'President') of the Comintern, assisted by four secretaries: Angelica Balabanova (also sometimes spelt 'Balabanoff'), Wacław Worowski (in Russia: Vatslav Vatslavovich Vorovsky), Jan Antonovich Berzin (born Jānis Bērziņš, alias 'Ziemelis') and Karl Radek,[9] only the first two of them attending the congress as delegates.

For many of the revolutionaries who gathered in Moscow, the world proletarian revolution seemed to be spreading even without the efforts of the Communist International, which they established under Lenin's dictate. Zinoviev, the Comintern chairman, forecast that within a year all Europe would become communist. Indeed, soviet republics were declared in Hungary on 21 March and in Munich, Bavaria, on 6 April. In Bavaria it was overthrown a month later and in Hungary in August. But to further promote the world revolution and to maintain contacts with its sympathisers, it was decided to open Comintern outposts outside Russia.

Initially, Lenin and other Bolshevik leaders didn't put much effort into distinguishing between the Comintern and Soviet foreign-policy objectives. Soon after the congress ended its work on 6 March, Mikhail Borodin was appointed by Lenin as the Soviet consul to the Mexican government and left the country using a complex route travelling through Germany to Switzerland and the United States. Borodin was born as Mikhail Markovich Gruzenberg in a Byelorussian village of the Vitebsk province to a Jewish family and joined the Bund aged 16. In 1906 he attended the 4th Congress of the Russian Social Democratic Labour Party in Stockholm and then, after having been detained by the Okhrana in St Petersburg, preferred emigration to exile in Siberia. He first moved to London but was promptly ordered out of the country and moved to the USA, residing in Boston and then settling in Chicago, where he opened a school for immigrants, coming back to Russia after the Bolshevik revolution. In July 1918 Borodin started working at the People's Commissariat for Foreign Affairs and by the end of March

1919 departed for Europe on the Comintern assignment. First, he arrived in Berlin with 500,000 Tsarist roubles (US$250,000, roughly equal to $25 million today) and another half-million dollars' worth of diamonds 'sewn into the lining of two bulky leather suitcases'.[10] From there he travelled to Geneva, Switzerland, where he deposited the money as 'Mr Gruzenberg' using a numbered and anonymous bank account 'payable to bearer' and then left the country, travelling to the United States. This account was allegedly frozen later on by the Geneva bank when an individual named Julius Fox turned up with the key, demanding access.[11] What happened to the deposit is anyone's guess.

The first South-eastern Bureau was set up in Kiev in April 1919 with Balabanova, Rakovsky and Sadoul as representatives. It was soon renamed the Southern Bureau.[12] This was later moved to Kharkiv with two sub-bureaus opened in Kiev and Odessa. Shortly after, it was decided to organise the Vienna Bureau under Steinhardt ('Gruber'), who received sufficient financial means to set it up but because of his arrest this was postponed until later. Since late January 1920 the Vienna Bureau began to function as the South-eastern Bureau responsible for Austria, Hungary, Czechoslovakia, Romania, Yugoslavia, Bulgaria, Greece and Eastern Thrace (European Turkey).[13]

On the same day, 14 April 1919, the Small Executive Committee of the Comintern, which consisted of the chairman and secretaries, decided to open the Scandinavian Bureau in Stockholm headed by Zeth Höglund with Fredrik Ström and Karl Chilbum as members.[14] When Lenin was passing through Stockholm in April 1917 on the way to Petrograd, Höglund was in prison for his revolutionary activities and Ström together with another Bolshevik supporter, Ture Nerman, and the mayor of Stockholm Carl Lindhagen were part of the small delegation of Swedish revolutionary socialists who greeted the future head of the first Soviet state. Nothing happened after the First Congress, with Höglund working hard to convince his friends from the Left Social Democratic Party to join the International and by June, largely owing to Bolshevik propaganda, the party had shifted its position substantially toward a programme very close to Comintern standards. A year later, in April 1920, the issue was raised again at the ECCI meeting. Two bureaus were opened: the Scandinavian Bureau in Stockholm with Höglund and Arvid G. Hansen, who at the time chaired the Norwegian Social Democratic Youth Association and was editor-in-chief of the Labour Party newspaper. He was included as a representative of Norway at the same time heading the Norwegian Bureau set up in Kristiania (Oslo) on the same day, 24 April. Yrjö Sirola was seconded to the Norwegian Bureau as an ECCI supervisor.

Parallel to that, shortly after the First Congress finished its work, Zinoviev opened an office in Petrograd which became the Petrograd Bureau located at the Smolny Institute, where he had his headquarters as Chairman of the Petrograd Soviet. Staffed by two young men with a turbulent revolutionary past, Victor Kibalchich (alias 'Serge') and Vladimir Lichtenstadt ('Mazin'), the bureau's task was to prepare propaganda material aimed at the European proletariat and Allied military personnel in Russia.

At the end of September 1919, the Comintern leadership decided to establish a branch in the Netherlands. Sebald J. Rutgers, the husband of Beatrice Rutgers, was sent to Amsterdam to open the West European Bureau. However, the internal situation of the Dutch Communist Party complicated his assignment. Like in Sweden, this small organisation was an offspring of the Dutch Socialist Party (SPD). The leading figures were David Wijnkoop and Willem van Ravesteyn, who were members of parliament and edited the party's newspaper, as well as the astronomer Anton Pannekoek, the poet Herman Gorter and the Socialist leader Henriette Roland Holst. Rutgers (alias 'G.L. Trotter', derived from 'globetrotter') became the bureau's secretary. The Comintern leadership placed the sum of twenty million roubles at their disposal. According to the Comintern documents in the Russian archives, Rutgers received the bulk of the amount in the form of precious stones.[15] The ECCI also allocated half a million roubles' worth of valuables for the communist propaganda activities in Western Europe and America and the organisation was renamed the Amsterdam Bureau.

In November 1919, another important West European Bureau started working in Berlin. Naturally, the inter-party squabbles began almost immediately because the KPD, which had over 100,000 members in autumn 1919, had little desire to share the turf with the Communist Party of Norway (CPN) with 2,400 members at most, and wanted to have Western Europe all to itself. For reasons explained in the next chapter, the Amsterdam Bureau ran into severe financial difficulties and soon Moscow was further disappointed because three of the its members broke their ties with communism.[16] The Berlin Bureau was transformed into the West European Secretariat (WES) according to the ECCI decision of 2 February 1920,[17] which also approved the establishment of the Balkans Bureau in Sofia. Partly because of the intrigues of the German communists, the ECCI decided to close down the Amsterdam Bureau after just six months, accepting the fact that its German counterpart had turned out to be more important organisationally, financially, and politically. The WES was to support, control and maintain close links with the communist parties of Germany, France, Belgium, Switzerland, Italy, Poland and – after the dissolution of the Amsterdam Bureau – with the fraternal parties of Great Britain and the USA.

On 13 March 1920 Finnish customs officials found and detained a Comintern courier by the name of Jim Gormley, who was hiding in a coal bunker of a ship. Taken to the police station he had to reveal his true identity. The man was identified as the American journalist John Reed travelling to the USA where he hoped to secure Comintern support for the Communist Labour Party of America (CLPA). During a thorough search of the passenger and his belongings, 102 small diamonds worth $14,000 were found together with photographs, letters and fake documents. Reed was arrested for smuggling jewels and later charged and convicted. Finally released in early June, he travelled to Petrograd and then Moscow. A few weeks later he attended the 2nd World Congress of the Comintern, this time held in both Soviet capitals, where Great Britain and the United States were represented by three different delegations each and where Reed was a delegate of the CLPA. In September 1920 he joined Louise Bryant in Moscow and together they visited Lenin, Trotsky, Kamenev and other leading Bolsheviks. Reed fell ill at the end of that month, was hospitalised and diagnosed with typhus. Due to the lack of proper treatment and antibiotics, it was a fatal illness and he died in Moscow on 17 October with his wife holding his hand.[18]

John Reed is one of the few Americans buried at the Kremlin Wall Necropolis in Moscow. Not far from Reed are the ashes of his political rival, C.E. Ruthenberg, an American Marxist politician and founder of the Communist Party of the USA (CPUSA), who died in Chicago in 1927. Their neighbour there is William Dudley 'Big Bill' Haywood, a founding member and leader of the Industrial Workers of the World. Haywood was tried for espionage in 1918, found guilty and sentenced to 20 years in prison. While on bail he escaped to the Soviet Union and became a labour advisor to the MOPR, better known as the International Red Aid.[19] Married to a Russian woman much younger than himself, he missed his native country, began to drink heavily and died in May 1928.

* * *

One year after the Bolshevik revolution, the governing circles of Britain came to the conclusion that its secret service machinery required reorganisation and retasking, with the focus firmly on Soviet Russia. Victor Madeira identifies four discernible factors that produced an immediate perception of danger in British official circles emanating from post-revolutionary Russia. 'One factor,' he writes, 'was fear of how Bolshevism would affect this nation following the war: bureaucrats worried about possible connections between working-class unrest and Bolshevik subversion.' Another factor, that became evident even before the Comintern was founded, was the considerable novelty of the perceived threat: never before had any foreign regime dedicated itself ideologically, politically and financially to upending the capitalist world system in which Britain had been playing a leading role irrespective of the enormous human and material losses of the Great War. Between the First and Second Comintern Congresses there was even a short-lived boom in the British economy caused by a rush of investments. The third factor – the threat to India, the 'jewel in the crown' of the British Empire – related closely to the second factor. While Britain was seeking to preserve the sanctity of India, the Comintern sought to undermine it.[20] The final and arguably most important factor, in Madeira's view, was the 'critical role that intelligence (both the community and the information it presented) played, unintentionally or otherwise, in portraying the scope and nature of the "Red Menace"'.[21] In other words, in spite of the seemingly successful missions of the British agents to Russia shortly before and after the Revolution, Walter Long, the First Lord of the Admiralty, pushed for urgent revision and re-organisation of the intelligence machinery, arguing that 'Unless prompt steps are taken, I am informed we shall find the Secret Service seriously crippled just when we shall need it most'.[22]

On 9 January 1919 Long forwarded a report to the Prime Minister:

I now find myself convinced that in England Bolschevism [sic] must be faced and grappled with, the efforts of the International Jews of Russia combated and their agents eliminated from the United Kingdom. Unless some serious consideration is given to the matter, I believe that there will be some sort of Revolution in this country before 12 months are past … At the present time the Secret Service receives reports from Switzerland, Holland, Scandinavia and Russia on Bolschevik activities, of agent being sent to France or England, of agitators and their schemes … Many will scoff at these ideas, yet how many 'extreme' British Bolsheviks are there, say 5,000! A bigger percentage in proportion to the population than Russia started with![23]

Soon afterwards the Cabinet set up a Secret Service Committee (SSC) under Lord Curzon, which included Long, Edward Shortt (Home Secretary), Winston Churchill (just appointed Secretary of State for War), and Sir Hamar Greenwood, Bt (Secretary for Overseas Trade).[24] At its third meeting in April 1920, the committee formally established a kind of a civilian secret service under Basil Thomson, until then responsible for Scotland Yard's Special Branch (SB), to combat sedition as well as monitor all forms of civil subversion, labour unrest, and revolutionary activity.[25] The new service, part of the Home Office, was called the Directorate of Intelligence (DI). In the course of that April meeting Curzon also informed the SSC that the Foreign Office had created a news section, a subdivision of which was the Political

Intelligence Department (established on 11 March 1918) to collect and analyse political, economic and military intelligence in both allied and enemy countries and to conduct propaganda overseas. William Tyrell was appointed the director of the department assisted by a British academic historian James Headlam-Morley who was involved in propaganda activity during the war and became a civil servant. Both were to liaise closely with Thomson.

With the benefit of hindsight one can say that the greatest flaw of this reorganisation was the division of counter-intelligence work between MI1c, MI5 and the new Directorate of Intelligence. At that time the SIS staff in London numbered 180 with some officers serving abroad under the newly-created Passport Control Officer cover, but Cumming agreed that after the end of the war that personnel (and funding) reductions were inevitable. While the Security Service (MI5) under Vernon Kell retained responsibility for counter-espionage, its funding decreased by nearly two-thirds between 1918 and 1920. In comparison, Thomson's new service was made responsible for the tracking of the Comintern activity and allocated generous funding which prompted falsified reports, distorted evidence and inflated information about subversive threats, sometimes based on badly assessed intelligence or even forgeries supplied by SIS – all of it passing on to the Cabinet, seriously eroding Thomson's personal credibility and that of his Directorate's.

The distinguished Russian physicist and future Nobel prize laureate Peter Kapitza (also spelt Pyotr or Piotr Kapitsa; in his native Romanian – Petre Capiţa) would become a target of such hyper-vigilance by the Security Service. Kapitza was born in Kronstadt to the family of a military engineer of Romanian descent and a Polish mother whose father, Hieronim Stebnicki, Kapitza's grandfather, was a Polish military cartographer serving in the Russian Imperial Army as General of Infantry. In Peter's family they communicated in Romanian although everybody could speak Russian. Peter's studies were interrupted by the 1914 war and he had spent two years at the Polish front as an ambulance driver. After demobilisation he returned to the Polytechnical Institute. An obviously talented young man, Kapitza graduated in 1918 and was appointed to a teaching post in the Institute. 'During these years,' David Shoenberg, who was Professor of Physics at Cambridge University and Head of the Low Temperature Physics Group of the Cavendish Laboratory, writes, 'a moving spirit in the physics world of Petrograd, and indeed Russia, was A.F. Joffé.'

Abram Joffé, who completed his PhD in physics at the University of Munich, was actively developing a physics school with an emphasis on research to keep abreast of scientific developments in the West. 'After 1918,' Professor Shoenberg notes, the research effort was concentrated in the newly established Petrograd Physical & Technical Institute, 'where Joffé succeeded in collecting a group of young and enthusiastic scientists around him who formed the nucleus of the enormous growth of Soviet physics in later years.'[26] After the chaos of war and the upheaval of the revolution, Joffé set up a 'Commission of the Russian Academy of Sciences for renewing scientific relations with other countries', which was provided with hard currency to buy equipment abroad. Joffé set out in February 1921 and as soon as he reached Berlin applied for an exit visa for Kapitza whom he included as a member of the purchasing commission. Germany, France and Holland refused to collaborate, but Britain was more accommodating and in May Joffé succeeded in getting Kapitza to London.

Early in June 1921 they started a round of scientific meetings which culminated in a visit to Ernest Rutherford, recently appointed Director of the Cavendish Laboratory in Cambridge. After some hesitation, Kapitza was accepted as a postgraduate research fellow in July. He spent another 13 years there working with Rutherford in the Cavendish Laboratory and founding the influential Kapitza Club. He had also become the first director of the Mond Laboratory in Cambridge and was elected a fellow of Trinity College.

Naturally, such a prominent figure from Bolshevik Russia attracted the attention of the Security Service, particularly because of several denunciations by some unknown informants in the college and because SIS reported, rightly or wrongly, that the Soviet trade organisation ARCOS, which began operations in London in 1920, had provided funding for Kapitza's research. An informant in Trinity College reported that the Russian scientist was in contact with the leading Cambridge communist Maurice Dobb and after Kapitza had proposed setting up a laboratory for low temperature and high magnetic field physics, another informant, perhaps prompted by professional jealousy, claimed that Kapitza was a Soviet spy.[27] The funding for the Mond Laboratory was obtained from the Royal Society Ludwig Mond Fund. Almost eight decades later, in its authorised history written by Christopher Andrew, the Security Service reluctantly admitted that 'though there were reasonable grounds at the time for suspicion ... it now seems highly unlikely that Kapitsa was engaged in espionage in the Cavendish Laboratory'.

October 1921 saw Thomson's last report thanks to his enforced resignation from his post. A document signed by a group of senior civil servants, which became known as the Fisher Report (named after Warren Fisher, Permanent Secretary to the Treasury and Head of the Home Civil Service, 1919–39), accused the DI of financial extravagance and overstepping its mandate. The report allowed William Horwood, Commissioner of the Metropolitan Police (and a long-time opponent of Thomson), to declare in a lengthy memorandum to the Prime Minister that the Directorate of Intelligence was 'expensive, wasteful and inefficient'.[28]

Thomson's replacement was Sir Wyndham Childs. As 1922 ended, marking the fifth anniversary of the Bolshevik revolution (and the Fourth World Congress of the Comintern held in Moscow and Petrograd between 5 November and 5 December), the Special Branch reports shifted focus almost entirely to the Communist Party of Great Britain (CPGB) and related groups. It was decided that the CPGB, but not Russia, presented the most significant threat and that its influence on the British establishment could not be underestimated. Those in power, even the Cabinet hardliners, were inclined to think that civilian unrest was more a reflection of post-war unemployment and privation than of foreign meddling. They reasoned that unemployment, after all, was 'a far more formidable peril that all the lunacies of Lenin'.[29] In July 2020 Parliament's Intelligence and Security Committee (ISC) would come to a totally different conclusion, identifying the Russia threat as a real and present danger. A century earlier, in the 1920s and for much of the interwar period, the Moscow-sponsored and controlled Comintern and its International Liaison Department, the secret OMS, had been the major conduit for Soviet intelligence operations. And like Putin's Russia today, Bolshevik Russia was a significant threat on a number of fronts – from espionage to interference in the democratic process and to serious crime such as murder on foreign soil, – a menace to civilisation.

* * *

Following the creation of the Comintern and the successful exposure of the conspiracy that became widely known as the 'Lockhart Plot', Dzerzhinky decided it was time to penetrate foreign bureaucracies and, most important, White Russian organisations abroad in order to get timely warnings of impending provocations. Reporting to the leadership, he proudly claimed that during the first 19 months of its existence the Cheka had discovered and neutralised over 400 anti-Soviet organisations.[30] The preferred method of dealing with such groups was shooting. According to Andrew (based on the Mitrokhin documents from the KGB archive), in the period of 1918–20 Cheka executions probably numbered as many as 250,000, and may well have exceeded the number of deaths in battle.[31]

During the civil war, the Special Department (Osoby Otdel) of the Cheka was tasked with guarding the Soviet borders and from 24 November 1920 it had also been involved in reconnaissance and subversive operations in the territories occupied by the White armies with Allied military forces supporting them. This included sending Cheka agents behind enemy lines.

The foreign section of the Special Department was charged with this work while the collection of foreign intelligence was of minor importance by comparison with the Cheka's role in assisting the victory of the Red Army over its enemies, both Russian and foreign,[32] and in eliminating 'counter-revolutionary elements' from post-revolutionary Soviet society.

Initially, all such operations had been controlled by Dzerzhinsky personally. He decreed that 'sending Cheka officials, or representatives, or secret agents abroad is categorically forbidden without my personal approval'.[33] On 11 June 1919 the All-Russian Central Executive Committee stated: '[We] have noted Comrade Dzerzhinsky's information concerning the necessity of leaving illegal political workers in the areas occupied by the enemy ...' It was proposed to set up a special department within the Cheka to handle such 'illegal political workers'.[34] With this, Dzerzhinsky realised that in order to successfully operate abroad, besides his or her revolutionary fervour an officer or agent needed certain qualifications.

In September 1920 Inessa Armand advised Dzerzhinsky to invite Yakov Davtyan (alias 'Davydov') to head the foreign section that would soon become known as INO – the Foreign Department of the Cheka and then the GPU/OGPU. Davtyan knew Europe well. From 1907 he had lived in Belgium, where he earned his university diploma as an engineer. In the course of his work with the Belgian Socialist Party, Davtyan became acquainted with Armand. Armand was born in Paris as Elisabeth-Inès Stéphane d'Herbenville. Her mother was half-French and half-English and her father a French opera-singer. Inessa, a Russian derivative of Inès meaning 'chaste', was brought up in Moscow by her aunt and grandmother living and working there as teachers, and at the age of 19 married Alexander Armand, the son of a wealthy Russian textile manufacturer. Arrested for revolutionary propaganda, she managed to escape and in November 1910 came to Paris where she met Lenin. For the next year in Paris she was involved with the work of the Bolshevik section and together with Lenin in the setting up of a school for underground party workers at Longjumeau.[35] Together with Lenin, Krupskaya and other revolutionaries she returned to Russia in April 1917 in what has since been described as the 'sealed train'.

After the revolution Armand served as an executive member of the Economic Council of the Moscow Region (Gubsovnarkhoz), where Davtyan was her deputy after his return to Russia in August 1918. Together with Armand he visited France as part of the Red Cross delegation. When Armand recommended him to Dzerzhinsky, Davtyan had been serving in the Commissariat for Foreign Affairs (NKID) as head of the department responsible for Poland and the Baltic states. In November 1920 he was transferred to the Cheka without leaving his NKID post.

On 20 December 1920, Dzerzhinsky signed Executive Order No. 169 establishing the Foreign Department (INO). Davtyan (using his alias 'Davydov') served as its interim chief until January, and then again from April to August 1921. In February 1922 he ultimately decided to return to the NKID, serving in Lithuania and then China, where he combined his diplomatic work with that of a formal head of station which at that time was a joint residency of military and political intelligence, which sometimes also housed a Comintern representative. From May 1925 he served in France as a councillor under plenipotentiaries Leonid Krasin and then Christian Rakovsky. Davtyan stayed in Paris until October 1927 and then also worked in Persia, Greece and Poland before his arrest in Moscow in October 1937. During his interrogation at the Lubyanka internal prison, the former intelligence chief confessed to having been a spy for Britain during all those years.[36]

In 1921 the INO, from 6 August headed by Solomon Mogilevsky, became part of the Secret Operational Directorate established in January that year to supervise the work of all operational departments.[37] On 13 March 1922, Meer Trilisser was placed in charge of the INO, now part of the Main Political Directorate (GPU) of the NKVD, while Mogilevsky was transferred to the Transcaucasian Cheka as the GPU plenipotentiary from 15 May. After a short spell of Yakov Davydov (Davtyan), Ruben Katanyan and Solomon Mogilevsky at this post, Trilisser was the longest serving Soviet intelligence chief and the first to make a mark on foreign intelligence operations.

'The priorities of Soviet intelligence under Lenin, and still more under Stalin,' Andrew writes, 'continued to be shaped by greatly exaggerated beliefs in an unrelenting conspiracy by Western governments and their intelligence agencies.'[38] In reality, the priorities of the Cheka and then the GPU/OGPU under Lenin and Dzerzhinsky were concentrated on countering anti-Bolshevik and anti-Soviet activities of what they called 'class enemies' (later 'enemies of the people')[39] engaged in counter-revolutionary campaigns or operations inside Russia and abroad. Only after the 'Lockhart Plot' it also included work against Western intelligence agencies who were assisting, financing and organising such anti-Soviet activities. It is true that all authoritarian regimes tend to see their opponents engaged in subversive conspiracy since they regard opposition as fundamentally illegitimate. But it is also true that whenever an authoritarian regime comes to power there is an opposition to it often, if not always, supported by the states who see themselves as democracies.

After the First World War and the Bolshevik revolution, both Great Britain and Soviet Russia rightly considered themselves as enemies, the term later changed to 'main adversaries'. The advantage of all British secret services

– SIS, MI5, GC&CS, Naval Intelligence, the Directorate of Intelligence of the Home Office and so on was their experience and, as a rule, much more superior education and qualifications of their staff and agents. Plus traditional secrecy and good organisation. When the British governments were not preparing an armed intervention, their secret services were secretly conspiring to subvert Soviet Russia from within. Unfortunately, they did not succeed.

Bolshevik ideology dictated that all capitalist regimes were their natural class enemies. Both Lenin and Trotsky were dreaming of the world revolution and if they could not even think of an armed invasion in Europe at the time (this became only possible almost three decades later), they, unlike their Western counterparts, were openly planning to subvert the capitalist world from within having, they believed, all 'poor and oppressed nations' on their side. This was the main reason for the creation of the Communist International. The aim of the organisation was to fight 'by all available means, including armed force, for the overthrow of the international bourgeoisie and for the creation of an international Soviet republic as a transition stage to the complete abolition of the State' as prescribed by Lenin's work *The State and Revolution*. By the 'armed force' the Comintern ideologues meant armed revolt or even civil war. In the twenty-one conditions of admission to the Comintern, suggested by Lenin and adopted by the Second Congress in 1920, it was clearly stated that all member parties were obliged, among other things, to create an illegal (in addition to the legal) organisation for subversive work. This is what so much frightened the powers that be in Europe and America.

In comparison with British secret services, INO had its advantages and disadvantages. One of the clear advantages was its permanently expanding staff and almost unlimited funds. Lenin, as head of state, was taking an active interest in INO's work although it is now known that, unlike Stalin after him, he was ill-informed in intelligence and counter-intelligence matters, judging by his comments on the intelligence reports and his advice to Dzerzhinsky. Another great advantage was a pool of potential agents and informers that were recruited not only from the fraternal parties but also from the 'fellow travellers' and 'useful idiots' in the West. These were assets willing to work for the Soviet government for ideological reasons, rarely accepting a monetary reward for their efforts.

Arthur Ransome, who was in contact with both Soviet and British intelligence and whose reports were assessed at least by the Soviets as 'very important', was one of the very few early sources for the Russians in what concerned Britain.[40] And this is not because others could not have been recruited. Primarily, this was because foreign intelligence collection was of minor importance for the Cheka and its successors in the early 1920s.

As William Ewer stated during his interrogation, the only assignment that he received from his Soviet contacts in London was 'the study of all organisations engaged in espionage against our country', that is, the USSR. Or, in his words, 'the remit was to ascertain British intelligence and counter-intelligence capabilities, and what countermeasures existed against Soviet and CPGB activities in Britain'. That is, 'purely counter', he said.[41] This, however, was not properly understood then and is still not fully comprehended by many intelligence historians and writers now. However, as at the time of writing we are living at the height of the Second Cold War, this may not be so important.

Chapter 5

The Looting of Russia

The Bolsheviks under Lenin obviously knew what they were doing when they took control of the largest and, as it turns out, one of the richest countries in the world back in 1917. As can be stated with absolute certainty more than a hundred years after the revolution,[1] the so-called 'dictatorship of the proletariat' had nothing to do with the declared workers', soldiers' and peasants' paradise in the country that would be proudly described for the next seven decades as nearly one-sixth of the Earth's land surface. The country known as the Soviet Union (or USSR) occupied this vast territory from December 1922 to December 1991. It was only the matter of who owned the enormous treasures of the country and controlled the printing press. Remarkably, in its comparatively short history there have been problems with both and things were always going on quite differently from what Lenin wrote in his pamphlet about the state after the proletarian revolution.

What made representatives of the communist, socialist and other parties flocking into Moscow join the Comintern? In his keynote address to the Third All-Russia Congress of Soviets (10–18 January 1918, O.S.), Lenin declared: 'We, the Russian working and exploited classes, have the honour of being the vanguard of the international socialist revolution; we can now see clearly how far the development of the revolution will go. The Russian began it—the German, the Frenchman and the Englishman will finish it, and socialism will be victorious.'[2] Thus, the immediate agenda was very clear: with Moscow's propaganda and financial backing to win elections or at least to get their candidates elected in order to achieve the primary aim of any political party, which is to attain power.

There are of course different ways to achieve this goal as well as different forms of the seizure of power – either by Lenin's violent overthrow of the state, in other words, revolution, or democratically, by popular elections. In the real political world, no party consists solely of office- or benefit seekers,[3] and for the world's first self-defined 'working class government' this was not of primary importance. Thanks to Sean McMeekin and others, we now have the key to the greatest mystery of the Russian Revolution: how the Bolsheviks, despite facing a world of enemies and producing nothing but economic ruin in their path, were able to stay in power. 'Surrounded by enemies both real and imagined,' McMeekin writes, 'the Bolsheviks needed to arm their supporters to their teeth, first to survive, and then to perpetuate their hold on power.'[4] Indeed, during the Comintern's first two years its programme of fomenting revolution in Europe and around the world went little beyond instructing and financing non-Russian revolutionaries and Soviet sympathisers.[5] The only instrument which could help them and their supporters in different parts of the world to survive was the Cheka. 'Without the Cheka,' its former archivist points out, 'there is no Soviet history.'[6] In its present incarnation, two decades into the twenty-first century, it is still all-important to the Kremlin.

* * *

By 1914, the delineations of the future Russian 'superpower' seemed to be clear to all who were in the position to know. Sir Arthur Nicolson, a former British ambassador to Russia now serving as Permanent Under-Secretary at the Foreign Office, blessed the fact that the two countries were allies. In July, as the crisis heated up in Germany, Chancellor Theobald von Bethmann Hollweg famously remarked about the seemingly unstoppable Russian juggernaut: 'The future lies with Russia, she grows and grows, and lies on us like a nightmare.'[7] And then he casually added: 'If the iron dice must roll, may God help us'. On that day, 1 August 1914, the German Chancellor had in mind the Great War.

What marvelled and at the same time scared him and others in the European capitals was the pace of economic growth in Russia which, in the last six years before the war, reached an average annual rate of 8.8 per cent (in January 2019, the GDP growth was 0.3 per cent, in May 2020 – minus 9.5 per cent, and in September 2021 – 4.9 per cent). By the time the war began, nearly every economic indicator showed Russia breaking through the limits of what had recently been believed possible. Her industrial production, according to one specific research study, 'measured in output of coal, iron, and steel, was now fourth in the world [11th in 2019], behind only Germany, Britain, and America, having shot past even France, Russia's key economic partner'. Russia's war industry as well as her railway network (into Poland, that is, to the west) were rapidly expanding. To complete the picture, by 1914 there were nearly a thousand factories in Petrograd alone, many devoted to producing arms.[8]

Russia's favourable trade balance and the real (or envisaged) returns from investments caused the exponential growth of British and French investors' interest in Russian corporate and government bonds. By the beginning of the war, the State Bank of Imperial Russia had accumulated Europe's largest strategic reserves, gold and foreign exchange, second only to the USA – 1,695 billion roubles worth, or 1,312 metric tons, in addition to the Treasury reserve worth 510 million. According to the Russian Gold Standard (forced upon a reluctant Tsarist government by Count Witte in 1895–7), 1 million golden roubles were worth exactly 774.20kg of pure gold. At the same time, the trade surplus that underwrote Russia's colossal gold reserve was beginning to erode in the last years before the war, as more and more imported components were needed to modernise Russia's rail network and her booming war industries.[9] In 1914 the government suspended the rouble's convertibility into gold.

For decades Soviet propaganda sought to convince its own people together with much of the world that the Bolsheviks inherited a poor, backward country and only the system of a centrally-planned economy together with the leading role of the Communist Party secured Russia's rise to world-power status. However, despite several potential trouble areas, one of which was a considerable dependence of the pre-war Russian economic boom on a constant influx of foreign capital, the impression Russia left on foreign visitors in 1914 was not one of backwardness and poverty. 'Considering the frequency of famines during the Communist era,' McMeekin notes, 'it is even more astonishing to be reminded today that pre-war Russia was the world's largest exporter of foodstuffs, shipping 20 million tons of grain abroad in 1913 alone – a surplus never remotely approached under Bolshevik rule.'[10]

Although the Russian Imperial Family, the Romanovs, may not have been the richest family in Russia, they are usually described as almost otherworldly in their opulence:

Atop the Imperial Sceptre was the Orlov diamond of 300 carats, 'said to have been prised from the eye of a Hindu idol in southern India'. The Great Imperial Crown, made for Catherine the Great's coronation in 1762, was 'encrusted with 4,936 diamonds weighing 2,858 carats', along with a single ruby weighing 400 carats. The crown jewels comprised '7 chains, 23 stars, crosses and emblems, 12 diadems, 16 necklaces, 6 diamond necklaces (rivières), 56 brooches, 10 clasps, 185 hair-pins, earrings, buttons, rings, lockets, bracelets, buckles, etc., 7 loose stones, 19 gold snuff-boxes and 60 sundry gold trinkets'. Altogether the 'Russian Crown Treasury', wrote the man later hired by the Bolsheviks to appraise it, contained '25,300 carats of diamonds, 1000 carats of emeralds, 1700 carats of sapphires, 6000 carats of pearls and many rubies, topazes, tourmalines, alexandrites, aquamarines, chrysoprases, beryls, chrysolites, turquoises, amethysts, agates, labradors, almandines'. This was not yet to count the famous Fabergé eggs (fifty-four of them), and hundreds of other Fabergé miniatures.[11]

After the February Revolution, the Provisional Government decided to move the former Tsar and his family to England but King George V, a cousin both to Nicholas II and to Alexandra Fedorovna, was frightened by the revolutionary events in Russia. 'George was "panick striken", Richard Aldrich and Rory Cormac write. 'He feared that bringing his cousin to Windsor, together with the reportedly pro-German tsarina, would be unpatriotic – even dangerous.' Whatever was the reason (some say his private secretary, Lord Stamfordham, feared an uprising against the monarchy), the King decided against it and categorically demanded that the government rescind the invitation. Soon, the British ambassador to Petrograd Sir George Buchanan was instructed to inform the Provisional Government 'that objections against allowing the emperor and the empress to come here are so strong that we will have to take the liberty of withdrawing the consent that was earlier given to the Russian government's proposal'. In the summer, however, the Kerensky government repeated its request but Sir George, who developed a strong bond with the Russian Tsar, 'came with tears in his eyes to inform the minister of foreign affairs that England had definitely refused to receive the former emperor'.[12] It seems other crowned heads of Europe also feared antagonising the new masters of Russia which, as some authors suggest, sealed the fate of Nicholas II and his family.

In December 2021, Olga Ivshina of the BBC News Russian Service in an article with a self-explanatory title claimed, without any documentary evidence, that in 1917 'British intelligence officers developed several options' for exfiltrating the former Tsar out of Russia.[13] This is wrong. According to the authors of *The Secret Royals* (2021), there was a kind of a turf war between Buchanan and 'C's organisation for the ambassador had been hostile to the British Intelligence Mission from the outset. Buchanan had arrogantly demanded, they write, that Cumming's networks in Russia be placed under his direct command. Quite clearly, this request received a rapid rejection from the War Office. Anyway, the Secret Service with all its Russian-speaking officers and agent networks on the ground never received instructions to get Nicholas and/or his family out of Russia. Their attention now switched from trying to save the Tsar to supporting the new Provisional Government in the struggle against Germany. In the absence of organised rescue activity by the Service, the plot was concocted by Oliver Locker-Lampson, 'an eccentric figure who commanded an armoured car squadron in Russia while simultaneously serving as member of parliament for Huntingdonshire'.

Locker-Lampson recruited a servant at the Alexander Palace, about 30 miles south of St Petersburg, where the Imperial Family had been held under house arrest since 15 March 1917, two weeks after Nicholas II abdicated the throne of Russia. This servant should have arrived at the palace, secretly cut the former Tsar's hair and shaved off his beard, donning a similar-looking false one himself while swapping clothes with the man who would then simply walk out unchallenged. Outside, Citizen Romanov disguised as a peasant would meet Locker-Lampson, joining up with the British military. They would move to Archangel in a lorry and from there to Britain by sea. In planning this swap, Locker-Lampson demonstrated his familiarity with Shakespeare's plays like *The Taming of the Shrew* or *King Lear* where such disguise plays an important role. Tellingly, the authors stress, Locker-Lampson received no green light from Britain while more enterprising amateurs filled the vacuum and made the situation worse.[14] Richard Aldrich and Rory Cormac preface this chapter with an epigraph taken from King George V's diary entry of 28 July 1918: 'Heard from Lockhart (our Agent in Moscow) that dear Nicky was shot.' As one of the Romanovs' biographers noted, 'George V's act helped doom Nicholas, his wife, and his five children'.

What happened to the last Russian tsar, his wife, children, relatives and people close to the royal household is now well known. In July 1917 the Provisional Government ordered them moved to Tobolsk, east of the Ural Mountains. Together with their retinue the Romanovs were place in the former house of the governor of Siberia. After the civil war began and the Bolsheviks took power in Tobolsk, on 2 May 1918 the Sovnarkom under Lenin's chairmanship decided to transfer the family with several servants to Yekaterinburg,[15] a large city (its population today is about 1.5 million) named after Catherine I (née Marta Helena Skowrońska), the widow of Peter the Great and Empress of Russia from 1725 until her death two years later, aged 43.

In July 1918, fearful that White troops might rescue them, the Executive Committee of the Urals Soviet decided to eliminate the whole family and all the retainers (a total of eleven people). Yakov Yurovsky, deputy Commissar for Justice and member of the local Cheka presidium who took responsibility for the captives on 4 July being appointed the commandant of the 'House of Special Purpose', where they had been kept prisoners, would also act as their chief executioner. Grigory Nikulin, a young party member recently transferred to the local Cheka, served as his deputy and assistant. He would later be promoted to head the Criminal Investigation Department of the Moscow Police, informally known as MUR. Nikulin lived well in Moscow in a spacious house with a separate room for a dog and after his death was buried at Novodevichy Cemetery, one of Moscow's most prestigious resting places. Across from his grave is that of Boris Yeltsin, the first President of Russia.

The names of all other executioners are also known. For example, Mikhail Medvedev (Kudrin), the only staff member of the Cheka who took part in the execution. He ended his career as a retired KGB colonel in 1964. The unconfirmed story goes that his son sent a personal letter to Nikita Khrushchev, then still a Soviet leader (but shortly to be deposed). 'On his deathbed, my dad asked me to congratulate you with your 70th birthday,' he wrote, 'to wish you good health and hand over to you on his behalf a historical relic of our family – a Browning pistol N389965, from which he [my father], on the night of 17 July 1918, shot the last Russian tsar Nicholas II (citizen Romanov N.A.) and his family in Yekaterinburg.'

One of the assassins, Alexey Kabanov, later served in the Cheka in Vyatka in western Russia and even, despite a total lack of any formal education, as a prosecutor of Feodosia Municipality in Crimea. Another, Pavel Medvedev (not a relative of Medvedev-Kudrin and not a Chekist), was appointed chief of external security of the Ipatiev house ('House of Special Purpose') when the Imperial Family was kept there, also taking direct part in the shootings. Petr Yermakov, yet another murderer, before the Revolution finished a parish school and played a role of a hitman in the local Bolshevik organisation, taking an active part in 'expropriations' or, as they were better known, 'exes'. This was part of a Bolshevik 'loot the looters' campaign officially announced in *Pravda* of 6 February 1918 but widely practised before the seizure of power by the Bolsheviks to collect money for the party. The idea was borrowed by Lenin from *Das Kapital* where Marx famously predicted that on the day of Communist reckoning, 'The knell of capitalist private property sounds. The expropriators are expropriated.'[16]

In November 1934, Richard Halliburton, an American travel writer, managed to interview Yermakov in Yekaterinburg (then Sverdlovsk). After the Revolution Yermakov served as a warden in a local prison, a post, Halliburton writes, 'he had received from the grateful Soviet nation for his glorious contribution to the cause of Communism'.[17] Yermakov recalled: 'I fired my Mauser at the Czarina – only six feet away – couldn't miss. Got her in the mouth. In two seconds, she was dead.' He also mentioned another member of the execution squad, Stepan Vaganov. 'Vaganof [*sic*] made a clean sweep of the girls. They were in a heap on the floor, moaning and dying. He kept pouring bullets into Olga and Tatiana.'[18] Vaganov did not leave the city before it was retaken by White troops – he was quickly found hiding in the cellar of his house and killed on the spot.

Victor Netrebin was the youngest of the executioners, aged only 17 then. Because his family was so poor, even free schooling was unaffordable and he was not able to get even primary education. All traces of Netrebin disappeared in 1935. Finally, Sergey Broido was employed as a Cheka driver arriving at the house together with Philipp (Shaya) Goloshchyokin, a local party functionary, member of the Central Executive Committee of the Ural Soviet, and Yermakov. Lacking enough men for the execution, Yurovsky included him as a member of the firing squad.

Jānis Celms was the only Latvian who agreed to take part in the murder, others refused. Little is known about him except that he had served in one of the Life Grenadier Guards Regiment in the service of the Tsar before the Revolution. Some sources say in the 1930s he had found a job working as a butcher in Mosnarpit, a public catering section of the Moscow city administration.

What was the Bolshevik haul from the Romanov family after Yurovsky's execution squad fired a ferocious hail of bullets into the bodies of Nicholas, the Tsarina, their daughters and the Tsarevich, their only son, the heir apparent to the Russian throne? (A week before, Nikulin shot Prince Vasily Dolgorukov, advisor to Nicholas II who accompanied the family to Tobolsk, as well as Count Ilya Tatishchev, Adjutant General to the Tsar. After the execution their bodies were thrown into a pit. And on 12 June, another group of Bolsheviks shot Grand Duke Mikhail Alexandrovich, the younger brother of the tsar, together with his secretary and friend Nicholas 'Koka' Johnson.)

So, what was the booty?

Yurovsky personally secured for the regime, by his own boast, some eighteen pounds of diamonds and other jewellery, sewn into the corsets of the tsar's daughters, along with a pearl strand belonging to the tsarina later appraised at some 600,000 gold roubles, or $300,000. (Because of the rapid advance of the Czech legion and the embryonic Volunteer Army of Siberia, which reached Ekaterinburg on 25 July 1918, all these items had to be hidden temporarily underground, being transferred to Moscow only after the Whites were expelled in 1919.) From the quarters in which the grand dukes had been housed in Alapaevsk, Yurovsky's men also discovered 'a number of valuables – more than a wagonload', most of it 'hidden in things down to their underwear'.

No matter how hard Yurovsky tried to micromanage the expropriations, however, the fabulous Romanov riches were too alluring to keep prying hands away. Andrei Strekotin, one of the guards, later recalled that his 'comrades began removing various items from the bodies, like watches, rings, bracelets, cigarette cases' ... Stories of buried treasure percolated around Ekaterinburg and Tobolsk for years, rumours thought to be fictitious until Soviet archives were opened in 1991. These reveal that as late as the 1930s, locals were being searched systematically by Cheka agents, who on one occasion turned up '154 valuable objects', including several brooches mounting 100-carat diamonds, altogether worth 3.2 million gold rubles, or $1.6 million.[19]

There were still the famous Romanov crown jewels that, quite by chance, remained in the Kremlin Armoury undiscovered by the Bolsheviks until March 1922. In July 1917, the Provisional Government decided to move the most valuable items like the Imperial Sceptre, the Orlov diamond and the crown regalia, along with thousands of other jewels and paintings to the Armoury after the first communist uprising in Petrograd, which became known as the 'July Days', failed. But even after they were finally located, the crown jewels proved nearly impossible for the Bolsheviks to sell.

In 1925, the four-book set entitled *Russia's Treasure of Diamonds and Precious Stones* was published in French, Russian, English and German by the People's Commissariat of Finances under the general supervision of Professor A.E. Fersman. The obvious motive was to lure wealthy foreign buyers. Today, this century-old catalogue is probably the most complete inventory of the Russian Imperial jewellery collection. After the Bolshevik revolution, the Cheka had been playing the leading role in 'expropriating' and selling the patrimony of Imperial Russia to anyone who would buy, dumping the bulk of it as fast as they could often at well below the market prices. Since then, many, although not all of the priceless objects from the Fersman catalogues have disappeared, perhaps forever.

* * *

In or around 1906, Nicholas II acquired a luxury automobile of French make, a Delaunay-Belleville 40hp, one of the most prestigious cars of the time. Perhaps it was the influence of Adolphe Kégresse, a French engineer who invented the so-called Kégresse track to modify normal motor vehicles into half-tracks and whom the Russian tsar had chosen as his personal chauffeur. Kégresse also headed the Mechanical Department of the Imperial Garage at Tsarskoe Selo near St Petersburg where there were other luxury limousines, like a German Benz or an American Packard. In 1914 Nicholas bought one of the last legendary Rolls-Royce models – a six-cylinder purple Silver Ghost, whose production was suspended during the First World War and its powerful engine was used in Rolls-Royce armoured cars developed in 1914 and Silver Ghost ambulances. It was a valuable addition to his other Rolls-Royce used by the Tsarina and their children.

There is a popular legend in Russia that the Old Bolsheviks, that is, those who made the revolution, were extremely modest individuals who dedicated their entire lives to reorganising the former empire into the world's first socialist state for toilers, people who work long and hard.

Lenin, a self-appointed leader of the Marxist party, awarded himself not only a primary role in the new proletarian state and in the international socialist crusade but also all the perks that came with the job. He helped himself to three imported luxury cars from the Imperial Garage, of which two were Delaunay-Bellevilles (a limousine and a touring car, better known today as a convertible, the Tsar's favourite) and one Rolls-Royce. At first, Lenin was driven around in a Delaunay-Belleville limo but after it was stolen from him at gunpoint on 30 March 1918 started using the 1914 Rolls-Royce Silver Ghost. The second Romanov Rolls-Royce was given to Trotsky. Thus, in 1919 there were only two British autos in the Sovnarkom garage that had previously belonged to the Tsar, but the commissars soon got a taste for luxury cars and in 1921 there were already thirteen Rolls-Royces, of which one belonged to Christian Rakovsky who at the time headed the Ukrainian Sovnarkom. Stalin, to his great disappointment, was given a less powerful Vauxhall D-type 25hp,[20] a staff car supplied to the British Army during the First World War.

As soon as the All-Russian Co-operative Society Ltd (ARCOS) was opened in London in October 1920, the flow of British cars to the Kremlin 'special' garage significantly increased. Altogether, the company made £1,970,000 worth of purchases during its first year,[21] with all payments made in gold traditionally via Reval (Tallinn), which was used as a breakpoint even after the lifting of the economic blockade. Very soon Moscow exceeded any other European capital in its number of Rolls-Royces.

* * *

Like the Nazis, the Bolsheviks obtained their gold, silver, diamonds and art treasures by looting banks and robbing museums, churches and monasteries, private collections, even countries and whole categories of people. It is now known that the Cheka looting of aristocrats, kulaks, other 'counter-revolutionary elements' and the Russian Orthodox Church between 1917 and 1922 was on a much larger scale. The Gokhran, or Soviet State Treasury, founded in February 1920 by the decree of the Sovnarkom as the depository of valuables, processed many thousands of tons of loot, including fine gold, high-quality precious stones and other valuables. Just between 6 April and 18 July 1920, for example, the Gokhran received 21,500 carats of diamonds, 20,000 carats of pearls, 6,300 carats in gold-plated jewels, plus 20 million tsarist roubles ($10 million) worth of fine gold ingots and coin.[22]

The Kronstadt rebellion against the government broke out on 1 March 1921, signalling that what had always been considered by the Bolshevik leadership as the most revolutionary group – sailors of the Baltic Fleet – were dissatisfied with the situation in the country and demanded fundamental reforms. Lenin decided that the economic and political system of war communism that existed during the Russian Civil War had outlived itself. On 14 March the Tenth Party Congress adopted a new, slightly more market-oriented economic policy sanctioning the co-existence of private and public sectors. Lenin would characterise this New Economic Policy, which became known by its Russian acronym NEP, as an economic system that included the elements of a free market under state control. The decree for the implementation of this new policy was signed on 21 March. In the meantime, long negotiations and manoeuvres led to the signature on 16 March of the Anglo-Russian Trade Agreement by the Soviet delegation headed by Leonid Krasin and the British coalition government of David Lloyd George.

During this period, the Cheka counter-intelligence and counter-revolutionary efforts were facilitated by the establishment of foreign sections in several Soviet cities and opening of new stations (rezidenturas) overseas in a number of bordering states and in Germany,[23] with Berlin becoming the largest station. All three Russian secret intelligence services – the Cheka foreign department (INO), the Registration Department of the Red Army (the future GRU), and the OMS of the Comintern – had their permanent representatives in Berlin. In January 1921 two large and important directorates were organised within the Cheka – Secret-Operational Directorate (SOU) headed by Menzhinsky, where he was also in charge of the 2nd Special Department with Yagoda acting as his deputy assisted by Artuzov. The department consisted of five special counter-intelligence sections.[24] Another important division was Economic [Intelligence] Directorate (EKU) headed by Nikolai Krylenko, with 15 special sections and 171 operational officers plus over 200 support staff.[25] Three days later another Special (Cypher) Department was organised headed by Gleb Bokiy.

Krasin's real goal, as Litvinov (then recently appointed Deputy Commissar for Foreign Affairs) made clear in his telegram, intercepted and decrypted by British intelligence, was 'to cajole Lloyd George into removing legal obstacles to the export of looted Russian gold while making only "platonic", that is, empty promises regarding repayment of Russia's colossal debt obligations'.[26] Krasin, far less known to Western historians than most Bolshevik leaders (the first book about him in English was only published in 1992), had been the true éminence grise of the Russian revolution.

Born in 1870, the same year as Vladimir Ulyanov (Lenin), Krasin was exposed to revolutionary ideas while studying chemical engineering in St Petersburg. In 1905 he was heading the so-called combat technical group formed by the Bolshevik leadership not for the revolution but for cash 'exes' (expropriations) and terrorist acts. Krasin set up a network for smuggling dynamite and weapons into Russia from Finland and helped design bombs, grenades and other hand projectiles. His underground weapons workshops 'would supply the explosives and arms used by Bolshevik bank robbers in Moscow, St. Petersburg, and most famously, in the Caucasian holdups in which the young Stalin first made his name'. Several Russian authors also speculate that Krasin had been involved in the murder (according to the official version, suicide) of the famous Russian millionaire Savva Morozov in Cannes in May 1905. The Morozov family was the fifth richest in Russia in the early twentieth century and a significant financial contributor to the Bolsheviks. Some even accuse him, for no apparent reason, of taking part in the assassination of the Russian prime minister Pyotr Stolypin, shot in Kiev in September 1911. And, which is probably not true, in counterfeiting pre-revolutionary banknotes.[27] This was the prerogative of Nikolai Krestinsky, the Commissar of Finance (Narkomfin).

Krestinsky's new mandate was announced in February 1920, when he was appointed director of a new Soviet 'State Treasury for the Storage of Valuables' (Gokhran). Now, apart from the financial matters, his responsibility was the 'centralisation and accounting of all valuables on the territory of [Soviet Russia], consisting of ingots of gold, platinum, and silver or articles [made from] them, diamonds, precious stones, and pearls'.[28] Naturally, there were other responsibilities to be delegated. Analysis of artefacts – to Lunacharsky's Narkompros (People's Commissariat for Education); budgeting and accounting – to Krestinsky's own Narkomfin; evaluation and sorting for export – to Krasin's Commissariat for Foreign Trade (Narkomvneshtorg); and financial security matters – to Stalin's new Workers and Peasants' Inspectorate, or Rabkrin. This was created in February 1920, alongside the Gokhran, specifically to root out corruption in the collection of loot.[29] As ever, the problem was recalcitrant local hoarders, traditional Russian drunkenness, rampant theft, bribery and lack of discipline.

Unsurprisingly, the situation demanded the establishment of several other Bolshevik bureaucracies. A lot of treasures and valuables collected throughout the country were lost, damaged or stolen. Only in Irkutsk, the Siberian city where Admiral Kolchak had been captured with the remainder of the imperial gold,[30] did the local Bolshevik committee with the help of the Cheka manage to organise proper transportation to Moscow. At monthly intervals between July 1920 and November 1921 they were sending boxes of loot to Gokhran.[31]

On 7 February 1921 the new State Fund of Valuables for Foreign Trade was established, which apart from gold and jewellery had under its management arts and antiques destined to be auctioned somewhere in Europe. On 10 August the Council of Labour and Defence (STO), an organisation responsible for the central management of the economy and the military production for the Red Army, created the new Cheka – the Extraordinary Commission for Export (Chrezkomexport) – headed by Mikhail Rykunov, a professional revolutionary albeit without any formal education. Remarkably, representatives of the Finance Commissariat were not included in this commission. Before they packed him off to the Directorate of Water Management in Turkestan in late 1922, parallel to his Chrezkomexport duties Rykunov had also been heading the Economic Directorate of the Narkomvneshtorg. The STO instructed Rykunov to arrange sales of Russian arts and antiques abroad or to foreign buyers for a sum exceeding 29 billion roubles.[32] It seems he failed in his mission because they soon kicked him out of the foreign trade business. In March 1927 Rykunov was put on trial 'for mismanagement and abuse of power'. Three years later he was acquitted but in May 1937 arrested again, sentenced to death, and executed in Omsk in January 1938.

In late August Krestinsky established yet another bureaucracy, the Safes Commission, formally subordinate to his Finance Commissariat but overseen by the Cheka. Its remit was to empty the bank safes confiscated by the authorities and hand over their contents to the Gokhran. The safecracking teams of the commission, McMeekin writes, 'were often struck dumb by the magnitude of their task. If we count simply by numbers, their progress was not insufficient: the fifty-man operation cracked open 17,166 safes between 10 September 1920 and 1 January 1921, or about 1,000 per week.' A new record was set in April 1921, when in two weeks the Gokhran took in 13,000 carats of diamonds, valued at over 50 million roubles (US$25 million, or some $2.5 billion in 2010).[33]

On 5 September 1921 the Central Party Committee adopted a secret resolution according to which the Gokhran together with the Cheka was to arrange a surreptitious voluntary-compulsory purchase of gold, platinum and foreign currency from the population. The Chekists, whose number would reach 280,000 by early 1921, were instructed to set up a secret network of buyers covering the whole country. Special gold trains were formed to bring treasures to the Gokhran, where they were to be sorted and evaluated by the experts together with the works of art and antiques.[34] Natalia Sedova, the wife of Trotsky, was one of these experts, having headed the museum section of the Narkompros (People's Commissariat for Education) from 1918 to 1928.

The castle gates will always open for gold-laden donkeys, says the Russian proverb. The Anglo-Soviet Trade Agreement of 1921, the Rapallo Treaty of 1922 and the Anglo-Soviet Treaties of 1924,[35] it is unanimously agreed, 'washed clean the stolen loot the Bolsheviks had previously had to launder, on the sly, in Estonia and Sweden'. Although the Soviets and their European and American 'business partners' were somewhat cautious at first in selling off Russian treasures in the auction houses and galleries of Europe, already in the autumn of 1922 the van Diemen Gallery in Berlin organised the first sales. Rudolf Lepke, the renowned German auction house also located in Berlin, soon followed in van Diemen's footsteps. From 1923 Lepke's experts could buy art and antiques directly from the Petrograd (later Leningrad) museums and depositories without any restriction and competition. In early 1928 Hans Karl Krüger arrived in Leningrad to personally select a collection for this auction house's 60th jubilee catalogue compiled by renowned German art historians Wilhelm von Bode and Otto von Falke. The major Russenauktionen (Russian Sales) started later that year, attracting international attention. The first auction at Lepke's was held on 7 November 1928 coinciding with the eleventh anniversary of the Bolshevik revolution. It included 447 objects attributed to Italian, Dutch and French schools featuring excellent bronze and marble sculptures (lots 313–349) as well as Old Master paintings (lots 350–447) by Rembrandt, Rubens, Bruegel the Elder, Van Dyck, Tintoretto, Canaletto, and other great artists. The catalogue also presented exquisite French furniture tapestries, splendorous decorations in bronze and silver, a collection of jewelled snuff boxes from Romanov palaces and a few Russian items. Art deals with Moscow continued until 1936,[36] that is, three years after the Nazis' rise to power.

A few days after the controversial Berlin auction (about sixty émigrés from Russia recognised their nationalised possessions among the lots and protested the sale of their former property), Vienna hosted another major sale organised by Dorotheum, one of the world's oldest auction houses. This well-publicised sale also caused protests from the former owners. Bernhardt Altmann, an Austrian textile manufacturer who later moved to London and after the war introduced cashmere wool to North America, is also said to have profited greatly from the Soviet largesse. Using a Moscow knitwear factory as cover, he exported to Vienna rare Caucasian- and Persian-style carpets captured by the Red Army.[37] With real fortunes to be made auctioning off such treasures, it was of course unlikely that private dealers in Stockholm, Berlin or Vienna would be able to keep the market to themselves for long. Indeed, one of the leading London auction houses Christie's ties to Russia stretch back to the eighteenth century, when James Christie famously negotiated the sale of Sir Robert Walpole's collection to Empress Catherine the Great. But contrary to expectations, the same Christie's pioneered the Russian auctions market only in 1934 with the first dedicated sale of Fabergé at their King Street premises.

> The Bolsheviks had much better luck dumping art and jewels in the United States, despite the fact that the Soviet Union was not officially recognised by Washington until 1933. In part, this was for the obvious reason that the richest American collectors simply had more cash to burn than their European counterparts. When Armand Hammer organised his famous department store auctions of 'Romanov treasures' in 1930, there was no shortage of wealthy women shoppers. Some of the items Hammer displayed, to be sure, were fakes, but not the dozen-odd Fabergé and imperial Easter eggs ... Steel magnate Andrew Mellon alone bought $6.6 million worth of paintings by Old Masters from the Hermitage in 1930 and 1931.[38]

By sheer coincidence, the 1928 United States' presidential election was held on 6 November, the first day of Rudolf Lepke's famous Russian Auction. On that occasion Mellon gave a radio address promoting Herbert Hoover, the Republican nominee. 'Russia is an example of what happens when credit values are destroyed,' he said. In the Soviet Union, the standard of living had collapsed, and 'large corporations' had 'ceased to operate'. By contrast in Italy 'the Bolshevik menace was met and vanquished'. Mussolini, he said, had not only rescued Italy from any possible danger of economic and social collapse, but had 'improved the well-being of the people of the country'.[39]

Thanks to the brilliant work of the writers, art historians, curators and academic scholars mentioned in this chapter, we now have a more or less full picture of the real heist of the century – the Bolshevik robbery of Russia in which the Cheka played a leading role. 'With breathtaking audacity,' one of them writes, 'they transformed the accumulated wealth of centuries into the sinews of class war: armoured airplanes, cars, trucks, and trains; colossal factories of agitprop; and most of all, a continent-sized army of enforcers possessed of warm clothing, boots, food, medicine, guns, and ammunition at a time when the economic catastrophe of War Communism meant such things were lacked by nearly everyone else in Russia.' Having emptied the banks, the churches and the Treasury, the Bolsheviks moved on to Russia's richest resource: her people. Having monopolised the country, they managed to reduce the once-wealthy land to bitter penury, which endures to this day.[40] But they never managed to build either a Socialism or a Communism. Instead, they created an ugly commonwealth of soviet states that collapsed on its feet of clay at the first opportunity.

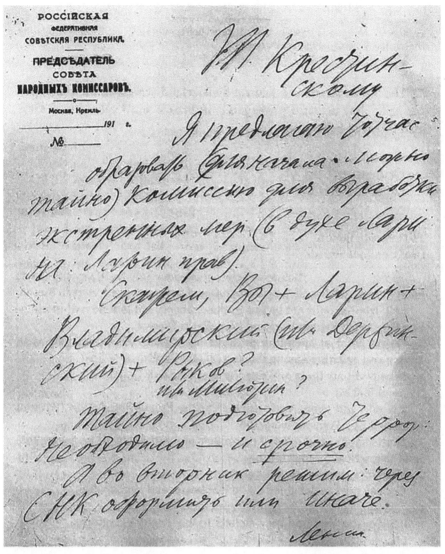

Lenin's note to Nikolai Krestinsky, at the time Secretary of the Russian Communist Party Central Committee, dated 3 September 1918. 'I propose to immediately form a commission (initially this can be done secretly) to work out emergency measures,' Lenin wrote. 'It is necessary secretly – and urgently – to prepare terror. And on Tuesday we will decide whether it will be through the SNK [Council of People's Commissars] or otherwise' (Richard Pipes, *The Unknown Lenin*, 56).

This was nothing new. Long before the revolution, in May 1901, Lenin already raised what he called 'the question of terror': 'In principle we have never rejected, and cannot reject, terror,' he declared. ('Where to begin', published in *Iskra*, No. 4, May 1901).

The looting of Russia – first by the Bolsheviks with the help of the Cheka and then by the Communist Party leadership and corrupt Soviet officials with the help of the KGB – never stopped. After the failed August 1991 coup in Moscow the office of the Russian Attorney General opened a case which became known as the 'Party Gold'. All 200 investigation files of the case remain classified to this day. The report by Kroll Associates, a corporate investigation and risk-consulting firm based in New York, commissioned by the Russian government in February 1992 to track down and find Soviet gold and the stockpile of foreign currency worth billions of US dollars that the Communist officials have moved overseas, disappeared and had never been found. In the meantime, Vladimir Putin, whose official net worth is a mystery, is reportedly the world's richest man. Anders Aslund, the author of *Russia's Crony Capitalism: The Path from Market Economy to Kleptocracy* (2019), estimates that through the practice of 'crony capitalism', Putin has amassed a net worth between $100 billion and $160 billion, which would make him richer than the officially wealthiest men in the world, whatever their names are – Jeff Bezos, Bill Gates, or both of them combined.

Chapter 6

Disinformburo and
Early Deception Operations

I t is probably accurate to assume that the West has never been particularly aware of what is really going on behind the Kremlin walls. And this is regardless of several major defections in the period shortly after the Bolshevik revolution and until a hundred years later when 'an intelligence source with access to the top-level decision-making' was successfully exfiltrated from Moscow by the CIA in 2017. The source, *The New York Times* reported, turned over compelling evidence for an important intelligence conclusion that the then US President Barak Obama made public shortly before leaving office. Namely, that Vladimir Putin himself was behind Russia's intrusion on the 2016 United States presidential election – information strongly denied by the Kremlin. This was part of the so-called 'active measures', a powerful and well-structured campaign of disinformation, denial and deception launched by Moscow with renewed vigour in 2000, when Putin succeeded Yeltsin as the President of Russia. This campaign continued during all Putin's terms and visibly intensified when Joseph 'Joe' Biden, who had served as vice-president under Obama, was elected the 46th President of the United States in January 2021 and shortly after his inauguration called Putin 'a killer'.

Deception can be found in any human activity. In everyday life it is usually punishable by law (or at least by some moral sanctions) like similar actions designed to subvert accepted rules for personal gain or advantage like cheating, fraud or fabrication. At the same time, in war, international politics and espionage the rules are different. All warfare is based on deception, Sun Tzu said some 500 years before Christ, and this proved to be perfectly correct.[1] 'Deception in international politics and more frequently in war,' Michael Handel writes, 'is rewarded by greater achievements and success.'[2] And, broadly speaking, espionage is part of both because any covert action, which includes obtaining secret information for the government, is the secret supplement to war and diplomacy. The Cheka realised it very quickly.

In December 1922 Dzerzhinsky's deputy Józef Unszlicht sent a proposal to the Politburo secretaries Stalin and Trotsky suggesting to set up a special bureau for disinformation attached to the GPU which had formally succeeded the Cheka earlier that year and was now part of the People's Commissariat for Internal Affairs (NKVD). Unszlicht stated, quite correctly, that after the Russian Civil War and foreign intervention the secret intelligence services of the bourgeois states, as he had put it meaning Britain, France, Japan and the USA, intensified their intelligence activities against Soviet Russia. First of all, they want to obtain information about the state of our industry, he stressed, about the political work of our Soviet and party organisations, the People's Commissariat for Foreign Affairs (NKID), and so on. Therefore, the young Soviet state should take advantage of this respite in class struggle with the capitalist world and use diplomatic negotiations to disorient and mislead its adversaries. 'Skilfully and systematically entangling our opponents in a web of disinformation will allow us to exert some influence on their politics in our interests,' Unszlicht wrote, 'forcing them to draw practical conclusions based on false calculations. In addition, our counter-intelligence efforts against belligerent foreign secret services will profit from disinformation, and facilitate the penetration of our agents into hostile intelligence organisations.' On behalf of the Cheka (now GPU) leadership, Unszlicht suggested the establishment of a special disinformation bureau with representatives from the GPU, Razvedupr (Red Army intelligence department) and NKID for 'systematic disinformation work'.

According to the Cheka planners, the priorities of the new bureau were:

- The identification of information collected by the GPU, Razvedupr and other [Soviet] agencies about the level of awareness of foreign intelligence services about Russia;
- The identification of information that may be of interest to the adversary;
- Assessing the levels of [knowledge, perception and] awareness of the adversary about us [that is, GPU, Razvedupr and NKID];
- The compilation and production of different false and misleading information and documents giving the enemy a wrong idea of the internal situation in Russia; of the Red Army organisation [command structure] and level of preparedness; of the political work of the leading [Bolshevik] party and Soviet bodies; of the NKID [People's Commissariat for Foreign Affairs], and so on;
- Passage of the above-mentioned [false] information and documents to the adversary via the GPU and Razvedupr;
- The writing of articles [newsletters, reports] and commentaries for popular periodicals preparing the basis for the release of fictitious materials.

In the last paragraph of the document the GPU asked the Politburo to approve the creation of the special disinformation service. The memo was signed by Unszlicht as the GPU deputy and Roman Pillyar as deputy head of the counter-intelligence department (KRO).[3] Two weeks later, on 11 January 1923, the Politburo passed a decree (No. 43) establishing the Disinformburo, an interagency body responsible for the production, coordination and dissemination of disinformation as proposed, with two important additions. Namely, that the membership also comprised representatives of the Party Central Committee and the Revolutionary Military Council (the supreme military authority of Soviet Russia), and that the newspaper articles and other materials for publication must first be approved by one of the Central Committee secretaries.

One of the first targets of the new bureau was White Poland – a much-hated neighbour especially after the Soviet defeat in the war of 1920–1, known in Poland as Wojna bolszewicka, or the Polish-Bolshevik War. Both Tukhachevsky and Stalin took part and both lost, feeling very humiliated because due to the Red Army losses in and after the Battle of Warsaw the Soviets had to agree to substantial territorial concessions. As a result, Poland added another 200km of territory east of its former border following a proposed demarcation line between the Second Polish Republic and Bolshevik Russia, the so-called Curzon Line, which had been discussed during the Paris Peace Conference after the First World War. The Peace of Riga, signed on 18 March 1921, partitioned the territories in White Ruthenia (Byelorussia) and Ukraine between Poland and Russia, and this border had remained undisputed for the whole interwar period.

One of the first disinformation campaigns against Poland began with the publication of articles in the Soviet newspapers *Pravda* and *Izvestia* seeking to provide evidence that Poland was preparing to attack Germany. This campaign backfired almost immediately because it coincided with the official policy statement of the Chief of the General Staff Władysław Sikorski, defining the main principles of the foreign and security policy of the Second Republic of Poland, published in January 1922. The document was entitled 'Foreign Policy from the Point of View of State Security' and was written by Ignacy Matuszewski, chief of the Second Department (intelligence) of the General Staff (Oddział II SG WP, also known as 'dwójka'). The central thesis of this declaration proclaimed that Poland was interested 'first of all in maintaining its status quo for as long as possible',[4] thus effectively contradicting the Soviet propaganda message and debunking Soviet disinformation. Later the Disinformburo decided to use foreign media to spread its elaborate hoaxes.

But even before the Bureau was officially established, the counter-intelligence department (KRO) of the Cheka was involved in active spy games against its Polish counterparts. First, Polish intelligence officers stationed in Tallinn, Estonia, were tasked to collect information about Soviet Russia through their network of agents and then the Polish Military Attaché Mission in Moscow, formally opened in August 1921, was to verify this information 'in place' and report. The intelligence station (ekspozytura) was headed by Lieutenant Colonel Romuald Wolikowski assisted by two officers and a typist.[5] The order of the day for the Cheka was to feed disinformation to both Polish intelligence outposts but primarily to control intelligence flowing from Moscow to the dwójka HQ in Warsaw. That was quite easily achieved because at the mission premises the security measures used to guard secret documents were staggeringly lax. Besides, agents and informers infiltrated by the Russians as well as the round-the-clock physical surveillance conducted by the Cheka watchers made the life of Polish intelligence officers in Moscow miserable.

In 1923 another disinformation operation mounted by the bureau was against Grand Duke Kirill Vladimirovich of Russia, who had managed to emigrate and settled with his wife in Coburg, Germany. With the murder of his cousins Tsar Nicholas II and his brother, Grand Duke Michael, Kirill became the head of the Imperial Romanov family and next in line to the throne, actively working for the restoration of the monarchy in Russia. The Grand Duke was supported by the Russian émigré monarchists who became known as the Mladorossy and who advocated a rather strange hybrid of the Russian monarchy and the Soviet system (the idea which also seems attractive to the Kremlin leadership of today), best evidenced by their 1920s motto 'Tsar and the Soviets' (later changed to 'Neither Reds, nor Whites, but Russian').

The Union of Mladorossy had probably been penetrated by the GPU agents from the first day when it was founded in 1923. The aim of the Soviet black propaganda was to show that Grand Duke Kirill supported the February Revolution and the Provisional Government, which was true. At the same time, it sought to undermine his reputation as the heir to the Russian throne and the leader of the monarchists by disseminating false claims. Nevertheless, after a London court order recognised Grand Duke Michael as legally dead in July 1924, Kirill assumed the title Tsar of All the Russias.[6] The Soviet disinformation campaign, however, did considerable harm to him and his wife, Princess Victoria Melita of Saxe-Coburg and Gotha, with accusations continuing until this day. The Soviet disinformation machine played the Mladorossy card again in 1957 when its founder and first president, Alexander Kazem-Bek, who had emigrated to the USA and from 1954 had been a lecturing professor at the Government of India School of Foreign Languages in New Delhi, unexpectedly returned to the Soviet Union. While in Moscow, *Pravda* published his letter of contrition with anti-American statements while he was given a solid job at the Department for External Church Relations of the Moscow Patriarchate, a Synodal institution that since its foundation in April 1946 has been working under the strict control of the NKVD and KGB.

Another anti-monarchist propaganda operation of the Disinformburo was to organise a 'secret' visit to the Soviet Union by the former politician Vasily Shulgin. Shulgin and Alexander Guchkov were the envoys of the State Duma who together with three other trusted persons gathered in the salon of the Romanov Imperial Train on 2 March 1917 where Nicholas II announced his decision to abdicate taken the day before. Just two weeks earlier, during the last session of the Duma, Shulgin called the Tsar 'an opponent of everything the country needs so desperately'.[7] Now he was present as this 'opponent' voluntarily renounced the throne of the Russian Empire on behalf of himself and his son.

After the Bolshevik revolution Shulgin participated in the White movement in the south of Russia. He moved to Odessa where he maintained close contacts with Emile Henno who presented himself as Consul of France as well as plenipotentiary and spokesperson for the Entente, and whom Shulgin much later identified as an officer of French intelligence.[8] He then moved to Kiev and Crimea, and in 1920 emigrated first to Constantinople and then to Europe, finally settling in the Kingdom of Serbs, Croats, and Slovenes (the future Yugoslavia).

Using his contacts with the White Russian All-Military Union (ROVS), founded by General Peter Wrangel in September 1924, Shulgin arranged a secret visit to the USSR allegedly to check the situation 'in-place' with the Monarchist Association of Central Russia (MOR). This was a fictitious monarchist underground invented by the Cheka in 1921 and used as a basis for a six-year deception that became known as Operation TREST ('Trust').[9] On 26 September 1925 it succeeded in luring Sidney Reilly, whom the Cheka and all its successors regarded as a British master spy after his Russian adventures, to Petrograd to a meeting with bogus MOR conspirators that quickly led to his arrest. Travelling in disguise with a forged passport in the name of 'Eduard Emilyevich Schmitt' and accompanied by GPU officers posing as anti-Bolshevik monarchists, Shulgin visited Kiev, Moscow and Leningrad (until recently Petrograd, now St Petersburg). His inspection of the MOR facilities was only a pretext because the main goal of Shulgin's visit to Russia was the search for his missing son, which was well-known to the Chekists. During his brief travels around Russia between 23 December 1925 and 6 February 1926, that is, after the arrest of Reilly, Shulgin was shown what every other foreign guest was permitted to see – Torgsin shops and

Potemkin villages whose sole purpose since pre-revolutionary times had been to provide an external façade to a country faring extremely poorly at the same time making foreign visitors and even some of its own people believe it was getting on pretty well.

Before he was permitted to leave the country, Shulgin was advised to write a 'truthful story' of what he had seen reflecting on his impressions about the New Economic Policy (NEP) and its achievements. His book *Three Capitals: Trip to Red Russia* (1927) was published in Berlin,[10] explaining how the NEP had reintroduced a measure of stability to the Russian economy and allowed the Soviet people to recover after the destitution of the war years. Although it contained some criticism, generally the book gave a positive impression of the new Soviet Russia.

Other foreign writers and journalists were used by the Cheka and its successors not only to disseminate Soviet propaganda and disinformation but also as the Comintern couriers, sources of intelligence and agents of influence.

* * *

One of them was the writer Arthur Ransome, whom Lockhart describes as 'a Don Quixote with a walrus moustache, a sentimentalist, who could always be counted on to champion the underdog, and a visionary, whose imagination had been fired by the revolution'. The British envoy also noted that Ransome 'was on excellent terms with the Bolsheviks and frequently brought us information of the greatest value'.[11] Ransome arrived in Moscow five days after Yurovsky and his team, following the decree of the Ural Regional Soviet, had executed the Tsar and his family in a dingy cellar of the Ipatiev house in Yekaterinburg fearing their release by the advancing Czechoslovak Legion and the White forces. Alighting from his train on 22 July 1918, he first visited Lockhart in haste to collect his passport in which Lockhart had been authorised to include Yevgenia Shelepina as Ransome's wife,[12] and then spent five days preparing for her departure to Stockholm. She was to become part of the secretariat of Vatslav Vorovsky, who had been named the Soviet government's representative in Scandinavia with a base in the Swedish capital. There, he had also acted as a secret liaison between the Bolshevik government and German officials. Vorovsky's first diplomatic mission would be terminated by the Swedish government in December 1918, following the expulsion of other Bolshevik envoys – Maxim Litvinov from London in September and Adolf Joffe from Berlin in November of that same year.

In the meantime, Ransome visited the NKID where he had a meeting with Chicherin, the recently appointed Commissar for Foreign Affairs, and via Petrograd and Helsingfors travelled to Sweden arriving in Stockholm on 5 August 1918, as his biographer notes, 'missing the Allied invasion and a mass arrest of British citizens by twenty-four hours'. Contrary to what he wrote to his London editors, his luggage did not contain 'a clutter of personal rubbish',[13] but instead there was three million roubles in cash that he had smuggled out for both the Vorovsky mission and the International Socialist Commission (ISC). In Stockholm, the ISC had been publishing a news bulletin in German known as *Nachrichtendienst*, the 44th and last issue of which came out on 1 September. Although its secretary, Angelica Balabanoff, tried to revive the influence of the ISC, arriving in Stockholm soon after Ransome, her efforts were not successful and she consented to its formal dissolution into the Comintern at its founding congress in March 1919, which she attended together with Vorovsky, who by that time had returned to Moscow.

It seems that Ransome's smuggling activities had not escaped the notice of British intelligence. Roland Chambers quotes a British agent's communication to the War Office dated 29 August 1918:

Mr Arthur Ransome, Petrograd correspondent of the *Daily News*, is reported to be in Stockholm, having married Trotsky's secretary, with a large amount of Russian Government money, and to be travelling with a Bolshevik passport. The alleged marriage we understand to be a 'put-up' job and so the Bolshevik passport may be of little account, but the fact that he has a large amount of Russian Government money is of interest to us, and we would like to have him watched accordingly.[14]

Another report followed soon, this time from John Scale, the MI1c station chief in Stockholm:

It certainly ought to be understood how completely he is in the hands of the Bolsheviks. He is living here with a lady who was previously Trotsky's private secretary, spends the greater part of his time in the Bolshevik Legation, where he is provided with a room and a typewriter, and he is very nervous as to the effect which his present attitude may have upon his prospects in England. I also know that he informed two Russians that I personally am an agent of the British government and said that he had this information from authoritative sources, both British and Bolshevik. He seems therefore to be working pretty definitely against us.[15]

These reports, obviously, had no effect and two years later Ransome, now living with Yevgenia in a small guesthouse with a view of Lahepea Bay about

40 miles from Reval where nobody cared if 'Mr and Mrs Ransome' were married or not, was as keen to continue his Russian adventure as before. In January 1920, in the middle of the Soviet-Polish War, he wrote to his friend Ted Scott, the son of the editor and owner of the influential *Manchester Guardian*, explaining that his coverage of the war would be a distant affair owing to 'an orgy of Anti-Bolshevism and Whiteness in Poland'. He was of the same opinion about Finland where the Whites, supported by Germany, were prevailing over the Reds led by Kullervo Manner. After the end of the civil war those of the communist supporters and sympathisers who, unlike Manner, Otto Kuusinen and other 'Red' leaders, could not escape to Soviet Russia were interned in concentration camps.

After the Treaty of Tartu was signed on 2 February ending the Estonian War of Independence, a direct rail link was established between the Estonian capital (previously known as Reval in the German, Swedish and Danish languages but now formally reverted to its Estonian name, Tallinn) and Moscow. Ransome was among the first to use this opportunity and together with two Norwegian journalists and Marcel Rosenberg, an NKID official in charge of the Entente sub-department who briefly headed the Soviet Press Bureau in Berlin, set off for Moscow. 'By the beginning of March,' his biographer writes, 'he was seated comfortably in his own office at the Commissariat for Foreign Affairs, hard at work on a new political pamphlet which would explain why Russia – the richest agricultural territory in Europe – was currently on the brink of starvation.' In January 1922 Ransome was in Finland meeting his friend Ernest Boyce who, after he had been expelled from Bolshevik Russia together with Lockhart, was posted as the British Passport Control Officer in Reval (Tallinn) before being appointed SIS head of station in Helsinki responsible for Russia and Scandinavia. In February Ransome was back in Moscow speaking to Chicherin, Litvinov and his friend Karl Radek, and in March his articles were published describing 'liberties, luxuries and sky-high prices' now in evidence in Moscow following the introduction of the New Economic Policy.[16] Reading this article today, one would probably ask whether the author really had in mind 1922 rather than 2022.

* * *

Another writer who, wittingly or unwittingly, lent his fame to the Bolshevik cause was Henri Barbusse, who became widely known after the publication of his novel *Le Feu* (*Journal d'une escouade*) in 1916. The story was based on his personal experiences as a French soldier – Barbusse was 41 when he volunteered – on the Western Front after the German invasion. The book had won the prestigious Prix Goncourt while the author became a pacifist and then a militant communist. After *Clarté* (1919), his literary works acquired a definite anti-war and anti-imperialist orientation much praised by Lenin who believed that Barbusse's novels demonstrated the development of mass revolutionary consciousness in Europe.[17] Indeed, his book *Light from the Abyss* (1919) and the collection of his articles and speeches *Paroles d'un combatant* (1920) contained calls for the overthrow of the capitalist system. A critic notes that from 1919 to 1922 Henri Barbusse tried to win leftist war veterans and intellectuals to the cause of the Third [Communist] International, 'while taking pains to publicise his political independence'.[18] According to Barbusse, communist doctrine was 'at the summit of the history of ideas' but he refrained from joining the French Communist Party until 1923. Then, for three years from 1926 to 1929 he had served as literary director of the communist newspaper *l'Humanité*.

Barbusse visited the USSR on several occasions but Wikipedia's claim that 'in January 1918 he left France and moved to Moscow, where he married a Russian woman and joined the Bolshevik party' seems an invention not confirmed by any source. However, as a 'cultural leader' (chef de file culturel) of the French revolutionary movement he was able to contribute a lot to the propaganda efforts of the Disinformburo for many years both in Russia and in the West until his death in 1935.

A decade earlier, in 1925, the German communist Willi Münzenberg, dubbed by some as the 'Comintern's clandestine minister for propaganda around the world',[19] put forward his idea of organising a big international cultural event related to the 10th anniversary celebrations of the Bolshevik revolution to the Comintern's Executive Committee. As head of the Workers International Relief, Münzenberg was experienced in arranging such events. In November 1927, an organising committee led by the Soviet and British Communist Party functionaries convened a world congress of friendship groups in Moscow. Thoroughly planned and prepared by the Disinformburo and Agitpropotdel (Agitation and Propaganda Department of the Comintern) officials who worked behind the scenes, an International Association of Friends of the Soviet Union was formed by the delegates from forty-three countries. Barbusse took part in all plenary meetings, sitting in the presidium with the elderly Clara Zetkin (Eißner), a German Marxist theorist and activist who since 1924 had lived in Moscow. In his opening speech, the British delegate Will Lawther (a Labour Party activist, future President of the TUC and Sir) said, 'I think that I express the desire of all attending this Congress when I call upon all delegates on their return home not only to proclaim "Hail to the October Revolution", but also to conduct an inspired and resolute struggle for the preparation of the World October'.

The audience responded by rising and singing the *Internationale*.[20] Since that time friendship societies would become an important and reliable base for Soviet intelligence, among other things for its disinformation and influence operations worldwide.

During the same year Münzenberg founded the League against Imperialism (which collapsed four years later) and in August 1932 the World Congress against Imperialist War based in Amsterdam which a year later became the World Committee against War and Fascism led by Henri Barbusse, André Gide and André Malraux as co-chairs. In January 1935 his Paris publisher Ernest Flammarion published Barbusse's last pro-Soviet propaganda book, *Staline: un monde nouveau vu à travers un homme* (published in English as *Stalin: A New World Seen Through One Man*) after which the author was invited to Moscow to write a biography of the Soviet dictator. There he fell ill with pneumonia and died in August 1935. In January 2003, half-jokingly but also half-seriously, celebrating the 80th anniversary of the creation of the Disinformburo, an article in one of the leading Russian newspapers admitted, based on the documents from the KGB archives, that 'ever increasing financial resources from the state treasury were allocated for the receptions of the French writer Henri Barbusse, which were fully paid off by his pro-Soviet publications'.[21]

* * *

John 'Jack' Silas Reed was an American journalist who served as a war correspondent during the Great War on assignment for *Metropolitan*, also contributing articles to *The Masses*, a socialist magazine published in the United States and edited by Max Eastman. Some of his writings like, for example, *Red Russia: The Triuph of the Bolsheviki* (1919) were also published by *The Liberator*, another monthly socialist publication founded by Eastman in 1918 to continue the work of *The Masses* which was shut down by the authorities. In August 1917 Reed and his journalist wife Louise Bryant travelled from New York via Finland to revolutionary Petrograd where they became witnesses of the Bolshevik coup d'état. Before they left, the Espionage Act 1917 was passed to prevent the support of US enemies during wartime and a few months later its extension, the Sedition Act, was enacted. According to the sworn testimonies of Reed and Bryant to the US Senate Sub-Committee on the Judiciary, they had both spent some time in the Winter Palace 'with the Kerensky officials and the Junkers [Yunkers]' and then in the Smolny Institute on the night of 25 October when the Winter Palace was attacked, the Provisional Government fell and they 'ran in [into the palace] with the first troops'.[22] That storming of the Winter Palace in

Petrograd was the symbolic event that started the revolution. Later, Soviet propaganda portrayed the attack as a savage battle, but according to the eyewitnesses, including Reed and Bryant, it was in fact a relatively bloodless event. The defenders of the Palace – Cossacks, a women's battalion and military cadets or Junkers – gave up with little resistance.

Reed became a great champion of the Bolshevik cause and supporter of the new regime. He volunteered to work for the People's Commissariat for Foreign Affairs translating documents into English and also collaborated in the gathering of material and 'distributing of papers to go into the German trenches', Reed later testified. He returned to New York in April 1918 worried that 'his vivid impressions of the revolution would fade' and eager to write a book about his first-hand experience in the workers' paradise. The book, *Ten Days that Shook the World*, became a classic that would come out again and again in all languages although his wife's book, *Six Red Months in Russia* (1918), appeared first. Max Eastman recalls meeting Reed in Sheridan Square in New York when he was working on his book: '[Reed] wrote *Ten Days that Shook the World* in another ten days and ten nights or little more. He was gaunt, unshaven, greasy-skinned, a stark sleepless half-crazy look on his slightly potato-like face – had come down after a night's work for a cup of coffee.'[23]

Lenin read the book, first published by Boni & Liveright in New York in 1919, and wrote an introduction to its 1922 edition: 'Here is the book that I should like to see published in millions of copies and translated into all languages. It gives a truthful and most vivid exposition of the events so significant to the comprehension of what really is the Proletarian Revolution and the Dictatorship of the Proletariat.'

In 1945, George Orwell wrote an introductory note to *Animal Farm*, one of his most famous books. This text was not printed and remained unknown until 1972 when it appeared in *The New York Times* under Orwell's original title 'The Freedom of the Press':

> At the death of John Reed, the author of *Ten Days that Shook the World* — a first-hand account of the early days of the Russian Revolution — the copyright of the book passed into the hands of the British Communist Party, to whom I believe Reed had bequeathed it. Some years later the British Communists, having destroyed the original edition of the book as completely as they could, issued a garbled version from which they had eliminated mentions of Trotsky and also omitted the introduction written by Lenin.[24]

Orwell was almost certainly referring to the 1926 hardback edition first published in London by the CPGB at the time of the General Strike and two years after Lenin's death. Albert Inkpin, General Secretary of the CPGB arrested shortly before Christmas, was serving a six-month term in prison – he was released just prior to the strike in May. The Trades Union Congress, which led the strike, was dominated by moderates who opposed any idea of revolution. Besides, in Soviet Russia now under Stalin the book was not welcome. In the eyes of the party leadership, Reed had committed the unpardonable sin of ignoring Stalin, who was mentioned only twice, while Trotsky was shown as one of the leaders of the revolution together with Lenin. With both of them out of the way – Lenin dead and Trotsky forced to resign from all his government posts – this was not to be tolerated any more.

Reed's biographer, Eric Homberger, believes that by the time of his death in October 1920, Reed had become strongly disillusioned by what he calls 'Soviet factionalism'. Homberger refers to the notes made of interviews with Louise Bryant in Riga in May 1921, and summarised in a letter from Colonel Matthew C. Smith, Military Intelligence Division, to J. Edgar Hoover at the US Department of Justice, dated 10 June 1921. 'She stated confidentially that her husband, John Reed, was carried away by Communism when he first went to Russia, but that she believes that, if she could have been with him, he would never have gone to the extremes that he did,' the letter claims. 'She stated, however, that he was much disappointed with what he found in Russia and that she believes this is what brought on his illness. He was so imbued with the idea of Communism, but when he got really in touch with the Russian situation, he found so few Communists and so many who used Communism as a means to get comfortable positions, extra food, homes, etc., that he was disappointed.'[25] John Reed's classic book was only allowed in the Soviet Union after Stalin's death.

* * *

On 30 November 1924 Artur Artuzov, chief of the counter-intelligence (KRO) department of the GPU's Secret-Operational Directorate (SOU), signed a Short Annual Report covering the activities of the KRO for 1923–4, classified 'Top-Secret'. The report was supplemented with an annex – *Spravka* No. 1 – on threats from espionage, terrorism and sabotage. In July 1922 Artuzov – a year before awarded one of the highest and most prestigious decoration of Soviet Russia, the Order of the Red Banner – was appointed to head the Soviet counter-intelligence service.

He was born Arthur Eugene Leonard Frauchi in 1891 in the Tver region of the Russian Empire. His father, Christian Frauchi, was from a Swiss cheesemaking family who came to Russia in search of a good income. Here, he married Augusta, one of the four sisters of the Didrikil family, which had its origin in Estonia, Latvia, Scotland and France. Remarkably, another sister, Nina, an old Bolshevik, got married to Nikolai Podvoisky, a Russian revolutionary and the first People's Commissar for Military and Naval Affairs, a post that he shared with two others before Trotsky replaced him in March 1918. Yet another sister, Olga, was married to Mikhail Kedrov, who joined the Bolsheviks in 1903 and in 1918 was appointed head of the military section of the Cheka. It is now well documented based on primary and secondary sources that the semi-qualified doctor and virtuoso pianist Kedrov 'would slaughter schoolchildren and army officers in northern Russia with such ruthlessness that he had to be taken into psychiatric care'.[26] According to the witnesses' testimonies, in the summer of 1920 local Chekists together with the Red Guards were executing 60–70 people every day in Archangel, including women and small children. Kedrov later remarried. His second wife, Rebecca Plastinina (née Meisel), a local Bolshevik official who used to be his mistress, assisted him in conducting mass executions in northern Russia (Archangel, Vologda, Kholmogory, Shenkursk, Solovetsky correctional labour camp), where she had personally shot more than a hundred, including the entire family of her husband, and then drowned another 500 on a barge.

From December 1917 to August 1919 young Arthur Frauchi had been working together with Kedrov in the north, where he married and acquired a new Russian-sounding name, becoming 'Artur Khristianovich Artuzov'. Back in Moscow, he also worked under Kedrov serving as the chief of the operational section of the Cheka Special (Osoby) Department from March 1920.[27] There he took part in the Cheka operation against the counter-revolutionary organisation that became known as the Tactical Centre.[28] This Centre united several underground anti-Bolshevik groups like the National Centre (Prince Sergey E. Trubetskoy), the Union of Regeneration (Sergey P. Melgunov),[29] the Action Centre,[30] the Military Commission and a few others maintaining contacts with the White armies of Admiral Kolchak and General Denikin and with other groups such as the Union for the Defence of the Fatherland and Freedom, founded by Boris Savinkov in March 1918. It is also claimed that the Tactical Centre supplied intelligence to Paul Dukes of the SIS, who was still operating in Russia at the time, using his agent and mistress Nadezhda Petrovskaya as a cutout. After her arrest, Petrovskaya testified that she had indeed arranged a few meetings for him with some low-ranking Soviet officials but that she only knew Dukes by his assumed name as 'Sergey Ivanovich Savantov', a Russia correspondent of a British socialist newspaper who was collecting information for his articles.

In January 1921 Artuzov was appointed assistant chief (later deputy chief) of the Special Department (Osoby Otdel) then headed by Menzhinsky but a few months earlier, in July 1920, he was sent to the Western Front to supervise all Cheka work against the Polish Military Organisation (Polska Organisacja Wojskowa, POW), formed during the war to gather intelligence and organise acts of sabotage against the enemy troops and installations. Artuzov's assignment also included counter-intelligence operations against the 'ekspozyturas' (stations) and agent networks of Polish military intelligence.

It has already been noted that Poland and especially its II (intelligence) Division of the General Staff as well as the POW were among the prime targets for Soviet counter-intelligence. As a result of the Cheka efforts, several Polish intelligence officers were arrested and successfully turned, including Ignacy Dobrzyński (group leader), Wiktor Marczewski, Wiktor Kijakowski, Maria Niedźwiałowska, Wacław Tabortowski and Leopold Czyllok, who were not only recruited as agents but became high-ranking Cheka/GPU and later NKVD officers. This, however, did not save them during the Great Terror.

On 18 June 1920 Soviet newspapers published an 'open letter' signed by Dobrzyński, explaining his and some of his former agents' decision to switch sides and join the Bolsheviks.[31] The text was distributed among Polish troops and prisoners of war.

Dobrzyński, known in Russia as Ignaty Sosnowski (his party alias), was a member of the POW with the pseudonym 'Świerszcz' (Cricket). After the war he served as a second lieutenant of Second Division, head of the intelligence department for Lithuania and East Prussia. From 1919 Dobrzyński was an intelligence resident (head of station) in Moscow. Arrested in June 1920 by the Cheka together with his fiancée, Jana Rzeplińska, Dobrzyński agreed to work for the Soviets after interrogations and talks with, among others, Feliks Dzierżyński and Julian Marchlewski, a Polish Bolshevik revolutionary. Dobrzyński betrayed his entire espionage network to the Cheka on the condition that the arrested Poles would not be sentenced but deported to Poland.

In Russia Wiktor Steckiewicz became Victor Kijakowski. In the spring of 1920, Lieutenant Steckiewicz, operational pseudonym 'Wik', a member of the POW, was sent by the Second Division to Soviet Russia with the task of setting up an intelligence network in Petrograd. There he was arrested and agreed to work for the Cheka. After the end of the Polish-Bolshevik war, documented as 'Kosiński', he operated in Helsinki and then Riga. In November 1921, Steckiewicz was one of the principal instigators of the disinformation operation code-named TREST, leading its first stage. During those years he made numerous trips abroad, mainly to the Baltic countries and Poland.

Leopold Czyllok fought with the 5th Polish Rifle Division against the Red Army in Siberia, surrendered to the Bolsheviks in early 1920 and was interned in a prisoner of war camp in Krasnoyarsk, from where he escaped.

Arrested by the Cheka on the border with Latvia, Czyllok was interrogated and agreed to change sides, operating against the POW in Ukraine. From 1921 he had served as a Cheka officer in Moscow using the name Karol or Karl Roller. In 1922 he was transferred to the KRO and, like Steckiewicz-Kijakowski, took part in Operation TREST.

Maria Niedźwiałowska (also known as Nawrocka, Niedźwiecka and Knoppe) had been a member of the Kiev POW organisation from 1918, collecting military intelligence in Ukraine. Arrested by the Cheka in 1920, she agreed to switch to the opposite side and was accepted to the staff of the KRO. In 1926 Maria was sent on an intelligence assignment to Italy and after coming back to Moscow worked at the GPU Lubyanka headquarters, released from active duty in 1933.

Wiktor Marczewski (in Russia Witkowski) was a member of the POW in 1914–15, then served in the Polish army. For some minor disciplinary violation, he was sentence to a term in prison, managed to escape, and defected to the Bolsheviks in 1920.

Wacław Tabortowski (in Russia Vatslav Ivanovich Gursky/Górski) also joined the Cheka, rising to Captain of State Security in the NKVD.

After the publication of the Dobrzyński declaration, the Cheka prepared a long and detailed appeal to the Polish Army and members of the POW, signed by nine former Polish intelligence agents who had served together with Dobrzyński-Sosnowski but decided to switch sides, persuading others who had been detained, arrested or interned, to surrender and cooperate with the Soviet security authorities.[32] Almost all of those who agreed became victims of the so-called Polish Operation of the NKVD in 1937–8, which resulted in the sentencing of about 140,000 people and summary executions of over 110,000 Polish nationals living in the Soviet Union.

* * *

After his relatively brief ten-month mission to Soviet Russia, Paul Dukes managed to escape with the help of his best agent Peter Sokolov (ST/65) and on his return to England in September 1919 was rewarded with a knighthood. 'Undoubtedly the most important part of his work,' Michael Smith writes in his unofficial history of MI6, 'was stitching together the agent networks left behind by Jim Gillespie and carefully tendered by John Merrett.'[33] These were led by Albert Hoyer, a Danish sea captain now working for MI1c. In September Hoyer was successfully reporting about the situation in Russia via John Scale in Stockholm and Raleigh Le May (ST/30), another member of the pre-revolutionary British community in Russia, appointed British vice-consul in Helsinki (former Helsingfors) to run the bureau there under Scale's direction.[34] In the meantime, 'on 18 September Dukes reported in person to both the Director of Military Intelligence and Sir Basil Thomson. Cumming also took him to see the Secretary for War, Winston Churchill, who gave him a "long interview over 1½ hours". On 20 September Cumming brought him to meet Lord Curzon at his private residence, 1 Carlton House Terrace.'[35]

In May 1920 Rex Leeper of the Foreign Office Political Intelligence Department was going to Poland and Dukes was to accompany him on behalf of the Secret Service which became known as SIS around that time. Something didn't work quite well and at the end Dukes went out alone, staying in Poland for six months attempting to establish a network of agents to work on Russia. According to the official history of the Service, his attempts did not have much success although his reports were nevertheless described back at the Office as 'very interesting'. While in Poland, Dukes was joined by Sidney Reilly.

Section 3 of Artuzov's Short Annual Report covering the activities of the KRO specifically dealt with espionage. The main accent was on deception operations. The report stated that the KRO organised its counter-intelligence work in such a way that the 'main European headquarters', that is, governments of the leading European countries, with the exception of Britain, received information and intelligence up to 95 per cent containing material concocted by the People's Commissariat for Military and Naval Affairs and the NKID. Therefore, the report claimed, 'they have as much knowledge and understanding of our military power as we want them to have'.[36] Using modern terms, the already very active Disinformburo had been using manipulation, distortion, falsification and even camouflage to induce foreign governments to react in a manner prejudicial to their interests. This desire to confuse or better to mislead the intelligence services of the adversary was fully justified. The problem was that Western governments more often than not didn't realise that they were being misinformed by their secret agents.

* * *

After his return from Petrograd following his first mission to Russia in October 1918, Sidney Reilly was sent there again with Captain George Hill, ostensibly attached to the Commercial Department of the British FO. They were instructed by the Chief to collect political information which was 'urgently needed from the whole of south of Russia'. Independently of Reilly and Hill, Cumming had another representative there, Lieutenant Commander Malcolm Maclaren (RS/1), who arrived in Odessa via Bucharest in early 1919 accompanied by Harold Gibson. Gibson was bilingual in Russian and was later appointed head of SIS station in Riga.

In the summer of 1920 Cumming launched an ambitious operation suggested by Reilly to form an international 'anti-Bolshevik intelligence service' by sending Vladimir Gregorievich [*sic*] Orlov, alias Orbanski, to recruit collaborators across Europe. Orlov had been a Tsarist intelligence officer and general criminal investigator under the Soviet regime before escaping from Russia. With Malcolm Maclaren, whom Cumming had summoned home from Istanbul in April 1920 'to take complete charge of our affairs in North Europe', Reilly, Orlov and Dukes toured east-central Europe spotting potential anti-Bolshevik agents, and signing them either for nothing, or for a regular stipend, or for an exchange of information. In Warsaw they recruited five; in Riga their haul was eleven; in Reval (now Tallinn), four; in Helsinki, three; and in Kovno (Kaunas), two. Most of these collaborators were exiled Russian former military and intelligence officers, but there was also a selection of officials of the various host countries' intelligence services, including some based in Berlin ... At the end of July 1921 Maclaren in Warsaw was instructed by London to close down his operation, although for some years a few of the contacts he and Orlov had made remained in touch with SIS through the Baltic stations. In the meantime, Orlov, Savinkov and Reilly continued their anti-Bolshevik crusade throughout Europe, but their links to SIS grew less close.[37]

After the last White forces left Russian soil late in 1920, many of those who had to emigrate against their will still believed in a possibility of mounting another serious challenge to Bolshevik rule. Among them were members of the Russian Imperial Family, White officers, business people, intellectuals of various professions, daredevils like Savinkov, and many of those Russian patriots who became known as first-wave émigrés opposed to the new regime.[38] Lenin, Trotsky, Dzerzhinsky and other Bolshevik leaders fully realised the danger, estimating that after the revolution there were roughly between one and two million anti-Bolshevik Russian émigrés abroad and an uncountable number of opponents of the regime inside the country. In the early and mid-1920s, the chief Cheka and then GPU/OGPU targets became the émigré White Guards, based mainly in Berlin, Paris and Warsaw, as well as in the Baltic countries and the Kingdom of Yugoslavia. The other 'counter-revolutionary' threat, according to the documents from the KGB archives, came from Ukrainian nationalists, who had fought both Red and White forces in an attempt to win their independence. The Cheka and later GPU were instructed 'not merely to collect intelligence on the émigré White Guards and Ukrainian nationalists but also to penetrate and destabilize them'.[39]

As a result of the Red Army defeat in the Polish–Bolshevik War (February 1919 – March 1921), Poland and its intelligence agencies (II Division of the General Staff and the POW) remained the main adversary of Soviet Russia. Besides, Polish authorities actively supported anti-Bolshevik groups either located on their territory or involved in sending emissaries through the corridors for illegal border crossings (known as 'windows') set up on the Polish border to Byelorussia and Ukraine. One of the first Cheka operations, codenamed SINDIKAT-1 ('Syndicate' or S-1), targeted various anti-Soviet groups like the Tactical Centre, National Centre and Action Centre, as well as the Savinkov's new People's Union for the Defence of Fatherland and Freedom, based in Warsaw since January 1921. All of these anti-Bolshevik groups ran agent networks inside Soviet Russia, planning risings and various subversive actions against the regime.

* * *

With today's access to research data including primary sources, it seems that a Cheka mole very seldom mentioned by intelligence historians had operated rather successfully against all three known British agents – Vladimir Orlov, designated Z/51, Boris Savinkov and Sidney Reilly (ST/1). He was also actively used in operations against several aforementioned anti-Bolshevik centres remaining uncovered until his hasty escape to Russia in 1928. Alas, only a few Russian publications are available to researchers (all of them originating from the KGB Press Bureau),[40] traditionally singing their agent's praises and always following the slightly paraphrased felicitous remark attributed to Einstein: 'If the facts don't fit your version of events, change the facts'.

The name of the agent was Nikolai Kroshko and he is often confused with Nikolai Klyshko,[41] who used to live and work in London before the revolution, was expelled as a dangerous Bolshevik and then returned as a member of the Soviet trade delegation headed by Krasin.[42] The delegation reached London at the end of May 1920.

Second Lieutenant (Poruchik) Kroshko was a walk-in who decided to change sides, offering his services to Soviet intelligence in Warsaw. Soon after formal diplomatic relations with Poland were established at the end of April 1921, a united residency of the Cheka and Razvedupr (the future GRU), then officially known as the Second (Intelligence) Directorate of the Red Army Staff, established its first 'legal' station in the Polish capital headed by the Pole Mieczysław Łoganowski (in Russia – Mechislav Antonovich Loganovsky). Loganovsky was officially accredited as Secretary of the Soviet mission, from September that years headed by Lev Karakhan, Envoy Extraordinary and Minister Plenipotentiary.

In November Loganosky was joined by another Pole – Kazimierz Barański (operational pseudonym 'Kobecki') – deputy resident responsible for penetrating Russian émigré circles and Polish intelligence.[43] Barański-Kobecki was the first handler of Kroshko, registering him in the card index as agent A/3.

When Kroshko visited the mission for the second time, both Loganovsky and Baranski (whom he knew only as 'Kobecki') talked to him at length, asking to provide detailed information on everything that he had learned about the émigré White Guards who were trying to overthrow the Bolsheviks and about 'their capitalist supporters'. This included the Polish branch of the Action Centre and its 'windows' on the border, activities of the Savinkov's organisation in Warsaw as well as a 'partisan headquarters' under Yurko Tyutyunnik. Later, Kroshko moved to Germany where he was in touch with the head of the united GPU-RU station Bronisław Bortnowski (introduced to Kroshko as 'Bronkowski) and his deputy Aleksey Loginov (alias 'Vladimir Bustrem'). The agent was instructed to penetrate the circle of Grand Duke Kirill Vladimirovich and the Mladorossy organisation headed by Kazem-Bek. His final assignment was the penetration of the forgery bureau that Vladimir Orlov set up in Berlin after he was barred from entering France in 1923. The bureau had been selling secret documents – genuine and forged – to anyone who was interested and able to pay. One of the regular customers was British SIS and those forged documents, shared with MI5, can now be found in the declassified files at the National Archives in Kew.

Russian sources claim, although without any proof, that a scandal involving Orlov, his associate Pavlunovsky (real name Mikhail G. Sumarokov) and their Berlin venture, which wrecked its reputation forever, was due to the fact that Kroshko managed to obtain evidence showing that documents sold by Orlov and Pavlunovsky to the American journalist Hubert Renfo Knickerbocker Jr. were fakes.

On 1 July 1929, a trial opened in the Berlin-Schoeneberg district court. The defendants faced charges of selling fraudulent documents purported to show that two US senators, William E. Borah of Idaho and George Norris of Nebraska, had each received $100,000 from the Soviets for their advocacy of pro-Moscow policies in Washington. This was a serious accusation, particularly in the case of Borah, the head of the powerful Senate Foreign Relations Committee and a man touted by many as a possible president.[44] Remarkably, Orlov's sensational memoirs, known in English as *The Secret Dossier: My memoirs of Russia's political underworld* (London: Harrap, 1932), first came out in Berlin in 1929 at the very moment that their author was standing trial for forgery.

This rare book was also published in Russia in 1998, edited by the former FSB General Alexander Zdanovich with Kroshko's memoirs as an addendum. A year before, a short monograph about Orlov's adventures inspired by Raymond Rocca of the CIA and written by Natalie Grant was published in Washington, DC.[45] The latest article about the man, aptly titled 'A Life Between Fact and Fiction', appeared in *Revolutionary Russia* in December 2008. Its author, Wim Coudenys, writes: 'Orlov's dramatic end – he was shot in the Berlin Tiergarten on 12 January 1941 by a person (or persons) unknown – can be considered the logical outcome of a life that hovered between fact and fiction and escaped every attempt at classification.'

* * *

Operations against Polish intelligence agents resembled those against the White Guards and Ukrainian nationalists, while the Cheka leadership was convinced – not without reason – that behind all anti-Bolshevik forces stood the governments and secret services of the USA, Britain and France plus similar structures of less important international players. By the beginning of 1921, in the Kiev region alone there were up to 100 rebel detachments focused on the restoration of the Ukrainian People's Republic (UNR). The total number of fighters in organised insurgent groups reached 40,000.

In these conditions the rebels needed experienced and competent leaders with solid military backgrounds. In January 1921 Simon Petlyura's Ukrainian government-in-exile established a coordination centre that became known as Guerrilla-Insurgent Headquarters (PPSh), first in the Polish city of Tarnów and then in Lvov (Lviv), headed by Tyutyunnik. During the Polish-Bolshevik war the UNR fought against the Red Army and Tyutyunnik, who commanded the 4th Kiev Rifle Division, its most combat-ready unit, was promoted to general-horunzhy (one-star general) of the Ukrainian People's Army.

Mitrokhin's notes reveal that the Ukrainian Cheka was ordered to collect intelligence on the Ukrainian nationalists' plans but also to penetrate the PPSh and get close to Tyutyunnik. The assignment was given to the young Ukrainian Chekist Sergey Danilenko (alias Karin), who visited Tyutyunnik's headquarters in Lviv posing as an emissary of one of the underground anti-Soviet groups operating in Ukraine. Danilenko-Karin was introduced to Tyutyunnik as 'Chernenko'. With their agent in place, the Ukrainian GPU began to devise a large-scale deception operation, codenamed D-39 (where 'D' stood for DELO/CASE). The purpose of the operation was to entice Tyutyunnik back to Ukraine.

On 2 July 1922 one of Tytyunnik's couriers by the name of Georgy Zayarny was caught crossing the Polish-Soviet frontier. He was interrogated and turned by the Cheka, becoming seksot – secret agent – No. 103 alias 'Gordienko'. According to the Cheka-GPU files, Zayarny was sent back to Tyutyunnik's headquarters with bogus reports that an underground Supreme Military Council (VVR) had been established in Ukraine and was anxious to set up a clandestine cell system of resistance fighters ready to wage war against the Bolsheviks authorities.[46] In November Agent 103 travelled to Chişinău, capital of independent Moldova, and invited Pyotr Stakhov, an associate of Tyutyunnik, to come and take part in the insurgent movement in Ukraine under the aegis of the new VVR. The cautious Stakhov first sent his brother Alexander to Kiev to investigate. The Chekists staged a show to the full satisfaction of Alexander who reported back to his brother. What followed was a pattern repeated by the Cheka-GPU many times in the 1920s to dupe leaders of the White Guard and nationalist movement, who had settled abroad and were plotting the overthrow of the Bolshevik regime.

The final stage of the operation D-39, also known in the internal documents as the operational game TYUTYUN (tobacco) is best described by Christopher Andrew:

Tutyunnik [sic] was too cautious to return immediately but sent several emissaries who attended stage-managed meetings of the VVR, at which GPU officers disguised as Ukrainian nationalists reported the rapid growth of underground opposition to Bolshevik rule and agreed on the urgent need for Tutyunnik's leadership. Like Zayarny, one of the emissaries, Pyotr Stakhov, a close associate of Tutyunnik, was recruited by the GPU and used as a double agent.

Attempts to persuade Tyutyunnik to return to Ukraine finally succeeded on 16 June 1923. The head of the Ukrainian KRO Nikolai Nikolayev-Zhurid led the operation. A day before Zayarny crossed into Romania to negotiate details of Tyutyunnik's return with his retinue. When Tyutyunnik accompanied by a bodyguard and aids arrived at a remote hamlet on the Romanian bank of the river Dniester, Zayarny met him with the news that the VVR leadership and Pyotr Stakhov were waiting on the other side. Still cautious, Tyutyunnik sent his bodyguard across to make sure that no trap had been laid for him. The unsuspecting bodyguard met Stakhov and 'his people' (all members of the Ukrainian GPU) and together they returned to Romania to reassure Tyutyunnik. According to the report in the file, 'Tutyunnik told him, "Pyotr, I know you and you know me. We won't fool each other. The VVR is a fiction, isn't it?" "That is impossible," Stakhov replied. "I know them all, particularly those who are with me [today]. You know, you can rely on me …" Tutyunnik got into the boat with Stakhov and crossed the Dniester.'[47] As soon as Tyutyunnik and his bodyguard set foot on the opposite bank, they were silently arrested. The shock was so great that the general passed out and they had to carry him away on a stretcher. The prisoners were first taken to Kiev, and then to Kharkov. On the same day Artuzov in Moscow received a telegram – 'Tea and tobacco ['tyutyun'] bought profitably'.

In his prison cell after arrest and interrogation, Tyutyunnik was prompted to write letters of recantation saying that the struggle was hopeless and that he had aligned himself irrevocably with the Soviet cause, after which he was released under an amnesty and given a job in a Ukrainian state trading company. While allowed to be at large, he wrote and published three books and even played the role of himself, that is, General Tyutyunnik, in a feature film directed by another GPU collaborator. On 12 February 1929, he was arrested in Kharkov and transported to Moscow. Yuri (Yurko) Tyutyunnik was sentence to death in December but shot almost a year later, in October 1930.

Agent 103 Zayarny was arrested in October 1938 and executed in February 1939. At the time of his arrest he had been serving as one of the guards at the NKVD dacha located in Skhodnya near Moscow.[48] Nikolayev-Zhurid, then recently appointed head of the 3rd (counter-intelligence) Department of the NKVD Chief Directorate of State Security, was also arrested in October 1938 and shot in February 1940. In August 1937 Sergey Danilenko (Karin) was arrested and after months of torture and abuse released in October 1939. He had almost completely lost his sight.

* * *

Two other elaborate deception operations codenamed S-2 (SINDIKAT-2) and TREST have become widely known although a good account of them is still to be written. Like D-39 and S-1 (there were also S-3, S-4, D-7, K-5, RDO, and a little-known operation codenamed KROT/MOLE in Byelorussia, a precursor to S-2), both SINDIKAT-2 (S-2) and TREST made imaginative use of what would become known as 'dangles', as well as double agents and bogus anti-Soviet underground organisations. S-2 was directed against Boris Savinkov aiming at luring him back to Russia to star in a show trial. Why? Winston Churchill, who met Savinkov and was greatly impressed by the man, noted that 'often single-handed, he fought the Bolshevik revolution. The Czar and Lenin seemed to him the same thing expressed in different terms, the same tyranny in different trappings, the same barrier in the path of Russian freedom'. Betrayed by his friends and loved ones, Savinkov crossed the Russian border and walked straight into a GPU trap. 'Tormented in his prison cell with false hopes and shifting promises, squeezed by the most subtle pressure,' Churchill writes, 'he was induced to write his notorious letter of recantation and to proclaim the Bolshevik Government as the liberator of the world ... They had reduced his life's efforts to meaningless grimace, had made him insult his cause, and had fouled his memory for ever.'[49] This would become the favourite pastime of the Cheka and its successors for many years to come.

In the Russian Far East, China and Japan the local OGPU mounted a series of elaborate deception operations, some of them similar to TREST and SINDIKAT, using plants, double agents, dangles and illegals. All of them targeted the Japanese secret police, the Kenpeitai (also known as Kempeitai); the Second Bureau (G-2, Intelligence) of the Imperial Army General Staff and specifically its Russia Section; and the émigré White Guards groups. One such operation, initially codenamed KHABAROVSK LINE and later MAKI-MIRAGE, was masterminded and controlled from Khabarovsk by Terenty Deribas, an experienced and ruthless Moscow Chekist who had served as deputy chief of the Secret-Operational Directorate and in 1929 was transferred as the OGPU plenipotentiary to the Far East. It involved a considerable number of the local OGPU officers plus several illegals who had operated in Japan and Manchuria for many years.

Operation MAKI-MIRAGE, which was hardly known until recently when some files from the regional FSB archives in Khabarovsk were partially declassified, is presented in Russia as a successful reconnaissance mission against the Japanese Kwantung Army in Manchuria.[50] Their intelligence element headed by Captain Kurazawa was based in the Chinese town then known by its Manchu name of Saghalien Ula hoton, pronounced 'Sahaliyan', now Hēihé. By 1930 the OGPU officer Lazar Izrailevsky, alias 'Leonid Ostrovsky' (codenamed LETOV), posing as a sales agent of the Soviet Far Eastern Trading trust Daltorg, speaking fluent Mandarin Chinese and able to travel abroad in his official capacity, appeared in Saghalien. Approached and quickly 'recruited' by the Japanese, Ostrovsky (codenamed STARIK/ OLD MAN by Kurazawa) soon reported that he managed to recruit a high-ranking officer of the Special Far Eastern Red Army. This completely fictional source, duly registered as Ōkina tokuhain ('Big Correspondent') by the Japanese, supplied bogus military information concocted by the OGPU in Moscow in order to deter Japanese expansion into China for several years until the operation was interrupted in 1937 by the arrest of Deribas and all its participants.

Operation TREST, invented by Artuzov in 1921 and used as the basis for a complex six-year deception, aimed at destroying the White Guards centres in Europe by sowing mistrust among their supporters from Western governments and their intelligence services.[51] According to the CIA study, 'the Trust was designed to accomplish two principal missions. The first was to penetrate, disrupt and ultimately destroy organised opposition to the Bolshevik dictatorship domestically and abroad. The second was to systematically delude the West as to the future course the communist regime would follow.'[52] Probably quite unexpectedly, the leading victim of the operation – to a great extent due to his own self-confidence and a tendency to self-deception – became the former SIS officer Sidney Reilly. The 'man from nowhere', born Sigmund Rosenblum, whose life motto was *Mundo Nulla Fides*.

On 3 December 1919 the Bolo Liquidation Club was founded in London with the avowed intention of putting the Bolsheviks out of business. Its members, Reilly among them, used to meet once a week for about a year. As the *Sunday Times* described the venture half a century later, 'they were quite serious about it, but it was a bit of a lark too'. It was an unofficial group but the members were all on the payroll of His Majesty's Government.

In October 1967 four of them met again. Major Stephen Alley, a fluent Russian-speaker born and brought up in Russia, who worked with Ernest Boyce in the Maikop oilfields and later ran intelligence operations in Russia and Norway, Brigadier George Alexander Hill, last time in Russia as the MI6 liaison and head of the SOE Mission in Moscow (codenamed SAM), designed to coordinate propaganda and sabotage in occupied Europe, Sir John Picton Bagge, Commercial Secretary 1st Grade to Russia in 1918 and Captain Alfred Ferdinand Hill of the Royal Highland Regiment, member of the British Intelligence Mission in Petrograd before and after the Bolshevik revolution. The meeting was convened by Robert Norman Bruce Lockhart, better known as Robin, the son of Sir Robert H. Bruce Lockhart and author of *Ace of Spies: The incredible story of Sidney Reilly, the most amazing secret agent in the history of Espionage*, the book just published in London by Hodder & Stoughton. They drank to absent friends, including Reilly and Sir Robert, and were not shy of being photographed. The Café Royal on Regent Street at Piccadilly, a London legend where they met, does not exist anymore. In the early twenty-first century the building was transformed into a luxury hotel.

Mundo Nulla Fides is translated into English as 'Put no faith in the world', or more simply, 'Trust No One'.

Chapter 7

First 'Illegals' and 'Rezidents'

'Successful war follows the path of deception', Sun Tzu said in the fifth century BC and in the twenty-first century AD it remains as true as it was then. The whole secret lies in confusing the enemy, so that he cannot fathom your real intent – 'in war, surprise is the key to victory'.[1] Nowadays deception and disinformation are integral parts of any intelligence operation. 'All intelligence collection methodologies are subject to deception,' Joseph Caddell notes.

> Signals intelligence (SIGINT) is susceptible to false signals, phony messages, bogus codes, and other forms of disinformation. Photographic or imagery intelligence (PHOTINT and IMINT) must deal with active and passive camouflage in a wide array of forms. Similar problems plague communications intelligence (COMINT), electronic intelligence (ELINT), acoustical intelligence (ACOUINT), and seismic intelligence (SEISINT). In any medium where information can be found, disinformation can be planted or devised.[2]

Governments and especially their intelligence organisations do their best to protect their secrets and capabilities. Therefore, even the oldest (and still the most difficult and valuable) method of intelligence collection, human intelligence or HUMINT, has to deal with a great variety of deception and disinformation strategies.

From the first years or its existence, Soviet intelligence became notorious for its use of agent provocateurs, dangles, plants, double agents and most famously 'illegals'. Because the Cheka and its successors always copied and adapted the operational methods and techniques of the Tsarist Okhrana on the one hand, and of the British Secret Intelligence Service on the other, the tradecraft of the first 'illegals' – officers and agents operating undercover often using false identities and disguising their true affiliation – did not differ much from that used by Paul Dukes, George Hill, Sidney Reilly, Stephen Tomes or Peter Sokolov. Those were intelligence operatives speaking two or more foreign languages, who had spent considerable time travelling between the

Old and the New World, and were ready to risk their lives for the cause. The principal operational method of illegals has always been based on deception.

The first Soviet illegals differed from modern-day Russian illegals in many ways. To operate underground using false identities, aliases and pseudonyms had been an old Bolshevik tradition born long before the revolution. Soon after the beginning of the civil war in 1918, the Cheka began sending its members – officers and agents – behind enemy lines in various guises to gather information. It had also been actively involved in recruiting and developing sources with access to secret intelligence who were usually given codenames for secret communications. Operatives who had been deployed without any official cover, that is, without any declared ties to the Soviet government for which they worked, became known in the Cheka jargon as 'illegals'.

This was (and still is) in contrast to the officers (and sometimes agents) sent abroad under an official cover, not necessarily diplomatic, which identifies them as persons employed by and working for their country on a temporary mission abroad. At the outset, but not before normal diplomatic relations were established between Soviet Russia and the outside world, there existed a customary rule that no state could be brought before the courts of another state for any matter, which meant that diplomats enjoyed full immunity and other official representatives partial or restricted immunity as well as privileges. Based on this principle, members of the Lockhart semi-official diplomatic mission and British Intelligence Mission in Russia after having been briefly detained by the Bolsheviks in August 1918 were released and expelled and the same happened to the members of the Litvinov mission in London.[3]

Remarkably, there is no word 'legal' in the Russian language as an antonym to the spy term 'illegal'. And Soviet illegals, according to the glossary of spy terms published by the International Spy Museum in Washington, are 'KGB/SVR operatives infiltrated into a target country without the protection of diplomatic immunity, having assumed new identities and even new ethnicities'. They are also sometimes described as the 'Soviet spies planted abroad under false or assumed identities, sometimes for decades' (BBC). Both of these definitions are wrong as much as the Wikipedia interpretations of 'sleeper agents' and 'illegals programme'.

Illegals and sleepers are different types of agents. Illegals can be posted on a specific mission for only a short period of time operating under 'deep cover', or for a longer time, sometimes years, using assumed or even their own identities and 'ethnicities' as well as their genuine profession or skills as a cover for their clandestine activities. This is known in the trade as working under 'natural cover'. Sleeper agents are seldom deployed, usually recruited in place, and do nothing else but wait for a signal from Moscow, otherwise living normal lives as ordinary citizens. They can also be placed in a target country having no or rare contact with the Service which deployed them until 'activated'. When and if a signal comes, they are usually given a simple task like sending a postcard, or emptying a dead letter box, or locating a person of interest. Both illegals and sleepers, when they are active as spies, are operating under non-official cover (NOC).

In the KGB spy lexicon, operatives who are sent abroad with official cover are said to be operating from the official or legal positions even if they are not members of the diplomatic service. Thus, according to the TASS report, Prague's decision to expel eighteen Russian diplomats in April 2021 involved a total of sixty-two people, counting their family members. Quite certainly not all of them were spies but should there be intelligence officers, agents or co-optees among them, they were operating uner official cover from legal positions. A good example from another camp is Janet Chisholm, an ordinary mother of three young children, who was married to a MI6 head of station in Moscow working undercover as the British embassy's visa officer. The best British (and American) agent-in-place at the time, GRU Colonel Oleg Penkovsky, was communicating with his handlers via notes he passed to Janet with his other material. When Penkovsky was detained and then arrested by the KGB, Mrs. Chisholm was simply asked to leave the country together with her PNGed ('persona non grata') husband.

By June 1919, only three months after the First Congress of the Comintern, the number of people of various nationalities secretly working for Soviet intelligence was sufficiently large to require the formation of the 'Illegals Operations Department' for 'illegal political workers operating in the areas occupied by the enemy', which was finally established in 1922. Years later it became Directorate S of the KGB and then the SVR.[4] Classified histories of the KGB as well as textbooks of the SVR Academy (the former Andropov Red Banner Institute) and the FSB Academy (the former Dzerzhinsky Higher School of the KGB) note that henceforth 'illegal' operations became 'an inseparable part of foreign intelligence'.[5] This is true for both the KGB with its many predecessors and successors, as well as for Russian military intelligence (GRU).

Apart from the already mentioned Alexey Filippov, one of the first Soviet illegals was Mikhail Adamóvich, born in Riga in 1898, who managed to survive the Great Terror. At the end of 1919, using the alias 'Kolesnikov' and posing as a former junior officer (ensign) of the Tsarist army, he was sent on a clandestine mission first to Saratov to infiltrate the anti-Bolshevik underground and then to Crimea occupied by the White Army of General Peter Wrangel. During the interwar period of 1932–9, already a commissioned

OGPU/NKVD officer, Adamovich operated as a Soviet illegal in Latvia, France, Switzerland, Spain and Czechoslovakia, being promoted to captain of State Security in March 1936.[6] It is claimed that he played a key role arranging an escape from Nazi-occupied Czechoslovakia of Zdeněk Nejedlý, who fled with his family to the Soviet Union. This may or may not be true because Nejedlý was not a big shot. He was a prominent music critic who in 1937 published a monograph on Soviet music, spent the war in the Soviet Union and in April 1945 became the first post-war Minister of Culture and Education of the Czechoslovak Socialist Republic. His ideas are said to have dominated the cultural life of his country for most of the twentieth century but there is nothing to justify or explain the risk and trouble of exfiltrating him.

About the same time, in late 1919, Józef Unszlicht, who had been an important member of the Revolutionary-Military Council (RVS) of the Western Front also placed in charge of intelligence, initiated the creation of the so-called Illegal or Underground Military Organisation (NVO), modelled on the Polish POW, to operate behind Polish lines. The purpose of the NVO was to inflict maximum damage on the enemy in the rear of the Polish army by organising terrorist acts, sabotage and insurgent activities. These clandestine operations were directed by Arthur Stashevsky (alias Verkhovsky), Bronislaw Bortnowsky (alias Bronkowski) and Samuel Pupko (alias Firin) with Stashevsky soon promoted to head the Registration Directorate (intelligence) of the Western Front. By the end of the Soviet-Polish War, the NVO had a staff of 169 operatives.[7] After the war several long-range patrols were formed commanded by the Byelorussian OGPU officers Stanislav Vaupshasov, Kirill Orlovsky, Nikon Kovalenko, Alexander Rabtsevich, Vasili Korzh, Nikolai Prokopyuk and others to reconnoitre in border areas and raid Polish outposts but mainly tasked with sabotage and subversion behind enemy lines in Western Byelorussia. Such operations were known in both OGPU and RU as *aktivka* or 'active measures' (aktivnye meropriyatiya). Parallel to destroying and damaging enemy facilities, communications and transport, this also included assassinations and terrorist acts. Pre-Second World War Soviet active measures (the Soviet-Polish War, Soviet-Japanese border incidents, the Spanish Civil War, and so on) must not to be confused with the term 'active measures' of Soviet Cold War propaganda, when it was (and still is) a form of political warfare.[8] It should also not be confused with what is now known as 'information disorder'.

In September 1918, a young Polish revolutionary named Lew Rosenthal volunteered for the Red Army and after joining the Bolshevik Party took the name Borovich. Lev Borovich fought against the White Army of General Denikin, was wounded, and after recovery sent to the commanders' course from where he was transferred to the intelligence department of the Western

Front. His assignment at the time was to smuggle secret agents across the border. When a Separate Special Purpose Brigade was formed to establish revolutionary law and order after taking control of Poland, Borovich became one of its first staffers. With plans to further move this brigade to Germany, Stashevsky was appointed its commander, Firin became his political commissar, and Woldemar Rose (Voldemārs Roze from Latvia) was chosen to head its signals unit. Jacob Faiwusch (Jakobas Faivušas from Lithuania), a future leading Soviet SIGINT and radio interception specialist, also served in this brigade as Rose's deputy. The brigade was composed mainly of Soviet intelligence personnel and German-Austrian prisoners of war. Many of them would become Soviet intelligence officers very active in Europe and Asia in the interwar period. All of those mentioned here would become victims of the Great Terror.

In April 1920, it was decided to open the Foreign Information Bureau inside the Special (Osoby) Department of the All-Russia Cheka (VeCheKa) to coordinate activities of the intelligence departments in the armed forces and in some provincial Chekas in areas close to the Soviet border. During the first months the bureau was headed by the 22-year-young Latvian Bolshevik Ludvig Skujskumbré.

After the Polish troops emerged victorious in the decisive Battle of Warsaw, the Soviets sued for peace and the war ended with a ceasefire in October 1920. In November the brigade was disbanded and all officers sent for retraining at the RU training facility near Moscow after which all of them were deployed to support Soviet propaganda, disinformation and counter-intelligence efforts abroad. According to the Politburo instruction, in those countries where Soviet Russia did not have its official representatives, the intelligence work had to be carried out by illegals.

* * *

For obvious reasons, Germany was the country of greatest interest to the Bolshevik leadership. It has long been observed that the existence of an independent Poland has been a cardinal factor in the relationship between the two great powers – when separated by a buffer state, Russia and Germany were friendly, whereas a contiguity of frontiers has bred hostility.[9] After the process of alienation was completed by the humiliation of Russian arms in the Great War of 1914–18, the Bolshevik revolution of October 1917 and the Treaty of Brest-Litovsk of March 1918, the first Soviet legation under Adolf Joffe was deported from Germany on 6 November on charges of preparing a Bolshevik uprising.[10] A week later the armistice ended the actual fighting although it took six months of negotiations to conclude a peace treaty. The

Treaty of Versailles was signed on 28 June 1919 in the Palace of Versailles in Paris, drawing Germany and Russia together as international pariah states with common grievances and ambitions.

The chief artificer of the early rapprochement between the two countries was General Johannes 'Hans' von Seeckt, who was a central figure in planning German victories in the East during the war. From 1919 to 1920 von Seeckt served as chief of staff of the Reichswehr and was then appointed commander-in-chief of the Reichsheer and Reichsmarine – the unified armed forces of the Weimar Republic, subjected to severe restrictions by the Versailles Treaty. 'Concerned purely with the preservation of the German military tradition,' John Wheeler-Bennett writes, 'von Seeckt set himself the task of circumventing the military clauses of the Treaty of Versailles which prohibited conscription and drastically manpower and armament.' Until his resignation from his post in October 1926, Hans von Seeckt engaged in the restructuring of the army and laid the foundation for doctrine, tactics and organisation, succeeding in making the Reichswehr (the word translated as 'defence of the realm') a volunteer professional force more formidable as most conscript armies.[11] But how could this force be supplied, equipped and trained? Naturally, by collaborating with the country that for years had been its major source of raw materials and other goods. By early 1921, a special group devoted to dealing with Russia, Sondergruppe R, had been created withing the Reichswehrministerium and within weeks it began setting up German war industry abroad, specifically in Soviet Russia.[12] The group's first chief was Colonel Walter Nicolai, the former head of the German secret service, a legendary figure in the world of pre-war espionage and a Russia specialist. And, as one researcher has put it, a mysterious but effective spy.

When Joffe and a small group of leading Bolsheviks tried to re-enter Germany to attend the Congress of Soviets, they were turned back at the border with only Karl Radek managing to get into the country. Together with two German Bolsheviks, Ernst Reuter (party pseudonym 'Friesland') and Werner Rakow (alias 'Felix Wolf'), he travelled via Wilna (Vilnius) and Königsberg by disguising themselves as Austrian prisoners of war, reaching Berlin in December 1918. Radek took part in a congress that led to the foundation of the German Communist Party (KPD) under the leadership of Liebknecht and Luxemburg who were both captured and shot during the January uprising. Radek was arrested on 12 February 1919 and put in Moabit prison.

In July 1919, dressed in a German soldier's uniform, a former member of the Joffe legation by the name of Victor Kopp illegally entered Germany, arriving in Berlin with a set of diamonds sewn into the lining of his soldier's greatcoat.[13] Kopp knew Germany rather well because he had spent three years there between 1915 and 1918 as a Russian prisoner of war before he joined Joffe's staff. The timing of Kopp's arrival coincided with the radical change of the German authorities' attitude towards the Bolsheviks with the idea of creating the alliance of nations who had suffered from the Versailles Treaty – principally Germany, Turkey and Russia – gaining currency in Berlin. In August Radek was transferred to a privileged room in the prison that became known as Radek's political 'Salon',[14] where he was allowed to receive a stream of visitors among whom were many prominent personalities from the Weimar Republic and abroad. Among other things, the possibility to form an international commission to visit Russia consisting of experts in agriculture and industry, a former Secretary of State as a specialist in administration and a chief of police from a large Swiss city as a law enforcement specialist was discussed with a view of placing them in positions of authority.

Kopp used to visit this 'Salon' once or twice per week to get some valuable business and political contacts. His presence in Berlin was tolerated as a Soviet government delegate to negotiate the release and repatriation of Russian prisoners of war, stipulated in the Treaty of Brest-Litovsk.[15] Unofficially, however, he was acting as a representative of both the NKID and NKVT, that is, serving as a diplomatic as well as trade agent of the Soviet government.

In January 1920 Radek was accompanied to the Polish village of Prostki at the border between Lithuania, Poland and Byelorussia and handed over to the Polish authorities.[16] A few weeks later the German Foreign Ministry recognised Kopp's status as an official Soviet representative in matters of prisoner exchange. He was allowed to have a staff of seven and signed his reports to Commissar Chicherin in Moscow as 'Plenipotentiary representative of the NKID and NKVT in Germany',[17] although this was not his official title.

On 11 July 1920, the British government under Prime Minister David Lloyd George sent a telegram to the Soviets that became known as the Curzon Ultimatum. Signed by George Curzon as Foreign Secretary it requested Lenin and his people's commissars to halt their offensive at the Curzon Line. In case of a refusal, the British threatened to assist Poland with all means available.[18] The Soviets refused. In early August Soviet and Polish delegations met at the Polish city of Baranowicze (today Baranavichy, Belarus) but without any result. By mid-August, Polish military intelligence managed to decrypt the Red Army's radio communications and the Bolshevik troops led by Tukhachevsky fell into a trap set by Piłsudski and the Polish General Staff. Tukhachevsky ordered a general retreat and the defeated Soviet troops retreated in panic with many taken prisoner or crossing into East Prussia towards Königsberg (now Kaliningrad, Russia). The victory at the Battle of Warsaw brought a lot of fame to the Polish troops and their commander. As Donald Rayfield has put it, 'the glory went to Poland's ruler Piłsudski, the disgrace to Dzierżyński and Stalin'[19] (because much of the controversy surrounding the Red Army's debacle at Warsaw focused on the actions of Stalin).

With all these developments in the background, in August 1920 the Russians used General Seeckt's friend Enver Pasha to sound out the Chief of the Weimar Republic's Army Command about possible military collaboration against Poland. In a letter dated 6 August, Baron Ago von Maltzan, one of the leading exponents of a Russo-German rapprochement, informed Count Ulrich von Brockdorff-Rantzau, soon to be appointed ambassador to Russia, that the Reichswehr had established close contact with the Soviet Army during the Polish-Soviet War.[20] This laid the foundation for amicable Russo-German and later Nazi-Soviet military and economic collaboration that lasted for two decades. As wisely noted by a historian, a cardinal factor in the relationship between Russia and Germany (or Prussia) has been the existence of an independent Poland. For, in general, 'it is true that when separated by a buffer state the two great Powers of eastern Europe had been friendly whereas a contiguity of frontiers has bred hostility'.[21]

Only after the turbulent 25 months of war between the Second Polish Republic and Soviet Russia, which ended with signing of the Peace of Riga on 18 March 1921, were both governments ready to continue negotiations. The Treaty of Rapallo, an important agreement between Germany and Soviet Russia, was signed on 16 April renouncing all territorial and financial claims against each other after the Treaty of Brest-Litovsk. An agreement concerning the repatriation of prisoners of war and interned civilians of both parties was concluded just three days later, on 19 April, followed by a Supplement signed together with the Interim Soviet-German Agreement on 6 May in Berlin by Gustav Behrendt, Director, and Ago von Maltzan, Councillor of Legation, both of the German Ministry for Foreign Affairs. The Soviet side was represented by Aron Scheinmann, deputy Commissar for Trade and Industry, soon to be appointed chairman of the State Bank (Gosbank).[22] In March 1929, on sick leave to Germany, Scheinmann announced that he had decided not to return to the USSR.

He was not alone. According to a memo of 5 June 1930 signed by the INO officer Ignaty Reif, the future recruiter of Donald Maclean, between October 1928 and August 1930 at least 190 members of the Soviet trade missions had chosen to stay abroad instead of coming back to the Soviet paradise,[23] despite the government decree of November 1929 imposing capital punishment for defection together with confiscation of property.

The already mentioned Interim Agreement with Germany, signed on 6 May 1921, expanded the powers of the delegates in charge of the prisoner of war exchange to safeguarding the interests of nationals of the sending states. This was the first step to consular functions and therefore – to full diplomatic recognition. It was also allowed to increase the delegate's staff to seven employees and was suggested that delegates should be joined by the trade missions for the development of economic relations between the two countries.

Soon, the Soviet trade delegation arrived in Berlin headed by the NKVT plenipotentiary Boris Stomonyakov, a Bolshevik of Bulgarian descent, who would soon become the official Soviet trade representative in Germany, remaining in this post until 1925. Because of Stomonyakov's intrigues and defamatory reports, supported by his friend Yuri Lutovinov, the counsellor of the delegation, Kopp was recalled, but the Control Commission in Moscow did not find any irregularities and he was allowed to go back, albeit only as a Soviet Red Cross representative. His role as a NKID delegate was taken by Pavel Levinson, known in Russia as Lapinsky-Mikhalsky,[24] who occupied it until 20 October 1921 when he was succeeded by Nikolai Krestinsky. One of his staff, arriving in Berlin together with Krestinsky, was Teodor Grikman, formally head of the mission's consular section in charge of repatriation of prisoners of war but in reality a Cheka officer.[25] It seems, however, that as an intelligence operative Grikman was quite mediocre or even worthless due to the lack of both talent and effort as well as education and experience, because after his return to Moscow he was transferred to the criminal police.

At the end of June, when Kopp was formally cleared of all wrongdoing, the Politburo secretly appointed him special envoy to Germany for the back-channel military and political negotiations,[26] although officially he was a mere representative of the Soviet Red Cross. As already mentioned, by that time Sondergruppe R ('R' for Russia) had been created within the Reichswehr as a result of Kopp's arrangements with General von Seeckt, and in late July-early August 1921 Lieutenant Colonel Oscar von Niedermayer visited Moscow again to meet with Chicherin. Previously, as a German General Staff representative, he had already been to Russia discussing Soviet-German military collaboration with Trotsky and Rakovsky.[27] He would then work at the Reichswehr office in Moscow.

Later that year, Narkompros, the People's Commissariat for Education headed by Anatoly Lunacharsky, gave David Stärenberg (aka 'Shterenberg'), the director of its Fine Arts Section (IZO), a mandate to organise an exhibition of contemporary Russian and new Soviet art in Berlin. The catalogue, designed by El Lissitzky, featured a foreword written by Shterenberg with contributions by Edwin Redslob in his capacity as Reichskunstwart and Arthur Holitscher, a journalist and writer who visited Radek in the Moabit prison to discuss joining the commission to visit Russia. When Radek left Germany, the commission was shelved but Holitscher went on his own in

September 1920, staying there for three months. This led to the publication of his book *Drei Monate in Sowjet-Rußland* in 1921 and invitation to take part in the catalogue in October 1922, writing that revolutionary artists have 'the power to shape the political and economic aspirations of the people'.

Historians and researchers have pointed out that the absence of diplomatic relations with foreign powers up to 1924 forced the Bolsheviks to contrive 'para-diplomatic' devices, involving 'the calculated use of non-diplomatic personnel, agencies and situations for covertly diplomatic purposes'.[28] Remarkably, one scholar argues,

> The unexpected success of the Berlin exhibition left an important legacy and proved a turning point in the Soviet cultural offensive toward Western societies and non-communist public opinion. It shook up Bolshevik dogmas and opened them to foreign practices of propaganda. Later developments, such as the creation of the All-Union Society for Cultural Ties Abroad [*sic*, Society for International Cultural Relations, Vsesoyuznoe obshchestvo kulturnoi svyazi s zagranitsei, VOKS] in 1925, Soviet participation in international exhibitions, cinema propaganda, subsidised émigré journals and so forth, sprang from this original momentum.[29]

The World Association of Russian Press (WARP) established by the First World Congress of the Russian Press (Moscow-Sochi, June 1999) had the same roots.[30] It seems that after the Russian invasion of Ukraine WARP is more dead than alive but their website still exists. Its aims and targets have been no big secret from the very beginning: penetration of Western society and media, propaganda, dissemination of misinformation and disinformation, establishing Moscow's presence in the information space, talent-spotting of potential agents (that is, intelligence sources and agents of influence) and so on. Plus various support functions to the Russian intelligence and security services providing necessary help in the target country. But we are looking ahead about a hundred years here. RT channels, also known as Russia Today, are closed in most countries and after twenty-one World Congresses of Russian Press in places like Moscow, Washington, New York, Berlin, Paris, Shanghai and so on, with the last congress in Ankara, Turkey, in October 2019, the organisation is virtually defunct. But back in the 1920s, while the Western public became fascinated with Soviet art and literature, Russian artists and intellectuals living abroad became, as Ewa Berard has put it, valuable agents of Moscow's outreach (but in fact, important agents of influence). With its cultural diplomacy oriented toward hostile foreign powers but aiming at 'fellow travellers', the Soviet Union succeeded in making the 'Russian world' well rooted beyond its borders.[31]

As soon as official relations with Germany were established, Berlin became the centre and most important base for Soviet intelligence operations in Europe, preserving the status quo for the next decade. Together with Stomonyakov, the first RIS (Russian Intelligence Service) agent representing both the OGPU and (G)RU arrived in Berlin to work under official cover of the Soviet trade delegation. This was none other than Artur Stashevsky (a Jew from Latvia born Artur Hirschfeld, party pseudonym 'Verkhovsky'),[32] and he would later play a prominent role in Soviet foreign trade and especially as a Soviet trade representative in Spain during the Civil War. For reasons not sufficiently well explained,[33] his first intelligence mission to Berlin did not last long and he was soon recalled.

Stashevsky's deputy in Berlin was once again Firin (born Samuel Pupko), who had been one of his subordinates during subversive raids against Poland in 1919. Pupko deserted from the Tsarist army during the war and then took part in the February Revolution in Petrograd and the October Revolution in Moscow. After serving as head of intelligence at the staff of the Western Front, Pupko/Firin was transferred to the (G)RU headquarters and sent to Lithuania where he was busy setting up intelligence networks in Kovno (now Kaunas) and Wilno (Vilnius). The country had been in turmoil since in the aftermath of the First World War both Poland and Lithuania regained independence and both were claiming Vilnius and its region. The dispute resulted in much tension in the relations between the two countries in the interwar period, with Kaunas becoming the temporary seat of government.

From Kaunas Firin moved to Berlin but, like Stashevsky, he had spent only a few months there having been transferred to Sofia, Bulgaria, as the controller of the illegal residencies run by Hristo Boyev (alias 'Fedor Rusev') in Burgas and Boris Shpak (who would become better known as 'Boris Bazarov') in Sofia. Firin returned to Germany in 1923 to help prepare the German October Revolution, more correctly remembered as the Hamburg Uprising. After a prominent career abroad as a military intelligence officer, Firin moved to the OGPU in 1930 and soon became one of the leaders of Stalin's GULAG serving as deputy chief of the White Sea-Baltic forced labour camp. Arrested in May 1937, he was shot three months later.

In 1921 Adolph Chapsky (Adolf Czapski) finished commander courses at the Academy of the General Staff of the Red Army (RKKA) and was sent to the INO and from there on a long-term undercover mission to Europe starting his tour of duty in Berlin. Chapsky was born as Abraham Abba Dawidowicz in Wieluń, central Poland, but changed his name to Czapski/Chapsky when he entered the Strelitz Polytechnic Institute in Germany. His intelligence career culminated in his being appointed the legal INO resident in Britain serving there under the official cover of the second secretary of the Soviet embassy, alias 'Anton Schuster'. His brother, Bernard Dawidowicz (codenamed GADAR), also operated in London running a branch of the Dutch textile waste rags firm Gada which served as a cover for Soviet illegals.[34] Dawidowicz resided in London for five years, returning to his native Poland in March 1938.

Herman Klesmet (born in 1897 in the Governorate of Livonia now divided between Latvia and Estonia) served as a rifleman in the Latvian Rifle Regiment and despite displaying heroic valour in combat was taken prisoner and transported to Germany. From December 1920 he joined the staff of Victor Kopp's delegation remaining in Germany until 1922 when, recruited as a Cheka undercover agent, he was sent to Sofia posing as an official of the Soviet Red Cross. His main task was helping to prepare a communist uprising in Bulgaria.[35] After the armed insurrection was supressed by the government, Klesmet was expelled. He was then sent to Manchuria working under diplomatic cover, turning up in Berlin before the war as an undercover operative where he was one of the controllers of Willi Lehmann, for several decades only known as Agent A-201 'Breitenbach', the most valuable Soviet mole in the RSHA. When working under official cover, Klesmet used the alias 'Alexander Nikolayevich Bitiyev'.

In February 1922, Stashevsky was succeeded as resident of the combined OGPU-(G)RU station by the 28-year-old Polish revolutionary named Bronislav Bortnovsky (spelt Bronisław Bortnowski in his native Polish). Bortnovsky was in Petrograd when an armed mob stormed the British embassy on 31 August 1918, the day after the shooting of Uritsky and Lenin. 'When their way was blocked by the Naval Attaché, Captain F.N.A. Cromie, the senior of the few British officials remaining in the building,' Richard Ullman writes, 'he was told to stand aside or be shot down. Cromie drew his pistol and killed two of the mob before their bullets killed him.'[36] It seems the description is not quite accurate because one of the two wounded was Bortnowsky, who survived although he was permanently crippled as his right arm was left paralyzed.

Bortnowsky operated in Berlin until December 1924 controlling networks and separate agents in other European countries and supporting underground activities of the Comintern, whose first representative in Germany, Jakob Reich (alias 'James Gordon', better known in the Comintern as 'Comrade Thomas'), arrived there in late 1919.

Reich recalled:

This was in the spring, no doubt in the beginning of May ... Lenin summoned me in the night and told me: 'You must go to Germany.' The activity of the Communist International had to be organised in the

West, and particularly in Germany. This could not be done without the assistance of veteran activists trained in clandestine work. They had to be sent from Moscow.

Lenin's instructions were brief: 'Take as much money as you can with you; send reports and, if possible, publications. In general, do what the situation allows. But do it.'

There and then, he drafted two notes, one for [Yakov] Ganetsky,[37] another for Dzerzhinsky. At the same time, he phoned Ganetsky, who at the time controlled the party funds, not the official funds relating to the Central Committee, nor the governmental funds appertaining to other services, but the secret funds which Lenin used as he saw fit without having to account to anyone. Ganetsky was the man to whom Lenin had entrusted its safeguarding and 'servicing'.

I had known Ganetsky for some years, and he greeted me like an old comrade. He handed me a million roubles in German and Swedish currency. Then he took me to the strongroom in which the secret funds were kept. It was in the basement of the same Palace of Justice in which the Congress of the Communist International had taken place.[38]

There, moving through a labyrinth of underground passages, they came into a secret room full of priceless treasures. Reich later testified that 'gold and gems were everywhere, precious stones were piled on the floor; someone had tried to put them in some order, but had given up'. Dzerzhinsky, he wrote, had had them deposited there for the secret needs of the Party. Lenin declared: 'All this was acquired by the capitalists by exploiting the people; now it must be used to expropriate the expropriators.' In this dimly-lit strongroom, Ganetsky (actually Jakub Hanecki, party pseudonym of Jakub Fürstenberg) offered Reich as many treasures as he could carry to take with him to Germany. 'Only those trusted by Lenin come here,' he said. 'Choose what you will at sight. Ilyich has said that you should take as much as possible.' Reich claims he had put gems in the suitcase given to him by Hanecki but left the gold as it was too bulky. 'I was not asked to make out a list of the gems,' he writes, 'but of course I made out a receipt for the currency.'

Angelina Balabanova, better known as Angelica Balabanoff, a Comintern secretary and one of Lenin's close associates, in her memoirs published in the USA remembered a similar case when a Comintern representative was sent to Austria with diamonds and jewellery, presumably from the same secret strongroom managed by Ganetsky on Lenin's instructions. Having arrived in Vienna with his luggage full of treasures, instead of spending them on communist propaganda he decided to open a jewellery shop,[39] no doubt somewhere in Vienna's antiques quarter near Dorotheum, a famous Austrian auction house at the heart of the First District.

Finally, Reich managed to reach Germany, documented by a 'foolproof passport' as a commercial attaché of the Mexican consulate, leaving the Soviet capital in panic while it was preparing to be occupied by the advancing White Armed Forces of South Russia (AFSR). Anton Denikin, a former lieutenant general of the Imperial Russian Army and now commander-in-chief of the AFSR, was convinced that the capture of Moscow would play a decisive role in the outcome of the Civil War. By the end of August, the AFSR took Odessa and Kiev and during September-October Denikin's plan had been carried out with exceptional success. To the Bolsheviks, everything pointed to an approaching disaster and as soon as the government agencies began evacuating to Vologda, the OGPU were ordered to form special stay-behind teams. 'Hiding places and caches were being set up in Moscow,' Reich recalled his last days in the Soviet capital, while 'gold, foreign currency and precious stones were deposited in safe locations'.[40] However, by the end of October, when he was safely in Germany, the Volunteer Army was defeated and began to retreat along the whole front pushed back all the way to the Black Sea by the Red Army.

Reich was not the only Comintern emissary sent to Germany in September 1919. Another ECCI representative was Abram Heifetz, also known as Samuel Guralski (alias 'August Kleine').[41] He was soon expelled but secretly returned in March 1921 together with Béla Kun to prepare the March Action, a failed communist uprising led by the KPD and other far-left organisations. Heifetz@Guralski@Klein took part in the 3rd World Congress of the Comintern (22 June–12 July 1921) and was elected to the KPD Central Committee. His wife, Käthe Pohl (née Lydia Rabinovitch), had been secretary of the KPD Politburo from 1922 to 1924 and together with her husband was a very influential figure in the party. In 1923 they divorced and he married Romana Wolf, better known in Russia as R.D. Yezerskaya.[42] At the time Yezerskaya had been working as secretary of the Presidium and Collegium of the Cheka (VChK-GPU). In August, Klein was elected member of the KPD Politburo and took an active part in the preparation of the Hamburg October Uprising in 1923 together with the Soviet (G)RU advisers. After two years operating undercover in France as a Comintern representative with a brief mission in Spain during the Civil War, Yezerskaya-Wolf was recalled to Moscow and shot in December 1937.

Soon, Reich was joined in Berlin by Mieczysław Broński (also known as Broński-Warszawski) from a well-to-do family of Polish industrialists who owned a cotton factory in Łódź. Arrested for his revolutionary activities in 1906, he emigrated to Switzerland and there joined a faction of the Social

Democratic Party led by Jakub Hanecki and Karl Radek. By 1916 Bronsky became an ally and near neighbour of Lenin in Zurich. In June 1917, he came to Petrograd, joined the Bolsheviks and worked in the Agitprop and then in the People's Bank later headed by Hanecki. From March to November 1918 Bronsky served as Acting Commissar for Trade and Industry and then worked in the Council of Foreign Trade until he was sent to Germany in November 1919. When Reich was instructed to organise the Western European Bureau (WEB) of the Comintern in Berlin, its first members were Radek (as long as he remained in Germany); Paul Levi, the leader of the German communists following the assassination of Rosa Luxemburg and Karl Liebknecht; August Thalheimer, a founding member of the KPD and its main theorist; Mieczysław Broński, Willi Münzenberg and Eduard Fuchs as treasurer. Fuchs had a doctor of law degree and practised as an attorney, later becoming a renowned scholar of culture and history, writer, art collector and political activist. Together with Kopp he was appointed by the Soviet government as their representative in charge of prisoner exchange with Germany after the war. He resigned from the party four years before the Nazis' rise to power and moved to France.

In 1920, after the signing of the Copenhagen Agreement, Broński was appointed Soviet representative in Austria for prisoner exchange arriving in Vienna in mid-July. His newly-wed wife Susanne Leonhard,[43] an active Austrian communist, worked at the mission as head of its press department. The Agreement was signed in the Danish capital after lengthy negotiations by Maxim Litvinov and the British Labour MP James O'Grady on 12 February. According to its terms, Britain would supply ships for the repatriation of prisoners of war held on Soviet territory. Later, similar agreements were signed in Copenhagen with Belgium, France, Hungary, Italy and Austria (on 5 July).[44] The Copenhagen Agreement is sometimes seen as the first step toward the normalisation of relations between Soviet Russia and the West after the Allied blockade of Germany was lifted and the Anglo-Soviet Trade Agreement was being negotiated to be signed early next year, ending the British blockade. It amounted to the de facto recognition of the Bolshevik government and opened a period of extensive trade.

As soon as Broński arrived in Vienna, he was immediately placed under permanent physical surveillance not only by the police watchers, their reports sent directly and without delay to the Vienna police chief, but also by the Evidenzbüro, the directorate of military intelligence. Contrary to many claims the Evidenzbüro still existed although its last director, Colonel Maximilian Ronge, was now deputy head of the prisoner-of-war and civil internment office. But apart from Johannes 'Johann' Schober (who would in 1923 become the founding president of Interpol, and for one year between September

1929 and September 1930 would lead the government as the Chancellor of Austria), and the agents of the Evidenzbüro, the Allied representatives in Vienna were likewise interested in the activities of the Bolshevik emissary and his team,[45] who were quite unwelcome from the first day of their arrival. There were good reasons for that.

To start with, Russia and its wartime prisoners of war and civilian internees from the beginning of the First World War were represented in Austria by the Spanish embassy, whose officials issued passports and travel documents, and occupied the imposing neo-renaissance palace of the former embassy of the Russian Empire in Reisnerstrasse, having no intention of giving it up.[46] This situation remained unchanged until the protocol between the RSFSR, Soviet Ukraine and Austria was signed on 7 December 1921 accepting diplomatic missions of these countries as the only legitimate representatives.[47] Before it happened, however, the police chief Schober insisted on expelling Broński for his communist propaganda activities, his support of political émigrés and his lack of interest in the problems of Russian prisoners of war, whose number in Austria was quite insignificant.[48] It was reported that Broński spoke fluent German but his command of Russian was poor and residing at the Hotel Regina he always refused to accept Russian visitors who needed his help. All his time was devoted to meeting his communist contacts and he was especially proud to have been able to set up a ROSTA bureau in Vienna.

The Russian Telegraph Agency ROSTA was established in the Austrian capital by Alexander 'Sándor' Radó in July 1920. Radó was a Hungarian cartographer, who fled to Austria following the collapse of the communist regime in his country. His Vienna team included individuals like György Lukács, a former member of the Hungarian Soviet government, Charles Reber of *l'Humanité*, Gerhard Eisler, an Austrian who would spy for the Soviet Union in the USA, and Konstantin Umansky, a future Soviet ambassador to the United States who was also appointed chief NKVD resident in North America.[49] Walter Krivitsky, a future spy and defector, was temporary employed by Radó as interpreter. Radó himself would become one of the most efficient and productive Soviet spies during the war controlling the group which became known as Rote Drei (Red Three).

Broński was succeeded in Vienna by Alexander Schlichter, a Ukrainian Bolshevik who after the revolution had served as People's Commissar for Agriculture and People's Commissar for Food first in Russia and then in 1919 in Ukraine. Next year, he would be sent to Tambov, Russia, where Schlichter became known for the suppression of the large peasant uprising challenging the Bolshevik regime. It is estimated that around 100,000 people were arrested and some 15,000 shot dead during the hostilities between the Red Army and the rebellious peasants. As a result (the rebellion became known in the Soviet historiography as Antonov's Mutiny), by the summer of 1921 the bulk of the peasant army was destroyed, Schlichter dismissed from his post and sent to work at the Commissariat for Foreign Affairs probably to get him out of sight. He arrived in Vienna in March 1922 but was officially registered only as the Soviet trade representative,[50] not plenipotentiary, taking over Broński's small office in Belvedergasse.

In late June 1922 Nikolai Krestinsky became the first Soviet Plenipotentiary and Ambassador to Germany, presenting his credentials in a formal ceremony on 8 July. Krestinsky's secretary and then counsellor was a Polish revolutionary Stefan Bratman-Brodowski (party pseudonyms 'Florian' and 'Floriański') who would also serve as chargé d'affaires staying in Berlin until 1929. He was later to be joined by Waldemar Aussem, former deputy chief of the (G)RU, also serving as a plenipotentiary of Ukraine. In May 1924 Aussem would be posted to Vienna as Plenipotentiary Representative of the Soviet Union in Austria.[51] The legation's first secretary was Ignaty Yakubovich (aka Ignaty Jakubowicz and Ignaz Jakubowitch), the former head of the Narkomindel's Western Department who arrived in 1923 and remained until 1932, from time to time replacing an ambassador and serving as chargé d'affaires. While in Berlin, Yakubovich often took part in important political and economic negotiations especially at the time of the so-called Shakhty case (and the following trial) in Ukraine, when several German specialists, who had been installing turbines and mining machinery in the Donbas, were arrested and accused of industrial espionage and sabotage.

On 7 March 1928 the German consulate in Kharkiv informed their Moscow embassy that five German engineers and technicians had been arrested and were awaiting trial on charges of wrecking and 'economic counter-revolution' (the wording approved by Stalin, Molotov and Bukharin, leading members of the Politburo).[52] Three days later, Felix Deutsch, chairman of the board of the company (AEG) four of whose employees had been arrested, announced that AEG would withdraw its entire operation from Russia unless his people were immediately released. Two engineers were released ten days later. On 22 March the Foreign Office informed Brockdorff-Rantzau of the AEG decision to continue its projects in the Soviet Union, and on 1 April *The New York Times* reported that in an interview to the German newspapers Deutsch expressed his rather naïve belief that the incarceration of his employees on unfounded charges would lead to the downfall of the OGPU and thus to the improvement of commercial relations with the USSR.[53] The next day the secretary of the German legation was granted permission to visit the prisoners and Yakubovich in his turn paid a visit to the Wilhelmstrasse to assure Herbert von Dirksen, head of the East European Division of the Foreign Office, that the Soviet government had nothing but goodwill for

Germany. At the end of the year Dirksen succeeded Brockdorff-Rantzau as ambassador to Moscow.

The position of the first secretary was given to Alexey Ustinov, the son of a wealthy landowner who studied in Switzerland at the Polytechnic School which by the time of his graduation became the Swiss Federal Institute of Technology (ETH Zurich), one of the driving forces behind the country's industrialisation. Active in the Socialist-Revolutionaries (PSR) Party, in the summer of 1907 Ustinov was sent to St Petersburg but was soon arrested after somebody denounced him to the Okhrana.[54] Having spent almost a decade in exile in France and Switzerland, he returned to Russia together with Lenin in April 1917 and was sent to Helsingfors. Invited to the Registration Directorate (Registrupr, future GRU) of the Red Army as assistant chief in January 1921, from there, in October, Ustinov was sent to Berlin as part of the Krestinsky mission (which was not an embassy yet), first as its Press Bureau chief.[55] He remained in Berlin until February 1924 with a short spell in the Krestintern (the Peasant International, formed by the Comintern in October 1923) before being appointed as Soviet plenipotentiary to Greece in May 1924.

Another officer of the Registration Directorate on the staff of the Soviet legation in Berlin was its military attaché entered on the Diplomatic Corps List as 'Mikhail Petrov'. The Petrov case, as it became known, generated considerable nervousness in Moscow and Berlin. 'On September 25 [1923],' a historian of the period reports,

> the *Vorwärts*, official organ of the Social Democratic Party of Germany, published an article in which it was asserted that a certain Petrov, an attaché of the Russian Embassy in Berlin, had purchased machine guns and ammunition. The article went on that documentary evidence also linked Petrov to two large arms caches found on premises occupied by German Communists. The Soviet Embassy issued an immediate denial of any involvement of its personnel, but admitted that several Petrovs worked in the Embassy, and that one of these concerned himself with military matters.[56]

The case was quickly hushed up, Major Niedermayer paid Petrov a very cordial visit when he lay ill while the case was still pending, the attaché was recalled and the case was considered closed by the end of January 1924. There were even rumours that 'Petrov' was in reality a French naval officer serving the Bolsheviks which was part of the usual disinformation campaign to confuse and mislead the public.

It turns out his real name was Jacob Fischmann (in Russian: Yakov Fishman) from Odessa. A former active member of the militant wing of the SRs (Socialist Revolutionaries), he was arrested by the Okhrana, exiled to eastern Siberia and after release emigrated to Italy where he studied chemistry specialising in explosives and poisons. In February 1921 Fishman was commissioned as a Red Army officer and invited to join the Registration Directorate, which in April was transformed into Razvedupr, the Intelligence Directorate of the Red Army Headquarters. Aged 35, he was sent to Berlin as an attaché of Krestinsky's first official Soviet legation.

A mixed group of Cheka agents and civilians who were not fully informed of the real aims of the mission went to Berlin in January 1921. The group was headed by Nikolai Alexeyev and its task was to penetrate the entourage of two prominent émigré leaders, Boris Savinkov and Nikolai Chaikovsky, the latter known as 'the grandfather of the Russian revolution'.[57] They were also tasked to gather information on anti-Bolshevik organisations. Many of them were active in both Berlin and Paris, therefore the final destination of at least several members of the group was Paris. Besides Alexeyev and his wife, Eugenia Weizmann, the group included Mikhail Gorb,[58] Ivan Zaporozhets, Vasili Zelenin, Leonid Zinchenko, Alexander Ulanovsky (nicknamed 'Aliosha') with his young wife Nadezhda (née Esther Fridgant), and the anarchist couple known only as Dukh and Rosa. Besides abundant amounts of dollars and pounds, the Ulanovskys were smuggling diamonds hidden in a leather belt worn under the shirt. The group was badly documented and after considerable difficulties and with a lot of luck only two couples were able to safely reach Berlin while others were arrested on the way. Cash and contacts eventually did their job and the lawyers soon managed to free them.[59] Ulanovsky and his wife, both of whom were not yet working for the Cheka, as well as Alexeyev with Eugenia returned to Moscow in February 1922. The anarchists stayed in France. It seems Gorb remained in Berlin until March 1924 working under cover of the Soviet legation registered as 'M. Chervyakov'.

After his mission was completed, Kopp returned to the NKID, actively participating in the development of Soviet-German relations and later served as the Soviet envoy in Japan and Sweden, succeeded there by Alexandra Kollontai following his sudden death during a business trip to Berlin.[60]

Boris Stomonyakov was promoted to Deputy People's Commissar for Foreign Affairs in 1934. On the night of 7/8 August 1938 he was sitting in his spacious office at Smolenskaya-Sennaya Square writing a letter to Stalin. He complained to the Master that Georgy Malenkov had summoned him and announced that the party had decided to transfer him to another post. Malenkov was one of the top party mandarins responsible for the party cadres, control and purges (cleansing of the party of perceived undesirables). Because he was closely associated with Stalin and heavily involved in the so-called treason trials (in 1938 Malenkov was one of the leading figures in bringing about the downfall of Yezhov, a degenerate whom Stalin placed in charge of the NKVD), Stomonyakov realised that his career was over. Shortly after midnight he shot himself twice in the heart with his semi-automatic Mauser pistol but missed.[61] Urgently transported to the NKVD clinic, Stomonyakov managed to recover only to be arrested shortly before Christmas. After two years of merciless interrogation, accused and found guilty of spying for Germany and Poland, he was sentenced to death and executed in October 1940.

* * *

Fast rewind: Skujskumbré was succeeded by Yakov Davtyan ('Davydov') who became chief of foreign branch of the Special (OO) Department in November 1920. Skujskumbré was then transferred to the Special Department's section dealing with secret agents. On 20 December Dzerzhinsky signed the VChK Decree No. 169, according to which: (1) the foreign branch of the Special Department was dissolved and replaced with the Foreign Department of the VChK, which became known as INO (inostrannyi otdel); (2) all staff of the foreign branch were transferred to the new Foreign Department; (3) the Foreign Department was subordinated to Menzhinsky, head of Special Department; (4) Davtyan/Davydov was appointed acting head of Foreign Departments and was obliged to present his staff recommendations to the VChK Presidium within a week; (5) henceforth, all VChK branches were to conduct their relations with foreign countries, NKID, NKVT and the Comintern only through the Foreign Department.

Davtyan headed the new INO until 20 January 1921 and invited Skujskumbré to supervise its Agents Section.[62] Davtyan was then briefly replaced by another Armenian, Ruben Katanyan, but on 10 April he was asked to return staying for another six months until Solomon Mogilevsky succeeded him on 6 August. Katanyan was sent to Germany as Consul General. Mogilevsky would occupy this post until 13 March 1922, when Trilisser took over. Trilisser previously served as chief of the overseas section of the foreign branch and would become the longest-serving Soviet intelligence chief.

* * *

After his return from Berlin, Bortnowski, also known as Bronkowski, Bronek and Petrovsky, a General Staff officer, worked at the Moscow (G)RU headquarters as head of its 2nd (agents) department before in 1929 he resigned for health reasons and was placed in the Polish section of the Comintern. From 1930 he was sent to Berlin again, this time by the Comintern's OMS, and after March 1933 – to Copenhagen. From 1934 Bortnowski headed the Polish-Baltic regional (Länder) secretariat of the ECCI until August 1935, when during the 7th Congress of the Comintern the ECCI was reorganised. The International Relations Department (OMS) was also reorganised and the Communication Service (Sluzhba Svyazi) was created in its place, headed by Boris Melnikov ('Müller') and his deputy Alexander Abramov-Mirov, both senior (G)RU officers.

In Berlin, Bortnowski's successor was Vladimir Bustrem, who arrived in August 1922. He worked under diplomatic cover at the Soviet legation with documents identifying him as 'Alexey Vasilyevich Loginov'. It is said that when Bustrem arrived, Trilisser was already there on an undercover mission,[63] probably inspection, which was no surprise given his new job. Bustrem returned to Moscow in December 1925 and as an old and trusted friend of Trilisser, the INO chief, who was together with him in custody and exile, was appointed assistant head of Soviet foreign intelligence. Six years later Bustrem was very lucky to be transferred from the OGPU reserve at the disposal of the CPSU Central Committee nomenklatura,[64] which secured him responsible jobs and comparative safety from persecution at the hands of his former colleagues. Thus, he managed to survive the Great Terror and died peacefully in his bed in Moscow in February 1943.

Before his arrest in July 1937, Fishman lived with his wife Natalia in the famous 'house of the Soviet elite' in Kalashny Lane, known then and now as the Mosselprom Building, and Firin, senior major of State Security, used to visit them when in Moscow. When they came to arrest Fishman, Firin was still in the GULAG system but then not as one of its chiefs but rather an unhappy prisoner accused of preparing a state coup. Fishman survived. Firin was shot on 14 August 1937.

Bortnowski was arrested in June 1937, and shot on 3 November; Abramov-Mirov – arrested on 21 May 1937 and shot on 26 November. Melnikov was arrested before them, on 4 May 1937, soon after his return from Spain, and shot on 28 July 1938.

Mikhail Gorb was arrested on 29 April 1937 as one of the close collaborators of the former NKVD chief Yagoda. On 20 August his name was entered in the Moscow-Centre list for capital punishment 'in the first category', meaning the verdict was signed personally by Stalin and his four loyal hangmen – Molotov, Kaganovich, Voroshilov and Kosior. On the next day he was shot in a summary execution without the benefit of a trial together with thirty-seven other prominent Chekists.

Chapter 8

Trade, Diplomacy and Famine

'As Russia's gold reserves began running down in winter 1921-22, it became increasingly clear to the Bolsheviks that there was no way to rob and loot their way out of the financial crisis.'[1] In the meantime, there was the question of the total human cost. A severe famine which began early in the spring of 1921 and lasted through 1922 put an estimated 32 million lives at risk in Russia, Ukraine and Georgia, killing at least five million people. Frank Lorimer's study estimated death for the period 1914–26 by comparing census figures and taking into account changes in territory and in the birth rate.[2] Quoted in what is probably the best book ever written on the Russian Civil War,[3] the result was a figure of 16 million, which Lorimer divided between two million military death and 14 million civilians. Subtracting 1.7 million killed in the World War and about five million who died in the 1921–2 famine would leave 9–10 million deaths, losses of innocent human lives, resulting directly or indirectly from the Bolshevik revolution during its first five years. If it is true, as one American historian has put it, that revolutions are conceived in fear and produce terror, then it is no surprise that fear and terror were everywhere in Russia, especially between 1917 and 1922 that saw the collapse of the economy.

Lenin's basic assumptions turned out to be wrong: Europe was not on the brink of proletarian revolution, the masses were not able to run the state and the economy, and his political vision proved to be just a dream. An evil dream as it soon turned out. The Bolshevik leadership, fearing for their power and the fate of the October Revolution, were forced by the economic situation and massive popular discontent – the Kronstadt mutiny together with large-scale peasant uprisings in Tambov, Siberia and elsewhere, plus unsuccessful communist revolts in Hungary and Germany – to change the destructive policy of War Communism.[4] World revolution became subordinate to more pressing tasks.

The 10th Congress of the Russian Communist Party (Bolsheviks) approved a turn to the New Economic Policy (NEP), cautiously proposed by Lenin to save the situation and adopted in March 1921. It was 'new' in comparison to the 'old Tsarist' economic policy. The original plan was to bring back elements of the free market and capitalism, all under state control as much as banks, foreign trade and heavy industry, until the economy was strong enough to start building socialism. For peasants and farmers, forced grain requisition was replaced by taxes payable in the form of raw agricultural commodities, while the main concern was the attraction of foreign capital. For the country's leaders, the major priorities of foreign policy became to negotiate trade agreements, persuade 'the capitalists' to provide loans and secure diplomatic recognition from the Western powers. The beginning of this process was the arrival of Soviet trade and, where possible, semi-diplomatic missions in various countries like Denmark, Germany, Great Britain, Norway, Sweden and Turkey. As every other empire, more often than not the Soviet rulers sought trade negotiations to realise not only economic but also political ends.

At least two Great Powers had to be almost immediately excluded from the Soviet plans – the United States and France – because both were categorically opposed to dealing with the Bolsheviks. The US Secretary of State Charles Evans Hughes Sr. was convinced that 'those in control of Moscow have not given up their original purpose of destroying existing governments wherever they can do so throughout the world'. His government colleague, Herbert Hoover, appointed US Secretary of Commerce at the same time as Hughes, in early March 1921 warned that 'we cannot even remotely recognise this murderous tyranny without simulating actionist radicalism in every country in Europe and without transgressing on every National ideal of our own'.[5] For France, where as a result of the revolution 'over one million small-scale investors saw their billions of francs in bonds and stocks go up in smoke as if by the stroke of some sadistic magician's wand', the situation was especially catastrophic. In March 1920, Maxim Litvinov, then Deputy Commissar for Foreign Affairs, told the French representatives that the Soviet government wanted trade relations and would 'pay its debts' when the war with Poland had ended. Wishing to drive a wedge between the two leading Western powers, Litvinov stressed that France, unlike Britain, should have an interest in a strong Russian state. Notwithstanding this, the French government rejected Litvinov's offer.[6] The same offer made later by Leonid Krasin was also rejected outright.[7]

When the Soviet delegation comprised of Krasin and his deputy Nikolai Klyshko arrived at 10 Downing Street on Monday afternoon, 31 May 1920, for a trade conference with the British prime minister accompanied by Mr. Bonar Law, Lord Privy Seal; Lord Curzon, Foreign Secretary; Sir Robert Horne, President of the Board of Trade; and Mr Harmsworth (probably Cecil, 1st Baron Harmsworth, Under-Secretary of State for Foreign Affairs), *The Times* correspondent reported from Paris:

The French government has always been most reluctant to enter into relations with any Soviet representatives ... M. [Edward Frank] Wise and M. [Vicomte du] Halgouët discussed trade questions with M. Krassin [*sic*] in Copenhagen at the beginning of April, and the impression made upon the French representative was that the negotiations could not be successful for the simple reason that Russia has practically nothing to exchange against our goods except gold, which the French rightly look upon as part of their security for loans and the precious stones which have been stolen. The French have made a formal protest against the contract entered into by some 15 Swedish houses who are about to trade with Russia and who are to receive payment of about 30,000,000f. (£1,200,000 at par) in gold of the Russian State Bank or of the Rumanian treasure which has fallen into Bolshevik hands.[8]

In his draft proposal sent to both London and Paris sometime after this meeting but before the Genoa Conference, Chicherin, People's Commissar for Foreign Affairs, indicated that the Bolsheviks might pay back at least Russia's pre-1914 debts. A month later Krasin, answering a question from the British trade union leaders and Labour Party officials about what guarantees could the Soviet government give if a loan of £100,000,000 were suggested, responded that 'the Soviet Government, faced with the present exhausted conditions of the country, cannot offer any immediate material guarantee in the shape of gold security or other pledged resources'. He added that his government was 'however prepared to grant, as security for such a loan, concessions for the exploitation of oil, mineral ores, forests, means of communications on certain conditions, and also to accord participation in the increased profit yielded by various undertakings'.[9]

Concessions of course would cost the regime nothing, and this idea was eagerly discussed by Lenin, Trotsky, Kalinin, Molotov and Stalin in October 1921. But the final conditions set by the Politburo before the conference stipulated that any Russian debt repayments would begin only 15 years later, and would not be made at all unless the Entente powers gave Moscow 'an immediate large loan (approximately one billion dollars)'.[10] With Britain, still one of the great world powers, that was unlikely to agree upon, especially having in mind that between the November 1918 Armistice and the Lloyd George speech exactly one year later (calling intervention in Russia untenable), Britain spent about £100 million (well over £1.5 billion in 2021) to topple the Bolsheviks.[11] Unaware of that but having no illusions about the British reaction, the Soviets decided to concentrate on Sweden, Italy and Germany, like themselves a pariah state, although back in January 1920, four days after the ratification of the Treaty of Versailles, Lloyd George proposed to end the blockade of Soviet Russia and resume trade with the former coalition partner and important Entente ally through the agency of the Russian Co-operative Societies (Tsentrosoyuz), allegedly a non-political trading organisation. The Japanese government was informed, but showed little interest. Swedish bankers and businessmen, on the contrary, were ready to offer their services. Olof Aschberg, in particular, was more than happy to step in yet again to play the role of middleman between the communist regime and Western capital.

'Neutral' Stockholm, Sean McMeekin notes, 'had been the Bolsheviks' preferred destination of illicit Romanov ruble sales in 1918 and gold dumping in 1920-21, so it was perhaps inevitable that it would be their first choice for credit now that there was no more cash and gold to launder'.[12]

Shortly after Christmas, Krasin sent two important reports to Moscow, both of which were shown to Lenin. In the first, dated 27 December 1920, the head of the Soviet trade delegation reported about the initiative of the Italian poet Gabriele D'Annunzio. A year before, he had led the seizure of the city of Fiume (today Rijeka, Croatia) and its occupation by the nationalist irregulars under his command, to the joy and cheering of the city's residents. D'Annunzio then declared it the independent Italian Regency of Carnaro, and appointed himself its Duce, forcing the withdrawal of the British, French and American forces. In November 1920 the Treaty of Rapallo was signed, creating the eternal 'Free State of Fiume'. D'Annunzio refused to acknowledge the document, and by the time his appeal reached Krasin in Berlin, the regular Italian army drove him out of the city which he proposed to the Bolsheviks to use as their trading port with the West.[13] The telegram was shelved.

Another report by Krasin dealt with the British reaction to Chicherin's note to Lord Curzon dated 4 December 1920.[14] During the final stage of trade negotiations that began on 12 September, the discussion centred on three main points. One was the preamble and consequent application of the agreement reached during previous meetings in May and June. Several experts suggest that the 29 June meeting was regarded by both sides as crucial, the principal issues being the cessation of propaganda, subversion and hostile acts, as well as Soviet recognition of former Russian debts. Others were the treatment of Russian gold on the London market and the security of Russian exports related to the debts and claims against Russia by pre-1917 creditors.[15] Having in mind Chicherin's telegram to Curzon, 'a new note to Great Britain' as the newspapers described it, Krasin expected the trade talks would founder on British rejection of the terms that Lenin insisted he must put forward. Krasin warned Lenin about the British intention to convene an international conference to deal with Russia.[16] One should have in mind that except a short break related to the loss of the Russian codes earlier in

1921, the Government Code and Cipher School (GC&CS) was able to decrypt, at least in part, the telegrams exchanged between Moscow and the Soviet delegation in London as well as between Moscow and Copenhagen so the British side was fully informed about Soviet plans, intentions and fears.[17] According to its Authorised History, GC&CS began in 1919 with twenty-eight clerical and twenty-four cryptologic staff supported by eighteen junior and six senior assistants.[18] Their SIGINT provided unique insights into Bolshevik actions by revealing information whose authenticity was considered to be beyond reproach while MI1c's human sources in several places including Tallinn (BP), Riga (FR) and Berlin (BN) turned out to be unreliable, in fact bogus.[19]

In early January 1921 Lenin discussed with Chicherin the appointment of Vatslav Vorovsky (Wacław Worowski) as the first Soviet trade representative in Italy. The Italian side agreed to accept Vorovsky having previously refused Jan A. Berzin (almost certainly because of his position as secretary of the Executive Committee of the Comintern). Berzin left the ECCI for a diplomatic career and from 1921 had served as Assistant Official Soviet Representative in London succeeding Adolf Joffe in Vienna in June 1925. Chicherin asked to postpone sending Vorovsky to Italy before he cleared this with Litvinov, then Soviet plenipotentiary (polpred) in Estonia. At the same time Lenin authorised Ganetsky (Jakob Hanecki), now Soviet polpred in Latvia, to start negotiations on the Russian-Latvian Railway Convention which was signed in Riga later that year.[20] It was a time, as one historian has described it, of change and compromise for Soviet diplomacy as the Narkomindel imperatives had to be realigned away from the world revolution towards the pursuit of stable diplomatic relations.[21] The revolutionary fervour was placed in the hands of the Comintern which continued to engage in communist propaganda and subversion.

In December 1920 Fritz Platten, a Swiss communist, close associate of Lenin and one of the founders of the Comintern, reported to Moscow that he had duly received credentials to act as the first Soviet trade representative in Turkey. The Soviet diplomatic mission in Angora, an old name for Ankara, the capital of Turkey, was established in October 1920 (the official opening was on 9 November) and for various reasons Soviet policy towards Turkey was quite ambiguous. This state of uncertainty was reflected in the choice of the first Soviet diplomatic representatives. The first chargé d'affaires, Latvian Jan Upmal-Angarsky (Janis Upmalis), had to be quickly recalled while the newly appointed polpred, Shalva Eliava from a noble Georgian family, was reassigned to Persia instead of going to Turkey. His successor, Budu Mdivani, another nobleman, stayed only for three months, when he was appointed People's Commissar of Trade in his native Georgia. Sergei

Natzarenus, former political commissar of the Moscow military district, with his allegedly 'inadequate conduct of the embassy's affairs' had to be replaced by a new chargé d'affaires, Boris Mikhailov.[22] Such was the situation when Chicherin decided to intervene.

In the first week of January 1921 Lenin devoted a lot of his time to foreign relations and together with Platten's report read Chicherin's letter to Krestinsky dated the same day, Tuesday, 7 December. Chicherin wrote about the situation in Turkey. In his letter, the Commissar for Foreign Affairs, a distant relative of Pushkin and a hereditary diplomat whose father served the tsars, stressed that relations with Turkey played an extremely important role in Soviet foreign policy. He insisted that the Soviet representative in Angora (Ankara) should have the political insight and diplomatic skills necessary for conveying Soviet foreign policy and political decisions properly. Chicherin proposed Karl Danishevsky (Jūlijs Kārlis Daniševskis, a Latvian communist) for this position.

It was a strange choice. Danishevsky was a die-hard communist, one of the leaders of the red terror in Crimea who in 1918–19 served as the first chairman of the revolutionary military tribunal. There, he became known for his interview, published in *Izvestia*, where Danishevsky claimed that military tribunals (court martials) should not be guided by any legal norms. These are punitive bodies, he said, created in the course of the most intense revolutionary struggle. That is, they have nothing to do with justice but their purpose is to punish and destroy the enemies of the revolution. This is exactly what happened to Danishevsky himself – arrested in July 1937, he was accused of counter-revolutionary and terrorist activities, sentenced to death and shot. Then, back in the 1920s, he did not accept Chicherin's proposal and asked to send him to a party post in Siberia instead. At the end of the day this did not help him and even if he agreed, he would hardly have survived because almost all Soviet diplomats of the first two post-revolutionary decades were executed during the Great Terror.

Remarkably, being completely in the dark on the scale of British intelligence activities and possibilities in Turkey, after Danishevsky refused to go Chicherin asked the Politburo to appoint Menzhinsky, a member of the Cheka Presidium who, he said, was well aware of the intricacies of Soviet Eastern policy.[23] Menzhinsky also didn't go to Angora and was soon appointed to head the Special (Osoby) Department which first included the overseas section and later the foreign department (INO) of the Cheka. From January 1921 Menzhinsky was promoted to controller of the Secret-Operational Directorate (SOU), which placed him in charge of all intelligence and counter-intelligence work – a position incomparably more responsible than that of a plenipotentiary in Turkey.

In the meantime, in January 1919 General Sir William Thwaites, the Director of Military Intelligence, a department of the British War Office, decided to concentrate wireless intelligence and the army's cryptography service (MI1b) in occupied Constantinople, with listening posts established in Baku, Batumi, and Baghdad, in addition to those in Cyprus, Greece and Egypt.[24] During the immediate post-war years Sir Mansfield Smith-Cumming, head of SIS (then MI1c), regarded his Constantinople operation as 'one of the most important, if not the most important, of all my agencies'. One of his colleagues at Head Office, probably Colonel Stewart Menzies, head of Military Section IV, asserted that 'a better service of information has never been organised regarding events in the Near East'. Besides members of MI1c posing under various guises, officers of the recently established Intelligence Corps as well as Naval Intelligence also provided a great deal of information. With all this, the most reliable and timely intelligence came from a very productive signals intelligence unit working under cover of the British occupation forces.[25] Remarkably, the Authorised History of GCHQ (former GC&CS) does not mention any of those achievements, but its author adds, in a different work, that 'in 1920 and 1921 the Istanbul [sic, Constantinople] station was among SIS's largest, with eight officers, six clerical staff, and representatives from the Army and Navy. It also was unusually well financed, receiving £2,200 per month for all operating expenses.'[26] British intelligence operations in Anatolia in the period of national struggle (1919–22), both SIGINT and HUMINT, are covered by other historians. With this, the work of the Intelligence Corps, initially commanded by Archibald Wavell (future Field Marshal Sir) a former British liaison to the Russian forces in the Caucasus during the First World War, remain largely unresearched.

Since the end of the war, the MI1c station in Constantinople had been headed by Rhys Samson, from October 1919 assisted by Harold 'Gibbie' Gibson. Samson's deputy was Valentine Vivian, seconded from the Indian police. The India Office intelligence agency, Indian Political Intelligence (IPI), liaised closely with Cumming's men. In March 1920 Cumming agreed with IPI that his Service would fund the IPI representative in Geneva to the tune of £1,500 a year and 'get from him all his non-Indian stuff in exchange' (by the end of the year this was cut to £500). Three months later, Rhys Samson proposed that he should be based in Switzerland to co-ordinate 'Pan-Islamic Intelligence in Western Europe' and from there run 'a certain Turkish Nationalist who would be in a position to get inside information on Turkish affairs'.[27] By September, he was appointed SIS Inspector of the Swiss Group and headed the station in Geneva, while Vivian succeeded him in Constantinople.

Another SIS production officer who had worked in Turkey at that time was Wilfred Dunderdale. In Constantinople, which after 1928 became known as Istanbul, both Dunderdale and Gibson worked against Bolshevik Russia, recruiting agents and forming agent networks from the Russian émigrés and the former Tsarist officers (called 'White Guardists' by the Soviets), of whom there was a great number after the exodus of the Wrangel army from Crimea. In mid-November 1920, some 150,000 people were loaded onto 126 warships and other vessels – 'anything that could float', and set sail mainly for Allied-occupied Constantinople.

There's a certain confusion among researchers and even intelligence historians about agents' codenames in Turkey because their identifications vary from HV to RV, JQ and MS. One agent, a former Tsarist officer, HV/109, whose personal file, quoted by Jeffery, describes his motives as 'finance, anti-Bolshevik and pro-British', moved with Gibson to Bucharest in December 1922. From there, his file asserts, he ran a large group of sub-agents in the Ukraine and Bessarabia. One successful agent, RV/5, gathered information in his men's clothing store, which was patronised by people associated with a secret revolutionary organisation known as the Committee of Union and Progress (CUP), whose leader was Talaat Pasha. When one of the agent's informants, a sub-agent in the Turkish Foreign Ministry, was caught red-handed, RV/5 was transferred to Egypt. According to the Authorised History of MI6,

> One 'very reliable' agent, JQ/6, a 'Turkman of European appearance', Russian education and a former Russian cavalry officer who spoke 'Turkman, Tartar [sic, Turkmen and Tatar], Turkish, Russian, Rumanian and fair English and German', with good contacts in Turkmeni, Caucasian and Azerbaijani circles, set up a coffee shop in Istanbul which became a centre of Kemalist gatherings [most former CUP members were able to join the Turkish nationalist movement led by Mustafa Kemal]. But by January 1923, having become known to many 'Azerbaijanis now working for Turks', he had to be got quickly out of Istanbul. SIS 'bought his a perfectly genuine Polish passport ... with all the necessary visas' and moved him to Romania.[28]

In his weekly reports to London Vivian described him as 'one of the very best agents we have got'. Never identified by name, JQ/6 later went on to Berlin where he remained in contact with the SIS station, headed by Frank Foley. In 1929 the agent was sent to Iraq but disappeared without trace between Marseilles and Baghdad.

In the immediate post-war years one agent run by Vivian had provided most of SIS's information on Kemal's intentions and activities. Codenamed 'Parsifal' in the station's reports, he was uncovered in 1921. In December 1919 Major Hay (no further details available, possibly Arthur Sidney Hay of the Royal Lancers)[29] reported to London that British Military Intelligence in Constantinople had recently succeeded in planting an agent in 'a small group of persons' in the Ottoman capital, who were apparently seeking, on behalf of the Soviet government, to establish contact with Mustafa Kemal and other nationalist leaders. According to the agent's report, Kemal was in touch with representatives of the 'separatist' Transcaucasian republics of Georgia and Azerbaijan.[30] However, a year later, in December 1920, a SIS report from agent MS/1 quoted a Bulgarian source close to Kemal as asserting that the Turkish leader was primarily a nationalist. It was suggested that if Britain were to back Turkey, this would at once 'put a stop to the unnatural collaboration between the Turks and the Bolsheviks'. Based on various reports but first of all on intercepts, SIS's analysis suggested that the Turks were more than happy to intrigue behind the backs of the Soviets in order to create a 'Moslem Federation' which would exclude Moscow's involvement.[31] In May 1920, noting that investigation revealed no connection and much mistrust between Turkish Nationalists and Bolsheviks, the SIS head of station in Constantinople (probably Samson) reported:

> I do not think we can say Bolshevism does not exist [in Turkey] because we can certify that no Bolshevist organisation exists. We are looking for something far more elusive and intangible than that, viz: tendencies and sympathies on the part of the Turks or any of the peoples of Turkey, which foreshadows a fusion with Bolshevism or may end directly or indirectly, morally or materially, in aiding the Bolshevik cause to our detriment.[32]

Whether Moscow was helping Ankara or vice versa did not really matter. The Turkish delegation headed by Yusuf Kemal Bey (later known as Tengirşenk) duly arrived in Moscow to sign the agreement with Bolshevik Russia on 16 March 1921. It was perhaps no coincidence that on the same day the Anglo-Russian Trade Agreement was signed in London.

The Turkish delegation, which apart from Yusuf Kemal, then Minister of Economy (he was elected Minister of Foreign Affairs shortly after return from Moscow), included Dr Riza Nur, Minister of Health and Public Assistance, and General Ali Fuat Cebesoy, the newly appointed ambassador to Moscow, represented the Grand National Assembly (GNA) of Turkey, whose leader was Mustafa Kemal.[33] The Lenin's government was represented by Chicherin and Jelal-Ed-Din Korkmasov, chairman of the new Soviet government of Dagestan, who came from a very noble and wealthy family of hereditary aristocracy. (Notwithstanding his revolutionary past and exemplary Soviet career, Korkmasov would be arrested and shot in 1937.) Kemal was assisting the Bolsheviks in Dagestan by sending military officers to help supress the uprising led by Said Bey. In its turn, the Moscow government was helping Kemal by providing military aid for the embattled Turkish Republic in its struggle with the common enemy, Britain and France, the imperialist Entente powers now opposed to both the Bolsheviks and the Young Turks. At that time both the Republic of Turkey and the Soviet Union were not yet established but after the signing of the agreement, which is also known as the Treaty of Brotherhood, active trade, military and political relations started to develop between Moscow and Ankara. The provisions of the agreement remain unchanged until this day.

As a result of the Treaty of Moscow and the following Treaty of Kars, signed in October, which established the borders between Turkey and the former Transcaucasian republics, now Armenia, Georgia and Azerbaijan, the Bolshevik government supplied Turkey with weapons, ammunition and money in gold bars and coins although in considerably smaller quantities. On 13 December 1921 Mikhail Frunze, commander of the Southern Front who took Crimea, pushing General Wrangel's forces out of Russia, and was recently elected to the Central Committee, arrived in Turkey as an envoy of Soviet Ukraine. He was received with great fanfare and shown around, staying until January 1922 when he signed the Turco-Ukrainian Agreement (2 January 1922).[34] Semyon Aralov, a new Soviet 'authorised representative' appointed by Chicherin shortly before Frunze's visit to Turkey, met him in Samsun where Aralov and his retinue arrived from Georgia by ship.

Aralov was a former Tsarist officer who had served in a grenadier regiment where some officers supported Socialist Revolutionaries (SRs). Carried away by Marxist ideas, he participated in the work of the Moscow committee of the RSDLP and after the split in the party joined the Bolsheviks. Sent to the Far East during the Russo-Japanese War, he was actively engaged in Bolshevik propaganda and subversion among the troops and soon had to return to Moscow to avoid arrest. During the First World War he was again in the army, took part in action, was awarded and promoted to Stabs-kapitan, a rank between senior lieutenant and captain. Shortly after the October Revolution he joined the Communist Party and began his Red Army career at the headquarters of the Moscow military district, soon promoted to the chief of Operational Department at the People's Commissariat for Military and Naval Affairs (Narkomvoyen) under Trotsky. In November 1918 Soviet military intelligence was created as the Registration Directorate of the Field

Headquarters of the Revolutionary Military Council of the Republic, and Aralov was appointed its chief, thus becoming the first director of what would be later known as the GRU. He remained at this post until July 1919, then briefly serving as deputy commander of the Ukrainian military district before Lenin recommended him to the NKID. In April 1921 Aralov was sent as the first Soviet plenipotentiary to Lithuania based in Kovno (now Kaunas), the temporary capital. It was his first diplomatic assignment before Turkey.

At the same time, as soon as the Moscow Agreement was signed in March 1921, Soviet representatives arrived. Alexander Golub, an old Bolshevik without any formal education sent by the party to the NKID, was appointed Soviet consul in Trebizond (Trabzon) arriving in April. He would later serve in Constantinople.

Although no separate trade agreement had existed between Russia and Turkey, the GNA government agreed with the Soviet proposal to open a trade mission in Angora representing the NKVT. In was inaugurated on 19 April 1922 with Aralov delivering a speech on behalf of the Soviet government. There, he announced that the struggle of Soviet Russia with the capitalist West was not over and that it simply shifted from the military to the economic sphere. Soviet Russia, Turkey, Persia, China, Afghanistan, Khiva and Bukhara (now both in Uzbekistan) must coordinate their economic policy, Aralov said, and create a united economic front in the whole East.[35] The Soviet trade mission in Turkey, according to the Soviet plan, was to serve as a barrier against Western capital. After Angora (Ankara), various Soviet trade missions were quickly opened in Trebizond (Trabzon), Samsun, Mersin and Inebolu, buying and selling various goods.

The trade mission in Constantinople established shortly after the signing of the Moscow Agreement was headed by Bronislav Kudish and initially consisted of himself, Yevgeny Filippovich and Vladimir Augenblick, all of them representing different branches of Centrosoyuz, an acronym for the joint board of the All-Russian Union of Consumer Co-operative Societies. They rented an office in the prestigious Galata neighbourhood separated from the old city by the Golden Horn, bought a green luxury automobile and quickly began to expand without doing any visible business. The Russian émigré newspapers in Berlin and Paris soon started publishing regular reports from Turkey mainly about how the Bolshevik emissaries were often reprimanded and even attacked in public places by the White officers and their wives for arrogant behaviour, and how, even at difficult times of famine back at home, they preferred to live comfortable wealthy lives of the privileged class, promenading along the luxurious Grande Rue de Péra and having meals at the famous and expensive restaurant of the prestigious Tokatlian Hotel.

In what concerned business, the delegation in Constantinople did not make any significant contribution to bilateral trade. Except for a few minor deals when some relatively small amounts of oil and its derivatives were exchanged for agricultural products, not a single import-export contract had been concluded between the two countries.[36] As the negotiations on the signing of a trade agreement began in October 1922, all Soviet trade delegations were temporarily closed.

Ever since the Armistice of Mudros, the British were able to intercept and read all telephone and telegraph traffic within occupied Turkey. According to the authorised history of GCHQ, Britain mastered the ciphers of all powers which had been involved in Middle Eastern affairs and solutions of Soviet and Turkish traffic showed their alignment was close, but strained.[37] Human intelligence supported this conclusion.

In June 1921 British military authorities organised a raid at the European part of Constantinople, Pera and Galata, detaining many people including those employed in various Soviet organisations. The House of Commons discussions in early July confirmed that on 29 June General Sir Charles Harington, Supreme Commander of the Allied Army of the Black Sea who also had under his command No. 3 Wireless Observation Group and the British 28th Division in Constantinople, ordered the arrest of fifty illegal aliens among whom were eighteen members of the Russian trade delegation as well as other Soviet subjects. Cecil Harmsworth, Under-Secretary of State for Foreign Affairs, explained to the MPs that a conspiracy had been uncovered whose aim was to assassinate the general and start a pro-Kemalist revolutionary uprising. Six years later, in 1927, such raids took place in eight different countries, including Turkey where, according to newspaper reports, one of the Soviet managers of the joint stock company RussoTurk was arrested for espionage in March.

Serious trade negotiations between Turkey and Soviet Russia began in April 1926. A limited most-favoured nation treaty of commerce and navigation, signed on 11 March 1927, became effective on 4 July to remain in force for one year.

At the same time, the semi-official history of Soviet foreign intelligence claims that in 1927 the OGPU established informal relations with the newly formed National Security Service of Turkey (Milli Emniyet Hizmeti, MEH, better known as MAH).[38] Officially formed in January 1926, the agency, headed by its first director Şükrü Âli Ögel (appointed on Christmas Day, Saturday, 25 December), began working in January 1927. The KGB historians suggest that the initiative came from the Turkish side and that the principal assistance to the MEH/MAH was in setting up a cryptographic service.

Among various Soviet representatives in Turkey, only Kudish, who at the time of the June 1921 raid was in London (coming back when the dust began to settle), had been described as a former Chekist allegedly active in the Crimea before they sent him to Turkey which, however, cannot be verified. But the RIS agents (Russian Intelligence Services that included military intelligence, RU; secret political police, VChK; and the secret service of the Comintern, OMS) were indeed rather active, of which the British side was well aware from both the intercepts and the human sources.[39] And although the real extent of Soviet involvement in the region was underestimated, this was of little importance.

* * *

Before Konstantin Zvonarev, the first military attaché, arrived together with Aralov in January 1922, a group of 'illegals' working for Soviet military intelligence had already been operating in Bulgaria and Turkey. Their principal target was the anti-Bolshevik forces of General Wrangel that had been successfully evacuated from Crimea and were now living as poor émigrés in these countries as well as in the Kingdom of the Serbs, Croats and Slovenes. Another important large group were Russian prisoners of war and other displaced persons temporarily resident in Turkey and Bulgaria, whom communist agitators did their best to persuade to join the Red Army instead of supporting the Whites. The Soviet Red Cross mission was urgently established in Bulgaria which together with the Union for Repatriation to the Motherland (cunningly abbreviated as 'Sovnarod') was conducting a massive propaganda campaign among Russian emigrants. By September 1922 the Bulgarian section of the Union for Repatriation had 5,300 members, with the Cheka effectively infiltrating and controlling the exiled community of White Russians. On 1 October 1920 the Bulgarian Foreign Ministry informed the War Ministry that all servicemen from the last echelon of the Russian troops sent to Odessa by the steamer *Sofia* were immediately enlisted into the Red Army upon their arrival.[40] In the Black Sea coast cities of Varna and Constantinople underground committees were set up by the Bulgarian Communist Party (BCP) where Bulgarian, Greek, Romanian and other communist agitators did their best to support the Russian Bolsheviks.[41]

One of the illegal (G)RU residents in Turkey was Nikola Traichev (in Russian: Nikolai Khristoforovich Traychev), alias 'David Davydov', who had been involved in revolutionary activities in Constantinople since 1908. Bulgarian by nationality, he joined the Red Army in 1919 and since 1920 had been placed in Constantinople controlling a large network of agents. In June 1921 he was arrested by the Intelligence Corps during a raid and spent a year in a British prison in Constantinople, after which he was expelled to Bulgaria. In 1924 Traichev returned to Turkey working for the Russian Trade Delegation, but a year later was arrested again. After his release he was sent to Greece but soon had to leave rather than risk exposure. In December 1931 Abramov-Mirov invited Traichev to join the OMS where, using the alias 'David Lazarevich Movanov', he controlled secret Comintern work in Odessa and Batumi.

Traichev's most active case officers in Turkey were Krastyu Katev, Gavrail Savov and Atanas Deverzhiyev who in turn controlled several sub-agents, all of them working for the (G)RU. Katev (in Russian: Khristian Toshevich Katev), alias 'Christo Traikov', operated in Varna in 1919–20, then fought with the Red Army in Crimea and was sent by the Intelligence Department of the Ukrainian Red Army to Turkey. In Constantinople Katev masqueraded as a businessman working for the Moshe Zhonte trading company to collect intelligence about the White troops. In 1923 he returned to Moscow, working in the Economic Department of the OGPU, and after the establishment of the shipping company Sovtorgflot (Soviet Commercial Fleet) served as its representative in Constantinople (1925–7). After a spell in the Directorate of Naval Forces of the Black Sea Fleet, Katev was arrested in 1937 and sent to the GULAG, but survived, living in Moscow until 1976 when he died aged 82. Ten years before that he was awarded the Kingdom of Bulgaria Order of Merit commemorating the Bulgarian coup d'état of 9 September 1944, his only decoration for service. In the summer of 2021, a large collection of such medals was offered at the Vienna Naschmarkt for 10 euros each.

Atanas Deverzhiyev was arrested in 1933 in Kiev and died five years later in the Chukotka GULAG. The Chukotka peninsula is Russia's most north-eastern expanse located less than 100km from Alaska. From the 1930s to the 1950s, Chukotka was part of the prison camp system, and became the graveyard of tens of thousands of prisoners. In 1916–18 Atanas served in the Bulgarian army and then joined the Red Army, taking part in the Russian Civil War operating behind enemy lines. Naturally, as an experienced underground operator he was sent to his native Bulgaria where he had worked for two years, from 1921 to 1923, preparing an armed communist insurgency which became known as the September Uprising. Backed by the Comintern, the goal was to establish 'a government of workers and peasants' in Bulgaria. After its suppression, the (G)RU sent him to Constantinople as a case officer controlling a group of sub-agents working for the illegal residency headed by Nikola Traichev. There he used the alias 'Dr. Vasil Kostov', operating under the commercial cover of an import-export business. During his several months in Turkey where he had been from February to December 1924, Deverzhiyev's intelligence work was limited to providing information about the former White troops stationed in and around Constantinople, disposition of military units, mood of officers and soldiers as well as about the general situation in the city. Upon his return, Deverzhiyev was sent to Kiev where he was employed as an editor for several Bulgarian communist printed media published by the Bulgarian Bureau attached to the Central Committee of the Ukrainian CP.

Gavrail Savov was born in 1900 in Greece to a Bulgarian family. From the age of 17 he took part in the Bulgarian revolutionary movement and after the September Uprising was arrested, but was soon released and emigrated to Turkey. Between December 1923 and March 1924, using the alias 'Petŭr Alekseev', he had been part of the (G)RU network in Constantinople controlled by Traichev, and was then recalled to Moscow for some basic training before his next assignment in Bulgaria. Arrested there again in connection with the terrorist attack on St Nedelya Church in Sofia, organised by the Comintern and the Bulgarian Communist Party with the technical assistance provided by the (G)RU. Released in February 1926, he had been working undercover for the Comintern in several countries including Austria, and from 1932 to 1940 had been deployed by the (G)RU in Greece and Turkey.

Like many other Soviet military intelligence officers of the time, including the (G)RU director Arvīds Zeibots appointed in April 1921, Zvonarev was born in Latvia in 1892 as Kārlis Krišjānis Zvaigzne. In September 1920 he joined the Registrupr and in April 1921 was sent to Kovno as assistant military attaché in Lithuania together with Aralov. In December, Aralov invited him to join his staff in Turkey as military attaché and Zvonarev moved to Anakara also appointed chief legal resident of Soviet military intelligence, at which post he remained until April 1923 succeeded by Semyon M. Mirny (alias 'Yuri Yakovlev', codenamed ABDULLAH). Mirny/Yakovlev operated in Turkey as deputy head of the Commission for Repatriation and Soviet vice-consul.

In his memoirs about his work in Turkey published during the period of the so-called Khrushchev Thaw, Aralov names several of his fellow workers but for whatever reason avoids mentioning others. For example, there is not a single mention of Ivan Zalkind, a former deputy of Trotsky in the Narkomindel who had served as consul general in Constantinople (1922–3).[42] In November 1928 Zalkind committed suicide by shooting himself in Leningrad. There was also a very able chief of the legation's press bureau by the name of Georgy Astakhov, who arrived in March 1922. Astakhov would serve in Turkey again as a counsellor in 1930–3, then in London (1934–5), and as the Soviet chargé d'affaires in Berlin where he played a key role in the Soviet-German negotiations that a few months later resulted in the infamous Molotov-Ribbentrop (Soviet-Nazi) Pact. Astakhov, who left a very interesting diary recording many important details of the secret talks that took place in Berlin in the spring and summer of 1939, was arrested in February 1940 and died in a GULAG two years later. In his memoirs Aralov does mention Golub, who later served as first secretary of the legation but forgets Anatoly Glebov, second secretary (1921–3), whose book about first Soviet diplomats in Turkey came out in Moscow at the same time as Aralov's own work. Among intelligence officers serving at his embassy Aralov carefully names only Konstantin Zvonarev, military attaché, and R.L. Ginzburg, member of the office staff. In reality, Rebecca Ginzburg (born in Vitebsk, Byelorussia, in 1898) had served as head of the cipher department of the (G)RU headquarters in Moscow and then as chief cipher officer with the 12th Army in central Ukraine (1919–21), where Aralov was head of intelligence in July 1920. In Ankara Ginzburg worked as secretary of the residency and cipher clerk. She and Zvonarev both left Turkey together with Aralov and Zalkind in April 1923.

Besides Rebecca Ginzburg, Zvonarev's small station (operating 'from the legal positions', that is, under the official cover of the Soviet legation) included Minzakir Absalyamov, a Tatar who had served in Turkey since June 1920 with a small Soviet military mission to the Turkish government, also employed as an interpreter. In October 1922 he was appointed assistant resident after graduating from the military academy (where he studied by correspondence). Absalyamov would eventually become a general and scholar serving as secretary of the Military Academy's Academic Council in the 1960s. Another Tatar, Halil Chingiz-oglu Takanaev, likewise a military intelligence officer, was also stationed in Ankara as an interpreter of the legation.

A Latvian, Vladimir Aboltin (Vladimirs Āboltiņš), alias 'Avarin', served with Zvonarev in Turkey (August 1921–June 1922) before the (G)RU leadership sent him to the military academy where, among other things, he was learning Turkish expecting to return soon. Alas, his knowledge of the country and its language turned to be of no use because already in January 1925 he was sent as a special representative of the NKID and at the same time chairman of the state acceptance commission to the Far East when Japan agreed to transfer the northern district of Sakhalin Island to the Soviet Union. He then served as the Soviet consul general in Harbin, China, which boasted a large Russian community, with its own newspapers, journals, libraries, theatres and two opera companies. The American scholar Simon Karlinsky who was born in Harbin in 1924 into a Russian-Jewish family, observed:

Nor was Harbin 'a lifelike reconstruction of pre-revolutionary Russia on Chinese soil'—it had been a Russian city all along, one that had escaped the Revolution, the civil war, and Stalin's collectivization and had managed to keep well into the 1940s the high standard of living that typified Russia during the decade that preceded World War I. The only difference was the presence of numerous Chinese shopkeepers, itinerant vendors, artisans and servants. But it was they who had to learn to speak Russian or, rather, the amusing Russo-Chinese pidgin called 'Moya-tvoya,' originated by Chinese peddlers in Siberia in the nineteenth century, which became the lingua franca for Russo-Chinese transactions in Harbin.[43]

Repressed at the time of the Great Terror as a Japanese spy, Aboltin managed to survive and was rehabilitated in 1946, comfortably settled until the end of his days as a section head at the prestigious Moscow Institute of World Economy and International Relations. In one of his books Sudoplatov mentions him claiming that 'one of the leading analysts of the Intelligence Directorate of the Red Army before the war … back in 1940 Aboltin prepared a note to the leadership of the People's Commissariat of Defence on the inevitability of a surprise attack by the Japanese fleet on strategic facilities of Great Britain and the United States in the Far East'.[44] As expected, nobody took any notice.

A secretary of the acceptance commission in Sakhalin headed by Aboltin was Fedor Gaidarov, a military intelligence officer who served together with him in Turkey in 1920–2 using the alias 'Haidarzhi'. After a tour of duty in China (1926–7), he was again sent to Turkey working undercover in Constantinople and Smyrna (now Izmir), and then again in 1932–4 before being redirected to the G(RU) residency in Vienna.

Two officers of the (G)RU rezidentura headed by Zvonarev were seconded from the Separate Caucasian Army headquarters in Tbilisi: Serb Milan Pogorelov until December 1922 based in the Eastern Anatolia Region, and Alexey Gotovtsev who arrived in Turkey in January 1921. Gotovtsev's spy career abruptly ended when he was arrested by the British during a raid in July and expelled to Russia. He had briefly served at the (G)RU headquarters but was soon invited as a lecturer to the military academy (but not because his superiors had ever read Bernard Shaw – remember: those who can, do; those who can't, teach). No, simply Gotovtsev was one of the rare 'old guard' officers who had graduated from the Imperial Nicholas Military Academy (of the General Staff) shortly before the First World War and had served the Bolsheviks with all his heart and soul ever since. This fact, however, does not explain how he was able to survive Stalin's purges. In 1944, still teaching at the Academy, Gotovtsev was awarded a second Order of the Red Star and the Order of the Red Banner, retiring with the rank of lieutenant general in 1945.

Even before any official Soviet representative arrived in post-war Turkey, the naval intelligence department sent scouts to Constantinople in April, June and August 1919 to collect information on the Allied forces occupying the then capital of the Ottoman Empire.[45] The activities of the Allied military administration and specifically of the British and French troops and their intelligence services were of primary importance. At the time nobody knew of course of the existence of the recently created Political Intelligence Department (PID) headed by Sir William Tyrrell where Arnold Toynbee was in charge of the Ottoman affairs. Toynbee, who during his war service in the Propaganda Department published *The Murderous Tyranny of the Turk* (1917), was assisted by Robert Vansittart, who later became Permanent Under-Secretary.[46] The department employed sixteen experts, two of whom were Russia specialists, but for various reasons by the end of 1920 it had ceased to exist.

On 2 December 1921, when the new structure of the foreign department (INO) was approved by the VeCheKa leadership, its overseas section headed by Meer Trilisser consisted of six controllerates or departments. Similar to their British counterparts, these controllerates were responsible for security, requirements, production and natural cover (in the Cheka parlance – 'illegals'). The intelligence work was carried out by the stations (in the Cheka – 'rezidenturas' or residencies) in six geographical areas:

1. Northern section controlled the main residency in Stockholm and sub-residencies in Copenhagen, Helsingfors, Reval (Tallinn), Riga and Libava or Libau (during the interwar period – the second major city in Latvia, now Liepāja).
2. Polish section – main residency in Warsaw plus sub-residencies in Danzig also covering East Prussia with Königsberg, Galicia (now part of the Second Polish Republic) and Carpathian Ukraine.
3. Central European section was one of the most important with the main residency in Berlin and sub-residencies in Paris, Rome, Brussels, and a residency in London also working against the USA.
4. Southern European and Balkan section – main residency in Vienna and sub-residencies in Prague, Budapest, Belgrade, Sofia and Bucharest plus a small residency in Constantinople covering two Arab North African countries Egypt and Algeria.
5. Eastern section – this section's work against Turkey and Persia was controlled by the plenipotentiary representatives of the VChK and later GPU in North Caucasus and Transcaucasia; and against China, Mongolia and Japan – by the foreign section (INO) of the

plenipotentiary representative of the GPU at the Far Eastern region (former Far Eastern Republic) established in November 1922.[47]

6. American section – residencies in New York and Montreal (although until at least 1927 no Soviet intelligence activity had been recorded in North America).

As has already been stated in this and other studies, in the early and mid-1920s INO's chief target was the émigré White Guards, based mainly in Turkey, Bulgaria and in the Kingdom of the Serbs, Croats and Slovenes. With many senior officers later moving to Berlin, Paris, Brussels and Warsaw, they continued to plot – although far less effectively than Lenin and the Cheka supposed – the overthrow of the Bolshevik regime with direct and indirect support of the intelligence services of the Great Powers opposed to this regime.

In the first volume of *The Mitrokhin Archive* Christopher Andrew provides a short list of several former Tsarist generals who for various reasons decided to collaborate with the new Soviet government. Thus, in 1922 the Berlin residency recruited General Yevgeny Zelenin, 'as a penetration agent within the émigré community'.[48] Indeed, in 1921 the general returned to Russia and in October 1922, together with three other senior White Guard officers published an appeal 'To the soldiers and officers of the White armies' urging them to change sides and join the Red Army. A later OGPU report, noted by Mitrokhin, claimed with obvious exaggeration that Zelenin had engineered 'a huge schism within the ranks of the Whites' causing a large number of officers to break away from Baron Wrangel. The rest of the file was not copied. A brief review of the available documents reveals that in Moscow Zelenin was employed as a junior clerk at Maslocentre, the All-Russian Dairy Cooperative Society, when he was arrested on 14 August 1930, accused both of espionage and preparing armed insurrection, sentenced to death and shot in April 1931.

Mitrokhin's notes also mention 'other OGPU moles praised for their work in disrupting the White Guards – General Zaitsev, former chief of staff to the Cossack Ataman A.I. Dutov, and ex-Tsarist General Yakhontov'.[49] No more details are given.

Discussions about the post-revolutionary career of General Ivan Zaitsev continue until this day thanks to the new declassified documents from his OGPU file and the efforts of the Russian scholar Andrey Ganin from the Moscow Institute of Slavic Studies. A full volume can be written about the general's life and adventures, probably much more colourful than those of the famous British political officer and explorer Lieutenant Colonel F.M. Bailey, one of the last protagonists of the Anglo-Russian strategic contest known as the 'Great Game', who was in Tashkent and Bukhara together with the general.[50] Zaitsev did not accept the Bolshevik revolution and from October 1917 had been fighting against the new regime. Leading a detachment consisting of 700 Cossacks, he took Samarkand, one of the oldest cities in Central Asia, and was moving towards Tashkent, the capital of Uzbekistan, when his troops were defeated by stronger Bolshevik forces who also actively relied on subversion and propaganda. Zaitsev managed to escape but was caught, imprisoned in the Tashkent fortress (the city's name means 'Stone Fortress') and sentenced to death. Four months later, on 1 July 1918, a breakout was arranged by the anti-Bolshevik Turkestan Military Organisation and after a lot of troubles, including another brief arrest, he joined the forces of Ataman Dutov and was appointed chief of staff of his Orenburg Army in October 1919. After a series of unsuccessful military operations against the Reds, Dutov led his army first to Zhetysu (today part of Kazakhstan) and from there moved to China with a small force.

In February 1920 Zaitsev, now a general, was sent to Peking while General Dutov and his men would be quartered in Shuiding. The 1911 *Encyclopædia Britannica* described it as 'Suidun, a military town, with provision stores, an arsenal and an arms workshop. Its walls are armed with steel guns.'[51] Later, as the plenipotentiary representative of his commander and head of a military-diplomatic mission, General Zaitsev moved to Shanghai. On 17 February 1921 he telegraphed from Peking about his plans to travel to Europe.[52] Only later Zaitsev learnt that Dutov had been murdered ten days earlier by a group of nine assassins sent by the Cheka.

General Zaitsev returned to China, staying there for another two years and watching, as he noted in his diary, the development of conflict between Soviet Russia and Britain. Anglo-Russian strategic rivalry in Asia was, of course, nothing new but in 1923 the first evidence that the Bolsheviks were interested in exporting the proletarian revolution to East Asia came when Joffe signed an agreement with Sun Yat-sen, promising the leader of the Chinese nationalist party, the Kuomintang (KMT), to provide arms, money and military advisers. The condition was that in return the KMT would agree to form a united front with the – then small and insignificant – Chinese Communist Party against British, American and Japanese imperialists, as proclaimed by the Comintern at its 4th Congress.[53] At the end of the year Zaitsev applied to the Soviet legation in Peking for an amnesty.

Adolf Joffe left his post as Soviet diplomatic representative to China in June 1923 and was succeeded by Lev Karakhan who had served and would again serve as Deputy People's Commissar for Foreign Affairs before he was arrested, sentenced to death and shot on the same day in September 1937. In December 1923 Karakhan's head of the consular section was Aristarkh

Rigin (alias 'Rylski'), the INO legal resident in China undercover as attaché of the legation. At the same time, Yakov Davtyan (alias 'Davydov'), former short-lived head of the INO, was also there in charge of the Far Eastern section as the chief resident in China operating under the diplomatic cover of a counsellor. They decided that the amnesty and the subsequent return of the former general to the Soviet Russia would only be beneficial to Bolshevik propaganda efforts and Zaitsev duly left for Moscow in May 1924. There, on 25 October, he was arrested by the OGPU.

After four years in the Solovki special forced-labour camp on the Solovetsky Islands in the White Sea, the 'mother of the GULAG' as Solzhenitsyn called it, where the conditions for prisoners were absolutely inhumane, Zaitsev managed to escape in August 1928. Using forged documents, he illegally crossed the Chinese border at the end of February 1929.

One account, supported by Russian intelligence historians, suggests that the general upon his arrival in Moscow started to collaborate with the OGPU and his escape was staged, aimed to establish him in China as a penetration agent.[54] Another, a much more reliable version, promoted by his biographer Dr. Andrey Ganin and based on the archival documents, follows Zaitsev to Shanghai where he settled after his escape from Russia until his tragic death in November 1934 aged 56. Zaitsev hanged himself in his room at 24 Route Dollfuss in a deliberate act of suicide.[55] After reviewing in detail the posthumous letters and materials of the late general, the Bishop of China and Peking Victor (Svyatin), formerly an officer of the Orenburg Army, wrote: 'I see that the deceased was a highly religious person and a patriot of exceptional staunchness and fidelity, who set the goal of his life to effectively fight the oppressors of our Motherland – the communists.'[56]

Tsarist General Victor Yakhontov died in Moscow aged 97. In 1907 he graduated with honours from the Imperial Nicholas Military Academy of the General Staff and, promoted to major-general (1916), was sent as the Stavka representative to Britain and France, where he was awarded the highest French order of merit, the Legion of Honour. From October 1916 General Yakhontov served as the Russian military attaché in Japan, welcoming the February Revolution. Yakhontov soon left for Petrograd where his friend, General Alexander Verkhovsky, was appointed Minister of War of the Provisional Government. Yakhontov became his deputy. However, after the October Revolution he returned to Tokyo and Verkhovsky joined the Red Army. In August 1938, accused of 'sabotage, participation in an anti-Soviet military conspiracy, and preparation of terrorist acts against the leaders of the party and government', he was sentenced to death and shot.

In April 1919 General Yakhontov arrived in the USA where he settled later travelling around the country giving lectures against foreign interference in Soviet affairs and for the recognition of the Soviet Union. In 1933, he made a flying visit to Shanghai, then returned to America and published a book entitled *The Chinese Soviets*. A reviewer noted that the book 'contained much misinformation and told the world exactly nothing that was not known before, but the Stalinists hailed it as "authoritative"'.[57] In 1947–52 Yakhontov worked in the United Nations Secretariat and then edited (1953–75) the pro-Soviet newspaper *Russian Voice*, 'a Russian daily with the highest circulation in the United States and Canada', as its editors claimed, published in New York since 1917. In 1975 Yakhontov's petition for Soviet citizenship was granted and he moved to Moscow. In the Soviet Union of 'developed socialism' headed by Leonid Brezhnev, the former Tsarist general became an active member of the Society for Cultural Relations with Compatriots Abroad known as 'Rodina' or 'Motherland',[58] a GRU front with branches in Minsk, Kiev, and other Soviet capitals.

There were many other former Tsarist generals who joined the Bolsheviks, like Lieutenant General Yevgeny Dostovalov, who had been twice wounded during the Civil War and in December 1920 was one of the commanding officers of the 1st Army Corps quartered in Gallipoli, Turkey.[59] 'By 19 December 1920,' Anatol Shmelev writes, '26,596 people were counted to have descended on the sleepy little town of Gallipoli and the army encampment – soon named the Valley of Death – located a few miles further down the peninsula. Of these 23,518 were officers and soldiers, the rest wives and children.'[60] At the end of 1922, seduced by Bolshevik propaganda and promises, Dostovalov returned to Mother Russia of which the local newspaper of Novorossiysk, then the capital of the Black Sea Soviet Republic, informed its readers on 1 February 1923. In the Soviet Union Dostovalov published his memoirs *About the Whites and the White Terror* (1924).[61] Then, the general disappeared. It is only known that he was executed in 1938.

In his book *The White Army in Exile* (2002), Paul Robinson explains that living conditions in Gallipoli were crude and the White officers with their families barely survived on rations donated by the French government and other sponsors. Yet they referred to this as the 'Gallipoli miracle' when a sense of a 'spiritual and moral resurrection' renewed their determination to fight the Bolsheviks.[62] One of the best tents in the camp was shared by General Nikolai Skoblin and a popular Russian folksinger.

In 1902 Dezhka Vinnikova married a Warsaw State Theatre dancer, one Edmund Plevitsky, and became Nadezhda Plevitskaya. Ten years later, after a visit to the French Riviera, they amicably divorced and in November 1917 Plevitskaya married a 25-year-old lieutenant, Yuri Levitsky, in spite of the fact that for the previous three years she had been engaged to another young army officer named Vladimir Shangin. By late 1919, she separated from Levitsky and took Captain Yakov Pashkevich, an officer in the Second Kornilov Shock Regiment, as her next lover although after the seizure of southern Russia by the Red Army in the summer of 1920 little hope remained for a White victory. Plevitskaya was one of thousands of civilians who were trapped on the Crimea peninsula during these months, her biographer writes. 'Sometime in the early autumn, she started volunteering in a hospital in Simferopol. It was probably here that she began her final romance with Nikolai Skoblin, a young major general in the same Kornilov Shock Regiment.'[63] General Peter Wrangel, Commander-in-Chief of the White Forces of South Russia, now also in Gallipoli with his troops, relied for support on his chief of staff General Pavel Shatilov and commander of the 1st Army Corps General Alexander Kutepov, Skoblin's superior officers.

According to her latest biographer, Plevitskaya married Skoblin in the Gallipoli camp in June 1921 in a modest wedding attended by the top brass, with General Kutepov presiding over the ceremony and playing the father of the bride. General Skoblin, tall and good looking, was over a dozen years younger than Plevitskaya. As a condition of their marriage, Skoblin asked his bride to promise she would avoid politics. By the end of the year together with many other Wrangel officers they moved to Bulgaria. After much thought and hesitation, on 3 November 1921 the Central Executive Committee (VTsIK) issued an amnesty to those participants of the White movement 'who had been tricked or coerced into fighting the Soviets and could now return in the status of prisoners of war'.[64] Together with active propaganda efforts of the Union for Repatriation to the Motherland (Sovnarod) those measures were intended to lure White army officers and soldiers back to Russia to serve in the Red Army. What would happen to them after is another story, but according to the recently declassified Cheka documents, a report to Vasili Mantsev, one of the leaders of the Red Terror in Crimea, states that out of 1,100 White Guardists detained in Feodosia, 1,006 were shot. The exercise was repeated again, exactly two decades later, now the victims being wounded members of the Wehrmacht, brutally murdered by Soviet marines and regular infantry.[65] It became known as the Massacre of Feodosia.

In her diary written in a French prison, Plevitskaya recalled that her husband had some doubts about this amnesty and their chances of returning to Russia. Indeed, a careful reading of the text of the VTsIK decree of 3 November makes it clear that the document had little or nothing to do with the army of Wrangel in Turkey.[66] 'To announce a full amnesty to persons who participated in the military organisations of Kolchak, Denikin, Wrangel, Savinkov, Petlyura, Bulak-Balakhovich, Peremykin and Yudenich as ordinary soldiers, drawn into the struggle against Soviet power through deception or by force and who are currently in Poland, Romania, Estonia, Lithuania and Latvia,' it said. Turkey was not mentioned.

Both Plevitskaya and Skoblin heard that General Yakov Slashchev, who lived in Constantinople and was at loggerheads with Baron Wrangel and his staff, agreed to return, and arrived in Sevastopol with his wife and several senior officers. From there they were promptly transported to Moscow in the personal railway carriage sent by Dzerzhinsky. Plevitskaya and Skoblin also read Slashchev's 'Appeal to the remnants of the White armies' of 21 November published in *Izvestia* and distributed among the Russian émigrés. In his address the former general demanded subordination to Soviet authorities in order to protect and safeguard the Motherland and its people from foreign invaders, which he considered his moral duty.

Until recently, no one knew what really happened to Slashchev and his people before and after they arrived in Russia.

* * *

After their retreat from Crimea, of which both the Cheka and (G)RU agents reported in detail in mid-November 1920, about 100,000 well-organised and disciplined Wrangel troops arrived in Constantinople. Here, they were reorganised into three army corps quartered at Gallipoli, the Greek island of Lemnos in the northern part of the Aegean Sea, and at Çatalca near Constantinople, a green area in East Thrace, on the ridge between the Marmara and the Black Sea. Part of the Imperial Russian Navy, warships of the Black Sea Fleet were interned in the French naval base of Bizerta in Tunisia. In Lenin's and Trotsky's view, this army still represented a formidable force and, backed by Britain and France, could mount a serious challenge to Bolshevik rule. 'A beaten enemy,' Lenin declared, 'learns much.' In his keynote address to the Comintern congress, speaking about the anti-Bolshevik Russian émigrés, Lenin stressed that 'these counter-revolutionaries are very well informed, excellently organised and good strategists'.[67] Therefore, the primary military strategies of the Bolshevik leadership regarding the Wrangel troops in Turkey were intimidation and subversion. The Cheka and Razvedupr were given the task of breaking the adversary's will to continue fighting using various means but first of all by luring their leaders back to Russia.

The Slashchev operation was one of the very first of this kind, its obvious success leading to many other similar setups including the well-known elaborate deception operations like TREST and SINDIKAT, described in detail in many published sources.[68] In the following years, the Cheka actions became bolder with the methods varying from threats and blackmail to kidnapping and assassination.

In the spring of 1921, a conference chaired by Menzhinsky was held at the Lubyanka headquarters with the top brass including Timofey Samsonov, Georgy Blagonravov, Genrikh Yagoda, Artur Artuzov (then still Menzhinsky's assistant) and Zinovy Katznelson.[69] The agenda was clearly formulated as subversion of the White Army in Turkey, that is, undermining of General Wrangel's authority, incitement of discontent and if possible rebellion against the leadership parallel to various communist propaganda activities. Judging by the Cheka officials present, the task was taken very seriously.

This conference was preceded by a report signed by Alexander Eiduk, an old revolutionary and former member of the Cheka Collegium.[70] Eiduk informed about two German refugees, Hans Homeyer and Emil Prosche, who were evacuated from the Crimea together with the Wrangel troops and were now sent by General Slashchev to Berlin to contact the Bolshevik representatives. Eiduk referred to the report by one Borodovsky at the Soviet trade mission in Berlin, who personally talked to them and with whom the German couriers were in contact.

General Slashchev's appeal soon reached the Politburo and after a while Berlin was instructed to inform Slashchev and his people that the Soviet government was ready to forgive repentant former enemies and give them the opportunity to atone for their guilt.

Based on agents' reports and information from the émigré newspapers as well as from Soviet legations in Berlin and Angora (Ankara), it had already been decided that a famed defender of the Crimea, a White army hero of the Battle of Perekop, Lieutenant-General Yakov Slashchev, would probably be the most promising candidate to lure back to Russia to achieve the best propaganda effect. Although Baron Wrangel had granted him general's rank and the honorary title 'Krymsky' (Crimean), he and Slashchev were in a state of permanent conflict because Slashchev considered his commander-in-chief the main culprit for the defeat of the White army. As a result, Slashchev was removed from the command of the corps, and under a far-fetched pretext tried by a military court of honour. This remarkable piece of legislation was first introduced by the Russian Tsar Alexander III in 1894 for the societies of officers in military units and detailed in a brochure published shortly before the war.[71] General Wrangel, who was particularly fond of images of knights and chivalry, re-established courts of honour in the White army in July 1920.[72] As a result, Slashchev was stripped of his rank and even denied the right to wear a military uniform. He was also excluded from the list of the Russian army which, among other things, deprived him of any financial support. Finally, he was strongly advised to leave Constantinople as soon as possible.

Slashchev, however, did not obey but instead started wearing his old colonel's uniform of the Moscow Life Guards Regiment, the rank granted to him by the Russian tsar, and refused to vacate his apartment in the Skutari (now Üsküdar) area. Senior officers close to the disgraced general continued visiting him and, according to some reports, they were discussing plans for the removal of the commander-in-chief. To add fuel to the flames, Slashchev continued working on the book, later published in the Soviet Union under the title *Crimea 1920* (Moscow-Leningrad, 1924) where he criticised the Volunteer Army which fought against the Bolsheviks on the Southern Front and the White generals, including Baron Wrangel.

Probably because it was one of the first operations (later repeated several times) considered to be very high profile, it was personally supervised by Jósef Unszlicht, Dzerzhinsky's deputy, on behalf of the Cheka and controlled by Trotsky as Commissar of Military and Naval Affairs with Chicherin in the know and even taking part.

In May, the Cheka intercepted a letter written by one Fedor Batkin from Constantinople and addressed to an actor friend who worked in Simferopol at the local theatre. Batkin was a former Socialist Revolutionary (SR), who in 1910 left Russia fearing arrest for his revolutionary activities. He then studied in Liège, volunteered for the small Belgian army known for its low pay, poor living and bad welfare conditions, taking part in the war where he was wounded several times, and returned to Russian in 1917 just before the February Revolution. Batkin again volunteered to the front and was awarded the Cross of Saint George 4th class. Sent by Admiral Kolchak to Petrograd at the head of a propaganda unit and from that time wearing the uniform of the Imperial Russian Navy, Batkin had also served at the OSVAG, the propaganda and information service of the Volunteer Army, before emigrating to Turkey together with his brother. Here he became a journalist close to General Slashchev and officers from his inner circle.

It turned out that the man to whom Batkin sent a letter explaining that Slashchev was ready to return to his homeland and voluntarily surrender himself to Soviet authorities together with his friends had been recruited by the Cheka. As soon as this information reached Moscow, Unszlicht sent one of his trusted officers, like himself a Pole named Jan Tannenbaum (alias 'Yelski'), to the Crimea to be secretly transported to Turkey to assist Slashchev and his men make their escape. At the same time, on 19 June 1921 the Politburo accepted Chicherin's proposal and decided 'to recognise as principally permissible the return of some members of the Wrangel army to the RSFSR and for that matter to set up a commission with powers to receive the applicants in Russia'.

It seems that parallel to the Cheka efforts, the (G)RU was also instructed to work on the same problem because on 6 October Trotsky was informed that a Ukrainian (G)RU officer arrived in Moscow with new proposals regarding the exfiltration of the Slashchev group from Turkey. To be on the safe side and demonstrate the success of his service, Zeibot, the (G)RU director, also sent a written report to Lenin informing him of the situation and asking for further instructions. In his turn, Lenin proposed to create a commission of Kamenev, Stalin and Voroshilov to discuss the matter with Dashevsky (the Ukrainian officer), in order to make the right decision.[73] All this had to be done on the same day without delay.

According to Soviet tradition, which is still strictly observed, Slashchev's return was timed to coincide with a memorable date. The group, which consisted of the general, his new wife Nina (the general's former orderly) with her brother, accompanied by Major General Alexander Milkovsky, Colonel Eduard Eberhard Hilbich, Colonel Mstislav Mezernitsky, Captain B.N. Voinakhovsky (Wojnachowski) and Batkin's brother Anisim, arrived in the Soviet Russia on 7 November 1921, the fourth anniversary of the Bolshevik revolution.[74] Three days later Slashchev was interrogated at the Lubyanka Cheka HQ for the first time.

An eight-point plan worked out by Trotsky and Unszlicht for Slashchev and two other senior officers included squeezing from them all useful military and political information, especially concerning British and French plans to collaborate with the Whites against the Bolsheviks, which could be further used by Chicherin's commissariat as a political lever in their diplomatic work. But most important was writing memoirs revealing ithe nsidious designs of the world bourgeoisie with scathing rebukes of General Wrangel's leadership, which was delivered in due course.

Slashchev was commissioned as an officer of the Red Army and soon became a lecturer at the Military Academy of the RKKA. However, due to multiple complaints from the cadets and staff, in June 1922 he was moved to the Vystrel officer training course, about 40 miles north-west from Moscow, teaching infantry tactics to future company commanders. The former White general met his inglorious end here, at the village of Solnechnaya Gora ('Sunny Hill'), on 11 January 1929. A young cadet from Moscow named Lazar Kohlenberg fired three shots point-blank at Slashchev right in his room. The body was cremated four days later. After they had investigated the case for six months, the OGPU found the assassin not guilty on the grounds that he was temporarily insane when he'd killed the general. Kohlenberg was released and the file sent to the archive.

* * *

Born Anna Louise Mohan, a young girl from rural Nevada began to use the last name of her stepfather, Bryant, rather than that of her real parent.

Leaving her first husband in 1915, Louise Bryant married a fellow journalist whose name was John Reed, and went with him to Petrograd and Moscow to witness the revolution. A collection of articles from her trip, dedicated to her husband ('that beloved vagabond'), was published in 1918 as *Six Red Months in Russia* by George H. Doran Company in New York. That was several months before her husband's first-hand account of the October Revolution, *Ten Days that Shook the World*, came out in January almost immediately to become a classic. Reed died of typhus in Moscow in 1920, disillusioned by what he saw in Russia after three years of proletarian dictatorship, as Louise put it in her book, and she returned to the United States, soon to become the mistress of William C. Bullitt. Bullitt was a US diplomat who took part in the Paris Peace Conference in 1919 but resigned from the Department of State in protest to the terms of the Versailles Peace Treaty and divorced his wife to live with Bryant.

While she had still been in Russia, Louise met several important Turkish personalities among whom were Ali Fuat Cebesoy, the ambassador, who arrived in February 1921 shortly before the Kronstadt rebellion, and Ismail Enver Pasha. Enver was one of the leaders of the Committee of Union and Progress (CUP) and served as the Ottoman Minister of War before he was dismissed in October 1918. When the Ottoman Empire capitulated after the defeat in the First World War, its leaders – Enver Pasha, Talaat Pasha and Cemal Pasha – fled into exile. Enver went to Germany where, according to Masayuki Yamauchi, he met Karl Radek in order to establish contacts with the Bolsheviks. In April 1919 he left Berlin for Moscow as one of the secret envoys of his friend, General Hans von Seeckt, who in 1917 used to serve as Chief of Staff of the Ottoman Army and was now eager to work with the Soviets. After a series of delays, 'involving air crashes, emergency landings and periods of imprisonment, he arrived in August 1920'.[75] But in between, starting from early January 1920 at least until the end of February Enver had been regularly meeting Major Ivor Hedley of the British Military Mission in Berlin.

While working hard to establish a military alliance between the Weimar Republic and Soviet Russia, Enver Pasha was also intriguing with the British. During his talks with Hedley, he admitted that he was going to Moscow to work with the Bolsheviks 'simply and solely to stir up insurrection against Britain throughout its Muslim possessions':

> However, he said, he had decided to delay his departure for a few days, as he was extremely anxious to work with Britain rather than with Bolshevik Russia. He wanted Egyptian independence to be extended to the Sudan, and an Anglo-Egyptian treaty concluded; self-determination

to be granted throughout Arabia, and the settlement of the Izmir and Thrace questions in Turkey's favour. If Britain came to terms with him, he would remain in Berlin until everything was finally settled. He would definitely break off negotiations with Moscow, and would then travel to the East where his presence would be essential if the feelings towards Britain were to be entirely changed.[76]

According to a secret British report dated 3 February 1920, in addition to helping General von Seeckt to establish contacts with the Bolsheviks, Enver was trying 'to unite the Arab, Turkish and Egyptian movements so as to consolidate all efforts before he undertook "the invasion" of Asia Minor and Azerbaijan with "Bolshevik army". He even sought the sympathy of Emir Feisal, who was amenable, but who would take no definite action until such time as "the independence of Arabia and Syria was recognised by Russia, and by the Sultan of Turkey"'.[77] The 'Bolshevik army' had been promised to Enver by Trotsky.

After one of the final meetings with Enver at the end of February, Hedley wrote to his superior, Major General Sir Neill Malcolm, Chief of the British Military Mission in Berlin: 'Even if we were prepared to stoop to treating with a man whom we regard as a criminal, it would do us no good. The CUP and the Bolshevists will work together, whatever Enver may say, and if we made terms with Enver, we should only give him more prestige to use against us.'[78]

In a letter to Cemal Pasha of 26 February, Enver said he was still hoping to be able to work 'for the salvation of the Turkish and Muslim world' but when the British bluntly turned him down he went to Moscow, staying there until spring 1921. During that time, he met Bryant and even taught her to count from one to ten in Turkish.[79] Whether he also used her as a courier is not known but it is recorded that before she left Russia she had visited Baku, Bukhara and Central Asia – all of them centres of Turkic activities. In her second book on Russia, *Mirrors of Moscow*, published in New York in 1923, Bryant devoted a chapter to Enver Pasha and the Mohammedans. 'No man I ever met lives so completely in the immediate moment as Enver Pasha,' she wrote, 'the past he puts behind him, the future he leaves to Allah.' Enver was not able to read what she wrote because according to a reliable report he was killed in a Red Army cavalry charge following a surprise attack on his military camp near Dushanbe,[80] Tajikistan, in August 1922.

The International News Service, a US news agency part of the Hearst Press empire, sent Bryant to Constantinople to report on Turkey and Bullitt decided to accompany her on this assignment. They travelled on the Orient Express from Venice, arriving in Constantinople on 22 April 1923. On the way to Venice, Bryant interviewed Benito Mussolini in Rome and then Gabriele D'Annunzio in Fiume, hoping to be able to interview Mustafa Kemal as well. After some weeks at the Tokatlian Hotel in Pera, Bullitt, who came from a prominent Philadelphia family (the law firm founded by his grandfather still exists and after its 2020 merger with another US law firm ranks among the largest law firms in the USA), moved with Bryant into a famed seventeenth-century mansion on the Asiatic shore of the Bosphorus. Louise kept a room at the Tokatlian as an office and here she met and befriended Ernest Hemingway, then reporting on Turkey as a foreign correspondent for the *Toronto Star* and residing in another of the best hotels in Pera, Hotel Buyuk Londra.[81] It is still there, now better known under its French name as the Grand Hotel de Londres. Meanwhile, Bullitt was busy writing his own book, which became a bestseller after it came out in 1926. Bryant and Bullitt were married in Paris in December 1923, their daughter Anne being born two months later in their rented Paris residence.

In early June 1923, Bryant briefly visited Angora (Ankara) hoping that after the publication of *Mirrors of Moscow*, Mustafa Kemal would be happy to meet her. Her friend and admirer from their days in Moscow, Ali Fuat Cebesoy, now lived alone in the capital and she believed he would be able to arrange an interview. She also met other important members of the National Assembly and visited the US chancery where she was welcomed by Consul Blake. Another fellow countryman whom Bryant could meet was Robert Whitney Imbrie, now in Angora with his young wife.

Imbrie served as vice-consul arriving in Russia in November 1917, and when the embassy moved to Moscow Consul General Maddin Summers ordered him to return to Petrograd to observe and report on the situation.[82] Thus, information for US intelligence and the Department of State had been collected by the agent networks formed and controlled by Kalamatiano in Moscow and by Imbrie in Petrograd. He arrived in the city on 5 April 1918, staying there for five months as a sole US representative in the Russian northern capital. At the end of August, having learnt of his imminent arrest, he managed to move to Viborg, Finland, where, under the diplomatic cover of vice-consul, Imbrie continued to collect political as well as military information.[83] In other words, as one of his biographers claimed, he established and operated 'a reconnaissance service for investigation in Soviet Russia',[84] also working to provide food relief to thousands of Russian émigrés.

Imbrie remained in Finland until June, leaving after his cover was blown. Following a brief assignment in Crimea and Constantinople, from March 1922 he was stationed in Ankara. Here, his mission was to establish American diplomatic and commercial influence and, according to Sir Horace Rumbold, the British High Commissioner for Constantinople, to combat

Soviet influence in Ankara and to pave the way for American economic penetration of Anatolia. Reports from Turkey suggested that 'he succeeded in gaining the confidence and good will of the Angora [Ankara] leaders in an unusual measure', demonstrating 'exceptional capacity for dealing with perplexing and perhaps dangerous situations in out of the way places'.[85] Allen W. Dulles, at the time chief of the Near East division of the Department of State, was especially proud of Imbrie whom he considered a personal friend.

In Ankara, Imbrie met Katherine Helene Gillespie, an American relief worker whom he married on Boxing Day, 26 December 1922. Shortly before Bryant reached the city, the American press reported: 'Robert Imbrie, described as "delegate of the American High Commission to Angora" lives with his wife in a railway passenger car, which he has converted into a "model apartment" … The wife of Mustapha [sic] Kemal Pasha is a frequent visitor to the perambulating residence of the United States Representative.'[86] The idea of transforming a railway passenger car into an off-grid home came to Imbrie due to Ankara's dire shortage of housing.

Whether Bryant and Imbrie ever met in Ankara is not documented although it is quite possible, almost certain, because regardless of her new status they had a lot of memories to share. Besides, his official position as a US representative and 'intelligence collector' would oblige him to meet such a prominent visitor. There could have been other considerations, too, as shortly after she took the train back to Constantinople on 19 June having stayed in Ankara for ten days, Imbrie was recalled to Washington 'to answer charges that he had endangered the life of Louise Bryant, widow of John Reed and wife of William Bullitt, by denouncing her to the Turks as a Bolshevik', as newly discovered documents reveal.[87] If true, he probably did it on his own initiative.

It had been noted that Imbrie often allowed his personal opinion to colour his reports. 'As with virtually all other Department of State officials in Russia in 1918,' David A. Langbart comments, 'he had an extreme, almost visceral, dislike of the Bolsheviks and expected their momentary collapse. His experiences in Petrograd did nothing to lessen that attitude. Indeed, they probably exacerbated it.' [88] Bryant's Moscow correspondence with Karl von Wiegand, another Hearst Press reporter based in Berlin during and after the First World War, was intercepted by GC&CS and shared with the US embassy from where it was sent to the Department of State and MID. One of the secret intelligence reports commenting her wireless dispatch to Wiegand in Berlin with details on the case of Marguerite Harrison describes Bryant as 'a well-known American radical agitator' and Wiegand as 'extremely pro-German, in fact, no more or less than a German agent'.[89] After meeting Bryant in Ankara Imbrie would not hesitate to report her to the authorities, being well-informed about her activities in Russia at the time of the Bolshevik revolution, as well as about her high-level contacts in Moscow. Anyway, nothing happed and after cooling his heels for some time, Imbrie was assigned to Tabriz, Iran, to reopen a consulate and build a network of reliable sources on the recently established Soviet Union.

Dulles, a future Director of the CIA who in 1921 had served at the US embassy in Constantinople, wrote that sending a man of Imbrie's rather impetuous disposition to countries like Iran was taking a certain risk. 'The only question is,' he reasoned, 'as to whether the advantages to be gained would justify this risk. I am rather inclined to think they would.'[90] The gamble failed and on 18 July 1924 Vice-Consul Imbrie was attacked and killed by a fanatical mob. 'Naturally, in view of his anti-Soviet background, the question of Communist complicity in the attack on Imbrie was raised,' Michael Zirinsky writes. 'Despite rumours that the Bolsheviks had put a $40,000 (gold) price on his head, the State Department could find no evidence of Bolshevik culpability. All the evidence pointed solely to Iranian responsibility, abetted by Imbrie's bad judgment.'[91] At the same time the historian notes the British government was informed that 'Mr. Imbrie was murdered at Bolshevik instigation'.

Bryant and Bullitt moved to Paris in December 1923. By 1926 she was drinking heavily suffering from Decrum's disease, a rare condition that can cause severe pain. In July that year the head of the Cheka known in Russia as 'Iron Felix' died. In her book Bryant calls him 'Fedore S. Dzerzhinsky, a man [who] can sign away life with an unruffled firmness'. Bullitt divorced her in 1930, winning sole custody of their daughter, and in 1933 President Roosevelt appointed him the first US ambassador to the Soviet Union. Bryant died in the suburbs of Paris in January 1936 and was not much remembered for five decades before a series of books about her life appeared including the latest, pretentiously entitled *Queen of Bohemia*, by Mary Dearborn.

* * *

The KGB historians still number among the greatest past triumphs of the Lenin's secret police deception operations against the White Guards after the Civil War. Several of them, including the two most praised – codenamed TREST and SINDIKAT – figure prominently in many published works related to the history of the KGB, its predecessors and successors, written by various authors and intelligence historians in many languages over the past hundred years. Describing those past achievements of the Cheka, many writers forget that the most dangerous foe the young Bolshevik state was facing at that time was not the White Guards, international counter-revolutionaries or

Russian émigrés scattered through foreign countries. Even before the March Action in Germany, the priority was not the spread of the Revolution but the saving of the Soviet regime at home. Lenin's announcement in his closing remarks to the delegates – 'I think the [10th] Party Congress will have to draw the conclusion that the opposition's time has run out, that's it, we want no more oppositions'[92] – was merely a propaganda ploy. By that time large areas of the Russian countryside were swept by famine, the worst Europe had ever known, the country's industry was close to collapse, more than 60 per cent of its railway network and over 80 per cent of the carriages and locomotives had been destroyed, and in February 1921 the Cheka reported 118 separate peasant uprisings quickly spreading through the country. The opposition had no hand in all that.

'The fiercest and most stubborn of these revolts,' Seth Singleton comments, 'occurred in the province of Tambov, 250 miles south-east of Moscow in the centre of Russia's bread-basket.'[93] In January 1921, bread rations were cut by as much as 30 per cent, angry and hungry workers of Petrograd went on strike, and demonstrations quickly turned into protests devolving into riots. One Cheka report from January described the famine sweeping over Tambov Province, attributing it to the unrestricted grain requisitioning of the previous year. The Tambov revolt, led by one Alexander Antonov, a former Socialist Revolutionary (SR) with a somewhat murky past, soon spread far and wide with a large number of volunteers joining his 'people's army'. In Petrograd, Cheka detachments had to be dispatched to restore order and in late February martial law was declared. A week before the 10th Communist Party Congress, the Kronstadt naval base near Petrograd rebelled against what they called the 'communist autocracy'; the revolt continued after the Congress closed on Wednesday, 16 March.

Both uprisings were ruthlessly supressed by the Red Army under the command of Mikhail Tukhachevsky. In February, the Plenipotentiary Commission for the Liquidation of Banditry in Tambov Province was formed, headed by Vladimir Antonov-Ovseyenko who had formerly been in charge of this province (guberniya). Born in Ukraine to the family of an infantry officer, he chose a military career, entering the St Petersburg Infantry Cadet School in 1902, where he soon joined the revolutionaries thanks to Boris Stomonyakov. John Reed mentioned Antonov-Ovseyenko in *Ten Days that Shook the World* as one of the leaders of the revolutionary uprising in Petrograd in October 1917. In his report to Lenin about his work in Tambov, Atonov-Ovseyenko stated: 'The Red Terror was harshly applied but the bandit terror was stronger still.'[94] An army of 100,000 under Tukhachevsky mounted a campaign of terror that included the use of heavy artillery and aircraft against what the Bolsheviks called 'bandits', mopping up the last pockets of resistance by the autumn of 1921.[95] Antonov himself remained at large for another year only to be killed in a Cheka ambush in June 1922.

The reprisals against the Kronstadt mutineers began early in the morning of 18 March. On the night of 29/30 March, a search all over the place 'yielded satisfactory results'. A report of the Kronstadt Special Section dated 30 March states that in Kronstadt, which is located on an island, 48 informers were recruited and 3,154 arrests made. The statistical communique of the Special Section of the Extraordinary Troikas of 1 May, according to the latest research by Israel Getzler of the Hebrew University of Jerusalem, gives the following figures: 6,528 arrested, of whom 2,168 had been shot and 1,955 sentenced to forced labour (with 1,486 getting a five-year sentence). Reportedly, some 1,272 were released. A later review of the mutiny raises the number of arrested to 10,026. Trotsky hosted the victory parade 'of the heroes of Kronstadt' with Tukhachevsky saluting the Red Army cadets who had acted as the Praetorian Guard of the regime in the Kronstadt events.[96] Around 8,000 people were able to flee across the ice to Finland. A hundred years later, writing about the crushing of the Kronstadt Uprising and the fate of those who remained, the Radio Liberty author described it under the self-explanatory title 'Shot like Partridges'.[97]

The Bolshevik leadership had been receiving Cheka reports of the monstrous famine sweeping the country since the beginning of 1921. In modern estimates, it ranked second among the ten worst famines of the twentieth century. The famine emanated from the traditionally drought-prone Volga region and reached east into the Urals, west into the Ukraine, and south into Transcaucasia covering the area with the population of approximately 37.5 million people.[98] Yet any official mention of it was forbidden at least until mid-July 1921. The 'investigation' ordered by the authorities concluded that only the central provinces – Ryazan, Kaluga, Oriol, Tula and Tsaritsyn governorates – faced real danger of famine.[99] On 17 February, without any official announcement, the All-Russian Central Executive Committee (VTsIK, the highest legislative, administrative and revising body of the country), created the 'behind-the-scenes' Commission for Famine Relief to Rural Population of the several famine-stricken provinces. In March, 'War Communism' was replaced by the NEP, which excited some Western observers while others noted that the key agricultural provisions of the NEP had nothing to do with direct famine relief. 'The replacement of grain requisitioning by a fixed taxation rate and the privilege of freely disposing of surpluses,' Charles M. Edmondson notes, 'meant nothing to those peasants faced with starvation ... Perhaps the NEP stimulated recovery in those areas unaffected by famine and eased urban hunger, but within the

famine zone itself the grim march of hunger and epidemic was unimpeded.'
According to Professor Edmondson:

> By promising to end grain requisitioning, however, NEP smoothed
> tempers and erased the most obvious causal link between the regime
> and the famine. In its relationship to the famine, then, NEP could best
> be characterized as a political *cordon sanitaire* thoroughly compatible
> with the refusal to attempt conventional famine relief.[100]

In June, several Russian public figures contacted Maxim Gorky (literary
pseudonym of Alexey M. Peshkov), a famous Russian and Soviet writer, five
times nominated for the Nobel Prize in Literature, with the suggestion to
form a public committee for famine relief. Among those figures were Sergey
Prokopovich, a well-known Russian economist, former minister of trade and
industry in the second coalition government and then minister for food in
the third coalition government (both chaired by Alexander Kerensky), and his
wife Ekaterina Kuskova.[101] They became acquainted with Gorky in Nizhny
Novgorod long before the revolution. In due course at the end of June Gorky
submitted his proposal to the Politburo. On 18 July 1921 the chairman of the
VTsIK Mikhail Kalinin signed a decree establishing the Central Commission
for Famine Relief as an expanded version of the previous commission.[102] CC
Pomgol, as it was known, was subject to oversight by the VTsIK.

A week earlier, the Patriarch of Moscow and All-Russia Tikhon (Vasili
Bellavin) addressed an appeal to the Archbishop of Canterbury (head of
the Church of England) and the Archbishop of New York. A great part of
Russia's population, he wrote, is doomed to death by hunger. Famine breeds
epidemics. Most generous aid needed immediately. All other considerations
must be cast aside, the Patriarch begged.

On 13 July Maxim Gorky (read: the Bolshevik government) through
the Narkomindel channels sent a telegram to Fridtjof Nansen, a famous
Norwegian polymath – explorer, scientist, diplomat and humanitarian –
serving as the League of Nations' High Commissioner for Refugees, soon
to be awarded the Nobel Peace Prize for his work on behalf of the displaced
victims of the First World War. Entitled 'To All Honest People', Gorky's
appeal described the Russian people as 'exhausted by war and revolution
which reduced considerably its resistance to disease and its physical
endurance'. Saying not a word about capitalist predators and exploiters of the
toiling masses, Gorky stressed that he believed 'particularly warm sympathy
in succouring the Russian people must be shown by those who, during
the ignominious war, so passionately preached fratricidal hatred, thereby
withering the educational efficacy of ideas evolved by mankind in the most

arduous labours and so lightly killed by stupidity and cupidity'. He ended his
telegram by asking 'all honest European and American people for prompt aid
to Russian people. Give bread and medicines!'

The texts of both appeals were immediately reported to the Department
of State by Albert Schmedeman, then serving as the US Minister to Norway.
After duly consulting the US diplomat, on the next day Dr Nansen sent a
reply to Gorky that was also attached to the report. It said:

> Have received your impressive telegram. Only people who can help
> materially now are Americans who have done unique charity work
> during and after war but serious obstacle will be that American citizens
> are retained in Russia and in Russian prisons. Must therefore most
> urgently advise that they are released at once otherwise I fear you cannot
> expect much help from America. I am doing all I can to send food at
> once. Signed: Fridtjof Nansen.[103]

Meanwhile, the Bolshevik leadership including Lenin, Trotsky and
Dzerzhinsky, but especially Lenin, were principally against the Commission
because it was public (only twelve of its delegates represented the authorities,
united in a 'communist cell', while sixty-one members were representing
non-Bolshevik intelligentsia and academia), and because it quickly became
apparent to the Commission members that effective famine relief depended
upon acquiring foreign assistance. For reasons explained in the next chapter
they thought Sweden would be their first port of call and even made
arrangements for a Pomgol Commission delegation to go to Stockholm.
However, the Cheka intervened and in the morning of 27 August 1921 the
Commission was disbanded on Lenin's demand.[104] His instruction to Stalin
and the Politburo in this regard first of all mentioned the 'impudent' proposal
by Nansen.

* * *

The story of how America saved the Soviet Union (actually, Bolshevik Russia)
from famine is largely forgotten, save for *The Russian Job* (2019) by Douglas
Smith and a couple of articles in academic journals. In the meantime, the
American famine relief efforts in Russia in the early 1920s were preceded by
a cobweb of intrigues, shifting alliances and political games.

From 1918 to 1920 the situation in Russia was becoming steadily worse
and by the spring of 1920 all signs of food shortages and devastating famine
had already been clearly in sight. As early as June 1918, a group of prominent
American politicians discussed a possibility of establishing a special 'Russia

Relief Commission'. They followed in the footsteps of the American Friends Service Committee (AFSC) composed of six women that arrived in Russia in July 1917. Travelling via Japan, they proceeded to Vladivostok and from there by the Trans-Siberian Railway to Buzuluk on the Samara River, where they joined British Friends already working there.[105]

The above-mentioned group of four American officials consisted of Vance McCormick, who began his career as a journalist and publisher, and later served as President Woodrow Wilson's 1916 campaign manager and Chairman of the War Trade Board, William Redfield from New York, an unsuccessful candidate for nomination as Vice President of the United States and appointed Secretary of Commerce, Robert Lansing, a conservative pro-British Democrat who served as Secretary of State from 1915 to 1920, and finally, Edward House from Houston, Texas, better known as Colonel House, an adviser, close friend and supporter of President Wilson. According to Charles M. Edmondson, they perceived the Relief Commission 'as an instrument of American influence, both political and economic, as an alternative to armed intervention in Russia, and as a means of preventing the spread of Bolshevism'.[106] Fear of Bolshevism and its expansion was one of the most prominent motives of their actions. In February 1919, William Bullitt accompanied by Lincoln Steffens, the journalist, made an unofficial tour of investigation in Russia commissioned by Colonel House who required first-hand information on conditions there. On 17 April, McCormick, Redfield, Lansing and House agreed that a 'neutral' relief commission, headed by Nansen and supplied by the American Relief Administration (ARA), could provide food for Russia. The brainchild of Herbert Hoover, the ARA, formed by the US Congress in February that year, had a budget of about US$200 million and all facilities and organisation in place to alleviate starvation in Russia. However, they said, food could be provided only upon specified conditions.

The proposal was sent by Nansen and reached Moscow on 4 May 1919. 'The Council of Four stipulated that Russian transport must be placed under the supervision of the "neutral" relief commission; the distribution of food must be vested not in the government but in the "Russian people of each locality"; and all hostilities, troop movements, and shipments of military supplies must be stopped.'[107] In the words of Charles Edmondson, to put it mildly these conditions were not designed to benefit the Bolsheviks and in his reply Chicherin castigated them as 'a perversion of charity'. In his turn, Lenin labelled these and similar proposals by Nansen as 'impudent' or 'brazen'.

Eventually, the American relief mission to Russia can be recognised as a purely humanitarian act. Whatever was initially planned or discussed, the US government did not intend to conduct a new intervention in Russia in the form of famine relief, which can be seen in Herbert Hoover's secret instructions to all ARA representatives there. In his letter to Walter Brown, the ARA's director for Europe, whose negotiations with Litvinov in Riga ended by an agreement and the Russian Famine Relief Act of 1921 passed by the US Congress in December, Hoover demanded that he abstain entirely 'not only from action but even from discussion of political and social questions'.[108] For two years, in what was (and still remains) one of the largest humanitarian operations in history, the ARA fed over ten million men, women and children across a million square miles of territory. Its efforts, the latest research seeks to prove, 'prevented a catastrophe of incalculable proportions – the loss of millions of lives, social unrest on a massive scale, and, quite possibly, the collapse of the Soviet state.'[109] As usual, there exists an opposite view, claiming that the charity funds set up by Hoover and the ARA to relieve the crisis in Russia were being covertly looted, at least partially, to help the anti-Bolshevik White forces restore the Tsarist regime in its previous incarnation.

The first part of this charge seems to be well founded. The evidence was produced by Senator Thomas E. Watson (D) in June 1922. During the discussion of the total children's relief deliveries paid for from the congressional fund for relief, Senator Watson asked to speak. 'It now appears,' he said, 'that England, France, and the United States entered into a secret agreement at the peace conference in Paris [1919–20] to support a revolution in Russia by equipping Kolchak, Youdenich [sic], and others with the necessary arms, equipment, and supplies. It appears that Mr. Herbert Hoover, as head of the American Relief Administration, was an active member in those intrigues and that the child's fund, contributed by Americans for the relief of the starving children of Europe, was at least in part converted for this purpose.'[110] As one example, the senator produced documents showing that in July 1919 Captain James B. Martin in command of the US ship *Lake Fray* then moored at the port of Bordeaux, France, was instructed to reload his ship with army trucks and supplies, which were sent by the ARA to General Nikolai Yudenich, Commander-in-Chief of the Russian forces on the North-west Front, for use in the offensive against Petrograd.

The second part of Senator Watson's accusations that the White armies were trying to overthrow the Soviet government in order to restore in Russia the regime of the Tsar, 'under which 49,000,000 Russian peasants were whipped with the scourge if they did not pay their taxes', does not seem justified. Many historians agree that although the White movement fought the Bolshevik regime, in many ways both the Reds and Whites were heirs to the Russian revolution of February 1917.[111]

In the meantime, the situation in Russia was going from bad to worse. On 6 February 1922, Patriarch Tikhon made a desperate appeal 'to all people of goodwill':

> We experience chilling horrors when reading the news about the situation of the starving people: 'The hungry no longer eat surrogates, all surrogates are gone.' Ravenous men and women scavenge for carrion, but this delicacy cannot be obtained any more. Dozens of people starve to death and their bodies are found in the snow in ravines along the roads. Mothers leave their toddlers in freezing cold. Cries, groans and screams are coming from all sides. Cases of cannibalism are not rare. A population decline is from 12 to 25%. Of the thirteen million hungry people, only two million receive food aid … 'Be ye therefore merciful, as your Father also is merciful' (Luke, 6:36).[112]

Contrary to some earlier publications, regardless of what the ARA staff did for the Russian people, the Soviet secret police officials were convinced that the presence of over 300 Americans represented a serious threat to the Soviet state. On 11 February, the Cheka, only days before being transformed into the GPU, the political directorate of the NKVD, issued an order to its agents to take all measures 'to purge the ARA organisation of undesirable elements'.[113] Arrests of its Russian personnel on bogus political charges were made in Tsaritsyn, Samara and Pugachyov near Saratov, seriously undermining the work of the ARA.

They also arrested Kuskova and Prokopovich and together with other members of the Commission exiled them to the Vologda governorate. In June 1922 the couple was expelled to Germany. By that time, the GPU had admitted in detail the scope of the catastrophe reporting the number of famine deaths in the provinces. According to their estimates, in Samara there were 3.5 million people dying of hunger and malnutrition, in Saratov – 2 million, in Simbirsk – 1.2 million, in Tsaritsyn – 651,700, in Penza – 329,700, in Tatarstan – 2.1 million, in Chuvashia – 800,000, and in the Volga German Workers' Commune – 330,000.[114] Kuskova and Prokopovich initially settled in Berlin but soon moved to Prague, and when the Second World War begantó Switzerland. Although both of them were dreaming about returning to Mother Russia, they probably realised how lucky they were to be able to live and die on the lovely shores of Lake Geneva, far from the GULAGs and torture chambers.

In April 1922, Patriarch Tikhon (who had openly condemned the murder of the Tsar and the Imperial Family and later protested against confiscations of ecclesiastical property) was placed under house arrest in

Donskoy Monastery.[115] In 1923 the Patriarch was formally 'deposed' by the Moscow Council of the so-called Living Church, a renovationist movement sponsored by the GPU. Vasili Ivanovich Bellavin (Tikhon of Moscow who had also served as Archbishop of North America) died two years later on 7 April, when the Orthodox Church celebrates the Feast of Annunciation.

Today, almost nobody remembers the ARA. Remarkably, during the great famine of the 1920s, among many other foreign countries and organisations Turkey, notwithstanding its own troubled situation, also contributed to the Russian relief effort, helping the famine-stricken Crimea and the Volga-Ural region. Known in Tatar as Idel-Ural, these are areas with large native Turkic populations where Turkish relief did significantly help those families who were fortunate enough to receive it.[116] Of course, the amount of aid from Turkey was obviously by no means comparable to that provided by the United States. For American people, the Russian relief operation and first of all the ARA relief mission was a truly unique undertaking, a story, as Douglas Smith writes, 'filled with political intrigue, violence, adventure, and romance' in a part of the world where the ruling regime by and large repressed, exiled and shot their critics and couldn't even resist putting spokes in the ARA wheels.

Chapter 9

The Raids

1 927 can probably be entered into the annals of intelligence history as the first international 'Year of the Spy'. In one of his classic volumes, *The Mitrokhin Archive* (I), Christopher Andrew writes:

> In the spring of 1927, there were dramatic revelations of Soviet espionage in eight different countries. In March, a major OGPU spy ring was uncovered in Poland; a Soviet trade official was arrested for espionage in Turkey; and the Swiss police announced the arrest of two Russian spies. In April a police raid on the Soviet consulate in Beijing [*sic*] uncovered a mass of incriminating intelligence documents and the French Sûreté arrested a Soviet spy ring in Paris run by Jean Crémet, a leading French Communist. In May Austrian foreign ministry officials were found passing classified information to the OGPU residency; and the British Home Secretary indignantly announced to the House of Commons the discovery of 'one of the most complete and one of the most nefarious spy systems that it has ever been my lot to meet'.[1]

An absolute sine qua non is that all sources, even primary, must be checked, double-checked and rechecked again. There's a lot of stuff in the archives that got there by chance, like a forgery accepted as a genuine document, or a report based on a biased interpretation or opinion but nevertheless duly filed. Sometimes a testimony, even of a seemingly credible witness or reliable defector, or a source described as 'a subject of undoubted loyalty', may be completely invented and include false claims which later leak into the books and articles.[2] There, as it happens, they are sometimes further misinterpreted or misrepresented. There are examples aplenty.

The above quotation is referred by the authors not to the KGB files copied by Mitrokhin, but to the earlier account written by Christopher Andrew with another Soviet defector, Oleg Gordievsky. When checked, it turned out the required citation was on a different page, which happens every now and then and is generally no big problem. In their first comprehensive history of the KGB, the authors claim that the above-mentioned spy ring uncovered in Poland 'was headed by the White Russian general turned OGPU agent,

Daniel Vetrenko'; that instead of a 'Soviet trade official' (from the previous quotation), 'a leading official in the Soviet-Turkish trade corporation in Istanbul was found engaged in espionage on the Turkish-Iraqi border'; and that in May 'there was a Special Branch raid in London on the premises of the All-Russian Co-operative Society (Arcos) and the trade delegation, following the discovery of what the excitable British Home Secretary, Sir William Joynson-Hicks, denounced with some degree of hyperbole, as ...' (see above).[3] Surprisingly, there is no mention of the original source of all this information.

Instead, the footnote points to yet another book written by Professor Andrew some time earlier and entitled *Secret Service*.[4] On the pages to which the reference is made, a fascinating story is unfolding, one of whose main protagonists is the very same Sir William Joynson-Hicks, 1st Viscount Brentford, popularly known as 'Jix'. As said, Joynson-Hicks was then the Home Secretary albeit 'with less sangfroid than Austen Chamberlain', his Cabinet colleague at the time serving as Foreign Secretary. Professor Andrew describes Jix, who before his Home Office appointment served as Minister of Health, as 'a Tory diehard who insisted on the complete redecoration of his room in the Home Office overlooking the Foreign Office quadrangle and the introduction of a new desk to symbolise, according to his admiring biographer, "the arrival of the new broom that would impart cleanliness to some neglected corners" ... Behind the resurgence of labour militancy Jix predictably detected the barely hidden hand of Moscow.'[5]

Like several other British officials involved in the defence of the realm, despite an obvious lack of evidence of Soviet espionage (but not of communist subversion or propaganda), Jix was anxious to bring matters to a head.[6] 'To make its charges against the Russian legation stick,' Professor Andrew explains, 'the cabinet decided to follow the appalling example of the 1923 Curzon ultimatum and quote intercepted Soviet telegrams ... The debate, on 26 May [1927], developed into an orgy of governmental indiscretion about secret intelligence for which there is no parallel in modern parliamentary history... Jix became quite carried away while accusing the Soviet trade delegation.'[7] 'They wanted to get—they have not got them yet, and I do not think they will—the plans of our two latest warships,' he said, answering the question of Liberal MP Lieutenant Commander Joseph Kenworthy, but giving no further details. 'I have had made out for me a list of all these things which this friendly Government, working through this friendly Trade Delegation, has been endeavouring to get by what I do not hesitate to describe as one of the most complete and one of the most nefarious spy systems that it has ever been my lot to meet.'[8] Again, Jix did not bother to explain specifically what 'nefarious spy systems' it could have been his lot to meet during his previous three years as Home Secretary. Perhaps he had in mind the case of Vivian Stranders, a former Royal Flying Corps officer who had been recruited by German intelligence. In 1926, now a Paris-based businessman, Stranders was discovered by SIS trying to persuade a Belgian national to provide him with both French and British military information intended for his German controllers. He was arrested in France, prosecuted as a spy and sentenced to two years' imprisonment.[9] However, if we put aside the Macartney case as harmless mischief, so far there were only two ongoing investigations of alleged Soviet espionage, at least one of them tempting but largely wrong and another raising plenty of questions and never completed. About each of them we can now say that it was an entirely false lead.

This third case, described in many books and academic articles, was opened shortly after the following advertisement was inserted in the *Daily Herald* on 24 November 1924:

SECRET SERVICE. – Labour Group carrying out investigation would be glad to receive information and details from anyone who has ever had any association with, or been brought into touch with, any Secret Service department or operation. Write in first instance Box 573, Daily Herald.

Both SIS and the Security Service reacted rather quickly. Less than a week later, on 29 November, an agent who figured in the internal correspondence as 'D', posted a letter to the above address offering his services and signing it as 'D.A. Reinmann'.[10] Using the language of the MI5 report on the case, 'several efforts which were immediately made to open up negotiations with the persons responsible for the insert of this advertisement failed, but eventually a contact was established between an agent of M.I.5 ['D'] and an individual calling himself 'BX' (who subsequently proved to be William Norman EWER)'.[11] In other documents related to this sting operation he would also figure as 'QX'. It was soon established that an office was rented at Room 50, Outer Temple, 222–225 Strand, on behalf of the Federated Press of America (FPA) although it had little to do with the FPA registered in the USA. Here, Ewer, who was the foreign editor of the *Daily Herald* and an active member of the West London branch of the CPGB, acted as a manager with one Albert Allen as assistant manager. The office also employed Walter Holmes, another active member of the CPGB who worked as a journalist for the *Daily Herald*; Walter Dale, dismissed from the Metropolitan Police in August 1919 and now responsible for security at the FPA London; and Mrs. Rose Edwards, a typist and office clerk. She appeared to be a daughter of Joe

Okhrana, St Petersburg Directorate, January 1905. (*Public domain*)

Nicholas II, tsarina and
HIH tsarevich Aleksey N.
Romanov. (*Public domain*)

Grand Duke Kirill Vladimirovich Romanov, 1924.

Carriage of the Imperial Train stationed in the town of Pskov where Nicholas II was forced by revolutionaries to abdicate the Russian throne on 2 March 1917 (Old Style).

Postcard with Bolshevik revolution heroes, Petrograd, October 1917 (top from left to right). Trotsky, Lenin, Lunacharsky, Spiridonova, Kollontai, Raskolnikov, Kamenev and Zinoviev. Papers of Sir Robert Hamilton Bruce Lockhart, Lilly Library, Indiana University, Bloomington, Indiana. (*Lockhart, R. mss., 1906-1969, Collection No. LMC 1674*)

GPU/OGPU special forces (OSNAZ) in training.

Bolsheviks, members of the Ural regional Soviet who sentenced the former Russian tsar and his family to death.

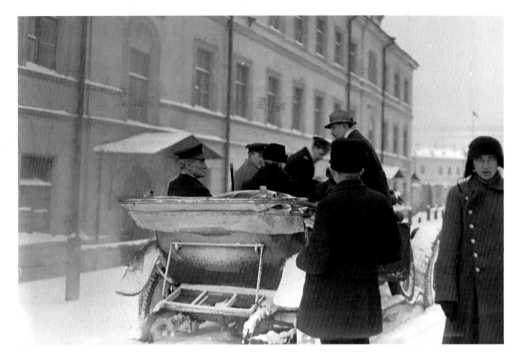

The British Naval Campaign in the Baltic, 1918–19. Rear Admiral Hugh Sinclair lands in Reval (Tallinn), leaving the landing stage in a car with Estonian officers, January 1918 ©Crown copyright. Director of Naval Intelligence in 1919, Sinclair became the second chief of SIS in 1923 and remained in this post until his death in November 1939. (*Public domain*)

American soldier in Archangel, 1918, and Archangel in 2022

Moscow, Lubyanka Square in 1900 and below – the OGPU headquarters in the same square in 1922.

Dzerzhinsky and first Cheka officers.

Бутырская тюрьма, 1909 год

Орловский каторжный централ, 1914 год

Центральная пересыльная тюрьма, г. Москва, 1916 год

Dzerzhinsky in various tsarist jails in Russia.

A draft of the Order of Dzerzhinsky for
Soviet intelligence personnel. It was not
approved by Stalin and never produced.

Dzerzhinsky chervonets 10 roubles.

Trotsky and Lenin, 1917. (*Public domain*)

Chicherin and Krestinsky, Berlin 1925.

Alexander Shliapnikov, Soviet trade-union leader, and Leonid Krasin in front of the Soviet embassy in Paris, 1924.

At least ten attempts were mounted by different revolutionary factions seeking to assassinate Pyotr Arkadyevich Stolypin. In April 1906, he was appointed Minister of Internal Affairs and in July Prime Minister of Russia. The anarchist revolutionary Dmitry Bogrov, an Okhrana double agent, assassinated Stolypin on 5 September 1911 (New Style: 18 September) at the Kiev Opera House in the presence of Nicholas II and his two daughters. Some have alleged that Bogrov was instructed to kill Stolypin by right-wing members of the Okhrana as they opposed Stolypin's reforms. The assassin was hanged while the investigation was stopped on Tsar' orders for reasons that remain unknown. (*Keystone/Getty Images*)

Boris Savinkov at the Supreme Tribunal in Moscow, 1924.

Robert H. Bruce Lockhart, 1920. (*Image UGC*)

Denys Norman Garstin, member of the British Intelligence Mission in St Petersburg 1917.

DeWitt Clinton Poole arrived as the US consul in Moscow in September 1917. Working under consul general Maddin Summers, Poole was instructed to control spy networks in Russia run by Xenophon Kalamatiano. After the sudden death of Summers from a brain haemorrhage on 28 April 1918, Poole was appointed consul general. (*Courtesy of the National Archives, photo No. 152776*)

Paul Dukes on an assignment in Moscow
disguised as a Russian, 1919.

Sir Paul Dukes, British Secret Service.

Paul Dukes' false pass identifying him as 'Alexander Bankau', an NCO of the transport department of
the VIII Red Army.

By the time this photo was published (March 1921), Xenofon Kalamatino, an American citizen and member of the US Consular Service, had been held prisoner by the Cheka. He graduated from the University of Chicago and in 1912 arrived in Russia as General Manager for Russia of the J.I. Case Company. In September 1917 Kalamatino became attached to the US consulate general in Moscow as a member of DeWitt Clinton Poole's staff and while in that service was arrested in September 1918 and thrown into prison charged with espionage. According to Poole's biographers, 'Poole was active in implementing U.S. policy, negotiating with the Bolshevik authorities, and supervising American intelligence operations that gathered information about conditions throughout Russia, especially monitoring anti-Bolshevik elements and areas of German influence'. Sentenced to death, Kalamatino was released in August 1921. He died in the USA two years later aged 41.

Lieutenant Colonel Ronald Meiklejohn, SIS station chief in Tallinn, Estonia, 1920.

Sidney Reilly, the so-called 'Ace of Spies', caught by Crowther Smith in RAF uniform.

Mikhail (Meer) Trilisser and the staff of the first Russian foreign intelligence section. (*INO*)

Boris Bazarov, legal OGPU resident in Vienna (1924–7).

Gleb Boky, revolutionary, paranormal investigator and one of the leading members of the Cheka and later the OGPU/NKVD.

Pyotr Ya. Zubov, OGPU legal resident in Turkey since 1928 under diplomatic cover as consul (alias 'Pyotr Ivanovich Grishin').

Dzerzhinsky's funeral in Moscow in July 1926 with all members of the Politburo including Stalin taking it in turns as coffin bearers. The 'Iron Felix' was buried in the Kremlin Wall Necropolis.

Dzerzhinsky and his deputies Vycheslav Menzhinsky (above) and Genrikh Yagoda (far right). Both would succeed him as Cheka/GPU/OGPU chairmen, Menzhinsky (Wacław Menżyński) from July 1926 until his death in May 1934.

Genrikh Yagoda (Enoch Gershon Yehudah) headed the NKVD, predecessor of the KGB, from July 1934 to September 1936. Stalin made him the first Commissar General for State Security. Arrested in March 1937, he was shot a year later.

The Metropolitan Police raid on the headquarters of ARCOS and the Soviet Trade Delegation at 49 Moorgate in London, in May 1927. (*Licensed photo M384366*)

Jacob Kirchenstein was born about 1890 in Latvia. In 1940, he was 50 years old and lived in the Bronx, New York, with his wife, Vallie, and son.

Rudolf Kirchenstein, brother of Jacob Kirchenstein, was an officer of Soviet military intelligence.

Sir Arthur Willert (second from left) in a gentlemen's club in London.

Vienna, Wallnerstrasse 8 in the First District where the British Passport Control Office and Consulate were located before the Second World War.

Above – Baron Falz Fein at home in Vaduz. (*Photo Elma Korac*) Below – meeting President Putin in Moscow at the Congress of Sootechestvenniki (fellow countrymen) in October 2001. He also participated in the First Congress in August 1991 together with Hans Georg Yurievsky, reportedly a heir of Alexander II.

FALZ-FEIN

Paul, ex-policeman and Head Detective of the Vigilance Detective Agency located in Clapton House in Clapton Common.

Thanks to the efforts of the penetration agent 'D' and a Home Office Warrant (HOW) imposed on the FPA correspondence, it was further established that regular reports were received from George Scolombe in Paris and Frederick Kuh in Berlin. Both were *Daily Herald* correspondents and Kuh was also in charge of the United Press of America bureau in Germany. A telephone check (imposed on 25 February 1925) revealed that Ewer, Allen, Holmes, Dale and Rose Edwards were in constant telephone communication with ARCOS, ROSTA (a Soviet news agency headed in London by Andrew Rothstein), the Soviet embassy, known as Chesham House, the trade delegation (Soviet House) and the Vigilance Detective Agency. Other individuals who were found from time to time to be assisting Dale in his work, the MI5 'History of a section of the Russian Intelligence Service under the management of Ewer' claims, were James Marston, a dismissed policeman from Scotland Yard (Agatha Christie's fans will remember A. James Marston, a villain and one of the main characters from her novel *And Then There Were None*) and George Alexander Pratt, also a dismissed policeman, now both employed at the ARCOS Bank. Sometimes, the watchers observed Rose Edwards visiting Chesham House and on occasions meeting Rose Cohen from the Soviet embassy's technical staff, 'in the middle of the day'.[12] Miss Edwards had earlier worked at the same embassy, regularly visiting Soviet Russia. All this, however, did not imply any wrongdoing. As leftist news outlets, both the *Daily Herald*, the only daily paper which had furiously championed militancy in both the women's and the labour movements (as one of its financial supporters pointed out), and the Federated Press would have been expected to have professional ties to all those institutions.

W.N. Ewer was quite obviously not a spy, but a willing and conscious collaborator eager to support the political course that he considered to be correct. It is possible, as Colonel Tsarev of the KGB Press Bureau claimed, that Ewer was referred to as B-1 ('B' for Britain), codenamed HERMAN, in the GPU/OGPU registry, but this cannot be verified and it does not mean that he was an agent. It is known, for example, that US President Franklin Roosevelt was identified as CAPTAIN and Winston Churchill as BOAR in the KGB correspondence and files, which was usual practice for reference purposes only. For SIS, MI5 and Special Branch it was another stab in the dark, like for example Nikolai Klyshko of the Russian trade delegation,[13] or the Russian émigré Boris Said, each of whom at one time was alleged to be 'head of the Bolshevik Secret Service in England'.[14] Likewise, Ewer was never managing 'a section of the Russian Intelligence Service operating in this country [Britain]', as MI5 surmised and Special Branch presumed.

Long after the ARCOS raid, thanks to an informant,[15] the Security Service was able to identify two Special Branch officers, Sergeant Charles Jane and Inspector Hubert van Ginhoven, who were followed to a meeting with Dale, where all three were arrested on 11 April 1929. Although Jix was still serving as Home Secretary, it was decided not to prosecute them. Why? Because there was no usable evidence of espionage.

* * *

By the spring of 1927, there were three simultaneous investigations of Soviet espionage activities in Britain. Besides the already-mentioned Macartney and Ewer/FPA cases, another was, as Gill Bennett has put it, 'a promising line of enquiry being pursued on an inter-Agency basis, relating to one Jacob Kirchenstein, alias "Johnny Walker", who was not only a senior ARCOS official but was thought to be one of the chief agents of the Third International in England and at the centre of revolutionary organisation in the UK'.[16] Miss Bennett had previously served as the Chief Historian of the Foreign and Commonwealth Office. In her book, enthusiastically quoted by many intelligence writers and even historians (including Keith Jeffery, the author of the authorised history of MI6), she refers, among others, to the unclassified Scotland Yard file on 'the Russian trade organisation and revolutionary organisations in the UK', compiled by Scotland Yard after the ARCOS raid. The document placed Jacob Kirchenstein at the head of Soviet intelligence-gathering in the UK. This case is so ridiculous that it will be dealt with in detail separately in Chapter 11.

In his introductory statement during the House of Commons debate, Jix boasted:

> The Secret Service of Great Britain is not so bad, after all. I happen to have in my possession not merely the names but the addresses of most of those spies. They have been traced in their nefarious plans. I have also in my possession a considerable number of the questionnaires which they have used, and which they have given to various people connected with the armed forces of this country to try to find out particular information in regard to the particular objects which are very rightly kept secret by our different Services.

Answering the question of another MP whether there was any other government whose representatives behaved as badly as the Russians, Joynson-Hicks said: 'There is no other trade delegation in this county and, so far as I know, there is no foreign Embassy in this country which has degraded itself in the manner in which that of Russia has.' The Home Secretary had probably forgotten about the espionage activities of the Japanese Naval Attaché's office in London and in particular the case of a British naval aviator who spied for the Japanese.

His name was Frederick Joseph Rutland, a squadron leader and one of Britain's most distinguished young officers of the Royal Naval Air Service. Rutland had served in the Great War, winning a medal for his part in the Battle of Jutland, the largest naval battle and the only full-scale clash involving battleships and the RNAS. 'His interest in working for the Japanese,' Antony Best writes, 'first came to the attention of the British authorities in 1922 through GC&CS's breaking of the Japanese naval attaché cipher, which revealed that he was willing to act as a technical adviser on naval aviation. Following this revelation MI5 and SIS kept Rutland under surveillance until he made his passage to Japan in 1924.'[17] Maybe the Home Secretary was not informed about this case.

Anyway, to the question whether there were any other agents of other countries in the UK, Jix responded: 'There is no other country which has anything like a similar spy system in this country to that which Russia had.'[18] Years later, an eminent British historian commented that Joynson-Hicks 'saw a communist [a Red] under every bed'.[19] Concerning the May 1927 reaction of the authorities to the revelations of the British secret services regarding allegedly hostile activities of Soviet agencies (including the Comintern) against the British Empire, Professor Andrew had to admit: 'Baldwin's government was able to prove its charge of Soviet dabbling in British politics, but the documents seized in the Arcos raid and the intercepted telegrams published in a white paper contained only a few cryptic allusions to the much more serious sin of espionage.' In other words, the Special Branch officers who conducted the search of the premises belonging to ARCOS and the Soviet trade delegation failed to find the document for which Jix had ordered the raid.[20] The summary of the documents obtained from ARCOS concludes that 'their only value was that they provided evidence of assistance given by ARCOS to the Communist Party of Great Britain'.[21] Thus, what the Home Secretary claimed in Parliament was a bluff.

> The cabinet found itself in a quandary when it met to discuss Anglo-Soviet relations on 23 May [1927]. Having decided to break off diplomatic relations, it had clearly to produce evidence to justify its decision. For this purpose, the papers seized in the Arcos raid were insufficient. A cabinet committee concluded that the Arcos haul did not even prove 'the complicity of the Soviet Diplomatic Mission ... with the propaganda activities of [the trade delegation].' Still lacking

usable evidence of espionage, the cabinet concluded that it must at least give public proof that the Soviet legation had breached the normal rules of diplomatic behaviour. The only proof available was the telegrams exchanged between the legation and Moscow decrypted by GC&CS. These were, as the cabinet minutes euphemistically observed, 'secret documents of a class which it is not usual to quote in published documents'.[22]

Today, many intelligence historians agree that the effect of the Baldwin government's publication of the Soviet intercepts from the British intelligence agencies was traumatic and yet at the same time it failed to produce public evidence to support Jix's charges. Quite groundless charges, one might add, and entirely based on wishful thinking. A study of Macartney's personal file PF 38661/Vols. 1-4, by now declassified and in the National Archives (KV 2/647-648), reveals that the whole 'spy case' involving him and George Monkton, who acted as an agent provocateur, had been fabricated by the Services. As early as 22 November 1926, an unidentified SIS officer, probably Major Desmond Morton, in his letter to then Captain Guy Liddell of Scotland Yard (who would eventually become Deputy Director General of MI5), wrote: 'Many thanks for all the trouble you have taken regarding MACARTNEY. After consultation with Colonel Menzies, however, we have decided that, in all the circumstances, he is no longer worth powder and shot from our point of view.' And the verdict: 'Both Macartney and Monkland are undesirables and liars.'[23] It seems that SIS rather quickly realised that Macartney was not for real – not a spy or agent, and even not a contact (to use professional slang), but rather a clown – and for various reasons decided not to do anything and let MI5 and Special Branch complete their work. Acting this way, the second 'C' (Hugh Sinclair, later full admiral and Sir) probably had another plan in mind, namely to demonstrate to his superiors in the Foreign Office and the Secret Service Committee the danger, as he had put it, 'which is caused by the absence of any central control or authority [over the Secret Services] in matters of this sort'.[24] He would later use the unfortunate ARCOS raid to prove the same.

Wilfred Macartney was arrested on 17 November 1927 and after two months (during which time, as before, they failed to establish any connection between him and Soviet intelligence) sentenced to 10 years imprisonment under the Official Secrets Act. He duly served this disproportionally severe sentence in HMP Parkhurst on the Isle of Wight, being discharged on licence in August 1935. In December 1936 Macartney volunteered to fight for the Republican cause in the Spanish Civil War and upon his arrival was appointed the first commander of the British battalion formed at the small village of Madrigueras 20km north of Albacete, the base of the International Brigades.[25] The man chosen as his political commissar was Douglas Springhall, better known as Dave. Unlike Macartney, he was a real Soviet agent.

Another person arrested (and released) at the same time as Macartney was a young German communist, Georg Hansen. But contrary to all published sources that mention them so far available, Macartney and Hansen are two completely different, unrelated stories. This is one of the reasons why the Authorised History of the Security Service (MI5) ignores this case and both men completely.

Other researchers, however, decided to get to the bottom of it. Timothy Phillips writes:

Macartney's story is worthy of a book in its own right – indeed, after his release from prison, he wrote one [*Walls Have Mouths*, with Prologue, Epilogue and Comments by Compton Mackenzie, 1936]. Racing at breakneck speed across Europe, surviving run-ins with Romanian princes and wealthy heiresses, and always returning to the Café Royal for what one observer described as large quantities of 'hot grogs', he was completely different from the typical 1920s socialist agent.[26]

Desmond Morton's leading role and personal interest in the Macartney case was highlighted by his new position, in addition to his current job as Head of Production. He was now in charge of yet another important new SIS department named Section VI. It was formed during 1926–7 to collect intelligence on industrial mobilisation of potential British enemies including Germany and the Soviet Union. This would later grow to become the Industrial Intelligence Centre (IIC) hidden at SIS headquarters and Major Morton was promoted to head it.[27] Morton's successful intelligence career continued in Whitehall where he had served as Winston Churchill's liaison with SIS.

Captain Compton Mackenzie, chief intelligence officer for the Middle East, had been Macartney's boss when young Macartney, then still aged 18 and Assistant Chief Censor in Athens, was transferred under his command to the Special Organisation (a euphemism for the Secret Service, then MI1c). When in December 1916 the political situation deteriorated in the Greek capital, Mackenzie had to move his headquarters, including Macartney, to the island of Syros (also known as Siros or Syra) in the Aegean Sea. Later, Macartney was appointed the governor of a small island named Kea or Tzia in the Cyclades archipelago about 40 miles south-east of Athens.

Mackenzie, who had already been a well-known novelist when he worked for 'C' in Turkey and in the Middle East, fully realised that the 1928 trial of his former Secret Service colleague was a farce and a staged event referring to Macartney as being in jail for 'comic opera espionage'.[28] In his introduction to Macartney's book, Mackenzie maintained that with this trial the government was attempting 'to impress upon the people of Great Britain that between them and being blown sky-high by naughty Bolsheviks there was nothing except the vigilance and acumen of a Secret Service, the devotion and patriotism of a Conservative Cabinet, and the determination of the Law to support both'.[29] Obviously, Mackenzie had his own reason to hold a grudge against the Establishment because he himself had been prosecuted under the Official Secrets Act when his book *Greek Memories* was published in October 1932.

The official charge was his inclusion in the book of some information acquired during his time as an intelligence officer in Greece. Although Mackenzie used similar material in two previous volumes of his memoirs without any problem, this time, according to the Official History of the UK's D-Notice system, the text contained 'criticism of inaccuracies in a contemporary book by the ex-Director of Intelligence, [Basil] Thomson'. The trial, most of which was held in camera, became an embarassement to HMG and Mackenzie was later able to retaliate by publishing his comedy spy novel *Water on the Brain* (1933), a bitter satire on the British secret services.

* * *

One did not need to be a diehard conservative like Sir William Joynson-Hicks at the Home Office, Lord Birkenhead, then Secretary of State for India, or Winston Churchill at the Treasury to decide that the Bolsheviks had only themselves to blame for their economic isolation. By repudiating Russia's debts and seizing the property of foreign nationals, Sean McMeekin comments, Lenin had ensured the enmity of Western governments, first of all Britain and France, but also Germany when the Treaty of Brest-Litovsk was nullified in November 1918. 'Only the wartime neutrals – Sweden, Norway and Denmark – remained relatively unperturbed by the ongoing Communist depredations against property,' he writes, 'in part because the Bolsheviks actively courted them, offering to exempt their nationals from Soviet taxes and nationalisation decrees if they would trade with Moscow.'[30]

Although Britain had always been an important trade partner and the most powerful economy before the war (preserving its status as a Great Power thereafter – in the 1920s, 400 million people lived under British rule and the British Empire had a huge impact on the world), the real target of the Soviet import-export and loan effort of 1921 was not Britain but Sweden. In late October 1921 a four-man mission was sent to Stockholm headed by Maxim Litvinov.

> The high priority the Politburo placed on exploiting the Stockholm loan market was evident in the personnel chosen for the mission in late October 1921, men who combined high Bolshevik rank with low international profile. Litvinov, who remained persona non grata in Entente countries, would lead the loan mission to Sweden ... Accompanying Litvinov were three men ... then largely unknown outside Soviet Russia and Sweden: the railway expert Georgi Lomonosov [sic]; Platon Kerzhentsev, president of the Soviet Trade Mission in Stockholm [sic]; and Aaron Sheinman, the most trusted official in the Finance Commissariat [sic].[31]

Their instructions were to enter negotiations with the Swedish government, banks and firms 'about the conclusion of a cash or commodity loan'.[32] 'There was a neat symmetry to the latest Stockholm mission,' McMeekin notes. 'Swedish bankers had been so successful in helping part the Bolsheviks from their money that it was only fitting that they also pony up the necessary loans when this money ran out. Stepping in yet again to occupy the role of Swedish middleman between the Communist regime and Western capital was Olof Aschberg, a long-time associate of Kerzhentsev, Lomonosov and Sheinman.'[33]

Yuri Vladimirovich Lomonosov, born in 1876, was a Russian railway engineer. His titles and achievements, summarised in an introductory note to his book published in New York in May 1919, were quite impressive but not full. Lomonosov is best known for design and construction of the world's first operationally successful mainline diesel locomotive, completed in 1924. Appointed professor of Kiev Polytechnic, the youngest full professor of the institute, he joined the social-democratic movement and became a Marxist. According to Russian sources, Lomonosov was also a secret member of the so-called combat technical group of the Central Committee of the Social-Democratic Labour Party (RSDRP). In June 1917 the Provisional Government sent Lomonosov to the USA as a representative of the Ministry of Railways. Some months before, in February, Ludwig Martens, a Russian engineer of German descent, who had emigrated to the United States where he became vice-president of the engineering firm Weinberg & Posner in New York, returned to Russia together with Trotsky and many other Social-Democrats.

In March 1919, to break the embargo against the first Soviet state, Martens was sent back to the USA to set up the Russian Soviet Government Bureau as the first, albeit informal, embassy of Soviet Russia, although it was not recognised by the State Department. Julius Hammer, a Jew from Odessa who emigrated with his parents to the United States in 1875 and settled in New York, served as the Bureau's director of the finance department. Julius, the father of Armand Hammer, was also one of the leaders of the Socialist Labor Party (SLP) of the USA, which split off to become the CPUSA of which Hammer senior was a founding member. According to one of the Hammers' biographers, the Soviet Bureau headed by Martens was funded by money accumulated from the proceeds of illegal sales of smuggled diamonds using his New York company Allied Drug and Chemical.[34] Another theory regarding the financing of the Bureau suggested that Lomonosov provided much of the original funding.

Martens appointed Lomonosov to the position of director of the railroad department. 'Committed to the Bolshevik course,' Tod Pfannenstiel's study reveals,

> Lomonossoff relinquished to Martens on 21 May 1919, all 'rights, titles and interests in and to all locomotives, car and freight car parts, rails and railroad equipment' as well as all 'contracts ... claims ... monies, office furniture, books, files, documents, papers and other personal property' previously held by the Ministry of Ways and Communications [*sic*, Ministry of Railways]. A significant portion of the financial assets Martens claimed to hold in America on behalf of the Soviet government included those forfeited by Lomonossoff when he renounced his affiliation with the Provisional Government and joined the staff of the Soviet Bureau.

Probably as a first example of the Soviet approach to the collection of industrial intelligence, something similar to Section VI of SIS, Isaac Hourwich (Gurvich), another Jewish émigré from Russia and graduate of Petrograd University, served at the Bureau as its director of the statistical department, a division intended to collect data on American and Russian businesses.[35] Prior to accepting his Soviet Bureau position, Hourwich had served as the chief statistician at the US Department of Labor.

Regardless of the sources, by early April 1919 the Bureau managed to get enough funding for Martens and his staff to begin operations in earnest. Back in Moscow, Lenin was very much interested in getting American goods, but first of all locomotives and wagons, to resolve the transport and food crises and help industrial modernisation. In an interview with Karl von Wiegand Lenin repeatedly stressed the Bolsheviks' willingness to offer American capitalists 'gold for machines, implements, etc., which may be of use to us in transport and production. And not only gold, but raw materials as well ... We shall require American goods, locomotives, automobiles, etc., more than those of any other country', he stressed.[36] It was said already after the government-sponsored raid put an end to the Martens Mission.

The Joint Legislative Committee to Investigate Seditious Activities, chaired by Senator Clayton R. Lusk, was established in March. The Committee's chief investigator was Rayme Finch, formerly an agent of the New York office of the Bureau of Investigation, forerunner of the FBI. On 12 June, the police and private detectives working for the Committee raided the Soviet Bureau. Several people were arrested and interrogated about Bolshevik propaganda in the United States, while witnesses and seized documents were used to demonstrate that the Bureau 'was planning a violent overthrow of the government'. Martens himself managed to escape, went underground and, according to Epstein, was often hiding in Hammer's home before he was detained by the police. On 10 January 1920, in response to charges brought by the Department of Justice, Martens stated that the accusations were unfounded and he as well as his Bureau had done nothing wrong. On the contrary, only three months before the raid, together with his credentials he sent a memorandum to the State Department where he announced Russia's readiness to purchase $200 million-worth of railway supplies, agricultural machinery, various electrical components, automobiles, shoes, clothing, medical equipment and food among many other products. Martens also emphasised his country's readiness to export to the United States flax, hemp, hides, furs, lumber, grain, and a variety of minerals. His commercial director, Abraham A. Heller, later reiterated Martens' claim, confirming that Russia had all the means necessary to pay for such purchases. Nevertheless, in December 1920 Ludwig Martens was deported to Russia.

In 1933 Martens wrote a letter to the OGPU leadership in support of the arrested Orthodox priest, theologian, philosopher and mathematician Pavel Florensky. He also took care of Father Flolensky's son. Regarding his own child, Wilhelm 'Willi' Martens, who the Russian sources claim was one of the founders of the National Committee Freies Deutschland (NKFD), established in July 1943, and a Soviet intelligence officer, this information cannot be confirmed based on the available documents.

Following the raid, Lomonosov returned to Moscow in September 1919, and Krasin introduced him to Lenin as one of the leading railway experts. He was soon appointed chairman of the High Technical Committee of the People's Commissariat of Railways (NKPS or Narkomput). In June 1920, Lenin drafted instructions to the Russian Railway Mission Abroad and Lomonosov was appointed its head in the rank of a people's commissar responsible for all railway purchases abroad.

Between Lomonosov's return from America and his appointment to the new post, in January 1920 the US Department of Commerce offered the Bolshevik government to buy 200 Decapod (2-10-0) steam locomotives that remained from the previous order. During the First World War, Imperial Russia ordered approximately 1,200 Decapods from American builders, 857 of which had already been delivered but more than 200 were either ready awaiting shipment instructions or in the process of construction.[37] For obvious reasons, this order was not completed. Instead, over 500 contracts were signed with European companies for the delivery of locomotives, wagons, rail tank cars, spare parts and other goods.

On 14 April 1921 Dzerzhinsky was appointed People's Commissar of Railways in addition to his other important posts as People's Commissar of Interna Affairs and chairman of the Cheka.

Lomonosov placed a large order for locomotives with the Swedish company Nydqvist & Holm AB (after 1916 abbreviated as NOHAB) based in Trollhätten. In 1865 the company made its first locomotive and in 1912 the 1,000th vehicle was proudly produced. Even for such a well-established manufacturer a one-time order for almost 1,000 units was considered to be very plum. In May 1920 NOHAB received an advance payment of 7 million Swedish krona (SEK) and after the contract was signed the Soviet side provided another 10 million SEK as an interest-free loan for NOHAB to expand manufacturing capacity.[38] On 22 January 1921 Lomonosov received a letter from the Swedish commercial bank Nordiska Handelsbanken: 'We hereby confirm the receipt of … 432 and 316 boxes of gold rubles weighing twenty thousand four kilograms seven hundred seventy-two grams of pure gold and ten thousand three kilograms one hundred twenty-three grams of pure gold.'[39] Alas, in spite of advance payment and prefinancing of further production, only 500 locomotives were delivered between 1921 and 1924.

As it happens, during all his time at the helm of the Russian Railway Mission Abroad there had been a wave of denunciations and complaints sent by telltales, mediocrities and the envious to the NKPS, the Cheka and to Dzerzhinsky personally accusing Lomonosov of embezzling money. 'There's a lot of talk about Comrade Lomonosov's grand living in Moscow and even more about his opulent lifestyle abroad,' letters from informers read. It was reported that all this time Lomonosov's wife resided with him in Stockholm, while his married daughter lived in Berlin and his only son studied in England, first at the old and famous Leighton Park boarding school for boys and girls and then at Cambridge University.[40] In March 1923 Dzerzhinsky was asking Lomonosov about various small presents that he was reportedly regularly bringing from his trips abroad (lingerie, stockings, shoes and so on). And in April Alexander Shlyapnikov, a trade unionist and leader of the

Workers' Opposition movement within the party, published a brochure where he accused several Soviet apparatchiks (Lomonosov was at the top of the list) of plundering funds from the state and depositing them abroad with the help of Aschberg, whom Shlyapnikov called 'a private banker of Soviet leaders'.[41] It seems that a hundred years ago it was all exactly like in Putin's Russia!

Soon Lomonosov moved with his wife to Berlin where he continued working on his project of creating the first diesel engine with electric transmission. By February 1925 his prototype passed all tests and became the world's first fully operational mainline diesel-electric locomotive built for Soviet Railways. Lomonosov continued working in Berlin as a teacher and consultant having decided not to return back to Russia. With his second wife Raisa he moved to Britain in 1938, eventually taking British citizenship. After the war Lomonosov relocated to Canada where his son Yuri settled with his family. There he fell ill and died shortly afterwards in November 1952.

* * *

A surprise raid on unregistered aliens, organised by the British military authorities in Constantinople in June 1921, had some long-term effects, if not on Soviet-Turkish political and trade relations then certainly on the Soviet personnel stationed there. At the time, parallel to the northern neutrals, the Bolsheviks were looking for suppliers and trade partners elsewhere, and one of the obvious targets was Turkey. Mustafa Kemal's domestic anti-communism was irrelevant for the Soviet government so long as his foreign policy remained anti-imperialist. This was calculated to provide multiple opportunities.

'The initiative in the Soviet-Turkish relationship,' David Stone reminds us, 'first lay with the Turks, as the Turkish national movement appealed for Soviet assistance in April 1920 in its ongoing struggle against Greece and the Entente powers.' 'The precise material nature of Soviet support for the new Turkish state remains obscure,' he adds, 'but seems to have involved substantial sums of gold from Soviet stores.'[42] According to the Soviet documents, the mission of Frunze, soon to be appointed commander-in-chief of the Red Army, combined both diplomatic and military goals. As a result, Turkey was granted an interest-free credit of 10 million gold rubles for an immediate purchase from the Red Army of significant consignments of small arms, machine guns, mountain guns and ammunition for them. In total, during 1920–2, 39,000 rifles, 327 machine guns, 54 howitzers, 63 million cartridges, 147,000 shells, many grenades, edged and bladed weapons, shrapnel, gas masks and other military equipment were delivered to Turkey through Novorossiysk, Tuapse and Batumi. In September 1920, two Turkish warships left from Samsun and Trabzon for Novorossiysk to transport weapons to the Turkish liberation forces. In addition, in May 1921 Kemal's request to build a gunpowder factory in Ankara was approved by the Politburo in addition to some equipment for a cartridge factory and the necessary raw materials supplied to Turkey.[43]

In July, following the raid, Bronislav Kudish was back in Constantinople meeting a Russian delegation headed by Alexander Serebrovsky, a prominent political figure, a former high-ranking official at the People's Commissariat for Trade and Industry and now chairman of Azneft oil company in Baku also authorised to make considerable purchases of various goods in Turkey. Serebrovsky recalled that during that visit he bought technical materials and consumer goods worth over half a million gold francs.[44] At the same time, he claimed (most likely grossly exaggerating his role) that he was also involved in some propaganda effort among Wrangel's former troops persuading them to return to Russia. But the main purpose of his visit to Turkey was to meet a Mr Day who had represented several large American manufacturers in Constantinople.

Henry Mason Day was an adventurous young man in his thirties.[45] After the war he arrived in Turkey as president of the American Foreign Trade Corporation and, following a trip to Russia in 1921, returned to the United States with a number of signed 'options' – preliminary agreements with the Transcaucasian authorities for oil concessions. Before long he interested the Barnsdall Oil Company from Oklahoma in the Russian opportunity and the International Barnsdall Corporation was soon formed with Mr. Day as president and a shareholder with a 25 per cent interest.

Because the Turkish economy was even more devastated than the Russian, Kemal had little to offer Moscow in return for the deliveries of arms and gold, besides cooperation in ejecting the British from the Caucasus. This he provided by urging Azeri Turks to cooperate with the Bolsheviks in Baku, which Turkish forces took in September 1918. The process of withdrawal of the British force began in March, with the last remaining British troops, who numbered some 950 men, leaving on 14 April 1919.[46] Until this day, the prevailing version among Russian historians has been that the massacre of the twenty-six Baku commissars, who escaped after the fall of Baku, was organised by the chief of the British Military Mission in Ashkhabad, Captain Reginald Teague-Jones. Teague-Jones changed his name in 1922 and all reference to him in Foreign Office files ceased after the end of 1922. For the next 66 years until his death in November 1988, he was known as Ronald Sinclair. As Sinclair he served as the British Vice-Consul in New York during the war, actively collaborating, his biographers say, with the US Office of Strategic Service (OSS), predecessor of the CIA.[47]

By the time the British soldiers were marching out of Baku and the Red Army was marching in, the United States had suddenly discovered that the long-term future of their oil supplies was by no means certain. It turned out that other countries, and first of all Britain, were about to acquire exclusive control of the world's oil resources. In a review article published shortly after the Second World War, Hans Heymann demonstrated how 'these fears and resentments spread a film of mistrust over the whole area of Anglo-American relations'. 'When Britain and France concluded the San Remo Agreement in 1920,' he wrote, 'providing for joint action with regard to petroleum concessions, American indignation became bitter. There followed a series of United States diplomatic manoeuvres, undertaken with the avowed objective of frustrating the further extension of British oil interests.'[48] As soon as it became clear that it might be possible to use oil as a powerful bargaining lever for diplomatic recognition and financial assistance, Krasin immediately arranged negotiations with Shell representatives in London.

In August 1921 Serebrovsky, who was negotiating with the Americans in Constantinople, received first proposals from Henry Dale regarding the potential interest of his International Barnsdall Corporation to commence operations in the Baku region. The initial discussion was about the equipping and pumping of old wells as well as about prospecting and drilling on undeveloped land, of which Serebrovsky immediately informed Lenin, Stalin, who was then in charge of the whole oil business, and Ordzhonikidze, the chairman of the Kavburo, the operational centre of the Soviet military-political forces in the Caucasus. Earlier that year, Ordzhonikidze together with Stalin played a decisive role in engineering the Red Army's invasion of their native Georgia, and now these two Bolshevik leaders, whose primary and secondary education was received in Tsarist prisons and exile, had to make decisions on international trade and business.

Arriving in Moscow later in the summer of 1922, Day and his party at first found negotiations with Soviet officials extremely difficult. The Russians rejected Day's initial proposal, causing some of the Americans to depart charging bad faith. Fortunately for Day, Lenin took a personal interest in the success of the International Barnsdall discussions. Whereas he had recently opposed Soviet ratification of a large mining concession agreement with a British capitalist, Leslie Urquhart [signed with Krasin, about whom Lenin once wrote that 'he is great hand in making promises and throwing dust in people's eyes'], Lenin favoured a small oil deal with the American entrepreneur.

As a result, at the end of September, Day succeeded in concluding two contracts with Azneft and by June 1923 the company had sunk fifteen new wells near Baku.[49]

After the signing of the Moscow Agreement with Turkey, Soviet officials responsible for international relations and trade did their best to supplement it with the trade agreement as soon as possible. However, in August 1921 Krasin informed Chicherin that there were still problems with the trade agreement, mainly due to the current status of the Soviet foreign trade which remained a state monopoly.[50] Nevertheless, international business in the region was gradually developing.

During his several visits to Constantinople in 1921, Serebrovsky established contacts with Turkish, British, French, American and Italian companies. In this work he was supported by Bronislav Kudish, the official Soviet trade representative in Turkey, and Philipp Rabinovich, at the time head of the NKVT Secretariate and plenipotentiary of the NKVT in Transcaucasia (and after 1922 director of ARCOS, London). This especially concerned oil trade and concessions. Together with Rabinovich, Serebrovsky also travelled to Sweden, Britain and the USA to negotiate naphtha contracts.[51] Because the capital of the Ottoman Empire was occupied by British, French, Italian and Greek forces, business representatives from Allied countries were very active and Moscow quickly realised that the newly minted Bolshevik oil dealers might play on their business interests using a divide and conquer strategy. After preliminary discussions with Anglo-Dutch Shell and American Standard Oil of New Jersey, it was decided to sign the first Azneft contract for petrochemical products with their French competitor, known in the Russian documents as SOCIFROS – Société industrielle, financière et commerciale pour la Russie – concluded on 9 May 1921.[52] This was quite a surprise for many especially because there was no trade agreement between France and Russia, which soon became the USSR, in spite of the much-publicised visit to Moscow of Édouard Herriot, leader of the Radical Party and future prime minister, in September 1922.

In the meantime, the staff of the Soviet trade delegation and many foreign trade, mixed-capital and joint-venture companies from Russia, Ukraine, Georgia, Armenia and Azerbaijan suddenly began to feel the consequences of the British raid. Parallel to the trade delegation, two major foreign trade organisations were ARCOS, which opened a branch office in Constantinople at the end of 1921 (according to other sources, in March 1922), and a joint-venture RussoTürk, but there were also the Grain Export Association, Petroleum Association, Transcaucasia Trade Office and many others with personnel and offices in Turkey that Russian intelligence operatives and agents also used as official cover. By 1922, Kudish had been replaced by Pavel

Anikeyev. The latter was forced to demonstrate vigilance and together with Varlaam Avanesov started purging all but a few staff members of various Soviet trade organisations, at the same time complaining to Krasin, People's Commissar for Foreign Trade, and begging to leave with him at least a few of the most valuable specialists.[53] These purges, of course, did not concern the Cheka, (G)RU or Comintern representatives and following the restructuring of the Soviet trade organisation in Turkey in May 1922, new trade agencies had been opened in Trabzon, Samsun, Inebolu and Mersin, an important port on the Mediterranean coast.

After the revolution, Avanesov (born Suren Martirosov) served as assistant and secretary to Sverdlov and played an active role in the prompt execution without trial of Fanny Kaplan, accused of attempting to assassinate Lenin in August 1918. From March 1919 Avanesov was a member of the Cheka Collegium and from August deputy head of its Special (Osoby) Department. He also combined his work in the Cheka-VChK with a senior position at the People's Commissariat of State Control (until February 1920 headed by Stalin).[54]

In October 1922, sharp disagreements arose between Turkey and Russia over Soviet trade activity in Turkey. On 24 October, the Turkish government raised the matter through a *note verbale* sent to the Soviet diplomatic mission in Ankara. The Turkish Foreign Ministry asked the plenipotentiary representation of the RSFSR to terminate all activities of the various Soviet trade agencies in Turkey until a trade agreement was concluded. On 1 January 1923, the Turkish side officially informed the Soviet government that it did not recognise the right of the Soviet trade mission to conduct trade operations in Turkey and denied it the right to issue permits for Turkish goods that were exported to Soviet Russia. In addition, at the beginning of 1923, the Grand National Assembly (GNAT) authorised the government to ban the import of Soviet goods into Anatolia.[55] Thus, trade relations between the two countries were practically broken off. And although the Soviet foreign trade company Naphtha Syndicate, established in July 1922, continued to operate in Turkey as a private firm, the GNAT refused to guarantee the rights of extraterritoriality for the trade delegate and the premises of the trade delegation. The trade agreement with Turkey was not signed until March 1927.

* * *

After several lengthy rounds of negotiations, the Anglo-Soviet Trade Agreement was finally signed in London on 16 March 1921, and it was only natural that the next move in this direction should be the Dominion of Canada. It took longer than one might have expected but in March 1924 Alexander Yazykov and his party reached Montreal. By that time the Red Scare, a perceived threat from the British and American labour movement, anarchism and political radicalism as by-products of the Bolshevik revolution in Russia had already been well present in the Canadian society. Already in 1920, the newly-formed Royal Canadian Mounted Police (RCMP), often referred to as the Mounties, charged with federal law enforcement as well as national security and intelligence functions, arrested about fifty revolutionary agitators. These were young people, most of them recent arrivals from Britain or the Continent, caught up in the revolutionary spirit and accused of possessing prohibited Bolshevik literature or of belonging to one of the illegal revolutionary organisations.

The conservative government of Sir Robert Borden, a former schoolteacher, lawyer and politician, at first ignored any suggestion that Canada might trade with Soviet Russia. The first such offer came from Martens, an unofficial Soviet representative to the United States based in New York, on 4 May 1920. Three weeks later, the Canadian Minister for Trade informed Martens that although there was no legislation prohibiting trade with Russia, the Canadian government would neither provide any guarantees for import contracts Moscow might make with Canadian firms, nor could it be responsible for the transportation of imported goods through Canada or to a point outside of Canada.[56] The minister, Sir George Eulas Foster, became known for coining the term 'splendid isolation' in January 1896 when praising Britain's foreign policy of isolation from European affairs.

In July 1920 Arthur Meighen succeeded Borden as Conservative leader and Prime Minister. Two months later he refused even to appoint a trustee to handle some $4 million worth of gold bullion which the Bolshevik government agreed to provide as the down-payment on the purchase of some railway equipment from the Allis-Chalmers Manufacturing Company, a US manufacturer of machinery.[57] At the end of November Krasin wrote to Sir George Perley, Canadian High Commissioner to the UK, formally requesting permission to send a Soviet commercial representative to Canada. 'The Prime Minister immediately referred the matter to the British Government,' a report maintains, 'and Lord Milner, the Colonial Secretary, advised him to stipulate to the Russians that they must desist from hostile propaganda against any part of the British Empire before trade arrangements were made with Canada. Meighen decided to consult his colleagues and postpone any decision on Russian trade until the outcome of the Anglo-Soviet negotiations.'[58]

In June 1921 David Lloyd George and the Dominions met at the Imperial Conference to determine a unified international policy. In London Meighen, who was accompanied by his Minister of Naval Service, was several times approached by the Russian trade delegation and although little aware of Russian matters he decided that the proposed trade would probably do more good than harm. Although the Imperial Conference was still under way, on 21 July he cabled to his ministers that he thought the Cabinet should adhere to the Anglo-Soviet Trade Agreement. The Cabinet concurred and two Canadian representatives were put on the staff of the British Trade Mission which opened in Moscow in August 1921 – the first official representation of a Great Power in the Soviet capital. As James Ullman has put it, 'Bolshevik Russia had taken its most important step toward full membership in the bourgeois community of states it so despised'.[59]

It looked as though Canadian-Soviet trade relations might start on a good note with a minimum of red tape but in December a general election brought to power a new leader, William Lyon Mackenzie King, and his Liberal Party which would eventually become the longest-governing political party in Canada of the twentieth century. It was Mackenzie King with whom Comrade Yazykov arranged the audience for the afternoon of 19 March. On 24 March 1924 he sent his carefully worded note to the Soviet representative: 'Following up my conversation of a few days ago, and with special reference to your letter of the 20th instant, I have the honour, in the best interests of both countries, to represent that Canada is prepared to recognise the Union of Soviet Socialist Republics.'[60] By that time the Soviet government had already concluded trade agreements with several key players. Great Britain was the first to act, having signed the agreement on 16 March 1921. Germany was next on 6 May with the recognition of the Soviet prisoner of war commission as its de facto consular and trade mission. Then came accords with Norway on 2 September, Austria on 7 December, and Italy on 26 December, followed by Czechoslovakia on 5 June 1922, and Denmark on 23 April 1923.

Acting in full conformity with Lenin's doctrine and the fundamental principles of the Communist International, which in slightly altered form would still be preached in Putin's Russia, Moscow believed that unless Soviet-style revolution swept Europe, the peace-loving first workers' and peasants' state would be crushed by the military might of world capitalism headed by Great Britain and the United States. From the very beginning, the Russians lost little time making themselves suspect in the eyes of the Canadian Government.

Already two weeks before Yazikov's [sic] arrival, Prime Minister King had been informed by an official of the C.P.R. [Canadian Pacific Railway] that a large consignment of books was en route to the Mission by sea. It was decided to intercept this shipment of some twenty crates and give it a thorough examination in case it contained propaganda. Customs officials in St. John, N.B. where the ship concerned was scheduled to dock on April 3rd, were instructed accordingly. Examination of the consignment revealed that the twenty crates and twelve parcels shipped from Moscow did contain literature that the authorities considered subversive. Altogether the shipment contained more than three thousand items including books, pamphlets and a small number of posters, and while most were harmless some contained material that vigorously propounded the Marxist-Leninist line.[61]

Therefore, on 12 April the Soviet trade delegate (who also acted as the official agent of his government) was summoned to Mackenzie King's office to comment. To the representative group of government officials that in addition to the Prime Minister consisted of the newly appointed Minister of Justice and Minister of Customs and Excise, as well as the High Commissioner of the RMCP Cortlandt Starnes (the traditionally used spelling of his name as 'Courtland' is wrong), Yazykov explained that it was his private library exclusively for his personal use. This was generally accepted and the final decision postponed until further notice. The discussion was still going on when the bottom dropped out in October.

The Zinoviev Affair, 1924

On the morning of Saturday, 25 October 1924, Thomas Marlowe, the editor of the *Daily Mail*, published an explosive story with a banner headline that read, 'Civil War Plot by Socialists' Masters'. As the same newspaper described it almost a century later, 'this really was dynamite, not least because the country was four days from a General Election, in which the Labour Prime Minister, Ramsay MacDonald, was hoping to retain power'. Over three columns on page nine the newspaper revealed the existence of a secret letter purportedly written (or at least signed) by Grigory Zinoviev, an important member of the Soviet Politburo and at the time Chairman of the ECCI, Executive Committee of the Communist International, otherwise known as Comintern.[62] In the letter, claimed to be sent the previous month to the British Communist Party, Zinoviev allegedly urged his British comrades to infiltrate and to gain power over the Labour Party – then in government – and to make it truly revolutionary, rather than allow it to remain 'under the thumb of the bourgeoisie'.[63] If this was not enough, the letter advised the CPGB leadership to rouse the British proletariat in advance of armed insurrection and class war. Marlowe never said who gave him a copy of the Comintern's missive.

Amazingly, questions about the origin of this notorious letter have been lingering for almost a century with sensational new publications coming out at regular intervals in various languages but without any definite answer ever offered to the public.[64] In their book about 'spies, secret intelligence and British prime ministers' Richard Aldrich and Rory Cormac almost entirely rely on the version suggested by Gill Bennett, the former Chief Historian of the Foreign Office. And instead of producing a fresh insight thanks to his privileged access to historical SIS files, the author of the authorised history of MI6 Keith Jeffery admits that he had 'drawn on Gill Bennett's careful and definitive study' for his account.[65] Aldrich and Cormac praise Jeffery's efforts saying that 'MI6 official historian sums up the suspicions nicely' while in their own account they, among other things, refer to a single article in *The Observer* suggesting that 'one of a team of four key White Russians suspected in the forgery, Alexis Bellegarde, had close links with MI6, and went on to become one of the service's most successful wartime double agents'.[66] In the meantime, this 'most successful agent' is not even mentioned in the authorised history of the Service.

The two authors also slightly misinterpret Jeffery's words, who actually said:

> Although it had been claimed that the Zinoviev Letter decisively contributed to Labour losing the election, their vote in fact went up, and the Conservatives under Baldwin won an absolute majority due to the collapse of the Liberal vote. The suspicion remains, nevertheless, that right-wing elements, with the connivance of allies in the security and intelligence services, deliberately used the letter (and perhaps even manufactured it) to ensure a Labour defeat.[67]

Two years later, Oxford University Press published Gill Bennett's latest version of the Letter affair with a self-explanatory subtitle *The Conspiracy that Never Dies* (2018). In her book, Mrs. Bennett indicates that while there are no definitive answers – yet – one of the plausible culprits is an ex-Russian Imperial Army officer Ivan Pokrovsky. Remarkably, his connection to the Zinoviev Letter was revealed by the *Daily Herald* as early as on 25 March 1929 and – what a wonderful coincidence! – the *Herald* story 'Red Letter Sensation' turned out to be almost identical with that published by Oleg Tsarev and Nigel West in *The Crown Jewels* (1998). The book, Gill Bennett believes, 'is based on KGB records'.[68]

The *Daily Mail* article of 12 October 2019 came out with a no less explosive banner headline, which this time read, 'Now, 95 years on, a new book poses a tantalizing question ... was the red plot letter that helped kick out Labour GENUINE after all?' The article quotes yet another new book, written by John Symons and published in London some days after the above-mentioned *Daily Mail* article and pretentiously titled *The Zinoviev Controversy Resolved*. Alas, the author uses old and well-known books by two Russian defectors, Georges Agabekov and Grigory Besedovsky, to support his argument that the letter was genuine and indeed came from Moscow.[69] There is no evidence to corroborate this theory and of course professor of philosophy at the University of Kansas should not necessarily be aware that whatever defectors say must never be taken for granted.

Sheila Kerr, a serious and reliable intelligence historian, devoted a long analytical article to *The Crown Jewels* by Tsarev and West, which she entitled 'Oleg Tsarev's Synthetic KGB Gems'.[70] In her analysis, Dr Kerr reminds the reader that Tsarev, a former lieutenant colonel of the KGB's foreign intelligence branch, played a role in persuading Robin Cook, the then Secretary for Foreign Affairs, to commission Gill Bennett to prepare a memorandum on the Zinoviev Letter using archival documents as primary sources. Mr Cook, the historian writes, celebrated Dr Bennett's study as a 'remarkable exercise in openness' and 'a unique exercise in international co-operation' with the Russian government. 'This important, complex book,' she explains, 'has much to offer historians, especially those inclined toward archeology, for Tsarev has skilfully choreographed his version of history to dance around the facts of some very well known intelligence and espionage cases.'[71] In her brief assessment of the Zinoviev Letter episode, Sheila Kerr reminds us that two MI6 officers were among those who had leaked the letter to the press and suggests that 'possible conduits were Desmond Morton of MI6 [then MI1c], Major Joseph Ball, an MI5 officer who joined the Conservative Central Office in 1927 [as the head of B Division, Ball also liaised with SIS on the matters of Soviet and Communist subversion], and Sir Stewart Menzies', whom she erroneously calls 'Head of MI6' (Colonel Menzies was appointed 'C' in November 1939; the chief of SIS in 1924 was Admiral Sir Hugh Sinclair).

Without any reference to the Secret Services' files, Keith Jeffery states that SIS was certainly involved, as 'the letter had been obtained by the Riga station, who had forwarded an English text to Head Office on 2 October [report no. L/3900]. The source cited was FR/3/K, Riga's star agent in Moscow. It took about a week to reach London and, having been evaluated by Desmond Morton, a copy was circulated by SIS on 9 October to the Foreign Office (directly to Sir Eyre Crowe, PUS, and John Gregory, Senior Clerk and Assistant Secretary) and other departments [Admiralty, War Office, Air Ministry, Scotland Yard and MI5]'. SIS categorically vouched that 'the authenticity of the document is undoubted'.[72] The unidentified source

FR/3/K (also FR/3/Moscow) was only known to be one of Rafael Farina's agents (Farina himself was FR/1, and his assistant FR/2), allegedly employed by the Comintern Secretariat and run through an equally anonymous cut-out, with over fifty reports from him remaining on file, which would probably be worth assessing today.

Remarkably, the Official Historian of the Security Service (MI5) Christopher Andrew states in his *Defence of the Realm*, that 'the Zinoviev letter came from the SIS Reval [now Tallinn] station, which appears to have been deceived once again by anti-Bolshevik White Russian forgers' (pages 148–9). One could think it was a slip of the pen, *lapsus calami*, but in *The Secret World* (2018) Andrew again repeated that 'it was a forgery obtained by the SIS station in Reval'.

Although Milicent Bagot's comprehensive MI5 history of the Zinoviev Affair written half a century ago remains classified, among many important documents that were sent to the National Archives after 2001 one file stands out. It contains a brief analysis drafted by G.E. Wakefield of MI5 on 5 May 1959 for Deputy Director General (DDG) Graham Mitchell. As the author of the report says, it is based on his cursory examination of S.Z. records in Archives pertinent to the case. S.Z. records are Scotland House files inherited from the police counter-subversion unit. These are primarily SIS letters to Scotland Yard of different dates all under CX/1174 referring to 'The Zinovieff Letter'. Wakefield's note may clarify some blind spots in the Bennett's and Jonathan Pile's versions of the affair.[73]

According to Wakefield, of the available SZ records only two folders are relevant to the case. The pertinent documents in these folders are:

(1) CX/1174 of 9.10.24 to Guy Liddell's department at Scotland Yard, sending a copy of the Zinoviev Letter dated 15 September 1924. [A manuscript note on this by Captain Hugh Miller of New Scotland Yard says that he spoke with William Strang, then a second secretary in FO's Northern Department, quoting as a confirmation a statement of informant that such a document had been received by the CPGB.] Wakefield writes that 'with regard to this "confirmation", it appears from a later Note dated 13.3.28 that it had been subsequently proved false'. He adds that 'it also appears from the same Note that some "subsequent amplification" of this false confirmation misled the Foreign Office in their assessment of the authenticity of the Letter'.

(2) A letter-copy dated 28 October 1924 makes it clear that the original Letter was a copy, and not a translation from Russian into

English – i.e., that the Letter, as sent to the C.P. (assuming there was such a Letter), was in English rather than in Russian.

(3)   CX/1174 of 17.11.24 to Scotland Yard, sending an alleged translation of the minutes (SNK Session, 25 October) where Chicherin states that Zinoviev had told him that the version of the Letter published in English was 'a deliberately distorted version' of a letter to the CPGB, drawn up by Arthur MacManus and dispatched to its destination.

(4)   CX/1174 of 16.12.24, Report on the SNK Session of 26 November with Chicherin saying, 'It would have been better had this letter not fallen into the hands of the British Secret Police … The original of the letter upon its receipt by the British Communist Party was destroyed by Comrade Inkpin'. British Communist leader Albert Inkpin denied the existence of the Letter, explaining that the document that MacManus had sent him and he destroyed was a copy of a speech by Zinoviev.

(5)   Missing.

(6)   CX/1174 of 9.1.25, which states: 'We now know the identity of every individual who handled it (the Zinovieff Letter) from the day the first person saw Zinoviev's copy to the day it reached us. With the exception of Zinoviev himself, they were all our agents'.

(7)   'Note on Zinovieff Letter for the D. of P.P.', undated, but marked 'ACSB has seen 15/6/27' [which probably means, Assistant Commissioner (of the Metropolitan Police) & Head of Special Branch Sir Wyndham Childs], setting out some of the facts relating to the disclosure of the Letter, mentioning that 'a copy of the text was received by Scotland Yard on the same date as by the Foreign Office'.

(8)   The *Daily Mail* editor's story of how he received his copies of the Letter from 'an old and trusted friend', and repudiating the allegation that it had been sold to him for £5,000 by J.D. Gregory, the official in the Foreign Office who signed the protest sent to the Russian Charge d'Affaires. Mr. Wakefield notes here: 'In this connection see later note on Mr. im Turn. There are also, in the CPGB HQ folder papers referring to some financial scandal in which Mr. Gregory was involved.' [Probably, a 1928 case is meant, known in the press as the 'Francs Case', in which Gregory with a Mrs Aminta Bradley Dyne and two other FO officials were accused of having used their position to speculate in foreign currencies – although Gregory was cleared of doing anything illegal, he was dismissed from the Diplomatic Service.[74]]

(9)   Various papers relating to the argument ... that the Letter is clearly a forgery since McManus [*sic*] was not in Moscow on the date on which he is said to have signed it.

(1?)   The problem of Mr. Conrad Donald im Thurn who first informed the *Daily Mail* editor Marlowe of the existence of the Letter (on 23 October, the day before the FO circulated in to the press). Marlowe described him as 'an old and trusted friend' and prime minister Baldwin described him as 'unconnected with office or politics or any of those things which make for conspiracy'. Im Turn stated that he had learnt of the Letter and obtained a copy of it, from 'a business acquaintance in touch with the Communist Party'. According to Wakefield, 'nowhere in the SZ file, or indeed anywhere else, it is revealed that <u>im Thurn was in M.I.5 during the war</u>'. 'I knew him well,' he adds. 'Whether any conclusion is to be drawn from this, I do not know. I have found no hint as to the identity of his "business acquaintance in touch with the Communist party", who provided him with a copy of the Letter.'[75]

Within a short period of time, however, it was established with considerable certainty that im Thurn did serve in MI5 during the war and that Baldwin was lying. To date, based on the well-established evidence, there is also no doubt that Donald im Thurn was directly connected with civil servants, and retired as well as serving officers of SIS, MI5 and Special Branch, as much as with 'office or politics or any of those things which make for conspiracy', to use the Prime Minister's words.

The prevailing theory since the publication of the Letter and until the end of the twentieth century had been, in the words of G.E. Wakefield, that 'there was an immediate and long-lasting controversy as to whether the Zinovieff Letter was genuine or (as alleged by the Communists and the Russian Government) a deliberate forgery, faked for the purpose of discrediting the Socialists and Soviets'. 'So far as I know,' the Security Service report states, 'this question has never been answered by the authorities publicly in a convincing way, and it is still [in 1959] considered one of those official "mysteries" which ... are liable to crop up years afterwards in heated controversy – with innuendos of official corruption etc.'[76]

Twenty years later, Christopher Andrew had to admit that a final verdict on the authenticity of the Zinoviev Letter was still impossible and the only thing possible was to weigh the balance of probability. 'If, however, the Zinoviev letter *was* forged,' Andrew deliberated, 'it follows that the "corroborative proofs", which the intelligence services claimed to have obtained from three wholly independent sources, were also forged. In that case the hypothesis that intelligence chiefs were simply taken in by one forged Comintern document appears hopelessly inadequate. It becomes necessary to assume instead either conspiracy or incompetence on a remarkable scale.'[77] With the benefit of hindsight one may now state with complete assurance that both – conspiracy and incompetence – were present in equal measure.

After a storm of publications analysing the Zinoviev affair in the 1960s and 1970s, including an article on its mismanagement by Gabriel Gorodetsky followed by an excellent book with a chapter analysing the case,[78] it seemed like after a while it was quite proper to speculate about this tricky business again. Before Gill Bennett's study appeared, a more balanced approach was that 'there is no field of modern history, in which the historian needs to tread more warily than in deciding the authenticity of secret documents'. And to illustrate how challenging it may be to separate the wheat from the chaff, especially in sensitive political issues, 'an impressive list of distinguished historians, including the leading British authority on Soviet Russia, E.H. Carr, have made notable errors of judgement in these matters'.[79] In the meantime, Carr, in his own brief comment on the Zinoviev Letter conundrum had rightly pointed out that intelligence officers (and, one may add, British intelligence officers in particular) are understandably reticent. 'Reports supplied by them to the Foreign Office for the use of ministers,' Carr notes, 'were marked by a strict economy of truth – how strict depended on their estimate of the minister in question.'[80] For example, Arthur Ponsonby (Baron Ponsonby), an old Etonian and a former Page of Honour to Queen Victoria, appointed by MacDonald as Parliamentary Under-Secretary of State for Foreign Affairs in charge of relations with Russia, was refused all access to intelligence intercepts and SIS reports. Remarkably, it seems he was quite happy about it. By his own admission, 'I was never allowed to come in, and I am glad it was so'.[81]

In her book Bennett refers to Gorodetsky's work *The Precarious Truce* where the author draws attention to the striking similarity between the 15 September letter, which caused such an uproar, and two other letters allegedly sent by Zinoviev earlier in 1924. The inevitable conclusion of the prominent historian and Russia expert was: 'It seems more than likely that all three letters emanated from the same source.' The letters, Gorodetsky explains, are similar both in style and content while most of the textual errors, which suggest that the notorious Letter was forged, occur consistently in all three letters. He further notes that 'the conceptual consistency of the letters and their deep familiarity with Soviet politics suggests that their authors were in fact Russians who managed to unite plausibility with "a tissue of absurdities"'.[82] Now, not every expert will come to the same conclusion and of course there is no way that the Letter or letters could have been forged by Red Russians, the GPU/OGPU or 'a group headed by Trotsky', as Bennett and a couple of other historians suggest. Regarding the first two letters, of 17 March and 7 April, allegedly signed by Zinoviev, Arthur Henderson, Home Secretary in the first-ever Labour government led by MacDonald and immediate predecessor of Joynson-Hicks in this post, when informed by the Special Branch emphasised the need for 'adequate evidence of the authenticity' of the document. And indeed, it was soon revealed that the source of the letter was SIS.[83] The required evidence never materialised and the file was shelved. The negotiations with Russia began on 14 April with MacDonald in the chair.

John Symons in his tiny book offers an interesting linguistic analysis of the text of the Letter – at least the one that became available to researchers – which on the one hand deepens the mystery of its provenance but on the other leaves no doubt that the original text from which the Riga SIS station's translation was made had been initially compiled in Russian by the White Russian émigrés. This original Russian draft seems never to have been found.

Mr Wakefield concludes his report to the MI5 DDG Mitchell with the following words:

> To sum the whole thing up, as far as I can on a hurried study of incomplete evidence, I cannot feel convinced beyond all reasonable doubt that the Letter was genuine; and as the original Letter, supposing it existed, was destroyed unseen by any living person and was never seen by anyone in Scotland Yard, the Foreign Office, or (so far as I can discover) even in S.I.S., there seems little likelihood that the problem will ever be satisfactorily solved.[84]

Leaving aside the Letter's provenance, all the rest is perfectly clear. As soon as the Riga station's copy reached Desmond Morton's Production Section at 54 Broadway, one of the SIS mandarins, probably Menzies, immediately contacted J. C. C. Davidson, until recently the Parliamentary Private Secretary (PPS) to Stanley Baldwin (and before him to Bonar Law). Lord Davidson, fully realising the impact the Letter was likely to produce, arranged for Donald im Thurn, a former MI5 agent, to get a copy.

It is said that Donald im Thurn enjoyed his time in MI5 during the war and when he returned to private life he missed the sense of belonging to an obscure but privileged gentlemen's club of Secret Service officers (at the time, SIS, MI5 and Special Branch were collectively referred to as Secret Services or S.S.). He turned to business and became involved in a variety of companies based in the City and run by Russian émigrés.[85] One of them was the London Steamship and Trading Corporation that collaborated with the Anglo-Russian Volunteer Fleet, since 1923 controlled by ARCOS.

Im Thurn was given a copy of the Zinoviev Letter on 9 October and upon reading the text became very indignant because, without questioning its authenticity, he saw that 'when the Labour government was proposing to lend good British money to Moscow, as part of a treaty which they had actually negotiated, Moscow was at that very moment engaged in fomenting sedition and revolution here'. In his testimony, signed by im Thurn personally and read to the House of Commons, he explained that he then handed this copy of the Letter (received from Davidson) 'not to the *Daily Mail* direct, but to a trusted City friend whom I knew to be in close touch with that newspaper, and requested him to arrange for its publication'.[86] This 'trusted City friend' was Guy Kindersley, a former stockbroker and major in the army. A Conservative Party politician, he was elected as MP for Hitchin, Hertfordshire in the 1923 general election and retained the seat in 1924. Unaware of im Thurn's connection with Davidson, he took the letter to the editor of the *Daily Mail* Thomas Marlowe. All the rest is more or less known with only one mystery remaining.

All three authors of official and authorised histories, Christopher Andrew (MI5), Keith Jeffery (SIS) and John Ferris (GCHQ), in their books refer to Gill Bennett's study of the Zinoviev Affair, themselves saying nothing relevant about the case. At the same time, we learn that Rafael Farina, who had been in charge of the Russian Section of MI5 before joining SIS, and as FR/1 was heading the Riga station as 'the sole representative of the SIS, directly under the orders of the Head Office in London and nobody else', was not only personally responsible for dispatching the Zinoviev Letter copy and a detailed report about it to London, but also:

> He was to provide Head Office with 'full particulars' of any agent or source he made use of 'in order that we may card them up for reference in PROD [Production Section]'. This should include 'the name of the individual, his nationality, social position, abbreviated past history, probably qualifications for employment, what lines he may be likely to be best on, and why, etc'. Any particulars 'likely to lead to the identification of the individual in case your letter got into the wrong hand should be put into code'. It was important that Farina supplied his list of sources 'at the very earliest opportunity' so that when an FR report came into Head office 'we shall at once understand who the author or authors are'. There were also 'brief hints on the form of reports' which confirmed that every report and letter to Head Office should be identified 'with lettered prefix and a serial number' [as already mentioned, in the Zinoviev Letter case it was report no. L/3900]. Three copies of all reports ... were to be submitted.[87]

Anyone familiar with this text would have serious doubts that all official historians with, as declared, 'unfettered and unrestricted access to secret files', were unable to identify a SIS agent (FR/3/K) who provided the Zinoviev fake.

Like the Freemasons, whose organisation, ritual and symbolism remain shrouded in mystery, the Bolsheviks and their followers and sympathisers in the West aroused both the hostility of the general public and the suspicion as well as fear of the authorities. This happened not merely because of their revolutionary potential and fervour (at least the former considerably exaggerated by their opponents) but also because they appeared as the agents of a hostile foreign power whose only aim was to destroy the existing order of things.[88] In the 1920s, the Cheka and then the GPU/OGPU, unlike the Comintern, were not able to or much interested in recruiting spies and secret agents in the UK, and even those who were happy to deliver whatever information mattered little when the Soviet Union posed no serious threat to a great world power like the British Empire. At least two of the British secret services, MI5 and Special Branch, hugely overestimated the danger of Soviet subversion and the significance of Soviet espionage. As Professor Andrew correctly showed many years ago, 'they remained curiously traditional in their search for it, concentrating their attentions on the labour movement, the armed services, the CPGB apparat and agents from abroad'.[89] Ironically, as it may now be stated with a very high probability, all their efforts were in vain and they were not able to uncover or get hold of a single Soviet intelligence operative, although they were a bit luckier with the Comintern.

* * *

In November 1924, the Soviet trade agent in Canada, Alexander Yazykov, who had by that time been in the country for eight months, received instructions from the newly established State Bank of the USSR, signed by its chairman Aaron Scheinmann (Sheinman), instructing him to obtain specimen sets of Canadian banknotes. Now it is difficult to say what Moscow needed sample Canadian paper money for. Earlier that year the Narkomfin started a monetary reform having decided to issue treasury notes (fiscal paper money) with the purpose of replacing the depreciating sovznak and the idea could have been to look at the Dominion banknotes as something in between British pounds and American dollars. In any case, this was not a particularly unusual request as foreign banks also needed such sets from time to time to protect themselves against the circulation of forged foreign banknotes. It is known that large amounts of Canadian dollars were coming to Soviet banks as a result of import-export operations, especially with Persia. This was probably one of the reasons that at the same time the Russian State

Bank (Gosbank) sent a $100 note issued by the Imperial Bank of Canada to Yazykov to verify whether the banknote was genuine or counterfeit.[90] It was immediately recognised as a crude forgery.

'Although counterfeiting was a federal offence,' a Canadian researcher notes, 'officials of the Imperial Bank did not consider the appearance of the Soviet note sufficiently serious to inform the R.C.M.P. even though the latter had requested that all such cases be reported immediately.'[91] But this bogus $100 note alerted the bank clerks that there might be more, and they were not mistaken.

In 1925 international money exchange facilities were not as simple as they are today, and Canadian money, like other foreign currencies, was usually collected by large London banking houses and routinely shipped back to the Dominion to be redeemed there by the issuing banks. Following the alert from Montreal, it was soon discovered that large amounts of fake Canadian banknotes were coming into the country and that the counterfeiting was so good that only an expert could tell the difference. The General Manager of the Imperial Bank called the RCMP and it was immediately assumed that because the counterfeiting was so good and on such a large scale, the only source of forged banknotes could be Soviet Russia. This was the first idea that came to their mind because there were persistent rumours circulating among some politicians and actively supported by conservative newspapers that the Bolsheviks planned to sabotage the economies of the capitalist powers by flooding them with counterfeit currency. For example, Frank A. Vanderlip, an American banker and journalist who used to serve as Assistant Secretary of the Treasury and president of the National City Bank of New York, sensationally announced to a group of US businessmen and Secret Service officials that the Bolsheviks had turned the talents of the Tsarist engravers, highly accomplished craftsmen, to counterfeiting British, French, Italian and American money.[92] The US Secret Service even produced a special *Counterfeiter's Glossary* for its officers.

In Canada, the Federal Department of Finance appointed one of its employees, a clerk named Walter Duncan, as a special investigator. After a series of interviews with the Imperial Bank of Montreal bankers, he found out that Yazykov had placed a request for specimen sets of Canadian banknotes. At once, the pieces of the puzzle began to fall into place – the Trade Agency was implicated in a Soviet scheme to flood Canada with professionally forged money and Yazykov's request was a key to it. 'Duncan was not a man to do things with circumspection', Ronald Adams writes. 'He swiftly went around to 212 Drummond Street and in an apparently overbearing manner demanded some explanations from Yazikov [*sic*]. When the Russian refused to show him the Agency's files on the original State Bank request and instead showed him the door, Duncan's suspicions were confirmed. He reported everything to the Prime Minister and suggested that proof could be obtained if a police raid was made on the premises of the Delegation.'[93]

An urgent and secret meeting was arranged at the Prime Minister's Office on Friday, 20 March 1925. The Commissioner of the RCMP, Cortlandt Starnes, was instructed by King to provide Duncan with several men and this force was scheduled to descend upon the Soviet Trade Agency on Monday, 23 March. According to the plan, all incriminating evidence collected during the raid was to be sent to Ottawa for inspection and evaluation. Fortunately, Oscar Skelton, Mackenzie King's most trusted adviser appointed Under-Secretary of State for External Affairs, who for whatever reason was not present at a meeting, managed to persuade the Prime Minister to contact London.

In the meantime, Canadian newspapers were running sensational stories on the forgeries in Britain and the Dominion in which Bolshevik Russia was named in no uncertain terms as the most probable force behind the economic aggression against the Dominion of Canada.

For two weeks nothing happened until on 6 April several coded telegrams arrived from the Colonial Office in response to King's request for advice. In them, Stanley Baldwin's government stated that the Soviet Trade Agency and its members were immune from search and arrest under the articles of the Trade Agreement. However, if the evidence of criminal activity was sufficiently strong the Canadian government could make the raid if it was prepared to accept sole responsibility for the consequences. In his letter Leo Amery, a former First Lord of the Admiralty now serving as Secretary of State for the Colonies, pointed out that if the search were to prove fruitless, Canada had better be prepared to meet Soviet protests with 'handsome apologies and redress on a generous scale'.[94] The second telegram advised King that enquiries made by the Foreign Office had established that a large number of the Canadian $100 banknotes had been coming from the Bank of Persia in Tehran.

After a year-long investigation involving a 24-hour surveillance of the Russian trade agency in Montreal, the RCMP had drawn a blank. A slightly more successful Scotland Yard effort concluded that a large quantity of counterfeit banknotes came from Rasht, the largest city on Iran's Caspian Sea coast, and from Hamadan, one of the country's oldest cities. From there the Imperial Bank of Persia forwarded them to London and from there back to Canada. Others came from Peking, Hong Kong, Harbin, Hamburg, San Francisco, Strasbourg, Berlin and Paris, so it was practically impossible to trace the original source.

Meticulously investigating the case, the Canadian scholar comes to the conclusion it is fortunate that Mackenzie King changed his mind and called off the planned raid on the Soviet trade delegation because 1925 was hardly the time and Canada certainly not the place to start dangerous political games.[95] (Two years later, Baldwin's Conservative government failed to follow their own good advice and ordered the raid on the London offices of ARCOS for similarly groundless reasons.) This, however, did not save Yazykov who was recalled because Moscow was not happy with the situation.

On his last visit to Ottawa, the Prime Minister was too busy to see him and it was Oscar Skelton who received the Official Agent to say thank you and goodbye. The Under-Secretary was informed that Ivan Kulik had been appointed temporary head of the trade mission until his successor was chosen. Skelton was also surprised (and probably even emotionally stirred) to learn that Yazykov had just completed the translation of a volume of Canadian poems into Russian.[96] He was obviously unaware that Yazykov came from a noble Russian family of diplomats, military leaders, scientists and scholars. When expelled from the St Petersburg Technological Institute for revolutionary propaganda, Yazykov went to Odessa where he took part in an attempt on the life of the Tsar, for which he was convicted and exiled to Siberia. In 1918, after the revolution, he became a member of the All-Russian Central Executive Committee (VTsIK), the highest legislative, administrative and revising body of Soviet Russia. When Yazykov was sailing off to Leningrad in early July 1925, he was 51 and it was his last diplomatic mission abroad.[97] He was eventually replaced by Longin Gerus, a former State Duma deputy who became a revolutionary and had lived for ten years in the USA, in exile becoming a farmer in Salt Lake City, Utah.

Gerus arrived in Montreal in October 1926 and there were no more problems with the Soviet trade delegation in Canada until May 1927.

* * *

On 3 May 1924, at about 4.00pm, Nikolai Krestinsky, the plenipotentiary of the USSR in Germany, composed and sent a long telegram to Litvinov, First Deputy People's Commissar for Foreign Affairs, with a copy to Chicherin. It was his first report of what later became known as the Bozenhardt or May Incident, which in fact was an unplanned and unexpected raid on the Soviet Trade Delegation (Handelsvertretung) in Berlin.

That Saturday morning, two officers of the Würtemburg Criminal Police with a German communist Johannes Bozenhardt in their custody missed a train to Stargard, an independent city now in Poland and formerly part of the German Reich with a predominantly German population, where they were supposed to deliver Bozenhardt. According to their later testimony, because their prisoner knew Berlin well having been employed by the Soviet Trade Delegation, they asked him to show them a place where they could get a decent breakfast. According to the generally accepted version, 'Bozenhardt led them to the headquarters of the Soviet Trade Delegation in the Lindenstrasse, pretending that it was a restaurant'.[98] This, however, raises some questions because in order to get from Invalidenstrasse 131, Mitte (formerly Stettiner Bahnhof) to Lindenstrasse 20–25, Kreuzberg (where the Trade Delegation was located at that time) one has rather a long way to go. And to any passerby, the gloomy grey building on Lindenstrasse looks like a government office, a prison or a bank but certainly not like a restaurant.

Anyway, the trio is said to have entered the building about 10:15 am and Bozenhardt, yelling out that he was a German communist under arrest, bolted and was helped by his colleague Lehmann, another German employee of the Trade Delegation, to escape via a side door, while the police officers were locked in the 'Director's room' and their names noted down by Alexander Postnikov, the house manager, Bozenhardt was spirited out of the building and hidden in a private apartment of his fiancée.

About two hours after the police officers were released and submitted their report, the chief of the Berlin 'Political Police' (Abteilung IA), Dr Bernhard Weiss, ordered a full-fledged assault by about 200 policemen on the Soviet Trade Delegation.

Dr Weiss was a lawyer from the family of Jewish merchants. He joined the Berlin police in 1918 and was promoted to head Abteilung IA two years later. After the large building at 20–25 Lindenstrasse was surrounded, seventy-five officers and men from Dr Weiss's department entered the premises and started a very thorough search. At the same time somebody managed to call the embassy saying that the building was surrounded by police and all employees, including both deputies (the official Soviet trade representative, Boris Stomonyakov, had just left, and his successor, Alexander Svanidze, Stalin's brother-in-law, not yet arrived), were being held in custody. Two deputy representatives were Vasily Starkov and Vladimir Turov. Starkov was an old revolutionary and one of the founding members of the League of Struggle for the Emancipation of the Working Class, a Marxist group headed by Lenin and established in St Petersburg in 1895. He got this well-paid job abroad as a reward for his former revolutionary activities. Another deputy, Turov, arrived in Berlin a year earlier and was probably an undercover INO officer.[99] Shortly before 2:00 pm the Soviet embassy telephoned the German Foreign Office, better known in Russia as the Außenamt, whose officials had not been informed of the police action, and demanded an immediate meeting with Gustav Stresemann, a former chancellor now serving as foreign minister. Half an hour later Krestinsky was received at the Wilhelmstrasse.

At the Soviet plenipotentiary's insistence, Stresemann, to whom the raid was also a surprise, telephoned the Prussian Ministry of the Interior requesting the search to be stopped immediately and the police withdrawn. At the same time, he reminded the Soviet diplomat that the building of the commercial mission was not extraterritorial, and that the agreement of 6 May 1921 provided diplomatic immunity only for the head and seven members of the Trade Delegation. When Krestinsky left the Wilhelmstrasse after a 50-minute discussion with the minister, the Außenamt sent a verbal note stating that the actions by the employees of the Trade Delegation constituted a severe breach of German laws. Following the raid, five persons who participated in the action against the police were detained, in addition two others – Postnikov, the house manager, and Kaplan, the chief of staff – were arrested and escorted out of the building because they resisted and insulted a police officer. In their note, the Foreign Office underlined that the matter was now in the hands of the German law-enforcement agencies.[100] However, by the late afternoon an official of the Eastern Department, Ernst von Druffel, had been dispatched by the Wilhelmstrasse to the Trade Delegation where he found that several desks had been broken into and heard complaints that the diplomatic immunity of some employees had been violated. The Soviet embassy was represented by Ivan Dmitriev, a counsellor, and Stefan Bratman-Brodowski, chargé d'affaires, who were sent to certify that the commercial mission had suffered significant material damage.[101] By 4:15 pm it was all over and the withdrawal of police from the premises was confirmed.

The German verbal note was published in the morning papers on Sunday, 4 May. On the same day Krestinsky ordered the Trade Delegation closed. On Monday, Foreign Commissar Chicherin told Ambassador Brockdorff-Rantzau in Moscow that the raid had demonstrated a complete change of Germany's policy toward Russia, in fact, a change of alignment.[102] Krestinsky was recalled to Moscow to report. In his absence, Bratman-Brodowski refused to talk about the incident. The German embassy in Moscow was informed on 7 May that the Foreign Office was assuming responsibility for acts committed in violation of extraterritoriality and suggested to discuss a settlement. Brockdorff-Rantzau was instructed to assure Chicherin that the pamphlets containing subversive propaganda obviously aimed at members of the Reichswehr and police (found during the raid) would not be released to the German press. A week later Dr Weiss, the chief of the political police, was suspended until the incident was cleared up.

On the day Weiss was furloughed, the ambassador telegraphed to Berlin that a new Soviet memorandum was being prepared. Indeed, he was duly summoned to the Narkomindel, then at No. 5 Kuznetsky Most Street, where Litvinov handed him a note signed by Chicherin verbally stating that it contained the minimum of Russian demands. Those included 'an immediate official apology, punishment of the guilty without delay and in a manner satisfactory to the Soviet government, compensation for the damages caused, and the acknowledgement by Germany that the whole Trade Delegation was according to the agreement of May 6, 1921, an exterritorial part of the Berlin Embassy'. Moscow further demanded 'a guarantee against future violations of the Trade Delegation headquarters'. This, however, was not all. Brockdorff-Rantzau complained about 'the complete cessation of economic activities, stoppage of all negotiations, the withdrawal of accepted contracts, an extremely vociferous propaganda campaign, and demonstrations and street processions of a provocative nature'.[103] Soviet grain and foodstuffs exports to Germany were stopped while Moscow refused to purchase German pharmaceutical and other products, placing orders elsewhere. Starkov, now in charge of the commercial mission, received unhappy German businessmen for only one hour a day, between 11 and 12, and only to revoke previously placed orders (totalling 8,140,000 gold dollars) and nullify Soviet export deals.[104] As if that were not enough, the Politburo sanctioned an assault on the German embassy in Moscow 'to demonstrate what must be done when an intruder violates the exterritoriality of a diplomatic mission'.[105]

The GPU arranged a rather clumsily-orchestrated attack on the embassy premises with one of its agents bursting in and making a scene in the course of which the guards promptly arrested him. The agent, named Kalashnikov, was quickly fired from his job and convicted of violation of exterritoriality of a foreign mission, all of which was duly reported in the newspapers. Because the only German reaction to the 'Moscow Incident' was a thank-you letter, several German specialists working in Russia were detained on espionage-related charges. In the meantime, Bozenhardt was arrested in Berlin together with his fiancée and his saviour Lehmann, and all three of them were sent to the old Stargard prison.

On 25 May, in his speech to the 13th Party Congress, Zinoviev declared that neither efforts by the German capitalists to prolong the incident nor attempts by the governing Social Democratic Party to precipitate a break had made the affair more than a passing episode. He stated that the German government would soon capitulate because it would realise that the Soviet Union had no intention of retreating from its demands. His confidence was partially based on the fact that earlier that month the German Reichstag federal election had increased the Communist Party strength from four to sixty-two seats (12.6 per cent),[106] and for Zinoviev this development spoke volumes since he attributed the success of KPD candidates to the efforts of the Comintern, of which he had been the chairman. Regardless of the election results in Germany, the decisive factor leading the Wilhelmstrasse to suggest a soft approach and propose a diplomatic settlement (not, however, yielding to all Russian demands) was the heralded Franco-Russian talks based on the results of the French legislative election (11 and 25 May), in which the left-wing Cartel des Gauches secured a victory. While negotiations continued in London (leading in August to a preliminary Anglo-Soviet agreement), as soon as Édouard Herriot was elected prime minister he immediately turned to the question of Soviet recognition. The German Foreign Office wanted amicable relations between Berlin and Moscow, so that it could keep being informed about these developments.[107]

The Bozenhardt incident was settled on 29 July, two weeks after the conference met in London to implement the Dawes Plan.[108] Although the settlement provided conditions for relatively normal relations to be resumed between Moscow and Berlin, the Kremlin was concerned that the Dawes Plan would move Germany into the Western orbit. Indeed, already in August the British Prime Minster, Ramsay MacDonald, in a letter addressed to the German Chancellor stated that he 'should be particularly happy ... to get Germany into the League of Nations'.[109] It was obvious, as the chief of the British Foreign Office Press Bureau wisely observed, that, although beaten, Germany was not going to be permanently crippled. Now it seemed the opportunity, for which the most prominent people in the German foreign service like Maltzan and Brockdorff-Rantzau had been waiting, had finally arrived and conditions could be made for both the West and the East.

With the conflict resolved, Krestinsky returned to Berlin where he would stay as ambassador until September 1930. Brockdorff-Rantzau left Moscow this to start a well-deserved three-month holiday. In December, Chicherin proposed to him the ingenious but somewhat far-fetched idea of enlarging the German-Soviet partnership into a 'Continental bloc' which would include France and be directed against Britain. The ambassador duly reported to Berlin but the proposal was rejected out of hand because of Germany's rapprochement with Britain whose support against France German leaders considered essential.[110] Brockdorff-Rantzau nevertheless managed to win Soviet agreement to sign the Treaty of Berlin in April 1926, under which Weimar Germany and the Soviet Union pledged neutrality should one of them be attacked by a third power. He remained in this post until his death in September 1928. Maltzan, since 1922 State Secretary and head of the Russian Department at the Foreign Office, shortly after these events would be sent to Washington as the new German ambassador. Praised as 'the most capable diplomat Germany has ever had', he would die in a plane crash in 1927 on the way from Berlin to Munich.

The Bozenhardt incident revealed a number of interesting aspects in German-Russian relations showing that the German security agencies, unlike their British or French counterparts, had their own ideas about the clandestine activities pursued by the Soviet agents in Germany. Primarily assigned to protect the state against political violence, crime and other harmful acts, various police departments and first of all political police (Abteilung IA) and Sicherheitspolizei (Sipo) or security police had served notice during 1924 that diplomacy and international relations should not overshadow domestic issues. Not at all concerned about espionage, which the German criminal law defined as pertaining solely to military targets and the penalty for which was extraordinarily light, the understaffed department under Dr Weiss regularly informed the Wilhelmstrasse about the continuing Comintern interference in German internal affairs. After the failure of the communist revolutionary uprising in Hamburg in October 1923, in which the role of the Comintern was obvious to the German authorities but the direct participation of Soviet political and military intelligence in the preparation and direction of the insurrection remained obscure, the situation did not improve. Dr Weiss reported that the overt expression of sympathy by the Bolshevik Moscow leadership with the German communists and the covert financial and propaganda support channelled to the KPD even increased during the Bozenhardt affair. Ironically, a leading article in *Izvestia* on 21 May accused Bozenhardt of being a police stooge. When he learned about it, Bozenhardt was so shaken that he tried to commit suicide in his prison cell.[111]

As if anticipating the scandal associated with the future notorious Zinoviev Letter to the CPGB of October, the echoes and reverberations of which continue to inspirate historians, in the spring of 1924 the leader of the Comintern Grigory Zinoviev in his several public statements called on the German workers to step up their efforts for the resumption of the revolutionary activity in their country.[112] This fact is properly documented. In the formal response, State Secretary von Maltzan instructed the German ambassador to ask the Soviet leadership to use all their influence to prevent the Third International from meddling in German affairs by advocating a violent overthrow of the government. Such actions, Maltzan stressed, might further damage the relations between the two countries and would have serious consequences.[113] No wonder the British officials accepted the Zinoviev letters as genuine when they surfaced.

Chapter 10

The Russians are Coming

Although Britain was the first country to accept a Soviet offer of a trade agreement signed in March 1921 and ended the economic blockade, opening Russian ports to British ships and international import-export business, the presumption of British enmity informed much of Moscow's diplomacy. After Lenin's death in January 1924, the rich Soviet harvest of diplomatic recognitions and established trade missions hardly went beyond legal formalities, and by the fifth anniversary of the formation of the USSR the country was still virtually isolated in Europe except for its close ties with Germany. 'And even this, Soviet officials feared, was being strained by Germany's *rapprochement* with Britain, a development,' an analyst noted, 'which might eventuate in an attack on the USSR by a united capitalist world.'[1] The Politburo Triumvirate of Stalin, Zinoviev and Kamenev, by now united against Trotsky, reasoned that the British would seek a European rather than Asian base from which to organise their anti-Soviet action.

During the previous years, based on Lenin's idea that a Russian revolution led by the Bolsheviks would be paralleled in Western Europe, the Soviet government was pursuing anti-colonialist and revolutionary goals in Asia. This strategic design had evolved in 1924 after the collapse of the proletarian revolutionary attempts first in Hungary and the previous year in Germany and by the precipitate decline in Anglo-Soviet relations after the Tory election victory at the end of October. While the new British government of Stanley Baldwin returned to its more comfortable anti-communist line and the NKID immediately changed its Western European focus from London to Paris and Berlin, the encouraging rise of national revolutionary movements in China and nearby areas induced Moscow to pin its hopes for the near future on the spread of Soviet influence in Asia.[2] In Europe, to forestall a united capitalist anti-communist bloc directed against Moscow, Krasin, by then the Commissar for Foreign Trade, was urgently dispatched to Paris as the first Soviet ambassador to France, while Chicherin sought to convert Germany's negotiations with Britain and France from a possible alliance against the USSR into mutually beneficial bilateral relationships. This plan, however, did not work out.

By sending Krasin as a plenipotentiary Soviet representative to France right after the government of Édouard Herriot recognised the USSR, Chicherin was trying to prevent a possible Anglo-French anti-communist alliance. Another important political goal was a rapprochement based on a lack of major conflicts of interest between the two countries. In late November he sent several requests to the Politburo asking to issue strict orders to Soviet personnel (that is, agents of the OGPU, Razvedupr and Comintern) working under various guises in France to avoid activities which could aggravate relations with Paris.[3] This, however, was too late to prevent the return from Moscow of Captain Jacques Sadoul, French renegade and communist sympathiser, the day before the arrival of Krasin, and the raising of the Red Flag with a hammer and sickle and a five-pointed star above them (a new design adopted in April), accompanied by playing of 'The Internationale', to celebrate the opening of the embassy. All this did not remain unnoticed by the anti-communist press.

Scandals related to Soviet intelligence activity in France were on the front pages of the French and international newspapers ever since the first 'illegal' resident, head of the joint GPU–RU residency Yakov Rudnik, was detained in Paris and then arrested and put into prison. With the help of the Comintern representative in Paris, the Bulgarian Stoyan Minev, Rudnik succeeded in recruiting one Joseph Tommasi, an official in the Car and Aviation Union. In December 1921 the Deuxième Bureau, one of several French military intelligence services, began to receive reports from Switzerland indicating that Soviet agents were targeting French armaments facilities. While the French agents were tightening their net around Rudnik, Tommasi skipped to Moscow one step ahead of the Sûreté detectives.

In November 1922 they were replaced by Semyon Uritsky, a future director of the (G)RU who represented intelligence department of the Red Army Staff and was assisted by Olga Golubovskaya, who soon returned to Berlin, and Maria Skakovskaya until his arrest in February 1924. Uritsky somehow managed to escape trial and hurriedly left for Germany. In March Jan Alfred Tilton (Alfrēds Tiltiņš in his native Latvian and Alfred Matisovich Tyltyn in Russian) came to Paris to replace Uritsky and take control of all agent networks. Because the Soviet government was still unrecognised in France, there were no official diplomatic representations which could serve as a reliable cover for RU officers so Tilton had to operate 'from the illegal positions'. Other members of his network were his wife Maria Tilton and brother Paul Tilton (Pauls Tiltiņš) as well as Vladimir Romm, a Lithuanian Jew who had also served with Aralov in Kovno as assistant military attaché. In November 1924 Romm would be transferred to the foreign department (INO) of the OGPU. He would later work under journalistic cover as a TASS correspondent in Tokyo, Geneva and Paris, and later in Washington writing for *Izvestia*. After his arrest, Romm testified as a witness against Karl Radek during the second Moscow show trial in January 1937.

The name Olga Golubovskaya (or Golubeva) says nothing even to the experts while her literary pseudonym 'Elena Ferrari' is rather well known. She was born in 1899 in Yekaterinoslav, Ukraine, as Olga Revzina. Her elder brother Vladimir Revzin would become a Soviet military intelligence officer. After joining the Bolsheviks and then the anarchists, Olga had served in the Red Army as a scout being often sent behind the lines on various reconnaissance missions in the rear of Denikin's army. At the same time her brother operated in Crimea on the Black Sea against Wrangel's troops. In May 1920 Aralov, then political commissar of the 12th Army, sent Olga to Moscow to the intelligence training course after which in March 1921 she was sent on a mission to Turkey. There, her brother Vladimir was serving as an OMS/Comintern representative at the same time controlling a group of (G)RU agents.

Aralov himself would soon arrive in Turkey as an official Soviet diplomatic representative. According to Maxim Gorky, Olga took part in the operation against Baron Wrangel in Constantinople when the Italian steamer *Adria*, sailing from Batum, rammed the yacht of the general. Wrangel, his wife and his aide-de-camp survived because they had just left the yacht and were on shore.[4] In November 1922 Olga returned to Berlin where she had been residing since April as 'Elena Ferrari', a Russian and Italian poet, while her brother was recalled to Moscow. In the GRU staff list he would be entered as 'Vladimir F. Volya'. Elena Ferrari was arrested during the Great Terror, sentenced in June 1938 and shot on the same day. After her trial, her brother was sacked from the Red Army, arrested and executed in March 1940.

Maria Skakovskaya (Skokowska) also spent considerable time in Turkey before she was recruited in France in 1921 as an agent of Soviet military intelligence. Maria was a daughter of a hereditary Polish nobleman, Wacław Skokowski. He had been exiled to Irkutsk, Siberia, where Maria was born in March 1878. Together with her sister she studied at the University of Geneva and later at the Sorbonne in Paris, where she was friendly with the famous Russian poet and critic Maximilian Voloshin. In Paris she also met Jelal-Ed-Din Korkmasov. A Kumyk by nationality (Kumyks are Turkic people indigenous to Dagestan and Chechnya), he had been arrested for his revolutionary activities in Russia, exiled to Siberia but managed to leave the country. Since 1908 Maria and Korkmasov lived together in a civil marriage first in Paris and then in Constantinople where they were close to the Committee for Union and Progress (CUP) and took part in the Young Turk revolution. Back in Paris in 1912, he continued his political work and she was managing a pension and a restaurant inherited from her mother where Russian revolutionaries used to meet. Later, her GRU biography claims, Maria got a position at the Russian military mission in Paris headed by Count Pavel A. Ignatiev. In 1915 Maria and Korkmasov separated and she married Semyon L. Boltz who, some sources suggest, would also become a Soviet intelligence officer.

Details of her recruitment differ. According to Valery Kochik, a GRU historian, she was recruited in Paris by Boris N. Ivanov, an illegal (G)RU resident who was an old friend of Korkmasov. However, in the early 1920s Ivanov was in Bulgaria (alias 'Boris Krasnoslavky') operating undercover as the first deputy director of the Soviet Red Cross. After a failed communist coup culminating in an attempt to assassinate the Tsar and leaders of the government by blowing up Sofia's Sveta Nedelya Cathedral during services in April 1925, Ivanov hurriedly left Bulgaria. Until 1927 he had operated in France, China and the USA before returning to Moscow. As so many other military intelligence officers, he was accused of spying, sentenced to death and shot in August 1938.

One of the members of the (G)RU network, a Russian émigré by the name of Grigory Zozovsky recruited like Skakovskaya in 1921, was arrested in Paris in April 1923. Three months later he was released without charge and expelled from France. Fearing arrest, Maria soon moved to Berlin and from there to Moscow.

When Pyotr Voykov arrived in Warsaw as the Soviet Envoy Extraordinary and Minister Plenipotentiary in November 1924, Grigory Zubov was appointed legal (G)RU resident in Poland operating under official cover as an attaché while Maria Skakowskaya was placed in charge of the agents' network officially registered as secretary of the embassy.[5] In June 1925 she was caught red-handed receiving classified documents and sentenced to four years' hard labour.

In France, as soon as the Soviet embassy was officially opened, the (G)RU sent to Paris an experienced intelligence officer of Polish origin named Stanislav Budkevich (Stanisław Budkiewicz), who had lived in Belgium, where he studied economics at the Free University of Brussels (ULB), and spoke fluent French. Budkevich arrived in Paris in April 1925 posing as an attaché of the embassy and using the alias 'Mikhail Petrovich Osovsky'). Until September the next year he controlled all Soviet military intelligence spy networks in France.

* * *

In the autumn of 1924, the INO leadership decided to do some reshuffling in the foreign residencies. The legal resident in Italy Grigory Yelansky (born

Hirsch Haim Lutsky) was transferred to France, and Adolf Chapsky, who was previously accredited at the Soviet trade mission in Stockholm, arrived in Rome (alias 'Anton Schuster') now appointed main OGPU resident in Italy and as in Sweden accredited at the Soviet trade delegation. This decision was not taken at random. It turned out that unlike other European nations, Italy replaced her provisional trade agreement with Russia with a trade and tariff treaty ratified on 7 March 1924. Within this treaty Italy even conceded to the Soviet trade delegation wider extraterritorial rights than it could ever hope to get, and her tariff treaty was the only one of its kind to be concluded with the recently-formed Soviet Union.[6] Thanks to these favourable conditions, even better than those granted by Germany, a more experienced operational officer was sent as resident agent.

Chapsky's period in Rome was marked by the great success of the residency because he managed to secure the first fully documented penetration of the British foreign service, although some evidence suggests that Soviet intelligence had at least one more human intelligence source right inside the Foreign Office in London in the early 1920s.[7] His name was actually mentioned in the KGB documents partially declassified for the book *The Crown Jewels* (1999), a collaboration project between Oleg Tsarev, a retired KGB colonel, and the British intelligence writer Nigel West, but the tip had never been followed up. Another high-level penetration, dating back to 1921, was in Vienna.

The penetration agent in Rome was an Italian messenger employed by the British embassy, Francesco Constantini (codenamed D2 and DUNCAN). The KGB archivists, who had access to his file, were only able to say that 'the residency officer credited by KGB files with Constantini's recruitment was Sheftel, codenamed DOCTOR'.[8] Neither Vasili Mitrokhin nor those who prepared summaries of the files for Tsarev for his book project with West could give further details on him.

The Russian Press Bureau was established in Rome in September 1917 with its headquarters at No. 66 via Due Macelli. It was directed by three very interesting Russian personalities – Konstantin Ketov, Vsevolod Shebedev and Mark Sheftel – all of whom had settled in Italy long before the revolution. Ketov (born in Saratov in 1880) had served as Rome correspondent of several Russian newspapers and in 1911 became the accredited correspondent of the St Petersburg Telegraph Agency in Italy. Shebedev, a native of Simferopol, had lived in Italy since 1907 and, being employed by the International Institute of Agriculture in Rome, collaborated with several Russian magazines and newspapers represented in Italy by his friend, Grigory Schreider. Both took an active part in the political and cultural life of the Russian colony in Italy and in 1914 co-authored a book on Italian culture published in Moscow as

Contemporary Rome. In May 1917 Schreider returned to Russia and was soon appointed the acting mayor of Petrograd, duly elected to this post in August.

Mark Sheftel was born in Taganrog to a well-to-do Jewish family in 1889. He studied philosophy, music and foreign languages under the guidance of his mother but in 1905 took part in the revolutionary events in Kharkov and was arrested and exiled to Siberia. Like many, he managed to escape in 1907 and came to France, enrolling at the Faculty of Law of the University of Paris ('the Sorbonne'). There, his primary task was not so much law studies but revolutionary agitation and propaganda among Russian students. Sheftel wrote in his memoirs that all this work in Europe had been supervised by Georgy Chicherin who emigrated in 1904 and became an active member of the Social Democratic Party living in Germany, France and Britain.[9] In 1911 Sheftel moved to Italy where he met his future wife, Ekaterina Stanislavskaya. The family moved to Liguria, the Italian Riviera, and he began to study medicine at the Instituto di Patologia Generale of the University of Genoa. Here, again, Mark was close to the politically active Russian émigré students.

After the February 1917 revolution in Russia, Sheftel and his wife returned to Rome where, together with Ketov and Shebedev, he headed the Relief Committee for Russian Political Emigrants located in the library named after Nikolai Gogol on via delle Colonette. The trio also set up the Russian Press Bureau (l'Ufficio della stampa russa) linked to the Russian embassy. The Bureau was considered the official news agency of the Russian Provisional Government. Its purpose was formulated by the embassy as 'the provision of truthful news of all aspects of Russian life, its current political and economic situation, at the same time informing the embassy of what the Italian press is writing about Russia'. The Bureau also published a daily *Information Bulletin*, whose boss and editor-in-chief was Konstantin Ketov of what now became the Petrograd Telegraph Agency, and its director Allegretti Alfredo di Pio, as stated in the documents, an employee of the Russian embassy. At the same time Sheftel completed his medical education and obtained a post of medical director at the Confederazione Generale del Lavoro.

In March 1915 Mikhail von Giers had been appointed Ambassador of the Russian Empire to the Kingdom of Italy and after the February Revolution of 1917 continued to represent the Provisional Government in Italy. The ambassy was quite satisfied with the work of the Russian Press Bureau and when the Italian authorities tried to expel the Sheftels, whom they considered dangerous revolutionaries, the embassy and especially its consul Ivan Persiani intervened to stop the extradition. The Bureau, however, ceased to exist in the autumn of 1918 because the embassy did not have funds to support its publications.

Although Mark Sheftel and his wife were allowed to remain in Italy, they were fired from the Ospedale San Giovanni in Rome where both of them had been working, and Ekaterina got involved in the campaign for the repatriation or exchange of Russian prisoners of war.

In 1920 Sheftel was employed as a medical doctor at the office of the socialist deputy Fabrizio Maffi and in July, together with Anton Geller (aka Antonio Chiarini), he accompanied the four-member delegation of the Socialist Party of Italy to the Second Comintern Congress in Moscow.[10] On 26 December 1921 a trade agreement was signed between Italy and Soviet Russia and since 1922 Sheftel had been accredited in Rome as the representative of the Soviet Red Cross. He was quite obviously not a Cheka operative but probably collaborated as an access agent. Such agents do not usually produce intelligence but can set up useful meetings and organise introductions to people considered for recruitment. This collaboration was provided at a price. After Sheftel became a Soviet official and before he started setting up informal meetings in his country house in Sant'Ilario with various individuals whom the local police considered suspicious,[11] Mark arranged that his mother, brother and daughter-in-law were allowed to join him in Italy. It is possible that during one of those informal parties his old friend Alfredo Allegretti, codenamed D1 by the OGPU, introduced the good doctor to Francesco Constantini. His formal recruitment was completed by Chapsky/Schuster.[12] In February 1925 Sheftel returned to the USSR but his wife remained in Italy working at the passport section of the Soviet embassy now headed by Konstantin Yurenev,[13] who was soon succeeded by Platon Kerzhentsev.

It is not known what Sheftel did during the whole year but in 1926 he started working at the People's Commissariat for Health headed by Nikolai Semashko. His wife was regularly visiting him in Moscow, always returning to Italy until at least 1927.[14] Later Sheftel worked in the USA as the Soviet Red Cross representative, a post usually reserved for intelligence officers although his name is not mentioned in any available list of the Soviet intelligence personnel. In 1935 he was arrested and died in the GULAG.

By January 1925 Constantini was providing, on average, 150 pages of classified material a week. Very mush satisfied, Moscow considered him their most valuable agent. 'Convinced of a vast, non-existent British plot to destroy the Soviet state,' *The Mitrokhin Archive* suggests, 'it counted on agent DUNCAN to provide early warning of a British attack, and instructed the Rome residency':

England is now the organising force behind a probable attack on the USSR in the near future. A continuous hostile cordon [of states] is being formed against us in the West. In the East, in Persia, Afghanistan and China we observe a similar picture … Your task (and consider it a priority) is to provide documentary and agent materials which reveal the details of the English plan.[15]

According to the documents provided by Mitrokhin, for more than a decade agent DUNCAN handed over a great variety of diplomatic papers and cipher material to his Russian handlers, but in 1936 he admitted that he had resigned from the British embassy (concealing the fact that he had been sacked for dishonesty). Not to lose the lucrative family business of selling information to foreign powers and, as it later became known, to the Italian Servizio Informazioni Militare (SIM), his brother, Secondo Constantini, codenamed DUDLEY, who had worked as a trusted servant in the embassy chancery for over 20 years, became a new source of British secret documents for Constantini's customers.

Since the Foreign Office had no security officer, it had to ask SIS for help. Secondo Constantini was promptly identified as a possible culprit but the embassy took little action. 'Instead of being dismissed,' Andrew reports, 'agent DUDLEY and his wife were – amazingly – invited to London in May 1937 as the guest of His Majesty's Government at the coronation of King George VI, as a reward for his long and supposedly faithful service'.[16] Another guest who had been invited to the coronation to represent the Soviet Union – one of the main consumers of Constantini's spying product – was Marshal Tukhachevsky. Known for summary executions of hostages and use of poison gas in his suppression of Russian peasant uprisings, Tukhachevsky was described by the British historian Simon Sebag Montefiore, already in this century, as having been 'ruthless as any Bolshevik'.[17] In June 2003, shortly after Montefiore's book was published, Russian President Vladimir Putin, a former KGB spy, was welcomed by the Queen at Buckingham Palace during the first state visit by a Russian leader in 130 years. Ecclesiastes was probably right and history merely repeats itself.

* * *

The OGPU's successful penetration of the British foreign service was overshadowed by an embarrassing series of intelligence failures that by 1927 became public. This happened primarily due to the total lack of experience of the first generation of RIS officers and agents. Many intelligence historians who write about this period allude briefly to dramatic revelations of Soviet espionage activities in different countries yet almost no one makes a reference to the initial source of this information.[18]

David Yulievich Levin was born in Byelorussia in 1889 and after two years at the University of St Petersburg was arrested for the first time for anti-Tsarist political activity. He spent two years in prison then emigrated to Germany, getting his doctorate of economics from the University of Heidelberg, and following the February Revolution of 1917 returned to Russia. Here he was elected to the Moscow City Soviet representing the Mensheviks, opponents of Lenin, was arrested by the Bolsheviks in 1920, and two years later went into exile fearing another arrest. Having spent some time in Germany and Poland, he moved with his family to the USA in 1939 where he became known as David J. Dallin.

In New York Dallin met Liliya 'Lola' Estrina (known in Russia as Lilia Yakovlevna Estrina). Born as Lilija Ginzberga in Latvia, she had studied in Moscow, like Dallin became close to the Mensheviks, emigrated to Berlin, married one Samuel (Semyon) Estrin, an émigré Social Democrat, and after moving to Paris in late 1933 began working as a secretary to Boris Nikolayevsky (erroneously spelt 'Nicolaevsky'), a well-known Russian political historian and archivist, former head of the Marx-Ebgels Insitute in Moscow. Nikolayevsky was deported from Soviet Russia by the Cheka and settled in Berlin but in June 1933 moved to Paris. There, Liliya soon befriended Trotsky's elder son Lev Sedov. Together with Mark Zborowski, an OGPU/NKVD agent (as it became known much later), Estrina was one of the closest collaborators of Trotsky and his son in Europe. After the death of Sedov, she moved to the United States where she met Dallin. Soon he left his wife, with whom he had a son, and started living with Liliya. At least two people – Sedov's mistress Jean Martin and the NKVD deserter Lev Nikolsky (aka 'Alexander Orlov') – publicly accused Liliya Dallin of being an NKVD agent. These charges, however, are refuted by the VENONA intercepts,[19] where both Dallin and Estrina figured under their own names and therefore could not be agents because under no circumstances could the real name of an agent or source ever be mentioned in correspondence.

David Dallin and his wife were much interested in Soviet affairs while he was working on the staff of *The New Leader*, a left-wing anti-communist magazine edited by yet another Russian Menshevik. For many years Dallin had been researching his probably most important book, *Soviet Espionage* (1955) published by Yale University Press. Collecting material for this book, his 'D Papers' as he called them, Dallin met with Soviet defectors like Alexander Orlov and Victor Kravchenko (whom he actually helped to defect having introduced him to William C. Bullitt) to discuss some aspects of Soviet intelligence operations abroad. Together with Eugene Lyons, Isaac Don Levine (the ghost writer of Krivitsky) and Max Eastman who had ghostwritten Kravchenko's bestseller *I Chose Freedom* (USA, 1947), Dallin was one of the important supporters and promoters of this collective work. The Information Research Department, a secret Cold War propaganda department of the British Foreign Office founded by Christopher Mayhew (later Lord Mayhew), the existence of which had been hidden from the British public for almost three decades, bought the foreign rights for the book and arranged its translation and publication in many countries. The IRD also arranged its active promotion worldwide.

Dallin also served as a vising professor of political science at the University of Pennsylvania and during his 23 years in the USA published a number of other works but none became so well-known and frequently cited as *Soviet Espionage*, dedicated to his wife Lilia and based exclusively on open sources like newspaper reports, public testimonies, interviews and books. Among Dallin's notes in the New York Public Library are summaries of interviews held between 1948 and 1951 with over fifty former Soviet political prisoners and notes on (published) primary and secondary sources relevant to his study of Soviet espionage and the NKVD.[20]

'During the year 1927,' Dallin writes, 'there occurred the first of the three major setbacks' that marked the course of Soviet intelligence operations in Europe and the Near East that had been in progress after the death of Dzerzhinsky and Stalin's coming to power. A crisis, he believes, was inevitable.

Late in 1926 Rudolph Gaida, celebrated hero of the Czechoslovak Legion, famous from its Siberian days, was arrested in Prague as a member of the Soviet secret service.[21] In March 1927 former White Russian general Daniel Vetrenko was arrested in Poland as the head of an important Soviet spy ring.[22] A week later compromising documents were found in the office of the Soviet-Turkish trade corporation in Istanbul; one of the corporation's chiefs, Akunov, was found to be connected with espionage on the Turkish-Iraq frontier.[23] Three days later the Swiss police announced the arrest of two Soviet spies, Bue and Euphony, who had worked under the ringleader Friedberg, a Dane, who managed to disappear.[24] In May of the same year, in Kovno, the Lithuanian general Kleszinski was arrested in the act of handing over secret military documents to an official of the Soviet legation.[25]

The next piece is especially interesting. According to *The Times*:

In Vienna, an employee of the Soviet legation, Bakony, was found to be the chief spy for Moscow. A Hungarian by birth, son of a prominent leader of the Kossuth party in Hungary and a naturalised Soviet citizen, Bakony had established contact in Vienna with employees of the Foreign

Office and was getting secret information for Moscow until the affair was discovered in May 1927.[26]

At the time the SIS representative in Vienna was Captain Thomas J. Kendrick, regarded by London as one of their best heads of station.[27] During his 13 years there, Kendrick was regularly sending voluminous but absolutely misleading information about Russian intelligence in Austria, Czechoslovakia and Hungary that was duly shared with MI5.[28] This happened almost certainly because, like in many other similar cases, his informants and 'reliable sources' were dishonest and double-dealing émigrés and local impostors who were feeding false intelligence to him in return for remuneration. Being unable to verify it, he took everything they said at face value and duly reported to London. Kendrick's most recent (and only) biographer devoted five long chapters of her book praising his intelligence exploits and achievements in Vienna, never bothering, like Kendrick's superiors in London, to check.

Remarkably, any mention of this 'sensational case of Soviet espionage in Vienna in May 1927', as most newspapers reported it, is absent in the available Secret Service files. This is probably because the Vienna station was temporarily closed down in 1927 following pressure from the Treasury.

This Vienna case is important not only because it contributed, albeit only to a very small degree, to the overall picture of Soviet intelligence failures ten years after the Bolshevik revolution. Although its role as the spy capital of the world will gradually develop to become 'a truth universally acknowledged' only at the time of the first Cold War (1947–91), Vienna showed the tendency to be used as a convenient 'city of spies' already in the 1920s. In this spy versus spy game, RIS have always been playing the first fiddle, leaving the United States, Britain and West Germany far behind (although at the time of writing other countries like China, Iran and North Korea were also active in Vienna). Ironically, not a single real Soviet spy case or operation is mentioned in the SIS station reports from Vienna in the period between 1922 and 1927.

Finally, the Austrian episode stands apart because following multiple foreign and local newspaper accounts of May 1927, the Office of the Austrian Federal Chancellor (Bundeskanzleramt) officially announced that 'von einer Spionagetätigkeit der beiden Entlassenen kann hiermit nicht die Rede sein'.[29] In other words, regarding two dismissed persons (whose employment at the Press Office had been abruptly terminated), 'there can be no talk of any espionage activity'.

The last episode of Dallin's chapter dealing with Soviet espionage failures of 1927 refers to the police raid of the Soviet premises in the Legation Quarter of Peking also mentioning that the French Sûreté arrested several members of the Soviet spy ring run by Jean Crémet, and the ARCOS affair.

The raid on the Soviet consulate in Peking, in which the police gathered rich booty, occurred on April 6, 1927. Four days later, the 'Bernstein'-Grodnicki-Crémet affair exploded in France. Finally, on May 12 another storm broke in England, where the Arcos affair, which revealed operations of Soviet espionage in Great Britain, led to the rupture of diplomatic relations between London and Moscow.[30]

Serious failures of Soviet foreign policy in Europe and Asia in 1926–7, described by experts on the period as 'renewal of suspicion and hostility', followed by dramatic press revelations of Soviet espionage in several countries was a result of the Communist doctrine of the inevitability of war. A Marxist-Leninist precept that wars are inevitable, based on the theory that revolutionary war is the highest form of class struggle, led Stalin and his associates to the firm conviction that if the Red Army was not yet able to destroy the capitalist world, Britain and other Western warmongers were plotting to attack the Soviet Union. Therefore, greater efforts were required from the Comintern and Soviet intelligence to penetrate the secret councils of foreign powers.

By 1926 Stalin had already firmly established himself as the leading figure within the Communist Party of the Soviet Union. In early 1926 Zinoviev and Kamenev drew closer to Trotsky, forming an alliance that became known as the United Opposition, but in October Stalin's supporters voted Trotsky out of the Politburo.[31] This way Stalin had outmaneuvered and defeated his principal rivals although it took him another 10 years to finally dispose of them. Now Stalin could exert greater influence on Soviet foreign affairs in which he was taking greater interest. Stalin's idea of 'socialism in one country', which he promoted as the party line, was based on his belief that before the Soviet Union became a great world power, that is, for at least 10 to 20 years, the Bolshevik-style proletarian revolution in the West could not be expected. At the same time, all nine members of the Stalin's Politburo – mostly from peasant families, poorly educated but with exemplary revolutionary records – began to emphasise with renewed vigour the danger of capitalist intervention. It had become crucial for them to better understand the secret plans of the adversaries, whoever they were, so Soviet intelligence was supposed to tell them everything they needed to know before choosing a course of action.

Alas, this was not exactly what David Dallin learnt from the newspaper reports and later wrote in his book.

General Gajda, Prague

Next to General Jan Syrový, Gajda was the most prominent former 'Russian legionary' in the Czechoslovak Army. This term (or, rather combination of words) is used in Czech historiography to describe members of the Czechoslovak Legion, the volunteer armed force composed predominantly of Czechs and Slovaks fighting on the side of the Entente powers during the First World War. In Russia, this 100,000-strong force took part in several victorious battles against the Central Powers. The Legion was also heavily involved in the Russian Civil War, fighting the Bolshevik Red Army and at times controlling several major areas in Siberia.

According to his biographer, Gajda was a Pan-Slav Czech and anti-German chauvinist born in 1892 at the Austro-Hungarian naval base of Cattaro (today Kotor, Montenegro) as Rudolf Geidl. Before the war, he changed his German name to the more Czech-sounding Radola Gajda and when conscripted into the Austro-Hungarian army served as a druggist in the sanitary corps on the Serbian front. After deserting to Montenegro in 1915, he made his way to Russia. There, after a series of adventures, Gajda came to serve as Admiral Kolchak's chief of staff and later commanded one of the large military units of the Czechoslovak Legion. Although described by his biographer as 'a man of limited education, unsophisticated and vain', Gajda possessed a natural intelligence and colourful personality that enabled him to rise rapidly in the Legion. General Charles Mittelhauser, the French chief of the Czechoslovak General Staff from 1921 to 1925, characterised Gajda as possessing all the advantages (and disadvantages) of a condottiere.[32] Even so, Gajda's cantankerous personality led him into repeated conflicts with his fellow officers and superiors both in Siberia and in post-war Czechoslovakia.

In 1918 in Yekaterinburg Radola met a young girl, Ekaterina Permyakova, whom he married the next year as soon as she turned 16. It was his second marriage. Back at home in January 1920, Gajda, then 28, bought a villa in Říčany, a small town about 20km south of the centre of Prague, where he settled with his wife. Their first son, Vladimir (Ivann), was born in March 1920 and his younger brother, Georgy (Jiří) in November 1921.

After his return from Russia Gajda expected to assume one of the key positions in the Czech army, but the French Military Mission, then in charge of the army's organisation and instruction, had other plans for him and Gajda was sent to the celebrated École de Guerre in Paris which prepared senior officers to assume staff responsibilities. After finishing his studies, Gajda was given a command position in the Košice district in eastern Slovakia. Although he was far from the capital, he continued to be one of the most important and popular military leaders because Czechoslovakia's legionaries, especially those who had served in Russia, were hailed as heroes in Czechoslovak society and politics.

In spite of his position in the province, Gajda remained very active and President Tomáš Garrigue Masaryk finally decided to transfer him to Prague where he thought it would be easier to control the general. In November 1924 Gajda was appointed first deputy chief of staff subordinate to Mittelhauser. Another French officer, General Louis Eugène Faucher, served as second deputy chief of staff.

In Prague, Gajda continued to be active in politics and late in 1925 became one of the founders of the Independent Union of Legionaries, a right-wing organisation. He also supported openly fascist groups such as the National Movement, which in 1926 grew into the National Fascist Community (Národní obec fašistická, NOF).

In the meantime, the country found itself trapped in political turmoil. Following the 1925 general election, a new cabinet was formed under Antonín Švehla, the leader of the Agrarian Party. A right-wing politician, Jiří Stříbrný, one of the 'founding fathers' of the Czechoslovak Republic, was appointed Minister of Defence. This cabinet fell in March 1926 and was replaced by a non-political cabinet under Jan Černý, a lawyer who had already served as prime minister in 1920–1 and several times as the provincial president of Moravia. The Stříbrný wing of the National Socialists, supported by other right-wing groups, tried to oust Edvard Beneš as Foreign Minister but President Masaryk refused to appoint a new cabinet without Beneš who represented his country at the 1919 peace conference in Paris and would become the longest serving foreign minister of Czechoslovakia.

Parallel to the political disputes of 1925–6, there were changes in the military leadership. On 1 January 1926 General Syrový replaced Mittelhauser as chief of staff. In February, Millethauser departed from Prague leaving Faucher in charge of the French Military Mission. He, in turn, pulled a few strings to place Syrový in the cabinet as a non-political expert for the French to be able to institute and control reforms in the Czechoslovak army. On 19 March Gajda was appointed chief of staff on an interim basis until a new cabinet was formed. Very soon rumours began to spread in the German areas of Bohemia that using his current position Gajda might attempt a fascist coup. A close ally of Beneš, the influential Social Democrat and journalist Rudolf Bechyně, attacked Gajda in the Social Democratic paper *New Freedom*, accusing the right-wing groups of searching for a formal Führer (leader), a general to lead a coup. 'Bechyně's, diatribe,' Jonathan Zorach writes, 'prompted a furious debate about Gajda in the Czechoslovak press ... Finally, on 2 July, Masaryk removed Gajda from his post, sent him on leave, and had him investigated for possible misconduct.'[33] The British military attaché Major Oldfield reported that surprisingly Gajda did nothing to refute these allegations.[34] In his turn Lewis Einstein, American Minister to Czechoslovakia, sent a detailed report to Frank Kellogg, the US Secretary of State.

The situation was aggravated by the announcement, immediately following his ouster, that Gajda, while a student of the École de Guerre in Paris, obtained and handed over to a Soviet agent a secret French military document. In early September even President Masaryk entered the fray by denouncing Gajda's behaviour in an interview to the liberal German newspaper *Prager Tagblatt*.

Despite general sympathy and solidarity with Gajda among the former members of the Czechoslovak Legion in Russia, Beneš was able to press his case against the general (he later admitted that he had great difficulty convincing army officers of Gajda's misconduct), and no high-ranking 'Russian legionaries' openly championed Gajda's course. In December, a military tribunal convicted him of having had contact with an unnamed representative of the Soviet government in 1920 (?!). His sentence was the retirement from the army with the loss of 25 per cent of his pension.

The records of the French Foreign Ministry, studied by Zorach, show that 'the French were as mystified as anyone else by the progress of the Gajda affair'. Relevant documents in the MAE (Archives du Ministère des Affaires étrangères) reveal that General Faucher reported to Paris that Gajda could not have had access to any secret military documents in France, as students were never given any privileged access to them. Gajda was eventually accused of having given French army manuals to a Soviet agent but, as one wit remarked, such 'secret documents' could have been procured from practically any Paris bookseller, not to mention the famous Bouquinistes of the Seine riverbanks where anything that had ever been printed could be found. The French did not make any statement and seemed not to have had any security problems with Gajda, speculating that perhaps Beneš and Vladimir Antonov-Ovseenko, appointed Soviet representative in Czechoslovakia in June 1924, might have instigated legal action against Gajda. It was known that the Soviets especially resented him for his daring exploits with the White forces in Siberia. This view was strengthened by the *Pravda* article of 11 January 1927 fiercely attacking the general. The Czechoslovak Communists and Socialists also raised their voices against him in the press and in parliament.

With all that, at least one curious aspect of this case cannot be ignored. General Faucher and the French Minister to Prague Fernand Couget were puzzled by the alacrity with which Antonov-Ovseenko was trying to persuade other diplomats that Gajda had indeed been in touch with the Soviets in 1920.[35] As Gajda was rabidly anti-Communist, the Soviets should have hated him. The Soviet role, if any, in the affair still appeared enigmatic to British, American and French diplomats in Prague.

The attempt of Masaryk and Beneš to discredit Gajda encountered difficulties in 1927 when Gajda used a civil court to sue the two main witnesses against him for libel. The charges against Gajda were not supported by documentary evidence but by the personal testimony of an old foe, Major Jaroslav Kratochvil (a Social Democrat and former Russian legionary who had opposed the Allied intervention in Siberia), and two other witnesses of dubious personal integrity, who held personal grudges against Gajda. Much to the embarrassment of the Hrad [Prague Castle, figuratively, country's rulers], the civil court upheld Gajda's suit in a decision announced in March 1927. There was no longer any danger that Gajda might recover his military post, but he threatened to become a powerful ally of right-wing forces in Czechoslovak politics.[36]

This, however, did not deter the country's leadership from further action. At the end of October 1927 members of the Czechoslovak Senate were presented with new 'evidence' of Gajda's alleged contacts with the Soviet government. This time it was a telegram dating back to October 1920, signed by Chicherin and addressed to Dr Solomon I. Gillerson, representative of the Soviet Red Cross in Prague in 1920–1 who was also in charge of the prisoner exchange and repatriation until they suspected him, wrongly, to be somehow involved in espionage.[37]

The text of the telegram suggests that Gillerson or a member of his mission might have been in contact with Gajda in or about September–October 1920 proposing to continue relations with him in Moscow, to which Chicherin responded: 'It would be interesting to know beforehand what offers he will make us; we have nothing to offer him and we await what he will say to us. Arrange it so that the initiative comes from him and not from us.'[38] On 6 October 1926 Sir George Clerk reported to the Foreign Office about Masaryk claiming that several telegrams, decoded in 1921, mentioned Gajda but it was incomprehensible that the president of the country and its foreign minister, Beneš, would wait for five years to make this information public tolerating their leading general's secret contacts with the Soviets. It is also doubtful that the Soviet NKID would send such sensitive information to its representatives through the official channels of the host country, as reported.

The telegram (or telegrams) had never been presented as evidence in court. Masaryk told the British minister that he was personally convinced of Gajda's guilt, complaining that Soviet officials refused to testify. Nevertheless, Gajda was tried again in a special military court of appeal and, in February 1928, the judge found him guilty on six charges. The first two of those were (1) negotiating with the Soviet government at a time when the Czechoslovak government was on unfriendly terms with Moscow; and (2) giving two books of information from l'École de Guerre to a Russian intelligence agent at the time of his two-year studies in Paris.[39] The appeal court upheld the decision made by the trial court: early retirement from the army with the loss of 25 per cent of his state pension.

After the court of appeal's decision was announced, General Faucher reported to his legation that the court was composed of two hand-picked legionaries and one former Austro-Hungarian officer who undoubtedly were willing to go along with the views of government officials eager to discredit Gajda. The fact that the defendant had won a civil suit against the two witnesses who charged him with stealing 'two books of information' (?!) from the French military school was disregarded by the judges of the appeals court. The proceedings were head 'in camera' with the public and press excluded and the doors of the courtroom closed.

After his conviction Gajda remained active in Czechoslovak politics until the German occupation of his country. Although he is said to have been investigated by the Gestapo, he was not imprisoned. Just days after Prague was liberated in May 1945, Gajda was arrested by SMERSH and interrogated while on remand, losing his eyesight as a result of cruel treatment. He died in Prague in April 1948.

General Vetrenko, Warsaw

Like in the 'spy case' of General Gajda, any reasonable explanation why the Polish authorities decided to accuse Russian General Daniel Vetrenko of espionage is missing.

Vetrenko, whose father was awarded the status of personal nobleman, was born in a small village in south-western Russia in December 1882. It would later become known as the Cossack Verdun for the opposition to the Bolsheviks. After two-year studies at the Faculty of Law of the Imperial University of Saint Vladimir in Kiev, Vetrenko joined the Tsarist army in August 1904. He was admitted to the Imperial Nicholas Military Academy (former General Staff Academy) in 1913 and after the first year sent to the front. Awarded several high military decorations for bravery, shortly before the Bolshevik revolution Vetrenko was promoted to the General Staff, serving with the Ukrainian People's Army (also known as the Ukrainian National Army, UNA) in the Ukrainian War of Independence. Having moved with his regiment to Pskov near Estonia, he joined the White forces of the Northern Corps. Raised to the rank of colonel, Vetrenko was soon promoted to major-general and was appointed commander of the 3rd Infantry Division consisting of six regiments, part of the North-Western White Army (SZA).

In the autumn of 1919, the SZA was successfully advancing on Petrograd under Generals Alexander Rodzyanko and Nikolai Yudenich.

The one and only logically inexplicable episode in Vetrenko's otherwise exemplary military and combat career happened during that autumn offensive. He was ordered to cut the Nikolaevskaya railway at Tosno in the vicinity of Petrograd and the Red Army was to quickly transfer numerous reserves from Central Russia to this area, allowing them to create a decisive superiority of forces in a north-west direction. After ten days of fierce fighting, with the number of the advancing Red Army troops growing to 60,000 men, the SZA began to retreat and on 3 November withdrew to the Estonian border in the Narva region. In Estonia, Yudenich was briefly arrested and in spite of his fiasco under Tosno,[40] Vetrenko was appointed temporary commander of the SZA in January 1920 having previously been awarded the Order of Saint Stanislaus 1st class. In a few days the North-Western White Army was liquidated.

General Vetrenko with his wife and two-year-old son Leonid settled in Estonia where he made his living organising groups of labourers for peat extraction. After a while the family moved to Poland. It is unclear what Vetrenko did there but in March 1927 he was apprehended in Warsaw, taken into custody, charged with espionage and put into prison.

The first RIS resident (head of station) in Poland representing both the INO and the RU was a Pole, Mechislav Loganovsky (Mieczysław Łoganowski) alias 'Luganetz', who arrived in April 1921, declared to the Foreign Ministry as First Secretary of the Soviet diplomatic mission. In September 1923 he was transferred to Vienna. His deputy in Warsaw was another Pole, Kazimir Baransky (Kazimierz Barański), operating undercover as Second Secretary of the legation alias 'Kazimierz Kobecki'. Baransky/Kobecki was placed in charge of the rezidentura after the departure of Loganovsky.

Unlike his predecessor, Baransky represented only the OGPU's foreign department (INO). The Intelligence Department of the Red Army Staff (Razvedupr or RU) started to operate in Poland on their own in November 1924, with the arrival of Pyotr Voykov as Minister Plenipotentiary of the Soviet Union to Poland. The first RU resident arriving with the staff of the mission was Grigory Zubov assisted by Elena Birenzweig-Balashova. The agents' network was controlled by Maria Skakovskaya (Skokowska), officially acting as secretary of the mission. After Zubov, the RU in Warsaw was represented by Vasily Talbov as chief 'legal' resident.[41] In 1925–6 Alexander Iodlovsky (Jodłowski) served as deputy resident, alias 'Jan Kowalski'. It is possible that General Vetrenko was one of his contacts.

Iodlovsy/Kowalski was arrested in late February 1926 during a secret meeting with his agents and in December 1927 sentenced to five years imprisonment. In June 1926 Skakovskaya was arrested and sentenced to six years. By that time Vetrenko had already been detained and interrogated in police custody. Iodlovsky later had his sentence reduced to four years. Released in March 1931 (together with Skakovskaya), back in Moscow he was appointed section chief (3rd section, statistics) at the (G)RU headquarters. Both Skakovskaya and Iodlovsky were awarded the Order of the Red Banner 'for extraordinary accomplishments, personal heroism and courage' in February 1933. Two years later, in July 1935, he was sent to Berlin as the (G)RU legal resident using the cover of deputy head of the press section of the embassy (alias 'Alexander M. Danilevich'). Summoned to Moscow in July 1937, Iodlovsky was arrested as a Polish spy, sentenced to death and executed a month later. Skakovskaya was shot in October of the same year.

Their INO colleague and fellow countryman, very active and feeling like a fish in water in his native Poland, Kazimir Baransky is credited with organising the attack on the Warsaw Citadel in October 1923 (28 killed, 48 severely injured and 110 hurt, according to the Reuters report). He is also said to having been involved in operations against Savinkov and Tyutyunnik, both of whom had been lured to the Soviet territory and arrested. A good recruiter, Baransky was able to set up agents' networks procuring valuable counter-intelligence information about the activities of various anti-Soviet émigré groups and Polish agents working against Russia.

A flop happened in the summer of 1924. Although the cause of the Citadel explosion was never clarified, the authorities suspected that Baransky/ Kobecki was somehow involved and routinely placed him on police watchlist. He was finally arrested in a sting operation organised by the State Police under Inspector General Marian Borzęcki. The spy was severely beaten, declared persona non grata and expelled.

His successor in Warsaw was Vasily Vysotsky (Wysocki), which was probably a mistake because he was born in the village of Strawieniki near Wilno (now Vilnius) and in early 1919 served as a commissar of the Bolshevik militia in the Lithuanian capital. Arrested after the city was captured by the Polish forces as a result of the successful Vilna offensive at the end of April 1919, Vysotsky was put in a Polish prison and after several months exchanged and sent to Soviet Russia. Years later he arrived in Warsaw as a Soviet diplomat and was immediately placed under covert police surveillance because compromising documents tend to live long. Especially those in the security services files.

Whether Vetrenko was detained as a result of this surveillance or for whatever other reason would remain a mystery. In April 1927 a Russian-language newspaper published in Reval reported based on information from

Warsaw that the investigation had been completed and the court hearing would begin either next week or in early May. It had been established, the report claimed, that Vetrenko had been involved in espionage in Poland for over three years having spent about three million zloty during his time as a Soviet spy. The investigators also found out, it was reported, that Vetrenko had been a Bolshevik agent even before he came to Poland, that is, while he was still serving with the North-Western Army (SZA), which could explain why he had ignored orders to cut the Moscow-Petrograd railway at Tosno that prevented the successful completion of the White Army offensive.[42] There was no mention of any spy ring and no any details were given about what exactly General Vetrenko did as a Soviet spy.

While Vysotsky continued to fulfil his duties as both the OGPU main resident and second secretary of the legation until 1930, after a year in a Polish prison Vetrenko was expelled to Soviet Russia where he was immediately arrested.

Released from prison in the early 1930s, he lived in some remote places in Siberia and the Far East working as a bookkeeper or an accountant while his son relocated to Leningrad where the seaport required more labour force.[43] He later used this opportunity to enrol at the university. Nothing is known about Vetrenko's wife except that her name was Maria and that none of them was persecuted during the Great Terror. After the war the former general settled with his relatives in Krasnodar Krai in the North Caucasus very near to where he was born and raised. In 1948, already seriously ill, Vetrenko moved to his son's family in Leningrad where he passed away peacefully aged 67.

Turkey, Switzerland and Lithuania

A prolonged collective effort of several colleagues – leading Turkish and British academics specialising in the period – did not bring any results. Comrade Akunov, a Soviet official 'connected with espionage on the Turkish-Iraq frontier', could not be found. It is known that parallel to the Soviet trade delegation two major foreign trade organisations in Turkey were ARCOS and a joint-venture RussoTürk, but there were also Grain Export Association, Petroleum Association, Transcaucasia Trade Office and many others that Russian intelligence operatives and agents used as official or semi-official cover. Among many Soviet agents working in Turkey in the 1920s under various aliases, one Akunov could have easily been lost. But there were others.

Dr Ephraim Goldenstein studied in the faculty of medicine at the University of Vienna founded in 1365, one of the oldest medical schools in the world. As a medical doctor working for the Russian Red Cross, he welcomed the February Revolution of 1917 and was elected chairman of the workers' and soldiers' soviet in Rovno, a city in western Ukraine. Four years later he was sent to Poland as part of the Soviet repatriation commission after the peace treaty between Poland, Russia and the Ukraine was signed in Riga in March 1921.[44] Lev Karakhan, the first diplomatic representative of the RSFSR arrived in Warsaw after Goldenstein in May, accompanied by Leonid Obolensky (the latter is often erroneously confused with Prince Obolensky).[45] Obolensky would succeed Karakhan and remain in Warsaw until October 1924. From August 1923 Goldenstein had served as a member of the non-diplomatic staff of the Soviet legation but in December 1924 he was transferred to Vienna as Second Secretary of the mission and at the same time INO resident in charge of the Austrian and Balkan operation. From December 1925 Goldenstein operated in Turkey as INO resident also under the familiar diplomatic cover of Second Secretary.[46]

Yakov Minsker was born in Kiev into a Jewish tailor's family and like Goldenstein welcomed the February Revolution and was elected chairman of the workers' and soldiers' soviet in Irkutsk. In 1921 he was part of the local ECCI staff responsible for Comintern work in the Far East but in February 1922 was transferred to Moscow and joined the INO. After several foreign postings under the diplomatic cover, he briefly served as a vice-consul in Shanghai from where, in December 1926, he was sent to Ankara operating under the cover of an embassy attaché at the same time appointed chief OGPU resident in Turkey. Three years later his tour of duty ended and he returned to Moscow.

When Minsker was still in charge of the OGPU in Turkey, Saul Saulov, another Jew from Ukraine, arrived in Ankara fresh from the Oriental Faculty of the Frunze Military Academy. In March 1927 he was transferred to the INO and joined the staff of the residency commanded by Minsker. In June 1928 Saulov was appointed vice-consul in Istanbul and at the same time the INO resident agent.

Another Cheka officer working in Turkey until March 1927 was Robert Gulbis, originally from what was then known as Livonia, a historical region on the eastern shore of the Baltic Sea, now part of Latvia. In 1922 Gulbis joined the INO operating undercover as a German businessman 'Grünfeld', the alias he also used for his Turkish mission, details of which are not known. Upon his return to Moscow Gulbis headed the INO section (polpredstvo) in charge of the Transcaucasian Republics (ZSFSR), later occupying responsible positions in the Central Party Committee of Azerbaijan. Appointed director of Azneft, which after the collapse of the Soviet Union would grow into the State Oil Company of Azerbaijan, commonly known as SOCAR, Gulbis committed suicide by throwing himself under a moving train in December 1937.

Pyotr Pavlenko was born in St Petersburg but as a boy lived in Tiflis and then studied at the Baku polytechnic college later serving as a political commissar in the Red Army. Working as a local party official in Azerbaijan and Georgia, Pavlenko agreed to be an unofficial collaborator of the OGPU and was sent to the staff of the Soviet trade delegation in Turkey in 1924. He had spent there three years but surprisingly from spring 1927 until his return to Russia in 1928 there is a gap in his biography. Having settled in Moscow, Pavlenko suddenly became a writer, publishing stories where he described life in Turkey. His first novel about the Paris Commune came out in 1932 and in 1937, together with Sergey Eisenstein, Pavlenko produced the script of what became one of the most famous Soviet movies of all time. Even today *Alexander Nevsky* (1938) is being hailed by Putin's propaganda as a cinematographic masterpiece. A fanatical Stalinist, Pavlenko was awarded the Stalin Prize four times in addition to the Order of Lenin, the highest Soviet decoration, and other prestigious Soviet medals. From 1939 he worked as a war correspondent covering the Soviet invasion of Finland in November and writing for *Pravda* until the end of the Second World War, moving to Crimea in 1945 where he lived for the rest of his life.

* * *

Like 'Akunov' in Turkey, 'Bue and Euphony' in Switzerland turned out to be another unsolved puzzle.

A tenuous relationship between Switzerland and the Soviet Union began in May 1918, when the Swiss legation in Berlin sent a letter to the President of the Swiss Confederation, Felix Calonder, describing a meeting with Jan Antonovich Berzin (born Jānis Bērziņš, alias Ziemelis) that lasted for over an hour. The legation reported that before the Great War Berzin had been in immigration in the West (France, Great Britain and the USA) as a journalist. He assured them, the report stated, that among his mission members there were no political agitators and the only aim of this mission was to establish good diplomatic, commercial and financial relations between the two countries. 'La Swisse n'aurait pas d'empêtements par son personnel', Berzin was said to assure Swiss diplomats that his people, like, for example his mission counsellor Grigory Shklovsky, doctor of natural sciences, intended to do their best to avoid any entanglement in the internal politics of Switzerland.[47] Permission was granted and on 17 May Berzin arrived in Bern with a staff of twelve people, three more coming later.

In November 1918, just hours before the Swiss general strike, the Soviet delegation was expelled and relations broken off. Carl J. Burckhardt, the author of the article in the *Encyclopaedia Britannica* (1926), wrote:

> The Soviet delegation acted mainly as an organ of propaganda and espionage, and the revolutionary tendencies of the general strike in that year were undoubtedly aggravated by its influence. The difficulties of the military in countering these tendencies, together with the suffering caused by a widespread epidemic of influenza, roused public feelings and the delegation was requested to leave the country.

There is no way to prove that any member of Berzin's mission had indeed been involved in espionage, but the idea of the strike organisers, SPS and trade unions to celebrate the first anniversary of the Russian October Revolution made the Swiss government decide it would be safer to get rid of the 'Reds' in the capital before anything serious happened. After a short delay, in the morning of 12 November a detachment of dragoons commanded by Colonel Diesbach escorted the Soviet Mission to the frontier. The assassination of Vatslav Vorovsky in Lausanne in May 1923 further deteriorated Swiss-Soviet relations severely disrupting any process of recognition or rapprochement.

Vorovsky's assassination hampered relations between the two countries for years to come. Accompanied by two other diplomats, Ivan (Iosif) Ahrens and Ivan Divilkovsky, Vorovsky arrived at the Lausanne Conference at the end of April. On 9 May he dispatched a warning to Moscow about the inadequate protection of the Soviet delegation. On the evening of 10 May, while he was dining with his colleagues in the restaurant of the Cecil Hotel, a Russian White émigré of Swiss ancestry named Maurice Conradi approached them, pulled a gun and shot Vorovsky dead. 'Because of a dispute over the exact nature of Vorovskij's [*sic*] mission to Switzerland,' Alfred Senn writes, 'the Swiss government insisted that Vorovskij had been in the country as a private citizen.'[48] This extraordinary declaration, the nationality of the assassin and above all the fact that having affirmed that Conradi and his accomplice were both guilty the Lausanne jury set them free became the basis for Chicherin's diatribe against the Swiss accusing the Bundesrat of complicity in the murder.[49] In June, the Soviet government imposed an economic boycott against Switzerland. The Swiss responded by closing the country's borders to all Russians, the Reds and the Whites, whether diplomats, bankers, commercial representatives or émigrés. When a court in Lausanne let the murderer go, the anger of the Soviets knew no bounds. As one Swiss-American historian noted, after the incident the two governments stood in a virtual state of war with each other.[50]

This hostile confrontation persisted until spring 1927 when the conflict was settled by diplomatic means. On 4 May the Soviet leadership announced the raising of the boycott against Switzerland as of 14 April. This cleared the way for sending a Soviet delegation to the World Economic Conference that met in Geneva between 4 and 23 May 1927. This time the Swiss provided the Soviet participants with thorough police protection. In the course of the conference Soviet delegates repeatedly formulated the necessity of working out a tenable relation between capitalist and communist systems which raised questions by some politicians and the Swiss press whether the next step would be the establishment of a permanent Soviet mission with the League of Nations. This criticism prompted Giuseppe Motta, head of the Political Department (now the Federal Department of Foreign Affairs) and former President of the League of Nations, to speak out against accepting the Soviet Union into the League. After a prolonged silence that had lasted for almost 30 years, full diplomatic relations between Switzerland and the Soviet Union were only re-established in March 1946.

Regarding 'the arrest of two Soviet spies, Bue and Euphony' in late March 1927, any information about this case is absent from the Swiss archives. In June, a new Swiss Military Penal Code (Code penal militaire, CPM) was adopted which entered into force in January 1928. Its article 93 read: 'Anyone who, on Swiss territory, collects military intelligence for a foreign state to the detriment of another foreign state or organises such a service, anyone who hires others for such a service or promotes such actions, will be punished by custodial sentence not exceeding three years or a monetary penalty.'

* * *

Information published by David Dallin and based on the newspaper reports was accurate in what concerned Lithuania. Indeed, under various headings like 'Traitor Caught', 'In Soviet Pay' or 'Lithuanian General Confesses' many newspapers, from Chicago to Auckland, reported about the arrest of the Lithuanian General Konstantin Kleszinski (Konstantinas Kleščinskis).

Kleszinki was born in the town of Elizebethpol (now Ganja, Azerbaijan's third largest city) and in May 1879, aged 22, graduated from the Moscow Military School. Four years later he was among the proud graduates of the Nicholas General Staff Academy in St Petersburg. Taken prisoner by the Germans in August 1915 when the Tsarist army surrendered following the siege of what is now known as Modlin Fortress in Poland, Kleszinki, after release from captivity, had briefly served in the Polish Army General Staff. However, willing to join the North-Western Army (SZA) of General Yudenich, he resigned and left for Finland.

On the way to Helsingfors in spring 1919 he briefly stopped in Kovno (Kaunas). There Antanas Merkys, who had also served in the Russian army during the war and was now Minister of Defence of the newly independent Lithuania, invited Kleszinki, with whom he had become acquainted through mutual friends, to join the Lithuanian army together with him. While Merkys was later decommissioned and became a lawyer, Kleszinski had been fighting against the Red Army in the Lithuanian-Soviet war from May 1919 and in November that year was invited to join the General Staff. Following a succession of several leading staff roles, he was appointed acting Chief of the Lithuanian General Staff in August 1920 and then commanded the 1st Infantry Division. Two years later, in January 1922, Kleszinski was promoted to lieutenant general.

In August 1923, aged 44, he submitted his letter of resignation, which was swiftly accepted. General Kleszinski retired from the army and settled near Kaunas with his second wife, a good military pension and about 30 acres (12 hectares) of land provided by the state. He had also applied and was granted Lithuanian citizenship. But there was an unsolved problem that tormented him.

Back in Russia, his former wife was terminally ill and his mother and brother were left without means in St Petersburg while his aunt lived with his 10-year-old son Boris in Moscow. After the death of his mother in 1925, the boy actually became an orphan. Kleszinski decided to do his best to bring what was left of his family to Lithuania. In his own words, his first contact with the Soviet legation in Kaunas was in July 1926.[51] Later there were several more meetings with Soviet representatives who agreed to help in every possible way, but there was a condition.

Although Kleszinski had already been discharged from military service, they knew that as a former Lithuanian general, albeit in the reserve, he continued to maintain personal contacts with senior army officers and political figures. From February 1926 the OGPU main resident in Lithuania was Pavel Zhuravliov posing as 2nd secretary of the legation assisted by N. Sokolov. The (G)RU was represented by the military attaché Ivan Klochko, a graduate of the Military Academy of the Red Army who had previously served as an adviser to the M-Apparat (secret military staff) of the German Communist Party (KPD) and was now controlling agent networks in all three Baltic republics: Lithuania, Latvia and Estonia.

Born in November 1898 into a poor rural family, after finishing a village school Zhuravliov joined the Red Army. Since 1919 he had been a Cheka operative in Tatarstan, Crimea and from spring 1925 deputy head of the Special (Osoby) Department of the Black Sea Fleet. In December he was invited to the INO and soon sent to his first tour of duty abroad in Kovno, the temporary capital of Lithuania. Zhuravliov became Kreszinski's controller and the agent was assigned an uncomplicated codename IVANOV-12. Whether the figure jokingly symbolised the 12 hectares of land that he possessed would remain unconfirmed. For the information that the former general would supply, the Cheka officers promised to pay 500 litas (about £60) per month and to improve the living conditions of his mother in Russia. They also promised to arrange Kreszinski son's travel to Lithuania.

While he started to supply secret documents to his new Soviet friends, the Directorate of Criminal Police, formed in January 1927 to investigate political (Section A) and criminal (Section B) offences, paid attention to the former Lithuanian general's regular contacts with the Russians. The political section was headed by Jonas Budrys (born Jonas Polovinskas) who had also served in the Imperial Russian Army, spoke perfect Russian and was a trained and experienced counter-intelligence officer. Budrys knew the former general well personally but had no scruples about putting him under surveillance. The result was not long in coming.

On 19 May 1927 police agents commanded by Budrys surrounded the house and detained Kleszinski red-handed as he was about to say goodbye to Sokolov who had about him a bunch of secret reports written by Kleszinski. During his trial, the general confessed to his crime but tried his best to downplay the damage he had done to national security, and regretted that he had been forced to do so because of his 'difficult situation'. On 25 May the newspapers reported Kleszinski's case to the world. Sentenced to death, Kleszinski wrote a pardon request to the president but it was declined. In the early hours of 1 June, he was shot at Kaunas Castle and the body buried in a pit. The newspapers reported that the execution took place on 31 May and that it was followed by a raid on the Soviet trade delegation and the Communist Party headquarters. The authorities had seized documents, one newspaper reported, compromising the Soviet government and the Cabinet was considering 'an absolute rupture of relations' with Russia.[52]

In reality, shortly after the execution, the Soviet plenipotentiary in Lithuania Sergey Alexandrovsky apologised on behalf of his government for the incident. He was recalled on 3 June and together with him all three Soviet intelligence officers – Zhuravliov, Sokolov and Klochko – left for Moscow. This way an international scandal had been averted. The official SVR biography of Zhuravliov trying to conceal this unpleasant episode of his early career, falsely claims that he joined the foreign intelligence department of the OGPU in 1926 and worked in Italy (1937) 'and other countries'. In reality, under the alias 'Pavel M. Drozdov' he was transferred from Kaunas to Prague as 2nd secretary of the Soviet legation and chief OGPU resident agent and from there to Istanbul, Turkey, in 1931. In July 1945 Zhuravliov was promoted to major-general but preferred early retirement soon after Stalin's death.

Red Vienna and Red Budapest

It seems that from October 1922 when Ernan Forbes-Dennis resigned as Passport Control Officer (PCO) and head of SIS station in Vienna, there was no one to replace him and run espionage operations in Austria and its neighbouring countries until at least December 1925. Then, Captain Thomas J. Kendrick arrived and settled at the Passport Control Office which in Vienna was housed separately from the Legation (that had always been at Metternichgasse 6 in the 3rd District) and the Consulate (Wallnerstrasse 8 in the 1st). Kendrick, the official history of the Service states, was a South African who had served in Field Intelligence Security during the Great War, and then with MI1c in Cologne after the war before moving to Vienna.[53] 'With no formal SIS training,' his biographer adds, 'Kendrick had to set his own rules and boundaries of operation.' Helen Fry suggests that 16 years after it was formed as the foreign section of the Secret Service Bureau, 'SIS was still an unexperienced organisation that relied on the gentleman amateur rather than trained intelligence professionals'. She recalls Prudence Hopkins, the daughter of Kendrick's SIS secretary Clara Holmes (known to insiders as 'Bill'),[54] as saying that it was not a particularly sophisticated network. 'You backed your own judgement,' Miss Hopkins revealed, 'and were thrown into the intelligence work with no rulebook. It had to be worked out on instinct.' The skill lay, another author quoted by Kendrick's biographer seeks to elucidate, in 'discovering the thing you should pay a spy to ferret out for you – that is among the more vital, fascinating long-term tasks of true security work'. 'Kendrick would prove adept in this', Ms Fry declares with full confidence.[55] However, the portrait that this biographer paints must be taken with a huge pinch of salt.

The Passport Control cover was useful in at least two ways. The fees collected for the British visas augmented the miserly annual sum, as one former officer put it, allocated by SIS for this work, and such premises *looked* as if they had an official status while in reality PCOs were rarely granted diplomatic immunity before the war. The rule was that SIS officers under the PCO cover could and did collect information about the country in which they were stationed but they were not allowed to operate against it. As the same former PCO officer explained, 'this gave them superficial protection and also made possible useful liaisons with local intelligence services'. Here they found support in the person of Johannes Schober, the long-time head of the Vienna Police Department who in the period between June 1921 and January 1932 twice served as the Austrian Chancellor and for over a year as Vice-Chancellor also in charge of the foreign affairs because the Ministry of Foreign Affairs of Austria-Hungary was dissolved after the First World War during the course of administrative reforms and the foreign policy portfolio had been assigned to two departments at the Federal Chancellery. Ironically, it was not before 1959 that the Federal Ministry for Foreign Affairs was established in Vienna, the historical capital of international diplomacy.

Most of the intelligence reports were coming to the SIS Vienna station from Czechoslovakia, Hungary and Italy. Following established practice, while stationed at PCO Vienna Kendrick and his assistants never operated against Austria also because, as one of them later confessed, 'there would not have been any intelligence worth getting there'.[56] This was probably said with tongue in cheek.

British secret services were rather well informed about the Cheka (and its successors, GPU-OGPU) and their work inside Russia but had little knowledge regarding foreign operations of the INO, (G)RU and OMS, their structure, personnel and agent networks. Both MI6 and MI5 only learned some details of Soviet intelligence techniques, operations and personnel abroad from the Soviet defector Walter Krivitsky as late as January 1940.[57] Although it is some sort of conventional wisdom among intelligence historians that Krivitsky's reports 'provided a unique insight into the inner workings of Soviet intelligence in the 1920s and 1930s', in reality the picture presented by this defector was so distorted that it hardly had any practical value. Nevertheless, it was accepted by both MI5 and MI6 as a revelation.

Desk officers at Head Office, according to the official history of MI6, had to learn on the job and having no agent-running experience and seldom visiting stations abroad 'knew very little about the realities of work in the field'.[58] All three services, SIS (MI1c), MI5 and Special Branch, considered the Comintern and its members' and fellow travellers' communist propaganda and other political activities equal to espionage and subversion. Therefore, one of the important tasks facing Kendrick, who had little specific briefing or preliminary training, was to concentrate on communist groups in Austria apart from other duties like spying on Austria's neighbours and establishing contacts among Vienna society. Before his only assistant arrived in the autumn of 1937, Kendrick had been helped in his intelligence work by three secretaries, Evelyn Stamper, Betty Hodgson and the already-mentioned Clara Holmes. They worked from a back room of the passport office then located in Wallnerstrasse 8 but separate from the consulate. The house, known in Vienna as Palais Caprara-Geymüller, was acquired by the Anglo Austrian Bank Ltd in 1922. Perhaps quite by chance in the early 1930s the Soviet embassy rented several rooms in the neighbouring building allegedly for their trade representative Nikolai Popov, an undercover intelligence officer who also had a spacious office at the legation. In the house at Wallnerstrasse 9 lived Ernst Rüdiger Starhemberg, the leader of the Austrian Heimwehr (Home Guard).

At the centre of the Vienna spy scandal mentioned by Dallin was Endre (András) Bakonyi, a Hungarian communist born in Karcag, then a small town in the Austro-Hungarian Empire, in November 1887. During the short-lived Hungarian Soviet Republic (March–August 1919) Bakonyi worked in the press office of Béla Kun's commissariat for foreign affairs. After the collapse of the communist regime at home, Bakonyi emigrated to Soviet Russia. He became a Soviet citizen and in May 1924 was sent with his wife to Austria together with the staff of the Soviet plenipotentiary Woldemar Aussem soon after the resumption of normal diplomatic relations between the two countries.

In Vienna Bakonyi's job was to monitor political news from Austria, Hungary and Italy and report to Moscow. He had also been working for the Comintern as a liaison to the KPÖ. Several Russian sources claim that at the time he was an agent of the (G)RU but this cannot be independently verified. On 29 April 1927 the Austrian newspapers reported that Bakonyi was arrested 'for deception and spying' ('wegen Betrügereien und wegen Spitzeldienstes') and expelled from the country.[59] He was first transported to Hungary and from there to Soviet Ukraine via the Chop-Tysa border crossing.

In the meantime, the state police of Budapest informed Vienna that in the papers found in his luggage were names of two Austrian civil servants. The Austrian Stapo immediately started to investigate and soon identified both suspects.

A typical confusion in the police and newspaper reports has not been clarified to this day. The two suspects were Robert Sawrzel and Rosa Fuchs, detained one after another on 30 April. Sawrzel is said to have been head of the chancellery of the press department of the Austrian Foreign Ministry, and Frau Fuchs the secretary of Ambassador Ludwig, director of the Federal Press Service (BPD, Bundespressedienst), to this day located on Ballhausplatz opposite the main building of the Bundeskanzleramt.[60] After interviews at the police directorate both were released, then forced into retirement and the case was promptly closed in spite of the obvious fact that it was just the tip of the iceberg. As usual, and in true Austrian style, nothing was pushed to its logical conclusion.

A brief historical background may be necessary to better understand all the intricacies of this case. The First Austrian Republic was established in September 1919, ending the Habsburg rump state of German-Austria. The new republican constitution was enacted on 1 October 1920. The old

Imperial Foreign Ministry was abolished and the new Federal Ministry for Foreign Affairs (Bundesministerium für Äußeres, BfÄ) was formed on 10 November 1920 (three years later, in 1923, it was incorporated into the Federal Chancellery as the Foreign Affairs section). Journalist Otto Pohl, who from 1918 until its liquidation in 1920 headed the Public Information section of the old Foreign Ministry was transferred to the BfÄ as chief of its press department. Rosa Fuchs, the wife of the Austrian journalist Ludwig Fuchs, became Pohl's secretary.

At the same time Dr Pohl was placed in charge of the Austrian Repatriation Commission to deal with prisoners of war and civilian internees. In 1921 the Federal Press Service (Bundespressedienst) was created as part of the Office of the Federal Chancellor (Bundeskanzleramt), and Pohl passed over his press and public relations duties to the new head of Bundespressedienst, Eduard Ludwig, together with his secretary, Frau Fuchs. During this transfer, as the police investigation later found out, she was able to steal from Pohl's desk a key to the so-called Chiffrentasche which gave her access to secret diplomatic correspondence. To all appearances, by that time she was already working for the Russians.

The first Soviet commission to take care of the Russian prisoners of war arrived in Vienna in July 1918 headed by Yakov Berman.[61] From the very beginning the Austrian authorities suspected that Berman and his co-workers would be engaged in communist propaganda which indeed happened because as a true Bolshevik Berman thought it was his duty to help in the formation of the Austrian and Hungarian Communist Parties. In December 1918 he was arrested in Budapest and interned in Szeged where he remained until March 1919 when Berman and his associates were freed by the workers' revolutionary soviet. Having moved to Budapest, he took part in the work of the local committee of the Russian Communist Party set up to support and coordinate the revolutionary movement. After the collapse of the Hungarian Soviet Republic, Berman fled to Austria together with Kun's 'people's commissars', arriving in Vienna by special train on 2 August 1919.[62] Two days later all of them were interned in Schloss Karlstein and in September Berman was expelled to Soviet Russia.

Among the group of Hungarian communist insurgents fleeing to Austria that August was a Pole, Jósef Rotstadt, who became better known under his revolutionary pseudonym Krasny ('Red'). He managed to settle in Vienna and soon Moscow placed him in charge of the South-eastern Bureau of the Comintern, set up in March 1919, which maintained relations with the Communist parties in Austria, Czechoslovakia and the Balkans.[63] Another bureau was established in Stockholm. In January 1921 the German-Austrian operational area was divided between Stashevsky, the main Cheka/GPU and (G)RU resident in Berlin, and Krasny in Vienna responsible for the intelligence work in Eastern Europe and the Balkans.

In February 1920 James O'Grady and Maxim Litvinov signed an agreement in Copenhagen for an exchange of prisoners of war between Great Britain and Soviet Russia and similar agreements were negotiated by the Bolshevik government with other countries. The treaty with Austria was signed by Litvinov and Paul Richter, member of parliament and vice-president of the Austrian State Commission for prisoners of war and civil internees, on 5 July 1920.[64] Soon Otto Pohl was placed in charge of the Repatriation Commission. Two years later, after the de facto recognition of Soviet Russia by Austria (7 December 1921), Pohl was sent to Moscow as the diplomatic representative of the First Austrian Republic. He also became the first Austrian ambassador (Plenipotentiary Minister) following the de jure recognition in February 1924. In Moscow Pohl was regarded as a friend of the Soviet Union and a personal friend of Chicherin and Litvinov which ultimately had a negative impact on his diplomatic career.

Ironically, just days before the July revolt, Pohl assured the Soviet foreign commissar of the stability of the political regime at home. Less than two weeks later a major riot broke out in Vienna culminating in the police forces firing at protesters angry over the acquittal of three nationalist paramilitaries for the murder of two left-wingers. 'Black Friday', 15 July 1927, began with the mob storming the Palace of Justice in Schmerlingplatz and setting it ablaze because for them it had become a citadel of right-wing injustice which they wanted to destroy. 'By the end of that "Bloody Friday", when the fighting died down as quickly as it had erupted,' Gordon Brook-Shepherd writes, 'there were eighty-four dead, nearly all of them demonstrators, and some five hundred wounded.'[65] In December, Otto Pohl was recalled despite Moscow's protests.

The recruitment of Rosa Fuchs was the first important penetration of a European government – the Austrian equivalent of the British Cabinet Office – by Soviet intelligence. She was recruited by Helena, the wife of Jósef Krasny, when still working as the secretary of Otto Pohl in 1921. During six years of spying, Rosa had been above suspicion, while her husband, the journalist Ludwig Fuchs, caught Stapo's attention because of his regular visits to the Soviet legation in Reisnerstrasse. His several trips to Paris where he met the Austrian diplomat Friedrich Bodo and a former publisher Imre Békessy now in exile in France were also noted.[66]

Remarkably, Rosa Fuchs was interviewed by the state police in Vienna before her name, as reported by the Austrian newspapers, was discovered in the Bakonyi papers and leaked from Budapest. According to the police protocol of 27 April 1927, she confessed that she had been regularly copying secret documents from her Chancellery and passing them over to her husband. She also admitted she had the key to diplomatic ciphers.[67] Whether her husband had been investigated and interviewed is unknown.

Jósef Krasny was arrested together with his wife, Elena Krasnaya (born Helena Starke in Krakow), while both were on a secret assignment in Prague in May 1922. After three months in custody awaiting trial, he was sentenced to eight days in jail for possessing a forged passport. Both he and his wife returned to Moscow in August. The chief of INO planned to send him to London as the main OGPU resident, but a visa was not granted and Krasny remained in Russia.[68] Having lost his ties with Soviet intelligence and the Comintern, Krasny was employed as the library director at the Socialist Academy of Social Sciences (from April 1924 renamed Communist Academy). He was later transferred to Krestintern, the so-called Red Peasant International formed by the Comintern in October 1923. Josef Krasny's book *Sibirien* with the subtitle 'New letters from exile' was published in Berlin in 1925. Unfortunately, no reliable information is available about his wife Elena Krasnaya who, unlike her husband, had allegedly been placed on the INO staff in Moscow after they returned from Vienna.[69]

In January 1927 Dr Ephraim Goldenstein, who had served in Vienna between December 1924 and December 1925 as chief resident agent of the INO in Austria under diplomatic cover of Second Secretary of the Soviet legation, moved to the same position in Berlin. In July, two officials of the Soviet trade mission in Berlin arrived in Vienna. Their names were Gyula Lengyel and Alexander Rapoport. The main aim of their visit to Austria was to negotiate a financial credit with the municipality of Vienna. Such a credit, as the then Soviet plenipotentiary in Germany Krestinsky explained to Chicherin, might 'set a precedent that would have a strong positive effect on German financial and political circles'.[70] On behalf of the Soviet government Anastas Mikoyan, People's Commissar for External and Internal Trade, not only issued a special permit to Lengyel to sign such an agreement but actually required him to do it by all means.

Lengyel (born Goldstein, pseudonym 'Pollák') was a Hungarian politician who, together with Béla Székely served as commissar of finance in the revolutionary governing council of the Hungarian Soviet Republic.[71] After the fall of the communist regime, together with Béla Kun and other commissars he fled to Austria. From 1922 Gyula Lengyel, also known as Julius, had been serving as an influential and authoritative member of the board attached to the Soviet trade mission in Berlin then headed by Karl Begge.[72] Lengyel's work in Berlin was highly valued because already during the war he was appointed professor first at the Academy of Commerce and then the College of World Economy and had been one of only a few specialists among the trade mission staff who understood the ins and outs of international trade. He would later be promoted to deputy head of the export department at the NKVT in Moscow.

The second member of the delegation was Rapoport, then aged 48, who headed the legal department of the Soviet trade mission in Berlin. Three years later, in 1930, summoned to Moscow, he decided not to return to the Soviet Union and remained in Germany, later moving with his large family to France.

After the recent spy scandal related to ARCOS in London followed by the rupture of diplomatic relations and expulsions of Soviet personnel, the Austrian authorities were quite nervous because their own mini spy case of April-May became public. They were very worried that the two Soviet representatives were perhaps communist agitators and could even be members of the Comintern. During the first years of its existence, the Third (Communist) International was viewed by many as 'the body charged with spreading the Soviet revolution abroad through, among other means, espionage and subversion'. It was this contagion that Western governments feared most.[73] While both Lengyel and Rapoport were detained by the police, Karl Hartleb, a former farmer recently elected vice-chancellor of Austria, spoke in the National Council reading out a document that allegedly confirmed suspicions against the two Soviet delegates. Following the British example, a police raid was ordered on the premises of two Soviet trade companies – RATAO and RUSAWSTORG.[74] As expected, nothing untoward was found during the search.

Krasny died in Moscow in December 1932. His wife survived him by four years – she was arrested and shot in September 1937. The Bundezkanzleramt in Vienna continued to attract attention of Soviet and later Russian intelligence during all those decades quietly moving into the new millennium. The latest case became officially known in January 2000 when some privileged information leaked to the Austrian press. Four years before, the British Secret Service shared sensitive documents with the Austrian directorate of public security then headed by Michael Sika identifying Soviet KGB agents in key government institutions like the state police, Foreign Ministry and the Office of the Federal Chancellor. As expected, although an internal investigation was launched, the Soviet mole in the Bundeskanzleramt, codenamed YERSHOV, has never been identified. There were rumours that later, following a tip from a friendly service, suspicion fell on one of the former Austrian ambassadors in China but no charges were ever brought.

Cheka in China

'By spring,' Victor Madeira reports, without doubt referring to Dallin's passage reproduced by Andrew, 'Soviet foreign and military intelligence – INO and IV Directorate, respectively – were reeling from the exposure of several networks worldwide ... In April [1927], Chinese authorities found compromising documents during a raid on a Soviet compound.'[75]

Owen Lattimore, who was born and raised in Tianjin and became a leading Far Eastern expert, believed that everyone who like himself was living in China in the period 1918–27,

> will remember the excitement, immediately followed by controversy, when in 1927 the henchmen of the warlord Chang Tso-lin, with the acquiescence of the Treaty Powers having privileges in the sacrosanct Legation Quarter of Peking, raided the Soviet embassy and seized quantities of documents. Many who remember the incident are likely to recall it now as a stale sensation and to wonder why it is worth rehashing such already hashed material.

It is an enlightening surprise to find, he adds, a fresh treatment,[76] referring to a collection of documents seized in the 1927 Peking raid published by C. Martin Wilbur and Julie Lien-ying How. Indeed, a fresh look always pays dividends.

A perfunctory examination of material related to the raid on the Soviet premises in Peking may conclude that (1) there was a raid on the Soviet compound, as stated in many accounts; and (2) the Peking government, concerned over the Kuomintang (KMT) and Chinese Communist Party (CCP) activities in the north, accused the Soviet representatives of disseminating communist propaganda and sheltering Chinese communists whom the authorities had a probable cause to prosecute. In other words, the spectre of Communism, predicted by Marx, caused legitimate fear that the same spectre was now looming to haunt China.

The first definite evidence of Soviet propaganda was obtained on 1 March, when the authorities detained a Soviet steamer officially carrying a cargo of tea, but in reality a large quantity of communist propaganda literature. Mikhail Borodin, chief Comintern adviser with the KMT since September 1923, together with a group of Soviet officials accompanied this secret cargo. Despite Soviet protests, the Chinese government refused to release the ship and several Soviet citizens were arrested on the grounds that the case was a breach of the Sino-Soviet Agreement of May 1924.[77] In reality, the situation with this agreement, which led to the immediate restoration of diplomatic relations between Soviet Russia and China, was not so unambiguous, and the general political situation in the country after the death of Sun Yat-sen was extremely complex, but this was not directly related to the government decision to carry out a search of the Soviet premises in Peking. Having in mind the recent Nanking Incident when the Revolutionary Army, the military arm of the Kuomintang, stormed the consulates of the United States, Great Britain and Japan,[78] the raid on the Soviet premises in early April may seem to have nothing to do with Soviet espionage.

In London, a House of Commons debate on 11 April 1927 sought to establish what really happened in the Chinese capital just a few days before, and whether HM Minister to China, Sir Miles Lampson, was in any way involved.[79] The Secretary of State for Foreign Affairs, Sir Austen Chamberlain, offered a preliminary report of the circumstances leading to the entry of Chinese troops into the Legation Quarter of Peking.

> The chief of the [Peking] Metropolitan Police called on the Senior Minister [William Jacob Oudendijk, the representative of the Netherlands] on 6th April, with a letter in duplicate calling attention to the subversive activities of Russians in the Legation Quarter, and requesting authority to search certain specified Russian property, namely the Dalbank, the Chinese Eastern Railway building not actually inside the Russian Legation itself, and the building belonging to the Russian Indemnity Commission. The original of this letter was duly countersigned by the Senior Minister, authorising ingress for the Metropolitan Police, and handed back to the authorities. The Senior Minister had previously consulted the representatives of the other Protocol Powers, who decided that the hospitality of the Quarter must not be used against the local Government ...

On the night of 6 April, the Chinese Government issued a communiqué with a brief statement of what happened during the previous day. As Chamberlain explained it to the MPs,

> The search began at 11 a.m. and continued throughout the day. It was effected by the Metropolitan Police, some gendarmes and many plain clothes detectives. An attempt was made by the Russians to burn some documents, but this was frustrated. The Senior Minister has informed His Majesty's Minister [Lampson] that among the captures was a list of names of 4,000 agents in Peking ready to stir up trouble and commit acts of violence at a given moment. Other seizures comprised one machine-gun, 30 rifles and a quantity of ammunition, together with a

number of flags with inflammatory slogans which were to be used for demonstrations.

Official seals were captured of the 'Anti-British Committee', whose special function appears to be agitation against Great Britain. The seals of similar committees for agitation against Japan and France were also seized. 22 Russians were arrested, and between 40 and 50 Chinese, for whom the authorities had long been searching, including the recognised leader of the Communist party of North China, who had taken refuge with the Russians.

The Russian Embassy itself, which is shut off by a high wall, was strictly respected.[80]

This report as well as the documents released after the search might well point to communist propaganda and subversion but still said nothing about Soviet espionage.

However, on 22 April four additional documents were made public. The subject of two of them was Soviet espionage in foreign legations (instruction to agents for hiring spies and the agreement signed by a Chinese who undertook to find the right people for this work); one was the estimate of funds required for military-political work in China for the first half of year 1925–6; and the last was minutes of a meeting of Russian military advisers in Canton on 1 July 1925.

The authorities were a bit more specific in their *Chinese Government White Book* with the foreword by the Metropolitan Police who also published a separate book *Soviet Plot in China* reproducing original Soviet documents.[81] These publications made clear that the Soviet embassy under Alexey Chernykh, the chargé d'affaires, had an extensive political and military network of agents and collaborators in China, which conducted espionage everywhere including foreign legations. It was established that Soviet advisers and instructors who had been working in the KMT and in the CCP councils were paid through the office of the Soviet military attaché, Roman Longva (Łagwa in his native Polish), a (G)RU officer who before coming to Peking also served as secretary of the Chinese Commission of the Politburo. Finally, the documents demonstrated that the Soviet government contrary to all agreements signed with China in the period of 1924–7, through its Peking embassy (as well as consulates) furnished arms, munitions and other war supplies to the enemies of the Peking government.[82]

The first official Soviet envoy, Alexander Paikes, who arrived in December 1921 as a representative of the Council of People's Commissars (SNK RSFSR), was quickly followed by Adolf Joffe, the first diplomatic representative of the Bolshevik government in China since July 1922. After less than a year Joffe was substituted by Lev Karakhan. Karakhan remained as semi-official diplomatic representative until full diplomatic relations were established and he presented his credentials as Plenipotentiary at the end of July 1924. Finally, in December 1926 Semyon Aralov, who had briefly served as the Soviet diplomatic representative in Turkey in the early 1920s, arrived in Peking representing the SNK while Chernykh was still in charge of the legation.

The first INO resident in Peking was Aristarkh Rigin who arrived with Paikes as a member of the delegation. In China Rigin was working undercover as 'Rylski'.[83] Using this alias, he was also entered on the diplomatic staff of first the Joffe and then the Karakhan missions as an attaché before being transferred to Copenhagen. Immediately upon arriving in China, Rigin started recruiting agents and helpers, many of them from the KMT and CCP ranks, and setting up networks for collecting political and military information.

The former chief of Soviet foreign intelligence, Yakov Davtyan, now on the staff of the Narkomindel, arrived in Peking in July 1922, officially accredited as counsellor of the Soviet diplomatic mission. As evident from his correspondence with the then INO chief Trilisser, Davtyan was also deeply involved in intelligence work combining his diplomatic duties with those of the main INO resident in China. However, contrary to several accounts published by Russian historians about Davtyan's successes in this country pointing to a network of consulates that he had allegedly set up all over China, apart from one consulate general in Harbin, headed by the (G)RU officer Dmitry Kiselev from November 1924 to May 1925, other Soviet consulates were opened in different Chinese cities only in 1925–6. By that time Davtyan had already been in Paris again as a counsellor with Rigin, his second-in-command, serving undercover as second secretary which, like the PCO for the British SIS, seems like a fixed position for Soviet intelligence officers in the interwar period.

By the time the Metropolitan Police raided and searched the Soviet premises in Peking, there were already seven Soviet consulates general and four consulates established in different operationally important centres and headed by OGPU and (G)RU officers.[84] Their main targets were White Russian officers who managed to flee to China and were now forming resistance and terrorist groups as well as various paramilitary units ready to be deployed to Soviet territory. In Manchuria, one Colonel M.G. Ktitorov, associated with the ROVS and representing the so-called Order of the Crusaders, operated as a recruiter of volunteers for the Russian battalion in the Shandong Army of the Chinese warlord Zhang Zongchang (nicknamed the 'Dogmeat General'). Ignoring the unpleasant consequences of the police raid in Peking with a months-long international scandal following revelations of Soviet espionage earlier that year, Soviet agents kidnapped Ktitorov in November and secretly transported him across the border to Russia.

In 1922 Fedor Karin arrived in Harbin first as deputy resident of the INO sub-station and later resident in this one of the most important cities of Northeast China, better known as Manchuria. Harbin was then considered China's fashion capital and home to one of the largest Russian diaspora communities in the world with over 120,000 Russians and other nationalities from the former Tsarist Empire.[85] Karin, alias 'A. Koretsky', successfully operated in Harbin until April 1927, turning it into the principal base for Soviet intelligence in China. One of Karin's assistants in 1924–5 was Vasily Zarubin who, during the Second World War would serve as the main resident of Soviet foreign intelligence in New York and then Washington (alias 'Zubilin'). Other INO officers at this time in Harbin were the German Erich Tacke, his future Polish wife Yunona, Russians Yakov Tischenko (alias 'Vasily Roschin'), Vasily Poudin (alias 'Shilov') and a group leader and recruiter (principal agent) Ivan Ivanov-Perekrest who had good contacts among the Japanese military. In the 1930s Karin would be appointed head of the 1st INO department responsible for intelligence operations in the USA and Europe and then, after transfer, chief of the II (Eastern) department of the (G)RU.

Sergey Velezhev studied at the Mining Institute in St Petersburg and during the Great War was a junior officer before joining the Bolsheviks in Siberia, where he was elected to the Central Executive Committee. Recommended by the party to the Cheka, Velezhev had served as assistant head of INO between 1923 and 1929. In 1925 he was sent to Peking (succeeding Davtyan as the main OGPU resident), working under the cover of an attaché of the Soviet legation and Consul General in Hankou (alias 'Vedernikov'). Velezhev remained at this post until mid-April 1927, when almost all INO staff were recalled as a result of the raid. Apart from Velezhev-Vedernikov, other officers returning to Moscow were Naum Eitingon (alias 'Leonid Naumov') and Yevgeny Fortunatov, the son of a well-known medical professor. In Peking Fortunatov used the cover of a legation doctor because before joining the Cheka in 1920 he graduated from the Faculty of Medicine of St Petersburg University. Back at the Lubyanka, Fortunatov was placed in charge of the Far-Eastern section of the INO. On 30 July, formerly part of the Secret-Operational Directorate under Genrikh Yagoda, INO became a separate department reporting directly to the OGPU Collegium.

Russian historians and writers usually point out that the most important achievement of the Far-Eastern section of INO in 1927 was a copy of what became known as the Tanaka Memorial, in which the Japanese Prime Minister Tanaka Giichi laid out for Emperor Hirohito a strategy of how to conquer or 'take over' the world. In 1940 Trotsky, while in exile in Mexico, explained that Soviet intelligence had obtained it from a highly-placed mole in Tokyo.[86] Six decades after the Tanaka Memorial was allegedly written, the American historian John Dower stated that based on his research in reality the document was a masterful anti-Japanese hoax. Its authenticity is not accepted by scholars today and Western historians agree that it was one of the most successful forgeries of the twentieth century.

Jean Crémet as the 'Little Redhead'@'L'Hermine Rouge' or 'The Red Stoat'

Despite ever-expanding technical and military collaboration with Germany, French military technology and industrial production were among the principal targets of Soviet intelligence in the interwar period. Jean Crémet seemed an ideal choice to be able to secure a steady flow of information. Deputy secretary of the Communist federation of Loire Inférieure, he was wounded in action in August 1914 and together with another communist began publishing the periodical *La Bretagne communiste*. In September-October 1923, then known as *La Bretagne communiste – Voix communiste et Germinal*, it published several articles describing Crémet's first trip to Soviet Russia, which he made earlier that year. It seems that he had been recruited as an agent of Soviet military intelligence during that visit to Moscow because already in 1924–5 he was involved in collecting military intelligence through the network of so-called rabkors (workers-correspondents) in Nantes, Marseille and Versailles. The information was supplied by the rabkors who were encouraged to report from their places of work answering the questions from the lists, known as questionnaires, distributed to them by Soviet agents like Crémet indicating what specific information Moscow sought. Crémet's associates Georges Ménétier, Pierre Provost, Jean-Marie Depouilly and Georges Sergent were also actively involved.

In 1925 Crémet left his wife and daughter in Brittany and moved to Paris. There he was soon elected a municipal councillor (PCF) for the quartier de la Santé in the 14th arrondissement, although after the raid on the Soviet premises in Peking, the OMS, the secret service of the Comintern, was instructed to be very careful in their contacts with communists abroad and special underground party cells were formed inside the important communist parties. For the INO and (G)RU legal and especially illegal residencies in Europe the recruitment of communists and fellow travellers was still tolerated.

In May Davtyan arrived in Paris officially accredited as counsellor of the Soviet legation (alias 'Davydov'), and in December his former assistant in Peking, Rigin/Rylski, joined him as the main INO resident in France, both operating from 'legal' positions and protected from arrest by their diplomatic passports. But Crémet and his people, among them his personal secretary Louise Clarac, who had been engaged in the 'underground work for the party' since 1923, and her sister Marie-Madeleine were reporting to the (G)RU station, every moment risking arrest. From April 1925 Stanislav Budkevich, attaché of the Soviet legation (alias 'Osovsky'), was the (G)RU man in France assisted by an illegal resident, Alfred Tilton. In March 1926, a new illegal resident arrived.

This was another Pole, Stefan Uzdański, better known to the security services of Poland and Austria as 'Jeleński', expelled three years earlier from Poland where he was collecting intelligence using the legal cover of the attaché of the Soviet legation in Warsaw. He then moved to Vienna again operating from legal positions under diplomatic cover. After a brief spell in Moscow, Uzdański arrived in Paris posing as a Russian artist 'Abram Bernstein'. His reports were reaching the Paris (G)RU station through his wife who was a member of the technical staff of the Soviet legation.[87]

The activities of the Crémet network could not escape the attention of the French security service. In January 1927, as soon as he returned from Moscow where Crémet had been working as one of the secretaries of the ECCI, Louise Clarac was moved from the 'underground party work' to a technical job at *l'Humanité* because it was decided that her name as an underground operative could become known to the police. In March the spy case started to unfold and she was forced to lie low for ten months because the police had already been looking for her. Indeed, after receiving tips from various sources, a Sûreté team led by Louis Ducloux and Captain Eugène Josset, head of the Russian desk at the Service de Renseignements, were following a number of leads into the case setting traps to catch the spies.

On 9 April 1927 Bernstein was arrested 'red-handed' in the process of receiving classified information. Other members of the spy ring including Stefan Grodnicki, Bernstein's assistant, were also detained and later sentenced to different prison terms from 16 months to five years which was the maximum penalty for spying (plus fines and deprivation of civil rights). Crémet and the Clarac sisters managed to escape to Moscow where Louise arrived in early March 1928.[88] Naturally, the loss of the Crémet group was not irreparable because by that time the Bulgarian Nikola Zidarov had already arrived in France travelling via Vienna and settled in Paris as a member of the Soviet trade delegation at the same time representing the International Red Aid (known as MOPR in Russia).[89] In reality, posing as a Croat 'Stanko Kuketz' and renting a room at the small hotel where Bulgarian émigrés lived, he was recruiting cadres for Soviet military intelligence. At the same time,

Pavel Stuchevsky ('General Muraille') succeeded Uzdański in Paris as the illegal (G)RU resident.

An experienced member of the Comintern secret apparat, after a year in Moscow Crémet was sent on a mission to China in 1929. At the same time another cadre of the Comintern's OMS, the German communist Richard Sorge, was invited to join the (G)RU and sent to Britain. Early next year Sorge was in Shanghai welcoming Crémet who by that time had already decided to break with both the Comintern and Soviet military intelligence.[90] He vanished at the beginning of 1931, was presumed dead and reportedly never seen again. In reality, with the help of the French writer André Malraux and his wife, Crémet managed to leave China in October the same year, and travelling via Japan and the United States arrived in Cherbourg in December. In Saint-Junien, a commune in the Haute-Vienne department of France, he obtained quasi-legitimate documents identifying him as 'Gabriel Pierre Peyrot' and settled in Belgium. Crémet used this name until his death in Brussels in March 1973.

Louise Clarac spent the war with her sister, Marie-Madeleine, now Mercier, in Vitry-sur-Seine in Île de France, less than five miles from the centre of Paris. At the end of 1946 she decided to join Crémet in Brussels but suddenly died of a stroke on the train taking her to Belgium. In her luggage the police found a passport with her photo but issued in the name of 'Marie-Thérèse Voisin'. Mystère et boule de gomme!

From London to Petrograd, October 1926 – October 1927

Two decades before Professor Andrew was appointed official historian of MI5, he penned an article about British intelligence and the breach with Russia, which is generally believed to have happened as a consequence of the police raid on the All-Russian Cooperative Society (ARCOS) located at 49 Moorgate, City of London. 'The British intelligence services,' Andrew wrote, 'were intimately involved in the breaking of Anglo-Soviet diplomatic relations in May 1927. They provided much of the evidence which led to the breach, and they were themselves one of the victims of it.'[91]

The article's somewhat contradictory conclusion suggests that although 'Baldwin's government was able to prove the charge of Soviet dabbling in British politics' (which even if demonstrated beyond any reasonable doubt, clearly not the case here, would not justify the rupture of diplomatic relations), 'the government contrived in the end to have the worst of both worlds'. Besides compromising the source of their most secret, valuable and reliable intelligence (GC&CS), the Conservative government under Stanley Baldwin 'failed to produce public evidence' to support Jix's dramatic charges

КРАСНЫЙ СЕВЕР   12 июля 1927 года № 156 (2444)

Трудящиеся губернии должны иметь в воздушном флоте самолет, созданный своими руками.

В „неделю обороны" поставим себе задачей--собрать средства на постройку самолета „имени тов. Войкова".

НАШ ОТВЕТ ТВЕРДОЛОБЫМ

построим самолет имени тов. Войкова

ДЕЛО ШПИОНА ДРУЖИЛОВСКОГО
в Верховном суде СССР.

ДРУЖИЛОВСКИЙ СОЗНАЕТСЯ В ПРЕСТУПЛЕНИЯХ.

МОСКВА, 8 июля. 8 июля в Верховном суде СССР начался слушанием дело Дружиловского.

ДЕЛО ДРУЖИЛОВСКОГО

8 июля в Москве в Верховном суде началось слушанием дело Дружиловского, известного ф-та фальшивок. На снимке — Дружиловский на суде

ПОКАЗАНИЯ ДРУЖИЛОВСКОГО.

РАБОТА В РИГЕ.

ПЕРИОДЫ ПРЕСТУПНОЙ ДЕЯТЕЛЬНОСТИ.

ШПИОНСКАЯ РАБОТА В ПОЛЬШЕ.

СВЯЗЬ С БЕРЛИНОМ И ПАРИЖЕМ.

ЦАНКОВСКАЯ ФАЛЬШИВКА.

Настоящий документ послужил началу Цанкову предлогом для расправы и массовых убийств коммунистов и других оппозиционных элементов. Сбоку надпись: „Этот документ написан мной фабрикантом подлога 1925 года. Сергей Дружиловский. Москва 16/VII 26 г.

ОТКРЫТОЕ ИЗГОТОВЛЕНИЕ ФАЛЬШИВОК.

Построим самолет!

Павел Смуров.

БУДУЩАЯ ВОЙНА И КРАСНАЯ ОБОРОНА.

Фронт и тыл.—Война потребует величайшего напряжения всех сил.—Решительная схватка двух систем.—Трудящиеся и Красная армия—повседневное внимание вопросам обороны.

Р. Эйсман.
Начальник Военной Академии РККА.

of 'the most nefarious' web of Soviet spies operating in London, nor any of the particular acts of espionage at all.

'Despite the fiasco,' Michael Smith writes in his unofficial history of MI6, 'the ineptitude of the entire affair was yet to reach its zenith' and indeed the consequences of the raid and the subsequent rupture of relations were much more traumatic.[92] They were unpredictable and multifaceted. First, the GC&CS lost the chance to decrypt high-grade Soviet government communications, this deficit of reliable intelligence lasting for over a decade, from 1927 to the beginning of the Second World War.[93] Second, the real Soviet spy network operating in Great Britain during that period was never uncovered.[94] Finally, less than a month after the raid, the SIS organisation in Russia suffered a devastating blow not mentioned in the official history of the service. On 12 June Soviet newspapers published information by the OGPU, reprinted by the world press, about mass arrests in Moscow and especially Leningrad of 'more than 23 persons working for the British Secret Service'. This time the claims of 'British spies' were genuine and the newspaper correctly named 'British intelligence officer Boyce [formerly] attached to the official British diplomatic mission in Helsingfors, and then in Reval'. Among his closest collaborators the article mentioned the former Tsarist Colonel Nikolai Bunakov 'who used to serve as a representative of the Grand Duke Nikolai Nikolayevich and was later on the staff of the British intelligence [station] in Finland. Peter Sokolov was also named as 'a former officer who during the Yudenich offensive on Petrograd [in the autumn of 1919] was placed by British intelligence at the Soviet-Finnish border being the right-hand man of Paul Dukes, a famous British secret agent'.

After a series of new arrests and trials between June and October 1927, where most of the defendants were charged with espionage for Great Britain and sentenced to death, two senior diplomats of the British Mission in Moscow were accused of setting up spy rings and recruiting agents. 'From the outset of their arrival in Moscow certain members of the British mission', the tribunal was told, having in mind Sir Robert Hodgson, chargé d'affaires since 1924 and Edward Charnock, commercial attaché and secretary, 'were utilising their diplomatic immunity to carry on spy work collecting information about the Red Army and Fleet as well as the Soviet aviation industry'.

In June, under the title 'The Soviet Union Defends Itself' the Comintern paper *International Press Correspondence* published in Vienna reported the arrest and execution of a group of twenty 'monarchist White Guardists in the pay and acting under the instructions of a foreign secret service'. Together with the former Duma member and one of the leaders of the Constitutional-Democratic Party, Prince Pavel D. Dolgorukov, who emigrated with the White Army to Turkey in 1920 but illegally crossed the Soviet border in

June 1926 to help the anti-Soviet underground movement, and Georg (Yrjö) Elfvengren, a Finnish officer who fought against Finnish and Russian Red Guards on the Karelian Isthmus and also entered the Soviet territory illegally in 1926, there were also several 'British spies and agents in the service of Hodgson and Charnock'.[95]

In October, among the accused sitting in the dock were the 'British agents' brothers Vladimir and Kirill Prové and Vladimir Korepanov. The brothers Prové came from the wealthy German family of Theodor Ferdinand Prové and his wife Sofia (née Schultz). Vladimir worked at the Central Aerohydrodynamic Institute (TsAGI) founded by the Russian aviation pioneer Nikolai Zhukovsky in December 1918. From 1925 the Institute hosted the first and only aircraft design bureau where Andrei Tupolev designed a twin-engined bomber, the TB-1, which made its successful maiden flight in November and was considered to be one of the most advanced designs of the time. Vladimir's brother Kirill Prové was employed as a clerk at the headquarters of the special battalion which was guarding the building of the Revolutionary Military Council (RVS). Their relative, former sworn attorney Korepanov served as a legal adviser at the same RVS.

Vladimir and Kirill Prové and their lawyer relative were sentenced to death and shot, while their parents and three younger brothers were exiled to Kazakhstan and Siberia for three years. The youngest, Vsevolod, was also later shot in spite of the fact that the court changed his sentence from execution to 10 years imprisonment. As Michael Smith wisely noted, the timing of the arrests of the Hoyer and Charnock spy rings might have had nothing to do with the ARCOS raid, although this seems unlikely.

At the end of October 1927 newspapers reported that Edward Charnock, formerly commercial attache and secretary of the British Mission, who was accused in recent dispatches from Moscow of being the master British spy in Russia since the revolution, declared in an interview in London that when the British Mission was called on to withdraw from Russia, not a single member dared to approach his dearest friend to say good-bye.

By sheer coincidence, this interview was exactly one year to the day when Bertie Maw of the SIS Production branch visited the chief. He told Hugh Sinclair that he might probably have evidence to prove that the Russians at ARCOS were really involved in espionage. Bertie's report, not taken too seriously at first, launched the operation that reverberates even now.

Chapter 11

Soviet House, British Spy Mania and SIS Activities in Russia: The ARCOS Tangle

Quite why things tumbled out of control in May 1927 now seems possible to explain in the context of the general political situation in Europe and the internal one in Britain. Based on new primary sources it seems obvious that there were reasons other than a mere departmental feud between Hugh 'Quex' Sinclair, the 'C' of SIS, and Sir Wyndham Childs, the Assistant Commissioner of the Metropolitan Police in charge of Special Branch. This well-known rivalry between two services is a usual explanation offered by historians, which is by far too little to be able to present an adequate picture of the events leading to one of the biggest intelligence flops of the interwar period.

By early 1927 relations between Great Britain and Soviet Russia continued to deteriorate in an atmosphere of mutual suspicion and recrimination, reaching breaking point by May. In January, Foreign Secretary Austen Chamberlain instructed Sir Robert Hodgson, British chargé d'affaires in Moscow, and his staff to destroy all non-essential ciphers and confidential papers, fearing a possible break-in at the embassy or interception of a diplomatic bag.[1] Whether Chamberlain remembered it or not, seven years earlier almost the same instruction was sent by Maxim Litvinov from Copenhagen to the Soviet delegation which was on its way to London for the second phase of Anglo-Soviet negotiations. Officially, conditions for a peace treaty and a trade agreement had to be agreed but since the very beginning the negotiations were troubled by controversies over communist propaganda and differences over the principles of repudiation of debts and nationalisation. The British side was unaware that the Soviet delegation also had a hidden agenda to put pressure on HM Government by means of propaganda among the workers to prevent British intervention in the Russo-Polish War.

Duly intercepted by the GC&CS, the text of Litvinov's missive of 24 July 1920 read in part: do not keep by you the decrypts of radio telegrams that 'might give grounds for being accused of propaganda', sagaciously adding that claims of diplomatic immunity would not stop the British.[2] It should be remembered that one of the two principal issues of the 1920 negotiations was hostile propaganda and subversion.

After Soviet trade unions provided funds to support the British miners' strike in May 1926, the British government sent a note to the Soviet government in the form of a letter addressed to the Soviet chargé d'affaires in London, Arkady Rosengoltz. Signed by Austen Chamberlain, the note referred to the Soviet government's official guarantee of 4 June 1923 not to support efforts to spread discontent or foment rebellion in any part of the British Empire. It also recalled previous British representations and denied all Soviet allegations of British hostile moves towards Russia. 'His Majesty's Government,' the note stated,

> are indeed well aware of the delusion under which M[onsieur] Chicherin and many of his colleagues are suffering that Great Britain is continually occupied in plotting against the USSR and for this purpose has never ceased to guide the policy of such countries as Poland and the Baltic states and Persia into an orientation directed against Soviet Russia ... [This] can only be based on a rooted, even perhaps temperamental hostility in the minds of the Soviet authorities themselves and a corresponding credulity in regard to false reports from interested informants.

Litvinov, then Deputy Commissar for Foreign Affairs, replied in the same spirit of cheekiness as the Foreign Minister Lavrov and his deputy Ryabkov would respond to a similar note a century later, in February 2022. In both cases, the answer meant to say: there is no agreement limiting the freedom of actions within the confines of the two countries. In short, we can act on our own territory as we see fit. At least Litvinov ended his answer in February 1927 by pointing to the benefits that Great Britain as well as Russia derived from the trade and diplomatic relations between the two states.[3] Unofficially it was added that Britain had been one of the three major trade partners of Russia alongside Germany and the USA,[4] which should not be forgotten.

Today historians agree that among the Cabinet ministers the Home Secretary Sir William Joynson-Hicks ('Jix') was one of Moscow's fiercest opponents. As had already been stated (see Chapter 9), much like Churchill, Curzon, F.E. Smith (Lord Birkenhead, Secretary of State for India) and others, 'Jix had no trouble using and misusing intelligence to expose CPGB and Soviet covert work'. While the Foreign Secretary felt the best way to deal with Moscow was to be indifferent, the Home Secretary believed the intelligence community was struggling with the challenge of communist propaganda, subversion and espionage. 'The question of the prosecution of Communist leaders, speakers and writers,' Joynson-Hicks proclaimed, 'is becoming a burning one. The old Conservative Party is getting very angry that nothing has been done …'[5]

It is probably with a good deal of surprise that intelligence historians have discovered that 'for over half a century after the Bolshevik revolution the term "subversion", though commonly used around Whitehall, was never officially defined'.[6] Three months before the breach of relations between Britain and Russia, in February 1927, the head of the British Mission pointed out in a memorandum from Moscow that a definition had never been provided.[7] It is therefore perhaps not so odd that much confusion still exists concerning the difference between the Comintern's seditious activities, communist propaganda and subversion versus active measures, espionage and terrorist acts.[8] When the Security Service (MI5) in addition to counter-espionage was dealing with subversion in the armed forces, and Special Branch had similar responsibilities in the civilian world, with SIS following their work, itself being engaged in both subversion and espionage in Russia and elsewhere, no wonder there was chaos in the British intelligence community.[9] It has already been noted that for many years the government had neither given subversion any precise meaning nor admitted using it as a basis for investigating or suppressing political views. Keeping the definition vague, some experts believe, had also maximised the scope of allowable activity within (and sometimes outside) security and intelligence mandates.[10] On the other hand, it also misled many of those whose job was to defend the realm.

* * *

Part of the Secret Service Committee sessions in March 1925 was devoted to examining co-operation or, rather, lack of such between SIS, MI5 and the Special Branch. Sinclair, who succeeded Cumming in September 1923, told the committee that it was 'impossible to draw the line between espionage and counter-espionage, for both were concerned solely with foreign activities'. Sir John Anderson, Permanent Under-Secretary of State at the Home Office, asked whether SIS currently employed any agents in the United Kingdom, as Commissioner Childs had reported. Because a special SIS organisation of domestic intelligence sources did exist and in Sinclair's opinion made a lot of sense, he answered somewhat evasively which made Anderson once again express 'concern at C's activities in this country, which he thought, if not curtailed, might sooner or later lead to trouble'.[11] Six years later nothing had changed concerning the 'casuals', as SIS agents and informants inside the UK became known within the British intelligence community, so in January 1931 Anderson summoned Sinclair to the Home Office and, as described by Jeffery, it 'turned out to be a very uncomfortable meeting about the Casual organisation'.[12] Back in Head Office at 54 Broadway, Sinclair circulated a summary of a meeting to Colonel Stewart Menzies (Military Section), Major Desmond Morton (Production) and Major Valentine Vivian (Counter-Espionage, CE), all of them directly involved in handling domestic sources including civil servants.

After leaving Constantinople in 1923, Valentine Vivian (V.V.) was based in Cologne serving as Regional Inspector for Western Europe before moving to London promoted to head of new Section V. The section, previously CE, was devoted to counter-intelligence and counter-communist work. It also took over the running of the 'casuals' together with Morton's existing network of agents. Morton, as head of Production at Head Office, 'retained a close interest in the work of the section, which overlapped with that of both Scotland Yard and MI5'. Following the recommendations of the Secret Service Committee made in March 1925, SIS endeavoured to improve liaison particularly with the counter-subversion experts, Captain Hugh Miller and Guy Liddell, in Scotland Yard's semi-autonomous section SS1,[13] later transferred to MI5 together with a similar unit, section SS2.

In October 1926, Bertie Maw, who worked in Morton's Production Section, went to 'C' reporting that a neighbour of his in Wimbledon had been employed as an accountant at ARCOS, widely regarded as a front for Soviet propaganda and subversion. This neighbour, without doubt one of the SIS 'casuals' (who was described by Morton as 'a British subject of undoubted loyalty'[14] and whose name is on record but still kept secret),[15] was willing to provide information on what was going on there, Maw said. In view of the recent Secret Service Committee discussions, Sinclair said the accountant should better go to Scotland Yard. There, one of chief inspectors interviewed him but was not quite so enthusiastic about what the informant said and let him go without taking any action. Nothing happened until the end of March 1927 when the accountant gave Maw a copy of the front page of a Signal Training pamphlet which, he claimed, had been copied at the ARCOS offices.[16] All three interested parties – Maw, the accountant (designated in secret files as 'X') and the man from the ARCOS photostat room (later designated 'Y') – immediately noticed that the front cover of the pamphlet carried the unambiguous warning: 'FOR OFFICIAL USE ONLY. THIS DOCUMENT IS THE PROPERTY OF HBM GOVERNMENT'.[17] Bingo!

Maw immediately reported to 'C' and they soon found out that one Edward Langston (to whom intelligence historians and even declassified secret documents always referred to as 'Y') was a low-ranking ARCOS employee working in the photostat room from October 1920 when it began operations in London.[18] At the end of January 1927, when it was already clear that

Langston was likely to lose his job because the personnel department had started laying off all non-communist foreign employees, a senior staff member, Iosif Dudkin, came down to his room in the basement of Soviet House at 49 Moorgate. Dudkin brought with him the Signal Training manual asking Langston to copy it, which he did. At the same time, he secretly made one extra copy of its cover for himself, just in case. In February, Langston was dismissed taking the photocopy with him. He then handed it over to 'X' to deal with.

Given that it was a War Office document (as it turned out, from the Aldershot military base), on 31 March Sinclair passed it on to Vernon Kell of MI5, whose responsibility it was to investigate such cases. Kell and Harker spent the next few weeks checking the reliability of SIS's information and conducting inquiries at Aldershot where the commanding officer confirmed that 'at least one' of the assigned copies was missing. Finally, Harker was put in touch with Maw and on 9 May arranged a meeting with Langston.[19] The interviews were held at The Dolphin, an old pub at Dolphin Bridge near the Grand Union Canal, and in Central London. For one of the meetings Oswald Harker's brother-in-law offered his flat on King's Bench Walk in the Inner Temple as an impromptu safe house. The MI5 officers were also thoroughly checking Langston and his story. Once satisfied, they drew up a report on the case for the Director of Public Prosecutions, Sir Archibald Bodkin. 'At 11 a.m. on 11 May,' according to the Authorised History of MI5, 'the DPP confirmed to Kell that the possession by ARCOS of the Signals Training document was an offence under the Official Secrets Act.'[20] Over half a year had passed since the agent approached Bertie Maw for the first time with his information.

Everybody remembered that during the Cabinet's February (1927) meeting they decided they needed an event comparable to the Zinoviev Letter in order to justify a sudden break of relations to the British public. Kell knew from the beginning that Langston's document was exactly what his boss and other hardliners had long sought, but the remainder of the morning of 11 May showed how much less well connected Colonel Kell was in Whitehall than the chief of SIS. After the meeting with Bodkin,

Kell tried and failed to secure appointments with, successfully, the PUS at the Home Office, the Directors of Military Operations and of Military Intelligence and the Chief of the Imperial General Staff. On his way back to the office from lunch, however, Kell had a chance encounter with the Secretary of State for War, Sir Laming Worthington-Evans, who agreed to see him at 5.15 p.m. Worthington-Evans in turn referred Kell to the rabidly anti-Soviet Home Secretary, William Joynson-

Hicks, who immediately took a note prepared by the Director [of Public Prosecutions] to the Prime Minister, Stanley Baldwin. Baldwin gave his permission to raid ARCOS in order to procure evidence of a breach of the Official Secrets Act.[21]

This is not quite correct. Jix did indeed go off to obtain the concurrence of the Prime Minister who passed him on to Austen Chamberlain. Answering Sir Austen's question, Jix assured him that 'on such information as he had before him, he would be prepared to raid any other English company'. This was later described in intelligence literature (by Roberta Wohlstetter and Frank J. Stech) as 'the tendency of policymakers to select estimates of the situation that suit their wishful expectations or preferences' – wishful thinking which is a dangerous form of self-deception. Chamberlain then agreed to the raid. Sir William Tyrrell, then PUS at the Foreign Office who had previously been head of the FO Political Intelligence Department, later stressed that 'Sir Austen Chamberlain's consent only covered the raid on Arcos: if the Trade Delegation had been mentioned Sir Austen would undoubtedly have hesitated and consulted the Foreign Office before agreeing to it.' In addition, with the confidence and authority of an experienced bureaucrat, Tyrrell 'was shocked to hear that Colonel Kell had direct access to the Home Secretary'. In his opinion, 'he ought to have seen Sir John Anderson and not Sir William Joynson-Hicks'.[22]

As should have been expected, the search which stretched over five days from Thursday to Monday (12–16 May 1927) was a disaster. First, it was poorly prepared and badly coordinated. Secondly, the fact that ARCOS shared the building with the Soviet Trade Delegation, which under Article 5 of the trade agreement was immune from search, was completely overlooked.[23] And finally, neither the Signal Training manual nor any other evidence of Soviet espionage was discovered. A Cabinet committee had to admit that the ARCOS haul did not even prove 'the complicity of the Soviet Diplomatic Mission' in the 'propagandist activities' of the Trade Delegation (this had not been conclusively demonstrated either).[24] Discussing the ARCOS raid at a June meeting of the Secret Service Committee, Sinclair said that he, Colonel Kell and Sir Wyndham Childs all knew that ARCOS and the Trade Delegation were in the same building and realised that raiding ARCOS meant raiding the Trade Delegation, which he, 'C', fully understood would raise serious political issues. 'Arcos,' he added, 'never appealed to him particularly: moreover, it was known that all Soviet agencies abroad had had orders to burn any compromising papers.'[25]

Already on 13 April, after Moscow's warning of the imminent raid on the Soviet premises, Rosengoltz telegraphed to the NKID:

I very much doubt the possibility of a raid on our Embassy. I would, however, consider it a very useful measure of precaution to suspend for a time the forwarding by post of documents of friends [Comintern and CPGB], 'neighbours' [RIS] and so forth from London to Moscow and vice versa. Telegraph your decision immediately. In the telegram sent in reply it is desirable to mention that the instructions emanate from the institutions concerned.

The last note was important for the OGPU, (G)RU and OMS representatives in London to understand that the instruction had been agreed with and approved by the leadership of their respective organisations.

Remarkably, although the telegram was duly intercepted and decrypted, no one paid attention to the apparent leak. Rosengoltz's message, like the previously intercepted telegram of 15 February, clearly suggested that the Kremlin had a source in the Foreign Office and this source was not one of the Constantini brothers in Rome. Albert Allen (whose real name was Arthur Lakey), a former Special Branch sergeant who had worked for Ewer and the FPA, during an interview with MI5 confirmed that 'a leakage of information comes from the Foreign Office owing to an individual who holds there an important position'.[26] The name of that individual was given by Allen to Harker at a subsequent interview. It was 'noted' by the Security Service but no action taken.

In May, Pyotr Zolotussky, an experienced INO officer, arrived in London to take care of the potentially dangerous situation. He had graduated from the Military Academy of the RKKA and had served as the (G)RU resident in Erzurum, Turkey, and later in Osaka, Japan, under official cover as secretary of the legation. In 1926 he was transferred to the foreign department (INO) of the OGPU and in early May urgently sent to the UK to deal with the crisis using the same diplomatic cover of a secretary. Shortly after the raid, Zolotussky (codenamed YAKOVLEV) reported: 'Your No. 126. There were none of our cyphers or very secret material at the Trade Delegation. On special instructions the Chargé d'Affaires [Rosengoltz] acquainted the Trade Delegate [Khinchuk] with the contents of certain cypher messages.'[27] Although this telegram was also intercepted, the Security Service overlooked the obvious fact that it had been sent by somebody other than the Soviet chargé d'affaires. In response to a Soviet request, the German government assumed the protection of Russian interests in Britain after diplomatic relations were broken off. Zolotussky remained in London until June. In 1930 he was sent to New York as a senior staff member of AMTORG.

Harriette Flory, who wrote a 'classic' account of the ARCOS affair back in 1977, asserted that in spite of the fact that 'the Arcos raid had not produced any firm proof of complicity on the part of the [Soviet] diplomatic mission at Chesham House ... the Foreign Office had secret evidence to that effect'.[28] Three decades later the Official Historian of MI5 agreed that 'the only proof available [of the complicity of the Soviet diplomatic mission] was the telegrams exchanged between the legation and Moscow decrypted by GC&CS'. Reference is made to the Prime Minister's statement of 24 May in the House of Commons.[29] It seems that since May 1927 no one either cared to read that statement or the documents in the government White Paper on the affair (Cmb. 2874, 1927) published later that year. It included (Part I) nine documents found during the search in Soviet House and (Part II) seven telegrams intercepted by the GC&CS during an intelligence operation against Soviet cryptosystems, to use the GC&CS vocabulary.

A careful study of all those documents (and four of the seven intercepts dealt with China) will lead an unbiased intelligence historian to the only possible conclusion that none of them contains anything even remotely related to Soviet espionage or Communist subversion.

The Prime Minister began his 24 May statement in the House of Commons with a false declaration that quickly coagulated into pure lies. 'For many months,' he said, 'the Police, in collaboration with the military authorities, have been investigating the activities of a group of secret agents engaged in endeavouring to obtain highly confidential documents relating to the Armed Forces of Great Britain.' Claiming that the unnamed 'agents' obtained their instructions 'from members of the Russian Trade Delegation working at Soviet House', he assured the MPs:

> These suspicions were confirmed when, early this year, a British subject employed in the Air Force was convicted of stealing two such documents as have been described. The documents were recovered and the individual is now undergoing imprisonment. The secret organisation on behalf of which he had obtained the documents is known and its connection with a similar Russian organisation has been established.

Alas, all this is pure invention. Whether he was fully aware of it or not, probably not, the British prime minister was lying to his Parliament.

Nonetheless, in the closing part of his statement Stanley Baldwin pointed out that the evidence now in the hands of the authorities proved that:

(1) Both military espionage and subversive activities throughout the British Empire and North and South America were directed and carried out from Soviet House.

(2) No effective differentiation of rooms or duties was observed as between the members of the Trade Delegation and the employés [sic] of Arcos, and both these organisations have been involved in anti-British espionage and propaganda.[30]

Unlike the Prime Minister, in his concluding remarks on the ARCOS affair Christopher Andrew tried to be objective and accurate. 'Baldwin's government was able to prove its charge of Soviet dabbling in British politics,' he writes. 'But the documents seized in the ARCOS raid and the intercepted telegrams published in a government White Paper contained only a few cryptic allusions to espionage' (even this is an exaggeration). Yet at the same time the government 'compromised its most valuable intelligence source', to which Moscow responded by adopting the virtually unbreakable 'one-time pad' for diplomatic and intelligence traffic.[31] Moreover, the government demonstrated its vulnerability to the charge that it had itself been engaged in espionage activities in order to obtain their 'evidence', which turned out to be misleading at best. 'The events between 12 and 24 May,' Harriette Flory sums up, 'made the cabinet appear foolish, inept and indecisive.'[32]

* * *

Just as had been the case before 1914, after the October Revolution 'the bear and the whale' remained potential adversaries, rarely using direct force against each other.[33] While Soviet Russia had been a primary target for SIS from 1917 to 1927, Great Britain (or 'England' as the Chekists wrote in their documents) became a primary target for RIS (Russian Intelligence Services) and Russia's main adversary during the Civil War. In 1919–20 SIS occasionally acquired – thanks to GC&CS intercepts or by other means – messages written by Lenin, which demonstrated the Bolshevik leader's hostility to Britain and his government's efforts to conspire with her enemies trying to manipulate British politics. 'But, of course, all this must be done absolutely unofficially and confidentially and the most prudent diplomacy must be maintained,' Lenin instructed his diplomats.[34] Well aware of that, Britain was the first country to accept Lenin's offer of a trade treaty and indeed the Anglo-Soviet Trade Agreement was finally signed on 16 March 1921 probably becoming one of the reasons why all intelligence activities 'on the ISLAND', as Britain began to be named in Soviet intelligence reports, were postponed for some time.

After Josef Krasny was refused a British entry visa in August 1922, a new GPU resident was selected among the INO staff. Although no records remain in the files, a possible candidate for the job is Robert Gulbis, a Latvian communist who fought in the Russian Civil War and joined the Cheka in 1921. Transferred to foreign intelligence (INO) in 1922, until 1928 Gulbis occupied different responsible positions at Moscow Centre, also serving abroad posted under commercial cover within Russian trade organisations. It is documented that Gulbis, using the alias 'Grünfeld', had operated in Turkey until 1927. Unfortunately, it has not been possible to find out whether he had been there attached to ARCOS or to another Soviet import-export company. Arthur Lakey testified that he knew a Soviet intelligence operator whom he only remembered as GRUNDFELD or GRINFELD and who had never been identified by MI5.[35] There are some grounds to believe that Gulbis-Grünfeld was initially assigned to the Anglo-Soviet Shipping organisation which became ARCOS Steamship Company in June 1923. It is also possible that in spring 1924 he left London travelling to Constantinople.

The next INO resident in the UK was also inconclusively identified by Lakey as VASSILOFF, or VASILTSEF, or VASILTSEV, an official of the Soviet diplomatic mission, and for easily understandable reasons neither MI5 nor the Special Branch ever followed up the tip. In the meantime, 'Vasiltsev' was an alias of Nikolai Alexeyev who in January 1921 was sent to Berlin with a group of other RIS operatives (see Chapter 7) to undermine Savinkov's efforts to form an anti-Soviet underground.

Alexeyev was born in the Russian town of Rzhev on the Volga. After his father died, the family moved to Kharkiv and there, aged 17, Nikolai joined the SR revolutionary movement. After a year at Moscow University Faculty of Mathematics and Physics, Alexeyev entered the Law Faculty of Kharkiv University but was arrested for his revolutionary activities. Active in Kharkiv during the revolution and civil war, he joined the INO in January 1921 and was sent to Berlin and Paris in charge of a mixed group of the Cheka and (G)RU officers. Recalled to Moscow in February 1922, Alexeyev occupied various posts in the Secret-Operational Directorate (SOU). In April 1924, using the alias 'Vasiltsev' (codenamed OSCAR), he was sent to London as a new 'legal' OGPU resident in the UK working under diplomatic cover as Assistant Head of the Consular Section of the Soviet legation at Chesham House. According to MI5, 'he arrived about May 1924 and remained for some two years',[36] which is different from what Soviet records suggest.

According to the Russian sources, Alexeyev returned from London in spring 1925 and in July was appointed first deputy head and later head of the Information Department (INFO) of the OGPU.[37] At the same time, in the autumn of 1924 a new INO resident in London was appointed. His name was Nikolai Rakow. Although perfectly Russian-sounding, his was actually a German name and he was born in Kreuzburg an der Düna (now Krustpils, part of the town of Jēkabpils, Latvia), then in the Russian Empire, as Nikolai August Wilhelm Rakow in August 1890. He was the eldest child in what would become a large family of three brothers and two sisters. His two younger brothers, Werner and Paul, would also be actively involved in different branches of Soviet intelligence apparat. When Nikolai was nine and his brother Werner six years old, the family returned to Germany for the boys to study at a German school.

Both brothers returned to Russia in spring 1914. They chose St Petersburg and Nikolai quickly found a job with the recently founded Russo-Asian Bank. During three years before the revolution, Nikolai and Werner became active in the Russian revolutionary movement joining the German section of the Bolshevik party. In July 1918 they moved to Moscow and in September Nikolai got a job at the German consulate as an interpreter thanks to his aunt who had also worked there and recommended him. In August 1919, now active communist militants, both brothers were in Germany again.

By the time Nikolai began his eight-year-long career with the OGPU, Werner Rakow (aka Waldemar Rakow, 'Karl Felix Wolff' and 'Vladimir Inkov/Inkow/Inkoff) had become one of the main organisers and later leader of the underground N-Apparat (intelligence service) of the KPD and an important foreign agent of the Red Army intelligence directorate (G)RU operating in Turkey, Austria and the USA. Before joining the INO staff, Nikolai had served as a local KPD secretary in Berlin, then was one of the secretaries of the Central European Bureau (CEB) of the Profintern, and a liaison officer between N-Apparat and the KPD Central Committee using the alias 'Krebs'. In June Nikolai came to Moscow, taking part in the establishment of the German section of the Comintern and joining the Russian Communist Party as 'Nikolai Bogdanovich Rakov'. He also became a Soviet citizen and was accepted into the INO at the end of 1923.

According to Markus Wehner, the author of a long and detailed article about the brothers Rakow, Nikolai was appointed the main INO resident in London in the second half of 1924.[38] He probably arrived in London in spring 1925 using the alias 'N.S. Skvortsov' (codenamed WOLDEMAR) and taking over from Alexeyev-Vasiltsev.[39] Tsarev claims (without any reference to any KGB document) that Moscow also sent one Belopolsky (codenamed MATVEI) as Rakow's assistant.[40] In London, Nikolai met Maria Runenko, employed as a secretary of the legation since December 1923, who became his second wife. The couple, both of whom had been working for the INO in London, was recalled to Moscow in January 1927. At the Moscow Lubyanka OGPU headquarters Nikolai was initially placed in the INO section dealing with China and East Asia where his brother Paul was working for the OMS, the secret service of the Comintern. In 1929 Nikolai Rakow was transferred to Tbilisi, Georgia, as the OGPU plenipotentiary representative in the

Caucasus. Maria was also there on the staff of the OGPU mission until in 1931 her husband was transferred to the OMS then headed by Alexander Abramov-Mirov.

Following the appointment of Rakow as a new OGPU resident agent in London, the first (G)RU representative also arrived there in July 1925 posing as an employee of the ARCOS Steamship Company. Like Rakow, he was a foreigner, a Pole named Stefan Zhbikovsky (Żbikowski), codenamed ALOIS. In January Rakow left to be succeeded by Pyotr or Peter Zolotussky, who came to sort out problems related to the raids about which Moscow had been forewarned. Zhbikovsky remained in London until May 1927. From there he was transferred to Berlin operating there undercover and joining the underground apparat of the KPD. Back in Moscow in August, he was appointed chief of Section A (special 'active' operations) of the Intelligence Directorate of Red Army Headquarters. According to his son, Zolotussky was sent to China and from there returned to Moscow to report about the situation directly to Stalin. He later operated in Sweden, Germany and the USA.

Judging by the official and authorised histories of British secret services (SIS, MI5, GCHQ and Special Branch) none of that had ever been known to them and, like most of the intelligence historians, they had been following false leads providing the political leadership and the government with bogus information, often specifically fabricated to serve their political masters. This inflated the British Cabinet estimates of Soviet intelligence capabilities and, as mentioned, resulted in a dangerous form of self-deception leading to the fearful overestimation but also to the sometimes dangerous underestimation of the adversary. Regarding the COMINT, considered the most reliable source of secret intelligence, the intercepts of the period were only dealing with the Soviet diplomatic and Comintern traffic. 'After December 1920,' John Ferris writes, 'the GC&CS rarely solved Soviet diplomatic traffic in Europe; the celebrated compromises of its successes against Soviet systems during 1923 and 1927 had little impact on that power in Europe.'[41] Nothing like the VENONA project existed before the Second World War. All this plus the lack of reliable information from Russia led to misinterpretations, fabrications, inventions and truly wild guesses that continue to fill books, academic articles and even doctoral theses.

Nikolai Klyshko

In the vast majority of published sources Nikolai Klyshko, the secretary of the Russian trade delegation and Krasin's deputy, is named as the first Soviet intelligence resident in London. When the head of the Russian section Captain Maurice Bray, one of MI5's Russian speakers, concluded in July 1918 that Klyshko was the 'most dangerous Bolshevik here', he clearly had in mind exactly what he said, that is, Klyshko's communist propaganda activities. Klyshko's security service files declassified in September 2003 correctly describe him as an 'early Russian revolutionary' and all Soviet and Russian documents so far available state exactly this while his alleged role as a Soviet intelligence agent, not to mention his being a 'resident', is a fantasy not supported by any evidence.

From 1907 until the Bolshevik revolution a decade later Klyshko lived in exile in London where he found well-paid work with the famous Vickers company that during the first decades of the twentieth century was going through several name changes, growing into a major warship and aircraft manufacturer. He married an English woman named Phyllis Frood, a manageress of a dressmaking business in London's West End described as tall, red-headed and very beautiful.[42] After 1917 Klyshko was especially close to Maxim Litvinov, who at that time was active in the International Socialist Bureau (representing Russia during its 15th Plenary meeting in London in December 1913) and was later made an unofficial Bolshevik diplomatic agent in the UK. Following the Lockhart scandal, Litvinov and his party were detained and held in Brixton Prison in September 1918. Exchanged for Lockhart and other members of the British diplomatic, trade and intelligence missions in Russia, he arrived in Moscow in November. Serving for over a decade as Chicherin's deputy, Litvinov was finally appointed People's Commissar for Foreign Affairs in 1930, holding this position until his dismissal in May 1939.

While in London in 1918, Litvinov even lived in Klyshko's house on Hampstead's High Street. Like Litvinov, Klyshko was interned as a hostage on 6 September but released two weeks later. On 26 September he left Aberdeen with Litvinov and others before returning to London in May 1920 as a member of the Russian delegation headed by Leonid Krasin. During this short spell in Moscow Klyshko served as first deputy director of the state publisher Gosizdat. In early February 1920 he was briefly posted to Estonia as the Russian diplomatic representative, succeeded there by Litvinov in December. Once back in London, this time as Assistant Official Agent of the Soviet government, Klyshko was kept under constant police surveillance. He had to leave Britain again in May 1923 as a result of Lord Curzon's Memorandum.[43] In Moscow Klyshko was appointed to head the Export Department of the NKVT. Between June 1924 and July 1926 he had served as a Soviet trade representative in China and later worked as manager of the technical bureau of the metal department of the Soviet trade mission in Berlin, visiting Britain four times for the purchase of machinery. On 2

September 1937 Nikolai Klyshko, who had never served in Soviet intelligence in any capacity, was arrested in Moscow and a month later shot.

It took MI5 almost five decades to come to the conclusion that is still being ignored by many historians:

> It is virtually impossible at this distance of time to determine with any accuracy what Klishko's [*sic*] role was in relation to the Russian intelligence service and the Comintern; certainly contemporary assessments, suggesting that he was the OGPU Resident or the U.K. representative of the Third International, are misleading. Klishko was not a trained intelligence officer; what he had to offer the Soviet regime in the post-Revolution period were his contacts [here] and an experience of conspiratorial work in the U.K. before the revolution ... Although we have detailed evidence of their own activities from both ALLEN [Arthur Lakey] and [Jacob] KIRCHENSTEIN ... the part played by Klishko remains somewhat obscure. It would be misleading to suggest that he controlled these operations; he was probably the channel through which much of the communications and reporting to Moscow passed, but his main role would seem to have been one of providing support and above all as paymaster.[44]

Even this early assessment is not quite correct because it is largely based on the sometimes inaccurate testimonies of Lakey and Kirchenstein, often a product of wishful thinking and overactive imaginations.

Jacob Kirchenstein

On 15 January 1952 J.C. Robertson, the head of MI5's B.2.a. division, which was responsible for counter-espionage, sent a note to Dick Thistlethwaite of B.1.f. It was about a lengthy report just sent by G.T.D. Patterson, the Security Liaison Officer (SLO) of MI5 at the British embassy in Washington, DC, and Thistlethwaite's successor in this post. The document in question was a 73-page-long protocol (serial 98a) of the FBI soft interrogation of Jacob Kirchenstein and Patterson strongly recommended Dick to read it carefully. 'I have only had time to skim the report,' he wrote, 'but it seems to me that a good deal of registry action is called for.'[45] Indeed, and this did not concern the MI5 registry only. In her turn, Evelyn McBarnet of B.2.b. also sent the protocol to Kenneth Morton Evans (B.1.a.) with the same recommendation.

This Security Service file covering the period of 36 years between January 1925 and December 1951 contains a great deal of other relevant documents including the B.2.b. comments on Kirchenstein's initial testimony (serial 99a) as well as material of the FBI agents' later interviewing him in New York in February 1952 (serial 106a) following MI5's request to reinterview him 'along certain lines' with comments, observations and conclusions by both the FBI and MI5 officers. Guy Liddell, then DDG of MI5, during his visit to Washington read the document (98a) mentioned by Robertson and decided that to the best of his recollection the statement was accurate (adding that he thought it might contain 'a few omissions of importance').[46] In reality, alongside true facts it contained a lot of inventions, guesses and hearsay that can now be easily spotted.

Jacob (Yakov Yakovlevich) Kirchenstein was born in Mazsalaca (in the protocol they use its German name Salisburg), Latvia, on 20 July 1887 to a Jewish family. By the time of the interrogation his parents had long been deceased. When he was attending a telegraph school in Riga in or about 1902, the young man became interested in politics, later joining the revolutionary Latvian Socialist Democratic Party. Having started his working career as a telegrapher for the Russian state railways in Riga, Kirchenstein took part in a strike, was arrested, exiled to Siberia (which may or may not be true), managed to escape and together with three others was put on board a vessel bound for England as a stowaway. In May 1908 he was in New York. There, he completed a wireless telegrapher course and met a Latvian woman, Vallie Waldman, whom he subsequently married but not before he had applied and was duly naturalised as an American citizen on 29 December 1914 at Bronx County, NY.

Kirchenstein explained that he became close to the Socialist Propaganda League of America (SPLA) especially when it moved to New York in spring 1917. On 1 March 1918 the *New York Times* reported about a mass meeting held in a New York City hall just a day before at which Louis Fraina, a young Italian-American radical, called for the establishment of a 'Red Guard' of draft-age men to be sent to Soviet Russia to fight for the Bolshevik government. In the interview Kirchenstein claimed that he was among the 2,000 people who had attended that meeting mentioning Fraina, whom he called 'Hugh Frayna', and saying that two other founders of the SPLA were Simon Berg and 'Gedus Beika, also known as Bernhard'.[47] In reality, Beika's name was David (Dāvids). He was indeed a Latvian revolutionary and political activist, one of the leading figures of the SPLA, who at one time was in America but returned to Russia after the February Revolution of 1917.

Among other people whom Kirchenstein said he had met in New York were Nikolai Bukharin and Jan A. Berzin (Jānis Bērziņš). Until early April 1917 Bukharin, the future General Secretary of the Comintern's Executive Committee (ECCI), lived in New York editing the newspaper *Novy Mir* with Trotsky (who left in March for Petrograd) and Alexandra Kollontai.[48]

Berzin, in turn, edited a Latvian social-democratic journal in Boston but also contributed to *Novy Mir*, leaving the United States after the February Revolution in Russia. Following Fraina's call, Kirchenstein and his wife sailed from San Francisco to Vladivostok arriving by the Trans-Siberian in Petrograd in early July 1917. A year later, disillusioned with what he saw in Russia, Kirchenstein said he went to the US consulate in Moscow seeking help to return to the United States but all his efforts and pleas for help were to no avail. 'From that time on,' he told the FBI 33 years later, 'I saw that I was trapped; Russia was surrounded by White Russian Armies and White armies were killing any and all political exiles, especially those [like he and his wife] bearing Figner Committee credentials [?!]. I saw no alternative other than to start to work actively with the then existent Bolshevik Government.'[49]

Jacob Kirchenstein was finally employed by the People's Commissariat of Railways (Narkomput, verbally translated in several publications as 'People's Commissariat of Communications Routes') and sent to Smolensk, where the Western Front field headquarters were until the front was disbanded in late 1918. He then claimed that he 'worked chiefly with General Tukhachevsky and General Kork, both anti-Communists at that time', and also met Stalin. However, Mikhail Tukhachevsky and August Kork were not 'generals' and not 'anti-communists' but were both serving the Bolsheviks diligently and faithfully as Red Army 'commanders'. When Kirchenstein was in Smolensk Stalin could have been there too, soon leaving for Tsaritsyn only to be recalled to Moscow in October.[50] In March 1920 Trotsky became Commissar for Railways and in May Arkady Rosengoltz, a future chargé d'affaires in London, was also placed in the Narkomput, occupying several important posts until 1922 when at the end of the year he was suddenly appointed acting commander and then commander and military commissar of the Red Army Air Force before being transferred to the army reserve in April 1925.

In his long testimony Kirchenstein gave a lot of details of how one day he went to Moscow 'filled with delegates of the 2nd Congress of the Third International', where he met his old friends Beika and Berg, and renewed his acquaintance with Nikolai Bukharin and Jan Berzin, all of whom were prominent Bolsheviks 'then very active organising the Third International'. All this is largely correct. The 2nd Comintern Congress was held in Petrograd and Moscow between 19 July and 7 August 1920. The receptionist who registered all delegates was Michael Borodin, according to Kirchenstein. Discussing the situation with Beika, who would be placed in charge of the OMS after the Congress, Kirchenstein said he had a plan how to evade the British naval blockade of the Soviet ports and according to his account was promptly dispatched to London together with his wife travelling via Vayda-Guba on the Kola Peninsula and Vardø-Trondheim-Christiania (now Oslo) in Norway. Finally, they arrived in Newcastle in the first week of November 1920 as stowaways on board the SS *Sterling* without visas, carrying a small case of Comintern literature. Their arrival as well as their later stay in the country was illegal in the sense that neither Kirchenstein nor his wife registered as aliens with the British authorities.

Until March 1921 Kirchenstein was doing some routine work, occasionally receiving Comintern literature from Oslo and sending reports to the OMS about the activities of British communists, some of whom he considered police informants. As it turned out decades later this suspicion was based on a correct assumption. In summer, he began receiving 'alarming news from Berg concerning the intrigues then going on in Moscow' and soon was informed that Beika had been removed from office and replaced by Osip Pyatnitsky, which happened right after the 3rd World Congress of the Comintern in July 1921. In the meantime, his initial task of breaking the British blockade had long been forgotten simply because it ended with the signing of the Anglo-Soviet Trade Agreement in March. The Soviet mission had already been established with its headquarters on New Bond Street and in July 1921 Jan Berzin, with whom Kirchenstein was acquainted in New York and whom he later met in Moscow, arrived as Krasin's deputy together with Peter Miller, the cypher clerk of the delegation. Krasin and his party arrived in May. During his FBI interview Kirchenstein all of a sudden accused members of the Krasin delegation of 'probably representing the OGPU as well as the Comintern', which was just a fantasy for which there was no evidence, then and now.

The secretary and shorthand typist of the Soviet mission, which Kirchenstein ironically called 'the Embassy', was Violet Lansbury, the daughter of the British MP George Lansbury who was elected chairman of the Labour Party soon after the ARCOS raid (he later became party leader following the collapse of the second Labour government). Fresh from school, Violet was briefly employed as her father's secretary. A journalist and political activist, Landsbury had been known as a pacifist and supporter of the Bolshevik revolution in Russia which prevented him being elected to Parliament in 1918 (he won a parliamentary seat in the 1922 general election and would hold it for the rest of his life). As soon as the Soviet delegation arrived in London, Andrew Rothstein recommended Violet to Krasin. After working there for almost five years, she travelled to Russia in October 1925 to study at the University of Sverdlovsk (now Yekaterinburg) perfecting her Russian, which she spoke rather well even before. Violet Lansbury became an interpreter and later a renowned translator of Russian literature. In her biography *An English Woman in the U.S.S.R.* (1940) she writes about life in the Soviet Union, providing her reflections about Russian society and politics. As soon as she settled in Moscow, she arranged her parents' visit there in 1926.[51] Violet stayed in the Soviet Union for 13 years, returning to Britain in February 1939.

Describing his life and work in Britain years later, Kirchenstein remembered Violet. He recalled that roughly in 1926–7 (*sic*) she fell in love with one Prigozhin who came to London allegedly 'to study research problems in the British museums', an obvious invention but based on a real fact. 'In the Embassy lobby,' Kirchenstein told the FBI, 'I once heard Prigozhin discussing the merits of his fiancée. One remark was that Violet Lansbury was very beautiful and that with training she would be first class material to circulate in the foreign diplomatic circles in Moscow. Prigozhin said that her only bad feature was that she did not drink, and added, however, that "We'll teach her". Shortly thereafter, Violet left for Russia with Prigozhin.'[52]

Although Kirchenstein mistook the dates, all the rest is probably correct. Abram Grigorievich Prigozhin worked in Kiev where he was in charge of the propaganda section of the local party committee. He took part in the suppression of the Kronstadt rebellion then, as a Cheka collaborator who proved his loyalty fighting the enemies of the revolution, was sent to Germany, and in 1924-25 was on the staff of the Soviet legation in London. Back in the USSR he joined the Department of Western History at the Leningrad State University soon becoming a professor there.[53] In 1937 Prigozhin was arrested and shot as a Trotskyite.

In Moscow Violet married Igor Reisner and they had two children, brothers Lev and Igor. In 1938 (according to other sources, in 1936) she married Clemens Palme Dutt, the elder brother of R. Palme Dutt who, like Rajani, was active in the Communist Party of Great Britain. Clemens worked as a journalist, translator and editor, in particular of the works of Marx and Engels. In 1930 he replaced Percy Glading as head of the colonial section of the party but a year later moved to Berlin and then to Moscow where he met Violet. During the Spanish Civil War Clemens was active collecting donations for the Republic. By the beginning of 1939 Palme Dutt, Violet and their baby daughter had returned to Britain permanently and settled in Cambridge. She published her book about Soviet Russia and he continued to work for the Communist Party, addressing meetings and writing articles.

Kirchenstein did not mention any of his contacts with Berzin in London but said he visited Andrew Rothstein who was sent to Britain as a correspondent of the Soviet news agency ROSTA and whose office was also there, at No. 128 New Bond Street, a narrow building now adjacent to the local branch of the HSBC bank. Andrew Rothstein's father, Kirchestein remembered, was deported from London together with Litvinov. According to Kirchenstein, in that office he also met Tom Wintringham who joined the

CPGB in 1923. Two years later Wintringham, together with eleven other CPGB officials, would be imprisoned for seditious libel and incitement to mutiny. Shortly after the beginning of the Spanish Civil War, he would be in Barcelona commanding the British Battalion of the International Brigades.

During one of the visits to Andrew Rothstein's home in Highgate in the summer of 1922, Kirchenstein said he met Borodin. 'Borodin berated me,' he recalled, 'for remaining idle in England stating that since the Comintern literature was now coming regularly to England by mail, my job was nothing but a sinecure.' Borodin arrived as the Comintern emissary which several informants immediately reported to SS2 of Scotland Yard. Acting under the aliases 'George Brown' and 'Art O'Connor', he was arrested in Glasgow and after serving a six-month sentence was deported in February 1923 for contravention of the Aliens Order.[54] Kirchenstein claimed that Borodin was a Latvian Jew – in reality, Borodin was born Moishe Grüsenberg in the Vitebsk region of Byelorussia.

The day after Borodin's arrest, Kirchenstein related, he went to see Andrew Rothstein, Jan Berzin and Nikolai Klyshko in the Soviet mission. 'They told me that if I were a legal resident of England, I would be given a very responsible and well-paying managerial position in Arcos.'[55] Therefore, in October 1922 Kirchenstein safely arrived in New York where his wife had already been staying for several months, and quickly obtained legal American passports and British visas for both of them. In early November they both sailed to Britain. Upon his return, Kirchenstein said, he was immediately given a job at ARCOS.

> Altogether during my legal residence in England from 1923 until June 1927, I held three positions: 1. Office Manager or Secretary of the Hides, Leather and Tanning Materials department of Arcos Ltd., 2. Manager, Forwarding Department of Arcos Steamship Company, also known as Ship Arcos and 3. One of the Russian Directors of the Russo-Norwegian Navigation Company, which was a joint enterprise organised by Bergenske, Inc., the largest Norwegian shipping company, and the Russian Northern Lumber Trust (Severoles). All these three institutions were strictly business concerns subject to British laws and my activities there were strictly legal.

As soon as Kirchenstein was established at ARCOS, he obtained a job for his former Latvian associates: Karl Bahn, as a recruiter of seamen crews for the ARCOS Steamship Company, and Robert Kaulin (Roberts Kauliņš), as an elevator operator in the ARCOS building at 49 Moorgate. Later Kaulin began his training as a photostat machine operator also serving as a courier carrying mail between ARCOS and the trade mission at Soviet House and the legation at Chesham House.

Originally a shoemaker from Riga without education, Kaulin-Kauliņš (he later changed his surname to the more English-sounding Koling) first came to the UK before the First World War. At the beginning of the war, he served as a crewman aboard a British vessel and married a British woman who kept a boarding house in Blyth in Northumberland.[56] According to Kirchenstein, Koling was recruited as a propaganda literature smuggler by Karl Bahn but did very little 'smuggling' as there was a very short supply of Comintern literature destined for Britain.

Karl Ansoff Bahn was born in Riga in February 1889 and first arrived in the UK from Antwerp in 1911 settling in Poplar in East London, the home borough of George Lansbury who was then active there in local politics helping to establish the *Daily Herald*, of which he became an editor. Bahn was serving as a seaman on British ships trading from South Shields. In May 1924 he was discharged from a cargo ship with an injured leg, came to the Seamen's Hospital in London for treatment and in September was picked up by Kirchenstein to run errands. As Kirchenstein correctly stated during his FBI interrogation, Bahn was later employed by the ARCOS Steamship Company at Beatley House, Masons Avenue, Coleman Street as a shore captain recruiting crews for the ships operated by ARCOS.[57] Both Bahn and Koling emigrated and lived abroad after the ARCOS raid. Nothing even remotely resembling espionage activities had ever been proved against them.

Kirchenstein recalled that about a week or 10 days before the raid on ARCOS,

> the strong rooms and safes in the Arcos building were cleared out, contents packed up, and shipped off as diplomatic baggage to Moscow. Anton Miller ... who was then employed as a cipher clerk in the Russian Trade Delegation in the Arcos building, told me that one machine, which had been stored in the Arcos vaults, had been dismantled and shipped in several bulky boxes to Moscow together with other material under diplomatic seal.

He believed this was the machine 'designed to counterfeit English ten-shilling notes'.[58] It is not possible today to verify this information but with the exception of the mysterious machine this seems exactly what several Russian sources claim the OGPU officer Zolotussky managed to accomplish as soon as he arrived in London.

In his testimony Kirchenstein repeated several times that one Radomsky was the OGPU resident agent in the Russian legation who had to leave London about three weeks before the raid. It is possible that after so many years his memory didn't serve him well because the only candidate for this role might be Stefan Zhbikovsky, who had operated in his native Poland as 'Jan Zasurski' organising the military section, so-called M-Apparat or Wydział Wojskowy of the Communist Workers' Party of Poland (KPRP). Arrested in 1919, he returned to Russia two years later, joining the military commission of the Comintern from where he was transferred to the (G)RU. In 1923 Zhbikovsky (ALOIS) was sent to Germany and from there to Britain as the main (G)RU resident.[59] Before his arrest in 1937, he operated in China.

Speaking about Comintern representatives in London, Kirchenstein demonstrated a certain degree of prevarication which could either be professional ignorance or an unwillingness to tell the truth. He described how, while passing through Oslo on his way to London after the Second Comintern Congress, he learned that John Reed had been appointed to represent the Executive Committee of the Third International (Comintern) in Britain. Kirchenstein had allegedly met both Reed and his wife, Louise Bryant, in Moscow but at the time he was in Norway preparing to depart to Newcastle Reed died (on 17 October 1920). 'About a year after Reed's death,' he said, 'one Stocklitzky was assigned to England as the Comintern political representative … He was discovered by the British authorities almost as soon as he reached the English shores as a stowaway.'[60] Finally, the third political representative of the Comintern was Mikhail Borodin who arrived in the summer of 1922 but was soon arrested and subsequently deported in February 1923.

According to the documents in the Russian archives, one of the first Comintern emissaries in Britain was Henry Robinson (born Arnold Schnee in 1897 in Brussels to a Lithuanian Jewish émigré father and a Polish mother). It is known that after the First World War Robinson was associated with Willi Münzenberg and the Swiss communist Jules Humbert-Droz and was operating in Europe on assignments from the KIM, known in English as the Young Communist International, a youth section of the Comintern. In April 1921 he was in Britain disbursing Comintern funds there.[61] Later, Henry Robinson became a Soviet intelligence operator who was one of the leaders of the large (G)RU spy ring in Paris, arrested there in 1942 by the Sonderkommando Rote Kapelle. The documents found in his possession when they were captured by the British after the liberation of Europe became known as the 'Robinson Papers'. After their assessment, it was concluded that the documents 'did not give any positive lead to spies in the UK; they do indicate that Robinson played an important part in running Russian operations in the UK in the 1930s'.[62]

However, the most significant Comintern emissary in Britain was A.J. Bennett, better known as David Petrovsky. Born in Ukraine as David

Ephraim Lipetz, he travelled the world using many aliases, posing as Max Goldfarb in the USA, Humboldt in France and Brown or Braun in Germany plus, as mentioned, Bennett in the UK and Petrovsky in Moscow. He had graduated from the University of Brussels in 1912 and then worked for the Bund, a secular Jewish socialist party, in New York joining the Socialist Party of America (SPA). After taking part in the Socialist Congress in Stockholm in 1917, he returned to Russia as Lipetz.

Like many Soviet, Red Army and Cheka officials with Jewish names, Lipetz officially changed his to David Aleksandrovich Petrovsky, working as a lecturer at various military educational establishments of the Red Army before he was transferred to the Comintern and appointed its permanent representative with the British Communist Party (CPGB), also working in France and the USA often spending long periods of time away from Britain. In 1926 he was briefly appointed the CPGB representative to the Comintern, a rather unusual role for a Russian, especially as he continued to 'control' the CPGB until his recall to the USSR in 1929.[63] In England he married Rose Cohen from a Polish émigré family. In 1920 she was one of the founders of the CPGB for many years headed by Harry Pollitt and had later worked as a Comintern courier officially registered as a member of the technical staff of the Soviet legation in London, travelling widely in Europe and Scandinavia.[64] She had also served as a cut-out to the Ewer/FPA group. The names of Bennett-Petrovsky or his wife had never been mentioned by Kirchenstein in the course of the FBI interviews. He only noted inter alia that personally he had nothing to do with the British Communist Party.[65]

During his sojourn in London between 1922 and June 1927 Kirchenstein visited the USA, where his son John was born, three times. After the ARCOS raid he and his family left Britain on 8 June sailing first to Hamburg and then proceeding by train to Berlin.

In his FBI testimony Kirchenstein presented a rather dubious story of his adventures in the German capital. There, he said, an unnamed 'Third Secretary' of the Soviet embassy who combined his position of the Comintern representative with that of the OGPU and SMI (his own abbreviation for Soviet military intelligence whose real acronym he didn't know) resident agent in Germany, suddenly received coded instructions from the OGPU to urgently arrange Kirchenstein's return back to Moscow. For whatever reason the man was also ordered to confiscate his genuine American passport and supply Kirchenstein with a false Czech or Polish document. This, as well as a physical description of the 'resident' ('a tall rugged man about 6" or 6' 1" in height, broad shouldered, with brown-blonde hair, then aged about 35') was obviously an invention because the INO OGPU legal resident in Berlin starting from January 1927 was Ephraim Goldenstein posing as Second

Secretary of the legation. He looked quite different and did not represent either the Comintern or the (G)RU, then known as the 4th Directorate of the RKKA Headquarters.

Despite the problems he allegedly encountered in Berlin, Kirchenstein with his wife and child returned to Hamburg and on 24 June sailed to North America. 'We arrived in New York about eight days later,' he explained to the FBI, 'and from that time on I have never been contacted nor have I been in touch with Soviet authorities, and since that date I have never engaged in any legal or illegal activities on behalf of the Comintern or the Communist Party', suddenly adding: 'God bless America'.[66]

After studying the FBI reports of their meetings and interviews with Kirchenstein, it is obvious, as one MI5 officer remarked, that 'a good deal of whitewashing has gone on here'. Aged 64 at the time, Jacob Kirchenstein demonstrated an amazing memory, recollecting names, places and facts dating back 33 years with meticulous attention to detail. However, as with practically all Soviet defectors before the war, he clearly exaggerated his role in London at the same time suffering from some curious lapses of memory when it was not to his advantage. With all this, the most important conclusion that MI5 counter-intelligence and counter-espionage sections came to regarding Kirchenstein was that 'it is extremely difficult to pin a hard case of espionage' on him.[67] Indeed, considerable efforts by MI5 failed to yield any conclusive evidence of spying, in fact no evidence whatsoever, and both their and their FBI colleagues' long-term investigations of Jacob Kirchenstein drew a blank despite a great volume of time, effort and paper spent on filing every tiny detail of his life and work. The forensic document experts from the FBI Laboratory were not even able to confirm that the handwriting from letters belonging to 'Johnny' or 'Jack Walker' discovered on board the SS *Sterling* and addressed 'to one of the chief agents of the Third International in Western Europe'[68] was identical to that of Jacob Kirchenstein, as had been previously believed. In October 1928, MI5 received a report from Scotland Yard with a copy of a denunciation written by an anonymous informant suggesting, 'If you want to find a Red Agent Jack Walker look for Jacob Kirkenstein in som [*sic*] Russian office London'.[69] A similar letter was sent to the New York City Police Department. The idea of Jacob Kirchenstein having been the head of the Soviet spy organisation in London must be dismissed as a long-lasting error.

Soviet Legation in London, 1924–1927

After his two years as official Soviet agent in London and a considerably shorter spell in Paris (14 November 1924–30 October 1925), Leonid Krasin arrived in Britain again as the Soviet plenipotentiary and head of the legation, presenting his credentials on 11 October 1926. In between, Christian Rakovsky had served as the Soviet chargé d'affaires in London. On his staff were five Counsellors: Jan Berzin (1921–4), Adolf Joffe (briefly in 1924), Arkady Rosengoltz (1926–26 May 1927), Ivan Maisky (1925–26 May 1927, never mentioned by Kirchenstein) and Mikhail Khloplyankin (1925–November 1926) also serving as a trade representative. In addition, Dmitry Bogomolov was registered as First Secretary and Eugène Berens, former Commander-in-Chief of the Soviet Naval Forces, as Naval Attaché.

Krasin died in London on 24 November 1926 and for a while his position was vacant until Rosengoltz was appointed chargé d'affaires ad interim with Maisky as Counsellor and Bogomolov First Secretary. Lev Khinchuk succeeded Khloplyankin as a trade representative, head of the Trade Delegation, and a new Second Secretary briefly appeared on the London Diplomatic List in August 1926. His name was Vladimir Lidin-Khrzhanovsky (spelt Khrjanovsky) and neither the officials of the Russian embassy in London nor the Russian Foreign Ministry historians and archivists were able to find any document mentioning this name.[70] He remains unidentified and it is very likely this man was the OGPU resident. Maybe the dates of Zolotussky's arrival in London are given wrongly and he arrived a bit earlier using this alias.[71] In December 1926 Alexander Yazykov, a former official Soviet agent in Canada, was registered as an attaché in London. All of them had to leave in June 1927 after diplomatic relations were broken off following the ARCOS raid.

Others from the Jacob Kirchenstein List

All persons mentioned in Kirchenstein's testimony may not be worth attention except perhaps three. Those are his cousin Rudolf Kirchenstein, Vasili Barabanov and Walter Krivitsky. 'Once,' Kirchenstein said, 'it is my recollection that General Walter Krivitsky visited there [Soviet House] for about three weeks.'[72] That was obviously a figment of his imagination because Krivitsky was not a 'general' and had never been in London before he was brought there as 'Walter Thomas' by MI5 in January 1940. It is clear that already in America Kirchenstein simply read about Krivistky in *The New Yorker* or Krivitsky's articles ghostwritten by Isaac Don Levine and published in *The Saturday Evening Post*.[73]

Barabanov's British visa application was supported by the note to the Foreign Office signed by Rakovsky, then Soviet trade representative in London, in April 1925. The note stated that 'Vassili Vassilievich Barabanov [*sic*], accompanied by his wife, was appointed accountant to the staff of ARCOS and his services were urgently required'. A letter from the British

Mission in Moscow confirmed that Barabanov was interviewed, proved to be a knowledgeable and experienced bookkeeper especially in the shipping business and should be granted a British visa. He arrived via Harwich with his wife and two sons in August to be employed as an accountant at ARCOS Steamship Company Ltd.

The man aroused no suspicion during his fairly short stay, leaving the UK before the ARCOS raid. But later, an unnamed informant reported that one Käthe Gussfeld arrested for allegedly having been 'engaged in espionage against a friendly foreign power [the USA]' was to get in contact with Barabanov upon her arrival in London. Miss Gussfeld was accused of travelling on a false passport in the name of 'Ethel Chiles' and some 'documents containing secret ink were found in her luggage' (according to Sir Wyndham Childs who testified at her trial) so it looked like a serious charge although Childs refused to produce any documentary evidence supporting his claims.[74] During his FBI interviews Kirchenstein confirmed that Barabanov was a Soviet military intelligence officer although he was not in the position to know it. Anyway, Barabanov and his family left London on 21 April and apart from this single anonymous reference to the Gussfeld-Chiles affair his MI5 file contains no evidence of any illegal activity on his part.

A much more interesting story, almost entirely ignored by MI5, was related to Jacob's cousin Rudolf.[75] Rudolf Kirchenstein, born in May 1891 like Jacob in Mazsalaca, Latvia, had been one of the senior officers of Soviet military intelligence in the 1920s and 1930s. His operational pseudonym was KNYAZ/PRINCE. Rudolf had served in Red Army field intelligence during the Civil War and then headed the intelligence department of the Petrograd military district from 1920, when his cousin Jacob was in Moscow mixing with delegates of the Comintern Congress. According to Jacob, he and Rudolf met in July shortly before the congress best remembered by historians for implementing '21 Conditions' required to join the Comintern. Jacob also recalled that at that time his cousin was 'in charge of military intelligence along the Finnish and Estonian borders'.

In 1922 Rudolf Kirchenstein was sent to the Caucasus where he headed the intelligence department of the Red Army headquarters. His first foreign assignment as an illegal (G)RU operative was in Germany between 1924 and 1926. He was later operating in Italy, Austria, Czechoslovakia and possibly France. Rudolf was sent to Great Britain in July 1930 as an undercover illegal resident of Soviet military intelligence. Back in Moscow in June 1931 he was promoted to assistant chief of the 2nd (human sources) Department headed first by Vladimir Tairov and then Boris Melnikov. The Service, at that time known as 4th Directorate, was then directed by Jan K. Berzin, a namesake of the diplomat Jan A. Berzin.

Rudolf Kirchenstein graduated from the special (intelligence) department of the Frunze Military Academy in 1935. He was then promoted to colonel and awarded the Order of the Red Banner which means he had been involved in an important operation abroad. As happened with almost all his (G)RU colleagues, despite his exemplary career he was arrested in December 1937, sentenced to death in August 1938 and shot on the same day.[76] During an interview Jacob Kirchenstein told the FBI that Rudolf visited him in London in the winter of 1924–25 arriving from Paris. 'He warned me,' Kirchenstein said, 'about the terrible carnage and intrigues going on in Moscow. He looked at my boy who was then about one-and-a-half years old, who had been born in New York in 1923, and also saw my American passport … He said that his wife and six-year-old son had been kept in Moscow as hostages to guarantee his return.'[77] According to Jacob, his cousin would flee if he could get his family out but, unlike Krivitsky who was lucky to escape with his wife and son, he never had the chance.

Other people mentioned by Kirchenstein were Yakov Zhilinsky, Michael Rudolf Birseneek-Nelson, Anton Miller (brother of Peter Miller of the Russian Trade Delegation, see KV-2/798 s.50a), Peter Silin, Lisa Wollstein and the already-mentioned Radomsky, as well as less important figures plus several known officials of the CPGB. Zhilinsky (spelt 'Jilinsky' in the files) is described as head of the Staff Allotment Department of ARCOS while he was actually head of Allotment and Registration Department of the Trade Delegation (he previously was chief of personnel at ARCOS until July 1925, before London having been employed at the Soviet Trade Delegation in Berlin as assistant director of economic department). It was Zhilinsky, with his rather frightening appearance of a stern proletarian revolutionary, who closely questioned Langston (source 'Y') on his political views shortly before the latter was sacked. The fact that he was not a member of the Communist Party, in Langston's opinion, might have accelerated his departure from ARCOS where his job was a photostat machine operator. Zhilinsky quit his post at the Trade Delegation on 6 April 1927, leaving for Moscow.[78]

Michael Birseneek is mentioned in several documents related to Kirchenstein's case. In London he had served as one of the managers of Russian Oil Products (ROP), a Soviet trading organisation which was established and registered as a British Limited Liability Company with the nominal capital of £100,000 in August 1924.

This capital was divided into 100,000 shares valued at £1 each, and at the time of registration ROP had two subscribers: Leo Rabinovitch, the company director with one share and Boris Malzman, a barrister and author of several monographs like, for example, *Legal Aspects of Industry, Commerce and Labour* (1923) at the time serving as vice-president of the Naphtha Syndicate, who also had one share. The Naphtha Syndicate was set up as a monopoly sales organisation for all Soviet oil products at home and abroad.[79] By the end of 1930 ROP already had four Soviet directors and, according to MI5, almost a thousand employees, about one-third of which were members of the CPGB. The company was said to have built up a network of thirty-three offices, deports and installations across the UK. When the matter was raised in the House of Commons about the trading companies under control of the Soviet government registered in the UK, it turned out that three years after the ARCOS raid there were twelve companies including ARCOS itself and two Soviet banks operating in the country.[80] In November 1930, Leo Rabinovitch was still its director. He was probably a relative of Philip Rabinovitch, since 1922 member of the management board of ARCOS and then its director who had also served as Rakovsky's deputy when the latter headed the Soviet Trade Delegation in London (July 1923–October 1925). After Rakovsky left, Philip Rabinovitch was briefly in charge, soon succeeded by Khloplyankin. Back in Moscow, Rabinovitch's latest post was head of the export directorate of the NKVT. Shortly before his arrest, he moved to Kotlass, a town between Moscow and Archangel (Arkhangelsk) on the White Sea, where he headed a local lumberyard. Arrested, he was sentenced in December 1937 and shot on the same day.

Concerning Michael Birseneek, known as Birseneek-Nelson, following the ARCOS raid, the rupture of diplomatic relations and the expulsion of Soviet personnel, he returned to the UK at the end of March 1928 still working for ROP and five years later applied for and was granted British citizenship.[81] The company, Russian Oil Products Limited, later registered at Heritage House, Kent, and incorporated in August 1924, was dissolved in January 2018. Its filing history at Companies House would make an interesting case study even today.

* * *

The particular interest of Special Branch and the Security Service in the Soviet Trade Mission and ARCOS could be easily explained by a simple fact that a good number of members of the British trade mission sent to Moscow in 1921 were agents of British secret services reporting either to the chief of SIS, with copies or summaries directed to MI5, or to the Director of Military Intelligence (later of Military Operations and Intelligence). Even earlier, shortly after the Bolshevik revolution when the official British intelligence mission, together with Lockhart and his party, were expelled from Soviet Russia, SIS established its stations in Latvia and Estonia as well as in Finland, forming SIS's Baltic Group.

Following British official recognition of the Soviet government in 1924, Sir Robert Hodgson became the chargé d'affaires and the British Trade Mission in Moscow was upgraded to a diplomatic mission, at the same time providing cover for intelligence operations and serving as a postbox for messages to and from agents although officially it did not have a Passport Control Office.[82] In fact, the need for a PCO for the diplomatic mission in Moscow was discussed in spring 1924 but this led to nothing.[83] Partly it may be explained by the Treasury's opposition to extra expense and partly to the fact that 'C' already had enough agents in place – officers formally attached to Baltic Group and other stations as well as local recruits – that it was considered unnecessary to have a separate Moscow station. Besides, any attempt to increase the number of British diplomats accredited in Russia would likely lead to a demand for a reciprocal increase from the Soviet side, which was to be avoided. In what concerns proper passport control functions, the work was duly done by the Mission. 'In a report on his visit to Moscow in 1925,' Phil Tomaselli writes, 'Owen St Clair O'Malley of the Northern Department of the Foreign Office advised that up to 50 visa applications a day were being handled by Mission staff and that fees for visas amounted to some £2,800 per year.'[84] This would have easily supported a PCO, an assistant PCO and some clerical staff.

For most of the period between 1920 and 1930 military and political information from Soviet Russia remained a priority for a number of SIS stations in Europe with Helsinki (where the original station had moved from Stockholm), Riga and Tallinn controlling most human sources and supplying the bulk of intelligence reports. This was based on a clear understanding that to Soviet leaders Britain was the main enemy and target. Reports from human sources inside the adversary were supplemented and often corrected by GC&CS intercepts. As the authorised history of GCHQ has put it, 'Comint had triumphs but its key partner was sources of less reliability'.

> Forgeries fooled British intelligence... Human sources on the USSR and its activities abroad were plentiful, with quality ranging from abysmal to excellent. Fortunately, Comint provided massive and reliable details which largely contained misapprehensions which Humint and stolen documents might otherwise have aroused.[85]

For its Baltic Group stations SIS appointed representatives with some Russian experience. In July 1920 Scale was replaced as the Group Inspector by Ronald Meiklejohn, who had served with the British intervention force in Murmansk the previous year and from April 1921 based himself in Tallinn after Britain recognised Estonia de jure in January.[86] The first British envoy in all three Baltic states was Sir Ernest Wilton, soon succeeded by Sir Tudor

Vaughan who remained until 1927, later serving as Envoy Extraordinary and Minister Plenipotentiary to Sweden. In the Estonian capital Meiklejohn was also assisted by Sydney Steers operating under cover of vice-consul, and a Russian interpreter Arseny Zhitkov.[87] Zhitkov belonged to the rare type of highly competent operators, known in the trade as principal agents, who are able to handle a network of other agents. One of his most important sources in Tallinn was Juhan Törvand who joined the Russian military in 1902, served as assistant chief operations officer with the 12th Siberian Rifle Division formed in Irkutsk in the summer of 1914 but from 1920 was serving as Chief of Staff of the Estonian Army. Meiklejohn visited him twice a week to get the latest updates.[88] Another source was a young officer of the Estonian General Staff named Roman Birk who regularly visited Soviet Russia because his uncle Ado Birk was in Moscow as the diplomatic representative of his country between 1922 and 1926 having previously served as Minister of Foreign Affairs.[89]

Meiklejohn arranged with Törvand that Birk was sent as an attaché to the Estonian legation in Moscow to get first-hand information from Russia. Here, the Cheka officers quickly noticed the young diplomat and involved him in the TREST deception, putting him in contact with two front-line agents, Eduard Opperput and Victor Kolesnikov. 'Kolesnikov' was an alias of a former Polish intelligence officer Wiktor Steckiewicz who changed sides (and name) and was now a Cheka-OGPU operative Victor Stanislavovich Kiyakovsky (Kijakowski), who played one of the leading roles in the TREST operation. Both Kolesnikov and Opperput were also engaged in apprehending Reilly. It was in Opperput's apartment that Reilly wrote a postcard to his friend Boyce on 26 September 1925. After leaving the house and posting the card Reilly got into the waiting car and instead of a railway station, as he expected, was taken directly to the Lubyanka. By that time Kiyakovsky had already recruited Birk as a fully-fledged agent who since 1923 had been delivering misleading information prepared by the Cheka to both his British and Estonian superiors. Meiklejohn also did not lose his time and managed to feed the Russians false telegrams and ciphers through the Soviet legation Counsellor Vladimir Shenshev and place his agent M.N. Anikin on the staff of the Soviet legation.[90] In 1926 Shenshev was transferred to Shenyang, better known by its Manchu name Mukden, as the Soviet Consul in north-east China. In 1927, afraid of being exposed as a Soviet agent, Birk moved to Vienna and became a first-year student, a 'Hunting Dog' as they were known internally, of the Vienna Consular Academy. He continued to work for the OGPU until his arrest in 1937.

Scale was based in Stockholm. The agent designation ST for those who were sent to Soviet Russia under his control meant 'Stockholm or Sweden

Travelling'.[91] The first to get this designation was Reilly who was ST/1 while Paul Dukes subsequently became ST/25. Two of the best SIS agents of the Baltic Group were Nikolai Bunakov (ST/28) and Peter Sokolov (ST/65).

The Baltic Group stations divided their intelligence priorities between themselves with Helsinki concentrating on naval intelligence since it was best placed to cover the Russian Baltic Fleet; Tallinn specialising on military intelligence; and Riga mainly focused on political and economic targets. The London Head Office also wanted to keep track of Comintern activities worldwide as well as of what was perceived as the Communist threat to the British Empire. The Baltic and other European stations depended almost entirely for Russian intelligence on émigrés, usually former Tsarist officers,[92] which ultimately had a negative effect on the results. According to the Service's historian, the three Baltic stations exchanged copies of the reports they sent to London.

Between March 1921 and November 1926 Ernest Boyce had been serving as Passport Control Officer in Helsinki and later also Tallinn. In November 1926 Boyce handed over control of the Tallinn station to Captain Alexander Ross. Without mentioning the name, Jeffery describes the new head of SIS station in Tallinn as an intelligence officer during the First World War and 'a Cambridge graduate, son of a British shipbuilder and a Russian mother [who] had served with army intelligence in Salonica and the Caucasus in 1916–19, spoke Russian and French fluently and had "moderate" Bulgarian'. Ross had a Russian wife whom he married in 1928 and was known as a lightweight who liked his drink. In Tallinn, he had served as an adviser to the Estonian Finance Ministry before moving to the PCO.

Unlike some other heads of SIS stations in Europe who were having much the same problem, that is, they were unable to check or verify information that they received from their sources, Meiklejohn was recalled because London had begun to express some concern about the material delivered by his principal agent BP/11 (Gregory), mistrust its provenance and suspect that his reports had been fabricated. Young Alec Ross seems to have been brought in to clean up the mess.

When Boyce left the Service in the summer of 1928, his deputy Harry Carr became first acting head and then head of the Helsinki station, and Brian Giffey was sent to take over the Tallinn station in December. Initially, he was expected to be 'under instruction of Capt. A. Ross'.[93] In the Estonian capital Giffey would be assisted by Sydney Steers. As his biographer has put it, although Brian was a heavy drinker and womanizer, 'London was obviously satisfied with his performance and left him in post until the fateful events of 1940',[94] when the Baltic States were occupied by the Soviet Union. The Riga station was opened in February 1921 when Rafael Farina arrived from London, having been appointed head of station with cover as British Passport Control Officer. He had been operating in Latvia for ten years. Other long-serving SIS officers under PCO cover were Thomas Kendrick in Vienna and Frank Foley in Berlin, who since October 1923 was assisted by Dick Ellis sent out to work on the Soviet target.[95]

The rupture of Anglo-Soviet diplomatic relations had a sinister sequel. Arkady Rosengoltz, the Soviet chargé d'affaires in London, on his way back to Moscow stopped in Warsaw on the morning of 7 June. Rosengoltz invited the Soviet Minister to Warsaw, Peter Voikov (sometimes spelt as Pyotr Voykov), to have breakfast together at the Central Station buffet, probably wishing to discuss the current political situation in Europe before returning to Russia. Voikov, who in 1918 served at the Urals Soviet, was one of those who was involved, albeit indirectly, in the murder of the Russian Imperial Family.[96] The British Foreign Office declared him persona non grata and he was not accepted as a Soviet diplomatic representative to Canada, but the Narkomindel somehow managed to place him as the envoy to Poland in 1924. Just before the train with Rosengoltz and his party left, Voikov was approached on the platform by a Russian exile, Boris Koverda, who shot him several times at close range. Arrested on the spot, Koverda exclaimed: 'I acted in the name of Russia, not Soviet Russia but our Motherland'.[97] As revenge for Voikov's assassination, the OGPU executed twenty randomly-seized members of the Russian nobility including, as already mentioned, Prince Pavel Dolgorukov. Koverda was released after 10 years in jail and died in the USA in February 1987, aged 79.

On the same day, 7 June, Litvinov handed a letter of protest to the Polish Minister in Moscow stressing that the murder of Voikov was 'the terrorist act of the reactionists' and described it as being directly linked to the series of raids against Soviet diplomatic missions in Peking, Shanghai and the Trade Delegation in London.[98] The Soviet government was quick to declare that 'a British arm directed the blow which killed Voikov' claiming that Britain was 'urgently conducting preparations for a war against the USSR', which was part of the war scare that swept the Soviet Union in late 1926 and 1927.[99] On the same evening, a bomb exploded in the Leningrad Party club, killing one person and injuring twenty-six and, as if by a prewritten plan, the head of the Byelorussian OGPU Iosif Opansky died in a handcar crash near Minsk which was also (falsely) presented as a terrorist act.

Early next month the Leningrad OGPU announced that they had uncovered 'a large espionage organisation directed and inspired by the well-known English intelligence agent Boyce, formerly officially attached to the British diplomatic mission in Helsingfors and later in Reval'. It was stated that Boyce's chief assistant there was 'a former White officer, Colonel Nikolai

Bunakov who had previously acted as a representative of the Grand Duke Nikolai Nikolayevich in Helsingfors'.[100] It was well known that Colonel Bunakov also represented General Kutepov in Finland and therefore, as part of the infamous operation TREST, he was used by the OGPU to arrange for Sidney Reilly's return to Russia, where Reilly was arrested and shot. Actually, Bunakov was rather skeptical of the Trust until Alexander Yakushev, one of its key players, got his brother out of Russia for a reunion in Helsinki in August 1925, which persuaded Bunakov that the Trust was a bona fide monarchist organisation with real power. The same newspaper article reported that the most active British agent in Russia was Albert Hoyer.

Albert Hoyer was a Danish sea captain who spoke fluent Russian and English and had worked for the Russian naval attaché in Copenhagen [according to the Russian sources – in Sweden] during the war. He was subsequently loaned to Stephen Alley in Murmansk before working for MI1c in Kirkenes, on the border between Norway and Russia. Hoyer was 'a man of extraordinary physique who could easily pass for a prizefighter', one British official said. After the revolution, he claimed to be a Bolshevik by persuasion and took a job as a ship's captain with the Russian merchant navy, the Sovtorgflot, using it as an opportunity to set up an agent network in Petrograd, focusing on naval, military and air force intelligence. By September 1919 Hoyer was already reporting, via John Scale, on the fate of the British sailors captured during the raid on Kronstadt as well as the low fuel stocks in Petrograd, plus full details of the damage to the Russian fleet.[101]

Hoyer was first detained by the OGPU in 1926 and it is suggested that they let him go because of insufficient evidence. According to Michael Smith, the OGPU then 'mounted a surveillance operation on him and his contacts, only waiting for the right moment to swoop'.[102] Under the pretext that Boyce still owed him some money, Hoyer even visited the British Consulate General in Leningrad asking to contact Boyce seeking the payment. Whether real or dictated by the OGPU, his plea was fully justified because early that year Lady Muriel Paget visited Leningrad and then wrote in *The Daily Telegraph* about fifty or so 'families of British nationality who are living in terrible conditions',[103] always in need of money. In fact, the Chekists hardly needed any extra evidence of British espionage and in July mass arrests followed, reported in the newspapers in a series of articles under the general title 'Liquidation of the British spy organisation in Leningrad'. They knew more or less all about the network and its members, and how intelligence reports were delivered from Russia to London. Apart from Hoyer, the OGPU

12 июля 1927 года № 156—(2444).   «КРАСНЫЙ СЕВЕР».

Ликвидация английской шпионской организации в Ленинграде.

Кто вдохновлял организацию?

В мае-июне с. г. ленинградским полномочным представительством ОГПУ раскрыта крупная шпионская организация, руководимая и вдохновляемая известным английским разведчиком Бойсом, состоящим на официальной службе в английской дипломатической миссии в Гельсингфорсе, а потом и в Ревеле.

Согласно старым данным английской разведки, сотрудник английской миссии Бойс использовывал антисоветские монархические группировки, а также услужливую финскую разведку.

Ближайшим помощником Бойса являлся представитель бывш. вел. кн. Николая Николаевича — бывш. полковник Н. Н. Бунаков, который впоследствии официально перешел на службу к английской разведке в качестве представителя таковой в Финляндии.

На самой советско-финской границе английская разведка имела представителя в лице б. офицера царского П. П. Соколова. Соколов во время Юденича состоял на службе у английской разведки и был правой рукой знаменитого английского агента Поль Дюкса.

Несмотря на короткий срок, прошедший со дня арестов, ленинградскому ГПУ удалось выяснить полную картину довольно обширной шпионской деятельности английской разведки на территории Ленинградского военного округа.

Следствием установлено, что, пользуясь содействием и помощью финской разведки и полиции, английская разведка наладила ряд переправочных пунктов для своих разведчиков на границе. Особые услуги оказывал им начальник териокской полиции Пентеля.

Крупные фигуры разведки.

Одним из крупных английских разведчиков являлся Антоний Хлопушин, который по заданиям англичан неоднократно переходил границу по налаженным переправам для организации шпионских резидентур, вербовки новых агентов и собирания сведений от существующей сети.

В один из переходов финской границы Антонием Хлопушиным совместно с финским разведчиком Виролайненом, последним был убит пытавшийся их задержать начальник заставы пограничных войск тов. Фадеев.

Независимо от поручений, даваемых Хлопушину английская разведка послала в СССР своего старого опытного шпиона-разведчика—капитана дальнего плавания А. И. Гойера.

А. И. Гойер работал в царское время в Швеции от русского морского штаба; после революции он переходит на службу к англичанам. Сначала он исполняет их задания в Западной Европе и на Балканах, а затем посылается Бойсом в Ленинград для создания разведывательного аппарата в Красном Балтийском флоте. В Ленинграде Гойер проживает до средины 1925 г. За это время он дает Бойсу целый ряд докладов, содержащих секретные сведения о Красном флоте. Сведения эти, а также и задания Бойса пересылались обычной почтой с применением тайных чернил. В особо важных случаях к Гойеру посылались нелегальным путем специальные курьеры. Таким курьером был, между прочим, Антоний Хлопушин, а также старый английский разведчик, бывш. морской офицер А. Старк, случайно убитый осенью 1925 г. в Ленинграде во время одного из походов к Гойеру.

После того, как Гойер наладил работу в Ленинграде, он был переброшен в Одессу, имея поручение собирать сведения о Черноморском флоте. По пути в Одессу Гойер создает в Москве специальную агентуру по наблюдению за внутренними водными перевозками, с каковой целью им вербуется сотрудник правления Совторгфлота — В. Валицкий. В Одессе Гойер устраивается на службу в Совторгфлоте и начинает создавать английскую разведку на Черноморье.

Распоряжением полномочного представителя ОГПУ в Ленинградском военном округе Гойер был арестован, при чем при обыске у него был обнаружен ряд писем Бойса и Бунакова, написанных тайнописью, химическими чернилами.

Победа империалистов и их белогвардейских наймитов несет возвращение помещичьей кабалы, капиталистического рабства национального гнета. Встанем на защиту власти советов. Не отдадим кровью добытых революционных завоеваний.

Чьи имена должны произноситься с негодованием.

Английская разведка усиленно интересовалась вопросами боевой мощи Красной армии, Красного флота и военно-химической промышленностью. Для получения сведений из указанных областей английской разведкой были привлечены в шпионскую деятельность нижеследующие лица:

1. Хлопушин, Георгий — служащий ленинградского табактреста; являлся помощником английского шпиона Антона Хлопушина и в его отсутствие заменял его, как резидент по связи со шпионской сетью своего брата. Георгий Хлопушин собирал военные сведения и через курьеров отправлял их в Финляндию. Георгий Хлопушин нелегально ходил в Финляндию, где имел тесную связь с Соколовым.

2. Куницын - Нерадов—б. морской офицер, служащий Балтфлота, старший химист «Марата». Предлагал англичанам ряд сведений секретного характера о Балтфлоте. Сведения передавались как через курьеров, так и через консульство в лице сотрудника такового Линдстета.

3. Груздев—б. офицер, служащий лаборантом на оптическом заводе. Передавал секретные сведения о Красной армии и военно-химической промышленности. Груздев имел на финляндской границе собственную дачу, которая служила главным явочным пунктом для английской разведки.

4. Пивоваров, Алексей — начальник отд. Мобчасти Управления Территориального Округа Имел связь с Антоном Хлопушиным, каковому передавал сведения о Красной армии.

5. Пивоваров, Сергей — б. офицер, военнослужащий. Принимал у себя Антона Хлопушина и оказывал услуги в сборе военных сведений.

6. Выржиковский — б. офицер, военнослужащий. Передавал сведения военного характера.

7. Глушаков—б. морской офицер, служащий брандмейстером на Ленинградском аэродроме. Давал для английской разведки сведения об авиации.

8. Никитин — доцент Лесного Института и зав. химической лабораторией госуд. оптического завода. Давал сведения о советской химической промышленности и о новых газах.

9. Червяков—сотрудник Волховстроя. Давал информацию английской разведке о Волховстрое.

10. Афанасий Хлопушин — ведал центральной явочной квартирой английских разведчиков и оказывал услуги по связи со шпионской сетью.

Следствием привлечен еще ряд лиц, помогавших английской разведке в сборе шпионских сведений.

Развернуть свою шпионскую деятельность и вербовку английской разведке не удалось. Эта деятельность была пресечена органами ОГПУ в момент, когда организация приступила к широкой вербовке агентов.

Всего по данному делу арестовано около 25 человек. Следствие заканчивается, и подлинные шпионы в ближайшее время предстанут перед судам.

statement published on 10 July named Nikolai Bunakov and Peter Sokolov as the main culprits who assisted Boyce in his devious spying and Anthony Khlopushin as the chief SIS courier who had been delivering messages from Leningrad to the SIS post at Terijoki on the Finnish-Soviet border for years. Both Anthony and his brother Georgy Khlopushin were Sokolov's teammates in the St Petersburg Unitas football club.

This route was established back in 1918 when Paul Dukes had to send his intelligence reports over the border using couriers, one of whom was Sokolov, previously a famous Russian footballer recruited after an interview with Boyce in Helsinki. Sokolov had probably been talent-spotted by Harry Charnock, a member of the Charnock family and a CEO at the Nikolskoe Textile Factory. Harry, a good friend of R.H. Bruce Lockhart, himself an avid football player, organised the first Russian football league in 1910 while the game was gaining popularity in Russia. At the time Sokolov was one of the best Russian defenders who, after joining Unitas, soon became the champion of Russia and was invited to join the national team. Duke's reports were transported by couriers to Terijoki, then part of the Republic of Finland with an imposing building of a local railway station. From there they were sent to Gillespie in Tornio/Torneå on the Finnish-Swedish border and then to Scale in Stockholm. There they were studied and prepared to be dispatched to London by John Scale and his new assistant Conrad O'Brien-ffrench (ST/36), recruited by Menzies in 1919, who succeeded Ernest Michelson, another old Russia hand.[104] Shortly before the war, O'Brien-ffrench was planted in Kitzbühel, one of the most famous and exclusive ski resorts in the world located in Tyrol, Austria. He was then working for Claude Dansey's Z Organisation as Agent Z/3 and masquerading as a businessman and owner of Tyrolese Tours. In March 1938 he was the first to alert his friends in Vienna that German troops were invading Austria,[105] which almost cost him his life.

From Stockholm SIS reports were delivered to Copenhagen and from there to London. There was also a backup route when couriers travelled by train from Riga to Kovno (Kaunas), then to Berlin and in Berlin Frank Foley took care of their safe delivery to the final destination.

The OGPU could not reach Boyce, Bunakov, Sokolov and Anthony Khlopushin who were all in Finland but arrested Hoyer and his network in Leningrad. Among those who fell into the clutches of the Cheka in July 1927 was Georgy Khlopushin who was an employee of the Tobacco Trust and often crossed the Soviet-Finnish border smuggling parcels with intelligence reports. He was in touch with his brother and with Sokolov. Another member of the Hoyer network, Eugen Kunitzyn-Neradov, was a former naval officer before arrest serving as a chemical weapons expert on the battleship, a dreadnought formerly known as *Petropavlovsk* of the Imperial

Russian Navy, now commissioned into the Baltic Fleet under the name *Marat*. Eugen's channel of communication with the Terijoki bureau was via Robert Lindtstedt, an employee of the Finnish consulate in Leningrad who was expelled from Russia in 1928. Eugen's second wife Ekaterina Kunitsyna and his brother Leonid Kunitzyn-Neradov were also arrested as British spies. Other members of the group were Vladimir Valitsky on the board of directors of the Sovtorgflot in Moscow who provided information on the volume and performance of transport on the Soviet inland waterway network; Aleksey Pivovarov, department head at the military mobilisation division of the local administration who collected information on various aspects of the Red Army mobilisation plans and was arrested together with his brother Sergey, a former Tsarist officer; and finally Afanasy Khlopushin who was named as a safe-house keeper. Altogether twenty-six persons were arrested.

The hearings lasted for weeks. On the last day the court deliberated for 12 hours and finally the verdict was announced. Eight of those charged were sentenced to death including Hoyer, Valitsky, Georgy and Afanasy Khlopushin, brothers Eugen and Leonid Kunitsyn-Neradov, one Alexander Gruzdev and a woman named Shorina-Stahl. Several defendants were found not guilty while others were sentenced to different terms in labour camps. One of them was Alexander Olshevsky, another footballer who played for Unitas.

When the diplomatic and trade missions were withdrawn in 1927, the Foreign Office noted, perhaps with too much confidence, that 'before the break our [Secret Service people] in Russia were extremely reliable, but now they have to send in much less staff'.[106] Now SIS had to rely almost exclusively on information obtained by the stations operating under the cover of Passport Control Offices (PCO), which had long been exposed and was wearing thin. Shortly before the war a new continental network of SIS, Claude Dansey's staff of secret intelligence agents, half-professional and half-amateur, that became known as the Z Organisation, was established but their primary targets were not Soviet or Communist machinations.

As usual, Peter Sokolov managed to avoid arrest. After 1927 the Soviet Union was not an intelligence priority for SIS anymore and he quietly retired to his family home, spending time in their country house near Terijoki engaged in peasant farming. He also set up the Terijoki football club, coaching youth football players. When the Soviets demanded his extradition, Sokolov moved to Helsinki and laid low while his wife Maria Nosova and aide Anton Yanushkevich remained in Terijoki until 1939. When the Soviet army invaded Finland three months after the outbreak of the Second World War claiming security reasons, Yanushkevich was captured and transported to Leningrad. His interrogation file is full of details about Sokolov's network of agents.[107] Following the Soviet invasion of Finland and the bombing of

Helsinki, the Finnish side invited Sokolov to join the war propaganda special radio unit. He was further involved in information warfare during the so-called Continuation War of 1941–4 against the Soviet Union. After the war he fled to Sweden afraid that SMERSH – the name coined by Stalin for an umbrella organisation of several independent counter-espionage agencies of the Red Army formed in 1942 – might grab him.

After the Finns signed a temporary peace agreement with Moscow in September 1944, the Politburo sent Andrei Zhdanov, one of the key figures of the Great Purge and the main architect of the Winter War, as head of the Soviet part of the Allied Control Commission (ACC) for Finland which occupied the Hotel Torni in Helsinki. Because the ACC was entirely under Soviet control it was semi-officially called the Allied Soviet Commission. With his network of informants in the capital and contacts in the headquarters of General Axel Erik Heinrichs, the chief of the Finnish Defence Forces at that time, Sokolov was certainly informed of the so-called 'Leino list'. Yrjö Leino, the newly-appointed Finnish Home Secretary, was summoned to Zhdanov's office on the evening of 20 April 1945 where General Grigory Savonenkov handed him a letter, signed by Zhdanov, demanding to immediately arrest twenty-two persons named in the attached list and hand them over to SMERSH officers. All mentioned individuals were allegedly guilty of war crimes, espionage for Germany, subversion and terrorist acts against the Soviet Union. Leino, a devoted Communist and son-in-law of Otto Wille Kuusinen, a former head of the Stalin's puppet Terijoki Government and member of the Soviet Politburo, followed Moscow's orders without a second thought.[108] It is said that among all those named in the list only Sokolov managed to avoid extradition to Moscow.[109] The SMERSH officers were operating in Finland and every other country occupied by the Soviets with impunity, arresting and kidnapping people at will.

Sokolov settled in the Swedish city of Enköping about 80km from Stockholm near a large freshwater lake. He married a Swedish woman and took her name, becoming Paul Sahlin. The place is famous for its football club, Enköpings SK FK founded in 1914, and guess where the world-class footballer found himself a job? Soviet intelligence soon located his refuge but were unable to lure him out of his safe home and the Swedes refused to extradite the man. Sokolov@Sahlin died in 1971 in Stockholm aged 80, survived by his two daughters from the first marriage. He first visited the Swedish capital almost six decades ago as one of over 160 players from eleven nations competing at the football tournament during the 1912 Summer Olympics in Stockholm. Then, Russia lost in the quarter-finals while the British team won the gold medals.

* * *

Spies and agents do not become known, even famous like Philby or Sorge, because of their proficiency, good tradecraft or extraordinary talents. Journalists, intelligence historians and writers do not always seem to realise that these two, like many others, were not successes but rather failures, making unforgivable mistakes, and the agents who have been caught are not heroes but losers. People know about them because they and their spy operations had been uncovered and perpetrators put into prison, expelled or exchanged, and even sometimes hanged or shot. Alas, nothing of the sort can be said about Sir Arthur Willert, born in May 1882 in Oxford, England. Sir Arthur left no secret memoirs, his several books contain not a single hint of his possible contacts with Russian agents (although there are chapters on Russian politics), his Security Service (MI5) personal file, even if it exists, has never been made public, and his only possible link to Soviet intelligence or Comintern networks was his son Paul Willert plus a few seemingly insignificant mentions in several secret files related to Soviet espionage in Britain in the interwar period. Nevertheless, there are reasons to believe that Arthur Willert had evolved from a major source of information inside the Foreign Office in the early 1920s into a fully-fledged Soviet agent codenamed ATTILA while his son was recruited as agent NACHFOLER, translated from German as successor, follower or replacement. All three definitions pass perfectly. This unsophisticated but quite appropriate codename was given by Dr Arnold Deutsch, the recruiter of Philby and two dozen other Soviet agents in London in the 1930s.

Arthur Willert joined *The Times* of London in 1906, soon becoming their chief correspondent in Washington, DC. Willert worked there for a decade, starting from 1910 with an interruption for one year when he was appointed Secretary of the British War Mission and the representative of the Ministry of Information in Washington in 1918. The archivists at Yale University Library where most of Willert's correspondence and papers are held, describe his work in America as follows:

While in the United States Willert's amiable personality and talent as a journalist won him a large number of contacts in influential government and private circles. Among those with whom he established friendships were: William Howard Taft, Elihu Root, Edward M. House, Robert Lansing, Frank Polk, and the young Franklin Roosevelt. During World War I Willert's contacts, combined with his firsthand knowledge of American public opinion, enabled him to supply the British government with valuable information on American politics, foreign policy, and public opinion. Of equal importance to Britain was Willert's skill in acting as an unofficial interpreter of the British viewpoint to American officials.[110]

As a result, Willert was appointed a KBE 'for valuable services rendered in connection with the War' in 1919. In November 1920 he left *The Times* to work at the Foreign Office News Department, a successor of the Ministry of Information which had handled wartime domestic and foreign propaganda, but it seems that until better times a place was found for him in the newly created British Library of Information (BLI) in New York City.

After the war William Tyrrell (future Lord Tyrrell) led the Foreign Office News Department's effort to establish a low-budget information agency in New York that would not be considered as a propaganda machine but would nevertheless serve as a tool to influence Americans by delivering and distributing official British information. The BLI seemed an ideal low-profile vehicle that could serve this purpose having in mind that there had already once been an agency in the form of the British Information Bureau, created in 1917, to provide information about the war.[111] Initially, the library was located within the British consulate-general at 44 Whitehall Street in Manhattan. The first director of the BLI from November 1919 was Charles Louis Des Graz (later Sir) soon succeeded by his deputy, Robert Wilberforce, who, like Willert, was educated at Balliol College, Oxford. Willert's short time at the library is not recorded anywhere and the only indirect mention of it can be found in an excellent but little-known academic book mentioning that 'during the war he had gained some experience of propaganda while serving in the British official organisation in the United States'.[112] In his memoirs Willert doesn't give it any comment either, only saying that his primary contacts were Tyrrell and Sir Maurice Hankey (later Lord) who was secretary both to the Cabinet and the Committee for Imperial Defence (CID). Willert names Wilberforce 'from our publicity office in New York' as his assistant, describing him as 'a good ally, quietly observant, outwardly nervous, inwardly tough, and liked by our clients'.[113] Willert later supported the library in every possible way.

When the library was set up, Lord Burnham, the owner of *The Daily Telegraph*, congratulated the Foreign Office on its decision to establish a vehicle for the regular supply of news and information to the press. After Percy Koppel succeeded Tyrrell as head of the News Department in early 1921,[114] it became clear that despite the efforts of first Tyrrell and then Koppel the Foreign Office was unable to find a man with the necessary qualifications who could be placed in charge of the newspaper propaganda. In the spring Arthur Willert joined the News Department and the problem was solved.

Having in mind his American experience and good contacts, Willert was immediately dispatched to the Washington Disarmament Conference to take charge of press publicity on behalf of the British delegation, sailing from Southampton to New York on board RMS *Olympic* at the end of

October.[115] After the conference, when the British publicity arrangements were praised as a great triumph, Willert wrote to his wife, 'It shows what can be done by telling nothing but the truth and not trying to have propaganda'. Upon his return, Willert assumed responsibility for the News Department's work with the British and foreign newspaper correspondents in London.[116] When Bonar Law succeeded Lloyd George as Prime Minister in October 1922, Willert also advised his office at 10 Downing Street on all press matters relating to foreign affairs, thus enjoying unlimited access to all internal correspondence and information necessary for his work. From his side, the grateful Wilberforce provided Willert with detailed information on the extent of the library's contacts since 1920 including a list of more than 200 academic institutions, newspapers, magazines, public libraries and individual writers.[117]

Willert was promoted to head the News Department in November 1925 while Percy Koppel was transferred to supervise the work of the newly created Dominion Information Service 'with responsibility for handling all information between the British government and the Dominions'. Remarkably, in his memoirs covering this period Willert never mentioned Koppel. In 1925 the staff of the News Department consisted of fourteen people which was quite a lot in comparison with other FO departments. During the following two years however Willert's staff was halved and its expenditure reduced from £80,000 in 1920 to £17,550 by the time of the ARCOS raid, that is, by May 1927, following the Treasury's policy of retrenchment.[118] A shortage of money caused anxiety which got worse over time.

Foreign Office officials who were generally responsible for the collection and distribution of political information to the media were also involved in the general administrative supervision of the News Department. Those were Willert, the head of the department; Clifford John Norton who served at Gallipoli during the war, like Willert entered the Foreign Office in 1921 and later became private secretary to Sir Robert Vansittart; Maurice Ingram, who had served as First Secretary in Berlin and Oslo and in 1927 was transferred as the chief clerk to the News Department, later joining the Ministry of Economic Warfare as diplomatic adviser; and George Steward. The latter, as Prime Minister Neville Chamberlain's personal press officer, became infamous for taking part in clandestine negotiations with Dr Fritz Hesse, press attaché of the German embassy in London and confidant of Joachim von Ribbentrop, the former ambassador now Hitler's minister of foreign affairs, in November 1938.[119] MI5 spotted Steward sneaking into the German embassy on Carlton House Terrace and duly obtained a copy of Hesse's telegram to Berlin describing the meeting after which the Security Service presented their report to the Foreign Secretary Lord Halifax.

Albert Francis Lakey, a former police sergeant, acted as an enquiry agent for Ewer and the Federated Press of America (FPA) between 1919 and 1927 using, as had already been mentioned, the alias 'Albert Allen'. Following the withdrawal of Russian funding after the ARCOS raid, Ewer tried to get some money for the FPA first in London and then in Paris, visiting the Soviet embassy there, but after his return told Lakey that Moscow wanted the entire operation closed down.[120] In November 1927, Lakey received his severance pay and was dismissed while the FPA office officially closed next year in March. Nevertheless, MI5 and SS1, one of the Special Branch secret departments, continued to keep a tab on the activities of its former employees and at the end of June John Ottaway of MI5's B.4 approached Lakey in Bournemouth where the former FPA office manager was now a proprietor of Dean's Café. Ottaway made a pitch 'under a false flag' posing as one 'G. Stewart of the Anti-Socialist Union'. He asked whether Lakey would consider selling some information about his former employers for money and Lakey promptly agreed, naming his conditions.[121] Four days later they met again at the same place.[122]

Among important things revealed during that second meeting with Ottaway, Lakey alleged that there were 'informants in most of the British Government Departments' and specifically, he added, 'a leakage of information also comes from the Foreign Office, and is obtained owing to one individual who holds there an important position and when dining with juniors occasionally mentions secret matters which are noted and sent to Moscow, through a London [OGPU] representative'.[123] Later MI5 produced a questionnaire for Lakey (codenamed ALLEN by MI5) and then made an assessment of his statements. Regarding Lakey's revelations about a source in the Foreign Office, it was noted that 'the name of Sir Arthur Willert was given by ALLEN to Mr. Harker at a subsequent interview'. To that MI5 commented that 'We known inter alia from correspondence addressed to EWER that Sir Arthur Willert is in the habit of entertaining press representatives to lunch'.[124] Indeed, as follows from his letter to Sir Charles Mendl, head of the press section at the British embassy in Paris, written in January 1929, Willert personally concentrated upon seeing 'as much as possible… the foreign editors of the big newspapers and the more important newspapers, British and foreign,' to discuss revevant issues in private in a relaxed atmosphere.[125] Whether he was also doing this to justify his occasional meetings with Ewer or a press officer of the Soviet embassy during which they could remain unobstructed at all times (for example, passing information and receiving money) remains unknown. However, it is established that in his role as head of the News Department Willert was in contact with Andrew Rothstein and many ROSTA-TASS correspondents.

Later, visiting the Foreign Office and seeing Willert, Harker 'lightly touched on William Norman Ewer and asked how he was behaving himself':

> Sir Arthur Willert assured me that, so far as they were aware, he [Ewer] was behaving himself most properly and was in fact regarded as persona grata at the Foreign Office.
>
> He asked me whether I still thought that EWER was in any way dangerous. I replied that I had no reasons to alter my opinion of EWER that had been mentioned to him in the past. I added that I considered him by far the most dangerous individual from an S.S. [Secret Services] point of view that the Russians had in this country, and that Sir Arthur Willert might rest assured that anything he told EWER would go straight to the Soviet Embassy.
>
> He then asked me whether by any chance I knew SLOCOMBE. I replied that SLOCOMBE was EWER's no. 2, and very nearly as dangerous.
>
> Sir Arthur Willert told me that he thought EWER and SLOCOMBE the ablest and most entertaining journalists he had ever met, and he then suggested that I might like to meet them. I said that, though nothing would please me more personally, I did not think it wise at this juncture that such a meeting should take place.
>
> D.C.D.S. informed as above.
>
> sd. O.A.H.[126]

From documents available today it is clear that Sir Arthur Willert himself was above any suspicion. Despite Harker's warning, Willert was not shy of mentioning Ewer's name in his 1972 memoirs published a year before his death. Writing that Ewer was one of those whose judgement he valued, Sir Arthur also described him as 'the able correspondent of the *Daily Herald* and a very good friend to me'.[127]

In the late 1990s British intelligence writer Nigel West was working with the KGB Colonel Oleg Tsarev on the book published in London as *The Crown Jewels* in 1998. In it they quote what they call '*The Report on the state of the London rezidentura as of 1 January 1927* [allegedly] written by Elena Krasnaya, who was working at that time as the special plenipotentiary of the external section of the Foreign Department of the OGPU'.[128] Alas, the OGPU Foreign Department (INO) did not have any 'external section' and the authors do not refer to any file from the KGB archives in their multiple quotes from this 'report'. A large part of this report deals with the work of William Ewer (the principal source of the London rezidentura codenamed B-1), who had a number of sub-sources 'with whom he maintained regular contact in his capacity as a journalist'. Among his contacts in the India Office, Home Office and Scotland Yard who provided information, there were also 'sub-sources' in the Foreign Office identified in the documents only by the letter 'F'. At least one of them was an unnamed typist, but two others, according to the authors, were 'two highly-placed Old Etonians, Sir Arthur Willert and John D. Gregory ... All the London *rezidentura*'s sources worked for money which varied from £25 to £60 per month'.[129] As stated in the documents from the KGB archives released by the Lubyanka for the joint Costello-Tsarev book project, agent ATTILA was paid £36 (about £3,000 in 2022) a month.[130] Although ATTILA remains unidentified, Arthur Willert was named at least twice as a Soviet intelligence source within the Foreign Office.

Two years after the restoration of diplomatic relations with the Soviet Union, Moscow decided it was high time to send a permanent OGPU resident agent to London. After the series of spy scandals and raids on Soviet premises in 1927, the INO leadership wanted to be on the safe side and opted for an 'illegal' rather than a 'legal' resident operating under the diplomatic cover. Yevgeny Mitskevich (Eugeniusz Mitskewicz), codenamed ANATOLY, was sent to London in 1931 and placed in one of the many Soviet trade organisations operating in the British capital. Mitskevich was informed about two groups of agents, neither of which was active, when he was leaving London in 1933.[131] One of these two groups is well known. It was headed by Percy Glading and operated in the Woolwich Arsenal. About the second group nothing has been established so far, but it was probably affiliated with the Soviet trading organisation Russian Oil Products (ROP), which was registered as a British limited liability company in 1924.

Mitskevich was succeeded as the illegal London resident by Ignacy Reif alias 'Max Wolisch', who was based in Copenhagen, visiting London occasionally for running agents and collecting information that he sent to Moscow by post. In February 1934 he was joined by another illegal resident agent, Dr Arnold Deutsch, who had previously operated in Paris and was sent to London under his own name to help Reif. Because both of them were foreigners, already in summer Moscow decided to reinforce the residency by sending yet another illegal, Lev Nikolsky, at the time staying with his family in Vienna after a botched operation in France. In his new mission briefing, signed by Artuzov, Nikolsky (SCHWED) was instructed 'to take over a group of sources previously handled by ANATOLY [Mitskevich]'. His main priority was to arrange for 'uninterrupted and regular' communication with MAR (Reif), and with Moscow Centre (Lubyanka HQ). MAR, according to the telegram, was waiting to get in touch with ANATOLY and be recalled home.[132] Artuzov planned to place Nikolsky in charge of the whole London operation but Nikolsky, who became later known as 'Alexander Orlov' first refused and then deserted his post. In the end Deutsch remained in London alone.

A quick recap: in February 1934 Deutsch went to London and Reif joined him there in April. They worked together until June when Reif left for Copenhagen again. By that time, they already had under Soviet control a considerably large network of sources: agents (in today's terms – intelligence agents, access agents, facilities agents and agents of influence) as well as talent-spotters, confidential contacts, couriers, and so on. In August or September Glading (GOT) introduced Deutsch to an important source whom Deutsch immediately codenamed ATTILA. He usually gave codenames to his assets by association. Thus, Kim Philby became SÖHNCHEN because he was the son of St John Philby, a famous British Arabist and explorer. Donald Maclean was WAISE ('Orphan') because his father, Sir Donald Maclean, a British Liberal Party politician and onetime leader of the opposition, died in 1932, two years before Maclean junior was recruited as a Soviet spy. Guy Burgess, a flamboyant homosexual, became MÄDCHEN ('Lassie') for obvious reasons. Margarete Moos was PFEIL ('Arrow') because she was used as a courier quickly delivering messages to their destination, while Edith Suschitzky's codename was simply EDITH. She had been an old acquaintance of Deutsch from their time in Vienna.

Agent ATTILA was given this unusual codename because he reminded Deutsch of a rather famous Austro-Hungarian actor by the name of Attila Hörbiger who was born in Budapest but then moved with his family to Vienna where his father set up a design shop. Hörbiger performed at the Raimund Theatre and in 1928 was accepted by the Theatre in der Josefstadt then under the direction of Max Reinhard, regarded as one of the most prominent theatre and film directors of his time. Attila Hörbiger was a Vienna celebrity and Deutsch knew him from popular theatrical performances and films.

Sometime after he was introduced to his new Soviet controller, whom he only knew as 'Otto', a postgraduate research student at the University of London, ATTILA was invited to a meeting with Reif, still the main resident agent in charge of the whole British operation. In his report to Moscow Centre Deutsch explained what happened:

> Reif's command of English was not good. On one occasion, ATTILA told Reif about his son and asked whether he should involve him in our work. Reif misunderstood him and said 'yes'. So, ATTILA brought his son with him to the next meeting. Reif became rather anxious when he saw him, and when he found out who the young man was, he upbraided ATTILA. I met him later to find out what exactly happened

and it turned out it was Reif's lack of proper knowledge of the English language that caused turmoil at that meeting. ATTILA's son turned out to be very useful to us and we began working with him.[133]

Deutsch gave him the codename NACHFOLGER which was appropriate for the son of a person knighted by the King of England who was at the same time a senior Foreign Office official. ATTILA's son proved to be very useful to Soviet intelligence, like his father receiving a monthly remuneration (£15) for his work.[134] At the time of the meeting described above Paul Willert was 25. A review of his biography will demonstrate that he was either a communist sympathiser or a so-called crypto-member of the Communist Party before the war, actively collaborating with RIS for many years.[135] In his letter to Moscow Centre originally written in Russian Deutsch mentioned that he was very happy to have acquired a valuable agent whom he cryptically called OTHELLO and his son HEIR.

According to Philip Taylor, Willert resigned in December 1934. 'It appears,' he writes, 'that Willert had not been happy at the Foreign Office for some time. Uncertainty concerning his future position and pension (he had remained a temporary counsellor since his appointment) was aggravated by illness, and the rows with Simon [appointed Foreign Secretary in November 1931] had forced him into an impossible position.'[136] However, from other sources it becomes clear that among other things Willert was sacked not only because of the mutual antipathy between him and Sir John Simon (even Simon's colleagues thought that he had been a disastrous Foreign Secretary) and a small skirmish between them during the World Disarmament Conference, but also because of his complaining about the reduction in his salary (£1,250 vs. £1,500) due to his not being a career civil servant. Whatever the reason, after a farewell dinner Willert left the Foreign Office in January 1935 and was succeeded by his second-in-command in the News Department, Reginald 'Rex' Leeper.

Rex Leeper previously served as head of the Russian section of the FO's Political Intelligence Department (PID) where his elder brother Allen held the same position in the Balkan section. In 1918, his office in Victoria Street, Westminster, was directly below the rooms used by Litvinov, the Soviet representative in London, and, according to Richard Ullman, Leeper was the only British official allowed to see Litvinov.[137] Leeper shared Willert's attitude towards Simon but he didn't have to endure him very long: six months after his appointment as head of the News Department Simon was replaced by Sir Samuel Hoare.[138] After his resignation, Arthur Willert devoted much of his time to writing and lecturing on British foreign policy leaving England for almost a year for a lecture tour in America that he clearly did not enjoy.

THE FOREIGN SERVICE
OF THE
UNITED STATES OF AMERICA

No. 901

AMERICAN EMBASSY
1, Grosvenor Square
London, W. 1
May 2, 1944

Dear Hart: Attn: Mr. R. H. Hollis

PF 41664

The Bureau advises that during the investigation of [Otto
Katz] with aliases, an individual reliably reported to be an
agent of the Communist International, information was received
that one PAUL WILLERT cooperated with Otto Katz in 1939 by taking
the funds raised by Katz from France to England for the purpose
of transmitting them to the Soviet Union. The funds referred
to were allegedly raised in Hollywood, California, and brought
to France by Katz himself.

Information was also received that PAUL WILLERT was the son
of a British nobleman and that during the period of his association with Katz he was connected with the British Intelligence
although simultaneously appearing to work for the Comintern.

Investigation has disclosed that PAUL WILLERT Was in Los
Angeles in the company of Otto Katz during 1940. It is also
known that WILLERT arrived on board the SS "Normandie" July 14,
1939. He previously resided at 14 Halsey Street, London, S.W.3,
England in 1937.

The files of the Bureau disclose that PAUL WILLERT on
December 25, 1939, was listed as one of the sponsors of the
national organization of the Abraham Lincoln Brigade. He was
also reported as the President of the Oxford University Press,
an organization issuing a high-type of anti-Fascist material.

Please advise me whether or not WILLERT was an employee of
British Intelligence and if so, I would appreciate such infor-
mation that he furnished to British authorities relative to
[Otto Katz] If WILLERT has had no connection with the British
Government, I would appreciate your furnishing me with such
information as you might have relative to his activities.

Sincerely yours,

M. Joseph Lynch

M. Joseph Lynch

H. L. A. Hart, Esq.
58, St. James' Str.
London, S. W. 1

He never failed to demand that his fee must be paid on time and to his bank account in Canada.

When the Second World War broke out, Willert joined the newly established (again) Ministry of Information (MOI) under Hugh Macmillan (Lord Macmillan) as minister. Macmillan, a distinguished Scottish barrister, during the First World War had served as Assistant Director of Intelligence in the first MOI (1918–19). The Ministry consisted of a number of divisions classified in four broad groups. The whole country was divided into twelve regional districts with the Ministry's regional offices responsible for each district. Willert was appointed the Chief Regional Information Officer for Region No. 9 – the Midlands, with an office in Birmingham.[139] He resigned in July 1945.

After all NKVD (formerly OGPU) illegal residents – Reif, Deutsch, Nikolsky and Maly – were recalled from London, all their sources were 'put on ice'. The story goes that in March 1940 Liza Zarubina was summoned to the Lubyanka NKVD Head Office and instructed to travel to the UK in order to reinstate contact with agent ATTILA who had not been in touch since November 1937. In April she was in Paris applying for a British visa using her genuine Austrian passport in the name of Elsa Hutschnecker. Who exactly interviewed her is not known but in late 1937 or early 1938 Major Geoffrey W. Courtney succeeded Maurice Jeffes as head of the SIS station in Paris operating under the PCO cover. In her report Zaubina mentioned that a person who talked to her was a typical British intelligence officer. She finally arrived in London in April seeking to meet ATTILA, according to the schedule agreed long before, in Madam Tussaud's wax museum in Marylebone Street. After the agent failed to show up, Zarubina allegedly bought the *Standard* and found out that ATTILA, a high-ranking Foreign Office official, had left the country with a government delegation. The mission being not accomplished due to reasons beyond her control, she returned to Moscow.[140] Turning a blind eye to obvious inaccuracies,[141] the story looks quite plausible and sticks well to Sir Arthur especially having in mind that he had been twice mentioned – by Lakey and Tsarev – as an important source in the Foreign Office. Anyway, he was never unmasked as a Soviet spy and never prosecuted.

Appendix: Lenin and the Cheka

Lenin's speech at a meeting followed by a concert for the members of the All-Russia Extraordinary Commission, 7 November 1918.

Comrades, in commemorating the first anniversary of our revolution, I would like to say a few words about the hard work of the extraordinary commissions [Chekas].

There is nothing surprising in the fact that we hear about the attacks on the Cheka's activities from both our enemies as well as quite often from our friends. We took on a challenging task. When we assumed control of the country, we could not avoid making mistakes and it is natural that the Cheka's mistakes are most striking. The narrow-minded intelligentsia picks up these mistakes not wanting to delve deeper into the subject matter at hand. What surprises me about the howls over the Cheka's mistakes is the inability [of some people] to see a bigger picture. What they do, they harp on some blunders committed by the Cheka, sob and make fuss about minor matters.

We say: we learn from mistakes. As in all other areas, so in this one we say that we learn by self-criticism. It is not about the structure and personnel of the Cheka, it is about the work they do where decisiveness, speed, and, most importantly, loyalty is required. When I look at the activities of the Cheka and compare it with attacks [on them], I say: this is philistinism, futile talk. It reminds me of Kautsky's sermons about dictatorship, which are tantamount to supporting the bourgeoisie. We know from our experience that the expropriation of the bourgeoisie comes after a long and arduous struggle, through the dictatorship [of the proletariat].

Marx said that the revolutionary dictatorship of the proletariat is the intermediate stage between capitalism and communism.[1] The more the proletariat puts pressure on the bourgeoisie, the more furiously the bourgeoisie resists. We know how France dealt with the workers in [the June Days uprising of] 1848, and when we are being accused of cruelty, we wonder how they can ignore the fundamental principles of Marxism. We remember the mutiny of the officer cadets in October, and we must not forget about a number of uprisings that are being prepared. We have, on the one hand, to learn how to be creative at work, and on the other, we must break the resistance of the bourgeoisie. The Finnish White Guards, for all their much-vaunted 'democracy', had no scruples about shooting workers. The need for the dictatorship [of the proletariat] has taken deep root in the minds of broad masses, despite its hardship and cruelty. It is clear that some unwanted individuals shall try to worm themselves into the Cheka ranks. Self-criticism will help us to kick them out. It is important for us that the Chekas are exercising the dictatorship of the proletariat [over other classes], and in this respect their role is invaluable. There is no other way to emancipate the broad masses of the people except by forcefully supressing the exploiters. This is precisely what the Chekas are doing and therein lies their service to the proletariat.[2]

Notes

Foreword and Acknowledgements

1. Boris Volodarsky, 'Nikolai Khokhlov, WHISTLER: Self-Esteem with a Halo', *Personal Files*, 1/1 (Spring 2005), xiv.
2. Christopher Andrew, *The Defence of the Realm: The Authorized History of MI5* (London: Allen Lane/Penguin Books, 2009), 220. Mrs Archer was sacked for insubordination by the acting director Jasper Harker in November 1940. She was then employed by Valentine Vivian in Section V of SIS.
3. Ibid., 266. The only one case was that of John Herbert King, who joined the British FO Communications Department as a temporary clerk in 1934 and was recruited by Henri Christian 'Han' Pieck, a Dutch artist, to work for Soviet intelligence. On 22 January 1946 Michael Serpell of the MI5 section B1c wrote in a minute to Maxwell Knight: 'It is remarkable how we seem to have been led to the detection and arrest of KING by three independent informants – H[ooper], Parlanti and Krivitsky' (TNA KV 2/811 s.213a).
4. Ibid., 268. As the historians of the Special Branch noted, 'he was wrong but the scale of Russian penetration of the British establishment was certainly not apparent as we now know, with the benefir of hindsight'. And why? Forgetting the extent of Russian penetration of the Special Branch itself and the total lack of experience of its officers in dealing with Russian espionage, they concluded: 'This was partly due to the Security Service's inability to cope with their task, given the resources available to them. Churchill regarded them as inefficient and by the end of the decade, when he became Prime Minister, he dismissed an aging and ailing Kell.' Ray Wilson and Ian Adams, *Special Branch: A History, 1883-2006* (London: Biteback, 2015), 208.
5. Interview with Mr [deleted], Security Service PF 47813/V2 (TNA KV 2/815) s.98a.
6. TNA, Tuesday, 28 November 2017, 'Security Service File Release November 2017'.
7. See F.A.C. Kluiters, 'Bill Hooper and Secret Service', Nationaal Archief, Den Haag, Onderzoeksarchief Frans Kluiters, nummer toegang 2.21.424, Inventarisnummer 103.
8. Karel Willem Leonard Bezemer, *History of the Dutch Merchant Navy in the Second World War*, in Dutch (1987), 240. According to Andrew, Hooper was 're-engaged as a SIS agent in October 1939' (246).
9. Andrew, *The Defence of the Realm*, 268. It is not surprising that intelligence historians, not to mention amateur intelligence writers, make errors. Mentioning Bill Hooper, for example, many call him 'Jack', although this was the nickname of Hooper's younger brother Herbert. Writing about his PCO chief in The Hague, Major Dalton, Nigel West calls him 'Hugh', while he was actually Ernest Albert Llewellyn Dalton. Ernest Dalton, aged 42, committed suicide on 7 July 1936, at 's-Gravenhage (The Hague), Netherlands. 'I have got myself into such a mess,' he wrote (Keith Jeffery, *MI6: The History of the Secret Intelligence Service 1909–1949* (London: Bloomsbury, 2010), 277), 'that this is the only way out.' Hugh Dalton (Baron Dalton) at the time served as Parliamentary Under-Secretary of State for Foreign Affairs (1929–31). In the authorised history of MI5 one can also read that after his dismissal from SIS in September 1936, 'Hooper volunteered his services to Soviet intelligence, which employed him as an agent during 1937 before

breaking contact with him – probably as the result of the defection of a GRU officer [?!] who knew of his recruitment.' In the light of the new documents, this assertion should probably be reconsidered.

10. Andrew, *The Defence of the Realm*, 268.

11. Half a century after the Bolshevik revolution, John Jones, the future DG and then head of MI5 F Branch (counter-subversion) finally rose to define subversion in similar terms.

12. David R. Stone, 'Ideology and the Rise of the Red Army, 1921-1929', in Robin Higham and Frederick W. Kagan (eds), *The Military History of the Soviet Union* (New York and Basingstoke, Hampshire: Palgrave, 2002), 51–63. In 1925 Voroshilov would succeed Frunze as People's Commissar for Military and Navy Affairs appointed by Stalin. David Stone notes that he was 'Frunze's clear inferior in terms of his administrative and intellectual gifts, but obviously outranked him in subservient loyalty to Stalin. Voroshilov would serve as Stalin's trustworthy implement for modernising the Red Army while keeping it under the party's complete political domination', which had been secured by both party activists and the Cheka-GPU-NKVD watchdogs.

13. John P. Sontag, 'The Soviet War Scare of 1926-27', *The Russian Review*, 34/1 (Jan. 1975), 66–77. 'Indeed,' the author concludes, 'the war scare represented the sort of interaction of foreign and domestic politics that Bolshevik leaders consistently perceived in the early years of Soviet rule. Genuine, if exaggerated fears of Western intentions in 1926 and 1927 were exploited by both sides of the party struggle in 1927, in turn influencing both Moscow's perception of Western intentions and Soviet domestic politics over the course of several years.'

Introduction: From the Okhrana to the National Guard

1. A.T. Vassilyev, *The Ochrana: The Russian Secret Police* (London: George G. Harrap & Co. Ltd., 1930), 38.

2. For personal memories about him, see the book by a famous Russian mathematician, Sofya Kovalevskaya (née Sophia Korvin-Krukovsky), *A Russian Childhood* (New York, NY: Springer-Verlag, 1978), chapter 6 'My Uncle Pyotr Vasilievich Korvin-Krukovsky', 111–23.

3. See, for example, Charles A. Ruud and Sergei A. Stepanov, *Fontanka 16: The Tsar's Secret Police* (Montreal & Kingston: McGill-Queen's University Press, 1999); Edward Ellis Smith, *The Okhrana: The Russian Department of Police* (Stanford, CA: Hoover Institution Press, 1967); and Fredric S. Zuckerman, *The Tsarist Secret Police Abroad: Policing Europe in a Modernising World* (Houndmills, Basingstoke, Hampshire: Palgrave Macmillan, 2003); Zinaida I. Peregudova, *Politicheskiy sysk v Rossii 1880-1917* (Moscow: ROSSPEN, 2000); and Rita T. Kronenbitter, 'Paris Okhrana 1885-1905', *Studies in Intelligence*, 10/3 (Summer 1966), 55–66, also reproduced in Ben B. Fischer (ed.), *Okhrana: The Paris Operations of the Russian Imperial Police* (Washington, DC: CIA's Center for the Study of Intelligence, 1997). Be aware of multiple factual errors in Kronenbitter's account.

4. 'Today's counter-intelligence methods and methodics,' according to the expert, 'are similar and even identical to those from the past, except that they have adapted to technological advances and societal changes; the methodology of counter-intelligence, however, remains unchanged.' For details, see Teodora Ivanuša, 'Some Counter-intelligence Methods', in Iztok Podbregar and Teodora Ivanuša, *The Anatomy of Counter-intelligence: European Perspective* (Bentham eBooks, 2021), 43–109.

5. Jean Longuet and Georges Silber, *Terroristes et policiers: Azef, Harting et cie. Étude historique et critique* (Paris: F. Juven, 1909; Nobu Press, 2012), 237–8.

6. Robert Henderson, *Vladimir Burtsev and the Struggle for a Free Russia: A Revolutionary in the Time of Tsarism and Bolshevism* (London & New York: Bloomsbury Academic, 2017), 151–4.

7. Ibid. See also Frederic S. Zuckerman, 'Vladimir Burtsev and the Tsarist Political Police in Conflict, 1904-14', *Journal of Contemporary History*, 12/1 (January 1977), 193–219.
8. See Rita T. Kronenbitter, 'The Illustrious Career of Arkadiy Harting', in Fischer (ed.), *Okhrana*, 31–46; Zuckerman, *The Tsarist Secret Police Abroad*, 151–65; and Ruud and Stepanov, *Fontanka*, 82–91, 94, 95.
9. Kronenbitter, 'The Illustrious Career of Arkadiy Harting', 45.
10. In his famous book *The Cheka* (1981), George Legett writes on page xxiv that 'when the legal Bolshevik newspaper, *Pravda*, was founded in St. Petersburg in 1912, the Okhrana obliged by providing the services of two of its agents to act, respectively, as editor (Malinovsky) and treasurer (Miron Chernomazov)'. This information, based on Bertram D. Wolfe's book, *Three Who Made a Revolution*, first published in New York in 1948, is wrong. For details, see Ralph Carter Elwood, 'Lenin and Pravda, 1912-1914', *Slavic Review*, 31/2 (June 1972), 355–80.
11. Ruud and Stepanov, *Fontanka*, 282–4.
12. Cf. Christopher Andrew and Oleg Gordievsky, *KGB: The Inside Story of Its Foreign Operations from Lenin to Gorbachev* (London. HarperCollins*Publishers*, 1990), 25.
13. Richard Aldrich, *The Hidden Hand: Britain, America and Cold War Secret Intelligence* (London. John Murray, 2001), 5.
14. See Ruud and Stepanov, *Fontanka*, 89. When Christopher Andrew, the first Western historian of KGB foreign operations, began his academic career in Paris working on the Entente Cordiale, he chose as the focus Théophile Declassé, who became the longest-serving foreign minister in the 70-year history of the French Third Republic. For the whole period of Rachkovsky's tour of duty in France, Declassé remained among his closest contacts, bypassing official channels and working through Rachkovsky when he arranged high-level contacts between the two countries.
15. Andrew and Gordievsky, *KGB*, 26. 'From 1898 to 1901,' Professor Andrew writes, 'Russia made repeated attempts to persuade Germany to sign a secret agreement on spheres of influence in the Turkish Empire that would recognise her age-old ambitions in the Bosporus. The attempts were abandoned at the end of 1901 because, as the Russian foreign minister Count Lamsdorf informed his ambassador in Berlin, decrypted German telegrams showed that the German government had no real intention of signing an agreement' (Ibid, 29).
16. See Richard H. Solomon and Nigel Quinney, *American Negotiating Behaviour: Wheeler-Dealers, Legal Eagles, Bullies, and Preachers* (Washington, DC: United States Institute of Peace, 2010), 96. See also Len Scott, 'Secret Intelligence, Covert Action and Clandestine Diplomacy', *Intelligence and National Security*, 19/2 (Summer 2004), 322–41.
17. T.G. Derevnina, 'Iz istorii obrazovaniya III otdeleniya', *Vestnik MGU, Istoriya*, 4 (1973).
18. Robert W. Pringle, *Historical Dictionary of Russian and Soviet Intelligence* (Lanham, MD: Scarecrow Press, Inc./Rowman & Littlefield Publishing Group, 2006), 181.
19. Christopher Andrew and Vasili Mitrokhin, *The Mitrokhin Archive: The KGB in Europe and the West* (London: Allen Lane, 1999), 735. There have been several classified histories of the KGB and its foreign operations written by the KGB staff for internal use only.
20. No relation to Matthew Vaughn and Karl Gajdusek.
21. From *The Internationale* by Eugène Pottier, 'Le monde va changer de base, nous ne sommes rien, soyons tout!'.

Chapter 1: Origins of the Cheka

1. December 7th according to the Julian (Old Style) Calendar then observed in Russia, but 20 December according to the Gregorian (New Style) Calendar used in most of the world. 'In 1918, after the Revolution, Lenin raised the question of calendar reform and, after an investigation of the subject, published a decree directing the adoption of

the Gregorian style "for the purpose of being in harmony with all the civilized countries of the world" ... Reference to the Russian Julian calendar must be made previous to 1918, from 1918 to 1923 the Gregorian calendar was in use, from 1923 to 1931 the five-day Russian Revolutionary calendar must be consulted, and from 1931 until 1940 the Russian calendar with the six-day week was in effect. From 1940 onward, official Russia returned to the Gregorian calendar with its seven-day week, using Sunday as a rest-day.' See Elisabeth Achelis, 'Russia's Difficulties', *Journal of Calendar Reform* (1954).

2. Robert P. Browder and Alexander F. Krensky (eds), *The Russian Provisional Government, 1917: Documents*, 3 vols (Stanford, CA: Stanford University Press, 1961), vol. 1, 194.

3. R.C. Elwood, 'Lenin's Testimony to the Extraordinary Investigatory Commission', *Canadian Slavonic Papers*, 41/3 (September–December 1999), 261.

4. One of the participants recalled, 'When leaving [the crime scene] I did not notice that a few steps from Sazonov lay the mutilated corpse of Plehve and the wreckage of his carriage'. See Boris Savinkov, *Memoirs of a Terrorist* [in Russian] (Leningrad: Lenizdat, 1990), 59; see also the same title in English (New York, NY: A & C Boni, 1931).

5. Paul Avrich, *Kronstadt 1921* (Princeton, NJ: Princeton University Press, 1970), 208.

6. Donald Rumbelow, a former City of London Police officer, crime historian and ex-curator of the City of London Police's Crime museum, in his book *The Houndsditch Murders and the Siege of Sidney Street* (1973), wrote that Peters was 'the man who should have been hanged' for murdering two sergeants and a constable.

7. In his book, Robert Bruce Lockhart remembered Peters, 'There was nothing in his character to indicate the inhuman monster he is commonly supposed to be. He told me that he suffered physical pain every time he signed a death sentence. I believe it was true. There was a strong streak of sentimentality in his nature, but he was a fanatic as far as the clash between Bolshevism and capitalism was concerned, and he pursued his Bolshevik aims with a sense of duty which was relentless'. See R.H. Bruce Lockhart, *Memoirs of a British Agent* (Barnet, S. Yorkshire: Frontline Books, 2011), 328.

8. For details, see David R. Stone, 'Soviet Arms Exports in the 1920s', *Journal of Contemporary History*, 48/1 (January 2013), 55–77.

9. RGASPI, f. 17, op. 9, d. 1709, and f. 613, op. 2, d. 59.

10. Andrew and Mitrokhin, *The Mitrokhin Archive I*, 31.

11. For details, see Earl F. Ziemke, *The Red Army 1918-1941: From Vanguard of World Revolution to US Ally* (London: Frank Cass/Taylor & Francis Group, 2004).

12. The issues that were to fall within the remit of the Commission (Cheka) were 'to radically suppress all counter-revolution and sabotage activities and attempts to commit them throughout Russia; bring before the Revolutionary Tribunal counter-revolutionaries and saboteurs, develop measures to counter such activities and mercilessly carry them out. The commission should conduct only a preliminary investigation.' The commission formed three sections: (1) Information (2) Administration (3) Counter-subversion and counter-sabotage. TsA FSB: f. 1, op. 1, d. 1, l. 1.

13. In May, when Trotsky was trying to make his way from New York to Petrograd, one of the agents of MI1(c) in Switzerland, codenamed SW5, reported from Berne that '40 Russian revolutionaries, fanatical followers of Lenin, including Lenin himself, [had] left for Russia via Germany' – this was the (in)famous 'sealed train' which brought the Bolshevik leader to Petrograd. Permission to travel was granted by the German government only after receiving Lenin's personal guarantee that 'every one of his 40 followers' favoured an immediate peace'. Jeffery, *MI6*, 108. For details about that 'train ride that changed the world' as well as the underground conspiracy and subterfuge that went into making it happen, see Catherine Merridale, *Lenin on the Train* (New York, NY: Metropolitan Books, 2017).

14. Vincent P. O'Hara, W. David Dickson, and Richard Worth (eds), *The Crown of the Waves: The Great Navies of the First World War* (Annapolis, MD: Naval Institute Press, 2013), Chapter 6: Russia.

15. About Filippov's Cheka career, see Vladimir Antonov (SVR historian), 'Aleksei Filippov – pervyi sovetskii razvedchik', *Nezavisimoe Voennoe Obozrenie*, 12 September 2008. See also Edward E. Roslof, *Red Priests: Renovationism, Russian Orthodoxy, and Revolution, 1905-1946* (Bloomington, IN: Indiana University Press, 2002), 30. Filippov, as the first Soviet intelligence agent sent on a secret mission abroad, is also mentioned in Andrew and Mitrokhin, *The Mitrokhin Archive I*, I, 31–2.

16. About Lenin's 17 years of émigré life in Paris, London, Geneva, Brussels and Munich, as well as his brief visits to Poland and Finland, where he first met Stalin during a conference in Tampere, see Helen Rappaport, *Conspirator: Lenin in Exile* (London: Hutchinson, 2009).

17. About Menzhinsky, see Donald Rayfield, 'The Exquisite Inquisitor: Viacheslav Menzhinsky as Poet and Hangman', *New Zealand Slavonic Journal*, Slavonic Journeys Across Two Hemispheres: Festschrift in honour of Arnold McMillin (2003), 91–109. See also idem., *Stalin and His Hangmen: An Authoritative Portrait of a Tyrant and Those Who Served Him* (London: Viking, 2004), Chapter 3. There is no 'official' or 'authorised' history of the KGB, its predecessors and successors either in Russia or in the West. One of the first attempts is the book by George Leggett, *The Cheka: Lenin's Political Police* (Oxford: Clarendon Press, 1981), which covers the first five years of its existence. Another important work is the book by Christopher Andrew written in collaboration with Oleg Gordievsky, a former KGB lieutenant colonel and MI6 agent, *KGB: The Inside Story* (London: Harper Collins, 1990). It was followed by two impressive volumes by the same author, Cambridge Professor Christopher Andrew, now in collaboration with the Soviet defector and former KGB archivist Vasili Mitrokhin, covering a wide spectre of Soviet foreign intelligence operations in Britain, Europe, America and around the world (and correcting several errors of the previous KGB history). A six-volume series entitled *Essays on the History of Soviet Foreign Intelligence* under the editorship of its former intelligence chiefs was written by the KGB historians and have little historical or academic value being a typical example of historical fiction (or historiographic metafiction – the style of writing that mixes fact with fiction). A much better four-volume series based on rare archival documents have been published in Russian by Vladimir Khaustov with a group of editors and its shorter version in English by Vladimir Khausov and David R. Shearer (see Recommended Reading). There also exist several classified histories of the Service from time to time written for the leadership or students of the KGB schools, like V.M. Chebrikov, G.F. Grigorenko, N.A. Dushin and F.D. Bobkov (eds), *History of the Soviet State Security Services: A Textbook* (Moscow: Dzerzhinsky Red Banner KGB Higher School under the Council of Ministers of the USSR, Special Department No. 9, 1977), Top Secret 2173. This so-called 'textbook' is nothing but a set of obsolete Soviet propaganda clichés.

18. There's an obvious error in *The Mitrokhin Archive I* by Andrew and Mitrokhin where it is stated that Ivan Serov 'blew his brains out in 1963' (p. 30). Serov, who was Beria's deputy and later successor of Abakumov as chairman of the KGB between April 1954 and December 1958, after his dismissal from the KGB also headed the GRU from 1958 to 1963. Serov was removed from his post primarily due to his friendship with Colonel Oleg Penkovsky, who was uncovered as an agent-in-place working for both the American CIA and British MI6. Arrested in October 1962, Penkovsky was tried and executed the following year. In 1965 General Serov was stripped of his party membership and died in disgrace on 1 July 1990.

Chapter 2: Lenin, Trotsky, and His Majesty's Secret Service

1. Jeffery, *MI6*, 99–100. See also Alan Judd (a pseudonym used by Alan Edwin Petty), *The Quest for C: Mansfield Cumming and the Founding of the Secret Service* (London: Harper Collins Publishers, 1999), 386; and Michael Smith, *Six: Murder and Mayhem 1909-1939* (London: Dialogue, 2010), 187.

2. Jeffery, *MI6*, 103. For Hoare's fascinating personal recollections of his intelligence mission in Petrograd, see Sir Samuel Hoare, *The Fourth Seal: The End of a Russian Chapter* (London: William Heinemann, 1930). For Hoare's recruitment and his first intelligence mission, see John Arthur Cross, *Sir Samuel Hoare: A Political Biography* (London: Jonathan Cape, 1977), 39–40.

3. Smith, *Six*, 195.

4. The Military Control Section was run by two officers, Alley in Petrograd and Lieutenant Commander Malcolm McLaren RNVR in Archangel. There were also sub-stations in Tornio in Lapland, a cross-border twin-town adjacent to Haparanda on the Swedish side, and in Vladivostok. Among those who worked for Alley was Gerald 'Jim' Gillespie, initially under consular cover in Kherson.

5. Jeffery, *MI6*, 95–6.

6. Ibid., 116–18. For Maugham's description of his adventures in Russia, see *Ashenden, or the British Agent: Mr. Harrington's Washing*, first published in 1928. See also Lorraine M. Lees and William S. Rodner (eds), *An American Diplomat in Bolshevik Russia: DeWitt Clinton Poole* (Madison, WI: The University of Wisconsin Press, 2014), Ch. 1. Among other things, Poole was sent to Russia to control the intelligence organization put in place by the US consul general Maddin Summers, which was then headed by the agent Xenophon Kalamatiano.

7. Still a schoolgirl, she met Nadezhda Krupskaya and by the time she graduated was already a seasoned revolutionary. 'Having abandoned socialism,' Roland Chambers write, 'Ariadna visited Krupskaya for the last time in 1908 in Geneva.' Krupskaya's husband, Lenin, was furious with Tyrkova for moving away from Marxism. She told him 'that she had no desire to live in a Russia ruled by illiterate factory workers. Lenin, smiling coldly, had told her this was exactly why, when the Revolution came, she would be amongst the first to hang from a lamp post'. See below.

8. Roland Chambers, *The Last Englishman: The Double Life of Arthur Ransome* (London: Faber & Faber, 2009), 90–2.

9. See TNA INF 4/11. Under H.H. Asquith (Prime Minister April 1908 – December 1916) propaganda was dispersed among different groups in departments such as the Home Office, the Foreign Office and the War Office. When Lloyd George became Prime Minister in December 1916, the war propaganda effort was restructured along more co-ordinated lines. Within three months, a Department of Information had been created (under the remit of the Foreign Office), which in turn became the Ministry of Information in February 1918. See also M.L. Sanders, 'Wellington House and the British propaganda during the First World War', *The Historical Journal*, 18/1 (March 1975), 119–46. At the same time, in January 1916, as part of the reorganisation of the Imperial General Staff, a new Directorate was created which became known as Military Intelligence Section 7 (MI7), where subsection (b) was responsible for foreign and domestic propaganda.

10. For details, see Hugh Walpole, 'Denis Garstin and the Russian Revolutions: A Brief Word in Memory', *The Slavonic and East European Review*, 17/51 (April 1939), 587–605.

11. According to Ullman's excellent study, 'The Anglo-French convention of 23 December 1917 was a wartime agreement which assigned to France responsibilities for direction of activities "against the enemy" in the territories west of the Don River – the Ukraine, the

Crimea, and Bessarabia – while the British were to take charge of operations "against the Turks" in the "Cossack territories" [?!], Transcaucasia, and Central Asia'. See Richard H. Ullman, *Anglo-Soviet Relations, 1917-1921, Volume 2: Britain and the Russian Civil War* (Princeton, NJ: Princeton University Press and London: Oxford University Press, 1968), 44–51. See also TNA: WO 161/5.

12. Appointed People's Commissar for Foreign Affairs after the Revolution, one of Trotsky's first acts of was to publish secret documents of the Treaty of London, signed on 26 April 1915 between the Triple Entente, that is, Great Britain, France and Russia, and the Kingdom of Italy. The secret treaty brought Italy into the First World War on the Allied side, promising her parts of Austria-Hungary in the north and in the east across the Adriatic as well as British financial help.

13. R.H. Bruce Lockhart, *Memoirs of a British Agent* (London: The Folio Society, 2003), 173–4. Baroness Maria Ignatievna Zakrevskaya aka Benckendorff aka Budberg is a legend. Her long life intersected with a brilliant cast of characters. Moura lived in the world of great events and was close to the men who shaped them. As a young woman she met the German Kaiser Wilhelm, and later in life used to have dealings with the top brass of Stalin's NKVD. For many years she had been suspected of working for the British SIS and the Russian GPU/NKVD and it seems she had indeed provided intelligence to both of them. Finally, she was the great aunt of Nick Clegg, the leader of the British Liberal Democratic Party (December 2007 – May 2015), and deputy Prime Minister (2010–15). For details, see Nina Berberova, *Moura: The Dangerous Life of the Baroness Budberg* (New York, NY: The New York Review of Books, 1988); Deborah McDonald and Jeremy Dronfield, *A Very Dangerous Woman: The Lives, Loves and Lies of Russia's Most Seductive Spy* (London: Oneworld Publications, 2015); and Andy McSmith, 'Was Nick Clegg's great aunt a Soviet agent?' *Independent*, 2 January 2015.

14. Jeffery, *MI6*, 136. Alan Judd gives 15 March 1918 as the date which Cumming recorded in his diary as their first meeting (*The Quest for C*, 384).

15. Diary of Mansfield Cumming, 15 March 1918. See also TNA: WO 106/6190 'History of the British Intelligence Organization in Russia', 26 February 1917.

16. See Jeffery, *MI6*, 136, and Norman Graham Thwaites, *Velvet and Vinegar: Autobiographical Reminiscences* (London: Grayson & Grayson, 1932), 181. See also Andrew Cook, *On His Majesty's Secret Service: The True Story of Sidney Reilly Ace of Spies* (Stroud, Gloucestershire: Tempus, 2002), 119–33. The author had worked as a foreign affairs and defence specialist, and was aide to George Robertson, former Secretary of State for Defence, and John Spellar, former Minister of State for the Armed Forces. According to his publishers, during his ten years researching the book on Reilly, Cook was only the fifth historian to be given special permission, under the 1992 'Waldegrave Initiative' by the Cabinet Office, to examine closed MI6 documents, not seen by any previous biographer of Reilly.

17. 'The Man from Nowhere' is the title of the second chapter of Cook's excellent biography of Reilly, *On His Majesty's Secret Service*. See also Robert Bruce Lockhart, *Memoirs of a British Agent* (London: Putnam, 1932) and Robin Bruce Lockhart, *Ace of Spies* (London: Hodder and Stoughton, 1967). There is of course the whole library of Reilly books, including his own 'memoirs': Sidney Reilly, *Britain's Master Spy* (London: Hippocrene Books, 1986), republished by Biteback as *Adventures of a British Master Spy* (2015) with the first part being Reilly's own account of his operations in Russia and the rest a story told by his last (but not only) wife, Pepita Bobadilla, an actress who married Reilly in 1923. Other books are Richard Spence's biography of Reilly, *Trust No One* (2002), and the famous *Iron Maze: The Western Secret Services and the Bolsheviks* (London: Macmillan, 1998) by Gordon Brook-Shepherd.

18. Jarrod Tanny, *City of Rogues and Schnorrers: Russia's Jews and the Myth of Old Odessa* (Bloomington, IN: Indiana University Press, 2011), 186–7.
19. Lockhart, *Memoirs of a British Agent*, 202–3. Lockhart spells the name 'Karachan'.
20. See, for example, TNA: WO 32/5669 OVERSEAS: Russia: CODE 0(AG): Organisation of new Red Army, CX 013592 of 12 May 1918.
21. Andrew and Gordievsky, *KGB*, 43–5.
22. Jeffery, *MI6*, 136–7.
23. Ian C.D. Moffat, *The Allied Intervention in Russia, 1918-1920: The Diplomacy of Chaos* (Houndmills, Basingstoke: Palgrave Macmillan, 2015), 1.
24. George Alexander Hill, *Go Spy the Land: Being the Adventures of IK8 of the British Secret Service* (London. Biteback, 2014), 97.
25. For details about Boyle, see the series of articles 'Who was Joe Boyle?' written by his daughter, Flora Alexander Boyle, and published in the American *Maclean's Magazine* in June 1938.
26. TNA: FO 371/3350, Russia: Code 38/Code W38, File 203967, Captain G.A. Hill's report on his work in Russia for DMI, 26 November 1918, with copies to Lieutenant General Sir Frederic C. Poole, then commander of the British expeditionary forces to Archangel; Lieutenant Colonel [Cuthbert] Thornhill, according to some sources GSO1 with the North Russia Expeditionary Force responsible, among others, for collecting intelligence; Bruce Lockhart; and MI1c.
27. See Paul Dukes, *Red Dusk and the Morrow: Adventures and Investigations in Soviet Russia* (London: Biteback, 2012), 1–3; and Jeffery, *MI6*, 137.
28. Dukes, *Red Dusk and the Morrow*, 5–6.
29. Semen K. Tsvigun and Yuri A. Akhapkin (eds), *V.I. Lenin i VChK: Collection of Documents, 1917-1922* (Moscow. Politizdat, 1975), doc. 48. See also, Andrew and Gordievsky, *KGB*, 46–7.
30. Jeffery, *MI6*, 180.
31. In his otherwise well-researched book, Andrew Cook writes that Starzhevskaya was 25 and that she worked for the 'Bolshevik Central Committee' (*On His Majesty's Secret Service*, 144). This is wrong. Olga Dmitrievna Starzhevskaya was born in 1890, that is, in July 1918 she was 28, and she worked for the VTsIK, the All-Russian Central Executive Committee, which was the legislative, administrative and controlling body of state power of the Russian Soviet Republic in 1917–18 and the RSFSR from 1918 to 1937. GARF, f. R-8419, op. 1, d. 321, ll. 60-61.
32. The Russian Foreign Ministry Cipher Bureau, a small unit headed by Vladimir V. Sabanin, was very successful in breaking foreign codes and ciphers. One of the Bureau's best experts was Ernest Constantine Vetterlein, the son of Carl von Vetterlein (a German language instructor at the Alexander Military Law Academy in St Petersburg), who started to work at the Ministry in November 1896. Even before the October 1917 Revolution, he had succeeded in breaking several diplomatic codes, including the British. In March 1918, Captain Wion de Malpas Egerton, British naval attaché in Helsingfors, cabled to the Director of Naval Intelligence (DNI), Rear Admiral Reginald Hall, describing 'Feterlein [*sic*], cipher expert to Russian F.O. for 25 years' as offering 'his services and full information on German position square Austrian military and diplomatic codes'. The British naval attaché added that Vetterlein was 'highly recommended' but needed 'financial aid for himself and wife to reach England'. Ernest and Angelica Vetterlein arrived in Britain on 17–18 May 1918 and in June he started working for the GC&CS. For the next three decades Vetterlein (and his family) would be of inestimable value to British SIGINT efforts and national security.

33. For example, Frīdrihs Briedis was a commander of one of the Latvian Riflemen Battalions who refused to join the Red Army and in 1918 became part of the anti-Bolshevist conspiracy in Moscow. In Savinkov's SZRS Lieutenant Colonel Briedis was responsible for intelligence, counter-intelligence and anti-Bolshevik propaganda. At the end of July 1918, he was arrested by the Cheka and four weeks later executed.

34. John W. Long, 'Sidney Reilly: The Lockhart Plot in Revolutionary Russia, 1918', *Europe-Asia Studies*, 47/7 (November 1995), 1227–8. TNA: FO 371/3287, Russia: Code 8/Code W38 File 6, papers 129986 and 131278, Lockhart (Moscow) to Balfour (London), 13 and 16 July 1918.

35. Long, 'Sidney Reilly', 1228. See also Richard B. Spence, 'The Tragic Fate of Kalamatiano: America's Man in Moscow', *International Journal of Intelligence and Counter-intelligence*, 12/3 (1999), 346–74, and David S. Foglesong, 'Xenophon Kalamatiano: An American Spy in revolutionary Russia', *Intelligence and National Security*, 6/1 (January 1991), 154–95. In most published sources, the name of the French intelligence agent is given as 'Henri de Vetrement', which is incorrect.

36. Long, 'Sidney Reilly', 1233–4.

37. SHD/T, 6 N 233 (all 'N' numbers are from the archives of the Ministry of War). Apart from being a *Figaro* correspondent, Marchand was also Agent officieux de Consulat Général de France à Moscou. He was shocked by what he had heard and after a discussion with Captain Jacques Sadoul of the French military mission decided to send a letter to the French president Raymond Poincaré describing every detail of the meeting. According to Marcel Body, Sadoul also advised him to inform Trotsky, the newly appointed commissar of war (see M. Body, *Un piano en bouleau de Carelie: Mes annees de Russia 1917-1927* [Paris: Hachette, 1981], 82). That was quite in line with the Ministry of War's ongoing support for a rapprochement with the Bolsheviks. For details, see Michael Jabara Carley, 'The Origins of the French Intervention in the Russian Civil War, January-May 1918: A Reappraisal', *The Journal of Modern History*, 48/3 (September 1976), 413–39. Marchand was not the only Frenchman in Moscow with pro-Bolshevik views. Sadoul, initially a socialist, had been assigned to the French military mission in Moscow and established close contacts with both Lenin and Trotsky to the extent of becoming a Red Army instructor. Both Marchand and Sadoul subsequently joined the Russian Communist Party and the newly created Groupe Communiste Français de Moscou, together with another member of the French Military Mission Pierre Pascal (RGASPI, f. 495, op. 270, d. 6147, ll. 63-65), who closely collaborated with the Cheka. Other prominent members were Henri Guilbeaux, Marcel Body and Suzanne Girault. For details about Marchand, see Yulia M. Galkina, 'The French Journalist René Marchand: Some Facts about "Soviet Russia's Friend"', *RUDN Journal of Russian History*, 18/1 (February 2019), 85–100. For details about Pascal, see Jonathan Beecher, 'Making and Unmaking of a French Christian Bolshevik: The Soviet Years of Pierre Pascal', *The Journal of Modern History*, 87/1 (March 2015), 1–35.

38. SHD/T, 6 N 221, Attaché Militaire à Ministre Guerre, Moscou, 10 Octobre 1918. Now the building is the Italian embassy in Moscow.

39. Smith, *Six*, 233.

40. TsA FSB, The Trust File no. 302330, vol. 37, page 241, quoted by Cook, *On His Majesty's Secret Service*, 151.

41. See Peter Day, *Trotsky's Favourite Spy: The Life of George Alexander Hill* (London: Biteback, 2017), 67, 73, 128.

42. Karsavina had been Benji's mistress since 1915 and their son Nikita was born in 1916. They were finally married in June 1918. See Tamara Karsavina, *Theatre Street: The Reminiscences of Tamara Karsavina* (London: Heinemann, 1930).

43. Smith, *Six*, 233–7. On 12 February 1919 Supplement to the *London Gazette* published His Majesty's rewards for distinguished services naming among others Lieutenant Ernest Thomas Boyce RNVR, Sub-Lieutenant Gerald James Gillespie RNVR, T/Captain Henry Landau (OBE Military Division), T/Lieutenant Ernest Albert Llewellyn Dalton (OBE Military Division), Lieutenant George Alexander Hill RAF (MC), and 2nd Lieutenant Sydney George Reilly RAF (MC).

Chapter 3: The Russian Civil War, Foreign Intervention, the Fate of the Romanovs, and British-American Intelligence

1. In his letter to Winston Churchill, then Minister of Munitions, Lloyd George argued, 'An expensive war of aggressions against Russia is a way to strengthen Bolshevism in Russia and create it at home'. The Prime Minister further stressed, 'We cannot afford the burden … if we are committed to a war against a continent like Russia, it is the road to bankruptcy and Bolshevism in these islands'. Lloyd George to Churchill, Churchill papers, 16/20, in Martin Gilbert, *Winston S. Churchill, Finest Hour 147: Coalition Foiled 1918, "A Plain of War Against the Bolsheviks"*, 24.
2. For details, see TNA FO 175/1-29, and WO 158/737-42.
3. Tsa FSB, d. 28253, ll. 2, 6-7, 35. See also V. Vinogradov, A. Litvin and V. Khristoforov, *The VCheka Archive* (Moscow: Kuchkovo pole, 2007), 677.
4. For the Soviet press coverage of the uprising, see *Izvestia*, 8, 9 and 10 July 1918. For details, see Alfred Erich Senn and Harold J. Goldberg, 'The Assassination of Count Mirbach', *Canadian Slavonic Papers*, 21/4 (December 1979), 438–45; and Lutz Hafner, 'The Assassination of Count Mirbach and the "July Uprising" of the Left Socialist Revolutionaries in Moscow, 1918', *The Russian Review*, 50/3 (July 1991), 324–44. The European newspapers immediately after the abortive rising reported mass executions in Moscow, which was an exaggeration. The reprisals, as Leggett noted, were relatively lenient. For Alexandrovich's personal details, TsA FSB: No. N-8, vols. 9 and 19.
5. Published in *Izvestia*, no. 141, 18 July 1918. Source: *Lenin's Collected Works*, 4th English Edition (Moscow: Progress Publishers, 1972), Volume 27, pages 534–5.
6. George Katkov, 'The Assassination of Count Mirbach', *Soviet Affairs*, 3 (1962), 53–93, in St Antony's Papers Number 12, edited by David Footman.
7. The Minister in Moscow (Mirbach) to the State Secretary (Richard von Kühlmann, Außenstaatssekretär), 25 June 1918, reproduced in Z.A.B. Zeman (ed.), *Germany and the Revolution in Russia, 1915-1918* (London: Oxford University Press, 1958), doc. 136, 137–8.
8. *Dnevniki imperatora Nikolaia II*, 625, quoted in Donald J. Raleigh (ed.) and A.A. Iskenderov (compl.), *The Emperors and Empresses of Russia: Discovering the Romanovs* (Armonk, NY: M.E. Sharpe, 1996), 396.
9. See, for example, Yakov Yurovsky, 'Confessions of an Executioner', *Istochnik* (historical supplement to *Rodina* magazine), 0 (1993), 108–16.
10. For example, Robert Wilton, *The Last Days of the Romanovs: From 15 March, 1917* (London: Thornton Butterworth Ltd, 1920), later published as George Gustav Telberg and Robert Wilton, *The Last Days of the Romanovs* (2013); Robert K. Massie, *The Romanovs: The Final Chapter* (New York, NY: Random House, 1995); Mark D. Steinberg and Vladimir M. Khrustalev, *The Fall of the Romanovs: Political Dreams and Personal Struggles in a Time of Revolution* (New Haven and London: Yale University Press, 1995); Wendy Slater, *The Many Deaths of Tsar Nicholas II: Relics, Remains and the Romanovs* (Abington, Oxon: Routledge, 2007); Helen Rappaport, *The Last Days of the Romanovs: Tragedy at Ekaterinburg* (New York, NY: St. Martin's Press, 2009), as well as *The Race to Save the Romanovs: The Truth Behind the Secret Plans to Rescue the Russian*

Imperial Family (New York, NY: St. Martin's Press, 2018); and, finally, Greg King and Penny Wilson, *The Romanovs Adrift* (East Richmond Heights, CA: Eurohistory and Kensington House Books, 2018).

11. Sir Thomas Preston had served as British Consul in Yekaterinburg, Vladivostok and Leningrad between 1918 and 1922. See his 'Reminiscences of ten years chaos in Russia', 1916-1928 (no date), with photographs, University of Leeds Special Collections, GB 206 Liddle Collection RUS 37.

12. For the English edition, see Nicholas A. Sokolov, *The Sokolov Investigation*, Translation and Commentary by John F. O'Conor (London: Souvenir Press, 1972). According to Robert Massie, one of the biographers of the Romanovs, the evidence collected by the Sokolov Commission was packed into a box, whose contents Sokolov referred to as the 'Great National Sacred Relics' having travelled with it across Siberia to Vladivistok. From there, he and his wife sailed for Europe with a White officer, Colonel Cyril Naryshkin, aboard the French ship *André le Bon* travelling 8,000 miles with the box under Mme Naryshkina's bunk. When they finally arrived in Venice, Sokolov and Naryshkin went together to the French Riviera to present the box to Nicholas II's cousin Grand Duke Nikolai Nikolayevich, whom most Russians in emigration regarded as the most suitable successor to the Russian throne. To Sokolov's dismay, the Grand Duke refused to accept the box. Sokolov then allegedly travelled to England, attempting to present the box to the former Russian tsar's first cousin King George V. In Massie's words, the king also did not want it. 'Eventually,' he writes, 'Sokolov gave the box for safekeeping to the Russian Orthodox Church Abroad.' See Robert K. Massie, *The Romanovs: The Final Chapter* (London: Head of Zeus, 2016), 133-5. Unfortunately, any reference to author's sources for these claims is missing. In his turn, refererring to the press conference at the TASS-Ural News Agency on 16 July 2008, Andrew Cook states that 'the Sokolov papers had been passed on by the investigator to Count Orlov'. In reality, Prince Vladimir Orlov inherited the archive after Sokolov's death in 1920 and they were later auctioned by Sotheby's. The auction took place in London on 5 April 1990 under the title 'The Romanovs: Documents and Photographs Relating to the Russian Imperial House', thirty-nine lots plus one describing the Sokolov archive estimated at £350,000 – 550,000. According to Cook, the records were acquired by Hans Adam II, Prince of Lichtenstein, who passed them on to the State Archive of the Russian Federation (GARF). See Andrew Cook, *The Murder of the Romanovs* (Stroud, Gloucestershire: Amberley, 2010), 225-6. Interviewed at his home in Vaduz in August 1998, Baron Eduard von Falz-Fein, one of Putin's admirers, told this writer that it was thanks to his efforts that these documents were handed over to Russia. Falz-Fein and Putin met in Moscow at the first Congress of Russian Compatriots Living Abroad in October 2001.

13. Slater, *The Many Deaths of Tsar Nicholas II*, 152–4. The author taught Russian history as a Fellow of Trinity Hall, Cambridge, and then as lecturer in Contemporary Russian History at the School of Slavonic and East European Studies, UCL.

14. See Andrei Pliguzov and Abby Smith, 'Nicholas and Alexandra: Unpublished Romanov Documents are in LC's Law Library', *Library of Congress Information Bulletin*, 55/2 (February 1996), 27–9. Georgy Gustavovich Telberg (September 1881, Tsaritsyn, Saratovsky Gub., Russia – February 1954, New York) deposited the documents at the Law Library in 1953.

15. Sergei Medvedev and Robert Coalson, 'Lenin at 150: Even Without COVID-19, Russia Was Set to Snub the Soviet Union's Founder', RFE/RF, 21 April 2020.

16. Cf. Jeffery, *MI6*, 172.

17. David S. Foglesong, *America's Secret War Against Bolshevism* (Chapel Hill, NV: University of North Carolina Press, 1995), 114–25. See also Susan M. Stein, *On Distant Service: The*

Life of the First U.S. Foreign Service Officer to be Assassinated (Lincoln, NE: University of Nebraska Press/Potomac Books, 2020), 71–94.

18. See Elizabeth Atwood, *The Liberation of Marguerite Harrison: America's First Female Intelligence Agent* (Annapolis, MD: Naval Institute Press, 2020). Liz Atwood is a former newspaper reporter and editor, later an associate professor of journalism at Hood College in Frederick, Maryland. In her excellent research on American journalist spies in the Soviet Russia of the 1920s, Dr Atwood wrote about Marguerite Harrison, who, like herself, worked for the *Baltimore Sun*, and several other lesser-known figures like Weston Estes, Albert Boni and Constance 'Stan' Harding.

19. Marguerite Harrison, *Marooned in Moscow: The Story of an American Woman Imprisoned in Soviet Russia* (Montpelier, VT: Russian Life Books/Russian Information Services, 2011), 232.

20. Harding was not the only foreign correspondent betrayed by Harrison. Her declassified files show, for example, that she also handed over to the GPU Weston B. Estes, an American who was indeed in touch with the MID, saying that while pretending to be a Washington reporter he was an American spy. The same concerns John Flick, his photographer, who was unaware of Estes's intelligence connection. See TsA FSB RF, combined file Marguerite B. Harrison R-47767 (21 October 1920 – July 1921). As a result, the GPU detained both. They were finally released on 6 August 1921, a year after their arrest.

21. See Melanie King, *The Lady is a Spy: The Tangled Lives of Stan Harding and Marguerite Harrison* (London: Ashgrove Publishing, 2019). See also Stan Harding, *The Underworld of State* (London: George Allen & Unwin Ltd., 1925). Two years after her release, speaking in the House of Commons, Sir Burton Charwick asked the Under-Secretary of State for Foreign Affairs 'whether His Majesty's Government is in possession of information to the effect that Mrs. Marguerite Harrison was arrested by the Soviet authorities as an American spy and obtained her release by consenting to act as a Soviet spy and, further, to the effect that in her capacity of Soviet informer she was responsible for the false imprisonment of Mrs. Stan Harding, a British journalist; and whether His Majesty's Government has taken any steps to secure redress from the United States Government for the misdeeds of its agent?' HANSARD, Volume 159: debated on Wednesday, 29 November 1922. Under the pressure of the British government, following her release Harding received £3,000 compensation from the Bolsheviks. See Russia No. 1 (1922), *Correspondence with the Russian Soviet Government Respecting the Imprisonment of Mrs. Stan Harding in Russia*, Presented to Parliament by Command of His Majesty (London: HMSO, 1922). Then, with the support of 200 cross-party MPs in the British Parliament, she attempted to sue the US government for employing Harrison, who had falsely denounced her.

22. G.A. Belov et al, *Iz Istorii Vserossiiskoi Chrezvychainoi Komissii, 1917-1921*. Collection of Documents (Moscow: Political Literature, 1958), 444, doc. 332.

23. NARA, Report 1807 dictated by agent "B" to T. Worthington Holiday, 2 August 1921; and Report 2190, 'Russia: Current conditions by B', 10 August 1921, both File 2070-2117, RG 165 (War Department General Staff), Military Intelligence Division, microfilm 1443.

24. Sheldon Bart, 'Remembering the Extraordinary American Woman, who Introduced Western Readers to the Transbaikal', in *Historical Development of the Border Region*, International Scientific-Practical Conference, 26 October 2018, Chita, Part 2, 163; and Svetlana A. Chervonnaya, 'Documentation of the Two Visits of Marguerite Harrison to Soviet Russia in the Archives of Moscow', in *Historical Development of the Border Region*, International Scientific-Practical Conference, 26 October 2018, Chita, Part 2, 159–62.

See also, Marguerite Harrison, *Marooned in Moscow: The Story of an American Woman Imprisoned in Russia* (London: Thornton Butterworth Ltd., 1921), and *There's Always Tomorrow: The Story of a Checkered Life* (New York, NY: Farrar & Rinehart, 1935).

25. Harrison's recollections about meeting Solomon Mogilevsky are also entirely false (*Marooned in Moscow*, 232). Since February 1919 all counter-espionage work was concentrated in the Special Department (Osoby Otdel or OO) VeCheKa, whose governing body was the Collegium. Before its new reorganisation in December that year, its 'active' operational department was headed by Vladimir Iosifovich (born Władysław) Platt (November 1919–August 1920), who was later sent as a GPU representative to the Soviet Far Eastern Republic before Harrison arrived there. Mogilevsky was neither a member of the VChK presidium, as Harrison claims, nor even part of the OO Collegium. After another reorganisation in January 1921, Mogilevsky would become deputy head of the 14th Special Section in charge of counter-intelligence work against the countries of the East. He was appointed chief of Soviet foreign intelligence (INO) on 6 August 1921 serving in this position until 13 May 1922. Two day later he was sent to Tiflis to head the Transcaucasian GPU. Although Mogilevsky is said to have briefly studied at Geneva University in 1905 after he was released on bail from the Okhrana prison, in reality he was spending his time with other Bolsheviks of the Lenin group on the Rue de Carouge in Geneva before returning to Russia at the same time as Lenin, in November 1905, to work undercover carrying out revolutionary propaganda at the Bryansky Metallurgic Plant in Yekaterinoslav, which in December became one of the epicentres of the revolutionary struggle. Mogilevsky quite certainly did not have a 'weakness', as Harrison claims, 'for old French literature' and for François Rabelais in particular. Her arrest warrant on 20 October 1920 was signed by Yagoda as chairman of the Special (Osoby) Department, and by Platt as head of the Secret Department which, like the INO until December 1920, was part of the OO. Harrison was not arrested by a soldier, as she writes, but detained by an OO officer named Glebov at her home, a former mansion of August Roerich at number 10 Maly Kharitonievsky lane now turned into the government guest house for foreign visitors.

26. Marguerite Harrison FSB combined rehabilitation file R-47767, also reproduced in *Marooned in Moscow* (2011), Appendix, 316, without any reference to the source.

27. John Ainsworth, 'Reilly's Reports from South Russia, December 1918-March 1919', *Europe-Asia Studies*, 50/8 (December 1998), 1448–9.

28. TNA: FO 371/3962, Russia Code 38/Code W38 File 93: Reilly's despatch from Sevastopol dated 28 December 1918, f. 364, and from Yekaterinodar, dated 11 January 1919. As John Ainsworth notes in his well-researched article, Allied forces actually were present in South Russia at the time, with troops of the French regiment commanded by Colonel Ruillier arriving on 26 December 1918 to replace 500 Royal Marines who had been landed there earlier. But the troops were never in any position to play the decisive anti-Bolshevik role advocated for them by Reilly.

29. Keith Jeffery, *The British Army and the Crisis of Empire, 1918-22* (Dover, N.H.: Manchester University Press, 1984), 135; Peter Day, *Trotsky's Favourite Spy: The Life of George Alexander Hill* (London: Biteback Publishing, 2017), 79–81. See also Andrew Cook, *On His Majesty's Secret Service: Sidney Reilly, Codename ST1* (Stroud, Gloucestershire, Tempus, 2002), 156–66.

30. TNA: FO 371/3962, Russia Code 38/Code W38 File 93, f. 128: Reilly's despatch no. 13 from Odessa dated 18 February 1919. On 5 March 1919, Walford Selby concluded on behalf of the FO that Reilly's reports (nos. 1-12) contained 'a fund of useful information on the subject of the whole situation in South Russia'. In his dispatch no. 15 from Odessa on 21 February 1919, Reilly requested to be recalled to London because 'only verbal reports can elucidate this intricate situation'.

31. Smith, *Six*, 234.
32. Ibid., 241. In the meantime, back in England in 1924, Gerald Gillespie's Russian wife Maria Andreyeva filed for divorce, TNA: J 77/2139/6988.
33. Jeffery, *MI6*, 175.
34. TNA T 161/30: letter of Paul Dukes to the Foreign Office's PUS Sir Eyre Crowe and Rex Leeper at the with a copy to the HM Treasury, May 1920.
35. In Harry Ferguson's *Operation Kronstadt* (2009), which has been advertised as 'a true story' of Paul Dukes, Petrovskaya is not identified, and in Michael Smith's *Six* her patronymic is erroneously given as 'Ivanovna' (p. 243) instead of 'Vladimirovna'.
36. However, by the decree of the Central Executive Committee (VTsIK) of 28 February 1922 Petrovskaya was pardoned and released because while in the Butyrka prison she had allegedly agreed to collaborate with the Cheka (namely with Agranov and Artuzov). See *Taktichesky Tsentr: Dokumenty i Materialy* (Moscow: ROSSPEN, 2012), 566; see also, GARF: f. 8409, op. 1, d. 233, l. 37. Kürz was also detained but after fully cooperating with the investigation was released. He lived in Moscow working for the foreign department of the State Bank when the OGPU, a successor of the Cheka, arrested him on espionage charges on 26 August 1930. Six months later he was shot.
37. Smith, *Six*, 259–60. See the whole chapter, 'A very useful lady', 257–72.
38. TNA FO 371/4017, Code 38/Code W38 Lockhart to John Duncan Gregory, Senior Clerk in the Foreign Office, 2 May 1919.
39. Jeffery, *MI6*, 174.
40. Victor Loupan and Pierre Lorrain, *L'argent de Moscow. L'histoire la plus secrète de PCF* (Paris: Plon, 1994), Documents 3, 4, 5. See also Chambers, *The Last Englishman*, 292.
41. Andrew and Mitrokhin, *The Mitrokhin Archive I*, 37.
42. Ibid.
43. Józef Unszlicht, who took part in the founding congress of the Comintern and from February 1919 had served as the War Commissar of the Lithuanian-Byelorussian Socialist Republic, was appointed Dzerzhinsky's deputy. Philip Medved, who before the revolution had worked as a construction technician at the Warsaw City Council, headed the Moscow GPU. Stanislaw Messing, a son of a musician and a midwife born in Warsaw, a professional revolutionary with only four classes of primary education, who used to serve as chairman of the Moscow Cheka, became head of the Petrograd GPU. Wacław Menżyński (Vyacheslav Rudolfovish Menzhinsky) studied in a St Petersburg gymnasium together with a future White General Alexander Kolchak, and before the Revolution had lived in France briefly working in the historic French bank Crédit Lyonnais. Between 1918 and 1922 Menzhinsky served as People's Commissar for Finances, member of the Petrograd Cheka, Consul-General in Berlin, and head of the Special (Osoby) department of the Cheka. In the new GPU Menzhinsky headed the so-called Secret-Operational Controllerate or Directorate, which included informational, secret, operational and foreign departments, established in January 1921 within the Cheka. Genrikh Yagoda took part in the Great War, rising to the rank of corporal. Yagoda was a friend of the writer Maxim Gorky and had served in the Petrograd Cheka; in 1919-20 he had been a member of the Collegium of the People's Commissariat for Foreign Trade (NKVT). In the GPU he was appointed head of the Special (Osoby) department. Gleb Boky, born to a good family in Tiflis, in the years after the 1905 revolution had been arrested twelve times for armed robbery. Boky was Lenin's personal friend and from March 1918 had served as deputy to the Petrograd Cheka chairman Uritsky before the latter was assassinated and Boky became his successor. In the GPU he was appointed head of the Special (Cipher) department. There, under great secrecy, Boky organised unconventional research in parapsychology – mind control and remote

influence – studying psychotronic effects on humans. Yakov Peters (Jēkabs Peterss) had served as Dzerzhinsky deputy in the Cheka and headed several prominent investigations of counter-revolutionaries like Savinkov's Union for the Defence of Motherland and Freedom, Ambassadors' (Lockhart) Plot and execution of the Grand Princes, members of the Russian Imperial family in Petrograd. From 1920 to 1922 Peters had served in Soviet Turkestan and was then recalled to Moscow to head the Eastern department of the GPU.

44. Cf. Andrew and Mitrokhin, *The Mitrokhin Archive I*, 37–8. See also, Lenin, *The State and Revolution* (London: Penguin Books, 1992), translated by Robert Service, xix, 80, 82, 89, 90.

Chapter 4: Comintern: Secret Soldiers of the Revolution

1. Before the collapse of the Soviet Union in 1991, both were extensively idolised as the first communist martyrs and revolutionary icons. About Rosa Luxemburg, see Klaus Gietinger, *The Murder of Rosa Luxemburg* (London: Verso, 2019). See also Annelies Laschitza, *Die Liebknechts: Karl und Sophie – Politik und Familie* (Berlin: Aufbau Verlag, 2007).

2. On 1 October 1918 Lenin wrote: 'The international revolution has come so close within the course of one week that we may count on its outbreak during the next few days ... We shall all stake out lives to help the German workers in expediting the revolution about to begin in Germany'. See Thomas T. Hammond and Robert Farrell (eds), *The Anatomy of Communist Takeovers* (New Haven and London: Yale University Press, 1975), 162.

3. Andrew and Gordievsky, *KGB*, 66.

4. James W. Hulse, *The Forming of the Communist International* (Stanford, CA: Stanford University Press, 1964), v–vi.

5. Ibid, 30–1.

6. Jakob Reich ('Comrade Thomas'), 'The First Years of the Communist International', *Revolutionary History*, 5/2 (Spring 1994). Jakob Reich (later Arnold Thomas Rubinstein) was one of the leading Comintern figures, heading its West European Secretariat (WES) in Berlin in 1921. See also Karl Steinhardt, *Lebenserinnerungen eines Wiener Arbeiters* (Vienna: Alfred Klahr Gesellschaft, 2013). Steinhardt was also a delegate at the 2nd, when he was elected member of the ECCI, and 3rd Comintern Congresses. Without doubt he was working for the Comintern's OMS collaborating with both the Cheka/GPU and Soviet military intelligence. In 1922–5 he had worked for the Soviet trade delegation in Hamburg, then in Berlin, and after his expulsion from Germany until November 1928 in Vienna (although this writer could not find supporting documents in the Austrian archives). In 1945–51 Steinhardt had served as a KPÖ deputy of the Vienna State Parliament (Landtag) and City Council (Gemeinderat).

7. For details of his early revolutionary career, see Christian Alexandru Voicu, 'The first communist under surveillance by the Siguranţa: Christian Rakovsky during the First World War (1914-1918)', *Arhivele Totalitarismului*, 14/3-4 (2016), 8–27.

8. Rayfield, *Stalin and His Hangmen*, 68.

9. Radek was born in the city of Lemberg, Austria-Hungary (now Lviv in Ukraine) as Karol Sobelsohn to a Lithuanian Jewish family. In 1917 he was one of the thirty-one revolutionaries who accompanied Lenin in the (in)famous sealed train from Zurich to Petrograd in April 1917. Lockhart's memoirs provide several portraits of the key Bolshevik figures of the time, one of the most colourful being Radek. 'He was in some respect a grotesque figure,' Lockhart recalled. 'A little man with a huge head, protruding ears, clean shaven face [...], with spectacles and a large mouth with yellow, tobacco

stained teeth, from which a huge pipe or cigar was never absent, he was always dressed in a quaint drab-coloured Norfolk suit with knickers and leggings. He was a great friend of Ransome, and through Ransome we came to know him very well. Almost every day he would turn up in my rooms, an English cap stuck jauntily on his head, his pipe puffing fiercely, a bundle of books under his arm, and a huge revolver strapped to his side' (pp. 183–4). Radek was one of the seventeen defendants at the second Moscow show trial in January 1937 – he and a former commissar for finance were sentenced to 10 years of penal labour while all others were shot. Both were later murdered in their prisons on Stalin's orders. For details, see Nikita Petrov, 'Stalinsky zakaz: Kak ubivali Sikolnikova i Radeka', *Novaya Gazeta*, 40 (5 June 2008) and N.V. Petrov, *The First Chairman of the KGB Ivan Serov* (Moscow: Materik, 2005), in Russian.

10. Dan N. Jacobs, *Borodin: Stalin's Man in China* (Cambridge: Harvard University Press, 1981), 60–1. See also, Lazar and Victor Kheyfetz, 'Mikhail Borodin: The First Comintern Emissary to Latin America (Part One)', *The International Newsletter of Historical Studies on Comintern, Communism and Stalinism*, 2/5-6 (1994–5), 145–9.

11. The document file relating to the incident is in the Swiss State Archive (Schweizerische Bundesarchiv, BAR) in Bern, Reference code E21#1000/131#10540 'Erhebung betr. bolschewistischen Finanzquellen, Herstellung von Falschgeld, Passfälschungen, falschen Arztzeugnissen', 1919 – 1920, File reference 06.2.3.2-1. I am grateful to Guido Koller from the BAR for helping to locate the documents.

12. RGASPI, f. 495, op. 1, d. 1, l. 29.

13. RGASPI, f. 498, op. 1, d. 1, ll. 1-4.

14. RGASPI, f. 495, op. 1, d. 1a, l. 12.

15. RGASPI: f .497, op. 2, d. 8, Rutgers (G.L. Trotter) to Jan A. Berzin (Winter), 9 March 1920.

16. About the Amsterdam Bureau, see Gerritt Voerman, 'Proletarian Competition: The Amsterdam Bureau and its German Counterpart, 1919-1920', *Jahrbuch für Historische Kommunismusforschung*, (Berlin: Aufbau Verlag, 2007), 201–20. See also Hulse, *The Forming of the Communist International*, 152–60.

17. RGASPI: f .499, op. 1, d. 1.

18. Eric Homberger, *John Reed* (Manchester: Manchester University Press, 1990), 202–15.

19. For details, see William D. Haywood, *The Autobiography of Big Bill Haywood: The story of his life and of the Industrial Workers of the World* (New York, NY: International Publishers, 1929), latest paperback edition May 2020. See also "Big Bill" Haywood Weds: Can't Speak Russian and Russian Wife Can't Speak English', *The New York Times*, 14 January 1927, 4.

20. Already at the First Congress the question of the liberation of the colonies was discussed. The Trotsky's view was that this liberation was conditional upon the political victory of the working class in the metropolis while Bukharin stressed that the rebellion in the colonies hastened the collapse of imperialism. See Sobhanlal Datta Gupta, *Comintern and the Destiny of Communism in India, 1919-1943* (Kolkata: Seribaan, 2006).

21. Victor Madeira, '"No Wishful Thinking Allowed": Secret Service Committee and Intelligence Reform in Great Britain, 1919-23', *Intelligence and National Security*, 18/1 (Spring 2003), 2. There was, of course, nothing new about it. Already at the end of the nineteenth century a number of influential men in the British government like, for example, Colonial Secretary Joseph Chamberlain and First Lord of the Treasury Arthur J. Balfour believed that it was not Germany but Russia that presented the greatest threat to the Empire. 'Russian imperialism,' Thomas Fergusson writes, 'was now perceived as a menace to British interests, not only in the Near East and India, but in the Far East as well'. However, it was not a big concern for the Foreign Office until the Russian

occupation of Port Arthur in December 1897. According to the same author and other experts of the period, 'the principal objectives of Britain's China policy, beginning in 1898, was to check the consolidation of Russia's control over Manchuria and to prevent her southward expansion'. Thomas G. Fergusson, *British Military Intelligence, 1870-1914* (Frederick, MD: University Publications of America, 1984), 198–9. See also, C.J. Lowe, *The Reluctant Imperialists: British Foreign Policy 1878-1902*, 2 vols. (London: Routledge & Kegan Paul, 1967), I, 230-3.

22. Long to Lloyd George, 18 Nov. 1918, Wiltshire Record Office, Long MSS, quoted in Christopher Andrew, *Secret Service: The Making of the British Intelligence Community* (London: Heinemann, 1985), 232.

23. Andrew, *Secret Service*, 232.

24. TNA: WO 32/21380 Secret service: revision of machinery. See also Gill Bennett, 'The Secret Service Committee, 1919-1931', in *The Records of the Permanent Undersecretary's Department: Liaison Between the Foreign Office and British Secret Intelligence, 1873-1939* (London: FCO, March 2005), 42–53.

25. TNA: KV 4/151, Security Service Organisation 1918-1939: Reports of the Secret Service Committee 1919-1923, Minutes of third meeting, 4 April 1919.

26. D. Shoenberg, 'Piotr Leonidovich Kapitza, 9 July 1894-8 April 1984', *Biographical Memoirs of Fellows of the Royal Society*, 31 (Nov. 1985), 326–74. See also, J.W. Boag, P.E. Rubinin and D. Shoenberg, *Kapitza in Cambridge and Moscow: Life and Letters of a Russian Physicist* (Amsterdam: North-Holland Elsevier Science Publishers, 1990).

27. TNA: KV 2/777, Personal File Pyotr L. KAPITZA PF3893, 1923 May 18 – 1940 Nov 1921, also quoted in Andrew, *The Defence of the Realm*, 167–8. The author erroneously states that Kapitza came to work at the Cavendish Laboratory in 1924.

28. Andrew, *Secret Service*, 282.

29. TNA CAB 21/173, Trading relations with Russia, 2 Sept. 1920. See also, Madeira, '"No Wishful Thinking Allowed"', 8–13.

30. Andrew and Mitrokhin, *The Mitrokhin Archive I*, 37.

31. Ibid.

32. Ibid.

33. TsA FSB (former TsA KGB), f. 1, op. 3, d. 13, l. 1.

34. The Papers of Vasiliy Mitrokhin, GBR/0014/MITN, Churchill College, Cambridge, vol. 6, ch. 5, part 1, n. 1, quoted in Andrew and Mitrokhin, *The Mitrokhin Archive I*, 752, n. 27.

35. Carter Elwood, *The Non-Geometric Lenin: Essays on the Development of the Bolshevik Party 1910-1914* (London and New York: Anthem Press, 2011), 118–19.

36. AP RF, f. 3, op. 24, d. 408, ll. 144-67, in V. Haustov, V. Naumov and N. Poltnikova (eds), *Lubyanka: Stalin i Glavnoe Upravlenie Gosbezopasnosti NKVD 1937-1938* (Moscow: Materik, 2004), 531.

37. By the VChK order no. 277 of 2 December 1921, its Foreign Department (INO) was reorganised as follows: Solomon G. Mogilevsky, head of INO; Ivan A. Apeter – deputy head; Roman A. Pillayr (Baron Romuald Ludwig Pilar von Pilchau) and Meer A. Trilisser – assistants to the head; foreign section – Trilisser, information (osvedomitelnaya) section – Lev B. Zalin (Zalman Markovich Levi), head, and Vasili F. Vysotsky – deputy head; visa section – Nikolai F. Ugarov.

38. Andrew and Mitrokhin, *The Mitrokhin Archive I*, 40.

39. As commented on the Quora site by Alexander Finnegan, 'The term "class enemy" or "enemy of the people" has a long origin, going back to Roman times. Later it was used during the French Revolution to refer to those who were on the side of the aristocracy and the rich against the rule by the people. In the Soviet Union the term was formalized

in the penal code to refer to people engaging in counter-revolutionary activities. These things ranged from sabotage to treason. Punishment for violating the laws also varied, depending on the crimes committed. In the U.S. an analogous term would be treason, which is punishable by death under federal law.'

40. In his comment to the Special Department (Osoby Otdel) report on the situation in England based on the information provided by Ransome, Lenin wrote: 'In my opinion, this is very important and probably basically true. Politically, no doubt, the main thesis is correct.' TsPA IML, f. 2, op. 1, d. 26237 quoted in Tsvigun et al, *Lenin i VCheka: Sbornik Dokumentov 1917-1922* (Moscow: Izdatelstvo politicheskoi literatury, 1975), 440. A note to Dzerzhinsky and comment on the Cheka report dated (on or after) 23 March 1921. About Ransome and SIS, see the previous chapter.

41. Victor Madeira, 'Moscow's Interwar Infiltration of British Intelligence, 1919-1929', *The Historical Journal*, 46/4 (December 2003), 919. See also TNA KV 2/1016 (PF 555,331).

Chapter 5: The Looting of Russia

1. When this chapter was first edited on 7 November 2020, Russia celebrated the 103th anniversary of the Bolshevik revolution with Gennady Zyuganov, Chairman of the Central Committee of the Communist Party of Russia and Member of the State Duma, making a speech in front of the Lenin Mausoleum in Moscow after a memorial flower-laying ceremony. The speech was entitled 'Great October – the most important public holiday of our planet'. 'There has been nothing more magnificent on the planet over the past 300 years than the Great October [25 October O.S. = 7 November 1917 N.S.]', Zyuganov said. 'The Russian Empire, disintegrated and burnt down in the First World War, reassembled thanks to the genius of Vladimir Ilyich Lenin. Nicholas II dragged Russia into this carnage only to protect the money and fortunes of the bankers in London, Paris and New York . . We must learn from those who managed to create our great powerful country. And the greatest Russia was under the leadership of Lenin and Stalin. Thanks to the reforms of Brezhnev and Kosygin. It was the most powerful, number one for aerospace, the best country in the world.'

2. Lenin, *Collected Works* (Moscow: Progress Publishers, 1972), vol. 26, 453–82.

3. See Joseph A. Schlesinger, 'The Primary Goals of Political Parties: A Clarification of Positive Theory', *The American Political Science Review*, 69/3 (Sept. 1975), 849. For a detailed and fascinating study of the revolutionary developments in Russia since 1825, see Feliks Gross, *The Seizure of Political Power in a Century of Revolution* (New York, NY: Philosophical Library, 1958).

4. Sean McMeekin, *History's Greatest Heist: The Looting of Russia by the Bolsheviks* (New Haven and London. Yale University Press, 2009), 6–7.

5. See Andrew and Gordievsky, *KGB*, 70.

6. Vasiliy Mitrokhin, *"Chekisms": A KGB Anthology* (London: The Yurasov Press, 2008), xviii

7. Norman Stone, *Europe Transformed, 1878-1919* (Hoboken, NJ: John Wiley & Sons, 1999), 143.

8. McMeekin, *History's Greatest Heist*, xvii.

9. Ibid., xvi–xvii. For the seven-year period after 2013, the Russian Central Bank has been the largest buyer of gold, moving Russia to the fifth place among countries with largest gold reserves. As usual, before sanctions were imposed on her for the invasion of Crimea, Russia would regularly turn to the West to compensate for its own dysfunctional machinery sector, putting serious constraints on her defence capabilities. In 2013 Russia imported dual-use goods worth 20 billion euros, according to the European Council for Foreign Relations. Remarkably, in 2019 Russia sold and Britain bought $5.33 billion

worth of Russian gold, or 93 per cent of Russia's total gold exports. Nevertheless, according to the World Gold Council, gold reserves in Russia increased to 2299.90 tons in July 2020 from 2206.99 tons in July of the previous year. By the time of the Axis invasion of the Soviet Union, the Soviet gold holdings reached their historical maximum of 2,800 tons. According to the head of the Chief Directorate of the Western Gold Industry, at the end of 1940 the total gold reserves of the USSR were the largest in the world. CIA, Office of Research and Reports, 'Soviet gold production, reserves and exports through 1954', CIA/SC/RR 121, 17 October 1955, 18–28 (p. 20).

10. McMeekin, *History's Greatest Heist*, xvii–xviii.

11. M.J. Larsons, *An Expert in the Service of the Soviet* (London: Benn, 1929), 61–2. The author of the book, also published in German and Russian, was a former deputy head of the foreign exchange department of the Narkomfin. Two months after Tsar Nicholas II's abdication from the Russian throne, on 12 May 1917, the *New York Times* published an article 'Won't Let Czar Go: Ex-Imperial Family's Wealth Put at $9,000,000' which, some believe, was probably an exaggeration (this would be the equivalent of nearly a trillion dollars today).

12. Donald J. Raleigh (ed.) and A.A. Iskenderov (compl.), *The Emperors and Empresses of Russia: Rediscovering the Romanovs* (Armonk, NY: M.E. Sharpe, 1996), 397, 402. See also Richard J. Aldrich and Rory Cormac, *The Secret Royals: Spying and the Crown, from Victoria to Diana* (London: Atlantic Books, 2021), 183.

13. See Olga Ivshina, 'To save important persons: How British intelligence tried to get Nicholas II out of Russia', BBC, 18 December 2021. The article was also published in English by Paul Gilbert.

14. Aldrich and Cormac, *The Secret Royals*, 186–9.

15. GARF, f. 130, op. 23, d. 13, ll. 58-59.

16. Karl Marx, *Capital: A Critique of Political Economy*, English translation 1887 (Moscow: Progress Publishers, 1977), vol. I, ch. 32.

17. Richard Halliburton, *Seven League Boots: Adventures Across the World* (London: Geoffrey Bles, 1937), 'The Massacre of the Romanovs', 79–121 (p. 83).

18. Ibid, 109–10.

19. McMeekin, *History's Greatest Heist*, 43–4. See also, Veniamin Alexeyev, *Gibel tsarskoi sem'i: Mify i realnost* (Yekaterinburg: BPI, 1993), 139–40; Yurovsky, 'Confessions of an Executioner', 112–13; as well as the latest and most comprehensive account based on the archival sources, V.N. Burobin (ed.) and L.A. Lykova (compl.), *Ubiistvo imperatora Nikolaya II, ego sem'i i lits ikh okruzheniya* (Moscow: Belyi gorod, 2015), 2 vols.

20. Yevgeny Zhirnov, 'O roli "Rolls-Roysa" v rossiiskoi istorii', *Kommersant Den'gi*, 10 (15 March 2004), 98.

21. 'The Work of Arcos', *Russian Information and Review*, 1/1 (October 1921), 19.

22. See the Gokhran files, Russian Government Archive of the Economy (RGAE), f. 7632, op. 1, d. 4, l. 8, cited in McMeekin, *History's Greatest Heist*, 235. The Russian State Treasury was established by a decree of Peter the Great dated 11 December 1719.

23. Mitrokhin, *"Chekisms"*, 4. On 18 March 1921 VChK foreign sections were established in Petrograd, Sevastopol, Astrakhan, Pskov, Smolensk, Kharkov, Kiev, Baku, Tashkent and other places. At the same time, the first overseas stations were opened in Poland, Lithuania, Latvia, Estonia, Finland, Turkey (following the Treaty of Moscow signed on 16 March), Afghanistan and Germany, where a special working group for Russia, Sondergruppe R, had been created within the Reichswehr Ministry and greatly expanded by early 1921, well before the Treaty of Rapallo.

24. A. Kokurin and N. Petrov (compilers), A.N. Yakovlev (ed.), *Lubyanka: Organy VChKa-OGPU-NKVD-NKGB-MGB-MVD-KGB, 1917-1991* (Moscow: MFD, 2003), 20–1. Administrative Order (AOU) no. 9 of 14 January 1921. The SOU consisted of three

departments – (1) operational, (2) special and (3) secret. Menzhinsky, Yagoda and Artuzov headed the special department comprised of four sections: (13) counter-intelligence work against Finland, Estonia, Latvia, Lithuania, Poland and Romania; (14) counter-intelligence work against the countries of the Middle East [including the South Caucasus]; (15) counter-intelligence work against the Allied Powers, known in Russia as the 'Big Entente'; (16) counter-intelligence work in the Red Army, section headed by Yakov Agranov; (17) counter-intelligence work against the former Tsarist officers. The task of Section 6 of the 3rd secret department was 'work against the clergy'.

25. Ibid, Order (UD) no. 19 of 25 January 1921. Special section 3 to deal with foreign trade and foreign concessions and special section 6 with gold, hard currency and other valuables.

26. McMeekin, *History's Greatest Heist*, 171. About the agreement, see M.V. Glenny, 'The Anglo-Soviet Trade Agreement, March 1921', *Journal of Contemporary History*, 5/2 (1970), 63–82.

27. About Krasin, see Timothy Edward O'Connor, *The Engineer of Revolution: L.B. Krasin and the Bolsheviks, 1870-1926* (London: Routledge, 1992), 86–9; McMeekin, *History's Greatest Heist*, 57–8, 168–84; Yuri Felshtinsky, *L.B. Krasin: Letters to his Wife and Children, 1917-1926*, 'Introduction' (2003), in Russian; Dmitri Volkogonov, *Lenin: A New Biography* (New York, NY: Free Press, 1994), 55; and S.S. Khromov, *Leonid Krasin: Unknown Facts of Biography* (Moscow: IRI RAN, 2001), in Russian. See also Mikhail V. Khodjakov, *Money of the Russian Revolution, 1917-1920* (Newcastle upon Tyne: Cambridge Scholars Publishing, 2014).

28. RGAE, f. 7632, op. 1, d. 1, L. 1, the decree signed by Lenin on 3 February 1920. Vladimir Anichkov, who headed the Volga-Kama Commercial Bank Yekaterinburg Branch before the Revolution, recalls that many famous Bolsheviks, including Krestinsky, were 'extremely ignorant' in finances. In his memoirs Anichkov mentions a meeting of Yekaterinburg bankers with Krestinsky, a local Soviet executive committee member at that time where the future People's Commissar of Finances admitted that he 'was never engaged in financial matters before'. Vladimir P. Anichkov, *Yekaterinburg-Vladivostok, 1917-1922* (Moscow, Russkiy Put, 1998), 64–5. After the murder of the Romanov family Anichkov moved first to Vladivostok and then via Shanghai to San-Francisco where he settled and opened the first Russian bookshop.

29. See McMeekin, *History's Greatest Heist*, 63–9.

30. Old Kazan gold reserves that became known in the Soviet historiography as the 'Kolchak gold' of about 270 tons, $210 million worth. Kolchak was then shot on 20 February 1920 after a brief interrogation and a proletarian trial.

31. RGAE, f. 7733, op. 1, d. 814, l. 10, report to Rabkrin, 14 February 1923, quoted in McMeekin, *History's Greatest Heist*, 68. See also N.G.O. Pereira, 'White Power During the Civil War in Siberia (1918-1920): Dilemmas of Kolchak's "War Anti-Communism"', *Canadian Slavonic Papers*, 29/1 (March 1987), 45–62.

32. N.P. Obukhov, 'Dvizhenie zolotogo zapasa Rossii v 1921-1933 godakh', *Finansy*, 6 (2002), 6870.

33. RGAE, f. 7632, op. 1, d. 12, l. 2 (verso), cited in McMeekin, *History's Greatest Heist*, 65–7.

34. Obukhov, 'Dvizhenie zolotogo zapasa Rossii', 68.

35. For details, see Arthur Ponsonby, 'The Anglo-Soviet Treaties of 1924: Recital of Events Which Led to Their Final Conclusion', *Journal of the Royal Institute of International Affairs*, 5/3 (May 1926), 150–4.

36. Anne Odom and Wendy R. Salmond (eds), *Treasures into Tractors: The Selling of Russia's Cultural Heritage, 1918-1938* (Washington, DC: Hillwood Museum & Gardens, 2009), 185–93.

37. See McMeekin, *History's Greatest Heist*, 216–7; Odom and Salmond (ed.), *Treasures into Tractors*, 190–3; and Waltraud Bayer (ed.), *Verkaufte Kultur: Die sowjetischen Kunst- und Antiquitätenexporte, 1919-1938* (Frankfurt-am-Main: Peter Lang, 2001).
38. 'In a curiously sinister twist,' McMeekin adds, 'Mellon was Treasury secretary at the time, responsible for enforcing American antidumping laws against the Soviet Union. Far from regretting this stunning display of hypocrisy, Mellon claimed his Soviet art purchases as charitable deductions on his income tax returns for 1931.' McMeekin, *History's Greatest Heist*, 218–20; Robert C. Williams, *Russian Art and American Money, 1900-1940* (Cambridge: Harvard University Press, 1980), 173. Probably, the 1933 sale in the New York department store Lord & Taylor is meant, and indeed the collection did contain at least some items which had belonged to the last emperor – in 1930 eleven Fabergé Easter eggs were issued to Hammer from the Kremlin Armoury. See Natalya Semyonova and Nicolas Iljin (eds), *Selling Russia's Treasures* (New York, NY: Abbeville Press Publishers, 2013), 260–88 (p. 268).
39. Matt Stoller, *Goliath: The 100-year War Between Monopoly Power and Democracy* (New York, NY: Simon & Schuster, 2019), 50.
40. McMeekin, *History's Greatest Heist*, 7.

Chapter 6: Disinformburo and Early Deception Operations

1. Also translated as 'Successful war follows the path of Deception'. And about using spies in deception operations, Sun Tzu preaches, 'When you find the enemy's agents spying on you, offer them bribes, lavish care on them and lodge them handsomely. Thus they may become converted spies and be of use to you. It is through these converted spies that you will be able to recruit local spies and internal spies. It is through them that your expendable spies will feed false reports to the enemy'. Sun Tzu, *The Art of War*, 11 and 95.
2. Michael I. Handel, 'Intelligence and Deception', *Journal of Strategic Studies*, 5/1 (1982), 122–54 (p. 122).
3. AP RF, f. 3, op. 58, d. 2, ll. 131-2, dated 22 December 1922.
4. Tadeusz Jędruszczak and Maria Nowak-Kiełbikowa (eds), *Dokumenty z dziejów polskiej polityki zagranicznej 1918-1939*, vol. I 1918–1932 (Warsaw, 1989), 183. Polish head of state Marshal Józef Piłsudski wrote about Matuszweski, one of his close collaborators at the time who, as the Polish intelligence chief, also took part in the talks leading to the 1921 Treaty of Riga: 'It was the first war since many centuries waged by Poland during which we [Poland] knew more about the enemy than the enemy knew about us.' In September 1939 Matuszweski, together with his wife and a friend, organised the evacuation of the 75 tons of Polish gold from the National Bank through Romania, Turkey and Syria to France where they handed it over to the Polish government in exile. Ignacy Matuszewski died in New York in August 1946.
5. See Marek Świerczek, 'Soviet CI activities against the Military Attaché of the Polish Republic in Moscow at the beginning of its functioning in the early twentieth as an exemplification of the Russian counter-espionage modus operandi', *Przegląd Bezpieczeństwa Wewnętrznego/Internal Security Review*, 17 [9] (2017), 393–406.
6. *Almanach de Gotha*, 182nd edition (London: Almanach de Gotha Ltd., 1998), 214. For Kirill's memoirs, see Kirill V. Romanov, *My Life in Russia's Service: Then and Now* (London: Seleyn & Blount, 1939).
7. Dmitry Igorevich Babkov, 'Political Activity and Views of V.V. Shulgin in 1917-1939', MPhil thesis, in Russian (Bryansk State University, 2008), 26. See also V.V. Shulgin, *The Years: Memoirs of a Member of the Russian Duma 1906-1917*, Introduction by Jonathan Sanders, translated by Tanya Davis (New York, NY: Hippocrene Books, 1984).
8. Documents from the FSB archive – investigation file R-48956 (7 Jan 1945 – 12 Nov 2001) and prison file 3569 of Shulgin were published in Moscow by Russky Put'

Publishers in 2010. See also Pascal Fieschi, 'L'intervention français à Odessa (décembre 1918 – mars 1919) vue à travers l'action du "Consul de France", Emile Henno', *Cahiers slaves*, 14 (2016), 161–72.

9. Andrew Cook tries to explain the name of the operation by claiming, without any source reference, that MOR's cover 'was a trust based in Paris by the name of the Moscow Municipal Credit Association' (see Andrew Cook, *On His Majesty's Secret Service*, 190), which doesn't seem a plausible explanation. First, there is no any mention or trace of l'Association de Crédit municipal de Moscou in Paris. Besides, in the 1920s there was only one Soviet financial institution in France – le Banque Commerciale pour l'Europe du Nord (BCEN). It was founded in 1921 by a group of wealthy Russian émigrés who, as a CIA report puts it, 'sold out to Soviet interests in 1925'. See 'Soviet-Owned Banks in the West', CIA Intelligence Report, Directorate of Intelligence, ER-IR 69-28 (declassified), 6.

10. In most sources, the year of publication is erroneously given as '1925'. The book was first published in Russian as *Tri stolitsy: puteshestvie v Krasnuyu Rossiyu* by the publishing house Medny Vsadnik (Bronze Horseman) founded by General Wrangel, Alexey von Lampe and Herzog Georgy Leuchtenberg during their meeting in Seeon in Bavaria in the summer of 1926.

11. Lockhart, *Memoirs of a British Agent*, 194.

12. TNA: KV 2/1903 Personal File PF R301 vol. 1 Arthur Mitchell RANSOME, 1917 Jan 01 – 1920 Dec 31, 'A very useful lady … In order to enable her to leave secretly, I wish to have authority to put her to Mr Ransome's passport as his wife and facilitate her departure via Murmansk', Lockhart to FO, 21 June 1918.

13. Chambers, *The Last Englishman*, 231.

14. Ibid.

15. TNA: KV 2/1903, Scale to SIS, CX 050167, 12 December 1918. Passing through Stockholm on his way home, Lockhart briefed Scale on what Ransom had been doing. Scale is said to have spoken to Ransome again and sent a fresh report to Cumming retracting his previous assessment. In March 1919, Clifford Dyce Sharp, a British journalist with the Secret Service designation S8, posted to Stockholm by the FO under his 'natural' journalistic cover, sent several memos to the head office about Ransome, stating that 'S76 may be regarded as absolutely honest'. Sharp concluded that Ransome's reports about conditions in Russia 'may also be relied upon absolutely with only the proviso that his view tends to be coloured by his personal sympathies with men like Litvinov and Radek', adding that 'he will report what he sees, but he does not see quite straight'. TNA: KV 2/1903 Memorandum from Sharp (S8) re Arthur Ransome (S76) of 17 March 1919. However, the Security Service continued to be suspicious about Ransome, see MI5 memo in the same file dated 27 March 1919. Lockhart wrote about Ransome in his memoirs first published in London in 1932, 'I championed him resolutely against the secret service idiots who later tried to denounce him as a Bolshevik agent' (Lockhart, *Memoirs of a British Agent*, 267).

16. Chambers, *The Last Englishman*, 312.

17. 'Henri Barbusse's novels *Le feu* and *Clarté*,' Lenin wrote, 'may be cited as particularly graphic corroborations of the mass phenomenon, observed everywhere, of the growth of revolutionary consciousness among the masses' (*The Complete Works of Lenin*, 5th ed., vol. 39, 106), in Russian.

18. David James Fisher, *Romain Rolland and the Politics of Intellectual Engagement* (Berkeley, CA: University of California Press, 1988), 89.

19. About Münzenberg, see Sean McMeekin, *The Red Millionaire: A political biography of Willi Münzenberg, Moscow's secret propaganda tsar in the West* (New Haven & London:

Yale University Press 2003). See also Christopher Andrew and Harold James, 'Willi Münzenberg, the Reichstag Trial and the Conversion of the Innocents', in David A. Charters and Maurice A. Tugwell (ed.), *Deception in East-West Relations* (London: Pergamon-Brassey, 1990).

20. Louis Nemzer, 'The Soviet Friendship Societies', *The Public Opinion Quarterly*, 13/2 (Summer 1949), 265–84 (p. 267).

21. Yevgeny Zhirnov, 'Disinformburo: 80 years of the Soviet disinformation service', *Kommersant*, № 2 (13 January 2003), 7, in Russian.

22. Testimonies of Louise Bryant and John Reed, *Bolshevik propaganda: Hearings before a Subcommittee of the Committee on the Judiciary*, United State Senate, Sixty-fifth Congress, third session and thereafter, pursuant to S.Res. 439 and 469, February 11, 1919, to March 10, 1919 (Washington, DC: GPO, 1919), 494, 568–70.

23. Max Eastman, *Heroes I Have Known: Twelve Who Lived Great Lives* (New York, NY: Simon and Schuster, 1942), 223.

24. *The New York Times*, 8 October 1972, Section SM, p.12.

25. Military Intelligence Division (G-2), *Surveillance of Radicals in the United States, 1917–1941*, 35 reels of microfilm, Frederick, MD, n/d, document 10058-94, 10 June 1921. Quoted in Eric Homberger, *John Reed* (Manchester: Manchester University Press, 1990), 237. See also, Daniel W. Lehman, *John Reed and the Writing of Revolution* (Athens, OH: Ohio University Press, 2002).

26. See Sergey Melgunov, *Red Terror in Russia, 1918-1923* (Berlin, 1924), 141; Rayfield, *Stalin and his Hangmen*, 67–8; and Natalia Golysheva, 'Red Terror in the North', BBC Russian Service, 25 December 2017 (in Russian).

27. TsA FSB, f. 1, op. 4, d. 12, l; 1+reverse.

28. About the Tactical Centre, see *Taktichesky Tsentr: Dokumenty i Materialy* (Moscow: ROSSPEN, 2012).

29. About the Union of Regeneration and other anti-Bolshevik underground organisations of the time, see Benjamin Wells, 'The Union of Regeneration: The Anti-Bolshevik Underground in Revolutionary Russia, 1917-1919', unpublished PhD thesis (Queen Mary, University of London, 2004).

30. The Action Centre (Tsentr Deistviya) is not very well known although it had been used in the Soviet disinformation, propaganda and deception programmes several times from 1924, after the first public trials of its members, and until today. The Action Centre was formed in Paris by Nikolai V. Chaikovsky, who arrived there in January 1919 to take part in the Paris Peace Conference. Its representative in Warsaw was Boris Yevreinov (alias 'Hussar'). He maintained contacts with Polish intelligence and arranged secret trips of the Centre's representatives to Soviet Russia and back. Its emissary, journalist Nikolai Vakar ('Zelo' and 'Zelinsky'), visited Russia undercover in March 1922 and set up three support groups of the Centre in Kiev and two in Moscow, returning back to Poland in June. Boris Savinkov and Vasily Shulgin were also collaborating with the Centre whose members in Russia and Ukraine were mainly academics, men of arts and letters, lawyers and generally intelligentsia. The Centre's groups in Russia broke up and ceased to exist after several failures and arrests in the spring of 1923. For details, see Mikhail Sokolov, *Soblazn Aktivizma: Russkaya respublikansko-demokraticheskaya emigratsyia 20'-30' godov XX veka i OGPU SSSR* (Moscow: Azbukovnik, 2011), 55–6; Alexander Zdanovich, *Polsky krest sovetskoi kontrrazvedki: Polskaya liniya v rabote VCheka-NKVD 1918-1938* (Moscow: Kraft+, 2017), 217–21.

31. Published in *POW po stronie rewolucji* (Warsaw, 1921), 10–16.

32. TsA FSB, Archival Criminal Case (AUD) No. R-8470, t. 3, ll. 33-38. For details, see Witold Rawski, 'Działalność Polskiej Organizacji Wojskowej w Moskwie, 1919–1920', part 2, *Przegląd Historyczno-Wojskowy*, 15/3 (2014), 133–54.

33. Smith, *Six*, 251.
34. See Juho Kotakallio, *Hänen Majesteettinsa Agentit: Brittitiedustelu Suomessa 1918-1941* (Helsinki: Atena, 2014), 15, 21.
35. Jeffery, *MI6*, 177.
36. The text of the Annual Report and 'Spravka No. 1 Espionage' is published in Vadim Abramov, *Counter-intelligence: Sword and Shield Against the Abwehr and the CIA* (Moscow: Yauza-Eksmo, 2006), in Russian. Artuzov also reported that the SIS budget for intelligence activities in Russia had been increased to £300,000, and that in the period 1923–4 the GPU detained more than 1,375 spies. The figure £300,000 is not a guess or estimate, but pretty exact information regarding British Foreign Secret Service accounts. The Official Secret Service vote decreased from £1,150,000 in 1918 to £300,000 in 1921. See Victor Madeira, *Britannia and the Bear: The Anglo-Russian Intelligence Wars 1917-1928* (Woodbridge: The Boydell Press, 2014), 75, 221.
37. Jeffery, *MI6*, 181–2.
38. See, for example, 'Zapiska o rabote po podgotovke, rukovodstvu i osuschestvleniyu sverzheniya sovetskoi vlasti v Rossii', 31 July 1923, Pavel Nikolaevich Shatilov Papers, Box 3, Folder: Correspondence with Grand Duke Nikolai Nikolaevich, Bakhmeteff Archive, Rare Books and Manuscript Library, Columbia University.
39. Cf. Andrew and Mitrokhin, *The Mitrokhin Archive I*, 41–2.
40. See, for example, Vasily Ardamatsky, *Nemesis* (1968), ch. 18, in Russian; Igor Damaskin, 'The King of Kremlin Spies', vol. 2, ch. 19, in *Essays on the History of Russian Foreign Intelligence* (1997), and *100 Great Spies* (2007), both in Russian; and Vladimir Antonov, 'In Search of a Fake Factory', *Nezavisimoe Voennoe Obozrenie*, 21 Aug. 2015. For Nikolai Kroshko's memoirs, see 'Iz vospominaniy N.N. Kroshko-Keith', in Vladimir Orlov, *Dvoinoi agent: Zapiski russkogo kontrrazvedchika* (Moscow: Sovremennik, 1998), 250–72.
41. Described in his TNA files KV 2/1410-1416, based on six volumes of his MI5 personal file PF 421 plus one supplement, as 'Nicolas KLISHKO, suspected OGPU officer'.
42. See Boris Volodarsky, *Stalin's Agent* (Oxford, 2014), 61, 62, 536. The actual confusion was due to the relevant passages in the book by Andrew and Gordievsky, *KGB*, 72–8. The Mitrokhin papers also include a short story of Kroshko as a GPU agent, but it seems Mitrokhin copied the material not from the KGB file but from the declassified memoirs, later published by General Zdanovich, which is why professor Andrew decided against including it into his book. See Mitrokhin, *"Chekisms"*, 391–3.
43. FSB Archive, Omsk region directorate, extract from the personal file of K.S. Baransky (Kazimierz Barański), 10/27/213 of 21 January 2016, quoted by Zdanovich.
44. See Richard B. Spence, 'Senator William E. Borah: Target of Soviet and Anti-Soviet Intrigue, 1922-1929', *International Journal of Intelligence and Counter-intelligence*, 19/1 (2006), 134–55. I am very grateful to Professor Richard Spence for sending his personal manuscript of the article despite the quarantine and lockdown in November 2020. For details about the Berlin 1929 process, see Karl Schlögel (ed.), *Russische Emigration in Deutschland 1918 bis 1941: Leben im europäischen Bürgerkrieg* (Berlin: Akademie Verlag, 1995), 169–73.
45. Natalie Grant, *Murder in the Tiergarten: The Political Life of Vladimir Orlov, Intelligence Agent and Disinformer* (Washington, DC: The Nathan Hale Institute, 1997). I am grateful to Jack Dziak for sending me his personal copy of this rare publication in April 2020. Natalie Grant was born Natalia Konstantinovna Mark in Estonia. In 1928–39 she had worked for the American legation in Riga, Latvia, as a translator and analyst and in the 1950s was employed by the US Department of State as a Sovietologist. Natalie Grant married Ryszard Wraga, also known as Jerzy Antoni Niezbrzycki.
46. Andrew and Mitrokhin, *The Mitrokhin Archive I*, 42.

47. Ibid. For a detailed account, see Mitrokhin, *"Chekisms"*, 83–93.
48. In the 1970s this house was a site of the KGB training camp for PLO terrorists in the use of small arms, explosives, and indoctrination, see William Claiborne, *Newsday*, 17 November 1980.
49. Winston Churchill, *Great Contemporaries* (Wilmington, DE: ISI Books, 2019), 126–7. Boris Savinkov was a former Socialist Revolutionary (SR) terrorist who had served as Alexander F. Kerensky's deputy in the second coalition cabinet with Kerensky as Minister-President and Minister of War and Navy. Savinkov's government service had lasted for slightly over a month after which he resigned and was expelled from the SR party. Savinkov was admired by many, including Winston Churchill and W. Somerset Maugham. 'When all is said and done,' Churchill wrote *Great Contemporaries* (first published in 1937), 'and with all the stains and tarnishes there be, few men tried more, gave more, dared more and suffered more for the Russian people.' Somerset Maugham, an amateur British spy and a popular playwright, novelist and short story writer, who in his intelligence reports to London predicted the fall of the Kerensky government, admitted, 'I suppose few remember his name now, but [it] is a name that might have well been as familiar to us all as that of Lenin, and if it had, Lenin's would have remained obscure. Boris Savinkov might easily have become a man of tremendous authority in Russia'. See John Whitehead (ed.), *A Traveller in Romance: W. Somerset Maugham Uncollected Writings 1901-1964* (London: 1984).
50. See Nikolai Choumakov, *Delo "Maki-Mirage"* (Khabarovsk: FSB Regional Directorate, 2013). The declassified files as well as the book were widely covered by the local media in 2013–14. Unfortunately, the OGPU documents do not specify against which Japanese unit the operation was targeted – was it Army General Staff's Second Section (Intelligence), or Tokumu Kikan, its special service, or their rivals the Kenpeitai?
51. Both deception operations, SINDIKAT-2 and TREST, were carried out by the officers and agents of the 4th and 6th sections of the KRO in close collaboration with the Disinformburo. The 4th section was headed by Viktor Stepanovich Kijakovsky (Wiktor Steckiewicz) handling counter-intelligence work against secret services of the countries of Central and Western Europe and the USA. From 15 October 1923 to 14 August 1924 this section was headed by the Latvian Vladimir Styrne (Voldemārs Stirne). Section 6 under Ignaty Ignatievich Sosnovsky (Ignacy Dobrzyński), was operating against the White émigrés and their armed units. Interestingly, Section 3, which was handling counter-intelligence work against Polish, Romanian, Hungarian, Czechoslovak, Bulgarian and Yugoslavian intelligence services was also involved in both operations. It was tasked with spreading disinformation to mislead them. The section was first headed by the Polish communist Jerzy Franciszek Makowski (in Russia – Yuri Ignatyevich Makovsky), then in February 1923 he was succeeded by another Pole, Jan Kulikowski (in Russia – Yan Kalikstovich Olsky), and then later that year by the Lithuanian Kazimir Juozas Naujokaitis who held this post until 1930.
52. Pamela K. Simpkins and K. Leigh Dyer (eds), *The Trust* (Washington, DC: Security and Intelligence Foundation, 1989), originally prepared by the Central Intelligence Agency, released for publication under FOIA.

Chapter 7: First 'Illegals' and 'Rezidents'

1. Sun Tzu, *The Art of War*, 11.
2. Joseph W. Caddell, 'Deception 101 – Primer on Deception', Army War College Monograph (Carlisle Barracks, PA, December 2004).
3. On 30 December 1917, Trotsky appointed Maxim Litvinov, who had lived as a Russian émigré in London since 1909, as Soviet chargé d'affaires in Great Britain. 'If we refuse to

receive him,' Sir George Buchanan, the British Ambassador in Petrograd wrote, 'Trotsky will retaliate by withdrawing our diplomatic immunities and by stopping all our cypher telegrams. As the Embassy could in such case be liable to search, we would have to destroy our secret archives and cyphers.' He urged London 'to come to some working arrangement' with Litvinov, which was duly done. TNA: FO 371/3298/3346, Russia Code 38/Code W38 File 1478 – 1869, date 1918.

4. In June 2017, the SVR celebrated the 95th anniversary of its top-secret Directorate S, now under the Deputy Director of Operations (DDO).

5. Cf. Andrew and Mitrokhin, *The Mitrokhin Archive I*, 36–7, 752

6. From July 1934 to December 1936 the Soviet foreign intelligence service was known as the INO, then from December 1936 to June 1938 as 7th department, and from June to February 1941 as 5th (Foreign) department of the Chief Directorate of State Security (GUGB) of the NKVD, first headed by Arthur Artuzov and then Abram Slutsky.

7. See A. Kolpakidi and D. Prokhorov, *Imperiya GRU*, vol. 2 (Moscow: Olma-Press, 1999), 55.

8. Volodarsky, *Stalin's Agent*, 187–8.

9. John W. Wheeler-Bennett, 'Twenty Years of Russo-German Relations, 1919-1939', *Foreign Affairs*, 25/1 (Oct. 1946), 23–43.

10. Until January 1918 Joffe headed the Soviet delegation at the peace negotiations at Brest-Litovsk, before he was replaced by Trostky, whom Joffe temporary replaced as People's Commissar for Foreign Affairs. In April 1918 Joffe was appointed Soviet representative in Germany with Menzhinsky, future head of the OGPU, as his deputy.

11. Wheeler-Bennett, 'Twenty Years of Russo-German Relations', 25. See also James S. Corum, *The Roots of Blitzkrieg: Hans von Seeckt and German Military Reform* (Lawrence, KS: University Press of Kansas, 1992), 79.

12. Akten der Reichskanzlei Weimarer Republik, die Kabinette Marx III/IV, Band I, Dokumente Nr. 138, Anlage 12.

13. AVP RF, f. 82, op. 2, d. 10, l. 1.

14. RGAE, f. 413, op. 2, d. 1379, l. 73 rev.

15. The subject of the repatriation of prisoners of war was regulated by a 'German-Russian Agreement Supplemental to the Peace Treaty' (Article 17) negotiated and signed at the same time as the Treaty of Peace of Brest Litovsk, on 3 March 1918, in accordance with Articles 8 and 12 of that Treaty. Source: Foreign Relations 1918, Russia, I, at 442; 1 Soviet Documents on For. Rel., 1917-1924, at 50. Remarkably, in this agreement the Bolshevik government gave the prisoners of war the option of refusing repatriation.

16. For details about Radek's stay in Berlin, see Otto-Ernst Schüddekopf, 'Karl Radek in Berlin. Ein Kapitel deutsch-russischer Beziehungen im Jahre 1919', *Archiv für Sozialgeschichte*, 2 (1962), 87–166. Already in mid-November 1919, Legationsrat Ago von Maltzan was asked to allow Radek to move to the house of Eugen Freiherr von Reibnitz at Sigismundstraße 5. In his telegram to Chicherin of 15 December Radek reported that he had already been staying at von Reibnitz's for a week. However, on the same day, he was transferred to the private apartment of Kriminalkommissar Müller in Berlin- Schöneberg, from where he was finally deported via Poland on 18 January 1920.

17. See, for example, Kopp's reports to Moscow Nr. 1029, 1030, classified 'secret', regarding his negotiations on maintaining the neutrality of Germany, dated 14 August 1920, in AP RF, f. 3, op. 64, d. 676, l. 3.

18. See Jerzy Borzęcki, *The Soviet-Polish Peace of 1921 and the Creation of Interwar Europe* (New Haven and London: Yale University Press, 2008), 79–81.

19. Rayfield, *Stalin and His Hangmen*, 88. 'In summer 1920,' Stephen Brown writes, 'Stalin was serving as a member of the revolutionary military council of the South-West Front,

one of two prongs of the Red Army's invasion of Poland.' For details, see Stephen Brown, 'Lenin, Stalin and the Failure of the Red Army in the Soviet-Polish War of 1920', *War & Society*, 14/2 (October 1996), 35–47.

20. Brockdorff-Rantzau Nachlass, 3445/9105/237050 ff. For details, see Hanz W. Gatzke, 'Russo-German Military Collaboration During the Weimar Republic', *The American Historical Review*, 63/3 (Apr. 1958), 565–97.

21. Wheeler-Bennett, 'Twenty Years of Russo-German Relations, 1919-1939', 23.

22. Aaron Scheinmann (in Russian: Aron Lvovich Sheinman) was born in the north-eastern Polish town of Suwałki near the border with Lithuania, then part of the Russian Empire. In July 1918, working for the Bolshevik government in Stockholm, Scheinmann together with Olof Aschebrg, a Swedish banker of Jewish descent, and Willi Münzenberg, set up several financial institutions to help the Kremlin launder money, gold and other valuables confiscated from Russia's rich and the Church, in order to buy machines and goods in the West (see McMeekin, *The Red Millionaire*, 135, 138, 296–7) and finance other governmental activities. In 1919 Scheinmann, together with Vorovsky, Litvinov and Mikhail Borodin, was expelled from Sweden. From October 1921 he had served as chairman of the Gosbank twice, until July 1928, when he left to spend a holiday in Germany and decided never to return. His MI5 personal file PF 1204 claims that Scheinmann 'resigned following a disagreement with Stalin but maintained good relations with the Soviet Union and remained in the West, finally becoming manager of Intourist in London' (TNA: KV 2/1978). Indeed, in January 1933 he was invited to manage the Intourist office. After the Second World War broke out in September 1939, Scheinmann resigned. During the same year he and his family became naturalised British citizens and he arranged for the family to leave for Australia. Scheinmann died in London in May 1944. See Vladimir Genis, 'Disgraced Dignitary' (in Russian: 'Opalnyi sanovnik'), *Politichesky zhurnal*, 10 (22 March 2004).

23. Vladimir Genis, 'Non-returners (nevozvraschentsy) of the 1920s and early 1930s', *Voprosy Istorii*, 1 (2000), 46–63, in Russian.

24. Paweł Lewinson (in Russia: Pavel Lyudvigovich Lapinsky-Mikhalsky) was born in May 1879 in Płock, Poland, to the family of a local attorney Ludwik Lewinson. From 1917 he was constantly in Russia before he joining the NKID combining diplomatic service with journalism and scientific work while on various assignments abroad. After his return to the USSR, he was arrested in June 1937. Levinson, who also the pseudonyms 'Andrzej Wolski' and 'Stanisław Łapiński', committed suicide in prison in September 1937.

25. Born in 1891 in Latvia as Teodors Grikmans, he came from a poor family. His father was a manual labourer and Teodors himself began his working career in manual labour at a farm and then at a local post office as janitor before moving to Petrograd and joining the militia. He was then lucky to be promoted to head several provincial Chekas. From May 1920 he had been in Moscow in the Special Department (OO) at the VeCheKa Lubyanka headquarters. It seems that from January 1921 he was in charge of the 17th special section (counter-intelligence work among former officers of the Russian Imperial Army) of the Secret-Operational Directorate (SOU). According to the available sources, Grikman worked in Berlin from October 1921 to May 1924. Soon after his return to Moscow he was appointed deputy head of the Moscow Criminal Police (MUR). He then headed the diplomatic courier service of the NKID, served as 2nd Secretary and Consul of the Soviet embassy in Romania (November 1934–August 1935) and was then appointed deputy chairman of Intourist in Moscow. Arrested in May and shot in August 1937 (RGASPI, f. 17, op. 171, d. 410, l. 259).

26. On 8 June 1921 the Politburo allowed Kopp to return to Berlin on a special assignment (AP RF, f. 3, op. 64, d. 644, l. 26). Two weeks later, on 25 June, Kopp was appointed secret political envoy to Germany (AP RF, f. 3, op. 64, d. 638, l. 4 copy).

27. AP RF, f. 3, op. 64, d. 644, l. 28. At the express request of Hitler, Oscar von Niedermayer (alias 'Neiman' in the secret Soviet correspondence, where his chief von Seecht was 'Siebert') would take up a teaching post at the Institute for Compulsory Military Doctrine in Berlin and in October 1939, promoted to colonel, would be transferred to the supreme command of the Wehrmacht (OKW). Arrested by the Red Army on 9 May 1945, he was deported to Russia, sentenced to 25 years in jail, contracted tuberculosis while in custody and died in the infamous Vladimir Central in September 1948.

28. Teddy J. Uldricks, *Diplomacy and Ideology: The Origins of Soviet Foreign Relations 1917-1930* (London: SAGE Publications, 1981), 54–5. For the so far best and most detailed study, see Ewa Berard's article, 'The "First Exhibition of Russian Art" in Berlin: The Transnational Origins of Bolshevik Cultural Diplomacy. 1921-1922', *Contemporary European History* (2021), 1–17. The article, the author asserts, explores unpublished Russian and German archival material to shed new light on the 1922 Berlin exhibition of Russian art. The researcher points out that these archival documents 'expose incoherent Soviet bureaucratic organization and the opposition of some leading Bolsheviks to the idea of publicizing Soviet Russia through art'. The article also re-examines Lunacharsky's 'claim to be the sole spiritus movens of the event', a claim subsequently repeated by the exhibition historiography. On the contrary, it shows the role played by the German Reichsministerium for Foreign Affairs and by Willi Münzenberg, the organiser, leader and general secretary of the Internationale Arbeiterhilfe (IAH) or International Workers' Aid (Mezhrabpom), formed on Lenin's instructions in August 1921, who later became known as 'the secret propaganda tsar' of the Comintern in the West. In addition, in March 1921 Victor Kopp sent a proposal to the German Foreign Ministry in which he outlined a plan for an official public exhibition of Russian art (Kopp to the German Foreign Ministry, 31/03/1921, PA AA, R 94534).

29. Berard, 'The "First Exhibition of Russian Art" in Berlin', 2.

30. According to data published by the WARP's Council, Russian newspapers, magazines, publishing houses, radio, television, web media groups and so on exist in more than eighty countries of the world. Many of them are members of the WARP. World congresses of the Russian press are held alternatively in one of the countries whose Russian media is represented in the WARP. Since its foundation in 1999, World Congresses were held in Russia (1999, 2008, 2015), USA (2000), Ukraine (2001, 2011), Germany (2002), Azerbaijan (2003), Bulgaria (2004), Finland and Sweden (2005), Kazakhstan (2006), France (2007, 2016), Switzerland (2009), Israel (2010), Italy (2012), Belarus (2013, 2017), and China (2014). With WARP Headquarters located in Central Moscow, it had registered representatives for Eastern Europe in Riga, Latvia; Central Europe in Prague, Czech Republic; Western Europe in Zurich, Switzerland; Western Asia in Baku, Azerbaijan; Middle East in Dubai, UAE; as well as Australia and Oceania in Sydney, Australia.

31. Cf. Berard, 'The "First Exhibition of Russian Art" in Berlin', 17.

32. About Stashevsky, see Volodarsky, *Stalin's Agent*, 610–11. Most of the Russian sources on Stashevsky give largely erroneous information about his career.

33. The only unreliable semi-official history of Soviet foreign intelligence, *Ocherki*, under the editorship of Yevgeny Primakov, states that because an unnamed traitor at the Soviet Berlin residency leaked information about Stashevsky's real role to the German press, the latter was urgently recalled, see vol. 2, 168.

34. See PF 46348 Vol 2 (TNA KV 2/1009 Paul HARDT/Mrs Lydia HARDT, s.60c). In his book *A Time for Spy* (1999) William E. Duff wrongly calls him 'Bernard Davidovich Gadar' (p. 81). See his MI5 file PF 73983 (TNA KV 2/2242).

35. The uprising would be staged in September 1923 by the Bulgarian Communist Party with full Comintern backing. The armed insurrection was supressed, and its leaders

328 The Birth of the Soviet Secret Police

Georgi Dimitrov and Vasil Kolarov fled to Soviet Russia via Yugoslavia leaving behind over 800 casualties.

36. 'The embassy was then searched, its archives and documents taken, and the other British officials imprisoned in the Fortress of Peter and Paul, where they were crowded together with Russian prisoners, twenty or more to a tiny unfurnished cell, and fed only with what could be brought them by the neutral legations.' Richard H. Ullman, *Anglo-Soviet Relations, 1917-1921, Volume 1: Intervention and the War* (Princeton, NJ: Princeton University Press and London: Oxford University Press, 1961), 288–9.

37. Jakub Hanecki (in Russian: Yakov Stanislavovich Ganetsky), was born in Warsaw as Jakub Fürstenberg to the family of a beer manufacturer of German descent who had adopted Poland as his homeland on 15 March 1879. Known as Kuba in the revolutionary circles, he had studied at Berlin, Heidelberg and Zurich universities and became a prominent revolutionary, a close associate of Lenin and Dzerzhinsky. It is said that through his good working relations with Parvus, Hanecki was one of the key figures helping to arrange secret German funding that ensured the Bolshevik victory in the October Revolution of 1917. In November 1918, he was appointed acting Chief Commissioner of the People's Bank of the RSFSR remaining at this post until January 1920 when the bank was abolished. On 2 November 1922 Hanecki/Ganetsky was a member of a high-profile nine-member delegation of the Narkomindel greeting the German Ambassador Count Ulrich von Brockdorff-Rantzau after he had presented his credentials to Kalinin at the Kremlin. Arrested with his wife and son in July 1937, Hanecki was tortured, then tried and sentenced to death in November as a Polish and German spy and shot on the same day. Volkogonov in his *Lenin: A New Biography* (1994) claims that Hanecki's wife and son were also executed. His house was thoroughly searched but reportedly nothing of value was found. About Parvus, see Z.A.B. Zeman and W.B. Scharlau, *The Merchant of Revolution: The Life of Alexander Israel Helphand (Parvus), 1867-1924* (New York, NY: Oxford University Press, 1965). See also, Gennady L. Sobolev, *Secret Ally: Russian Revolution and Germany 1914-1918* (St Petersburg: St Petersburg University Press, 2009), in Russian.

38. Jakob Reich ('Comrade Thomas'), 'The First Years of the Communist International', *Revolutionary History*, 5/2 (Spring 1994).

39. Angelica Balabanoff, *Impressions of Lenin* (Ann Arbor, MI: University of Michigan Press, 1968), 16.

40. Jakob Reich ('Comrade Thomas'), 'The First Years of the Communist International'.

41. Guralski(y)/Kleine was born in Riga on 10 April 1890 as Abraham Jakob Heifetz to an Orthodox Jewish family. His father was a teacher at the Jewish school. Abraham attended a commercial school in Riga where he joined the Bund movement and was later active in the Latvian social-democratic Cultural Centre in Riga using the alias 'Samuel Guralski'. First arrested for his revolutionary activities in 1908, he had worked in Byelorussia and Russia before coming to Austria and entering Vienna University. From Vienna Guralski moved to Lausanne. Together with Lenin, he returned to Russia in 1917, was involved in the Odessa Bund and after the Red Army captured Kiev occupied several responsible posts in Ukraine before the Comintern sent him to Germany as an ECCI representative. After the 1921 March Action he was in Germany again, elected to the KPD Central Committee in January 1923 (as August Kleine) and later that year to the Politburo preparing what became later known as the Hamburg Uprising but had initially been planned as the October Revolution in Germany. About Guralski-Kleine, see Volodarsky, *Stalin's Agent*, 596–7; Hermann Weber and Andreas Herbst, *Deutsche Kommunisten: Biographisches Handbuch 1918 bis 1945* (Berlin: Dietz, 2008), 375.

42. She was a Polish communist born in December 1899 in Warsaw as Romana D. Wolf. During her underground communist work, she used the pseudonym 'Helena Jezierska'

and later became known in Russia as Romana Davydovna Yezerskaya. See, for example, RGASPI, f. 5, op. 1, d. 2603, l. 13.

43. Susanne Köhler's first marriage to Rudolf Leonhard did not last long before she got married for the second time, to Mieczysław Broński. With Rudolf they had a son named Wladimir, who would become a German historian of Communism better known as Wolfgang Leonhard. Broński was in Germany during the Communist uprising of March 1921 (the so-called März Aktion) but then came back to Vienna where he had been under permanent surveillance since his arrival in July 1920. In 1924 he returned to Moscow. The first official Soviet plenipotentiary, Woldemar Aussem, arrived in Vienna in May 1924. He was succeeded by Adolph Joffe in December that year.

44. See Jonathan D. Smele, *Historical Dictionary of the Russian Civil Wars, 1916-1926* (Lanham, MD: Rowman & Littlefield, 2015), 296.

45. Niederösterreichisches Landesarchiv (NÖLA) St. Pölten, Präs. „P" 1920, Zl. 1160/I/1. See also ÖSTA/KA, AOK-Evidenzbüro. Die Kommunistische Bewegung 1920-1921. Berichte Sowjetrußland: Die Resultate des Bolschewismus, Karton 3678.

46. AVP RF, f. 066, op. 3, p. 101, d. 1, l. 26.

47. From the Russian side, the document was signed by Broński, from the Ukrainian by Mikhailo V. Levitsky, who was born in Austrian Galicia, in 1920 took part in the 2nd Comintern Congress and at the time served as the Ukrainian plenipotentiary in Prague (and then in 1923–4 in Vienna). On behalf of the Austrian government, it was signed by Johann Schober, the chancellor.

48. According to the information provided by the Austrian authorities (Kriegsgefangenen Amt), between 19 July 1920 and 3 October 1921 less than 800 Russian PoWs chose to return home. ÖSTA/AdR, BKA/KGF 1922: VI. Ende der Heimkehrbewegung. About Broński in Vienna, see Barry McLoughlin, Hannes Leidinger and Verena Moritz, *Kommunismus in Österreich, 1918-1938* (Wien: Studien Verlag, 2009), 41–51.

49. Volodarsky, *Stalin's Agent*, 538–9.

50. Archiv der Bundespolizeidirektion Wien, Schoberarchiv, Schachtel 47, Ausländer 1922, Pr. Z. IV-788. Schlichter remained in Vienna until March 1923 after which he was sent as the NKID plenipotentiary to Ukraine. In Kiev he made a successful career in academia rising to vice-president of the Ukrainian Academy of Sciences and director of the Ukrainian Institute of Marxism-Leninism. One of the streets in Kiev was named after Schlichter but in 2015 it was decided to rename it after Bethlehem, the biblical birthplace of Jesus.

51. In Russia named Vladimir Khristianovich Aussem, he was of Flemish descent. In January 1920 the party sent Aussem to the Razvedupr as assistant chief, then promoted to deputy chief and even acting chief of the Registration Directorate (intelligence) of the Field Headquarters of the Revolutionary Military Council of the RSFSR, as the GRU was then called. In June, after a disagreement with Stalin, Aussem submitted his resignation letter and in August was transferred to a post at the Supreme Council of the People's Economy. He mysteriously disappeared without trace in 1937.

52. Kurt Rosenbaum, *Community of Fate: German-Soviet Diplomatic Relations, 1922-1928* (Syracuse, NY: Syracuse University Press, 1965), 253. According to other sources, Chicherin invited the Germany ambassador Brockdorff-Rantzau to visit him privately on 6 March, late in the evening, to discuss the news. See S.A. Krasilnikov, A.I. Savin, and S.N. Ushakova, *The Shakhty Trial of 1928: Its Preparation, Conduct and Results* (Moscow: ROSSPEN, 2011), 2 vols, in Russian

53. See Rosenbaum, *Community of Fate*, 256–8. 'Upon his return to Berlin,' Rosenbaum writes, 'Senior Engineer [Franz] Goldstein reported to the Wilhelmstrasse on the background of the arrests. In his considered opinion, the catastrophic decline of production, as well

as the numerous accidents and disturbances in the Donetsk Basin area, was due to the Soviet system and not to sabotage' (p. 254). The engineer saw a problem in the fact that control of production was left to inept party members and the overall control to poorly educated apparatchiks while non-party specialists were under constant fear of arrest.

54. GA RF, f. 63 (Moscow Okhrana), op. 22, d. 499. Sent as the Soviet ambassador to Estonia in January 1934, Ustinov died at his post in Tallinn on 26 September 1937.

55. Between August 1920 and April 1921 Registrupr was headed by Jan Lenzman (Jānis Lencmanis), a Latvian Bolshevik. Ustinov was probably not lying when he wrote in his memoirs that 'in connection with the most severe form of asthma, which in the end confined me to bed, the Central Committee sent me to be treated abroad for 2 years'. In Berlin he decided to combine medical treatment with work. At the legation Ustinov also served as a party secretary between 1922 and 1923. In summer 1923, together with Gorb and Vladimir Potyomkin, he was sent to Marseilles to negotiate the repatriation of the Russian Expeditionary Corps prisoners and in March 1924 to Vienna as part of the delegation headed by Krestinsky to negotiate with Romania (RGASPI, f. 17, op. 100, d. 75280, ll. 6-12). After the war, relations between the two countries were tense and the Vienna meeting was to improve them. During the talks the Soviets immediately raised the question of Bessarabia, proposing a plebiscite. On 2 April, the Romanian delegation rejected the proposal and ceased negotiations.

56. Kurt Rosenbaum, *Community of Fate: German-Soviet Diplomatic Relations, 1922-1928* (Syracuse, NY: Syracuse University Press, 1965), 72. See also pages 73, 76, 83.

57. Like the Union of the Revival of Russia, Tactical Centre and Action Centre, which Chaikovsky chaired from 1920 before its dissolution in the summer of 1923. He was also one of the founders of the Masonic lodges Astrea No. 500 and Nothern Lights No. 524 and reportedly became one of the officers of the Grande Loge de France, one of the Scottish Rite lodges which still exists in Paris. He moved to London in 1925 and one can still find an entry in the 1922 *Encyclopædia Britannica* on 'Tschaikovsky, Nicholas Vasilievich', who died in April 1926 and is buried in Harrow Cemetery.

58. Moses Rojzman (in Russian: Moisei Sanelevich Roizman) was born in 1894 in Chudniv, a city in Zhitomir oblast, Ukraine. The Jewish population was important in the town and many emigrated to the United States and Palestine between 1900 and 1920. However, at the time of writing Wikipedia records only two notable people from Chudniv – Menachem Ribalow, newspaper editor, and Schloimke Beckerman – a well-known klezmer soloist in New York. Roizman took an active part in the revolutionary movement from 1914, supporting Left SRs. He later joined the Bolsheviks using the party pseudonym 'Gorbunov' for his underground activities, which was later shortened to Gorb with his name and patronymic changed to 'Mikhail Savelyevich'. In February-March 1920 Gorb was appointed chairman of the Odessa Cheka and a year later was invited to the newly formed INO. His career peak was deputy department head at the State Security Directorate (GUGB) of the NKVD.

59. See Nadezhda and Maya Ulanovskaya, *The Story of my Family* (St Petersburg: Inapress, 2003), ch. 3, 42–50, in Russian.

60. Victor Kopp died in Berlin on 27 May 1930. For details about Kopp, see Vasili L. Chernoperov's doctoral thesis, 'Diplomat V.L. Kopp and his role in the formation of Soviet policy towards Germany, 1919-1924', State University of Nizhny Novgorod, 2006. For Kopps's correspondence with the NKID, see AVP RF, Referentura po Germanii (reference file Germany), secret fund 082, opis 3, papka 3, delo 1. For Kopp in Japan, see George Alexander Lensen, *Japanese Recognition of the U.S.S.R.: Soviet-Japanese Relations 1921-1930* (Tokyo: Sophia University, 1970), 211-15, 218-22. Grigory Besedovsky, counsellor of the Soviet embassy in Tokyo in 1926-7, wrote of Kopp: 'Very intelligent,

with a European education, [and] speaking foreign languages, Kopp has by nature little in common with revolutionary political activity. He is rather a political realist ...' G.Z. Besedovsky, *Na putyakh k Termidoru* (Paris: Mishen, 1930), vol. 1, 225.

61. TsA FSB, no. 105731, ll. 75-76, Report to Stalin of 8 August 1938, signed by the head of the NKVD 3rd Department (counter-intelligence, KRO), 1st Directorate, Commissar of State Security 3rd Rank Nikolai G. Nikolayev-Zhurid.

62. In 1922 Skujskumbré was sent on a secret mission abroad and upon return served in military counter-intelligence before reinstating himself in the Cheka, by then renamed the OGPU and later the NKVD, as a senior officer of its Economic Department.

63. See Primakov (ed.), *Ocherki*, vol. 2, ch. 20, 169–70.

64. About the nomenklatura, see Bohdan Harasymiw, '*Nomenklatura*: The Soviet Communist Party's Leadership Recruitment System', *Canadian Journal of Political Science*, 2/4 (Dec. 1969), 493–512.

Chapter 8: Trade, Diplomacy and Famine

1. McMeekin, *History's Greatest Heist*, 199.

2. See Frank Lorimer, *The Population of the Soviet Union: History and Prospects* (Geneva: League of Nations, 1946), '3. Estimated Loss in Wars, Revolution, and Famine', 36–9.

3. Evan Mawdsley, *The Russian Civil War* (Edinburgh: Birlinn, 2017), 399.

4. While the 10th Bolshevik Party Congress was in session in March 1921, the sailors of the Kronstadt garrison, formerly described by Trotsky as 'the beauty and pride' of the Revolution, rebelled against the political repression and economic hardship imposed by the Bolshevik regime. The manifesto of the Kronstadt rebels singled out the Cheka. 'The power of the police-gendarme monarchy passed into the hands of the communist usurpers who,' it stated, 'instead of bringing freedom to the workers, instilled in them the constant fear of falling into the torture-chambers of the Cheka, which in their horrors far exceeded the police rule of the Tsarist regime' (Andrew and Gordievsky, *KGB*, 712). Writing about the rebellion, the authors failed to mention that one of its top leaders, Stepan Petrichenko, chairman of the Kronstadt revolutionary committee (Revkom), who after the defeat of the uprising escaped to Finland, soon became a Soviet agent. Petrichenko had been working for the (G)RU in Finland from 1922 until his arrest in 1941. After the Moscow armistice was signed between Finland on one side and the Soviet Union and Great Britain on the other in September 1944, Petrichenko was expelled to the USSR. There, he was arrested by SMERSH, sentenced to 10 years and died in June 1947.

5. Douglas Little, 'Anti-Bolshevism and American Foreign Policy, 1919-1939: The Diplomacy of Self-Delusion', *American Quarterly*, 35/4 (Autumn 1983), 376–90. Hoover had served as one of President Wilson's advisers at Versailles.

6. M.A. Mikhailov, agent of the French trading firm SOCIFROS (Copenhagen), to SOCIFROS, Paris, 2 March 1920, MAÉ, ancienne série Z-Europe, 1918-1940, Russie et URSS, volume 69, folio numbers 83-91; and Henri Martin, French minister in Copenhagen, nos. 109-112, 13 March 1920, ibid, ff. 106-109, in Michael Jabara Carley, 'Episodes from the Early Cold War: Franco-Soviet Relations, 1917-1927', *Europe-Asia Studies*, 52/7 (2000), 1275–1305.

7. MAÉ, Correspondance politique et commerciale, 1914-1940, Z-Europe, Russie et URSS, 421, 81-84, Memorandum of plan by L. Krassin and L.B. Kameneff, representatives plenipotentiary of the Soviet Government. Enclosure in Krassin to Vicomte du Halgouët, Délégué du Ministère du Commerce à Londres, London, le 8 août 1920. Enclosure in Aimé-Joseph de Fleuriau, Chargé d'affaires de la République Française, Londres, à Millerand, le 10 août 1920, no. 280, Très confidentiel.

8. 'No Political Dealings with Krassin', *The Times* (from our own correspondent), Paris, 31 May 1920. E.F. Wise was a British economist, civil servant and Labour Party politician, acting as the British representative on the Supreme Economic Council. Jobic de Poulpiquet du Halgouët, the French representative on the Permanent Committee of the Supreme Economic Council, in London at the time of the Soviet British trade conference, was appointed by President Millerand to represent France at the conference 'purely as commercial delegate' accompanied by Joseph Avenol, finance expert at the French embassy in London. In 1915–18 Vicomte du Halgouët served as counsellor of the embassy and commercial attaché in Petrograd and from 1921 to 1937 as commercial attaché in London. Italy, invited to participate in the opening talks with Krasin's delegation, sent only its chargé d'affaires in London who attended one session (DBFP, VIII, 280; Nos. 25, 242).

9. *Trade with Russia: The Facts* (interview with Mr. Krassin, head of the Russian Trade Delegation in London, on November 29, 1921), published by the 'Hands off Russia' Committee, London, 1921.

10. McMeekin, *History's Greatest Heist*, 199–200.

11. Curtis Keeble, *Britain, the Soviet Union and Russia* (Basingstoke, Hampshire: Macmillan Press, 2000), 69.

12. McMeekin, *History's Greatest Heist*, 200.

13. RGASPI (former Central Party Archive of the Institute of Marxism-Leninism, TsPA IML), f. 2, op. 2, d. 16770.

14. Chicherin's note to Curzon on Trade Agreement, December 4, 1920, DVP USSR, vol. 3, no. 207, pages 367–9.

15. See, for example, M.V. Glenny, 'The Anglo-Soviet Trade Agreement, March 1921', *Journal of Contemporary History*, 5/2 (1970), 63–82; and Stephen White, *Anglo-Soviet Relations, 1917-1924: A study in the politics of diplomacy* (unpublished PhD thesis, Glasgow University, September 1972).

16. RGASPI, f. 5, op. 2, d. 158, ll. 20, 21, 23, 24, 26, 28. See also Report by Director of Intelligence, Scotland House, 29 June 1920, Parliamentary Archives, LG, The Lloyd George Papers, F/202/3/17.

17. See Christopher Andrew, 'The British Secret Service and Anglo-Soviet Relations in the 1920s, Part I: From the Trade Negotiations to the Zinoviev Letter', *The Historical Journal*, 20/3 (Sept. 1977), 688–91. See also, Victor Madeira, 'Because I Don't Trust Him, We are Friends: Signals Intelligence and the Reluctant Anglo-Soviet Embrace, 1917-24', *Intelligence and National Security*, 19/1 (Spring 2004), 28–50.

18. John Ferris, *Behind the Enigma: The Authorised History of GCHQ, Britain's Secret Cyber-Intelligence Agency* (London: Bloomsbury, 2020), 78.

19. From April 1921 SIS head of station in Tallinn was Ronald Meiklejohn who succeeded Ernest Boyce (BP/1). According to the Official History of the Service, of all the SIS stations in the Baltic, Riga was the most productive, opened in February 1921 when Rafael Farina (FR/1) came from London to be head of station with cover as British PCO. Because he did not have any preliminary training, he was instructed, once he had settled in, to go to Tallinn and 'spend 10 days or a fortnight there with BP/1, seeing how he does intelligence work'. In October 1919 Captain Henry Landau (BN/1) was sent to Berlin under cover as the chief PCO, but soon got into financial difficulties and had to leave the Service in 1920. In April he was succeeded first by Lieutenant Colonel Norman G. Thwaites and then by Major Timothy Breen, until Captain Frank Foley who had served as assistant chief was installed as head of station in April 1923. For some interesting details, see Henry Landau, *All's Fair: The Story of the British Secret Service Behind the German Lines* (New York, NY: G.P. Putnam's Sons, 1934) and *Spreading the Spy Net: The Story of a British Spy Director* (London: Jarrolds Publishers, 1938); Norman

Thwaites, *Velvet and Vinegar* (London: Grayson & Grayson, 1932). See also C.G. Mckay, 'Our Man in Reval', *Intelligence and National Security*, 9/1 (January 1994), 88–111.

20. RGASPI, f. 2, op. 1, dd. 16776 and 16783.

21. Cf. Alastair Kocho-Williams, 'Soviet Diplomacy and the Comintern, 1921-1927', November 2013. 'For over half a century after the Bolshevik revolution,' Christopher Andrew writes, 'the term "subversion", though commonly used around Whitehall, was never officially defined. Even the Security Service (MI5), though it had the lead role in counter-subversion for most of this period, was reluctant to attempt a definition.' However, Sir John Jones, who would become the Director General (DG) of MI5 in 1981, rose to the challenge, defining devised subversion as 'activities threatening the safety or well-being of the State and intended to determine or overthrow Parliamentary democracy by political, industrial or violent means'. See Madeira, *Britannia and the Bear*, ix.

22. See Gözde Somel, 'Soviet Russia's Foreign Affairs with Turkey in 1923: Reports of Ambassador Surits', *Journal of Balkan and Near Eastern Studies*, 22/2 (2020), 222–39.

23. RGASPI, f. 159, op. 2, d. 57.

24. TNA WO 33/965 Telegrams, European War: Constantinople, Nr. 3371 Director of Military Intelligence to General HQ, British Forces, Constantinople. For details, see Daniel Joseph MacArthur-Seal, *Britain's Levantine Empire, 1914-1923* (Oxford: Oxford University Press, 2021), 234.

25. Jeffery, *MI6*, 203–4. See also, Keith Jeffery and Alan Sharp, 'Lord Curzon and the Use of Secret Intelligence at the Lausanne Conference: 1922-1923', *The Turkish Yearbook of International Relations*, 23 (1993), 79–87.

26. John Ferris, 'Issues in British and American Signals Intelligence, 1919-1932', *Center for Cryptologic History*, volume 11 (2015), 27.

27. Jeffery, *MI6*, 196.

28. Ibid, 204–5. Regarding the Committee of Union and Progress (CUP), the FO noted that its leaders were 'without exception freemasons' while the SIS station in Constantinople reported that 'Jewish Free Masonic elements' dominated the CUP. TNA: FO 373/5/6 'The Rise of Islam and the Caliphate The Pan-Islamic Movement', Jan. 1919; FO 371/4946, E 11702, FO Political Departments, Caucasus Code 58, File 1, 'From our representative, Constantinople', Memorandum 676/V, 12/8/20.

29. Major Hay was an officer of the Intelligence Corps serving tour of duty in Turkey. Various records also mention Norman N.E. Bray from the 18th King George's Own Lancers, who, in September-December 1920, produced several intelligence reports on the causes of unrest in Mesopotamia on the instruction of the Political Department, India Office. See, for example, TNA FO 141/433/3, 'Middle East. Turco-Bolshevik Activities: Note by Political Intelligence Officer attached to India Office', Very Secret, B. 360, 10/12/20.

30. Much of the information regarding British intelligence and the Turkish national movement can be found in the multivolume edition, Bilâl Niyazi Şimşir, *British Documents on Ataturk, 1919-1938* (Ankara: Türk Tarih Kurumu Basimevi, 1992) in Turkish and English. For more details, see the articles by the British historian Alexander (A.L.) Macfie: 'British Intelligence and the Causes of Unrest in Mesopotamia, 1919-21', *Middle Eastern Studies*, 35/1 (January 1999), 165–77; 'British Intelligence and the Turkish National Movement, 1919-22', *Middle Eastern Studies*, 37/1 (January 2001), 1–16; and 'British Views of the Turkish National Movement in Anatolia, 1919-22', *Middle Eastern Studies*, 38/3 (July 2002), 27–46. See also, Masayuki Yamauchi, *The Green Crescent Under the Red Star: Enver Pasha in Soviet Russia, 1919-1922* (Tokyo: Institute for the Study of Languages and Cultures of Asia and Africa, 1991).

31. Jeffery, *MI6*, 206.

32. TNA, FO 371/5178, E 4689 Turkey, Code 44 Files 322-345, 'Connection of Nationalists and Pan-Islamists with Russian Bolshevists', SIS CX/3452 of 05 May 1920.

33. General Cebesoy was one of three Turkish leaders who 'made the revolution' and founded the Turkish Republic. He was appointed Turkish ambassador to Moscow on 21 November 1920, arriving at the Soviet capital on 27 February 1921, just days before the Kronstadt revolt. It is suggested that after Cebesoy's arrival in Moscow, Stalin, then Commissar of Nationalities, with Lenin's approval urged the Turkish ambassador to use his influence as a Turkish military hero and a Muslim to persuade the Tatar divisions in Russia, one in Moscow and one in Kazan, to participate in the suppression of this dangerous uprising (see Ivar Spector, 'General Ali Fuat Cebesoy and the Kronstadt Revolt, 1921: A Footnote to History', *International Journal of Middle East Studies*, 3/4, October 1972, 491–3). The Turkish ambassador had to leave Moscow after, on 21 April 1922, the Cheka broke into the apartment of his military attaché and interpreter Major Ziya Bey, led away his assistant and confiscated some documents. Unable to obtain an explanation or excuse from the Narkomindel, Cebesoy left Moscow on 10 May, returning to Ankara on 2 June 1922. Mustafa Kemal did not want a break with the Bolsheviks and the matter was settled by a compromise.

34. For interesting details about Frunze's visit to Turkey, see Alexander D. Vasiliev, 'Mikhail V. Frunze's mission to Ankara as reflected in archive documents, references of the participants, and researchers', *Journal of the Institute of Eastern Studies, Russian Academy of Sciences*, 2 (2018), 60–9.

35. Ramil Zalyaev, 'Soviet Trade Missions in Turkey', *Academic Journal of Kazan State University*, 151/2/2 (2009), 162–7.

36. V.N. Koptevsky, *Rossiya-Turtsiya: etapy torgovo-ekonomicheskogo sotrudnichestva* (Moscow: Institute of Oriental Studies, Russian Academy of Sciences, 2003), 69–70.

37. Ferris, *Behind the Enigma*, 130–1. See also, John Ferris, 'The British Empire vs. The Hidden Hand: British Intelligence and Strategy and "The CUP-Jew-German-Bolshevik combination", 1918-1924', in Keith Neilson and Greg Kennedy (eds), *The British Way in Warfare: Power and the International System, 1856-1956. Essays in Honour of David French* (Farnham. Ashgate, 2010), 325–46.

38. Yevgeny Primakov (ed.), *Ocherki istorii rossiiskoi vneshnei razvedki* (Moscow: Mezhdunarodnye otnosheniya, 1997), vol. 2: 1917-1933, 269. In his memoirs *Zapiski Chekista* (Berlin: 1930, 218–19), a senior Soviet defector Georges Agabekov contradicts this statement, writing that cooperation proposals of the Turkish intelligence service were declined by the OGPU leadership.

39. For example, during the Chanak crisis, both General Harington and the Whitehall knew from the intercepts that the Soviet diplomatic representative in Angora (Ankara) Semyon Aralov in his reports outlined his attempts to manipulate the Turks into hostilities with Britain, explaining how he was going to do it. They were also aware that the NKID advised Turkey to attack Britain (TNA: WO 106/1441, telegram from Sir Horace Rumbold, High Commissioner to Constantinople, to FO, no. 474 of 28.9.1922). See also Ferris, *Behind the Enigma*, 138.

40. State Military Historical Archives of Bulgaria (GVIAB), f. 1919/40, op. 1, d. 2804, l. 330.

41. Krastyu T. Katev, 'V zashchita na sovetskata vlast', *Bulgarian-Soviet Friendship*, 5 (1960), 10–11.

42. Moscow communicated with its consulate in Constantinople via the legation in Angora (Ankara). For example, on 30 May 1923 deputy foreign commissar Karakhan asked Zalkind to provide an approximate estimate of the costs for the 'repatriation of all Russian citizens from Constantinople'. AVP RF, f. 04, op. 39, papka/folder 2110, d. 53226, l. 8.

43. Robert P. Hughes, Thomas A. Koster and Richard Taruskin, *Freedom from Violence and Lies: Essays on Russian Poetry and Music by Simon Karlinsky* (Boston: Academic Studies Press, 213), 312–13.

44. Pavel Sudoplatov, *Days of Secret War and Diplomacy, 1941*, in Russian (Moscow: Olma-Press, 2001), 54.

45. For details, see Oleg Karimov, 'Soviet naval intelligence during the Russian Civil War', in Russian, *Voprosy Istorii*, 7 (2004), 131–8.

46. For details about the PID, see Erik Goldstein, 'The Foreign Office and Political Intelligence 1918-1920', *Review of International Studies*, 14/4 (Oct. 1988), 275–88. Note that some of the author's TNA references need to be rechecked. See also, Douglas Newton, 'Disillusionment in the "Academic Garrison": The Political Intelligence Department of the British Foreign Office and the German Revolution of 1918-1919', in Andrew Bonnell, Greg Munro and Martin Travers (eds), *Power, Conscious and Opposition: Essays in German History in Honour of John A. Moses* (New York, NY: Peter Lang, 1996), 45–73.

47. It was established that intelligence work had in fact been conducted from early 1921 from the two residencies, one at the Manchuria railway station and another in the city of Harbin, both controlled by the State Political Okhrana (GPO) of the Far Eastern Republic. For details, see O.M. Shinin, 'Organizatsyiya organami gosudarstvennoi bezopasnosti Dalnevostochnoi respubliki razvedyvatelnoi deyatelnosti v 1920-1922 godakh', *Istoricheskii Journal: Nauchnye Issledovaniya*, 3 (May 2013), 289–301.

48. Andrew and Mitrokhin, *The Mitrokhin Archive I*, 43.

49. Ibid.

50. For details, see Peter Hopkirk, *Setting the East Ablaze: Lenin's Dream of an Empire in Asia* (London: John Murray, 1984) and *The Great Game: On Secret Service in High Asia* (London: John Murray, 2006). See also, F.M. Bailey, *Mission to Tashkent* (Oxford: Oxford University Press, 2002). About F.M. Bailey, see TNA: WO 106/61; Royal Society for Asian Affairs, London: RSAA/SC/BAI, as well as 'Obituary: Lieutenant-Colonel Frederick Marsham Bailey, C.I.E.', *Journal of the Royal Central Asian Society*, 54/2 (June 1967), 223–5.

51. *Encyclopædia Britannica*, 11th ed., vol. 26, 51.

52. GA RF, f. 5881, op. 2, d. 985, l. 76.

53. This goal was in line with the 'General Theses on the Eastern Question' that had been adopted at the Comintern's congress in November-December 1922. See Antony Best, '"We are virtually at war with Russia": Britain and the Cold War in East Asia, 1923-40', *Cold War History*, 12/2 (May 2012), 205–25.

54. See, for example, Eva Merkacheva, 'The most loyal traitor', *Moskovsky Komsomolets*, no. 27383 (28 April 2017).

55. See A.V. Ganin, 'The Great Game of Major-General I.M. Zaitsev', Almanac *The White Guard*, no. 8, 'Cossacks of Russia in the White Movement', (Moscow: Posev, 2005), 193–207, and '"I gave an oath of promise to relentlessly fight against the executioners and tyrants of Russian people ..." New material on the General I.M. Zaitsev', *Journal of Ancient Technology Laboratory*, 13/3 (2017), 109–21.

56. Quoted in Ganin, 'The Great Game of General Zaitsev'.

57. Li Fu-jen, 'A Liberal in China', *New International*, 4/3 (March 1938), 89–90.

58. GA RF, f. R-9651, op. 2, d. 848. From 1975 to 1984 the society, which had its branches in all Soviet republics, was formally headed by a Soviet party official Vsevolod N. Stoletov, whose career spanned six decades from the editor of the journal *Soviet Cotton Growing Review* (1929), to the assistant president of the Agricultural Academy (1939), where he supported Trofim Lysenko, a Stalinist charlatan who denied that genes existed. A

recent article in *The Atlantic* (19 December 2017) claims that his 'spurious research prolonged famines that killed millions' in the Soviet Union and China, which is a considerable understatement. Ten years later, in 1949, Stoletov was appointed director of the Moscow Academy of Agriculture, then deputy minister of agriculture, minister of higher education, deputy minister of culture, and so on to the president of the Academy of Pedagogical Sciences.

59. GA RF, f. 5826, op. 1, d. 6, ll. 313-314 rev.

60. Anatol Shmelev, 'Gallipoli to Golgotha: Remembering the Internment of the Russian White Army at Gallipoli, 1920-3', in Jenny Macleod (ed.), *Defeat and Memory: Cultural Histories of Military Defeat in the Modern Era* (Basingstoke, Hampshire: Palgrave Macmillan, 2008), 195–213.

61. RGASPI, f. 71, op. 135, d. 193, ll. 1-159.

62. Paul Robinson, *The White Army in Exile, 1920-1941* (Oxford: Clarendon Press, 2002), 32.

63. Pamela A. Jordan, *Stalin's Singing Spy: The Life and Exile of Nadezhda Plevitskaya* (Lanham, MD: Rowman & Littlefield, 2016), 69–70.

64. See Vasili S. Khristoforov, *Istoriya strany v dokumentakh arkhivov FSB Rossii* (Moscow: Moscow's Main Archive Directorate, 2013), 24. This was a Soviet response to two Turkish cargo ships that arrived in Odessa in the spring of 1921 bringing several thousand former Wrangel troops who wanted to remigrate. At the time the Soviets were not prepared and on 5 April 1921 the Central Committee adopted a resolution ordering Dzerzhinsky and his Cheka to prevent the return of Wrangel men to Russia (TsA FSB, f. 1, op. 5, d. 454, l. 14).

65. About the shooting of the former Wrangel soldiers, see TsA FSB, f. 38, op. 1, d. 454, l. 14 (report to Mantsev of 8 December 1920). From July 1920 Vasili Mantsev had been a member of the VeCheKa collegium and from August served as the head of the Special Department (OO) of the South-Western and Southern Fronts, also chairing Cheka troikas, a group of three officials including himself who used to issue death sentences to people after simplified speedy investigations and without any trial. In 1921–2 Mantsev served as the chairman of the Ukrainian VeCheKa (later GPU), in March 1922 he was appointed People's Commissar for Interior of Ukraine, and from 1936 to 1937 served as deputy chairman of the Supreme court of the RSFSR. Arrested by the NKVD in October 1937, in March 1938 Mantsev testified at the last Moscow show trial, the Trial of the Twenty-One, charging so-called 'old Bolsheviks' (like, for example, Nikolai Bukharin, Alexey Rykov, Nikolai Krestinsky, Christian Rakovsky, Arkady Rosengoltz and Dmitry Pletniov – a prominent medical scientist and physician, who had been severely tortured and shot later, in 1941 – as well as Genrikh Yagoda, former head of the NKVD, plus others, less well-known figures). After the trial, Mantsev himself was sentenced to death in July 1938, and executed at the Kommunarka shooting ground in August. About the Massacre of Feodosia between 29 December 1941 and 1 January 1942, see Alfred M. de Zayas, *Die Wehrmacht-Untersuchungsstelle für Verletzungen des Völkerrechts: Dokumentation alliierter Kriegsverbrechen im Zweiten Weltkrieg* (Beltheim-Schnellbach: Lindenbaum Verlag, 2012).

66. See TsA FSB, f. 1, op. 5, d. 454, l. 39 and f. 2, op. 3, d. 673, l. 10.

67. *V.I. Lenin i VChK: Collection of Documents, 1917-1922* (Moscow: Iz-vo Politicheskoi Literatury, 1975), 480-5, 'Report to the III Congress of the Comintern on the tactics of the Russian Communist Party', 5 July 1921, no. 437.

68. Regarding TREST, SINDIKAT and SINDIKAT-2, one of the best accounts remains Andrew Cook's book, *On His Majesty's Secret Service* (2002). See also Andrew and Mitrokhin, *The Mitrokhin Archive I*, ch. 2, and Volodarsky, *Stalin's Agent*, 452–5.

Remarkably, the account originally prepared by the CIA and then released for public distribution under the FOIA, see Pamela K. Simpkins and K. Leigh Dyer (eds), *The Trust* (Arlington, VA: Security and Intelligence Foundation, 1989), is riddled with factual errors and distortions.

69. Samsonov had recently been appointed head of the SOO (special-operational department), Blagonravov headed the TO (transport department), Yagoda was Menzhinsky's deputy at the OO and head of the UD (administration department), Artuzov was soon to become head of the KRO, counter-intelligence department (July 1922), and Katznelson was deputy chief of the powerful AOU (administration directorate), soon to head the financial department of the reorganized EKU (economic directorate).

70. Alexander Eiduk (Aleksandrs Eiduks) came from a teacher's family in the rural community of Odziena, Latvia. From a young age he joined the revolutionary movement and in January 1906 was sent to Odessa to participate in the underground party work. In November he emigrated to Germany and in June 1908 moved to Vienna where, among other things, he studied at the higher agricultural school (Höhere Landwirtschaftsschule). Eiduk had spent the war in Austria as a civilian internee and was only able to return to Russia in January 1918, joining the Cheka in October. On 27 March 1919 the Council of People's Commissars (SNK) approved him as one of the members of the Cheka Collegium and in July he headed the newly formed secret-operational department (SOO) at the Cheka HQ in Moscow. By the time when the staff of the new Collegium, the Cheka's governing body, was approved by Lenin in July 1920, Eiduk was no longer chairman of the Central Collegium for Prisoners and Refugees which was soon reorganised as the Central Office for the Evacuation of Population, Tsentoevak (part of the Cheka and then GPU, see GA RF, f. R-3333, op. 28, d. 2904). Later he served as head of the department in charge of all trade agents abroad of the Main Customs Directorate of the NKVT and then, from 11 November 1921 as a Soviet representative at the American Relief Administration (ARA). In 1923 he was dismissed from all responsible posts from October 1932 serving at the various sections of the GULAG. In July 1938 Eiduk was arrested, and in August accused of spying for Germany and shot.

71. See P.A. Shveikovsky, *Sud chesti I duel v voiskakh rossiiskoi armii*, 3rd ed. (St Petersburg: Izdatel V. Berezovsky, 1912).

72. Paul Robinson, 'Courts of Honour in the Late Imperial Russian Army', *The Slavonic and East European Review*, 84/4 (Oct. 2006), 725. General Wrangel's order no. 3402, 12/25 July 1920.

73. 7 October 1921. RGASPI, f. 2, op. 1, d. 24643.

74. What happened to his wife, Nina Nechvolodova, is unclear. According to one version, she had worked in the theatre and cinema. General Milkovsky used to serve as an aide of the minister of war at the Crimean government and the Inspector of Artillery of the 3rd Army Corps commanded by General Slashchev. After his return, Milkovsky was accepted to the Red Army. He was executed during the Great Terror. In 1920 Colonel Hilbich served as the military commandant of Simferopol and was shot by the Bolsheviks in April 1931. Fedor Batkin illegally returned to the Crimea in 1922 only to be executed in July. His brother Anisim was also executed. After his return to Russia, Colonel Mezernitsky became a secret agent of the counter-intelligence department of the Cheka, later GPU/OGPU. In 1924 he took part in Operation TREST. As an OGPU officer he later served in Siberia and was sent on secret assignments to China and Mongolia. Arrested in June 1937 in Ulan Bator (now Ulaanbaatar). Sentenced to death and shot in August. Mezernitsky's memoirs were published in New York in 1996. The Chekist Jan Tanenbaum was shot on 29 December 1937.

75. Macfie, 'British Intelligence and the Causes of Unrest in Mesopotamia', 173.

76. Salahi R. Sonyel, 'Mustafa Kemal and Enver in Conflict, 1919-22', *Middle Eastern Studies*, 25/4 (Oct. 1989), 507. About the first or one of the first meetings with Major Hedley in Berlin, see Ferris, 'The British Empire vs. The Hidden Hand', 325. See also, TNA: WO 32/5620, INTELLIGENCE: General (Code 69A): Turkish nationalist intrigue; Interviews with and reports on Enver Pasha in Berlin related to Bolshevik ambitions in Europe and Asia, Memorandum by Hedley, 6 Jan. 1920.

77. See Sonyel, 'Mustafa Kemal and Enver in Conflict', 506-7, TNA: FO 371/5137, Turkey, Code 44 File 113, secret dispatch, India Office to FO, 13 Feb. 1920 (attaching a report of 03/2/20).

78. TNA: FO 371/5211, Turkey, Code 44 File 1311, Major Ivor Hedley to Major-General Neill Malcolm, Berlin, 23 Feb. 1920.

79. See George S. Harris and Nur Bilge Criss (eds.), *Studies in Atatürk's Turkey: The American Dimension* (Leiden & Boston: Brill, 2009), 85.

80. See Admiral Sir Reginald 'Blinker' Hall, *A Clear Case of Genius: Room 40's Code-Breaking Pioneer* (Stroud, Gloucestershire: The History Press, 2017), 192.

81. Howard A. Reed, 'Turkey and Her Nationalist Leaders as seen in the 1923 Reports of Louise Bryant', in Harris and Criss, *Studies in Atatürk's Turkey*, 86. See also Neriman Kuyucu, *Hemingway in Turkey* (unpublished Master's thesis, University of Michigan, 2013).

82. See David A. Langbart, 'Five Months in Petrograd in 1918: Robert W. Imbrie and the US Search for Information in Russia', *Studies in Intelligence*, 52/1 (March 2008), web supplement 1. After Summer's sudden death on 4 May 1918, Imbrie reported to acting Consul General DeWitt C. Poole.

83. See David A. Langbart, '"Spare no expense": The Department of State and the Search for Information about Bolshevik Russia, November 1917-September 1918', *Intelligence and National Security*, 4/2 (1989), 316–34. See also, David S. Foglesong, *America's Secret War Against Bolshevism* (Chapel Hill, NC: University of North Carolina Press, 1995).

84. Michael P. Zirinsky, 'Blood, Power and Hypocrisy: The Murder of Robert Imbrie and American Relations with Pahlavi Iran, 1924', *International Journal of Middle East Studies*, 18/3 (Aug. 1986), 275–92.

85. Ibid., 277 and 288.

86. The article continued: 'Angora has no decent hotels and there is a dearth of houses; so when 35 representatives of European business interests in Turkey announced their intention of going to Angora to settle directly the economic clauses of the peace treaty, the Turkish Government was worried. The Imbrie scheme gave them an idea. They are fitting up a train of passenger cars as living quarters for the busy business delegates. The Imbries are the center of much admiration in Angora social circles. The wife of Mustapha Kemal Pasha is a frequent visitor to the perambulating residence of the United States representative. She has even expressed a desire to have the apartment given to her in the event that Mr. and Mrs. Imbrie be unfortunately compelled to leave!' *TIME*, Monday, May 28, 1923, Vol. I, No. 13, Foreign News: A Box Car.

87. NARA, General Records of the Department of State, RG 59, personnel record of Robert W. Imbrie, Central Decimal File 123 Im 1, 70, 75, see Zirinsky, "Blood, Power and Hypocrisy: The Murder of Robert Imbrie', 277.

88. Langbart, 'Five Months in Petrograd in 1918', 2.

89. Secret Report R-10783 of 11 January 1921 with the intercept of 4 January 1921 Bryant (Moscow) to Wiegand (Berlin) dispatch re Harrison. I am grateful to Elizabeth Atwood for sharing this document with me.

90. NARA, RG 59, File 123 Im 1, 48. Zirinsky comments that Dulles came to know Imbrie in Istanbul, where Dulles was aide to Admiral Mark Lambert Bristol, U.S. High Commissioner to Turkey.

91. Zirinsky, 'Blood, Power and Hypocrisy: The Murder of Robert Imbrie', 277.
92. 10th Congress of the RCP(b), 8–16 March 1921 (Stenographic report, full version, Moscow, 1963), Lenin's closing remarks to the Report of the Central Committee, 9 March. One hundred years later, the same slogan was repeated almost word for word by the Putin clique during the Russian Duma elections in September 2021.
93. Seth Singleton, 'The Tambov Revolt (1920-1921)', *Slavic Review*, 25/3 (Sept. 1966), 499.
94. The report of V.A. Antonov-Ovseyenko, chairman of the commission (February-July 1921), to Lenin and the Central Committee 'About the bandit movement in Tambov Province' (in Russian), dated 20 July 1921. Trotsky Archives, Harvard University, doc. #686. For details, see Singleton, 'The Tambov Revolt', 497–512.
95. See Douglas Smith, *The Russian Job: The Forgotten Story of How America Saved the Soviet Union from Famine* (London: Picador/Macmillan Publishers, 2019), 15–16.
96. Israel Getzler, 'The Communist leaders' role in the Kronstadt tragedy of 1921 in the light of recently published archival documents', *Revolutionary Russia*, 15/1 (June 2002), 24–44. On 5 March Trotsky, as chairman of the Revolutionary-Military Council (RVS), ordered to reform the 7th Army and 'to supress the uprising in Kronstadt' appointing Tukhachevsky as its commander. On 7 March, Kronstadt *Izvestia* published Trotsky's ultimatum: 'I am giving the immediate order to get ready to crush the revolt.' Remarkably, as has already been mentioned, in his memoirs General Ali Fuat Cebesoy claims that as the Turkish ambassador in Moscow at the time, he took part in the events when Stalin allegedly urged him to use his influence 'to persuade the Tatar divisions in Russia, one in Moscow and one in Kazan, to participate in the suppression of this dangerous uprising' (Spector, 'General Ali Fuat Cebesoy and the Kronstadt Revolt', 492), which is almost certainly the general's later invention. For a detailed study of the Kronstadt campaign, see Neil Croll, 'The Role of M.N. Tukhachevskii in the Suppression of the Kronstadt Rebellion', *Revolutionary Russia*, 17/2 (December 2004), 1–48.
97. Amos Chapple, RFE/RL, 28 February 2021.
98. Charles M. Edmondson, 'The politics of hunger: The Soviet response to famine, 1921', *Soviet Studies*, 29/4 (October 1977), 506–18.
99. Later research conducted by Western experts revealed that the most severely stricken gubernias were, in addition to those mentioned, Astrakhan, Samara, Saratov, Simbirsk, Volga German Workers' Commune, Tatarstan (according to several researchers the famine here was man-made), Vyatka, Ufa, Uralsk, Orenburg, and Penza.
100. Edmondson, 'The politics of hunger', 509.
101. Kuskóva (née Yesipova), became an orphan at 15 and married her gymnasium teacher right after finishing her studies. The couple had two children but her husband soon died and she moved to Moscow where she soon got carried away by the revolutionary movement. In 1891 she was living in Saratov actively participating in underground revolutionary activities. Arrested, she had spent a year behind bars and then three years on probation. In Saratov, she entered into a sham marriage with a student, whose name was Kuskov, in order to get him out of prison. After this episode she became known as Kuskova. In 1894 she moved to Nizhny Novgorod where she became interested in Marxism and met the already famous writers Vladimir Korolenko and Maxim Gorky, economist, statistician and journalist Nikolai Annensky, as well as her future husband Sergey Prokopovich. Together, they left Russia and settled in Brussels, Belgium where in 1899 Kuskova produced a document which was not intended for publication but somehow became widely known under the title 'Credo'. In the document, Kuskova argued that the struggle of the Social Democrats for the creation of a proletarian party and the seizure of political power has no prospects in the political conditions of Russia. This thesis was severely criticised by Lenin and both Kuskova and Prokopovich became

disillusioned with Marxism. After the Bolshevik revolution they stayed in Russia, opposing both the Red and the White Terror. In 1918 Kuskova together with Gorky's wife and human rights activist, Ekaterina Peshkova, and a former minister for state charities of the Kerensky government, Nikolai Kishkin, organised the Save the Children League. In 1920 Kuskova and Kishkin on behalf of the League asked the Sovnarkom to let them apply for aide to the foreign relief organisations. Because it was a public and non-party organisation, the authorities did not like this initiative and soon the state took control of the League.

102. GARF, f. 1235, op. 96, d. 4, l. 115. For details, see Vladimir Makarov and Vasili Khristoforov (both of the FSB department of registration and archives), 'To the History of All-Russian Committee for Famine Relief', *Novaya i Noveishaya Istoriya*, no. 3 (2006), 198–205. Kalinin himself was made the chairman of the Commission with three deputies: Peter Smidovich (Piotr Smidowicz in his native Polish) – a Russian and Soviet revolutionary from an aristocratic Polish family, in 1920 he was chief of supplies for the 5th Army of the Southern Front and chairman of the Revolutionary Tribunal of the Southern Front, took part in the liquidation of the Antonov Uprising, and in 1921 of the Kronstadt Uprising; Alexey Rykov – deputy chairman of the Council of Labour and Defence, soon to become chairman of the Sovnarkom; and Lev Kamenev – chairman of the Moscow Soviet. There were also four members of the Presidium, and ten members of the Commission representing various commissariats, including Lev Krasin who represented NKVT and Stepan Popov, member of the NKVD Collegium (but not VChK).

103. US Department of State, *Papers Relating to the Foreign Relations of the United States*, 1921, Volume II: The Minister in Norway to the Secretary of State, Christiania, July 15, 1921, No. 1869.

104. Pomgol is a Russian acronym for 'pomoshch golodayushchim', that is, help the hungry. On 26 August Lenin sent a directive to Stalin, then People's Commissar of Workers' and Peasants' Inspection (RKI), previously the People's Commissariat for State Control. Referring to the Commission as 'Kukish' (a rude gesture indicating contempt and a desire to humiliate an opponent, 'a fig' in English), Lenin formed this acronym from the initial letters of the names of two commission members: Kuskova and Kishkin = 'Ku-kish'. The Bolshevik leader ordered to immediately dissolve the commission, arrest Prokopovich for three months 'for anti-government statements' while an investigation was on the way and expel other members from Moscow to the countryside. They must live there under supervision and preferably without any access to the railway, Lenin wrote. 'We will give orders to the newspapers: do your very best to ridicule and bully them at least once a week for two months.' Do not hesitate, he concluded, the Politburo must put an end to it at once. Lenin, *Complete Works*, 5th edition (Moscow: Iz-vo politicheskoi literatury, 1970), volume 53, No. 229, 141–2.

105. John Forbes, 'American Friends and Russian Relief, 1917-1927 (Part I)', *Bulletin of Friends Historical Association*, 41/1 (Spring 1952), 39–51.

106. Edmondson, 'The politics of hunger', 509–10.

107. US Department of State, *Papers Relating to the Foreign Relations of the United States, 1919, Russia*, 108–9. See Edmondson, 'The politics of hunger', 511.

108. Hoover to Brown, August 9, 1921, in Herbert Hoover Archives, The Hoover Institution on War, Revolution and Peace, Stanford, CA, box 17, folder 6.

109. Smith, *The Russian Job*, 5. See also, Benjamin M. Weissman, 'The Aftereffects of the American Relief Mission to Soviet Russia', *Russian Review*, 29/1 (Oct. 1970), 411–21.

110. Statement of Senator Watson of Georgia, Congressional Records – Senate, 6 June 1922, 67th Congress, 2nd Session, 8251.

111. See, for example, Liudmila Novikova, *An Anti-Bolshevik Alternative: The White movement and the civil war in the Russian north* (Madison, WI: The University of Wisconsin Press, 2018), 221.

112. RGASPI, f. 17, op. 163, d. 244, ll. 30, 31.

113. Smith, *The Russian Job*, 124.

114. Victor V. Kondrashin, 'Year 1922 in the Soviet village through the eyes of the GPU', History Seminars at the FSB Lubyanka HQ, 1999 (keynote address).

115. Although Tikhon was not sentenced, they forced him to collaborate with the GPU. That summer, the general fiasco of the famine effort with the Chekists trying to split the clergy on Lenin's orders exacerbated the splits in the Orthodox Church which had already been evident before the revolution. This resulted in the creation of the new, or Living Church (in Russian 'Obnovlenchestvo' or Renovation), staffed with GPU agents and collaborators, a practice which continues until this day. This renovationist movement consisted of several groups and formally ended with the death of its leader in 1946. For details about the relations between the Russian Orthodox Church and the GPU at the period, see Rayfield, *Stalin and His Hangmen*, 119-24. For a documentary collection from the Russian archives, see N. Pokrovsky and S. Petrov, *Politburo and Church, 1922-1925*, in 2 vols. (Moscow: ROSSPEN, 1997), I, 249–304, in Russian.

116. For details, see Hakan Kirimli, 'The Famine of 1921-22 in the Crimea and the Volga Basin and the Relief from Turkey', *Middle Eastern Studies*, 39/1 (Jan. 2003), 37–88.

Chapter 9: The Raids

1. Andrew and Mitrokhin, *The Mitrokhin Archive I*, 48.

2. For documented examples of completely false testimonies of such well-known Soviet defectors as Walter Krivitsky and Alexander Orlov, see Volodarsky, *Stalin's Agent* (2014). For misinterpreted and largely unaccepted information provided by another defector, see idem, 'Unknown Agabekov', *Intelligence and National Security*, 28/6 (2013), 890–909.

3. Andrew and Gordievsky, *KGB*, 110-11.

4. Andrew, *Secret Service*.

5. Ibid., 318.

6. The irrational actions of the alleged 'Soviet spy' Wilfred Macartney, encouraged and inspired by such unsavoury provocateur as George Monkton, 'an undesirable type of man about town' (KV 2/647 serial 169a memo of 26.7.27) acting in close conjunction with Special Branch and MI5(b), both answerable and accountable to the Home Office, Macartney himself later described as 'cretin-like stupidity'. 'One of Moscow's harshest opponents in Cabinet was Home Secretary Sir William Joynson-Hicks,' Victor Madeira writes. 'Much like Churchill, Curzon, [Admiral Sir Reginald 'Blinker'] Hall, [Walter] Long, [Admiral Sir Hugh] Sinclair, [Basil] Thomson and others, Jix had no trouble using and misusing intelligence to expose CPGB and Soviet covert work ... Of the six Home Secretaries in the period covered in this book [1917-29], Jix was the boldest advocate of using fascist groups to roll back Communism' (*Britannia and the Bear*, 132–3).

7. Andrew, *Secret Service*, 332.

8. Russo-British Relations, House of Commons Debate, 26 May 1927, vol. 206, cc. 2301-2302.

9. TNA KV 2/1290.

10. For the history of the Ewer group operation, see his MI5 personal file PF 655331, s. 809a now at The National Archives as KV 2/1016. For the introductory letter of agent 'D' to the *Daily Herald*, see PF 38299/Supplement Vol. 2 (TNA KV 2/1102) s.18a.

11. TNA KV 2/1016, s. 809a. This is the first page of what MI5 called 'History of a section of the Russian Intelligence Service, operating in this country, under the management of

William Norman EWER, 1919-1929' with a cover letter to the War Office, Directorate of Military Operations and Intelligence (DMO&I) signed by C.D.S. and dated 8 January 1930.

12. TNA KV 2/1016, s. 809a.

13. See Volodarsky, *Stalin's Agent*, 61, 62 and especially 536.

14. In his Authorised History of MI5, Christopher Andrew is desperately trying to find a documented link between the FPA and Soviet intelligence missing in all other accounts. He writes that 'tapping the FPA telephone line produced "immediate results", revealing calls to ARCOS, to prominent Communists and *to at least one suspected Soviet intelligence operative*' (p. 153, italics added). The footnote refers to three alleged sources: Minute of 7 Feb. 1925 in TNA KV 2/1101; 'History of a Section of Russian Intelligence' in TNA KV 2/1016, s. 809a of 8 Jan. 1930; and 'Synopsis of main telephone conversations', n.d. in TNA KV 2/1101 s. 46a. Alas, all three are false leads. Three minutes of 7 Feb. are (1) HOW on The Federated Press of America and (2-3) GPO reports about lack of letters at 28 Hova Villas, Hove, East Sussex. Serial 809a in TNA KV 2/1016 is a 14-page 'History of a section of the Russian Intelligence Service, operating in this country, under the management of William Norman Ewer 1919-1929'. And s.46a in KV 2/1101 is a 'Personal & Secret' letter from Major Morton, SIS, to Major Ball, MI5, CX 5327/Prod of 19 Feb.1925. The telephone check had been working since 27 February 1925. TNA KV 2/1101 s.59a mentions a telephone call 'to our old friend Boris Said, now in Berlin', wrongly (and anyway not quite seriously) suspected by MI5 to be 'head of the Bolshevik Secret Service in England' (P.F.R. 7484).

15. Who turned out to be Albert Allen, deputy manager of the FPA, codenamed ALLEN by MI5. His real name was Arthur Francis Lakey, a Special Branch sergeant until his discharge for going on strike in 1919. See his PF 38426/V1-2 at TNA KV 2/989-990.

16. Gill Bennett, *Churchill's Man of Mystery: Desmond Morton and the World of Intelligence* (London and New York: Routledge, 2007), 96.

17. See Antony Best, 'Intelligence, Diplomacy and the Japanese Threat to British Interests, 1914-41', *Intelligence and National Security*, 17/1 (2002), 86-7. See also TNA HO 45/25105 WAR: Defence Regulation 18B detainee: RUTLAND, Frederick Joseph; pre-war agent for Japanese secret service. Rutland's declassified MI5 personal file PF 37966 is KV 2/328-339.

18. Russo-British Relations, House of Commons Debate, 26 May 1927, vol. 206, cc2299-2303.

19. A.J.P. Taylor, *English History 1914-1945* (Oxford: Oxford University Press, 2001), 242.

20. Andrew, *Secret Service*, 332. (There is a footnote to this quotation referring the reader to a mysterious Cmd. 2874. To spare the time of a future researcher, this is a 31-page brochure *Documents illustrating the Hostile Activities of the Soviet Government and Third International against Great Britain*, London: HM Stationery Office, 1927). See also, Christopher Andrew, 'British Intelligence and the Breach with Russia in 1927', *The Historical Journal*, 25/4 (December 1982), 957-64.

21. TNA, KV 3/35. The file contains a collection of ARCOS documents provided by an informant (probably source 'Y') with access to its photographic room over the period 1924-7.

22. Andrew, 'British Intelligence and the Breach with Russia in 1927', 963.

23. TNA, KV 2/647 (from the M.I.5 B file PF 38661, Volume 1), serial 20A and KV 2/647 (part 3, page 31) s.164a with reference to 10.6.27, s.101a.

24. TNA, FO 1093/73, Secret Service Committee, 1927, Miscellaneous Papers, letter from 'C' (Sinclair) to Sir William Tyrrell, FO, no. C/2523 of 28 June 1927.

25. For Macartney's time in Spain, see Richard Baxell, *Unlikely Warriors: The British in the Spanish Civil War and the Struggle Against Fascism* (London: Aurum, 2012), 119–25. See also Volodarsky, *Stalin's Agent*, 184–5, 492; and TNA: KV 2/655 serial 507a.
26. Timothy Phillips, *The Secret Twenties: British Intelligence, the Russians and the Jazz Age* (London: Granta, 2017), 321.
27. Jeffery, *MI6*, 230. See also Peter Davies, *The Authorised History of British Defence Economic Intelligence: A Cold War in Whitehall, 1929-90* (London: Routledge, 2020), 31.
28. TNA KV 2/647 part 3, n.d. no serial number (page 77 between s.16a and s.20a). See also Jeffery, *MI6*, 126–7. Captain Mackenzie, who had been serving as an intelligence officer in Gallipoli during the Great War, was sent on sick leave to Athens and ended up being seconded to work under Samson, Jeffery writes. After Samson was transferred to head the Eastern Mediterranean Special Intelligence Bureau in Alexandria, a joint SIS (MI1c) and MI5 headquarters, Mackenzie took charge. Instructed to move to the Island of Syros and provided with considerable funds by Cumming, by the early summer of 1917 Mackenzie had created a lavishly resourced Aegean Intelligence Service with a staff of thirty-nine officers.
29. Compton Mackenzie, in Macartney, *Walls Have Mouths* (London: Victor Gollancz, 1936), 21–2.
30. McMeekin, *History's Greatest Heist*, 123.
31. Ibid., 201. Lomonosov's first name and patronymic were Yuri Vladimirovich but when he published his *Memoirs of the Russian Revolution* in New York in 1919, he signed them as 'George V. Lomonossoff'. Platon Kerzentsev's real name was Lebedev. He was a Soviet state and party official, journalist, diplomat, playwright and a leading figure in the Proletkult movement, also serving as the director of ROSTA (Russian Telegraph Agency). In 1921 Kerzhentsev was appointed the plenipotentiary (ambassador) to Sweden. In January 1919 Scheinmann (Sheinman) was expelled from Sweden together with other 'dangerous Bolsheviks' such as Vorovsky, Litvinov and Mikhail Borodin. On 13 October 1921, Scheinmann was appointed chairman of the newly established State Bank of the RSFSR.
32. Minutes of the Politburo meetings 1919-1952, RGASPI, f. 17, op. 3, d. 224, para 3, Politburo meeting of 28 October 1921.
33. McMeekin, *History's Greatest Heist*, 201.
34. Erward Jay Epstein, *Dossier: The Secret History of Armand Hammer* (New York: Random House, 1996), 40. J. Edgar Hoover's investigation of radical activities in 1919 and 1920 provided some credibility for the 'diamonds' theory, Todd Pfannenstiel writes in his interesting research article. In his book, *Master of Deceit* (1958), Hoover recalls an episode when customs officials began searching seamen aboard the SS *Stockholm* when she docked in New York City. When one sailor turned back and ran down the pier, officials detained him for further investigation. A package found on him revealed several envelopes, one inside another, with the smallest holding over 200 uncut diamonds worth about $50,000. In addition, the package contained a typewritten letter addressed to 'Comrade Martens'. 'The smuggling of diamonds,' Hoover wrote, 'was one of the early Bolshevik techniques of financing operations in the United States.' J. Edgar Hoover, *Masters of Deceit: The Story of Communism in America and How to Fight It* (New York: Henry Holt & Co., 1958), 292. See Todd Pfannenstiel, 'The Soviet Bureau: A Bolshevik Strategy to Secure U.S. Diplomatic Recognition through Economic Trade', *Diplomatic History*, 27/2 (April 2003), 171–92.
35. Pfannenstiel, 'The Soviet Bureau', 178.
36. Karl Wiegand, 'An Interview with Lenin', *New York Evening Journal*, February 21, 1920.
37. George H. Drury, *Guide to North American Steam Locomotives* (Waukesha, WI: Kalmbach Publishing Company, 1993), 176.

38. RGAE, f. 413, op. 4, d. 307, ll. 203, 204, 206.
39. RGAE, f. 413, op. 4, d. 307, l. 154.
40. RGASPI, f. 76, op. 2, d. 76, ll. 23, 24, dated July 1921.
41. Alexander A. Igolkin (historian, Russian Academy of Sciences), 'Lenin's Narkom: At the origins of Soviet corruption', in Russian, *Novyi Istorichesky Vestnik*, 1 (2004), 1–17. Despite his obvious achevements, critical publications about Lomonosov continued to come out in Russia. In the West, besides Lomonosov's books and scientific works, of note are his manuscripts which make up part of the collection of the Leeds Russian Archive. The collection also catalogues the history of many other Russian nationals forced to flee their country for social and political reasons, notably the revolutions of February and October 1917, the Civil War, and the subsequent formation of the USSR.
42. David R. Stone, 'Soviet Arms Exports in the 1920s', *Journal of Contemporary History*, 48/1 (2012), 57–77.
43. Victor N. Koptevsky, *Russia-Turkey: Etapy torgovo-ekonomicheskogo sotrudnichestva* (Moscow: Rzussian Academy of Sciences, 2003), 70–1.
44. A.P. Serebrovsky, *Na neftyanom fronte* (Moscow: Neftyanoe khozyaistvo, 2015), 78.
45. The *New York Times* of 1 July 1923 described Mr. Day as follows: 'He is a young man, 37, but older in looks. He is a big man, 6 feet 2, weighing 190 pounds. His complexion is swarthy. In the crowd in the Levant the natives would not observe him as a foreigner except for his propelling energy. He rides camelback as easily as in an automobile, and he is as good at golf as at international dickering.'
46. See McMeekin, *History's Greatest Heist*, 123. See also Michael Sargent, *British Military Involvement in Transcaspia, 1918-1919* (Camberley, Surrey: Defence Academy of the UK/Conflict Studies Research Centre, April 2004), 33. McMeekin asserts that 'the British withdrew their last troops in March 1919'.
47. For details, see Reginald Teague-Jones, *The Spy Who Disappeared: Diary of a Secret Mission to Russian Central Asia in 1918* (London: Victor Gollancz, 1991); Peter Hopkirk, *On Secret Service East of Constantinople* (London: John Murray, 1994), especially pages 352–99; and Taline Ter Minassian, *Most Secret Agent of Empire: Reginald Teague-Jones, Master Spy of the Great Game* (London: Hurst & Co Publishers, 2014).
48. Hans Heymann Jr., 'Oil in Soviet-Western Relations in the Interwar Years', *The American Slavic and East-European Review*, 7/4 (Dec. 1948), 303–16.
49. Philip S. Gillette, 'American capital in the contest for Soviet oil, 1920-23', *Soviet Studies*, 24/4 (1973), 477–90. For details about the Urquhart deal, see Thomas S. Martin, 'The Urquhart Concession and Anglo-Soviet Relations, 1921-1922', *Jahrbücher für Geschichte Osteuropas*, Neue Folge, 20/4 (Dec. 1972), 551–70.
50. RGAE, f. 413, op. 2, d. 1686, ll. 5, 7-8.
51. Serebrovsky, *Na neftyanom fronte*, 79. From June to November 1921 Philipp Yakovlevich Rabinovich, previously a deputy, served as the NKVT plenipotentiary in Transcaucasia; in 1922 he was appointed member of the board and then promoted to Director of ARCOS in London and deputy trade representative. In October 1925 he succeeded Rakovsky as the official Soviet trade representative in the UK. Very soon, however, Rabinovich was recalled and Mikhail Khloplyankin was appointed, serving until November 1926. The last Soviet trade representative in London before the break of diplomatic relations was Lev Khinchuk, occupying this position from November 1926 to May 1927.
52. Ibid., 72, 293. See also Stanislas Jeannesson, 'La difficile reprise des relations commerciales entre la France et l'URSS (1921-1928)', *Histoire, économie et société*, 19/3 (2000), 411–29. For details, see Centre des Archives du Monde du Travail, Banque Nationale du Commerce et de l'Industrie, archive group 120 AQ 587. After this agreement the Russian-French trade turnover in petroleum products was constantly

growing amounting to approximately 15 per cent of French imports by 1928 and reaching 29 per cent in 1932 (Michael Jabara Carley, 'Five Kopecks for Five Kopecks: Franco-Soviet Trade Negotiations, 1928-1939', *Cahiers du Monde russe et soviétique*, 33/1 (Jan.-Mar. 1992), 23–57).

53. RGAE, f. 413, op. 2, d. 1850, ll. s. 52-59. See Anikeyev's letter to Krasin of 5 April 1924 s. 59. See also, Erdal Bilgiç, '1927 The Trade Agreement Between Soviet Union and Turkey: A Milestone in Economic Relationship?', *Journal of Modern Turkish History Studies*, 21/42 (Spring 2021), 237–67. I am very grateful to Dr. Bilgiç for his friendly help and for sending copies of the original documents from the RGAE related to the case. Krasin headed the NKVT until his appointment as plenipotentiary to France, at which position he had served from 14 November 1924 before moving to London in October 1925, where he succeeded Christian Rakovsky. For interesting details about Krasin, see Yu. Felshtinsky, G. Chenyavsky and F. Markiz, *Krasin's letters to his wife and children* (Moscow: Direct-Media, 2014), in Russian. See also Semion S. Khromov, *The Unknown Krasin, 1920-1926* (Moscow: Russian Academy of Sciences, 2001), in Russian, and Michael Glenny, 'Leonid Krasin: The Years before 1917. An Outline', *Soviet Studies*, 22/2 (Oct. 1970), 192–221.

54. The commissariat was transformed into Rabkrin – Workers' and Peasants' Inspection – again under Stalin, and Avanesov became his deputy. When Krasin left for France in November and was succeeded by Alexander Tsyurupa, Avanesov was appointed deputy commissar for foreign trade probably because of his experience before the revolution and command of foreign languages. From 1907 to 1913 Avanesov had lived in Switzerland and graduated from the University of Zurich Faculty of Medicine.

55. For details, see Ramil Zalyaev, 'Soviet trade offices in Turkey', *Scholarly Research Articles of Kazan University, Humanitarian Sciences*, 151/2 part 2 (2009), 162–7. In 1924 Naphtha Syndicate, a state monopoly for oil sales at home and abroad, had the audacity to set up its own subsidiary, Russian Oil Products Ltd (ROP) in London, with offices and depots throughout Britain (TNA KV 5/73), for Russian oil and petroleum products exports to the UK. Although MI5 hugely exaggerated its role as 'a cover for Soviet subversion and intelligence gathering', also suspecting 'that its facilities and staff would be used, or at least had the potential to be used, to bring about acts of sabotage in the event of hostilities with the USSR', it was indeed used as a cover for some Soviet intelligence activities and personnel.

56. *Dokumenty vneshnei politiki SSSR* (Moscow: Politicheskaya Literatura, 1958), Vol. 2, No. 332, 499–500.

57. Library and Archives Canada, Arthur Meighen fonds, Series 2: Correspondence of Rt. Hon. Arthur Meighen as Prime Minister of Canada and Secretary of State for External Affairs, file 187, no. 026754, as quoted by Ronald A. Adams, *Mackenzie King and the Soviet Trade Mission to Canada, 1924-1927* (unpublished MA thesis, University of Ottawa, 1970), 21.

58. Adams, *Mackenzie King and the Soviet Trade Mission to Canada*, 21.

59. James Ramsey Ullman, *Anglo-Soviet Relations, 1917-1921*, Volume 3: The Anglo-Soviet Accord (Princeton, NJ: Princeton University Press, 1972), 453.

60. William Lyon Mackenzie King, Primary series correspondence (J1), no. 94398.

61. Adams, *Mackenzie King and the Soviet Trade Mission to Canada*, 43–4.

62. He was born in Yelisavetgrad (Fort St Elisabeth, Central Ukraine, built in 1752) as Yevsey Gershon Radomyslsky to a well-to-do Jewish family. His father was Aaron Radomyslsky and his mother's name before marriage was Apfelbaum. The name Radomyslsky comes from the Polish name of the town Radomyśl, a centre of Jewish settlement, annexed by the Russian Empire in 1793 and included in the Kiev Governorate. During his early

revolutionary years Gershon lived in exile in the German-speaking canton of Bern, Switzerland, and used the name Hirsch Apfelbaum for the convenience of German pronunciation because nobody could pronounce his name given at birth. 'Grigory Zinoviev' was his revolutionary pseudonym.

63. Guy Walters for *The Mail on Sunday*, 12 October 2019. For the full text of the Letter that was sent by SIS to the FO (John D. Gregory), see 'The Zinoviev Letter', *Advocate of Peace Through Justice*, 86/12 (World Affairs Institute, Dec. 1924), 695–8.

64. The 'Zinoviev Letter' library is truly impressive if we only take the names of eminent historians and intelligence historians and limit ourselves to the twentieth century. A short list will include W.P. Coates, *The "Zinoviev Letter": The Case for a Full Investigation* (London: The Anglo-Russian Parliamentary Commission, May 1928), with a preface by J. Maxton (a Labour MP who took an active part in the 'Zinovieff Letter' debates in the Parliament in March that year); A.J.P. Taylor, *English History 1914-1945* (Oxford: The Clarendon Press, 1965); two early articles by Christopher Andrew, 'The British Secret Service and Anglo-Soviet Relations in the 1920s, Part I: From the Trade Negotiations to the Zinoviev Letter' (1977) and 'More on the Zinoviev Letter' (1979) plus the whole chapter 'Zinoviev Letters and the Breach with Russia' in his important work *Secret Service* (1985) plus, of course, a piece in *The Defence of the Realm* (2009), the authorised history of MI5; a book by three journalists Stephen Fay, Lewis Chester and Hugo Young, *The Zinoviev Letter* (Philadelphia, PA: Lippincott & Co., 1967); Natalie Grant, 'The "Zinoviev Letter" Case' (1967); Paul W. Blackstock, ch. 6 'The British Zinoviev Letter: An Intelligence Evaluation' in his book *Agents of Deceit: Frauds, forgeries and political intrigue among nations* (Chicago, IL: Quadrangle Books, 1966); Sybil Crowe, 'The Zinoviev Letter: A Reappraisal' (1975); John Ferris & Uri Bar-Joseph, 'Getting Marlowe to hold his tongue: The Conservative Party, the Intelligence Services and the Zinoviev Letter' (1993); and finally Gill Bennett, *'A most extraordinary and mysterious business': The Zinoviev Letter of 1924* (1999), not to mention at least two classified intelligence histories (one of them by Milicent Bagot of MI5, in 1970).

65. Jeffery, *MI6*, 761, note 14.

66. Richard J. Aldrich and Rory Cormac, *The Black Door: Spies, Secret Intelligence and British Prime Ministers* (London: William Collins, 2017), 49.

67. Jeffery, *MI6*, 216.

68. Gill Bennett, *The Zinoviev Letter: The Conspiracy that Never Dies* (Oxford: OUP, 2018), 143.

69. See John Symons, *The Zinoviev Controversy Resolved* (London: Shepheard-Walwyn, 2019), 80 pages long. About Agabekov, see Volodarsky, 'Unknown Agabekov', *Intelligence and National Security*, 28/6 (2013), 890–909. See also, Volodarsky, *Stalin's Agent* (OUP, 2014), and a chapter on early Soviet defectors in the upcoming second volume of this new KGB history. Although John Symons refers to the above-mentioned article in *Intelligence and National Security*, where this writer states that both SIS and MI5 did not take Agabekov seriously for various reasons, and hugely underrated his potential contribution to the understanding of Soviet intelligence, its structure, personnel, operations and agent networks, Agabekov's two books are full of factual errors and inventions and this defector was in no way in any position to confirm the authenticity of the Zinoviev Letter. Take, for example, his descriptions of his 'personal and professional contact with a GPU officer who had served in London and so had witnessed the Zinoviev scandal at first hand' (Symons, 59–60). Here, John Symons uncritically repeats Agabekov's inventions because in reality Agabekov's 'Braun, a GPU officer', is a mixture of Nikolai Alekseyev, head of station in London in 1924, and Peter Zolotussky, who had briefly served there in 1927 (February-May) before the rupture of diplomatic relations. Before London, in 1924, Zolotussky was head of station in eastern Anatolia, and Agabekov, who had a lot

to do with Turkey as a senior officer of the Oriental Section of the Cheka/GPU (posted to Constantinople in 1929 as an 'illegal' resident agent), could have professionally met him.

70. Sheila Kerr, 'Oleg Tsarev's Synthetic KGB Gems', *International Journal of Intelligence and Counter-intelligence*, 14/1 (2001), 89–116.
71. Ibid., 89.
72. FCO, History Notes, *The Zinoviev Letter of 1924: 'A Most Extraordinary and Mysterious Business'*, Issue 14 (February 1999). See also Jeffery, *MI6*, 217–18. About the authenticity of the document – Assistant Secretary John Gregory's copy of this note, and of the Letter, are in TNA FO 371/10478 (N 7838/108/38).
73. Jonathan Pile, the author of *Churchill's Secret Enemy* (2012), with quotations from G.E. Wakefield's report, describes himself as a self-employed 'author, researcher and investigative historian' from Wakefield, West Yorkshire.
74. For details, see HANSARD, HC Deb 19 March 1928 vol 215 cc47-109 (column 77).
75. TNA KV 2/501 (from MI5 file ZINOVIEV, G.E. PF P.P. 200, Volume 1) s. 57a. 'P.P.' in the original file number stands for 'Peace Propaganda'.
76. TNA KV 2/501, s. 57a, Letter to DDS of 5.5.59.
77. Christopher Andrew, 'More on the Zinoviev Letter', *The Historical Journal*, 22/1 (March 1979), 213–14.
78. See Gabriel Gorodetsky, *The Precarious Truce: Anglo-Soviet Relations 1924-27* (Cambridge: CUP, 1977), 35–52. A short time before, Gorodetsky published a more detailed work specifically on the subject: 'The other "Zinoviev Letters" – New Light on the Mismanagement of the Affair', *Slavic and Soviet Series*, 1/3 (1976), 1–30.
79. Andrew, *Secret Service*, 302.
80. E.H Carr, 'The Zinoviev Letter', *The Historical Journal*, 22/1 (March 1979), 210.
81. HANSARD, HC Deb 26 May 1927 vol 206, column 2258.
82. Gorodetsky, *The Precarious Truce*, 41. See also Bennett, *The Zinoviev Letter*, 232. Professor Gorodetsky, a former student of E.H. Carr and at the time of writing a Quondam Fellow of All Souls College at Oxford University, when *The Precarious Truce* was published, had been director of the Cummings Centre for Russian Studies at Tel Aviv University.
83. TNA PREM 1/49 Soviet Union: propaganda activities of Trade Missions in the United Kingdom, Sir John Anderson (1st Viscount Waverley), Permanent Under-Secretary of State at the Home Office, to the Foreign Office, 3 May 1924. See also, Andrew, *Secret Service*, 302–3.
84. TNA KV 2/501 s. 57a.
85. See Hilary Richardson, 'Conrad Donald im Thurn', unpublished obituary at https://butleigh.org/Obituaries/Donald_im_Thurn(2).pdf, last accessed on 10 November 2021.
86. HANSARD, *HC Deb 19 March 1928 vol 215* cc47-109.
87. Jeffery, *MI6*, 189. 'A sub-source introduced in late 1924 by FR/3/Moscow, whose name was known and who was said to be a fully conscious and paid agent,' Jeffery further explains, 'provided minutes of Sovnarkom (the Soviet of People's Commissars) meetings. Regarded as particularly valuable by SIS and its customers, Head Office Circulating sections subjected them to careful scrutiny and concluded they were probably genuine.' Alas, these were also fakes.
88. 'But if this is so,' Tolstoy wrote, 'if it is true that it depends on us to destroy the existing order of life, have we the right to destroy it, without knowing clearly what we shall put in its place? What will become of the world if the existing order of things is destroyed? "What will be there, beyond the walls of the world which we leave behind?" (Herzen's words.) "Terror seizes us, – the void, expanse, freedom ... How can we go, without knowing whither?"' Leo Tolstoy, *The Kingdom of God is Within You* (New York, NY: Cosimo Classics, 2007, originally published in 1893), 368.

89. Andrew, *Secret Service*, 338.
90. The State Bank acknowledged the receipt of the bills in a letter to the Royal Bank of Canada in Montreal on 21 January 1925.
91. Adams, *Mackenzie King and the Soviet Trade Mission to Canada*, 67.
92. *The New York Times*, January 5, 1920, quoted by Adams.
93. Adams, *Mackenzie King and the Soviet Trade Mission to Canada*, 71–2.
94. L.S. Amery to the Governor General of Canada, Field Marshal Julian Byng (1st Viscount Byng of Vimy), 6 April 1925, Governor General's Papers, file 34691, vol. 2(b).
95. Adams, *Mackenzie King and the Soviet Trade Mission to Canada*, 97.
96. In his 'Memorandum of Interview with Mr. Yazikov' of 2 July 1925, O.D. Skelton noted about Yazykov's successors, 'It is to be hoped that all their activities will prove equally innocuous', King's Papers, no. C104226.
97. For details, see Svetlana A. Chervonnaya & Donald J. Evans, 'Left Behind: Boris E. Skvirsky and the Chita Delegation at the Washington Conference, 1921-22', *Intelligence and National Security*, 29/1 (2014), 19–57.
98. Rosenbaum, *Community of Fate*, 87.
99. Vladimir Turov (born Wolf Zalman Ginzburg), an elder brother of Semen Ginzburg (a future high-ranking Soviet state official, awarded five Orders of Lenin), was an active revolutionary who at the age of 22 was appointed a member of the Council of People's Commissars of the Socialist Soviet Republic of Lithuania and Belorussia (Litbel), a short-lived Soviet puppet state established in February 1919. He is suspected to be an undercover INO officer seconded to the NKVT and placed in Germany as deputy trade representative. In reality, his role was to deliver money, gold and diamonds to secretly finance foreign communist parties. After Berlin, he served as a member of the NKVT Collegium (1925–6) and was then placed at the Communist Academy. Turov was murdered at a small railway station by some unidentified persons in June 1927. According to one of the versions, he was transporting a large sum of money and other valuables as a usual routine, but something went wrong.
100. Rosenbaum, *Community of Fate*, 89.
101. AP RF, f. 3, op. 64. D. 679, l. 1.
102. Brockdorff-Rantzau to Aussenamt, Berlin, 5 May 1924, 2860H/1407/553 822-3, quoted by Rosenbaum.
103. Rosenbaum, *Community of Fate*, 93–4.
104. DVP SSSR (Documents of Soviet Foreign Policy, Moscow: Gospolitizdat, 1963), vol. 7, doc. 142, page 286. With this, Rosenbaum notes, 'the Soviet government overlooked the fact that Germany's share in Russian imports amounted to 41.3 per cent in 1923, but that was only 1.9 per cent of Germany's total exports. The same disproportion held true for exports. In that case 32 per cent of all Russian exports went to Germany, but, again, this was only 2.2 per cent of Germany's imports' (p. 99).
105. AVP RF, f. 04, op. 13, folder 82, d. 5019, l. 61.
106. See Dieter Nohlen and Philip Stower (eds), *Elections in Europe: A Data Handbook* (Baden-Baden: Nomos, 2010), 762. See also Rosenbaum, *Community of Fate*, 97.
107. Rosenbaum, *Community of Fate*, 97. See also Michael Jabara Carley, 'Episodes from the Early Cold War: Franco-Soviet Relations, 1917-1927', *Europe-Asia Studies*, 52/7 (2000), 1282–4.
108. Published in April 1924, the plan proposed by Charles G. Dawes, an American banker, called for instituting annual payments of reparations on a fixed scale. Dawes also recommended the reorganisation of the German State Bank and increased foreign loans. The Dawes Plan was initially a great success.
109. Nachlass Brockdorff-Rantzau, Serial 9101H, roll 3432/H226 973, MacDonald to Chancellor Wilhelm Marx, 22 August 1924, quoted by Rosenbaum.

110. For a detailed analysis, see Harvey L. Dyck, 'German-Soviet Relations and the Anglo-Soviet Break', *Slavic Review*, 25/1 (Mar. 1966), 67–83.
111. Rosenbaum, *Community of Fate*, 96. This information was also reprinted by other newspapers, see for example *Krasnoe Znamya*, Tomsk, of 1 June 1924, page 1.
112. RGASPI, f. 324, op. 1, d. 55, ll. 26 and 35. The German Foreign Office pointed to three public statements made by Zinoviev: (1) his public speech in Leningrad on 1 March where, contrary to the usual claims he said that the Comintern and the Soviet government are one and the same; (2) his public speech in Leningrad on 8 April where, on the eve of German federal election, he called on the German masses to get ready to fight on the barricades; (3) his letter to the KPD published in *Pravda* on 24 April where he recommended arming the workers and setting up Red Hundreds with the aim of organising an uprising against the government.
113. AP RF, f. 3, op. 64, d. 676, ll. 55-6, minutes of the meeting between Chicherin and Brockdorff-Rantzau concerning public statements of Zinoviev with a call to the German communists for an uprising, 2 May 1924, Top Secret.

Chapter 10: The Russians are Coming

1. Dyck, 'German-Soviet Relations and the Anglo-Soviet Break', 69.
2. See ibid., 68; and Carley, 'Episodes from the Early Cold War: Franco-Soviet Relations, 1917-1927', 1283. See also R.P. Morgan, 'The Political Significance of German-Soviet Trade Negotiations, 1922-5', *The Historical Journal*, 6/2 (1963), 253–71.
3. AVP RF, f. 136, op. 7, d. 67, p. 103, ll. 15-16, Chicherin to Politburo, no. 1408/ChS, 18/11/1924; and AVP RF, f. 04, op. 4, d. 157, p. 27, ll. 191-4, Chicherin to Politburo, no. 1423/ChS, 21/11/1924, quoted by Carley. Chicherin obviously had in mind the arrest of the first Soviet intelligence officer in France, Yakov Rudnik, who had been in charge of the joint GPU–RU station from February 1921. A year later he was arrested in Paris and was expelled from the country after spending two years behind bars. From May 1925 Rudnik was registered as a temporary editor at the press section of the Soviet embassy in Vienna. Semyon Uritsky, his successor, was also detained in February 1924 but managed to escape and settled in Germany.
4. For details, see Boris Volodarsky, *The KGB's Poison Factory: From Lenin to Litvinenko* (Barnsley, South Yorkshire: Frontline Books, 2017), 56.
5. Piotr Kołakowski, 'Z działalności sowieckiego wywiadu wojskowego przeciwko II Rzeczypospolitej', *Dzieje Najnowsze*, 32/4 (2000), 24.
6. Malcolm W. Davis, 'Soviet Recognition and Trade', *Foreign Affairs*, 5/4 (Jul. 1927), 650–62.
7. For details, see Madeira, *Britannia and the Bear*, 241n30.
8. Andrew and Mitrokhin, *The Mitrokhin Archive I*, 46 and 754n63. Mitrokhin's records reveal that 'Constantini was recruited in 1924 by the OGPU residency with the help of an Italian communist, Alfredo Allegretti, who had worked as a Russian embassy clerk before the revolution'. West and Tsarev, *The Crown Jewels*, 96, mistakenly refer to the agent as Costantini claiming that he had been recruited to work for the Soviets in 1924 'by an officer of the Rome *rezidentura* named Sheftel through D1, another Italian who had been employed at the pre-Revolutionary Russian Embassy in Rome', giving incorrect references to the KGB file DUNCAN throughout their Chapter V.
9. For interesting details about Chicherin's early life, see Baron Alexander Meyendorff, 'My Cousin, Foreign Commissar Chicherin', *The Russian Review*, 30/2 (Apr. 1971), 173–8.
10. The Italian delegates were Nicola Bombacci, Antonio Graziadei, Luigi Polano and Giacinto Menotti Serrati.
11. ASMAE, AP. 1919-1930. B. 1540. F. Ufficio sorveglianza russi.

12. Chapsky remained his handler until 1927 when he was succeeded by Ivan Kaminsky (codenamed MOND). West and Tsaev, *The Crown Jewels*, 351n10, mistakenly state that after Chapsky Constantini's contact was 'Umansky'.
13. Ambassador Yurenev (born Konstantin Krotovsky), provoked a scandal when he invited Mussolini to a reception celebrating the 7th anniversary of the Bolshevik revolution. The PCI fiercely protested and the Comintern representative in Italy, a former Swiss pastor Jules-Frédéric Humbert-Droz, demanded Yurenev's dismissal. For more details, see Alexander Barmine, *One Who Survived: The Life Story of a Russian under the Soviets* (New York, NY: G.P. Putnam's Sons, 1945), 154–5.
14. For biographical details about Mark Sheftel, see Agnese Accattoli in Antonella d'Amelia and Daniela Rizzi, *Russkoe prisutstvie v Italii v pervoi polovine XX veka*. Encyclopaedia (Moscow: ROSSPEN, 2019), 723–4.
15. Andrew and Mitrokhin, *The Mitrokhin Archive I*, 47.
16. Ibid., 68.
17. See Simon Sebag Montefiore, *Stalin: The Court of the Red Tsar* (London: Weidenfeld & Nicolson, 2003), 222.
18. See, for example, Richard Deacon, *A History of the Russian Secret Service* (London: Grafton, 1987), 204; Andrew and Gordievsky, *KGB*, 110–11; Andrew and Mitrokhin, *The Mitrokhin Archive I*, 48; and Madeira, *Britannia and the Bear*, 161–2.
19. VENONA, New York to Moscow, No. 594 of 1 May 1944. See also, Volodarsky, *Stalin's Agent*, 410–16.
20. The New York Public Library, Rare Books and Manuscript Division, David J. Dallin Papers, Accession Sheet, Accession # 84 M 23 and 72 M 21.
21. *New York Times*, Jan. 9, 1927 and Aug. 4, 1929.
22. *New York Times*, March 3, 1927.
23. *New York Times*, March 13, 1927.
24. *New York Times*, March 17 and 18, 1927.
25. *New York Times*, May 25 and 26, 1927.
26. *The Times* (London), May 17, 1927.
27. Jeffery, *MI6*, 202.
28. See TNA KV 3/230 Russian Intelligence in Austria, Czechoslovakia and Hungary. Intelligence reports, mostly from SIS, on the file's subject between 1923 and 1929 (shared with MI5, their ref. SF 450-0065).
29. 'Spionage in Ballhausplatz', *Wiener Allgemeine Zeitung*, Sechs-Uhr-Blatt, No. 14692 vom 17. Mai 1927. Eduard Ludwig, chief of the Federal Press Service (Bundespressedienst, BPD, 1921–36) to the newspaper. The BPD in the Austrian Federal Chancellery, usually headed by a senior diplomat, was responsible for the public relations work of the Austrian federal government. Today it is still part of the Bundeskanzleramt with its role considerably expanded.
30. David J. Dallin, *Soviet Espionage* (New Haven: Yale University Press, 1955), 39–40.
31. Full members of the 14th Politburo of the All-Union Communist Party (Bolsheviks) of the USSR (in the period from 1 January 1926 to 19 December 1927) were: Bukharin, Kalinin, Molotov (also member of the Secretariat), Rudzutaks, Rykov, Stalin (General Secretary), Tomsky, Trotsky, Voroshilov, Zinoviev. In the 15th Politburo (19 December 1927 – 13 July 1930), Zinoviev was replaced by Kuybyshev and Trotsky expelled.
32. Jonathan Zorach, 'The Enigma of the Gajda Affair in Czechoslovak Politics in 1926', *Slavic Review*, 35/4 (Dec. 1976), 683–98 (684). See also Radola Gajda, *Moje paměti* (Karlín, 1920).
33. Zorach, 'The Enigma of the Gajda Affair', 689.

34. TNA FO 371/11227 C 8296/32/12, Czechoslovakia, Code 12 File 83, Major Oldfield to Sir George Clerk, British Minister to Prague (1919–26), 22 July 1926, D/19, enclosure in Sir George Clerk to Sir Austin Chamberlain, same date.

35. MAE, T-9, No. 173, Couget to Aristide Briand, 13 July 1926. Diplomatic exchanges between the Soviet Union and Czechoslovakia began with the formal establishment of relations between the two countries in June 1922. The first Soviet diplomatic representative, Pavel Mostovenko, was appointed in December 1922 and remained until February 1923 (he briefly studied in the Military Medical Academy in St Petersburg in 1901 but was expelled for his revolutionary activities, since then occupied various party posts including such exotic positions as member of the All-Russian commission for the repair of transport before he was sent as Soviet diplomatic representative to Lithuania in March 1921). He was succeeded by Konstantin Yurenev (February 1923–March 1924) and then Otto Aussem (March–June 1924).

36. Zorach, 'The Enigma of the Gajda Affair', 691.

37. Solomon Isidorovich Gillerson (born 1869 – died after 13 April 1939 in France) was a medical doctor who before the revolution worked in hospitals in Moscow and Harbin. In 1917 he joined the Bolshevik party and served as a medical doctor and a party organiser in the small town of Nikolsk-Ussuriysk near the Chinese-Russian border. In the summer of 1920 Gillerson was sent to Prague in charge of the Soviet Red Cross mission. In June he was joined by Roman Jakobson, one of the mission's officials who would become a prominent American linguist working for two decades at Harvard and in his last decade as honorary professor at the Massachusetts Institute of Technology. Because Gillerson and other members of his mission were actively involved in communist propaganda, which was part of his remit, he was accused of espionage and left Prague in 1921. Eventually, as in other countries, the mission was later used as a Soviet trade representation with consular functions. The first INO resident, Maxim Belsky, alias 'Beletsky' (born Moishe Mintz), arrived in 1924 operating undercover as 2nd secretary of the Soviet legation. In 1925 he was succeeded by Nikolai Samsonov, alias 'Golst'.

38. The text of the decrypted telegram presented to the Czechoslovak Senate was reported by John S. Gittings, chargé d'affaires ad interim (a.i.) to secretary of state on 5 November 1927, USSD 860f.22/24. On 1 July 1927 Lewis Einstein, American Minister to Czechoslovakia, departed from Prague on leave of absence. Diplomatic secretary Gitings assumed charge of the Legation, see *The American Foreign Service Journal*, 4/8 (Aug. 1927), 248.

39. Zorach, 'The Enigma of the Gajda Affair', 692–3.

40. First, instead of moving to the north he ordered his troops to turn to the south in the direction of Petrograd, capturing the town of Luga, and then did not comply with the order to take Tosno putting friendly troops in danger and giving the enemy forces an advantage.

41. Karol Grünberg, *Szpiedzy Stalina: Z dziejów wywiadu radzieckiego* (Warsaw: Książka i Wiedza, 1998), 37–8.

42. 'The Vetrenko Spy Case', *Poslednie Izvestiy* (Latest News), Reval, Sunday, 24 April 1927, p. 2. See also, William Lincoln, *A History of the Russian Civil War* (New York, NY: Simon and Schuster, 1989), 296–9.

43. His textbook *Seaport Management* was last published in 2000. Professor Leonid Vetrenko made a notable career mentioned in a presidential awards list (September 1996) as Chairman of the Scientific and Technical Commission of the Association of Sea Ports, St Petersburg. He is also one of the founders of the Faculty of International Transport Management at State University of Maritime and Inland Shipping and author of several other textbooks.

44. For details, see Zbigniew Karpus, 'Soviet prisoners of war 1919-1921', Institute of National Remembrance, 18 August 2020. The Treaty was signed in Riga on 18 March 1921.

45. Archive of the State Hermitage (AGE), f. 1, op. 13, d. 616, ll. 50-51.

46. In January 1927 Goldenstein moved to Berlin as the chief INO resident (codenamed DOCTOR) using the same diplomatic cover of 2nd secretary. After his return to Moscow in March 1930 Dr Goldenstein was working for the Comintern's Executive Committee. Volodarsky, *Stalin's Agent*, 17–18. See also, Freddy Litten, 'Die Goldštajn/ Goldenstein-Verwechslung: Eine biographische Notiz zur Komintern-Aktivität auf dem Balkan', *Südost-Forschungen*, 50 (1991), 245–50.

47. DODIS (Diplomatic Documents of Switzerland), Swiss Legation in Berlin to the Foreign Ministry, 10.5.18, B. 429. Like all the rest, what Berzin said was not true. Born Gersh Ber Leiba Schklovsky near Bobruisk to the family of a Jewish cobbler, Shklovsky was a professional revolutionary, a close associate of Lenin. Shklovsky took part in the III Congress of the RSDRP in London in 1905 and four years later was exiled to Siberia for his revolutionary activities. Having fled to Switzerland later that year, he participated in party work even more actively taking part in the Basel Congress of the Second International (1912) representing the Leninists and in the Bern Conference of Bolshevik groups abroad (1915). In Switzerland Shklovsky served as a trusted cashier keeping secret party funds. Lenin and his wife often visited him in Bern and in Lenin's *Collected Works* (1958–66) there are thirty-one letters addressed to Shlovsky between 1910 and 1922. Shklovsky is also known to have coined the phrase: 'In a revolution, revolutionaries make up only a very small percentage'.

48. Alfred Erich Senn, 'The Soviet Union's Road to Geneva, 1924-1927', *Jahrbücher für Geschichte Osteuropas*, Neue Folge, 27/1 (1979), 69–84. Also by the same author, *Assassination in Switzerland: Murder of Vatslav Vorovsky* (Madison, WI: University of Wisconsin Press, 1981).

49. The leading newspaper of the city, *Feuille d'Avis de Lausanne*, explained the situation: the accused were declared guilty by five jury members out of nine and therefore benefited from a minority rule since the Vaudian criminal code requires a majority of six 'yes' and three 'no' for the accused to be declared guilty.

50. Senn, 'The Soviet Union's Road to Geneva', 69. See also Annetta Gattiker, *L'Affaire Conradi* (Frankfurt am Main: Peter Lang, 1975).

51. Manvydas *Vitkūnas*, 'Sušaudytas už šnipinėjimą Rusijos naudai', *Savaite*, 28 July 2017.

52. 'A Lithuanian General Shot – Break with Russia Possible', *The Advertiser* (Adelaide, South Australia), Friday, 3 June 1927, p. 14, based on the report from Riga.

53. Jeffery, *MI6*, 202.

54. In his article (see below) Kenneth Benton calls her Margaret. Lest there be any misunderstanding, her full name was Clara Marguerite Lockington Holmes, née Bates, DOB: 28 Jan. 1895, see TNA HS/9/733/4. She rejoined the Vienna PCO team in 1930 after her husband died.

55. Helen Fry, *Spymaster: The Man who Saved MI6* (New Haven and London: Yale University Press, 2021), 25. To show Kendrick's proficiency, his biographer claims that 'a precise and detailed picture of Russian agents and communist activists functioning in and out of Austria was being efficiently tracked by Kendrick' (p. 31). 'Kendrick went a step further', Ms Fry writes, 'and secretly tapped into the telephone cables of Russian intelligence in Vienna' (p. 34). This extraordinary achievement immediately yielded a rich harvest of intelligence information. For example, 'Nadia Zachariova posed as a Russian refugee, but in fact she was an agent from the counter-espionage section of the Comintern in Moscow. Another agent, known in the files simply as Swagens, was

from the same department and had been dispatched to Vienna to uncover British intelligence organisations [*sic*] and networks in the capital' (p. 34). Neither these people nor such a section of the Comintern ever existed. Under the headline 'Tracking Russian Agents' Helen Fry further elaborates that 'by the latter half of the 1920s, Kendrick had become an expert for SIS on Comintern and Bolshevik activities'. 'Such was his successful penetration work that, by the autumn of 1927 [it should be reminded that by that time the Vienna station had been temporary closed down], he had compiled a complete list of Bolshevik sympathisers and activists for MI5 to track if they entered Britain. He discovered that the Soviets had engaged a German (or Austrian) named Comrade M. Schmidt, whose task was to track Sonia Alberovaya, an agent engaged by the Italian secret service on anti-Soviet espionage. Not only was Soviet intelligence following Alberovaya, but Kendrick was monitoring the Soviet tracking of her' (p. 36). Finally, 'the interception of [Soviet] mail continued throughout the 1920s and, in early June 1928, Kendrick's network gained access to a letter written by Stanislas Kalina of the "special section" of the Soviet embassy in Vienna. The section was of particular interest to Kendrick, because it was believed to be directing espionage on behalf of the Soviet Union' (pp. 36–7). Needless to say, all this was sheer invention. Nevertheless, as already noted, in the interwar years Kendrick was regarded by SIS 'as one of their best heads of station' (Jeffery, *MI6*, 202). Finally, and concerning only one of Kendrick's agents, 'by the early 1930s London had begun to mistrust the source and suspect that his reports had been fabricated' (ibid).

56. Kenneth Benton, 'The ISOS Years: Madrid 1941-3', *Journal of Contemporary History*, 30/3 (Jul. 1995), 359–410. Benton had been working for 'C' in Vienna from autumn 1937 to late August 1938 when he was transferred to Riga. For more about Benton, see Christopher Andrew's Introduction to 'The ISOS Years: Madrid 1941-3', *Journal of Contemporary History*, 30/3 (Jul. 1995), 355–8.
57. See TNA KV 2/840 (PF R4342/SAV 1). See also Volodarsky, *Stalin's Agent*, 74–7.
58. Jeffery, *MI6*, 195.
59. 'Bakonyi aus Wien ausgewiesen', *Innsbrucker Nachrichten*, No. 96 (Friday, 29 April 1927), p. 3.
60. OÖLA, Nachlass Mayer, GVf1-3, a typed copy from *Wiener Allgemeine Zeitung*, 17 May 1927, Nr. 14692. I am grateful to Dr Josef Goldberger of the Upper Austria Landesarchive in Linz for providing this document.
61. Yakov A. Berman was born in January 1869 and in 1890 graduated from the Faculty of Law of Moscow University. Already an active Marxist as a student, in 1905 in Moscow he was a member of the Menshevik military organisation, moving to St Petersburg in March 1906. After the Bolshevik revolution Berman worked at the Presidium of the Moscow Soviet and in December 1917 was elected chairman of the Moscow revolutionary tribunal. In July, the Sovnarkom sent him to Austria to negotiate the repatriation of the Russian PoWs. See also, RGASPI, f. 495, op. 65a, d. 2767, l. 1.
62. Volodarsky, *Stalin's Agent*, 516n15.
63. Verena Moritz und Hannes Leidinger, 'Wien als Standort der Kommunistischen Internationale bis Mitte der Zwanzigerjahre', in *Jahrbuch für Historische Kommunismusforschung* (JHK 2004), 32–63.
64. HHStA/NAR/F 36, Der Vertrag von Kopenhagen, 5. Juli 1920.
65. Gordon Brook-Shepherd, *The Austrians: A Thousand-Year Odyssey* (London: Harper Collins Publishers, 1997), 260–1. Eric Gedye, often cited as G.E.R. Gedye, also described the Justizpalastbrand in his most famous book *Fallen Bastions* (London: Victor Gollancz, 1939). Gedye had been accredited in Vienna as the *News Chronicle* reporter before *The Daily Telegraph* hired him as their Central Europe correspondent. Kendrick's biographer

Helen Fry claims that while in Vienna Gedye was co-opted as a SIS agent, which may or may not be true although he had indeed operated as an intelligence officer in Germany after the war (1918–19). Among his papers in the Imperial War Museum there are documents relating to his Intelligence Corps training and exams. During 1925–6 Gedye had been *The Times* correspondent in Vienna and the Balkans and spent a year in Moscow as a correspondent for *The New York Times*. In Vienna Eric lived with his local PA, Alice ('Litzi') Lepper Mehler, who would later become his second wife and it was Eric who in 1934 introduced Kim Philby to his future first wife, by coincidence also named Alice-Litzi. In January 1941 together with the former Vienna SIS secretaries, Evelyn Stamper and Clara Holmes (known as 'Medames'), Gedye was on the staff of the Austrian Section of the British SOE. This was a sub-section of the German and Austrian Section (Section X, see TNA HS 6/692) and he later operated together with Alice in Istanbul and the Balkans for the rest of the war (IWM, Private Papers of George Eric Rowe Gedye, Documents.22580). Gedye's only son by his second marriage, Robin Gedye, a foreign correspondent of *The Daily Telegraph*, was expelled from Moscow in a tit-for-tat retaliation for the British government's decision to declare persona non grata thirty-four KGB and GRU officers working in London under the diplomatic cover as a follow-up of the Gordievsky operation.

66. Edgard Haider, *Die Österreichisch-Sowjetischen Beziehungen 1918-1938* (unpublished PhD thesis, Vienna University, July 1975), 176–7.

67. HHStA/NPA/Geheimliassen Personalia Fasz 481, Bericht der Pol.Dion Wien vom 27. April 1927.

68. Information about 'Joseph J. Krasny alias Rothstadt' in West and Tsarev, *The Crown Jewels*, 8–9, is incorrect.

69. In both the English and Russian versions of the book by West and Tsarev published in London by Harper Collins as *The Crown Jewels* (1998), there's a long story of Krasnaya's reading a kind of consolidated report of the OGPU London station some time in 1927. The report presumably covers the period from May 1924 to January 1927. Alas, the authors provide no reference to any archival document but even with such a reference there is no possibility of independently rechecking their information.

70. AP RF, f. 3, op. 64, d. 653, ll. 97-99, Plenipotentiary Krestinsky (Berlin) to Foreign Commissar Chicherin (Moscow), 'On the financial situation of Germany and Soviet-German economic relations', 10 July 1927, Secret.

71. Gyula Lengyel (Goldstein), DOB: 08-Oct-1988, should not be confused with József Lengyel, DOB: 04-Aug.-1896. Like Gyula, József became a communist. During the Soviet Republic he had worked as a journalist for the communist newspaper *Vörös Ujság* ('Red News'), also editing *Ifjú Proletár* ('Young Proletarian'). After the fall of the Soviet regime he fled to Austria in October 1919, was arrested on the border and interned in Karlstein. From 1920 to 1927 József lived in Vienna having joined the KPÖ and briefly studied at Vienna University but then moved to Berlin. In 1930 as a foreign correspondent of the newspaper *Berlin am Morgen* he came to Moscow where he settled, acquiring Soviet citizenship. He is known in Russia as the Soviet writer Iosif Pavlovich Lengiyel. His daughter Tatiana published memories of her father's years in the GULAG.

72. Karl Begge was born in the port city of Libava (now Liepāja), Latvia, in 1884. Since 1902 he was an active party member taking part in the revolutionary movement. After the revolution he occupied various positions in the NKVT and in December 1924 was elected member of the Foreign Trade Bank (VTB) advisory board. In Berlin Begge succeeded Alexander Svanidze who became General Agent/Representative of the People's Commissar of Finance in Germany. In October 1927, still head of the Soviet trade mission in Germany, Begge was promoted to the Board of Directors of the VTB

and representing the bank in Germany. Arrested in October 1937, he was executed in January 1938. For Begge and Lengyel in Berlin, see, for example, AP RF, f. 3, op. 64, d. 653, l. 16 and other documents in G. Sevostianov (ed.), *Policy and Diplomacy of the Kremlin, 1920-1941*. Collection of Documents (Moscow: Nauka, 2011), vol. 2 (1927–1932), in Russian.

73. Judd, *The Quest for C*, 446.
74. Haider, *Die Österreichisch-Sowjetischen Beziehungen 1918-1938*, 192. RUSAWSTORG (Russisch-österreichische Handels- und Industrie AG) was a public company established in Vienna on 3 July 1923. It was soon followed by RATAO (Russisch-österreichische Handels AG), a likewise public company registered on 25 August with a share capital of 300,000 gold rubles divided into 2,000 shares, of which 50 per cent belonged to the Soviet government and the rest 50 per cent to an Austrian group. For details, see ibid., 90–121. The bank accounts of RUSAWSTORG were opened at the Dresdner Bank in Leipzig (Sächsisches Staatsarchiv, 21018 Dresdner Bank in Leipzig, Nr. 0093). Remarkably, in 1993 Dresdner became the first Western credit institution in Russia to open a universal bank. Its first office in St Petersburg, headed by Matthias Warning, started operations at the end of 1991. Warning was a former East German spy, a Stasi 'officer for special purpose' (OibE), deployed in West Germany undercover as a trade representative (codenamed ARTHUR). A close friend of Putin, since 2003 he would also become a member of the board of directors of the VTB, the second largest credit institution in Russia nicknamed 'the bank of Putin's lackeys'.
75. Madeira, *Britannia and the Bear*, 161–2.
76. Owen Lattimore's review of C. Martin Wilbur's and Julie Lien-ying How's important book *Documents on Communism, Nationalism, and Soviet Advisers in China, 1918-27* (1956) in *The Journal of Modern History*, 30/2 (Jun. 1958), 152. Lattimore, born and raised in Tianjin (also known as Tientsin), China, was a leading Far East scholar who during the Second World War was an adviser to Chiang Kai-shek and the US government. Professor of Chinese studies at the University of Leeds (1963–70), Lattimore was accused by Senator Joseph McCarthy of being 'the top Russian espionage agent in the United States', an accusation not based on any evidence except the testimony of the Soviet defector Alexander Barmin, the value and credibility of which was zero.
77. For details, see Qihua Tang, 'The Sino-Soviet Conference, 1924-1927', *Journal of Modern Chinese History*, 1/2 (December 2007), 195–218. See also, Bruce A. Elleman, 'The Soviet Union's Secret Diplomacy Concerning the Chinese Eastern Railway, 1924-1925', *The Journal of Asian Studies*, 53/2 (May 1994), 459–86.
78. For the British reaction 'to the outrages at Nanking', see TNA CAB 23/54/23, Conclusions of a meeting of the Cabinet held in the Prime Minister's Room, HC, on Monday, 4 April 1927.
79. Sir Miles Lampson (1st Baron Killearn) was Acting British High Commissioner in Siberia in 1920, and served as British Minister to China between 1926 and 1933.
80. HANSARD, Police Search Peking, HC Deb 11 April 1927 vol 205 cc5-9.
81. *Soviet Plot in China*, Issues 1–28 (Peking: Metropolitan Police Headquarters, April 1927).
82. *Chinese Government White Book*, 'Foreword', 153–5; *Soviet Plot in China*, iii–iv. See also C. Martin Wilbur and Julie Lien-ying How, *Documents on Communism, Nationalism, and Soviet Advisers in China, 1918-1927: Papers seized in the 1927 Peking raid* (New York, NY: Columbia University Press, 1956), 8–19. See also, TNA HW 12/95, Chernykh Peking-Moscow, 6 April 1927.
83. For details about Rigin-Rylski, see Victor Usov, *Soviet Intelligence in China, 1920s* (Moscow: Olma-Press, 2002), 325–6, in Russian.

84. The consulates-general and consulates were opened in Kashgar, headed by the Latvian Max Dumpis (OGPU, previously INO resident agent in Afghanistan); Mukden (Shenyang), until 1926 headed by Arkady Krakovetsky (OGPU); Urumchi (Ürümqi), with consul general Alexander Bystrov, main OGPU resident in Western China in 1926; Hankou, headed by Alexey Bakulin, (G)RU officer, deputy head of the group of Soviet military advisers in China while the INO resident there was Sergey Velezhev (alias 'Vedernikov'); Harbin, where Boris Legran, former chairman of the Revolutionary Military Tribunal in 1919–20, was probably the only party official not affiliated with Soviet intelligence, but in 1928 he was succeeded by Boris Melnikov, a high-ranking (G)RU officer; Shanghai, headed by Consul General Friedrich Linde (Latvian Fricis-Aleksandras Linde, February 1926–April 1927), former prosecutor of the Supreme Revolutionary Tribunal; Kalgan (Zhangjiakou), where consul Anatoly Klimov, (G)RU, also served as military adviser of the Kalgan group; Canton (Guangzhou), with Consul Boris Pokhvalinsky, later sector head of II department of the (G)RU, then known as IV Directorate.
85. See Mara Moustafine, 'Russians from China: Migrations and Identity', *Cosmopolitan Civil Societies Journal*, 5/2 (Aug. 2013), 143–58. See also by the same author, *Secrets and Spies: The Harbin Files* (Sydney: Vintage Books/Random House Australia, 2002).
86. Trotsky, 'The Tanaka Memorial', *Fourth International*, 2/5 (June 1941), 131–5 (article written in August 1940, just days before he was murdered by an NKVD assassin).
87. Volodarsky, *Stalin's Agent*, 19–22. Stefan Uzdański, son of Tadeusz, was born in Warsaw in February 1898. He joined the Red Army and the Bolshevik party in 1918 and after the revolution graduated from the Frunze Military Academy. According to the Russian sources, in March 1921 Uzdański took part in the suppression of the Kronstadt rebellion. After joining the (G)RU, he was sent to Warsaw in April 1922 as assistant resident under diplomatic cover as an attaché alias 'Jeleński'. Expelled from Warsaw but transferred to Vienna in April 1924 as an acting resident using the same diplomatic cover and alias. In Austria for only a few months, from April to December 1924, Uzdański-Jeleński collected military and political information from the local sources and from the Balkans. Back in Moscow between December 1924 and March 1926, he was placed in charge of the 3rd technical bureau of the information and statistics department at the (G)RU headquarters during which time he published several analytical articles and brochures about the French armed forces and tendencies of their future development. In March 1926 the (G)RU leadership sent Uzdański to Paris as illegal resident. After his arrest and trial, Uzdański-Bernstein was sentenced to three years in prison, returning home in November 1931. In 1933 he was awarded the Order of the Red Banner and until 17 June 1937 served as deputy chief of the 1st (Western) department at the HQ. He was sentenced to death as a Polish spy and shot in November the same year (RGASPI, f. 495, op. 252, d. 8914). See also Mikhail Alekseyev, Alexander Kolpakidi and Valery Kochik, *Encyclopedia of military intelligence, 1918–45*, in Russian (Moscow: Kuchkovo Pole, 2012), 778–9. For details about Crémet and Louise Clarac, see Jean Maitron and Claude Pennetier, 'Jean Louis Aimé Marie Crémet' and 'Louise Clarac (née Madeleine Thibault)', in *Le Maitron, dictionnaire biographique mouvement ouvrier et movement social* (maitron.fr, version mise en ligne le 19 avril 2021).
88. RGASPI, f. 495 op. 270 d. 6639, l. 16, Autobiography of Louise Clarac in the Comintern archive.
89. Born in Bulgaria as Nikola Popvasilev Zidarov in August 1888, he was known in Russia as Nikola Vasilev Zadirov. Information about the Crémet spy ring in Raymond W. Leonard, *Secret Soldiers of the Revolution: Soviet Military Intelligence, 1918-1933* (Westport, CT & London: Greenwood Press, 1999), 71–4, is to a large extent incorrect.

90. For details, see Roger Faligot and Rémi Kauffer, *L'Hermine Rouge de Shanghai* (Rennes: Les Portes du Large, 2005). In the vast majority of Western publications interwar Soviet military intelligence is referred to as 'IV Department'. In reality, after a complete restructuring the Red Army intelligence organisation formed in November 1918 (secret decree of the Revolutionary Military Council no. 197/27 dated 5.11.1918) was established as the Intelligence Directorate (RU) of the Red Army Headquarters in 1924. Only for a period between September 1926 and August 1934 it was known as the 4th Directorate of the RKKA HQ.

91. Christopher Andrew, 'British Intelligence and the Breach with Russia in 1927', *The Historical Journal*, 25/4 (1982), 957–64.

92. Smith, *Six*, 319.

93. Specialists from the Cheka Special (8th) Cipher Department, since May 1921 headed by Gleb Bokiy, changed their codes and ciphers several times already in the 1920s as a result of British indiscretion, gradually progressing to more sophisticated systems. In May 1927, given the lack of incriminating material found during the raid, the Baldwin government bolstered the required 'evidence' by six telegrams, several of them from the Moscow-Peking traffic, that had been intercepted and then deciphered by GC&CS. As a result, the OGPU responded by adopting the completely unbreakable one-time pad encryption technique for diplomatic communications.

94. Instead, there were three ongoing investigations. One was a sting operation by both SIS and MI5 which involved the Lloyd's underwriter George Monkland acting as a decoy and a former SIS operative Wilfred Macartney, who was not a spy but from the very beginning to the very end behaved like a fool. Another was a promising lead with two main protagonists, a left-wing journalist William Ewer and the London office of the Federated Press of America which paid several people for information which would today be considered fairly harmless – there were no prosecutions and the case was soon closed. Finally, British Secret Services followed by the journalists, writers and even some intelligence historians created the imaginary spy ring of a totally fictitious spy, Jacob Kirchenstein, which allegedly operated from within the London offices of ARCOS. Amazingly, not a single person mentioned in the files related to this case was a spy, including poor Jacob, mistakenly identified as 'one of the chief agents of the Comintern', alias 'Johnny Walker'. When the scandal erupted, the man, an American citizen of Latvian origin, quietly immigrated with his wife to the United States and later collaborated with the FBI. All relevant documents have long been declassified and are in the National Archives, but no one ever cared to check.

95. 'The Soviet Union Defends Itself: Communications of the United State Political Administration of the Soviet Union', *Inprecor*, 7/35 (16 June 1927), 728. Among the 'British agents' were Vladimir Evreinov, a former chief of the Tsarist secret service in Persia and later employee of the State Bank of the USSR, who allegedly supplied financial and military information to Hodgson; Konstantin Malevich-Malevsky, 'sent by British secret service into Soviet Union in 1927 to organise espionage and terrorism'; Alexander Skalsky, accused of providing secret information concerning the Soviet air service and the armament industry to Nikolai Bunakov, a 'British spy in Finland'; Boris Naryshkin, who allegedly 'carried out espionage for a number of foreign representatives in Moscow'; Nikolai Lytchev, agent of Charnock 'to whom he supplied military and political information'; Nikolai Koropenko, 'spy of the British Chargé d'Affaires Hodgson'; and Sergey Mazurenko, employed in the Central Administration for marine transport and likewise 'one of Hodgson's secret agents'. All of them were shot on the night of 9/10 June 1927 in retaliation for the murder of Pyotr Voykov in Warsaw. Starting from 1923 the editorial office of *Inprecor* was located in Vienna on Berggasse 31 in the 9th

District. By sheer coincidence, the wife of the Russian banker Alexander Smolensky opened her luxury shop V.T.D. nearby on the same street when her husband was accused of laundering millions of dollars received as international aid to Russia from the IMF in the 1990s.

Chapter 11: Soviet House, British Spy Mania and SIS Activities in Russia: The ARCOS Tangle

1. TNA FO 371/12589, Russia Code 38 File 209 (paper 229), 18 January 1927.
2. TNA HW 12/12, Decrypts of intercepted diplomatic communications, Soviet Union, 3507-3510, 24 July 1920. The Soviet delegation was now headed by Kamenev, a senior member of the Politburo, with Krasin and Klyshko as his deputies. Two extra members, Vladimir Milyutin, then vice-chairman of the VSNKh and member of the Council of Labour and Defence (STO), and Theodore Rothstein were added to reinforce the delegation which by 20 July had reached Reval on the way to London. They were stopped here by the British note warning the Soviet government against advancing into Poland and threatening to break off the trade talks (*DBFP, 1919-1939*, Vol 8, HMSO, 1960, 649–50). A week later Lloyd George managed to persuade the Cabinet that it would be better to have the Soviet delegation to hand. Kamenev and Krasin reached London on 1 August, where the delegation's address was officially registered at 128 New Bond Street. For details, see M.V. Glenny, 'The Anglo-Soviet Trade Agreement, March 1921', *Journal of Contemporary History*, 5/2 (1970), 63–82. See also Davis, 'Soviet Recognition and Trade', 655.
3. Xenia Joukoff Eudin and Harold H. Fisher, *Soviet Russia and the West, 1920-1927: A Documentary Survey* (Stanford, CA: Stanford University Press, 1957), 342–3. For the text of the British note of 23 February 1927, see *A Selection of Papers Dealing with the Relations between His Majesty's Government and the Soviet Government, 1921-1927* (Cmb. 2895), 45–50. For Litvinov's answer of 26 February 1927, see *Sovietskaya Sibir*, 49 (1 Mar 1927), 1.
4. This was an accurate estimate. If we compare Russian exports and imports for the first quarter of the fiscal years 1926–7 (in millions of gold roubles), we shall see that Russian exports to Germany were 49.8, Great Britain 59.2 and the USA 7.7, while Russian imports were 29.2 (Germany), 26.5 (Great Britain) and 32.6 (United States). Accordingly, German, British and American shares in Russian imports in 1926 were: Germany 26 per cent, Great Britain 19 per cent and the USA 18 per cent. Figures taken from *Soviet Union Review* (April 1927), as compiled by People's Commissariat of Trade and Industry, quoted in Davis, 'Soviet Recognition and Trade', 650–62.
5. Madeira, *Britannia and the Bear*, 132–3.
6. Christopher Andrew, Foreword to Madeira, *Britannia and the Bear*, ix.
7. TNA FO 371/12589, Russia Code 38 File 209 (paper 791), Sir Robert Hodgson's report about Anglo-Soviet relations, 23 February 1927.
8. Which is usually defined as consisting of three components: (1) the use or threat of action including, inter alia, 'serious violence'; (2) the use or threat must be designed to influence the government (of the UK or any other country); and (3) the use or threat is made for the purpose of advancing, inter alia, a political or ideological cause.
9. For details, see Hugh Sinclair's letter to William Tyrrell (PUS for Foreign Affairs, 1925-28) in TNA FO 1093/73 C/2523 of 28 June 1927, nine typed pages.
10. See Peter Gill and Mark Phythian, *Intelligence in an Insecure World* (Cambridge: Polity Press, 2018), 182. See also, Madeira, *Britannia and the Bear*, 135.
11. TNA FO 1093/67-68, Secret Service Committee 2nd, 6th and 8th meetings (March 1925).

12. See Jeffery, *MI6*, 226–36.
13. Jeffery, *MI6*, 207, 227. During a meeting of the Secret Service Committee on Tuesday, 22 March 1927, it was suggested 'that the duties of S.S.1. and S.S.2., while ultimately directed by "C", might in some way be combined with those of M.I.5.', TNA FO 1093/71, 3.
14. Andrew, *The Defence of the Realm*, 154.
15. Under the Foreword to Keith Jeffery's official history of SIS/MI6, signed by John Sawers (Chief of SIS, Nov. 2009 – Nov. 2014), there's an unsigned anonymous statement to the effect that 'SIS does not disclose the names of agents or of living members of staff' (p. viii).
16. Smith, *SIX*, 316.
17. HBM stood for His Britannic Majesty. Beneath was a NOTE in small letters: 'The information given in this document is not to be communicated, either directly or indirectly, to the Press or to any person not holding an official position in His Majesty's Service' (TNA KV 3/15, Signal Training, Volume III, Pamphlet No. 11, Descriptions of and Instructions for Wireless Telegraph, Set 'C', Mark II, 1926). The credit for discovering Langston's name in the files must be given to Michael Smith although Timothy Philipps claims in *The Secret Twenties* (2017), first published seven years later than Smith's work, that he separately identified Edward Langston while working with the names in ARCOS staff list in TNA HO 144/8403 'POLICE: Participation of members of Russian Trade Delegation and Arcos Ltd in anti-British espionage: police raid on premises'.
18. 'The Work of Arcos', *Russian Information and Review*, 1/1 (Oct. 1921), 19. His full name is mentioned in *The Yorkshire Post*, Thursday, 26 May 1927, p. 11. I am very grateful to Michael Smith for providing this document.
19. TNA FO 1093/71 Minutes of the 4th meeting of the Secret Service Committee held on Thursday, 30 June 1927, pp. 3–4. Maw figures as 'C²', Harker as 'K²' and Langston as 'Y'.
20. Andrew, *The Defence of the Realm*, 154.
21. Ibid.
22. TNA FO 1093/71 Minutes of the 3rd meeting of the Secret Service Committee held on Friday, 24 June 1927, p. 4.
23. In an attempt to rectify this damaging omission, the Home Secretary met with G.R. Warner, head of the FO Treaty Department and H. William Malkin, Legal Adviser to the FO together with police representatives who had participated in the raid. Warner concluded that the Trade Representative (in this case, Lev Khinchuk, from November 1926 to May 1927) was indeed personally immune from arrest and search and this immunity would logically extend to his office in Soviet House. And to make matters worse, among more than 1,000 staff members of ARCOS and the Trade Delegation briefly detained by the police was the wife of Rosengoltz, the chargé d'affaires, who certainly had full diplomatic immunity. See Harriette Flory, 'The Arcos Raid and the Rupture of Anglo-Soviet Relations, 1927', *Journal of Contemporary History*, 12/4 (Oct. 1977), 707–23.
24. TNA CAB 23/55/2, Attendees: Baldwin, Chamberlain, Cave, Churchill, Amery, Hoare, Bridgeman, Chamberlain, Percy, Peel, Balfour, Salisbury, Joynson-Hicks, Worthington-Evans, Gilmour, Cunliffe-Lister, Guinness, Steel-Maitland, Cecil, Hogg. Agenda: (2) Russia – The police search of 'Arcos', 19 May 1927.
25. TNA FO 1093/71 Minutes of the 4th meeting of the Secret Service Committee held on Thursday, 30 June 1927, pp. 5–6.
26. MI5 PF 38426/R 0401 Volume 1, LAKEY, Arthur Francis (TNA KV 2/989), ALLEN's statements and MI5 comments. To Mr. Ottaway, 27.6.28.

27. For the telegram of 15 February 1927, see TNA HW 12/91 'Decrypts of intercepted diplomatic communications, Soviet Union: 25478-25482'. For the telegrams of 13 April and 18 May 1927, see *Documents illustrating the Hostile Activities of the Soviet Government and Third International against Great Britain*, Russia No. 2 (1927), Cmd. 2874, p. 31.

28. Flory, 'The Arcos Raid', 719.

29. Andrew, *The Defence of the Realm*, 155.

30. Hansard, HC Deb 24 May 1927 vol 206 cc1842-54.

31. Andrew, *The Defence of the Realm*, 156.

32. Flory, 'The Arcos Raid', 721.

33. Cf. Keith Neilson, *Britain, Soviet Russia and the Collapse of the Versailles Order, 1919-1939* (New York, NY: Cambridge University Press, 2006), 56. See also by the same author, *Britain and the Last Tsar: British Policy and Russia, 1894-1917* (Oxford: Clarendon Press, 1995), 110–46. Great Britain fought three wars with Russia: in 1807–12 during the Napoleonic Wars; in 1854–6 during the Crimean War; and during the Allied intervention in the Russian Civil War in 1918–20. In August 1917 (O.S.) a British armoured-car squadron commanded by Oliver Locker-Lampson and dressed in Russian uniforms participated in the failed Kornilov coup in Petrograd. See Richard Ullman, *Anglo-Soviet Relations, 1917-1921*, Vol. 1: Intervention and the War (Princeton, NJ: Princeton University Press, 1961), 12.

34. Ferris, *Behind the Enigma*, 144, referring to GC&CS, No. 003934, 20.8.20, HW 12/13.

35. LAKEY, Arthur Francis, Security Service file PF 38,426 Vol. 1 (TNA KV 2/989), serial 69b. See also, Alexander Kolpakidi and Valentin Mzareulov, *Soviet Foreign Intelligence, 1920-1945: History, Structure and Personnel* (Moscow: Rodina, 2021), 247.

36. TNA KV 2/989, serial 69b.

37. Nikita Petrov and Konstantin Skorkin, *Kto rukovodil NKVD, 1934-1941* (Moscow: Memorial, 1999), 53. The INFO was headed by Georgy Prokofiev from 4 February 1924 to 15 July 1926, when Alexeyev, who for two weeks after his return from London had been appointed Prokofiev's deputy, was promoted to head the department. From July to November 1925 Prokofiev had also been acting head of the PK (Political Control) before PK was joined with INFO.

38. Markus Wehner, 'Kaderkarrieren der Weltrevolution: Die deutsch-russische Geschichte der Brüder Rakow', IWK, *Internationale wissenschaftliche Korrespondenz zur Geschichte der deutschen Arbeiterbewegung*, 30/1 (March 1994), 29–67.

39. TNA FO 371/40233 Code 34 file 5183.

40. Oleg Tsarev and Nigel West, *KGB in England* (Moscow: Tsentropoligraph, 1999), 20, in Russian.

41. Ferris, *Behind the Enigma*, 142.

42. See Ivy Litvinov papers 1911-1997, Hoover Institution Archives, Collection number 87075. See also David Burke, *Russia and the British Left: From the 1848 Revolutions to the General Strike* (London: Bloomsbury Academic, 2020), 177–8.

43. Following the British Note of 8 May 1923 and anticipating HM's Government hostile action, Moscow decided to recall Klyshko, see RGASPI, f. 17, op. 3, d. 346, l.1. See also, George Bingham's (The Earl of Lucan) explanation to Viscount Bertie of Thame, Hansard, House of Lords debates, Tuesday, 17 November 1931, vol 83, columns 50-53. The relevant paragraph of Lord Curzon's Memorandum in the Command Paper read as follows: 'In the same year (1922) a number of bank notes of £100 each, issued through Lloyds Bank and the Russian Commercial and Industrial Bank in London to Nikolai Klishko [*sic*] in June, 1921, were cashed in India on behalf of a revolutionary Panjabi in touch with other seditionaries who are known to have been closely associated with the Russian representative in Kabul.' As a result of that Memorandum Klyshko had to leave Britain.

44. MI5 PF 421 V/6 KLISHKO, Nicolas Clementievitch and KLISHKO Phyllis (TNA KV 2/1415), s.319a (Part V 'Conclusions', paragraphs 58, 60).
45. MI5 PF R.3984/V1-V2-V3 (TNA KV 2/1391) KIRCHENSTEIN Jacob, page 3.
46. TNA KV 2/1391, Patterson's letter to DG (Percy Sillitoe), 27 September 1951.
47. Simon Berg would later head the Riga Soviet. See Marina Germane, 'Pēteris Stučka and the National Question', *Journal of Baltic Studies*, 44/3 (Sept. 2013), 375–94.
48. In spring 1925 Kollontai, then the Soviet Minister to Norway, visited London to discuss some commercial and economic issues involving Norway. During her negotiations Kollontai was assisted by Philip Rabinovitch of ARCOS and Christian Rakovsky, the Soviet trade representative in the UK (between August 1923 and October 1925). For details, see A.M. Kollontai, *Diplomatic Diaries, 1922-1940* (Moscow: Academia, 2001), I, 241–4. Remarkably, in his later very detailed account of his life and work in London at this time, Kirchenstein never mentioned Kollontai.
49. TNA KV 2/1391, s.98a, page 6.
50. For details, see Timothy J. Colton, 'Military Councils and Military Politics in the Russian Civil War', *Canadian Slavonic Papers*, 18/1 (March 1976), 36–57.
51. Her first husband was Igor Mikhailovich Reisner, whom a recent publication modestly calls 'Igor Reussner, Professor of Agriculture', see Keith Laybourn and John Shepherd (eds), *Labour and working-class lives: Essays to celebrate the life and work of Chris Wrigley* (Manchester: Manchester University Press, 2017), 194–216. In reality, Reisner became a professor already after he and Violet divorced and she married Clemens Palme Dutt, brother of the communist intellectual Rajani Palme Dutt who briefly served as General Secretary of the CPGB. Igor Reisner was born in December 1898 to the family of a law professor. His elder sister was Larisa Reisner about whose incredible life and adventures a book was only published in Moscow eight decades after her tragic death at age 30. In 1917 Igor served as secretary to Dmitry Manuilsky in the Petrograd Duma, in 1919–21 he was a secretary at the Soviet diplomatic mission in Afghanistan, where his sister also arrived at the end of his term as a wife of the Soviet plenipotentiary Fedor Raskolnikov. After Afghanistan Igor Reisner studied part-time at the (special) Eastern Faculty of the Frunze Military Academy being on the staff of the Narkomindel and in 1923–5 operated undercover in Scandinavia and Germany for Soviet military intelligence. After his tour of duty Reisner was a lecturer at the same faculty of the Frunze Military Academy whose graduates were prepared to work abroad as military diplomats and intelligence officers. He was also teaching a course at the Moscow Institute of Oriental Studies. In 1935 he became professor of Moscow State University (MGU) and three years later was elected to the Russian Academy. His second wife was psychologist Dr Maria Pevzner.
52. TNA KV 2/1391, s.98a, p. 49. Remarkably, Kirchenstein never mentioned another daughter of George Lansbury, Dorothy, who was not a communist but nevertheless obtained a job as an accountant at ARCOS in early 1925. See Kevin Morgan, *Labour Legends and Russian Gold – Part 1: Bolshevism and the British Left* (London: Lawrence & Wishart, 2006), 100.
53. About Prigozhin, see Igar Halfin, *Stalinist Confessions: Messianism and Terror at the Leningrad Communist University* (Pittsburgh, PA: University of Pittsburgh Press, 2009). See also the archives of St Petersburg State University at (last visited on 8 March 2022) https://bioslovhist.spbu.ru/person/3148-prigozin-abram-grigorevic.html.
54. TNA HO 382/2, and MI5 PF 589/SAV1 (KV 2/3037) no serial number, report dated 14.8.22.
55. TNA KV 2/1391, s.98a, pp. 33–7.
56. For details, see MI5 PF R.4003/Volume 1 (TNA KV 2/806). See also TNA KV 2/1391, s.98a, p. 38.

57. For details, see MI5 PF 3934/V1 (TNA KV 2/645). See also TNA KV 2/1391, s.98a, p. 39.
58. TNA KV 2/1391, s.98a, p. 56.
59. Ludwik Bazylow and Jan Sobczak, *Encyklopedia rewolucji październikowej* (Warsaw: Wiedza Powszechna, 1977), 487.
60. At the Second Comintern Congress Alexander Stocklitzki together with Fraina represented the Communist Party of America but nothing had been heard about his mission to London.
61. RGASPI, f. 495, op. 100, d. 23, n/p, Robinson to Kobetsky, 4 April 1921, quoted in Andrew Thorpe, 'Comintern "Control" of the Communist Party of Great Britain, 1920-43', *The English Historical Review*, 113/452 (June 1998), 637–62. Since August 1920 Mikhail Kobetsky was a member of the so-called Small Bureau of the ECCI (later presidium) and in April 1921 headed its Secretariate. In 1921–3 he was deputy chairman of the ECCI then headed by Zinoviev. He later joined the Diplomatic Service (NKID).
62. The Security Service Subject File SF 441-0313-2 Vol. 1 s. 4x and 5x (TNA KV 3/137).
63. Bennett-Petrovsky was the sixteen CPGB representative to the Comintern, for details see John McIlroy and Alan Campbell, 'The British and French Representatives to the Communist International, 1920-1939: A Comparative Survey', *Internationaal Instituut voor Sociale Geschiedenis* (IRSH), 50 (2005), 203–40. At the Comintern 9th Plenum in 1928 Petrovsky and Robin Page Arnot were elected candidates to the ECCI Presidium.
64. Rose Cohen was a good-looking young woman bringing her lively personality to her Communist work. According to his own words, Pollitt was in love with her, proposing marriage on a number of occasions. For details about Petrovsky, Rose Cohen and many others, see Francis Beckett, *Stalin's British Victims* (Stroud, Gloucestershire: Sutton Publishing, 2004). The book contains several technical errors and typos (editor's fault) but otherwise is a useful source. See also TNA KV 2/1396-1397, which is part of Rose Cohen's MI5 personal file PF 38437.
65. TNA KV 2/1391, s.98a, p.62. With this, Kirchenstein continued to describe himself as a former Comintern representative at the same time stressing that 'I should like to state here that I never engaged in any sabotage in my entire career as a Comintern representative or as a representative of the Soviet Union'.
66. TNA KV 2/1391, s.98a, p. 73.
67. TNA KV 2/1391 s.99a, Comments on KIRCHENSTEIN interrogation, TsT/B.2.B., 26.11.51. Admitting that a certain confusion existed at that time between the Comintern and Soviet intelligence organisations, an unknown officer however erroneously attributed this fact not to MI5's own lack of information, knowledge and experience but to the alleged chaos in Moscow.
68. Several authors writing about the period refer to New Scotland Yard's Supplementary Report No. 2 'The Russian Trade Delegation and Revolutionary Organizations in the United Kingdom' dated 7 Dec. 1925 (TNA KV 2/1392, pp. 1–2) produced by its SS branch. According to the report, 'these letters, now identified as being of KIRCHENSTEIN's (vide Appendix M) were from an individual styling himself "John or Jack Walker" in England. From two letters partly in Latvian partly in English attached in Appendix M it is impossible to identify a person and the FBI experts later refused to confirm that they belong to Kirchenstein. The report further claims that this 'Walker' was 'a self-confessed enemy agent [?!] residing in the United Kingdom as an unregistered alien; and that he was there engaged at the head of an organization for distributing Bolshevik propaganda and for facilitating the passage of Bolshevik agents to and from Russia as stowaways. He was also cognisant of, though not hopeful about, the organization of a Red Army in this country.' Nothing of the sort had ever been proved against Jacob Kirchenstein except his so-called self-confession which happened exactly 26 years after this report.

69. TNA KV 2/1391 s.18a Liddell (NSY) to Harker (MI5), 28 October 1928. See also 19a.
70. Russian Foreign Ministry to the author, No. 12797/udd, dated 28.10.2021. See also TNA KV 2/799 personal file JILINSKY, letter from the Soviet Embassy to the Trade Delegation dated 19 August 1926 and signed by Lidin.
71. Different Russian sources provide different dates of his stay in London. In his famous book, *Jews in the KGB* (2008), Vadim Abramov writes that Zolotussky was in London between February and May 1927. Kolpakidi takes it from Abramov and Igor Zolotussky, his son, offers three different versions. In a memo for the Sakharov Centre, he completely omitted his father's work in London; in his memoirs (magazine *Zvezda*, St Petersburg, November 2021) he first referred to the book by Kolpakidi and Prokhorov, *Vneshnyaya Razvedka Rossii* (2001) that mentions Feb.– May 1927 but later quoted a letter from the Russian Foreign Ministry No.890/au, dated 31.8.1956 stating that Peter Zolotussky served as 'a secretary of the General Consulate in London from May to June 1927'. All this information may be wrong except that he left London together with all other diplomats in June. From 1930 Zolotussky had been employed by Amtorg in New York under the alias 'Semen Filin-Myshkin'.
72. TNA KV 2/1391, s.98a, p. 44.
73. See Harold Ross and Philip Hamburger, 'Krivitsky', *The New Yorker*, December 2 (1939), 21. Between 15 April 1939 and 1 June 1940 the *Saturday Evening Post* published eight articles by Krivitsky.
74. Katherine 'Käthe' Gussfeld (DOB: 19 May 1899 in Berlin) aka 'Ethel Chiles' had a false British passport no. 416668 issued in London on 28 February 1927 and a false German passport in the name of Edith Blazer. She was arrested on charge of conspiring to obtain a false British passport but was actually suspected to be spying for the Soviets against the USA. See MI5 PF 38764/V3 (TNA KV 2/592). Unfortunately, other volumes of this file are not available.
75. It seems that much later the Security Service (MI5) opened a file, PF 707824, on Rudolf Kirchenstein but by the time of writing it has not been declassified.
76. His brother, Professor August Kirchenstein, also returned to his native Latvia from political exile in 1917 and was accepted to the University of Latvia founded in September 1919. In 1923 he was elected professor of microbiology and in 1940 was promoted to prime minister. In July 1940 President of Latvia Kārlis Ulmanis retired and transferred executive powers of the head of state to Kirchenstein. When the Red Army occupied the country in August, Kirchenstein was appointed chairman of the Supreme Soviet of Latvia.
77. TNA KV 2/1391, s.98a, page 44.
78. For details, see MI5 PF R.4019 (TNA KV 2/799).
79. 'Frustrated in its efforts to obtain foreign credits and assistance, the Soviet government now began to concentrate its forces on the development of domestic production for export in order to obtain the foreign exchange with which to purchase vitally needed imports.' Hans Heymann Jr., 'Oil in Soviet-Western Relations in the Interwar Years', *The American Slavic and East European Review*, 7/4 (Dec. 1948), 303–16. By 1924 the Naphtha Syndicate was ready to launch a bold offensive to expand its sales on the world markets setting up its own subsidiary in England – Russian Oil Products Limited (see ibid., 308–9).
80. Hansard, Trading Companies in Great Britain, Volume 245: debates on Tuesday, 25 November 1930, the matter raised by Edward Marjoribanks, MP. About ROP, see TNA KV 5/71-72. See also Andrew, *Defence of the Realm*, 166–7, and Volodarsky, *Stalin's Agent*, 125.
81. TNA HO 144/17721, Certificate AZ2786 issued 5 May 1933.

82. See, for example, Smith, *SIX*, 289; and P. Tomaselli, 'C's Moscow station – The Anglo-Russian Trade Mission as Cover for SIS in the Early 1920s', *Intelligence and National Security*, 17/3 (Autumn 2002), 173–80. I am very grateful to Phil Tomaselli for his everlasting help during the work on this volume.

83. TNA FO 371/10480 Code 38 File 171 Paper 2277.

84. Tomaselli, 'C's Moscow Station', 177. To compare, the annual fees collected by PCOs in the key cities of the SIS Baltic group were: £1,000 in Helsinki, £607 in Riga and £71 in Tallinn. Figures for passport control offices to year-end 31 March 1923 as quoted in FO 336/808.

85. Ferris, *Behind the Enigma*, 142–3.

86. In his unofficial history of SIS (1909–39), Michael Smith writes that 'the Reval office was run, under Meiklejohn, by S.G. Goodlet, also a member of the pre-war British community in Russia, and between 1920 and 1922 by Sydney Turner, whose real name was Stephen Tomes, under which name he had previously worked for MI1c in Petrograd and Torneå [Tornio, a city and municipality in Lapland, Finland]'. See Smith, *SIX*, 288.

87. About Zhitkov, see Andrey Ganin, 'Russian sailor from the British intelligence station', *Rodina*, 5 (May 2016), 113–16, in Russian. In his book *Near and Distant Neighbours* (OUP, 2015, 33), Jonathan Haslam erroneously calls him 'Zhidkov' without providing any further details and confuses high-ranking Estonian politician and diplomat Ado Birk (see Note 89 below) with his nephew Roman Birk, an Estonian officer and a Soviet agent. It was Roman Birk who together with Professor Julius Patzelt from the Vienna Consular Academy founded the American-European Information Agency (AMEIA) in 1929 later moving to Hamburg and using this agency for 'false-flag' operations.

88. General Törvand was arrested by the Soviet occupation authorities and deported to the USSR in 1941. He died during a preliminary investigation in the Vyatka prison camp in May 1942.

89. Like General Törvand, Ado Birk was arrested by the Soviet secret police in 1941, sentenced to death but died before the execution in the Sosva prison camp in February 1942.

90. National Archives of Estonia, Tartu, ERAF.129SM1.26760. V1 p. 209.

91. Michael Smith to author, 29 June 2020. I am very grateful to Michael for this and other valuable comments and explanations.

92. Jeffery, *MI6*, 184–5. According to one researcher, by August 1921 Meiklejohn had recruited some thirty-eight agents. See C.G. McKay, 'Our Man in Reval', *Intelligence and National Security*, 9/1 (January 1994), 88–111.

93. Director of Passport Control to Giffey, 18 Dec. 1928, Stockholm collection quoted by Tina Tamman (see below). By that time the Passport Control head office had moved into 21 Queen Ann's Gate, adjoining Broadway Building were both SIS and GS&CS moved in the spring of 1926.

94. Tina Tamman, *Portrait of a Secret Agent* (Layerthorpe, York: Thousand Eyes Publishing, 2014), 83–107.

95. Jeffery, *MI6*, 184–203. Agents controlled from Helsinki were identified in CX reports as ST (for Stockholm), from Riga FR, Tallinn BP, Berlin BN, and Vienna V. According to Tomaselli, other agents working in Russia or the Baltic states were identified as D (Copenhagen), N (Norway), S (Sweden) and HV (Turkey).

96. 'I went to Voikov, supply director for the Urals, to obtain gasoline or kerosene, sulphuric acid for disfiguring the faces, and a shovel. I obtained all of these' – from the chief executioner, Yurovsky, note now at the State Archive of the Russian Federation (GARF), quoted in Andrew Cook, *The Murder of the Romanovs* (Stroud, Gloucestershire: Amberley, 2010), 197.

97. See the book *Ubiistvo Voikova, Delo Borisa Koverdy* (Paris: La Renaissance, 1927).

98. *DVP USSR*, vol. 10 doc. 154, Note of 7 June 1927 No. 243/ch (Moscow: Iz-vo Politicheskoi Literatury, 1965), 289.

99. For details, see John P. Sontag, 'The Soviet War Scare 1926-27', *Russian Review*, 34/1 (Jan. 1975), 66–77. According to the author, this war scare has been treated in Western historiography as largely a sham, fabricated in the heat of Stalin's conflict with Trotsky and Zinoviev. This interpretation is based on a number of elements. 'Among these,' Sontag writes, 'are the absence of a direct threat of attack against the USSR, the crude and intemperate manner in which Stalin hounded his foes by claiming disloyalty at a time of extreme national danger, and the manipulation of the fear of war by Stalin to enforce total subservience upon the Comintern.' See also Andrew, *Secret Service*, 333.

100. The official OGPU information published in several Soviet newspapers was reprinted by the Russian-language Paris newspaper *Vozrozhdenie*, 3/772 (14 July 1927), 2.

101. Smith, *SIX*, 251.

102. Ibid, 322.

103. Lady Muriel Paget, 'Some pictures of Soviet Russia V: Hospitals and Clinics', *The Daily Telegraph*, 5 February 1927, p. 7.

104. See Smith, *SIX*, 244–5.

105. For details, see Chris Parker, 'The Gentleman Badass: Conrad O'Brien-ffrench was the Real James Bond', *Adventure Journal*, 28 January 2021. See also Anthony Reed and David Fisher, *Colonel Z: The Secret Life of a Master of Spies* (London: Hodder and Stoughton, 1984), 184. In Vienna Dansey's men were Frederick Voight, the Central European correspondent of the *Manchester Guardian*, and Patrick Maitland, a 'young, enthusiastic, and raw-boned Scot', whom R. Selkirk Panton, a foreign correspondent for the *Daily Express* in Europe, hired as his assistant. In 1943 Maitland joined the Political Intelligence Department of the Foreign Office where he remained until the end of the war, later being elected MP for Lanark. Patrick Maitland subsequently became the 17th Earl of Lauderdale. The official SIS stations in Europe and elsewhere had never been informed about the existence of the Z Organisation and operated quite separately.

106. Simon Ball, *Secret History: Writing the Rise of Britain's Intelligence Services* (Montreal, Quebec: McGill-Queen's University Press, 2020).

107. Archive of the FSB Directorate for St Petersburg and the Leningrad Region, PF P-76654 YANUSHKEVICH, Anton Alekseyevich. Juho Kusti Paasikivi, who served as prime minister and president of Finland, later commented that the Soviet attack without a declaration of war violated three non-aggression pacts: the Treaty of Tartu of 1920; the Non-Aggression Pact between Finland and the Soviet Union signed in 1932 and again in 1934; and the Charter of the League of Nations, whose only reaction was to expel the aggressor.

108. For details, see Vadim J. Birstein, *SMERSH: Stalin's Secret Weapon* (London: Biteback, 2011), 296–301.

109. Peter Bazanov, *Brotherhood of Russian Truth* (Moscow: Posev, 2013), 29, in Russian.

110. See Arthur Willert Papers (I. Correspondence; II. Writings; III. Personal and Memorabilia), Yale University Libraries, Sterling Memorial Library, Call Number. MS 720.

111. David A. Lincove, 'The British Library of Information in New York: A Tool of British Foreign Policy, 1919-1942', *Libraries & the Cultural Record*, 46/2 (2011), 156–84. 'By 1920,' Lincove writes, 'budget cuts and reorganizations had reduced the propaganda efforts of the Foreign Office News Department to informing domestic and foreign press writers in London of government foreign policy news and distributing government policy information in other countries', ibid., 158.

112. Philip M. Taylor, *The Projection of Britain: British overseas publicity and propaganda 1919–1939* (Cambridge. Cambridge University Press, 1981), 22.

113. Arthur Willert, *Washington and Other Memories* (Boston: Houghton Mifflin, 1972), 152.

114. Both Tyrrell and Koppel had served in the Political Intelligence Department (PID) of the Foreign Office. Tyrrell was its first head assisted by James W. Headlam-Morley (later Sir), a noted historian who later became historical adviser to the Foreign Office. Among well-known figures on the staff of the PID were Rex Leeper and his brother Allen, Lewis Namier, Arnold Toynbee and during the last weeks of the war Harold Nicolson and Robert Vansittart were also assigned to the PID. For details, see Goldstein, 'The Foreign Office and Political Intelligence 1918-20', 278.

115. See Willert, *Washington and Other Memories*, 153.

116. Taylor, *The Projection of Britain*, 22–3.

117. Lincove, 'The British Library of Information in New York', 161.

118. Taylor, *The Projection of Britain*, 23–5.

119. TNA FO 1093/107. Steward was probably not followed but one of MI5's static surveillance units (A Branch) was installed watching the German embassy at 9 Carlton House Terrace, the so-called Prussia House, where he 'conducted private negotiations with the Nazi regime'. The Security Service also had an informant inside the embassy who reported that Steward visited as 'a representative of the PM'. MI5 obtained a complete version of the report Hesse prepared for von Ribbentrop. It explained that George Steward had offered concessions that could 'serve as the basis for a General Anglo-German understanding'. Steward said that these should be negotiated 'direct between the Fuhrer and Chamberlain'. Dr Hesse reported that 'Great Britain in now ready ... to accept practically everything from us and to fulfil our every wish'. For details, see Tim Luckhurst, 'How Neville Chamberlain's adviser took spinning for the PM to new and dangerous levels', *The Conversation*, 8 October 2020.

120. In October, Ewer went to Paris again and was given the sum of £575 to distribute to Dale and Allen.

121. In his book *Britannia and the Bear* (2014), Victor Madeira writes: 'John Ottaway first approached Allen on 25 June 1928 in Wallington, Surrey ... He asked if Allen would consider selling information for money. He did, for £75 a meeting' (p. 245n111). Madeira makes a reference to 'Federated Press of America, Supplementary, p. 6, TNA KV 2/1432; and Lakey, p. 1, serial 2A, TNA KV 2/989'. Unfortunately, all this is rather inexact. In 'The Federated Press of America' MI5 file PF 38299 Supp. A, Vol 1 (TNA KV 2/1432) serial 12a page 6 incorrectly describes the first meeting between John Ottaway and Albert Allen @Arthur Lakey as having been on 25 June 28. It also doesn't mention any remuneration. In reality, MI5's watcher Ottaway first visited Lakey in Bournemouth on Friday, 22 June 1928. They had a talk and then Lakey accepted Ottaway's invitation to dinner. During the dinner he agreed in principle to share some information provided his name was not mentioned and he would not expose the names of one or two very close friends. Lakey told the MI5 agent a lot of very interesting things but this is outside the scope of the present volume. Ottaway concluded: 'His manner I was impressed with and feel sure he would give genuine and most useful information if generously paid, but I do not think that anything less than £200 would tempt him to talk' (see TNA KV 2/989 s. 1A, Ottaway's report of 25 June 1928). They met again at the same place in Bournemouth four days later. Now Lakey said that the sum of £1,500 seemed a reasonable figure for his information and if the Union didn't have this money, he advised to get in touch with Colonel Kell's department (MI5) 'who would best be able to deal with the matter' and arrange with him the payment.

122. TNA KV 2/989 s. 2A, Ottaway's report on meeting ALLEN/Lakey again on Tuesday, June 26, dated 27.6.28. See also 77a of 10 September 1928.
123. TNA KV 2/989 s. 2A, Ottaway's report 'Re Federated Press of America' of 27 June 1928. Lakey also revealed that 'Macartney [in the TNA document the name is deleted] upon his liberation from prison for shop breaking applied for work with Arcos, but was not employed as they suspected some ulterior motives. Allen afterwards had his movements kept under observation' (p. 3).
124. TNA KV 2/989 s. 76a 'ALLEN's statements and M.I.5 comments' [to Mr. Ottaway's report of 27.6.28].
125. TNA FO 395/435, General Code 150, File 57, Paper 1457, quoted in Taylor, *The Projection of Britain*, 26–7.
126. MI5 PF 655,331 EWER, William Norman (TNA KV 2/1016, s. 892a) dated 22 August1930 and signed by O.A.H. (Oswald Allen Harker).
127. Willert, *Washington and Other Memories*, 183 and 195. William Norman Ewer's case was quite uncritically revisited by Victor Madeira for his article 'Moscow's Interwar Infiltration of British Intelligence, 1919-29' (2003) based almost exclusively on the old MI5 files, and later by John Callaghan and Kevin Morgan. In their article 'The Open Conspiracy of the Communist Party and the Case of W.N. Ewer, Communist and Anti-Communist' (2006) they present a critical analysis of Madeira's work and correctly point to the common shortcoming of such accounts. Ironically, it is identified in the epigraph of Madeira's article. 'If all records told the same tale,' Madeira quotes George Orwell, 'then the lie passed into history and became truth.' Nevertheless, Ewer himself admitted quite openly that in the 1920s he and his organisation collected political information for the Soviets which included spying on SIS, MI5 and Special Branch. Ewer declared that to him such activities were 'purely counter'. He explained that it was done to ascertain British intelligence and counter-intelligence capabilities as well as British Secret Services' possible actions against his party (CPGB), the Comintern and the Soviet Union.
128. West and Tsarev, *The Crown Jewels*, 10. The role should be described as Chief Operative of the overseas section of the INO (there was also a visa section and a foreign travel section).
129. Ibid., 11–12. John Duncan Gregory joined the Diplomatic Service in 1902. From 1907 to 1909 he was assigned to the British embassy in Vienna as 2nd secretary, later served as chargé d'affaires in Bucharest and was posted to the Holy See in 1915. Since 1920 Gregory served at the Foreign Office in London as Senior Clerk and Assistant Secretary promoted to Assistant Under-Secretary of State for Foreign Affairs in 1925. Together with Aminta Bradley Dyne and a number of his civil service associates, Gregory was accused of speculating in foreign currency in what became known as the 'Francs Case' in 1928. Although cleared of any criminal wrongdoing, he was dismissed from the Diplomatic Service. Gregory was the author of two well-received books, *On the Edge of Diplomacy* (1929) and *Dollfuss and His Times* (1935). He died in January 1951.
130. Volodarsky, *Stalin's Agent*, 103. Copies of the relevant documents are in this writer's personal archive. The Wikipedia biographies of both Sir Arthur Willert and John Duncan Gregory are surprisingly short in comparison with their colleagues of the same age and social status.
131. Ibid., 80–1 and 544n7.
132. For details, see ibid., 78–80.
133. This report is also quoted in West and Tsarev, *The Crown Jewels*, 124.
134. Volodarsky, *Stalin's Agent*, 103, quoting original KGB documents.
135. MI5 PF 302011 V1, 1939 Oct 20 1950 Jan 05 (TNA KV 2/3840). At the time of the meeting, Paul Willert had just married or was about to marry his first wife, The

Hon. Brenda Ruby Pearson, a daughter of the 2nd Viscount Cowdray. They divorced in November 1948 and he married Kate O'Malley, one of the two daughters of Sir Owen St Clair O'Malley, a British diplomat and intelligence officer. In 1936 Paul Willert was sent as vice-president and manager of the Oxford University Press (OUP) office in New York. According to the official history of OUP, while there he 'offered accommodation to members of the Soviet secret police'. See *History of Oxford University Press*, vol. III (1896–1970), footnote on p. 617.

136. Taylor, *The Projection of Britain*, 28.
137. Ullman, *Anglo-Soviet Relations, 1917-21*, I, 60.
138. Taylor, *The Projection of Britain*, 29.
139. For details, see Cedric Larson, 'The British Ministry of Information', *The Public Opinion Quarterly*, 5/3 (Autumn 1941), 412–31. See also, *Birmingham Mail*, Friday, 8 September 1939, p. 8.

Appendix

1. Actually, in Marxist philosophy, between a capitalist economy and a communist economy.
2. Semion Tsvigun et al (eds), *V.I. Lenin and VCheKa: Collection of Documents, 1917–1922* (Moscow: Political Literature Publishers, 1975), 117–18, doc. 83, originally published in Russian in Lenin, *Complete Works*, vol. 37, 173–4. Translated by this writer. Army General Tsvigun had served as the First Deputy Chairman of the KGB from 1967 to 1982.

Я счастлив, что дожил до того дня, когда стало возможным познакомить русского читателя с воспоминаниями моего деда — генерала Николая Алексеевича Епанчина. Умирая вдали от Родины, в солнечной Ницце, он сказал мне: «Эта рукопись теперь твоя, сохрани ее. Когда кончится власть большевиков и Россия снова станет Россией, верни ее на Родину и опубликуй».

Воля старого генерала исполнена, и я благодарен всем, кто принимал участие в подготовке к выходу в свет духовного завещания Н.А.Епанчина — книги «На службе трех Императоров».

Вадуц, Лихтенштейн
Осень 1995 года

Барон Эдуард фон Фальц-Фейн

FALZ-FEIN

Falz Fein book inscription to Boris Volodarsky to commemorate the meeting in Vaduz, Lichtenstein, on 16 August 1998.

Recommended Reading

Aldrich, Richard J., and Rory Cormac, *The Secret Royals: Spying and the Crown, from Victoria to Diana* (London: Atlantic Books, 2021).

Andrew, Christopher, 'British Intelligence and the Breach with Russia in 1927', *The Historical Journal*, 25/4 (1982), 957–64.

——, 'Governments and Secret Services: A Historical Perspective', *International Journal*, 34/2 (Spring 1979), 167–86.

——, 'Historical Attention Span Deficit Disorder: Why Intelligence Analysis Needs to Look Back Before Looking Forward', in Carol Dumaine and L. Sergio Germani (eds), *New Frontiers of Intelligence Analysis: Papers Presented at the Conference on New Frontiers of Intelligence Analysis – Shared Threats, Diverse Perspectives, New Communities*, Rome, Italy, 31 March–2 April 2004 (Rome: Link Campus University of Malta, 2005), 63-79.

——, 'The British Secret Service and Anglo-Soviet Relations in the 1920s Part I: From the Trade Negotiations to the Zinoviev Letter', *The Historical Journal*, 20/3 (September 1977), 673–706.

——, 'Whitehall, Washington and the Intelligence Services', *International Affairs* (The Royal Institute of International Affairs), 53/3 (July 1977), 390–404.

——, *Secret Service: The Making of the British Intelligence Community* (London: Heinemann, 1985).

——, *The Defence of the Realm: The Authorised History of MI5* (London: Allen Lane/Penguin Books, 2009).

——, *The Secret World: A History of Intelligence* (London: Allen Lane/Penguin Books, 2018).

——, with David Dilks, *Missing Dimension: Governments and Intelligence Communities in the Twentieth Century* (London: Macmillan, 1984).

——, and Julie Elkner 'Stalin and Foreign Intelligence', *Totalitarian Movements and Political Religions*, 4/1 (2003), 69–94.

——, and A.S. Kanya-Forstner, *The Climax of French Imperial Expansion, 1914–1924* (Stanford, CA: Stanford University Press, 1981).

——, and Jeremy Noakes (eds), *Intelligence and International Relations 1900-1945* (Exeter: Exeter University Press, 1987).

——, and Vasili Mitrokhin, *The Mitrokhin Archive* (I): *The KGB in Europe and the West* (London: Allen Lane/Penguin Books, 1999).

——, and Vasili Mitrokhin, *The Mitrokhin Archive* (II): *The KGB and the World* (London: Allen Lane/Penguin Books, 2005).

——, Richard J. Aldrich and Wesley K. Wark, *Secret Intelligence: A Reader*, second edition (Abingdon, Oxon: Routledge, 2020).

Andreyev, Alexander, *Soviet Russia and Tibet: The Debacle of Secret Diplomacy, 1918-1930s* (Leiden • Boston: Brill, 2003).

Bagley, Tennent H., *Spy Wars: Moles, Mysteries and Deadly Games* (New Haven and London: Yale University Press, 2007).

Bainton, Roy, *Honoured by Strangers: The Life of Captain Francis Cromie CB DSO RN, 1882–1918* (Shrewsbury, Shropshire: Airlife Publishing Ltd., 2002).

Beckett, Francis, *Stalin's British Victims* (Stroud, Gloucestershire: Sutton Publishing, 2004).

Berberova, Nina, *Moura: The Dancing Life of the Baroness Budberg* (New York, NY: The New York Review of Books, 1988).

Berkeley, Roy, *A Spy's London* (Barnsley, S. Yorkshire: Pen & Sword, 2014).

Brandenberger, David, and Mikhail Zelenov (eds), *Stalin's Master Narrative: A Critical Edition of the History of the Communist Party of the Soviet Union (Bolsheviks) Short Course* (New Haven and London: Yale University Press, 2019).

Brook-Shepherd, Gordon, *Iron Maze: The Western Secret Services and the Bolsheviks* (London: Macmillan, 1998).

Bruce Lockhart, R.H., *Memoirs of a British Agent* (London: Putnam, 1932).

Bulgakov, M.A. 'Benefit Lorda Kerzona' [Lord Curzon's Benefit Performance], *Collected Works in 10 volumes* (Ann Arbor: Ardis, 1982), vol. 1, 314.

Bunyan, James, and Harold H. Fisher (eds), *The Bolshevik Revolution, 1917-1918: Documents and Materials* (Stanford: Stanford University Press, 1961).

Carley, Michael Jabara, 'A Soviet Eye on France from the Rue de Grenelle in Paris, 1924-1940', *Diplomacy and Statecraft*, 17 (2006), 295–346.

Chambers, Roland, *The Last Englishman: The Double Life of Arthur Ransome* (Jaffrey, NH: David R. Godine, 2012).

Charters, David A. and Maurice A.J. Tugwell (eds), *Deception Operations: Studies in the East-West Context* (London: Brassey's, 1990).

Coates, W.P. (compl.), *Raid on Arcos Ltd. and the Trade Delegation of the USSR: Facts and Documents* (London: Anglo-Russian Parliamentary Committee, May 1927).

Cook, Andrew, *On His Majesty's Secret Service: Sidney Reilly Codename ST1*, paperback (Cheltenham, Gloucestershire: Tempus Publishing, 2002).

——, *The Murder of the Romanovs* (Stroud, Gloucestershire: Amberley Publishing, 2010).

Corera, Gordon, *The Art of Betrayal: Life and Death of the British Secret Service* (London: Weidenfeld & Nicolson, 2011).

Count de Marenches, Alexander, and Christine Ockrent, *The Evil Empire: The Third World War Now – By the former head of the French Secret Service* (London: Sidgwick & Jackson, 1988).

Curry, John Court (ed.), *The Security Service, 1908–1945: The Official History* (London: Public Record Office, 1999), with introduction by Christopher M. Andrew.

Dallin, David J., *Soviet Espionage* (New Haven: Yale University Press, 1955).

De Graaff, Bob, and James M. Nyce with Chelsea Locke (eds), *The Handbook of European Intelligence Cultures* (Lanham, MD: Rowman & Littlefield, 2016).

Deacon, Richard, *A History of the Russian Secret Service*, paperback (London: Grafton Books/Collins Publishing Group, 1987).

Deriabin, Peter, *Watchdogs of Terror: Russian Bodyguards from the Tsars to the Commissars* (Bethesda, MD: University Publications of America, 1984).

——, and T.H. Bagley, *The KGB: Masters of the Soviet Union* (London: Robson Books, 1990).

Dorril, Stephen, *MI6: Inside the Covert World of Her Majesty's Secret Intelligence Service* (New York, NY: The Free Press, 2000).

Dukes, Paul, *Red Dusk and the Morrow: Adventures and Investigations in Soviet Russia*, paperback (London: Biteback Publishing, 2012).

——, *The Story of "ST25"* (London: Cassell, 1938).

Elkner, Julie Clair, *Constructing the chekist: The cult of state security in Soviet and post-Soviet Russia* (unpublished PhD thesis, University of Cambridge, 2009).

FCO Historians, *The Records of the Permanent Under-Secretary Department: Liaison between the Foreign Office and British Secret Intelligence* (London: FCO, March 2005).

Fergusson, Thomas G., *British Military Intelligence, 1870-1914* (Frederick, MD: University Publications of America, 1984).

Ferris, John Robert, *Men, Money and Diplomacy: The Evolution of British Strategic Foreign Policy, 1919-1926* (Ithaca, NY: Cornell University Press, 1989).

——, 'Whitehall's Black Chamber: British Cryptology and the Government Code and Cypher School, 1919-29', *Intelligence and National Security*, 2/1 (1987), 54–91.

——, *Behind the Enigma: The Authorised History of GCHQ, Britain's Secret Cyber-Intelligence Agency* (London: Bloomsbury, 2020).

Fischer, Ben B. (ed.), *Okhrana: The Paris Operations of the Russian Imperial Police* (Washington, DC: Center for the Study of Intelligence, 1997).

Foglesong, David S., *America's Secret War Against Bolshevism: US Intervention in the Russian Civil War, 1917-1920* (Chapel Hill, NC: University of North Carolina Press, 1995).

Haider, Edgard, *Die österreichisch-sowjetischen Beziehungen 1918-1938*, unpublished doctoral thesis (University of Vienna, May 1975).

Harris, George S. and Nur Bilge Criss (eds), *Studies in Atatürk's Turkey: The American Dimension* (Leiden & Boston: Brill, 2009).

Haynes, John, and Harvey Klehr, *In Denial: Historians, Communism, & Espionage* (New York, NY: Encounter Books, 2003).

——, and Alexander Vassiliev, *Spies: The Rise and Fall of the KGB in America* (New Haven and London: Yale University Press, 2009).

Hill, George A., *Go Spy the Land: Being the Adventures of I.K. 8 of the British Secret Service* (London: Cassell, 1932).

Hill, Elizabeth, and Jean Stafford Smith (ed.), *In the Mind's Eye: The Memoirs of Dame Elizabeth Hill* (Sussex: The Book Guild, 1999).

Hingley, Ronald, *The Russian Secret Police: Muscovite, Imperial Russian and Soviet Political Security Operations 1565-1970* (Abingdon, Oxon: Routledge, 2021).

Höhne, Heinz, *Der Krieg im Dunkeln: Die geschichte der deutsch-russischen Spionage* (Munich: Bertelsmann/Sonderausgabe für Gondrom, 1993).

Jacobs, Dan N., *Borodin: Stalin's Man in China* (Cambridge, MA: Harvard University Press, 1981).

Jansen, Marc, and Nikita Petrov, *Stalin's Loyal Executioner: People's Commissar Nikolai Ezhov, 1895-1940* (Stanford: Hoover Press, 2002).

Jeffery, Keith, *MI6: The History of the Secret Intelligence Service 1909-1949* (London: Bloomsbury, 2010).

Johnson, Richard J., '*Zagranichnaia Agentura*: The Tsarist Political Police in Europe', in George L. Mosse (ed.), *Police Forces in History* (Ann Arbor, MI: University of Michigan, 1999).

Jordan, Pamela A., *Stalin's Singing Spy: The Life and Exile of Nadezhda Plevitskaya* (Lanham, MD: Rowman & Littlefield, 2016).

Joukoff Eudin, Xenia, and Harold H. Fisher in collaboration with Rosemary Brown Jones, *Soviet Russia and the West, 1920-1927: A Documentary Survey* (Stanford, CA: Stanford University Press, 1957).

Joukoff Eudin, Xenia, and Robert C. North, *Soviet Russia and the East, 1920-1927: A Documentary Survey* (Stanford, CA: Stanford University Press, 1957).

Judd, Alan, *The Quest for C: Sir Mansfield Cumming and the Founding of the Secret Service* (London: HarperCollinsPublishers, 1999).

Kern, Gary (ed.), *Walter G. Krivitsky: MI5 Debriefing and Other Documents on Soviet Intelligence* (Riverside, CA: Xenos Books, 2004).

Khaustov, V.N., Naumov, V.P., and Plotnikova, N.S. (eds), *Lubyanka, Stalin i VChK-GPU-OGPU-NKVD January 1922 – December 1936* (Moskva: Materik, 2003).

Kokurin, Alexander I. and Nikita V. Petrov (compl.), A.N. Yakovlev (ed.), *Lubyanka: Organy VChKa-OGPU-NKVD-NKGB-MGB-MVD-KGB, 1917 – 1991* (Moscow: MFD, 2003).

Kolpakidi, Alexander and Valentin Mzareulov, *Soviet Foreign Intelligence, 1920-1945: History, Structure and Personnel* (Moscow: Rodina, 2021), in Russian.

Kotkin, Stephen, *Stalin: Paradoxes of Power, 1878-1928* (London: Allen Lane/Penguin Press, 2014).

Kronenbitter, Rita T., 'Paris Okhrana 1885 – 1905', *Studies in Intelligence*, 10/3 (Summer 1966), 55–66.

Leggett, George, *The Cheka: Lenin's Political Police* (Oxford: Clarendon Press, 1981).

Lensen, George Alexander, *Japanese Recognition of the U.S.S.R.* (Tokyo: Sophia University in cooperation with Tallahassee, FL: The Diplomatic Press, 1970).

Lomonossoff, George V. [Yuri Vladimirovich Lomonosov], *Memoirs of the Russian Revolution* (New York, NY: The Rand School of Social Science, 1919).

Macartney, W.F.R., *Walls Have Mouths*, with the introduction by Compton Mackenzie (London: Victor Gollancz, 1936).

Macfie, Alexander (A.L.): 'British Intelligence and the Causes of Unrest in Mesopotamia, 1919-21', *Middle Eastern Studies*, 35/1 (January 1999).

Madeira, Victor, 'Because I Don't Trust Him, We are Friends: Signals Intelligence and the Reluctant Anglo-Soviet Embrace', *Intelligence and National Security*, 19/1 (Spring 2004), 28–50.

——, '"No Wishful Thinking Allowed": Secret Service Committee and Intelligence Reform in Great Britain, 1919-23', *Intelligence and National Security*, 18/1 (Spring 2003).

McDonald, Deborah and Jeremy Dronfield, *A Very Dangerous Woman: The Lives, Loves and Lies of Russia's Most Deductive Spy* (London: One World, 2015).

McMeekin, Sean, *History's Greatest Heist: The Looting of Russia by the Bolsheviks* (New Haven and London: Yale University Press, 2009).

——, *The Russian Origins of the First World War* (Cambridge, MA: Belknap Press of Harvard University Press, 2011).

——, *The Russian Revolution: A New History* (New York, NY: Basic Books, 2017).

McLoughlin, Barry, Hannes Leidinger and Verena Moritz, *Kommunismus in Österreich 1918-1938* (Innsbruck: Studien Verlag, 2009).

Merridale, Catherine, *Lenin on the Train* (New York, NY: Metropolitan Books Henry Holt and Company/Macmillan Publishing, 2017).

Merlen, Éric, and Frédéric Ploquin, *Carnets intimes de la DST: 30 ans au cœur du contre-espionnage français* (Paris: Fayard, 2003).

Mitrokhin, Vasili, *KGB Lexicon: The Soviet Intelligence Officer's Handbook* (Abingdon, Oxon: Routledge, 2004).

——, *"Chekisms": A KGB Anthology* (Self-published – The Yurasov Press, 2008).

Moffat, Ian C.D., *The Allied Intervention in Russia, 1918-1920: The Diplomacy of Chaos* (Basingstoke: Palgrave Macmillan, 2015).

Moustafine, Mara, *Secrets and Spies: The Harbin Files* (Sydney: Vintage Books/Random House Australia, 2002).

Neilson, Keith, '"Pursued by a Bear": British Estimates of Soviet Military Strength and Anglo-Soviet Relations, 1922-1939', *Canadian Journal of History*, 28 (August 1993), 189–221.

——, *Britain, Soviet Russia and the Collapse of the Versailles Order, 1919-1939* (Cambridge: Cambridge University Press, 2006).

Nekrich, Alexander M., *Pariahs, Partners, Predators: German-Soviet Relations 1922-1941*, edited and translated by Gregory L. Freeze, with a foreword by Adam B. Ulam (New York, NY: Columbia University Press, 1997).

Odom, Anne, and Wendy R. Salmond (eds), *Treasures into Tractors: The Selling of Russia's Cultural Heritage, 1918-1938*, paperback (Washington, DC: Hillwood Museum & Gardens, 2009).

Önnerfors, Andreas, *Freemasonry: A Very Short Introduction* (Oxford: Oxford University Press, 2017).

Orlov, I.B. and A.D. Popov, *Skvoz "zheleznyi zanaves": See USSR! Inostrannye turisty i prizrak potemkinskih dereven* (Moscow: High School of Economics, 2018).

Orwell, George, *Nineteen Eighty-Four: The Annotated Edition*, paperback (London: Penguin Classic, 2013).

Osokina, Elena, *Zoloto dlya industrializatsyi: Torgsin* (Moscow: ROSSPEN, 2009).

Papi, Stefano, *The Jewels of the Romanovs: Family and Court* (London: Thames and Hudson, 2013).

Pipes, Richard (ed.), *The Unknown Lenin: From the Secret Archives* (New Haven and London: Yale University Press, 1996).

Plotke, A.J., *Imperial Spies Invade Russia: The British Intelligence Interventions, 1918* (Westport, CT • London: Greenwood Press, 1993).

Pyman, Avril, *Pavel Florensky – A Quiet Genius: The tragic and extraordinary life of Russia's unknown Da Vinci* (New York, NY: Continuum, 2010).

Rayfield, Donald, *Stalin and His Hangmen: An Authoritative Portrait of a Tyrant and Those Who Served Him* (London: Viking/Penguin Books, 2004).

Reilly, Sidney, *Adventure of a British Master Spy: The Memoirs of Sidney Reilly*, paperback (London: Biteback, 2014).

Rosenbaum, Kurt, *Community of Fate: German-Soviet Diplomatic Relations, 1922-1928* (Syracuse, NY: Syracuse University Press, 1965).

Ruud, Charles A., and Sergei A. Stepnov, *Fontanka 16: The Tsar's Secret Police* (Montreal & Kingston: McGill-Queen's University Press, 1999).

Scott, Len, 'Secret Intelligence, Covert Action and Clandestine Diplomacy', *Intelligence and National Security*, 19/2 (Summer 2004), 322–41.

Semyonova, Natalya, and Nicolas V. Iljine (eds), *Selling Russia's Treasures* (New York, NY: Abbeville Press Publishers, 2013).

Shukman, Harold (ed.), *Redefining Stalinism* (London: Frank Cass Publishers, 2003).

Sibley, Katherine A.S., *Loans and Legitimacy: The Evolution of Soviet-American Relations, 1919–1933* (Lexington, KY: The University Press of Kentucky, 1996).

Slater, Wendy, *The Many Deaths of Tsar Nicholas II: Relics, Remains and the Romanovs* (Abington, Oxon: Routledge, 2007).

Smith, Douglas, *Former People: The Destruction of the Russian Aristocracy* (London: Pan Books, 2013).

Smith, Edward Ellis, *The Okhrana: The Russian Department of Police* (Stanford, CA: Hoover Institution Press, 1967).

Smith, Michael, *Six – A History of Britain's Secret Intelligence Service, Part 1: Murder and Mayhem, 1909-1939* (London: Biteback, 2010).

Sokolov, Nicholas, *The Sokolov Investigation*, translated by John F. O'Connor (London: Souvenir Press, 1972).

Sokolov, Nikolai, *Ubiistvo tsarskoi sem'i* (Berlin: Slovo, 1925; Moscow: Algoritm, 2007).

Sonyel, Salahi R., 'Mustafa Kemal and Enver in Conflict, 1919-22', *Middle Eastern Studies*, 25/4 (Oct. 1989).

Spence, Richard B., *Trust No One: The Secret World of Sidney Reilly* (Port Townsend, WA: Feral House, 2003).

Stech, Frank J., 'Self-Deception. The Other Side of the Coin', *The Washington Quarterly*, 3/3 (Summer 1980), 130-40.

Sun Tzu, *The Art of War* (London: Amber Books, 2014), translated by James Trapp.

Thomas, Gordon, *Secret Wars: One Hundred Years of British Intelligence Inside MI5 and MI6* (New York, NY: Thomas Dunne Books/St. Martin's Press, 2009).

Tomaselli, P., 'C's Moscow station – The Anglo-Russian Trade Mission as Cover for SIS in the Early 1920s', *Intelligence and National Security*, 17/3 (Autumn 2002), 173–80.

Tomaselli, Phil, *Tracing Your Civil Service Ancestors*, paperback (Barnsley, S. Yorkshire: Pen & Sword Books, 2009).

Tzouliadis, Tim, *The Vorsaken: An American Tragedy in Stalin's Russia* (New York, NY: The Penguin Press, 2008).

Ullman, Richard Henry, *Anglo-Soviet Relations, 1917-1921, Volume I: Intervention and the War* (Princeton, NJ: Princeton University Press, 1961).

——, *Anglo-Soviet Relations, 1917-1921, Volume II: Britain and the Russian Civil War* (Princeton, NJ: Princeton University Press, 1968).

Vassilyev, A.T., *The Ochrana: The Russian Secret Police* (London: George G. Harrap & Co. Ltd, 1930).

Vatlin, Alexander, *Agents of Terror: Ordinary Men and Extraordinary Violence in Stalin's Secret Police,* edited, translated and with an Introduction by Seth Bernstein (Madison, WI: University of Wisconsin Press, 2018).

Volodarsky, Boris, 'Unknown Agabekov', *Intelligence and National Security*, 28/6 (December 2013), 890–909.

——, *Stalin's Agent: The Life and Death of Alexander Orlov* (Oxford: Oxford University Press, 2014).

White, Christine A., *British and American Commercial Relations with Soviet Russia, 1918-1924* (Chapel Hill, NC: The University of North Carolina Press, 1992).

Wilbur, C. Martin and Julie Lien-ying How (eds), *Documents on Communism, Nationalism, and Soviet Advisers in China, 1918-1927: Papers seized in the 1927 Peking raid* (New York, NY: Columbia University Press, 1956).

Wilton, Robert, *The Last Days of the Romanovs*, including the depositions of eye-witnesses, preserved and translated by George Tellberg (London: Thornton Butterworth Ltd., 1920).

Zeman, Z.A.B., *Germany and the Revolution in Russia, 1915-1918: Documents from the Archives of the German Foreign Ministry* (London: Oxford University Press, 1958).

——, and W.B. Scharlau, *The Merchant of Revolution: The Life of Alexander Israel Helphand (Parvus), 1867-1924* (New York, NY: Oxford University Press, 1965).

Znamenski, Andrei, *Red Shambhala: Magic, Prophecy, and Geopolitics in the Heart of Asia* (Wheaton, IL: Theosophical Publishing House, 2011).

Zuckerman, Frederic S., *The Tsarist Secret Police Abroad: Policing Europe in a Modernising World* (Houndmills, Basingstoke, Hampshire: Palgrave Macmillan, 2003).

Index

Marx, Karl 33, 74, 241, 269, 298
Masaryk, Tomáš Garrigue 221, 222–3
Massino, Konstantin Pavlovich, *see* Reilly
Masterman, Charles 13
Matuszewski, Ignacy 87, 320
Maugham, William Somerset, cover name 'Somerville' 12–13, 21, 324
Maurras, Charles xlvi
Maw, Bertie 251, 255, 256
Mayhew, Christopher Paget 217
McAlpine, Robert 15
McBarnet, Evelyn 265
McCormick, Vance C. 166
McMeekin, Sean 69, 70–1, 80, 133, 178–9
Mdivani, Budu 134
Medvedev, Dmitry Anatolyevich 49
Medvedev, Pavel 74
Medvedev, *see* Kudrin 74
Meighen, Arthur 188
Meiklejohn, Ronald Forbes 279, 280–1, 332
Melgunov, Sergey Petrovich 97
Mellon, Andrew William 82
Melnikov, Boris Nikolayevich, alias 'Boris Müller' (Comintern/OMS) 129, 276, 356
Mendl, Sir Charles Simon 291
Ménétier, Georges 246
Menzhinsky, Vyacheslav (Wiesław Mężyński) 8, 49, 56, 78, 97, 128, 135, 154
Menzies, Sir Stewart Graham 136, 176, 192, 197, 255, 285
Merkulov, Vsevolod Nikolayevich 9
Merkys, Antanas 232
Merritt, John 44–5, 47
Mezernitsky, Mstislav 156
Mikhail Alexandrovich, Grand Duke, youngest brother of Nicholas II 34, 75
Michelson, Ernest 285
Mikhailov, Boris Danilovich 135
Mikoyan, Anastas Ivanovich 239
Milkovsky, General Alexander 156, 337
Miller, Anton 271, 277
Miller, Hugh 193, 255
Miller, Peter 268, 277
Milli Emniyet Hizmeti (MEH and MAH), National Security Service of Turkey 141

Milne, Field Marshal George 43
Minev, Stoyan 209
Minsker, Yakov Grogoryevich 228
Mirbach-Harff, Graf, *see* von Mirbach
Mirny, Semyon Maksimovich, alias 'Yuri Yakovlev' 144
Mitchell, Graham Russell 193, 197
Mitrokhin, Vasili Nikitovich (often wrongly spelt 'Nikitich') 5, 49, 64, 104, 148–9, 158, 170, 212, 214–15
Mitskevich, Yevgeny Petrovich 293
Mittelhauser, General Charles 220–1
Mogilevsky, Solomon Grigoryevich 66, 128, 312
Molotov, Vyacheslav Mikhailovich 125, 129, 132, 144
Monkland, George 176, 357
Montefiore, Simon Sebag 215
Moos, Margarete Charlotte 294
Morozov, Savva Timofeyevich 79
Morton, Sir Desmond 176–7, 192, 197, 255
Motta, Giuseppe 231
Münzenberg, Wilhelm 'Willi' 93, 94, 123, 272, 326–7
Mussolini, Benito 82, 159

Nansen, Fridtjof 164–6
Nathan, Sir Robert 21
Natzarenus, Sergei 135
Nejedlý, Zdeněk 112
Nelson, James Carl 29
Nerman, Ture 58
Netrebin, Victor 74–5
Nicholas I, Emperor of Russia, King of Congress Poland and Grand Duke of Finland xlvii, xvii
Nicholas II, Nikolai Aleksandrovich Romanov, the last Emperor of Russia xliii, 1, 22, 33, 34–7, 72–6, 88–9
Nicolaevsky, *see* Nikolayevsky
Nicolson, Arthur (1st Baron Carnock) 70
Niedźwiałowska, Maria (aka Nawrocka, Niedźwiecka and Knoppe) 98–9
Nietzsche, Friedrich 9
Nikolai Nikolayevich, Grand Duke 250, 283, 310